W9-CLI-832

REVOLUTION IN HISTORY

Edited by

ROY PORTER

Senior Lecturer in the Social History of Medicine, Wellcome Institute

and

MIKULÁŠ TEICH

Emeritus Fellow, Robinson College, Cambridge

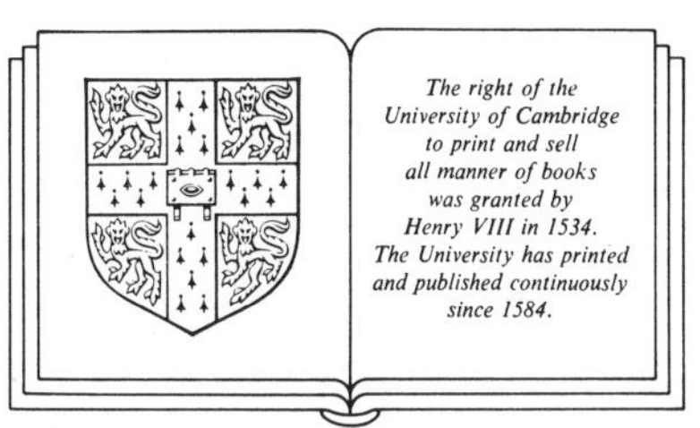
The right of the
University of Cambridge
to print and sell
all manner of books
was granted by
Henry VIII in 1534.
The University has printed
and published continuously
since 1584.

CAMBRIDGE UNIVERSITY PRESS

Cambridge
London New York New Rochelle
Melbourne Sydney

Published by the Press Syndicate of the University of Cambridge
The Pitt Building, Trumpington Street, Cambridge CB2 1RP
32 East 57th Street, New York NY 10022, USA
10 Stamford Road, Oakleigh, Melbourne 3166, Australia

First published 1986

Printed in Great Britain at the University Press, Cambridge

British Library cataloguing in publication data

Revolution in history.
1. Revolutions – History
I. Porter, Roy, 1946– II. Teich, Mickuláš
909 JC491

Library of Congress catloguing in publication data

Revolution in history.
Includes index.
1. Revolutions – History. I. Porter, Roy, 1946–
II. Teich, Mikuláš.
D32.R44 1986 909 86-6085

ISBN 0 521 25978 9 hard covers
ISBN 0 521 27784 1 paperback

CE

Contents

Notes on contributors *page* vii

Introduction 1

1 Revolution 5
E. J. HOBSBAWM

2 Revolution in antiquity 47
M. I. FINLEY

3 Social devolution and revolution: Ta Thung and Thai Phing 61
JOSEPH NEEDHAM

4 The bourgeois revolution of 1848–9 in Central Europe 74
ARNOŠT KLÍMA

5 Socialist revolution in Central Europe, 1917–21 101
T. HAJDU

6 Imperialism and revolution 121
VICTOR KIERNAN

7 Socio-economic revolution in England and the origin of the modern world 145
ALAN MACFARLANE

8 Agrarian and industrial revolutions 167
WILLIAM N. PARKER

9 On revolution and the printed word 186
ELIZABETH L. EISENSTEIN

10 Revolution in popular culture 206
PETER BURKE

11 Revolution in music – music in revolution 226
ERNST WANGERMANN

12 Revolution and the visual arts 240
RONALD PAULSON

13 Revolution and technology 261
AKOS PAULINYI

14 The scientific revolution: a spoke in the wheel? 290
ROY PORTER

15 The scientific-technical revolution: an historical event in the twentieth century 317
MIKULÁŠ TEICH

Index 331

Notes on contributors

PETER BURKE was educated by Jesuits, and at St John's College – taught by Keith Thomas – and St Anthony's College, Oxford. He went to the University of Sussex soon after its foundation and taught in the School of European Studies for sixteen years before moving to Emmanuel College, Cambridge. His books include *Popular Culture in Early Modern Europe* (1978) and *History and Sociology* (1980).

ELIZABETH L. EISENSTEIN was born in New York City and educated at Vassar and Radcliffe. Her study of Filippo Buonarroti: *The First Professional Revolutionist* appeared as a Harvard Historical Monograph in 1959. Her 1965 critique of Georges Lefebvre: 'Who Intervened in 1788?' has been reprinted in several collections. Her series of preliminary articles on the impact of printing, issued in the 1960s and 70s, culminated in *The Printing Press as an Agent of Change*, 2 vols. (Cambridge University Press, 1979, 2 vols.-in-one edn, 1981). An abridged illustrated version, *The Printing Revolution in Early Modern Europe*, was published in 1984. Since 1975, Mrs Eisenstein has served as Alice Freeman Palmer Professor of History at the University of Michigan.

SIR MOSES FINLEY (b. 1912) is Professor Emeritus of Ancient History, University of Cambridge; he was Master of Darwin College, Cambridge from 1976 to 1984. He is author or editor of twenty volumes, several hundred articles and book reviews. His most recent books include *Ancient History: Evidence and Models* (Chatto and Windus/Viking Press, 1985) and *Politics in the Ancient World* (Cambridge University Press, 1983).

TIBOR HAJDU was born in 1930 in Budapest, Hungary, where he attended the university and has lived since. An archivist at the Institute of Party History for twelve years, he was later appointed to a research post. Since 1975 he has been at the Institute of History of the Hungarian

Academy of Sciences as a research adviser. He has published various books on the Hungarian revolutions after the First World War, for which in 1970 he was awarded a National Prize. In 1978 he published a biography of Count Michael Károlyi.

ERIC HOBSBAWM is Emeritus Professor of Economic and Social History of Birkbeck College, University of London, and author of various works on a wide range of historical subjects, mainly in the period since the late eighteenth century.

V. G. KIERNAN was born in 1913 and, after attending the Manchester Grammar School, studied History at Cambridge and in 1937 became a Fellow of Trinity College, Cambridge. He spent some years in India, and in 1948 joined the History Department of Edinburgh University, of which he is now an Emeritus Professor. He has written on a variety of subjects connected with modern European and Asian history, imperialism, Marxist theory, and English literature.

ARNOŠT KLÍMA (b. 1916) was Professor of History at the Charles University, Prague, until his retirement in 1981. He has published seven monographs (in Czech) on nineteenth-century Czech history, dealing especially with the labour movement, and numerous articles besides in journals such as the *Economic History Review*. He is now working on a monograph *Der lange Krieg*. From 1962 to 1982 he was a member of the Executive Committee of the Economic History Association, visiting Professor at the University of Leipzig, University of Wisconsin, Madison, University of Bielefeld and University of Vienna.

ALAN MACFARLANE was born in Assam, India, in 1941 and educated at Oxford and London. He is currently Reader in Historical Anthropology and Fellow of King's College, Cambridge. He is author of nine books, including *The Origins of English Individualism* (1979) and *Marriage and Love in England* (1985).

JOSEPH NEEDHAM (b. 1900) was trained at Cambridge as a scientist and in 1928 became a Demonstrator in Biochemistry (subsequently, in 1933, Sir William Dunn Reader in Biochemistry). Having spent much of the Second World War in China as head of the British Scientific Mission, he has devoted much of his subsequent career to the multi-volume work *Science and Civilization in China* (1954–), which is still in progress. He has besides published many volumes of essays dealing with issues in the history of science East and West. From 1966 to 1976 he was Master of Gonville and Caius College, Cambridge.

WILLIAM N. PARKER is Philip Golden Bartlett Professor of Economics and Economic History in Yale University (New Haven, USA). A collection of his essays on European economic history has just been published under the title *Europe, America, and the Wider World*, vol. 1, *Europe and the World Economy* (Cambridge University Press, 1984).

AKOS PAULINYI (b. 1929) is Professor of the History of Technology and of Economic History at the Technische Hochschule Darmstadt. His publications cover the fields of the economic history of Slovakia in the eighteenth and nineteenth century, of the history of technology in iron-making and metal-working and of the transfer of technology in the nineteenth century.

RONALD PAULSON teaches English Literature at the Johns Hopkins University. He is the author of books on Hogarth, Swift, Rowlandson and on various aspects of eighteenth-century literature and art.

ROY PORTER is Senior Lecturer at the Wellcome Institute for the History of Medicine, London. After working early on the history of the earth sciences, and writing *The Making of Geology* (1977), he has subsequently researched in parallel into social history (publishing *English Society in the Eighteenth Century* with Penguin in 1982), and into the social dimensions of the history of medicine. He is currently working on the early history of psychiatry in Britain, on quackery, and on the lay experience of illness and doctors.

MIKULÁŠ TEICH first studied medicine in Prague. Thwarted by Hitler he eventually obtained a Ph.D. in chemistry (Leeds, 1946), and a C.Sc. in history (Prague, 1959). He is now Fellow Emeritus at Robinson College, Cambridge. His publications deal with wide-ranging topics of scientific history in different periods. Returning to Britain in 1969, he has edited (with Robert Young) *Changing Perspectives in the History of Science* (1972), and (with Roy Porter) *The Enlightenment in National Context* (1981). His *A Source Book in Biochemistry c.1770–c.1940* (with Dorothy M. Needham) is completed. *Bier, Wirtschaft und Wissenschaft in Deutschland 1800–1914* is nearing completion.

ERNST WANGERMANN was born in 1925 in Vienna, and read history at Balliol College, Oxford. His doctoral thesis was on Jacobinism and the Jacobin Trials in Austria (1953). He taught history for many years at the University of Leeds, where he was promoted to a Readership in 1977. He has held Visiting Professorships at Cornell University, the University of Wisconsin at Madison and the University of Linz, Austria. Since 1984 he has held the Chair of Austrian History at the University of Salzburg, Austria. His principal publications are *From Joseph II to the Jacobin*

Trials (1959; 2nd edn 1969); 'The Habsburg Possessions and Germany', in *The New Cambridge Modern History*, vol. VIII (1965); *The Austrian Achievement 1700–1800* (1973); *Aufklärung und staatsbürgerliche Erziehung: Gottfried van Swieten als Reformator des österreichischen Unterrichtswesens 1781–1791* (1978).

Introduction

When Marx wrote that people make their own history but not under circumstances of their own choosing, by 'make their own history' he was referring to actions in the world of affairs. But the sentiment could apply no less well in another sense; to the circumstances in which people 'make history' by conceptualizing the past. There have been distinguished attempts to trace the rise of true historical scholarship out of the history-as-myth and history-as-legitimation which once held sway. But – viewed from a particular angle – these interpretations themselves all too easily look like refurbished, higher-order myths, ones perhaps serving the interests of the historical profession. Indeed, once we remember that the breakthrough into true historical scholarship is supposed not to have been made till the nineteenth century, and admit that the age of romanticism was a peculiarly fertile age for breeding myths of origins and antiquity, it is hard to escape the conclusion that the more we pride ourselves upon the acuteness of our historical vision, the more we also need therefore to humble ourselves by seeing this as a product of the particular times in which we live.

And who can deny that these are confused? Today when the future of mankind under nuclear threat looks less assured than formerly, it is hardly surprising that the clear lines of the past as well disappear before the eyes. Can historians see any historical pattern? The liberal West has hardly produced a secular philosophy of destiny since positivism, evolutionism, and their surrounding aura of progress theory collapsed amid their own ambiguities in the century of Total War. For its part, Marxism continues to guide fields of historical interpretation. But there are many Marxisms. And, moreover, the capacity of Stalinist regimes to 'forget' or 'rewrite' inconvenient pasts has hardly boosted the credit of Marxism as a vision of the dynamic linking of past and present, thought and action.

Then, for its part, yesterday's Structuralism told us to forget (for the present at least) about dichronicity in favor of synchronicity, study slices of time not changes. And now today's Deconstructionism goes further, and writes off everyday notions of a 'real' history back there in the past by insisting that there is no reality outside the texts. And so, with the clear contours of the past dissolving before their eyes, it is small wonder then that today's professional historians are a cautious bunch, alert to complexity, singing the praises of pluralism, and sensitive to the snares lurking in the very words and concepts they use, waiting to trap the unwary user.

At the thick of these problems – indeed one of their most notable casualties – lies the idea of revolution. On the one hand, the concept has increasingly been overworked, debased and almost done to death. By a process of the inflation of historians' vocabulary, what formerly might have been termed a 'shift', or a 'change', becomes a 'revolution' in the mind of the historian needing to win a place in the sun for his own specialized wedge of research. On the other hand, so many of the great revolutions of the traditional historical canon – the French Revolution, the Industrial Revolution and Russian Revolution will serve as illustrations – have been subjected to withering factual, conceptual and terminological scrutiny.

In some quarters, this onslaught on 'revolution' has been ideological, an attempt to discredit Marxism as a theory of society by showing that the revolutions which form its historical props are no such thing. In part, however, it has followed from more genuinely penetrating and critical scrutiny of our concepts and their adequacy for depicting the thick texture of historical processes. What sort of criteria should we use if we are to make precise and helpful distinctions between (say) a revolution, a transformation, a revolt, a rebellion, or mere change?

It is the importance of questions like this, and the urgency of not simply settling into a cosy Anglo-Saxon semantic scepticism ('it all depends on what you mean by revolution') that has led to the launching of this book, and encouraged its contributors to engage with the key questions in the fields in which they are acknowledged experts. They have taken it as central to their brief critically to survey the existing scholarship, both empirical and conceptual, in their respective specialities, and to show the strengths and weaknesses of of historians' concepts of revolution in fields as diverse as economic history, the development of the visual arts, and power politics.

One volume cannot be expected to cover all the various aspects of such a wide-ranging theme. The next best thing to that, however, is to have an essay such as the one here by Eric Hobsbawm which 'does not set out to establish a general theory of revolution, but to sketch out, as it were, the landscape within which historical study of revolutions ought to be set'.

The other contributors have explored the particular ways in which historical thinking in revolutionary terms is (or is not) applicable to special fields of history. Moses Finley's and Joseph Needham's contributions, for instance, suggest a negative finding, the apparent absence of revolutions in traditional Marxist terms in antiquity and China before 1911 respectively. Yet this in itself is extremely positively revealing as to the real configuration of societies at that time.

Arnošt Klíma's and Tibor Hajdu's contributions are essentially studies of defeats of revolutions in the same geographical area, separated in time by about seventy years. The revolutionary movements in Central Europe of 1848–9 and 1917–21 were, of course, about different issues: establishment of bourgeois democracy and, later, socialist democracy. And their effects were also different. As Klíma points out, the military and political defeat of the revolution of 1848–9 did not prevent the post-revolutionary society of Central Europe from becoming essentially bourgeois. Nothing like socialist society is, however, discernible in Central Europe after 1917–21.

From Klíma's and Hajdu's accounts, nationalism emerges as one of the powerful forces that affected the bourgeois and socialist Central European revolutionary movements of 1848–9 and 1917–21 respectively. It goes without saying that nationalism imbued the revolutionary struggles against colonial rule which are tracked down in Victor Kiernan's essay. Reminding the reader that 'national consciousness always takes a jumble of forms ... it could be either westernizing and modernizing, or ... reactionary', Kiernan's contribution ranges over several overlapping social, economic, political and religious levels.

Many of these essays pose the question of wherein precisely lies the revolutionariness of certain dramatic transformations. For example, Paulinyi's contribution focusses attention on technology. Is it with the great inventions (the steam engine and the like) that we see the true revolutionary break? Or do we find that other, more subtle transformations, involving social relations as well as machines, are the ones that truly deserve the term revolutionary? Or (and this is what Peter Burke's and Alan Macfarlane's essays discuss) might there be certain levels of history in which the vocabulary of revolution is almost certainly bound to prove misleading, except perhaps with very special connotations, as in the idea of a 'long revolution'?

And through these inquiries some general clarifications begin to emerge. It is thus the argument of many of the essays in this collection that events build up their own evolutionary momentum; hence the historian's true yardstick for interpreting the nature and quality of past change is often the revolutionary break which constitutes the outcome rather than the origin of transformation. Thus it would be misguided and myopic, suggests Porter's essay, to abandon the idea of the scientific revolution of early modern times merely because it appears to have fed on the past even at the same time as it rejected it, and to have begun by a gradual process rather than cataclysmically.

Lastly, in putting forward positive suggestions for the role of the concept of revolution and the interpretation of revolution as a historical force, the contributors consider the dynamic interconnections of phenomena which acquire the character of a revolution, occurring in different spheres. For those concerned with comparing revolutionary accomplishments in agriculture and industry, William N. Parker's essay has particular interest. He finds that 'change' in one generally seems to have facilitated, and sometimes to have been a consequence of, change in the other. The revolution which was the coming of the printed book (argues Elizabeth Eisenstein) culminated, to some degree, in that transformation of the political world we call the French Revolution and the bourgeois state. Eighteenth-century music and aesthetics, as Ernst Wangermann's essay shows, had powerful affinities with contemporary political impulses towards radical change. And the French Revolution called up in turn, argues Ronald Paulson, a revolution in art, though one which – acknowledging the complexity of history – we must see in purely art-historical terms as reactionary. Germane to these issues is M. Teich's discussion of the modern scientific-technological revolution in the context of the unparalleled 'socializing' impact of science and technology in the twentieth century.

We live in confused times, but times in which change has more and more revolutionary consequences for us. Only if we can appreciate the diverse, subtle, yet essential nature of revolution in the course of our history, will we have the insight and courage to confront and contribute to the transformations of our own times.

1

*Revolution**

E. J HOBSBAWM

I

To judge by the subject catalogue of the Library of Congress, the literature on 'revolution', stable in the 1950s, grew at an extraordinary rate between 1960 and the mid-1970s. Surveying 'a lively and disorderly' field, Zagorin (1973, pp. 28–9) observes that there are three possible ways of attacking the problem of revolution. Practically all we know about them comes by the investigation of particular revolutions. Those who practise comparative study, or seek to establish a general explanatory theory of revolution, have been almost entirely parasitic on the first group of students. No attempt can be made here to survey the enormous bulk of their productions, but three observations can be made about the relation of the historiography of actual revolutions to comparative and general study.

First, the revolutions about which we possess abundant and serious literature are those recognized by contemporaries as prodigious and influential upheavals. They are the 'great revolutions', e.g. the French, Russian and Chinese (cf. Skocpol 1976, 1979a, 1979b) and those classified as such by analogy with them at the time retrospectively and prospectively. Thus we know more about anti-Bourbon insurrections in nineteenth-century Italy than about Carlist wars in Spain, though the latter were considerably larger than the former. *Second*, since the 'great revolutions' have *de facto* provided the criteria for the rest, their influence on historiography has been profound. It has operated prospectively on revolutionaries, counter-revolutionaries and social scientists, and retrospectively on both practitioners and historians of revolution. In short, they have provided analytical models. From 1799 onwards revolutions have been searched for analogies to Jacobinism, Thermidor and Bonaparte (Brinton 1938; Bahne 1967, pp. 74–6; Cordova 1975, p. 92), and

* This paper is based on a report given to the XIV International Congress of Historical Sciences, San Francisco, 1975.

since 1917 for seizures of power as in Russia, for disciplined parties of the Bolshevik type, for Stalinist tendencies. The Chinese and some colonial revolutions drew attention to peasants and protracted guerrilla approaches to power, which had played little part in the analyses before the Second World War. Thus Brinton (1965 ed., pp. 59–60) had devoted only a single page to peasants.

Moreover, analytical models were derived from the arbitrary selection of revolutions which happened to form part of the analysts' intellectual universe. The Chinese tradition of revolutionary change played no part in Western analysis, though Mao was clearly influenced by it (Schram 1967, pp. 127–8; Schram 1969; Mao Tse Tung III, 1954, pp. 73–6). The Mexican Revolution passed the world by. There appears to be no reference to it in Debray's influential pamphlet (Debray 1967). Theory and practice were – temporarily – overshadowed by the much smaller but internationally more 'visible' Cuban events of 1956–9. Critical observers have since used Mexico, now recognized as the first 'great' revolution of this century, to question received models (Aya 1979, p. 44; Goldfrank 1979).

Third, the actual historiography of revolutions is of very uneven quality and quantity, so that the basis for comparison and generalization is skewed. The ideal of a revolution satisfactorily and accessibly documented, with a long and mature tradition of study, and sufficiently emancipated from contemporary passions of government and public opinion to be safe from the pressures of both, is still rarely realized. Hence the French Revolution, though by no means recollected in political tranquility, continues to stand out as the model to which, speaking historiographically, all the others aspire. Time may remove the three major obstacles in the way of historians: a public opinion committed to myths about the formative events in national life; government authority and policy committed to particular (and not always unchanging) interpretations of the historical past; and the inevitable, and sometimes lengthy, time-lag between the occurrence of a revolution and the possibility of dispassionate, if not uncommitted, historical analysis. The historiography of Ireland since 1960 is proof of what chronological distance can achieve. However, since so many of the revolutions which form the basis for generalization and comparative analysis are rather recent, the problem is serious.

In short, extensive comparative study, though indispensable, as Skocpol rightly argues (1979a), is rarely based on comparable knowledge or satisfactory criteria of comparability.

The present paper is not a survey of work in the field of comparative revolutionary studies, still less a bibliographical guide to it.[1] While critical of most of the earlier social science literature on the subject, which has been often and of necessity repetitively surveyed,[2] it does not set out to establish a general theory of revolution, but to sketch out, as it were, the landscape within which historical study of revolutions ought to be set. It will be evident that I find some work of the 1970s congenial, illuminating or useful, notably the line of inquiry which leads from Moore 1966 to Skocpol and the explorations of Tilly and his followers. I share with them the belief that such questions as 'why men rebel' (Gurr 1970) or 'when men rebel and why' (Davies 1971) are an inadequate approach to revolution; the belief that the question of 'violence', a term which is usually left ambiguous and ill-defined (see Hobsbawm 1973, ch. 21; Hobsbawm 1974, pp. 378–9; G. P. Meyer 1976, p. 129) may be inseparable from revolution but is peripheral to it;[3] and the belief that, in spite of the proven inadequacies of much Marxist writing on revolution, 'the marxist theory of society, frequently upgraded into a theory of revolution, remains one of the most stimulating models for the analysis of revolutionary processes of transformation' (G. P. Meyer 1976, p. 167). However, it will also be clear that I pay rather less attention to the much-studied causes (long-term or short-term) of revolutions than they do, believing that they are far from exhausting the interest of the subject. Conversely, the present paper stresses the neglected problem of how and when revolutions finish.

The present paper thus proposes to pick certain strands out of the web of historical debate. It is concerned particularly with revolutions as incidents in macro-historical change, i.e. as 'breaking-points' in systems under growing tension, and with the consequences of such ruptures. It will not be particularly concerned with revolt and insurrection and still less with revolutionary organisation as putative makers of revolution. The author's approach should emerge from the text, but for the sake of clarity three points should be made at the outset: (1) the historical study of revolutions cannot usefully be separated from that of the specific historical periods in which they occur; (2) it can never be separated from the history of the period in which the scholar studies it, including that scholar's personal bias; (3) I wish specifically to disclaim as unhistorical any version of the view that 'revolution is always avoidable if the creative potential of political organization can be realized' (Chalmers Johnson, cited in Stone 1972, p. 14), as well as the opposite proposition.

II

There is little point in discussing at length the numerous definitions of revolution proposed by social scientists, though an analysis of their underlying assumptions might be profitable. How much is the analysis of revolutions distorted by the view that they are deviations from a social equilibrium which is taken to be the norm (Johnson 1964: 1968), or by the organicist view of society which underlies the familiar metaphor of revolution as a 'fever'? (Sorokin 1925, 3, p. 403; Brinton 1938, crit. by Dahrendorf 1961; Eckstein 1965; Wertheim 1974, pp. 176–7). Social science definitions are both unrealistic and tend to assume the existence of a universal class of revolutions (or a single ideal type of revolution), criteria for whose membership are to be established. Definition may be so broad as to tell us nothing of interest about actual revolutions. At best it establishes that historical change implies discontinuity as well as continuity, at worst the word becomes a synonym for any sufficiently noticeable change which takes place at an observably faster rate than others.[4] On the other hand, arbitrary selections from the total complex of phenomena most of us think of as 'revolution' are of little use to historians, though they may provide the illusion that revolutionary phenomena can be quantified, compared and correlated non-trivially on a 'scientific basis'. Selection may define it simultaneously as 'change which is characterized by violence as a means and a specifiable range of goals as ends' (Zagorin 1973a, p. 27) and as 'a fundamental change in social structure which is accomplished in a short period of time' (Galtung in Jänicke 1973, p. 121), two formulae which have nothing in common except the word 'change'. Without entering into their merits, their omissions are obvious. Zagorin does not enable us to distinguish the Mexican Revolution from the Chilean coup of 1973, while Galtung does not enable us to distinguish between the Russian Revolution and the social changes which occurred in Jamaica as the result of the abolition of slavery. All such definitions, broader and narrower, assume chronologically and geographically almost universal applicability of the concept.

But historians (Geiss and Tamchina 1974; Moore 1967) are doubtful about such universal applicability. They are much more likely to confine the phenomenon to the period of the transition to global industrialization, i.e. the period covered by the historiography of the 'neuzeitliche Revolutionsbegriff' (Griewank 1973; Koselleck 1969). Whether even the Netherlands revolt should be included (as by Smit in Forster and Greene 1970; see also Zagorin 1976, 1982) has been doubted. Even narrower chronological definitions have been suggested, as by Bauman 1971. A less extreme view would at least divide the phenomenon of 'revolution' into two phases: the period of 'modern revolution' in the full sense which belongs to the era of Polanyi's 'great transformation' (Polanyi 1945) – whether or not we regard this as completed – and a less far-reaching mode of socio-political change, which also occurs in earlier periods.

Nonetheless it seems clear that the attempt to extend the 'system-changing' revolutions too far into the past breaks down. The thesis that the transition from classical antiquity to feudalism was due to a 'slave-revolution' (for which, incidentally, there is no warrant in the texts of Marx or Lenin) was abandoned in Soviet Marxism.[5] If the term retains any value when applied to such periods, as has been maintained (Heuss 1973), it must be used with considerable care.

The most useful definitions have been descriptive or synthetic. That is to say they have started by describing what the term 'revolution' has actually come to mean, as in Griewank (1973, pp. 21–2):

> Hitherto revolutions has come to be used quite unambiguously only for certain total historical phenomena which combine three features. *First*, a process which is both violent and in the nature of a sudden shock – a breaking through or overturning, especially as regards changes in the institutions of state and law. *Second*, a social content, which appears in the movement of groups and masses, and generally also in actions of open resistance by these. *Finally*, the intellectual form of a programmatic idea or ideology, which sets up positive objectives aiming at renovation, further development or the progress of humanity.

We may note the presence of the element of mass mobilization, without which few historians would identify a revolution as such. The value of this type of definition is diagnostic. It treats revolution as a syndrome, to be recognized by a *combination* of 'symptoms' rather than by the separate occurrence of one or more of them. It also helps to separate the revolutions about whose character there is likely to be substantial consensus from those (such as the Nazi era in Germany) which are not universally accepted as such. On the other hand its analytical value is small, nor is it sufficient to describe the specifically 'modern' revolutions which take place during the transition to an industrial world, still less more specific phases of these.

Limited as the synthetic type of definition is, it allows for the crucial duality of the revolution as studied by historians. This consists of two interlocked but rather different types of phenomena. They are a series of events, generally associated with 'revolt' and capable of transferring power from an 'old regime' to a 'new regime', though not all revolutions achieve such a transfer.[6] Normally they consist of a nest of Chinese boxes of such episodes, ranging in length from those measured in days ('les trois glorieuses', 'ten days that shook the world') to those measured in months ('February', 'October'), years (1789–99) or decades (e.g. in China 1911–49). Where the revolutionary process is interrupted by 'restorations' or other peripeties, the time-scale may be even longer, as indeed it may be if we take as terminal dates not the actual collapse of the old regime and the transfer of power to the permanent victors, but some suitable point in the 'crisis of the old regime' which precedes its fall, and the point at which the convulsions of the transitional era give way to history within a new and fairly permanent framework, i.e. when 'revolution' turns into a new 'evolution'. (Cf. the title of Cline 1962.) This generally occurs some time after the transfer of power.

Lengthy though these 'revolutionary eras' may be, they are to be distinguished from the historic macro-phenomena in which they are embedded, such as the change from pre-capitalist to capitalist societies. The revolutions which interest historians lie at the intersection of these two types of phenomena. We are unlikely to class them as revolutions if they do not involve potential transfers of power in the characteristic manner. On the other hand, if most of us did not regard the context of historical transformation as essential to the phenomenon, the comparative history of revolutions would not tacitly have dropped out of sight most members of the largest class of events known by that name, the 115 successful revolutions of nineteenth-century Latin America (Lieuwen 1961, p. 21; there are other estimates). Many political systems periodically generate crises, at all events among the ruling elite, e.g. because of the absence of a foolproof mechanism for transferring office, which make the succession of any woman or minor in some hereditary monarchies or that of any Ecuadorian president for long periods an almost automatic occasion for conflict. Historians of revolution neglect them when they lead to no more than dramatic episodes in the national history of events, as in sixteenth-century England. Not so when they act as triggers to more far-reaching changes, as in sixteenth-century Scotland.

If we omit the context of historic transformation we may be left with analyses based on static dichotomies such as 'internal peace/internal war' (Eckstein 1965), violence/non-violence (Zagorin 1973), or more generally 'social dysfunction'. These neither explain why the attitude of old regimes to revolution changed after 1789 (Sorel 1908, pp. 53f, 543f), nor the difference between the 1917 revolutions and the assassination of Tsar Paul I in 1801. We may therefore find ourselves analysing not revolution, but some more restricted phenomenon, though one normally associated with it, such as, say, 'rebellion'.

On the other hand, however we define the macro-phenomenon of historical transformation it is neither identical with nor, except in a very general sense, does it imply the micro-phenomenon of actual revolution. Following Marx, who provided the most powerful guide to it, we may call the macro-phenomenon 'an epoch of social revolution' (Marx 1859). Marx's analysis of such a period, 'when the productive forces of society come into conflict with the existing relations of production', may apply to a wide range of areas, though the maximum region involved in a productive system (i.e. under capitalism the capitalist 'world economy') is more readily defined than the smallest unit of such epochs.[7] To accept this type of analysis is to recognize that at certain periods specific kinds of drastic historical change are inevitable, and that therefore historic forces beyond the control of will must 'break asunder the integument' of the old systems and regimes in one way or another. Such a view is not confined to Marxists, but has been the basis of most conservative, including counter-revolutionary, thought since the French Revolution, including much that goes under the head of 'modernization theory'.

It has long been recognized that much 'counter-revolutionary' theory aims to protect a social order against one form of drastic change by meeting the demand for such change in another manner. 'Revolution' and 'counter-revolution' may share much of the same analysis, and revolutionaries may pass from favouring one form of transformation to the other, as in the career and writings of Cuoco in eighteenth-century Naples, or they may be keenly aware of the one as a surrogate for the other, as in Gramsci's concept of the 'passive revolution' (Cuoco 1929; Gramsci 1971, pp. 59, 106ff). Anti-revolutionary 'modernizers' like Huntington (1968) are counter-revolutionary in this sense. The two terms are not simply opposed (as Mayer 1971 seems to suggest) but dialectically related.

Thus, social revolution in this sense, and *a fortiori* any specific form of insurrectionary transfer of power, is only one form among several of such changes. However, it may be argued that since 1789 the other options have generally been secondary to revolution. They require a prior model of revolutionary transformation which they imitate (Moore 1967, p. 414), or they are attempts to avoid some consequences of revolution by bringing about the necessary changes in other ways.

Nevertheless, there can be no serious dispute about the two propositions that, since the sixteenth century, some functionally revolutionary changes have been inevitable, and that some actual revolutions have been avoidable, if only because they have in fact been avoided. Both propositions have met with strong emotional resistance, but this does not make them less true. We may also note that, while Marx was prepared to specify fundamental changes which *must* take place on the basis of his general analysis of capitalist development (e.g. the 'expropriation of the expropriators'), he allowed for a variety of forms of transition, including peaceful transition (Storia 1978, ch. 8; Marek 1966, pp. 125ff). In so far as he predicted one form of revolution, this was based on concrete political analysis. It was not simply inferred from the occurrence of 'epochs of social revolution'. Whether a certain type of property relation and the ruling groups associated with it are bound to disappear is a different order of question from the one whether, e.g., ruling classes are disposed to resist their overthrow or capable of doing so. The two kinds of question ought not to be confused.

For the present purposes the argument need not be taken further. However, three general observations may be made. *First*, that an 'epoch of social revolution' without a number of actual and crucially significant revolutions is both hard to conceive in theory, and most implausible in practice, given the historical record since 1776. *Second*, that even the alternatives and surrogates for revolution in such periods must, in de Tocqueville's terms (Tocqueville 1861, 1, p. 423) aim at 'transformation' and not mere 'modification' of society. They imply drastic and radical changes which, since 1776 at least, have taken place in a general context of revolution and sometimes, as in Germany, in partial combinations with them.[8] *Third*, various ways of achieving these transformations, revolutionary or otherwise, produce rather different socio-economic and political results, and the possible variants have begun to receive historical analysis (Moore 1967). They will not be discussed here.

III

Irrespective of their general character as phenonema of historic rupture, concretely revolutions are also episodes in which groups of people pursue intended goals, whatever the causes and motives which make them act or the – inevitable – difference between their intentions and the results of their action. They belong to the realm of politics as well as to that in which political decisions are unimportant. The element of conscious action and decision cannot be left out of the analysis, though both the strategists of revolution and (perhaps because they control more power) especially those of counter-revolution, tend to overestimate its scope.[9] As events showed, success in controlling a revolutionary outbreak in the Dominican Republic in 1965 provided no argument for the practicability of such control in Vietnam. This applies also to the role of individuals. The fact that Lenin cannot be written out of the scenario of 1917 by some reductionist hypothesis or otherwise should not encourage the now conventional exaggerations of his personal responsibility for the October Revolution.[10] History is made by men's actions, and their choices are conscious and may be significant. Yet the greatest of all revolutionary strategists, Lenin, was lucidly aware that during revolutions planned action takes place in a context of uncontrollable forces.

The actual situation may be so structured as to leave little choice except between making or failing to make the 'right' decision; and sometimes not even that choice. Moreover, revolutions are themselves in some senses 'natural phenomena', if only because in their course masses are mobilized and institutions, conventions and political forces break down and are overwhelmed, which normally set certain limits to what may happen. This uncontrollability of revolution has been recognized since 1789 both by its opponents, who used it as perhaps the chief argument against them (see Burke 1790, Lacqueur in *IESS* 1968, 13, p. 505), but also by Jacobins like Georg Forster (cited in Griewank 1973, pp. 196ff). Hence the future course of the 'great revolutions' has rarely been predicted with any appreciable success, except for limited aspects.

Consequently, theories which overstress the voluntarist or subjective elements in revolutions are to be treated with caution. If a simile be permitted, the evident importance of the actors in the drama (single or collective) does not mean than they are also dramatist, producer and stage-designer. From the historians' point of view the organized forces of revolutionaries and their strategies are clearly secondary, except in special circumstances, most of which occur *after* revolution has turned revolutionaries into governments or where the two are the same. Even where significant organized revolutionary movements exist (as was not the case at the outset of several major revolutions, e.g. the French or Mexican), their capacity, as Lenin saw, rarely suffices to dictate the course of events; their achievement lies in turning a changing situation to their advantage. Attempts to plan the outbreak of revolutions from below have almost invariably failed. (For a good discussion, see Lewis 1974, Introduction.)

Similarly, with an exception to be noted below, the study of so-called 'revolutionary populations' (Zagorin 1973, p. 35) in general has a more limited significance than is allowed by those who 'increasingly ... seek the relevant conditions of revolution in those which touch and energize the actor' (Schwartz in Davies 1971, p. 132). This is not to deny its importance, though approaches which seek to identify specifically 'revolutionary behaviour' or a 'revolutionary personality' are of little historical interest, even when not vitiated by the assumption – once widespread in the literature – that revolutionaries are by definition deviants from a norm of personality and behaviour. (This is rightly criticized by Johnson 1968, pp. 75ff.) Like armies and wars, revolutionary movements and revolutions breed identifiable behaviour-patterns and tend to recruit those to whom they appeal, among others. Yet, as in conscript wars, in revolutions such specialized behaviour is not confined to specifiable groups of individuals. Actual mass participation in such periods is difficult to study,[11] but Lenin was undoubtedly right in seeing an enormous explosion of public activity among the masses as characteristic of revolutionary situations. At such times people who are not normally revolutionary, become so. The criteria for detecting potential 'troublemakers' in the German or Russian navies in 1914 become irrelevant when the words 'sailor' and 'revolutionary' become almost interchangeable in Kronstadt or Kiel (Trotsky 1936, pp. 440ff; Carsten 1972, p. 33; Getzler 1983).

Such arguments may also apply to larger social groups, though obviously recruitment and participation in political movements, like electoral support, are decisively influenced by membership of class or other social groups. (See Lipset 1960 for a conspectus of data.) What is at issue is rather the assumption, not only confined to the left, that the political attitude of any class or group, as prescribed by its character and place in society, can be ranked on a scale ranging from the 'consistently revolutionary' to the 'reliably conservative', peasants being cast in the latter role by nineteenth-century conservatives, in the former more frequently since 1945 (see art. 'Bauerngut', in *Handwörterbuch* 1899, Wolf 1971), workers in one role by classical Marxism, in another by critics (cf. Landsberger in Lipset and Solari 1967, Jean A. Meyer 1970). The fact that the place of various groups on such scales is uncertain and shifting should give the analyst pause.

In fact, such procedures replace the specific problem of revolution by macro-social analysis, exaggerating *structure* and devaluing *situation*. The general question what type of socio-economic order is desired by, compatible with, or in the long run corresponding to the interests of some social group is *not* identical with the question how such a group will behave in a given historical situation or what its prevalent subjective attitude will be. Bodies of students of comparable social composition have recently shifted political attitudes in many Western countries, or have participated in varying degrees in politicial outbreaks, e.g. in Russia 1905 and 1917 (Trotsky 1973, pp, 85ff, 101ff, 269; Trotsky 1936, p. 1040). The same considerations may move skilled metalworkers at one time to moderation, at another to support of the revolutionary left (Hinton 1973, Hobsbawm 1984). The effect of unchanged group behaviour is transformed by the situational context. Ordinary cost-of-living riots, which for most participants imply no intended or immediate challenge to the existing order (Thompson 1970), may become the starting-point of revolution when they occur in 1917. Structure and situation interact, and determine the limits of decision and action; but what determines the possibilities of action is primarily situation. At this point the analysis of forces capable of mobilizing, organizing and moving into action groups of people on a politically decisive scale become relevant, though it must not be isolated (J. W. Lewis 1974, p. 14), as is often done in the study of that most formidable tool of social engineering, the revolutionary 'vanguard party'. Yet even if, as sometimes – e.g. after lengthy periods of guerrilla war – a nationally manoeuvrable revolutionary force exists, the situation may well (as in Europe 1943–5) determine what it does or can decide.

IV

For understandable reasons, comparative students of revolution in the past generation have concentrated their attention overwhelmingly on its causes and the circumstances determining its outbreak or success. To this large literature there is little to add except a note of scepticism. The value of generalizations rests both on the questions behind them and on their capacity to provide illumination in concrete cases, in this instance of revolution. Those based on the assumption that revolution is primarily a form of (undesirable) *instability* or *civil strife* (e.g. Feierabend and Feierabend 1966, Gurr in Graham and Gurr 1969) will only reveal conditions of likely strife. Theorists exclusively concerned with *predicting* outbreaks, which, *pace* Davies, 1962, was not Lenin's major concern (cf. Davies 1971, p. 9), are likely to concentrate on causes and lose interest when revolutions actually have occurred or been avoided. At the same time the degree of abstraction may be excessive, as in the discussions of 'relative deprivation' and 'J-curves' (Davies 1962, Stone 1966, Gurr 1970), which in itself tells us nothing about what may cause 'deprivation', or about the significantly different reactions of different groups (e.g. workers, middle strata) to it in particular historical contexts, or the different consequences of their reactions (e.g. towards Fascism or communism in the 1920s–30s). Generalizations rooted in objective historical realities, even very widespread ones such as the town/country dichotomy, are less likely to suffer from these disadvantages, which is why Marxist approaches have been found useful (cf. the use of Gramsci 1949 by Tilly 1974).

Analysis has generally attempted to distinguish between 'preconditions' or long-run underlying causes which make the occurrence (or success) of revolutions possible (Forster and Greene 1970, pp. 13–17) and 'precipitants' or 'immediate incidental factors ... which trigger the outbreak' (Stone 1966), and which are sometimes regarded as indispensable (Johnson 1964). This distinction, though useful, has three disadvantages. (1) It tends to assume that no revolution is in the long run inevitable. If it were to be, the problem of what match dropped into the accumulating pile of explosives might be quite secondary. (2) In practice no clear distinction between 'pre-conditions' and 'precipitants' is often possible, inasmuch as the accumulating tensions within the system (Dahrendorf's 'analogy of the steam-boiler' which he rightly finds more illuminating than Brinton's 'fever' (Dahrendorf 1961)) may actually produce or facilitate the production of certain precipitants such as economic crises and wars, and encourage certain situations of political vulnerability in old regimes, such as financial crises. However, (3) attempts to construct models of the automatic generation of revolutions accordingly, along Labroussian or other lines (Labrousse 1948) overlook the crucial mingling of structural/conjunctural and situational factors already noted. Though the distinction has been used to excellent effect (e.g. Stone 1972), we must be careful not to become its victims.

In this sceptical light, two aspects of the prodrome of revolution may now be briefly discussed; 'historical crises' and 'revolutionary situations'.

At least since Burckhardt (1929) historians have been aware of 'historical crisis' (Starn 1971), a concept which has recently attracted the attention of political scientists (IESS 1968, 3, p. 510ff; Jänicke 1973a and literature cited there), though these generally concentrate on 'acute situations of decision' rather than on 'longterm systemic disturbances' (Jänicke, pp. 10–23). Since 1973 it may be once again attracting the attention of economists. The term 'crisis of the old regime' as applied to a more or less lengthy period preceding and generating a revolution is familiar in France (Mathiez 1921, 1, ch. 1). The wider concept of a system or 'world' whose crises and revolutions must be analysed as a whole is established (Palmer and Godechot 1955, Palmer 1959, 64, Aston 1965). The concept of a 'general crisis' – an epoch of restructuring in the evolution of a system – may have entered historiography both through Marxism and the inter-war depression which, perhaps via Abel (1955), led to discussions which could be formulated as being about a 'general crisis of feudalism' (IX Int. Hist. Congr. 1, pp. 224ff; X Int. Hist. Congr., 6, p. 950; Génicot 1966). The links of such a systemic crisis with revolt were soon argued (Graus 1955, pp. 565–70). Indeed, the occurrence of 'contemporaneous revolutions' (Merriman 1938) helped to stimulate the debated concept of a seventeenth-century 'general crisis' (Hroch and Petráň 1982). Such crises may be identified with Marx's 'epochs of social revolution', though this term is very general. Contemporaneous ruptures may be analysed accordingly.

The study of contemporaneous ruptures has perhaps been excessively diverted into comparative case-studies (Robertson 1952, Carsten 1972, Forster and Greene 1970), which assumes a comparability of cases and therefore seeks for analogies. But the comparability of the English Revolution, the Fronde and the Catalan–Portuguese–Neapolitan revolts of the 1640s does not rest on any assumed similarity between these areas as societies or political structures, and hence we need not be surprised at the 'seemingly totally separate and distinctive character of the ... events considered' (Forster and Greene, p. 2). It rests on common membership of a system, and to the vulnerability of states to some factor disturbing it, or to the effects of some general 'contradiction' within the system, many of whose components may have different structures, functions and histories.

There is no *a priori* reason to seek for a 'bourgeois revolution' in France or Naples of the 1640s, even if we believe one to have occurred in England. Similarly there is no reason to assume *a priori* that the numerous countries launched into political independence by the collapse of the European colonial systems were necessarily similar in any other respect than their dependence on the metropolitan countries.

Membership of a common system is indeed likely to produce certain types of component with similar structure (e.g. industrialized capitalist economies), though always with significant variations, but not a single standard type of component. What it does provide is common factors of disturbance, common sensitivity to these and intercommunication, from which superstructural similarities may spring. Such are, e.g., the general prevalence at a given time of ideological and programmatic 'models' ('the Enlightenment', liberalism, Marxism, representative democracy, nationalism, etc.) and the 'demonstration effect' of particularly striking revolutions which may be widely copied, e.g. the French and the Russian, or which, occurring at a suitable moment, may spread rapidly over large areas (as from Paris in 1848) or stimulate remote rebellion through the diffusion of news-media (Diaz del Moral 1929; 1967, p. 277, for the effect of the Russian revolution in Andalusia). Communication links the most improbable contemporaries.[12]

The diffusion of common patterns through ideology, the market or naked power is thus characteristic of a system, and where it does not exist the mere sensitivity to common disturbance is probably not enough to constitute one: China in the present century is part of a global system, as – despite argument to the contrary (Adshead 1970) – it probably was not in the seventeenth. It may also be argued – by both 'modernizers' and Marxists in different ways – that the development of all components of the system, though visibly uneven, is, or is destined, to converge towards a single type of goal, or proceed in a single direction. Historians as such need not discuss the merits of these arguments. Whether true or not, the actual structural, historical and other differences between the components (let us call them 'countries' or groups of countries for convenience) have until the present been decisive.

Nevertheless, the concept of 'general crisis' is useful as a reminder that particular revolutions or other ruptures occur within systems, which pass through periods of breakdown and restructuring, and at the same time as a corrective to the tendency to generalize about revolution in the abstract while reducing the concrete analysis of revolutions to an aggregate of case-studies. It also confirms doubts about the separability of 'preconditions' and 'precipitants' or 'triggers'. The general long-term crisis through which the world system has been passing since the early 1900s[13] contains four periods of system-wide shock which have acted as triggers to contemporaneous ruptures, revolutionary or otherwise: the two world wars, the slump of 1929–33, and the world depression of the 1970s, which has produced a crop of revolutions and regime-changes in three continents, though, with the exception of Iran, and perhaps Ethiopia, not in any major country.[14] Yet the trigger-mechanism was certainly a product of system-wide, and presumably system-immanent 'contradictions' in the case of economic crisis, and arguably in that of world wars. Moreover, during this period contemporaneous ruptures also occurred without equally obvious general triggers, or more than some element akin to chain-reaction. Such was the breakdown, between 1905 and 1911, of the ancient and by then, semi-colonial monarchies of Persia, the Ottoman empire, Morocco, China, to which the Mexican Revolution may be added, under the tension generated by global capitalist expansion. The coincidence of these conflagrations, and their implications, were already noted by Lenin in 1908 (Lenin 1936–8, 4, pp. 297ff).

The profitable historical analysis of this 'epoch of social revolution' as a whole has been inhibited on the non-Marxist side by a failure to recognize it as a system-wide crisis at all, or by a tendency to see its various ruptures as incidental to a rather simplified and unilinear process of 'modernization',[15] possibly leading towards a single pattern of revolution-proof 'maturity' (cf. Rostow 1960, Lipset 1960, ch. 13). On the Marxist side the existence of a period of global crisis has indeed been recognized and since Lenin (cf. Meyer 1957, ch. 12) formed the basis of a global strategy and expectations of 'world revolution'. Though this has never implied a single episode of overthrow (Marek 1966, pp. 121ff), the historic experience of dramatic accumulations of contemporary ruptures has at various moments since the early nineteenth-century encouraged more extreme hopes or fears (see Kriegel and Salvadori in Agosti 1974). On the other hand, the belief that this transformation must also be in some sense unilinear – towards 'socialism', often, until recently, defined in rather specific ways – and the excessive preoccupation of revolutionaries with strategic calculations, as well as their built-in optimism, have made most Marxist analyses of the period considerably less than adequate. Hence, though useful collections of case-studies of twentieth-century revolutions exist (Wolf 1971 for Mexico, Russia, China, Vietnam, Algeria, Cuba; Dunn 1972 for the same plus Yugoslavia and Turkey; Leiden and Schmitt 1968 for Mexico, Turkey, Egypt, Cuba), as well as collective studies of other ruptures such as Fascism (Nolte 1965, 1975; *Journ. Contemp. Hist.* 1966; Woolf 1968), a comprehensive analytical study of this entire crisis-period and its ruptures would be very helpful to historians of revolution, but may still be impracticable.

A 'revolutionary situation' may be defined as that variant of a short-term crisis within a system with long-term internal tensions, which offers good chances of a revolutionary outcome. Whether it exists is thus debatable until revolution has actually occurred.[16] That such a situation can be identified before or as it occurs, is implied. 'Revolutionary situations' are thus about possibilities, and their analysis is not predictive. The classic analysis of them is Lenin's, which comprises (1) a 'crisis in the policy of the ruling class which causes fissures through which the discontent and the indignation of the oppressed classes burst forth'; (2) a sharpening of the discontent of the lower classes, and (3) a 'considerable increase in the activity of the masses' (Lenin 1936–8, 5, p. 174).[17]

Lenin's analysis is thus not concerned with either 'preconditions' or 'triggers', nor does he fall into the error of those who have, since Brinton (1938) and Gottschalk (1944) drawn up lists of sometimes 'nebulous', (Zagorin 1973, p. 29, Johnson 1968, p. 61) sometimes analytically miscellaneous or even tautological[18] 'conditions' whose coincidence is supposed to create revolutionary situations or even revolutions. His object was not to predict or even bring about revolutionary situations (for his scepticism on this point, see Lenin 1936–8, 5, 145) but the more modest one of teaching Bolsheviks to recognize opportunities. His modesty holds lessons for comparative analysts of revolution.

Curiously enough, the formulation of this eminent applied theorist has not figured much in the social science literature. Thus Johnson does not refer to it, though discussing Lenin under the heading of 'coup d'état' strategy (Johnson 1968, pp. 150–9). It assumes no unilinear or automatic relation between the situation and its long-term or structural causes, allows for various combinations of what others might call 'precipitants' or 'triggers', but above all it brings out the *political* element in it and combines structural and situational analysis. 'International and world-historical circumstances' (Skocpol 1979b, p. 290) are, of course, a crucial component of the situation – often the decisive one, as Skocpol has argued in one of the most interesting and illuminating of recent contributions to the literature, though the omnipresence of an international situation need not lead us to conclude that it is always decisive, even for great revolutions. The Iranian revolution, a 'great revolution' by any objective standards, does not seem to fit well into Skocpol's model derived from Franco-Russo-Chinese experience.

However, the core of the Leninist analysis lies in the interplay between an indispensable 'crisis of the upper classes' and rebellion of the masses, drawn into independent historical action, both being necessary and intertwined elements in it. Each may precipitate the other, or both may appear independently, though Lenin regards the latter possibility as unusual.[19] Lenin adds that the conjuncture of the two phenomena is 'independent not only of the will of separate groups and parties, but even of separate classes' (Lenin, *loc. cit.*). This suggests that a revolutionary situation is not controllable, at least from within, by deliberate policy or 'crisis-management'. In fact, relative uncontrollability is one of its main characteristics.

That not every such situation has a revolutionary outcome is obvious. Indeed, the infrequency of revolutions compared to potential revolutionary crises suggests that the odds are against such an outcome. (Gurr in Jänicke 1973a.) The absence of one or more constituents of a 'revolutionary situation' may be fatal to its prospects. In no country was the rebellion of the masses more impressive than in Colombia 1930–48, for it reached the point of spontaneous combustion: the assassination of a charismatic popular leader led to an immediate insurrection of the capital, joined by the police, which destroyed large parts of the city, while in the provinces revolutionary committees seized power in various towns and held it for some weeks without quite knowing what to do. Yet, for reasons still hotly debated by the few historians to take an interest in that remote country, or recognize its significance for the analysis of modern revolutions, the outcome was not a transfer of or even a serious challenge to power, but almost twenty years of unstructured civil strife and massacre, known (for want of a more specific term) as *la violencia*.[20] When the outcome is likely to be a revolution it cannot be determined retrospectively, as the outcome is then known. Counter-factual exercises to this effect should not be confused with the assertion that another outcome than that which occurred was actually available. Nevertheless, an analysis of realistic contemporary estimates, e.g. of the unlikelihood of revolutionary outcome of the 1929–33 crisis in the industrial countries, or the expectation of revolution in tsarist Russia, may advance historical understanding. More generally, it may be suggested that a comparative analysis of crises which might have been expected to lead to revolution but did not, and of 'failed' revolutions, is at present more useful than further collection of case-studies of actual revolutions.

V

I do not propose here to discuss the political evolution or 'stages' of revolutions after their outbreak, though this evidently forms the bulk of actual historical work done in the field (e.g. *c.* 86 per cent of Furet and Richet, 1973, *c.* 80 per cent of Soboul 1962), and attempts to establish 'stages' – mostly cyclical – have sometimes been made (Brinton 1938, Stone 1972, pp. 20–2). Variations are too numerous for other than empty generalization, though we may note in passing that the differentiation between 'Eastern' and 'Western' types, depending on whether the transfer of power comes early or late (Huntington 1968) does not seem fundamental. It may be more useful to set work in this field in the context of the consequences of revolution. This implies discussing their 'conclusion'.

How they end seems to have interested recent students much less than how they begin, though there is a large literature about revolutions which have failed – e.g. 1848–9, 1918–19 – which inevitably considers their end. However, except in so far as 'failure' implies a definition of 'success', this leaves the problem of the outcome of successful revolutions open. Obviously, the minimum condition of success is the establishment and maintenance of state power or its equivalent. Recent studies, increasingly – and rightly – stressing the role of the modern territorial state as the defining element of any kind of historical development, and perhaps an important or even essential motor, have concentrated on the role of revolutions, or for that matter revolutionary parties which tend to transform themselves into power-structures, as generators of strong state power. (See Dunn 1972, p. 249; Lewis 1974, p. 15; and especially Skocpol 1979a, pp. 7–15; Skocpol 1979b *passim.*) Nobody could possibly underestimate the state-generating and state-strengthening functions of revolutions. Yet they do not exhaust the question of their outcome, except where the objects and functions of a revolution are defined merely as the establishment of state power where previously none existed ('national independence') or the re-establishment of functioning state power after a period of breakdown.

What any of the lists of 'great revolutions', such as Skocpol's (1979b, p. 287),[21] have in common specifically is not state power, but state power devoted to creating a 'new framework' and orientation for its society. The arguments about whether some 'great revolution' was 'necessary' (e.g. Runciman 1983) hinge not on a denial that it generated or strengthened state power, but on a denial that, considering pre-revolutionary trends, developments in society would in any significant way have been different even without a revolution. A revolution which cannot claim to have at least attempted to establish such a 'new framework' is not likely to be listed. Such a framework may be defined for our purposes, in the modern era, as a stable set of institutional arrangements within an effective state, based upon forces capable of maintaining both the regime and their control of it, and imposing a certain character and orientation upon subsequent autonomous national development, subject to the state's power and resources.[22]

Are these system-carrying forces social groups, defined ethnically or otherwise (e.g. 'classes')? Can they also be institutions (e.g. armies, parties, etc.) which replace social groups in situations of balance or weak class development? To what extent do institutionally defined elites themselves become social groups with their own interests – as suggested by Djilas (1957)? These are ideologically sensitive and highly controversial questions into which there is no need to enter, though one may note in passing that a comprehensive Marxist treatment of such questions appears to be lacking, in spite of some concrete case-studies (Abd el Malek 1968, Rodinson 1972, esp. pp. 623ff). Whatever the nature of the system-carrying forces, the point is that when most protracted revolutionary processes begin (e.g. at the moment when the old regime ends), such forces are rarely in being, at least for practical purposes. They gradually emerge from the ruins of the old regime, as in China and Mexico in the course of the first half of the present century. Those who seek for a self-conscious, let alone organized 'bourgeoisie' seeking to make a 'bourgeois revolution' *before* such a revolution, are likely to be disappointed. In extreme cases, such as Mexico, not even hindsight can detect the effective agents of revolutionary transformation in the early phases of the revolution. As Vernon observes (Vernon 1963, p. 63), 'No disciplined cadre existed to play the role of the Bolsheviks; no common philosophy prevailed in revolutionary circles; no military group was altogether dominant.'

From some successful revolutions no dominant force, orientation, or effective state institutions have emerged, either because the dominant social group may not require a state policy of national development, or because no post-revolutionary force establishes decisive supremacy over the rest.

The first case may arise when the major thrust of the revolution is negative, as when its primary object is to eliminate an objectionable (often foreign) superstructure, political or socio-economic, and no other changes are believed to be requisite. In such – usually archaic – situations a ruling class, e.g. of landowners, may rest content with a *de facto* national anarchy which allows its members to control, or to compete for control over, the regions and territories which are of immediate interest to them. Much more rarely, a population of peasants and small independent producers believes that it needs only to remove a superstructure of exploiters and oppressors which appears to be irrelevant to its economy or communal organization (see Womack 1969, ch. 8, for such a short-lived emergence of a regional peasant democracy.) At state level the result may be the familiar caricature regimes of much of nineteenth-century Latin America, characterized by formal constitutional innovation, rhetoric, little social and economic change, and endemic political instability at the top. Such negative revolutions may even, as in Great Colombia

1819–30 and Central America 1821–39, lead to the fragmentation of states.

The second case produces the more interesting result of compromise solutions or 'incomplete revolutions'. Familiar examples occur when, for instance, new regimes like Kemalist Turkey are unable to establish effective control over the agrarian sector in largely rural countries (cf. Dunn 1972; R. D. Robinson 1963). Thus the Bolivian revolution of 1952 was undoubtedly a major and successful social revolution, but no post-revolutionary force has been able to establish unquestioned control. All, including even the revived army, have been able to do no more than to manoeuvre between politico-economic groups, none of which can be eliminated from the contest, but none of which is able – or, in the case of the peasantry, willing – to establish a stable hegemony alone or in coalition.[23] What the Bolsheviks succeeded in doing in the 1920s and 1930s no force has been able to achieve in the not wholly dissimilar Bolivian situation after 1952.

Compromise solutions may not necessarily be incomplete or truncated revolutions. They need not therefore inhibit the substantial reorientation of historical development and the construction of a positive new framework. It is quite possible that, in the course of the unpredictable and uncontrollable mass mobilizations which are so characteristic of revolutions, and so essential for preventing defeat and the relapse into restored old regimes (see Bergeron 1968, p. 602), a force capable of controlling development may nevertheless emerge. A group or interest may establish hegemony over allies remaining subaltern, such as the Mexican working-class in the Mexican Revolution (see Jean A. Meyer 1970). Or, as in France, it can settle for concessions to other groups, such as the peasantry which, while possibly distorting or slowing down the new developments, do not actually prevent them (see Lefebvre 1933; Furet and Richet 1966, 2; Chevalier 1967). This is highly relevant to the problem of what would today be called 'land reform', both after and perhaps before revolutions, in both would-be capitalist and would-be socialist regimes. As we shall see, 'bourgeois' revolutions are probably better suited to compromise settlements than others are. However, it may be argued that historically such solutions are probably usual, even when theoretically inadmissible. The abandonment of wholesale collectivization in the agrarian sector of parts of Eastern Europe after the middle 1950s may be regarded in this light.

Whatever the nature of the revolutionary solution, there comes a time when the period of convulsion gives way to post-revolutionary history. It cannot do so unless the (or a) revolutionary regime survives and no longer risks overthrow from within or without. Revolutions cannot be said to 'conclude' until they have either been overthrown or are sufficiently safe from overthrow. When this moment has been reached is sometimes difficult to establish. Almost certainly the Cuban revolution of 1959 was internally safe from the start, but, though the Bay of Pigs (1961) confirmed this, it would hardly have led us to suppose that the USA would abandon serious attempts to overthrow it by force for the next quarter-century. At most it demonstrated that such an overthrow would henceforth imply a fairly substantial war. Can we say that the Cristero civil war of the 1920s seriously put the Mexican revolution of 1911 at risk (cf. Jean A. Meyer 1974)? Probably not, but one can hardly consider a regime stable which has to face a substantial and lengthy counter-revolutionary civil war over a large part of its territory. Still, the end of effective threats to the new regime provides us with a minimum criterion for ending the period of revolution. A maximum criterion is the establishment of the 'new framework' within which the country's historical evolution henceforth takes place. Here, as we shall see, dating may also be problematic. Perhaps this is one reason why historians and political scientists have been as reluctant to ask questions about the conclusion of revolutions as they have been eager to ask questions about their origins and outbreak. And, indeed, there has been much uncertainty in this matter, as witness the different dates chosen on varying grounds by historians of the French revolution: mainly 1794 (Mathiez 1921, Thompson 1944, Goodwin 1953, Sydenham 1965) or 1799 (Lefebvre 1963, Soboul 1962, Furet and Richet 1973; see also Schmitt in Schieder 1973).

Where the aim of revolution is merely negative, as in the case of risings for national independence or the overthrow of tyranny, the problem may seem simple. The Irish revolution 'ended' with the defeat of the Republicans in the Civil War of 1922–3, which confirmed the Treaty of 1921. Yet even in such apparently transparent cases, some caution is advisable. Liberation may lend itself to official dating (especially in countries given to naming their streets after such dates), but it rarely exhausts the content or history of revolutions.

Though dating is fuzzy and uncertain, we are on relatively firm ground when revolutions 'end' because they can visibly go no further, i.e. when they have come up against the limits of their capacity to secure change, given the post-revolutionary configuration of forces.

In this sense the Bolivian revolution 'ended' sometime between 1952 and the coup of 1964, the Algerian revolution a few years after independence, with the victory of Colonel Boumedienne. Both these events clearly mark the end of period of socio-economic experimentation and the opening of a new era in their country's history – of endemic political instability in the first case, of stable government in the second. Only the historian's ultimate weapon, hindsight, enables us to call such dates 'terminal'. They did not seem so at the time, and argument about them is always possible. However, in long retrospect we can detect analogous limits to revolutionary transformation more confidently. Thus it can be argued that all the instability and the upheavals of Spanish nineteenth-century history took place within the general type of socio-economic and institutional regime established by the 1820 revolution, and did not seriously modify it, even though the victory of liberalism was abortive (Carr 1966). Most historians would also agree, against Fontana (Fontana 1971, p. 291), that the chances of a great or more permanent triumph of 'bourgeois liberalism' in Spain after 1820 were negligible.

The problem of dating is more intractable, where the limits of the revolution's historical achievement are not so clearly defined, i.e., when the revolutionary transformation is clearly not complete, and continues after the moment when the actual survival of the new regime is no longer in doubt. It is of course possible to date the 'end' of the Russian or Mexican revolutions in this manner – e.g. at the conclusion of the Russian civil war (Chamberlain 1935) or the triumph of President Obregon (Atkin 1969). Yet at these dates neither the permanent pattern of the new society and its institutions, nor the lasting re-orientation of its subsequent development had yet emerged. Of course from this moment on there may be unbroken political continuity, and subsequent development is embedded within a permanent state and party organization for ruling the country (as in Russia, China or Cuba), though the situation in Mexico remained rather more undefined for a number of years after 1920. Yet there can be no doubt that the mere establishment of a permanent structure of power is not an adequate criterion. The Russian Revolution, in the sense of the lasting transformation of Russian society and its institutions, had hardly begun at the moment when it became clear that the regime was secure, and that no force other than the Communist party would henceforth determine it.

Moreover, even where the revolution henceforth continues, as it were, exclusively, 'from above', a purely political criterion is inadequate. For, even where an all-powerful authority sets out to implement a preconceived programme (e.g. the construction of a socialist society), the process will almost certainly produce unintended results. The most controlled and planned construction of a new framework – as e.g. in Soviet Russia – leads to consequences which are far from the intentions of the constructors, but which can, in retrospect, be seen to be highly characteristic of that new framework. The enormous all-pervasive control by party/state power concentrated at the apex of the system, was demonstrably not what Lenin had in mind (cf. Barfield 1971). In any case, as the history of the USSR, and even more clearly, China demonstrates, there may be profound disagreements among the constructors about what the pre-conceived and agreed policy-objectives imply, and the means of carrying them out. There are also cases, both of socialist and non-socialist revolutions, in which the actual nature of the transformation they achieve is initially quite unclear, and largely, or even entirely, determined by developments after the transfer of power. This is so, it has been argued, in the case of Cuba after 1959 (J. and V. Martinez-Alier 1972, pp. 67–73, ch. 5; O'Connor 1970), and demonstrably so in Mexico (Cumberland 1952). In short, the subsequent transformation of a country is not the simple corollary of establishing a permanent, effective or even irremovable new regime. To this extent there may be, historically speaking, no fundamental difference between revolutions presided over by a continuous body of new rulers (e.g. the Russian communist party) and a protracted and intermittent process, as in France after 1789.

However, there may be a fundamental difference between the revolutions of the era of bourgeois liberalism (and perhaps earlier revolutions, if they are accepted as such), and the revolutions of the twentieth century.

By now some consensus about the revolutions of the bourgeois-liberal period is perhaps possible. Their consequence, at all events in Europe, was a general orientation towards a capitalist type of economy, which was developed with varying degrees of success. The policy-determining or hegemonic group (using the word in its Gramscian sense, see Gramsci 1971) was likely to be an actual class of entrepreneurs, since the operations of such an economy rested on a body of individuals of this kind (cf. Hobsbawm 1975, ch. 13), whatever the role of state protection and state promotion in economic development. (Cf. Gerschenkron 1962, pp. 21–2).

This does not mean that we need to accept the simple-minded model of 'bourgeois revolution' as a conscious political operation by a 'bourgeoisie', conscious of itself as a class and formed as such under the old regime, which struggled for power against an old ruling class standing in the way of the establishment of the institutions of a 'bourgeois society'. As the never-ending debate on the French Revolution shows, this model is plainly inadequate. Paradoxically, it may tell us more about later nineteenth-century revolutions, taught by the French Revolution what a 'bourgeois revolution' should be like, and in which self-conscious entrepreneurial groups of liberal bourgeois, with something like a coherent politico-economic programme, played a part – e.g. in Germany in and after 1848. How far such classes were already in existence, how far created or formed into self-conscious groups in the course of, or after, the actual revolutions which may be regarded as functionally 'bourgeois-liberal', are questions to be settled case by case.[24] It is equally impossible to generalize *a priori* about the degree to which the older elites or ruling classes had actually to be eliminated or extruded from the process of decision-making, or how far they could adapt to the functions of a bourgeoisie in the new economy – an adaptation from which they might derive considerable advantages. In fact, such adaptation, and a consequent symbiosis between, e.g., a landed aristocracy and an entrepreneurial bourgeoisie or liberalism and ancient monarchy, was common, and quite compatible with the hegemonic status of 'bourgeois' ideas (cf. for France, Zeldin 1973, ch. 1). Britain in the eighteenth–twentieth centuries is an obvious case in point. It is a mistake to see such symbioses necessarily as a 'persistence of the old regime' (Mayer 1981) or as necessarily indicating a functional failure to complete the 'bourgeois programme'.

In fact, since in a 'bourgeois' society the operations of the economy and of 'civil society' (Gramsci 1965, pp. 481–2) were largely independent of state power, though relying on conditions which the state alone was capable of establishing, a certain heterogeneity was to be expected. 'Dual power' (to use Lenin's phrase about the coexistence of soviets and the provisional government in 1917, which he rightly saw as incompatible) could, as it were, be permanent. A plainly bourgeois society – nineteenth-century Britain – could, without serious problems, be governed by hereditary peers. How far or when (if ever) the bourgeoisie actually took the place of the specialized personnel of rule and administration therefore also requires specific case-study. (Cf. for Britain, Guttsman 1963, Vincent 1966.)

It may also be agreed that a largely 'self-acting' capitalist economy and 'civil society' required a set of institutions broadly definable as 'liberal' (cf. Moore 1966, p. 429), within the political limits which protected the system from jeopardy. The most obvious aim of revolutions in the bourgeois-liberal era was the construction of states with such systems of institutions (typically embodied in a constitution and suitable systems of law). Why the political system best suited to such societies should have been universally identified with assemblies of elected representatives is not altogether clear: other arrangements are quite compatible with bourgeois society. There are, of course, powerful historical reasons, deriving from the struggles against monarchs and a hereditary nobility, why elected assemblies, being organs for the control of governments rather than for government, should have become crucially important. Given the relatively modest role of executive government in the bourgeois-liberal era of capitalism, such constitutions seemed both desirable and practicable and, indeed, provided an important element of political flexibility.

The unlimited extension of election and civic rights was widely recognized as being implicit in liberalism, not least by de Tocqueville (1835–40, 1, Preface), and 'bourgeois democracy' therefore came to be accepted as a preliminary to their own by such socialists as thought in political terms. By the same token, in the classical bourgeois-liberal period the actual 'democratic republic' was considered politically risky, and therefore remained rare. Constitutions with more limited electorates were the norm until the late nineteenth and early twentieth centuries. Nevertheless, in so far as 'bourgeois society' was instituted by revolutions and in the light of the experiences of revolutions from the seventeenth to the mid-twentieth centuries, an ideal type of such a revolution and of the subsequent regime or framework could be constructed, and actual ones could be at least notionally measured against it. Revolutions aiming at any result other than a 'bourgeois society' and its characteristic form of economic development were unlikely to be recognized as belonging to the genus. They could be excluded as negative rebellions, like the Carlist wars in Spain (Carr 1966, pp. 184–5), extruded into the realm of deviancy and the *fait-divers* (Hobsbawm 1959; Tilly in Lewis 1974, p. 284), or simply fitted into some relation to the main process (Hertz-Eichenrode 1966). What a revolution was supposed to achieve, and the sort of institutions it was supposed to create, seemed to be generally understood. Conversely, it also seemed clear what changes – often profound enough to be regarded as a 'revolution from above' (cf. Engelberg 1974) – had to be undertaken by statesmen who wished to adapt an old regime to the nineteenth century rather than to fall victims to revolution.

The revolutions which have taken place during the general crisis of the twentieth century belong to a period when the 'great transformation' of the globe (Polanyi 1945) could no longer take place, or continue, primarily through the market-mechanism of liberal-bourgeois society. Even in so far as such revolution remained committed to maximum techno-economic growth as the source of socially beneficent results, neither the free-market liberal, nor any other single recipe for ensuring the wealth of nations, was any longer universally accepted. Moreover, between 1905 and 1917 the formerly general view among socialist and communist revolutionaries, that bourgeois-democratic revolutions and regimes were necessary preconditions for post-bourgeois ones, was abandoned. Neither the revolutions of this century nor the regimes which came out of them can be judged against a single idea type. Indeed, there is not even much agreement about whether the most influential revolutionary family of the century, the 1917 revolution and its descendants, has established a new kind of social order, or whether they have merely carried on the industrializing and 'modernizing' transformations, as it were, minus a bourgeoisie. Moreover, the old common ground of 'economic development' has itself recently been put into question in the richest countries, and perhaps also by the apparently strongly utopian component in Chinese revolutionary thought which has sometimes prevailed (Meisner in Lewis 1974). How significant these trends are, is unclear. Since Saint-Just's idealization of austerity, periods of temporary hardship, not to mention policy failure, during revolutions have occasionally been interpreted by ideologues as short-cuts to utopia: one thinks of episodes during Russian 'war communism' (cf. Roberts 1970) and the 'simultaneous construction of socialism and communism' in the Cuba of the late 1960s. Still, there is probably rather more than sour grapes in the anti-industrialism of current revolutionary ideologies, and it cannot be so easily neglected as its occasional nineteenth-century predecessor (Paniagua Fuentes 1974).

Historical judgement on these revolutions, and indeed on the variously mixed economies and regimes which have emerged from the turmoil of the twentieth century, is thus unusually difficult. It is complicated by the fact that most twentieth-century revolutions have occurred in economically backward or dependent countries (cf. Geyer 1967). Only three generalizations can be safely made about them. First, that *some* of these regimes, namely those which have eliminated private employment from the economy, except for peasant agriculture and the self-employed, cannot reasonably be called 'capitalist' or 'bourgeois' in any sense. To this extent some of the new societies must be described as non-capitalist. Second, in the great majority of them the political pattern of representative democracy has proved neither lasting nor viable.[25] Third, in countries under new revolutionary regimes the official machine of state or state/party institutions has usually played a decisive role, even where the societies eventually produced by revolution are clearly based on the private accumulation of wealth (Mexico). This applies not only to its control and economic functions, but to its functions in assisting the emergence of, or generating new elites, or absorbing old ones. In states which permit or encourage private enterprise, the 'public sector' may function as an organ of primary accumulation, which is distributed among those in a position to divert it to private use. In states where private accumulation is not permitted or recognized, the role of the state in generating new elites is even more direct. Where (for a time?) the entire set of a country's elites is expected to belong to a single organization, such as a state-party, as in the USSR, post-revolutionary changes in the composition of that organization become highly significant. (Cf. Carr 1950–78, 6, pp. 177–230; Procacci 1974.)

The criteria for establishing the end of the revolutionary period are therefore different in each of the two main types, or phases, of modern revolution.

The 'conclusion' of liberal-bourgeois revolutions may be said to have been the moment when, the permanency of the new regime being assured, the politico-legal conditions were established which permitted and encouraged a largely informal development through the play of private forces to proceed. The state and state action were no doubt essential, and in fact a nation-wide state, usually stronger than that of the old regime, normally resulted from such revolutions, though the emphasis was on the internal limits of state power and state action, so that historians have sometimes paid little attention to the actual increase in the liberal state's scope and efficiency. The state was perceived as an ancillary to civil society. By the same token, the construction of a politico-legal system was the most clearly perceived objective of such revolutions – typically, in the form of a 'constitution', which allowed the more or less free play of post-revolutionary politics, seen as a sort of counterpart to the free play of the market and such other unofficial mechanisms as determined the operations of civil society. The main outlines of such a system could emerge very quickly. 'Free enterprise France was born' in 1790–1 (Furet and Richet 1973, p. 124), and 1791, broadly speaking, sketched out the framework to which France tended to revert, in a more or less restricted or extended form, throughout much of the nineteenth century, after the various peripeties of its revolutionary history. More precisely, the French Revolution 'had done its work' when we can determine which of its consequences remained substantially permanent or proved irreversible, e.g. when it had created the institutional framework of state administration, as shaped by Napoleon, and the element of constitutional electoral politics which never disappeared from sight after 1815. Our judgement of nineteenth-century French society would not be fundamentally different if its regime had remained that of Louis XVIII which was a weak version of 1791. But our judgement of the Russian Revolution of 1917 or the Mexican Revolution of 1911 would be very different indeed if they had not been followed by the Stalin or Cardenas periods, or some equivalent phase of translating revolutionary potentiality into post-revolutionary actuality. And, for want of sufficiently long retrospect, it is still not possible to tell whether the post-Maoist phase of Chinese development represents 'the end' – i.e. the lasting post-revolutionary shape – of Chinese society.

Liberal-bourgeois revolutions, then, paid enormous attention to the elaboration of political constitutions, but otherwise left development to itself. Post-liberal revolutions, on the contrary, even when not dedicated to the construction of non-capitalist societies, have needed to develop elaborate institutions of public power, administration, planning and national development from the outset. But the precise nature of their tasks and of the means required to carry them out was unclear because unprecedented, or because revolutionary regimes, like others, tend to repeat the failures of their predecessors under the impression that they were, or must lead to, successes. Consequently the permanent shape of the post-revolutionary society was more likely to emerge only after a period of experiment, groping, and changing of courses. In this sense post-liberal revolutions, whatever their various natures, require a good deal more by way of development after the transfer of power to be considered 'at an end'. Nineteenth-century France was largely implicit in the institutions of 1791, but the USSR of Brezhnev and Chernenko was not equally discernible in 1918, or indeed at any time before the middle or later 1930s.

On the other hand, post-liberal revolutions have normally downgraded, or neglected the politico-legal framework of constitution and politics, on which liberal-bourgeois revolutions concentrated their attention. Constitutions themselves may be of little importance, as witness the irrelevance of Soviet state and party constitutions to much of what has happened in that country, or the long-lasting uncertainty about the very formal constitutional structure of, say, China and Cuba. The actual structure of political decision may be quite obscure, even when it is known that there are recognized mechanisms for it, as witness the uncertainty, even of political scientists, about the actual way in which Mexican presidential candidates are chosen, before they are triumphantly elected by a pre-established majority. Post-liberal revolutions have usually made no attempt to institutionalize the politics of competition, bargaining and debate, though they have generally found it unavoidable to institutionalize the balance between such groups as nationalities (as in the USSR and Yugoslavia). In this respect post-liberal revolutions are not so much incomplete as deficient. The space of politics is left void. In the most rigid one-party or confessional regimes, there is no formal place for them at all. Politics naturally persist, as they must, but they take place and evolve either behind the scenes, within the ruling party or in the manner of court intrigues, or else in a way reminiscent of what happens during revolutions, i.e. as a series of confrontations and compromises between more or less irresistible forces and more or less immovable objects. (One might regard the Maoist perspective of a secular evolution of such regimes through an endless series of post-revolutionary revolutions as a special case of this.)

In fact, such regimes acquire their own established pattern of politics. Pluralist bargaining may be institutionalized within a one-party system by the representation of corporate interests, as in the Mexican Institutional Revolutionary Party.[26] Within the 'democratic centralism' of state parties, the emphasis may – at least on occasions – shift away from centralism to allow the nominal democracy to emerge or re-emerge, as in Czechoslovakia, 1968. Or else, as for long periods in Poland, *de facto* direct action, active or passive, may be recognized as capable of changing government policy, so long as it operates within the system or the international constraints upon it. The fact remains that while such regimes pay enormous and constant attention to the policies of national development, to their institutions, and to the selection of their personnel ('cadres decide everything', as Stalin said), their politics have been left to work themselves out by processes whose very obscurity and lack of formalization, reminiscent of court, ecclesiastical and corporate office politics, are significant.

I have so far considered the 'end' of revolutions in terms which require some sense of their historical functions. Is it possible to devise criteria so objective as to convince a hypothetical observer who is uninterested in the historical changes they bring about, but merely wishes to measure or date, the social equivalent, as it were, of an earthquake? Where revolutions have led to major social and economic disruption, the time when this has been overcome – e.g. when population and production regain their pre-revolutionary level – may help in dating the change. Thus in Mexico population appears to have recovered between 1930 and 1940,[27] while the Soviet population seems to have regained its pre-revolutionary level by 1930. Fortunately not all revolutionary periods are so destructive.

More directly relevant may be the date when the first adult generation of 'children of the revolution' emerge on the public scene, those whose education and careers belong entirely to the new era. This is both more visible and more easily measured in the great state-planned revolutions of our century, especially when combined with dramatic events such as the Soviet purges of the 1930s or the Chinese 'Cultural Revolution' of 1965–75. (Both, it will be noted, occurred about twenty years after the transfer of power.) Such changings of the guard are not confined to revolutionary regimes, though revolutions normally accentuate them. They may play an unusually important role in revolutions which require both substantial and accelerated social mobility, and to transform revolutionary organizations and movements originally recruited for different roles, and in different circumstances, into organs of government and national leadership. The USSR is a case in point (see Rigby 1968; Fitzpatrick 1979a, 1979b). For the 'children of the revolution', the finished revolution is, by definition, a historical datum. It is where they start from. Its events come to them through others, even its aspirations reach them only in the forms mediated by the historical record, and the official doctrine and rhetoric of the regime and its critics or opponents, and distanced by the ideological selection of memory. It is in the highest degree unlikely that the Jacobin Republic, the famous 'Year II' could have become an inspiration to any large movement of French democrats not born well after its defeat. It is historically apposite that Stalin should have published a tissue of evident fictions about the Russian Revolution as its offically canonical history, twenty-one years after 1917. The revolution is plainly 'over' when a generation has taken charge which knows of the revolution only at second hand.

In the last analysis, however, the historian anxious to determine the length of revolutions, and the point at which they give way to post-revolutionary development, can only fall back on hindsight. We know that a new regime is permanent, when it has demonstrated the capacity to resist internal challenges, and has not been overthrown for a sufficient time. We know revolutions are over, when the general pattern or 'framework' set up at one point in their history has not been fundamentally altered for a sufficiently long time, though this need not exclude quite significant changes within it. The 'rules of the game' in this sense have been unchanged for half a century in both the USSR and Mexico. If either system were to be overthrown now, it would be the outcome of tensions generated within a post-revolutionary society.

By the same token, the historian must, to some extent, fall back on empiricism or tautology in judging the historical achievement of revolutions. In so far as some responsibility for subsequent changes can be assigned to a revolution, what it achieves is what actually emerges after it, irrespective of intention. Indeed, some of the most obvious consequences of revolution are quite specifically *not* part of anyone's programme, as notably when pre-revolutionary characteristics are, as it were, preserved against subsequent change by its intervention. This curious dialectic of revolution and conservation is familiar: 'traditional' Germany is in many ways more recognizable in the German Democratic Republic than in the Federal Republic. In short, Balzac's France may not have been in the mind of those who made the French Revolution, but that is what came out of it, and must therefore be regarded as its historical result. Intention and programme are relevant to the historian only in two ways: in so far as they provide a theme for political discourse in post-revolutionary society, and in so far as we ourselves wish to assess the feasibility of the revolutionary programme and the extent to which it was, or could have been, realized. As for the second question, intentionality is merely a special case of such an inquiry. We may analyse, for example, the failure of the Risorgimento to attempt or achieve the historical results of other comparable sets of historical events, without judging the intentions of its participants (Gramsci 1975, pp. 2010–34, 2035–46, 2048–54; Caracciolo 1963;

Salomone 1971). As for the first, it is an evident result of revolutions that subsequent politics cannot but refer back to them, and are often largely fought out in terms of the political and ideological positions then formulated. In this sense the nineteenth century cannot be understood except in terms of the political discourse established by the French Revolution, the twentieth century except in terms of the Russian Revolution.

VI

A final question may be briefly raised. In so far as a choice is conceivable, what difference does it make whether the transformation of 'an epoch of revolutions' takes place through revolution in the Griewank sense (see above p. 9), i.e. something like insurrectionary upheavals, or otherwise. For it is evident that the most drastic and far-reaching measures to change institutions or reorient policy and development can be, and have been, brought about by decree from above, whether by established rulers (as in the Meiji Restoration in Japan), by conquerors (as by the US occupying authority in post-1945 Japan), or by post-revolutionary governments (as by Stalin in the period of collectivization and the first Five Year Plan). Whether we choose to call such changes 'revolutions from above' or not, and how far, in any given situation, such changes are more likely to be undertaken, are questions which need not be considered here. Nor need we consider if or under what circumstances equally drastic and far-reaching changes may be achieved by processes of gradual transformation, though it is clear that these must operate on a different time-scale.

Changes achieved by revolution are indeed likely to aim at a more radical transformation, and to be much more uncontrollable, but this does not prove that revolutions are indispensable. They are, however, probably unique in one respect: in the subjective effects of mass mobilization on those whom they mobilize. This subjective effect of revolutions on those involved may be so profound that it may, at least for a time, achieve wholesale changes of values, and efforts to achieve new goals, which are not otherwise practicable (see Wertheim 1974, p. 220; Lipset and Solari 1967, pp. 37, 40). Indeed, in our time even traditional types of mobilization, such as the religious and the military (see Nettl 1967, p. 125), have tended – as in nationalism – to fuse with, and to adopt the modes of revolutionary mobilization. This suggests that in societies characterized by mass participation, or requiring active participation in carrying out drastic changes of structure and goals, revolution is not merely one means of achieving such breakthroughs, but in some ways uniquely suited to this purpose. At this point the analysis of revolutions as moments of historical change and the analysis of revolutionary movements and individuals coincide. It is probably the only point at which they necessarily do.

The most profound effects of revolutionary expectation on human personality – utopian or millennial confidence in the possibility, indeed the actuality, of total change (Hobsbawm 1959, ch. 4) – clearly do not often occur on a vast scale, and tend, in general, to be short-lived. They are generally confined to particular groups of the population, and especially to a relatively small cadre of political activists. Where the revolutionary struggle is one of minorities amid a largely passive, though perhaps sympathetic, population – as in Ireland (see Bowden in Elliott-Bateman 1974; Townshend 1983) – the inspiring force of revolution can hardly be expected to extend beyond such cadre-groups. Still, the revolutions of France, Vietnam and Iran certainly transformed the military effectiveness of mass armies in those countries, to the surprise of their adversaries. Nor would it be wise to underestimate the element of genuine, though by no means universal, mass enthusiasm for the construction of a new and better society, which helped to achieve some striking results in Eastern Europe in the decade after 1945.[28]

In one way or another this inspiration is likely to get lost as post-revolutionary regimes leave their original impetus behind. Where it does not evaporate, the 'revolutionary spirit' is nevertheless routinized and institutionalized, if not reduced to the rhetoric of civic anniversaries. How far, and to what extent, the change of values and their capacity to mobilize citizens are maintained – especially when the more utopian expectations are revealed as impracticable – requires historical analysis. What remains of the original revolutions, when the transformations they have brought about are taken for granted, and they have become components of a country's history? There is a wide range of possibilities, stretching from the revolutions which are no longer even rhetorically remembered – when did British politicians last refer to the 'Glorious Revolution'? – to those which remain permanent points of reference, as perhaps in the USA, or important elements in current political and ideological debate, as perhaps in France. Such investigations need not imply any belief in the realizability of the utopian hopes which inspire active revolutionaries, and at times whole peoples, and through which transformations are achieved which are no less historically significant for failing to be those expected and hoped for by the men and women who made, or set out to make, revolution. 'All historical experience', wrote Max Weber (cited in Meyer 1976, p. 176), 'confirms that men might not achieve the possible, if in this world they had not, time and again, reached out for the impossible.'

NOTES

1 For convenient guides, see Gurr 1970; Dunn 1972, v. Beyme 1973; G. P. Meyer 1976; Skocpol 1979b.

2 Cf. Dahrendorf 1961; Stone 1966; Rittberger 1971; Freeman 1972; Kramnick 1972; Zagorin 1973; G. P. Meyer 1976; Aya 1979.

3 If revolutions are 'violent' by definition, violence can be subsumed under other analytical headings in the case of historical breaks thus defined. (Cf. Bauman 1971, p. 27.) In any case, as Tilly, Tilly and Tilly (1975, p. 282) rightly note, 'the violent events are generally routine collective actions in which a second group – especially representatives of the state – intervenes to counteract [them]'.

4 Purely metaphorical or rhetorical uses of the term are not considered.

5 For the dogma, see Kuusinen 1961, p. 158; for its abandonment E. M. Staermann in Kossok 1971, pp. 19ff.

6 No clear line divides successful revolutions from situations in which power is seriously at risk but survives, but this causes problems only for those who wish to take censuses of revolution, mainly for the purpose of often rather trivial statistical compilation. (Cf. Calvert 1970a; Feierabend 1966; Feierabend, Feierabend and Nesvold 1969, 1973; Gurr in Graham and Gurr 1969.)

7 Galtung (Jänicke 1973a, pp. 121–2) is right in arguing that the belief in a 'society' (mostly meaning a nation-state) as the basis unit of revolution rests on the dual assumption that such a society is internally homogeneous and that structural change and subsequent defence and maintenance of the new system require the capture of power within whatever is the *de facto* unit of political decision-making. He is also right in arguing that in the last analysis whatever constitutes 'the world' is always the framework within which revolutionary phenomena must be analysed. But he is almost surely wrong in denying that there is a lower limit to the unit of possible revolution, short of 'any group of two'.

8 Germany (or both Germanies) provides an example of transformations achieved by a variety of often catastrophic events: wars won and lost, revolutions – 1848–9, 1918–19 – the Nazi period, etc.

9 'The principles of effective organisation are thus held to be more important than the appeals of Communist ideology or the frustrations of social and economic conditions' (Millikan in Pike 1966, p. vi). For an extreme example of this manipulative literature, inspired by the Vietnam war, see Leites and Wolff 1970.

10 W. Pietsch (1969) – see also T. H. Rigby (1974) – has shown the inadequacy of a view based on excessive preoccupation with the internal discussions within the Bolshevik Party.

11 It is not adequately studied by concentration on activist strata (e.g. Soboul 1964), institutions (e.g. Anweiler 1958), or even explosions of activity (Rudé 1959, 1964; Lefebvre 1933, 1973). Lags in participation, as by peasants (see Landsberger ed. 1974, p. 59), fluctuations and changes of alignment (as noted for ex-Zapatistas in the 1920s by Jean A. Meyer 1974) may not be clearly brought out even in brilliant monographs (cf. Womack 1969). For useful approaches see e.g. Ferro 1967, Malefakis 1970, Hufton 1971, Rougerie 1971, Shorter and Tilly 1974, Michelle Perrot 1974. R. Cobb's suggestion that 'popular militancy should not be defined only in its positive forms' (Cobb

1970, p. 104), like Lenin's reference to people 'voting with their feet', should not be neglected.

12 Cf., for the Irish revolution as a model for Burmese revolutionaries *c.* 1930–1, J. Badgley in Lewis 1974, p. 152, and as model of British assistance to continental resistance movements in the Second World War, M. R. D. Foot in Elliott-Bateman *et al.* 1974, p. 185; for French left-wing thought as a model in New Granada, Urrutia Montoya 1969, pp. 17ff.

13 Given the absence of major ruptures, there seems little point in taking it back to the 1870s, though a case can be made for this in terms of the breakdown of a liberal market economy and its corresponding 'civilization of capitalism'. Cf. Lichtheim 1972, pp. 29–30, Polanyi 1945, pp. 207–8.

14 For the international repercussions of this wave, see Halliday 1983, esp. pp. 86–104.

15 'Much of the recent literature on political development reflects to some degree or other the view that societies can be historically classified according to some variation of the three basic categories of "traditional", "transitional" and "modern".' L. Pye in Binder 1971, p. vii. For 'modernization' literature, see *IESS*, 10, art. 'modernization'; Weiner 1966.

16 For typical discussions, àpropos Italy 1943–5, see Kolko 1969, pp. 436–8; Claudin 1972, 2, pp. 402ff; Del Carria 1970, 2, ch. 20; Sereni 1971; Secchia 1971.

17 Lenin subsequently modified this formulation slightly, but not insignificantly (a) by omitting 'increasing misery' from his 1920 version (Marek 1966, p. 111), (b) by stressing the subjective readiness and determination of the activists among the workers for major change, (c) by stressing the necessity of the upper-class crisis to draw into action even the most backward sections of the masses, (d) by underlining the necessity of a strategy capable of neutralizing 'the inevitable oscillations' of intermediate classes and (e) by insisting on a significant degree of disintegration within the armed forces of the old regime (see Salvadori in Agosti 1974, p. 43), a point he had already stressed in 1905.

18 Brinton (1965, pp. 250ff) safeguards himself by calling these conditions 'prodromal symptoms', but, while some can probably claim to be no more than that (e.g. the 'transfer of allegiance of the intellectuals'), others are clearly envisaged as causal in the long or short term.

19 Where the bulk of the population remains outside the conflict, as in the Engish revolution (see Stone 1972, p. 145), or most revolutions for Latin American independence (see Lynch 1973, pp. 340–1), the term 'masses' can be used only for the active sectors of the population. However, the inactivity of larger sectors does not necessarily imply lack of involvement or sympathy (see Townshend 1983). Whether it does or not, requires concrete investigation.

20 For some general background, Dix 1967; on the insurrection, its aftermath and *la violencia*, Guzman *et al.* 1962; Guzman 1968; Alape 1982; Réndon 1983; Sanchez 1983; Sanchez and Meertens 1983.

21 France, Russia, China, Mexico, Yugoslavia, Vietnam, Algeria, Cuba, Bolivia, Angola, Mozambique, Guinea-Bissau, Ethiopia – to which, presumably, Iran would be added.

22 Such a 'new framework' may of course be imposed from outside by conquest, formal or informal domination, or economic dependence, and so may the orientation of development. This concerns us only in so far as it limits the

capacity of revolutions in small and weak countries to construct their own framework, or distorts it.

23 For a lucid summary, see Puhle 1970; for pre-revolutionary aspects of the problem, Lewis 1974.

24 For changes and recruitment during the revolution in France, the formation of group consciousness and transitional stages of group development, see Sentou 1969, 1970; Daumard 1970; Tudesq 1964.

25 In fact, the Irish Republic is the only example of a state born of twentieth-century revolution which has maintained such a pattern without any break. Even in Austria it was interrupted.

26 But cf. Gonzalez Casanova 1965, chs. 2–3, as against the official view in Cline 1962; see also Chirot 1980.

27 Global population had apparently more than regained the 1910 level by 1930 (Cline 1962, App., Table IV), but local studies are less sanguine (cf. Gonzalez y Gonzalez 1968, pp. 248; Cook and Borah 1968, Table 14; Perez Lisaur 1975).

28 Wajda's film *Man of Marble* catches this element even in the unpropitious environment of Stalinist Poland with great perception.

BIBLIOGRAPHY

Abd el Malek, Anouar: 1968. *Egypt, Military Society* (New York, Random House)

Abel, Wilhelm: 1955. *Die Wüstungen des ausgehenden Mittelalters* (2nd ed., Stuttgart, G. Fischer)

Adshead, S. A. M.: 1970. 'The Seventeenth Century Crisis in China' (*France-Asie*, 24/1, pp. 251–65)

Agosti, A., ed.: 1974. *Problemi di Storia dell'Internazionale Communista* (Turin, Einaudi)

Alape, Arturo: 1982. *Antecedentes y consecuencias historicas del 9 de abril* (11 vols., Bogotà)

Anweiler, O.: 1958. *Die Rätebewegung in Russland 1905–1921* (Leiden, E. J. Brill)

Aston, Trevor, ed.: 1965. *Crisis in Europe 1560–1660* (London, Routledge)

Atkin, Ronald: 1969. *Revolution! Mexico, 1910–1920* (London, Macmillan)

Aya, Rod: 1979. 'Theories of revolution reconsidered' (*Theory and Society*, 8/1, pp. 39–100)

Badgley, John: 1974. 'Burmese communist schisms' (in Lewis ed. 1974)

Bahne, Siegfried: 1967. 'Trotzkismus in Geschichte u. Gegenwart' (*Vierteljahrshefte f. Zeitgeschichte*, 15, pp. 58–86)

Barfield, R.: 1971. 'Lenin's utopianism: state and revolution' (*Slavic Review*, 30/1, pp. 45–56)

Bauman, Z.: 1971. 'Social dissent in east european politics' (*Archives Eur. de Sociologie*, 12/1, pp. 25–51)

Bergeron, L.: 1968. 'Une relecture ... de la Révolution française' (*Annales ESC*, 23/3, pp. 595–615)

v. Beyme, K., ed.: 1973. *Empirische Revolutionsforschung* (Opladen, Westdeutscher Verlag)

Binder, L., ed.: 1971. *Crises and Sequences in Political Development* (Princeton, N. J., Princeton University Press)
Bowden, Tom: 1974. 'Ireland: background to violence; decay of control; the impact of terror' (see Elliott-Bateman 1974)
Brinton, Clarence Crane: 1938. *The Anatomy of Revolution* (1965 ed., New York, Vintage Books)
Burckhardt, Jacob: 1929. 'Die geschichtlichen Krisen', in *Weltgeschichtliche Betrachtungen* (Gesamtausgabe 7, Munich, Rupprecht-Presse)
Burke, Edmund: 1790. *Reflections on the Revolution in France* (London, J. Dodsley, 1790, 1793)
Calvert, Peter: 1970a. *Revolution* (London, Macmillan)
1970b. *A Study of Revolution* (London, Pall Mall Press)
Caracciolo, Alberto, ed.: 1963. *La formazione dell'Italia industriale* (Bari, Biblioteca di Cultura Moderna)
Carr, E. H.: 1950–78. *A History of Soviet Russia*, 7 vols. (London, Macmillan)
Carr, Raymond: 1966. *Spain 1808–1939* (Oxford, Clarendon Press)
Carsten, F. L.: 1972. *Revolution in Central Europe, 1918–1919* (London, Maurice Temple Smith)
Chamberlain, W. H.: 1935. *The Russian Revolution, 1917–1921* (2 vols. London, Macmillan)
Chevalier, François: 1967. *The Ejido and Political Stability in Mexico* (see Veliz 1967)
Chirot, D.: 1980. 'The Corporatist Model and Socialism' (*Theory and Society*, 9, pp. 371–3)
Claudin, Fernando: 1972. *La crise du mouvement communiste* (2 vols., Paris, Maspero)
Cline, Howard, F.: 1962. *Mexico. Revolution to Evolution, 1940–1960* (Oxford, Oxford University Press)
Cobb, Richard: 1970. *The Police and the People: French Popular Protest 1789–1820* (Oxford, Clarendon Press)
Cook, Sherburne F., and Borah, Woodrow Wilson: 1968. *The Population of the Mixteca Alta 1520–1960* (Berkeley and Los Angeles, University of California Press)
Cordova, Arnaldo: 1975. *La formación del poder politico en México* (4th ed., Mexico, Ediciones Era)
Cumberland, Charles C.: 1952. *Mexican Revolution: Genesis under Madero* (Austin, University of Texas)
Cuoco, Vincenzo: 1929. *Saggio storico sulla rivoluzione napoletana nel 1799*, ed. F. Nicolini (Bari, Scrittori d'Italia)
Dahrendorf, Ralf: 1961. 'Uber einige Probleme der soziologischen Theorie der Revolution' (*Archives Européennes de Sociologie*, 2/1, pp. 153–620)
Daumard, Adeline: 1970. *La bourgeoisie de Paris au XIXe siècle* (Paris, Flammarion)
Davies, James C: 1962. 'Towards a theory of revolution' (*Amer. Sociol. Rev.*, 27, pp. 5–19)
1971. *When Men Revolt and Why. A Reader in Political Violence and Revolution* (London, Collier-Macmillan)
Debray, Régis: 1967. *Révolution dans la révolution? Lutte armée et lutte politique en Amérique Latine* (Paris, Maspero)
Del Carria, Renzo: 1970. *Proletari senza rivoluzione* (2 vols., Rome, Savelli)

Diaz del Moral, Juan: 1929. *Historia de las agitaciones campesinas andaluzas – Cordoba* (1967 ed., Madrid, Alianza editorial)
Dix, Robert H.: 1967. *Colombia: The Political Dimensions of Change* (New Haven and London, Yale University Press)
Djilas, Milovan: 1957. *The New Class* (London, Thames and Hudson)
Dunn, John: 1972. *Modern Revolutions: An Introduction to the Analysis of a Political Phenomenon* (Cambridge, Cambridge University Press)
Eckstein, Harry, ed.: 1964. *Internal War. Problems and Approaches* (London, Collier-Macmillan)
1965. 'Towards an etiology of internal wars' (*History and Theory*, 4/2, pp. 133–63)
Elliott-Bateman, Michael, *et al.*: 1974. *Revolt to Revolution: Studies in the 19th and 20th Century European Experience* (Manchester, Manchester University Press)
Engelberg, E.: 1974. 'Über die Revolution von oben', (*Ztschr. f. Gesch. wiss.* 22/2, pp. 1183–212)
Feierabend, Ivor K. and Rosalind L.: 1966. 'Aggressive behaviour within politics, 1948–1962: a cross-national study' (*Journ. of Conflict Resolution*, 10, pp. 249–71).
Feierabend, Ivor K., and R. L., and Nesvold, Betty K: 1969. 'Social change and political violence: cross-national patterns' (see Graham and Gurr 1969, pp. 632–870)
1973. 'The comparative study of revolution and violence' (*Comparative Politics*, 5, pp. 393–424)
Ferro, Marc: 1967. *La révolution de 1917* (2 vols., Paris, 'Collection historique')
Fitzpatrick, Sheila: 1979a. 'Stalin and the making of a new élite' (*Slavic Review*, 38/3, pp. 377–402)
1979b. *Education and Social Mobility in the Soviet Union (1921–1934)* (Cambridge, Cambridge University Press)
Fontana I. Lazaro, Josep: 1971. *La quiebra de la monarquia absoluta, 1814–1820* (Esplugues de Llobregat, Ediciones Ariel)
Foot, M. R. D.: 1974. 'Revolt, rebellion, revolution, civil war: the Irish experience' (see Elliott-Bateman 1974)
Forster, Robert, and Greene, Jack O., eds.: 1970. *Preconditions of Revolution in Early Modern Europe* (Baltimore, Johns Hopkins University Press)
Freeman, Michael: 1972. 'Review article: theories of revolution' (*Brit. Journ. of Polit. Science*, 2, pp. 339–59)
Furet, François, and Richet, Denis: 1965–6. *La Révolution* (2 vols., Paris, Fayard)
1973. *La Révolution française* (Paris, Fayard)
Galtung, Johann: 1973. 'Eine strukturelle Theorie der Revolution' (see Jänicke ed. 1973a)
Geiss, Imanuel, and Tamchina, Reiner eds.: 1974. *Ansichten einer künftigen Geschichtswissenschaft 2: Revolution – ein historischer Längsabschnitt* (Munich, Hanser)
Génicot, L.: 1966. 'Crisis: from the middle ages to modern times' (*Cambridge Economic History of Europe*) (2nd ed., 1, Cambridge, Cambridge University Press)
Gérard, Alice: 1970. *La Révolution française: mythes et interprétations, 1789–1970* (Paris, P.U.F.)

Gerschenkron, Alexander: 1962. *Economic Backwardness in Historical Perspective* (Cambridge, Mass., Harvard University Press)

Getzler, Israel: 1983. *Kronstadt 1917–1921. The Fate of a Soviet Democracy* (Cambridge, Cambridge University Press)

Geyer, Dietrich: 1967. 'Die russische Revolution als zeitgeschichtliches Problem' (*Vierteljahrshefte f. Zeitgeschichte*, 16, pp. 36–47)

Goldfrank, Walter L.: 1979. 'Theories of Revolution and Revolution without Theory: Mexico' (*Theory and Society*, 7/1 and 2, pp. 135–66)

Gonzalez Casanova, Pablo: 1965. *La democracia en Mexico* (Mexico D.F., Era)

Gonzalez y Gonzalez, Luis: 1968. *Pueblo en vilo, microhistoria de San José de Gracia* (Mexico D.F., El colegio de Mexico)

Goodwin, Albert: 1953. *The French Revolution* (London, Hutchinson)

Gottschalk, Louis: 1944. 'The causes of revolution' (*Amer. Journ. of Sociol.*, 1, pp. 1–8)

Graham, Hugh Davis, and Gurr, Ted Robert, eds.: 1969. *Violence in America: Historical and Comparative Perspectives. A Report Submitted to the National Commission on the Causes and Prevention of Violence* (New York, Signet Books)

Gramsci, Antonio: 1949. *Il Risorgimento* (Turin, Einaudi)

1971. *Selections from the Prison Notebooks*, ed. Quintin Hoare and Geoffrey Nowell-Smith (London, Lawrence and Wishart)

1975. *Lettere dal carcere*, ed. S. Caprioglio and E. Fubini (Turin, Einaudi)

Graus, F.: 1955. 'Die erste Krise des Feudalismus' (*Zeitschr. f. Geschichtswissenschaft*, 3/4, pp. 552–92)

Griewank, Karl: 1973. *Der neuzeitliche Revolutionsbegriff* (Frankfurt-am-Main, Suhrkamp)

Gurr, Ted Robert: 1970. *Why Men Rebel* (Princeton, N.J., Princeton University Press)

1973. *Vergleichende Analyse von Krisen und Rebellionen* (see Jänicke ed. 1973a)

Guttsman, W.: 1963. *The British Political Elite* (London, MacGibbon and Kee)

Guzman, German: 1968. *La violencia en Colombia* (Bogotà, Ediciones El Progreso)

Guzman, German, Fals Borda, O., and Umaña Luna E.: 1962. *La violencia en Colombia* (2 vols., Bogotà, Ediciones Tercer Mundo)

Halliday, Fred: 1983. *The Making of the Second Cold War* (London, Verso)

Handwörterburch d. Staatswissen schaften, 2nd ed. 1899. vol. II. art: Bauerngut (Jena, Gustav Fischer)

Haupt, Georges: 'La commune comme symbole et comme exemple' (*Le Mouvement Social*, 79, Apr.–June 1972, pp. 205–26)

Hertz-Eichenrode, D.: 1966. 'Marx über das Bauerntum und die Bündnisfrage' (*Int. Rev. of Social History* 11, pp. 382ff)

Heuss, A.: 1973. 'Das Revolutionsproblem in Spiegel der antiken Geschichte' (*Hist. Zeitschr.*, 216, pp. 1–72)

Hinton, James: 1973. *The First Shop Stewards' Movement* (London, Allen and Unwin)

Hobsbawm, E. J.: 1959. *Primitive Rebels* (1971 ed., Manchester, Manchester University Press)

1973. *Revolutionaries* (London, Weidenfeld and Nicolson)

1974. 'Labor History and Ideology' (*Journ. of Social Hist.*, 7/4, pp. 371–81)

1975. *The Age of Capital, 1848–1875* (London, Weidenfeld and Nicolson)
1984. *Worlds of Labour* (London, Weidenfeld and Nicolson)
Hroch, M., and Petráň, J.: 1982. *Das 17. Jahrhundert. Krise d. feudalen Gesellschaft* (Hamburg, Hoffmain und Campe)
Hufton, Olwen: 1971. 'Women in Revolution 1789–1796', (*Past and Present*, 53, pp. 90–108)
Huntington, Samuel: 1968. *Political Order in Changing Societies* (New Haven and London, Yale University Press)
IX International Congress of Historical Sciences, 1950, 1: Rapports
X International Congress of Historical Sciences, 1955, Relazioni, 5: Storia contemporanea
X International Congress of Historical Sciences, 1955, 6: Relazioni generali e supplementi
IESS: *International Encyclopedia of Social Sciences*, 1968 (New York, Macmillan)
Jänicke, Martin, ed.: 1973a. *Herrschaft und Krise: Beiträge zur politikwissenschaftlichen Krisenforschung* (Opladen, Westdeutscher Verlag)
1973b. *Krisenbegriff und Krisenforschung* (in Jänicke ed. 1973a)
Johnson, Chalmers: 1964. *Revolution and the Social System* (Stanford, Stanford University Press)
1968. *Revolutionary Change* (London, University of London Press)
Journal of Contemporary History, 1, 1966: International Fascism
Kirkham, James F., Levy, Sheldon G., Crotty, William J., eds.: 1970. *Assassination and Political Violence*: A Report to the National Commission on the Causes and Prevention of Violence (New York, Praeger)
Kolko, Gabriel: 1969. *The Politics of War: Allied Diplomacy and the World Crisis of 1943–45* (London, Weidenfeld and Nicolson)
Koselleck, R.: 1969. 'Der neuzeitliche Revolutionsbegriff als geschichtliche Kategorie' (in *Studium Generale*, 1, pp. 825–38)
Kossok, M., ed.: 1971. *Studien über die Revolution* (Berlin, Akademie-Verlag)
Kramnick, I.: 1972. 'Reflections on Revolution: Definition and Explanation in Recent Scholarship' (*History and Theory*, 11, pp. 26–63)
Kriegel, Annie: 1974. 'La crisi rivoluzionaria 1919–20: ipotesi per la costruzione di un modello' (see Agosti 1974)
Kuusinen, O. ed.: 1961. *Fundamentals of Marxism–Leninism* (London, Lawrence and Wishart)
Labrousse, E.: 1948. 'Comment naissent les révolutions' (*Actes du Congrès Hist. du Centenaire de la Rev. de 1848*, Paris)
Landsberger, Henry: 1967. 'The labor elite: is it revolutionary?' (see Lipset and Solari 1967)
ed.: 1974. *Rural Protest: Peasant Movements and Social Change* (New York and London, Harper and Row)
Lacqueur, Walter: 1968. *Revolution* (in *IESS* 1968)
Langer, William, L.: 1969. *Political and Social Upheaval, 1832–1852* (New York and London, Harper and Row)
Lefebvre, Georges: 1933. 'La Révolution française et les paysans' (in *Études sur la Révolution française*, Paris, P.U.F., 1954)
1963. *La Révolution française* (Paris, Peuples et Civilisations)
1973. *The Great Fear of 1789* (London, New Left Books)
Leiden, Carl, and Schmitt, Karl M: 1968. *The Politics of Violence: Revolution in the Modern World* (New York, Prentice-Hall)

Leites, N., and Wolff, Charles Jr: 1970. *Rebellion and Authority* (Chicago, Markham Publishing Co.)
Lenin, V. I.: 1936–8. *Selected Works* (12 vols., London, Lawrence and Wishart)
Lewis, John Wilson, ed.: 1974. *Peasant Rebellion and Communist Revolution in Asia* (Stanford, Stanford University Press)
Lichtheim, George: 1972. *Europe in the Twentieth Century* (London, Weidenfeld and Nicolson)
Lieuwen, Edwin: 1961. *Arms and Politics in Latin America* (New York, Praeger)
Lipset, S. M.: 1960. *Political Man. The Social Bases of Politics* (London, Heinemann)
Lipset, S. M., and Solari, Aldo, eds.: 1967. *Elites in Latin America* (New York, Oxford University Press)
Lynch, John: 1973. *The Spanish American Revolutions, 1808–1826* (London, Weidenfeld and Nicolson)
Malefakis, Edward E.: 1970. *Agrarian Reform and Peasant Revolution in Spain: Origins of the Civil War* (New Haven and London, Yale University Press)
Mao Tse-Tung: 1954. *Selected Works*, 3 (London, Lawrence and Wishart)
Marek, Franz: 1966. *Philosophie der Weltrevolution. Beitrag zu einer Anthologie der Revolutionstheorien* (Vienna, Europa Verlag)
Martinez-Alier, Juan and Verena: 1972. *Cuba: economía y sociedad* (Paris, Ruedo Ibérico)
Marx, Karl: 1859. *Preface to A Critique of Political Economy* (Berlin)
Mathiez, Albert: 1921. *La Révolution française* (Paris, Armand Colin)
Mayer, Arno: 1971. *Dynamics of Counterrevolution in Europe 1870–1956* (New York and London, Harper and Row)
1981. *The Persistence of the Old Regime. Europe to the Great War* (New York, Pantheon)
Meisner, Maurice: 1974. 'Utopian socialist themes in Maoism' (see Lewis 1974)
Merriman, R. B.: 1938. *Six Contemporaneous Revolutions* (Oxford, Clarendon Press)
Meyer, Alfred, G.: 1957. *Leninism* (Cambridge, Mass., Harvard University Press)
Meyer, Georg P.: 1976. 'Revolutionstheorien heute. Ein kritischer Überblick in historischer Absicht' (see Wehler 1976)
Meyer, Jean A.: 1970. 'Les ouvriers dans la révolution mexicaine: les Bataillons Rouges' (*Annales ESC* 25/1, pp. 30ff)
1974. *La cristiada* (3 vols., Mexico, Siglo Veintiuno Editores)
Moore, Barrington, Jr: 1967. *Social Origins of Dictatorship and Democracy: Lord and Peasant in the Making of the Modern World* (London: Allen Lane)
1972. *Reflections on the Causes of Human Misery* (Boston, Beacon Press)
1978. *Injustice* (New York, Sharpe)
Nettl, J. P.: 1967. *Political Mobilization: A Sociological Analysis of Methods and Concepts* (London, Faber and Faber)
Nolte, Ernst: 1965. *Three Faces of Fascism* (London, Weidenfeld and Nicolson)
1975. *Die faschistischen Bewegungen* (Munich, Dt. Taschenbuch Verlag)
O'Connor, James: 1970. *The Origins of Socialism in Cuba* (Ithaca, Cornell University Press)
Palmer, R. R.: 1959, 1964. *The Age of Democratic Revolution: A Political History of Europe and America, 1760–1800* (2 vols., Princeton, N.J., Princeton University Press)
Palmer, R. R., and Godechot, J.: 1955. 'Le problème de l'Atlantique du XVIIIe au XXe siècle' (X International Congress of Hist. Sciences, 5)

Paniagua Fuentes, Xavier: 1974. 'La ideologiá económica de los anarquistas en Catalũna y el País Valenciano' (*Saitabi, Revista de la Facultad de Filosofía y Letras de la Universidad de Valencia*, 24, pp. 151ff)
Papcke, Sven: 1973. *Progressive Gewalt: Studien zum sozialen Widerstandsrecht* (Frankfurt-am-Main, Fischer)
Perez Lisaur, Marisol: 1975. *Poblaciòn y sociedad: cuatro comunidades del Acolhuacan* (Mexico D.F., SEP-INAH)
Perrot, Michelle: 1974. *Les ouvriers en Grève, France 1871–1890* (Paris, La Haye: Mouton)
Pietsch, Walter: 1969. *Revolution und Staat* (Cologne, Verlag Wissenschaft und Politik)
Pike, Douglas: 1966. *Viet Cong: The Organization and Techniques of the National Liberation Front of South Vietnam* (Cambridge, Mass., London, MIT Press)
Polanyi, Karl: 1945. *Origins of Our Time* (London, Victor Gollancz)
Procacci, Giuliano: 1974. 'Il partito nel sistema sovietico 1917–1945' (*Critica marxista*, 12/1, Jan.–Feb., pp. 59–125; 12/2, Mar.–Apr., pp. 49–95)
Puhle, H.-J.: 1970. *Tradition und Reformpolitik in Bolivien* (Forschungsinstitut der Friedrich-Ebert-Stiftung, Vierteljahresberichte, Special issue 5)
Rendon, Gloria: 1983. *Bibliografía sobre Gaitàn, 9 de Abril y violencia* (Bogotà, Centre Cultural Jorge Eliecer Gaitàn)
Rigby, T. H.: 1968. *Communist Party Membership in the USSR 1917–1967* (Princeton, N.J., Princeton University Press)
1974. 'The first proletarian government' (*British Journ. of Polit. Sci.*, 4/1, pp. 37–51)
Rittberger, V.: 1971. 'Über sozialwissenschaftliche Theorien der Revolution. Kritik u. Versuch eines Neuansatzes' (*Politische Vierteljahresschrift*, 12, pp. 492–529)
Roberts, P. C.: 1970. '"War Communism": A Re-examination' (*Slavic Rev.*, 29/2, pp. 238–61)
Robertson, Priscilla: 1952. *Revolutions of 1848: A Social History* (Princeton N.J., Princeton University Press)
Robinson, R. D.: 1963. *The First Turkish Republic: A Case Study in National Development* (Cambridge, Mass., Harvard University Press)
Rodinson, Maxime: 1972. *Marxisme et monde musulman* (Paris, Editions du Seuil)
Ross, S. R. ed.: 1966. *Is the Mexican Revolution Dead?* (New York, Knopf)
Rostow, W. W.: 1960. *The Stages of Economic Growth* (Cambridge University Press)
Rougerie, J.: 1971. *Paris Libre 1871* (Paris, Editions du Seuil)
Rudé, George: 1959. *The Crowd in the French Revolution* (Oxford, Clarendon Press)
1964. *The Crowd in History. A Study of Popular Disturbances in France and England, 1730–1848* (New York, John Wiley and Sons)
Runciman, W. G.: 1983. 'Unnecessary revolution: the case of France' (*Arch. Europ. de sociologie*, 24, pp. 291–318)
Salomone, A. W.: 1971. 'The Risorgimento and the political myth of "the revolution that failed"' (in A. W. Salomone, ed., *Italy from the Risorgimento to Fascism*, Newton Abbot, David and Charles)
Salvadori, Massimo: 1974. 'Rivoluzione e conservazione nella crisi del 1919–20', (see Agosti 1974)

Sanchez, Gonzalo: 1983. *Los días de la revolución: Gaitanismo y 9 de abril en provincia* (Bogotà, Centro Cultural Jorge Eliecer Gaitàn)
Sanchez, Gonzalo, and Meertens, Donny: 1983. *Bandoleros, gamonales y campesinos: el caso de la violencia en Colombia* (Bogotà, El Ancora Editores)
Schieder, T., ed.: 1973. *Revolution und Gesellschaft* (Freiburg-im-Breisgau, Herder)
Schmitt, E.: 1973. 'Die französische Revolution' (see Schieder 1973)
Schram, Stuart: 1967. *Mao Tse-Tung* (London, Allen Lane)
1969. *The Political Thought of Mao Tse-Tung* (London, Pelican)
Schwartz, David C.: 1971. 'Some dynamics of revolutionary behaviour' (see Davies 1971)
Secchia, Pietro: 1971. 'La resistenza: grandezza dei limiti oggettivi' (*Rinascita* 19/2, 1971)
Sentou, Jean: 1969. *Fortune et groupes sociaux à Toulouse sous la Révolution (1789–1799)* (Toulouse, Edouard Privat)
1970. *La fortune immobilière des Toulousains et la Révolution française* (Paris, Bibliothèque Nationale)
Sereni, Emilio: 1971. 'La scelta del 1943–'45' (*Rinascita* 29/1, 1971)
Shorter, E., and Tilly, C.: 1974. *Strikes in France, 1830–1968* (Cambridge, Cambridge University Press)
Skocpol, Theda: 1976. 'France, Russia, China: A Structural Analysis of Social Revolutions' (*Comparative Studies in Society and History* 18/2, pp. 175–210)
1979a. 'State and Revolution: Old Regimes and Revolutionary Crises' (*Theory and Society*, 7/1-2, pp. 7–96)
1979b. *States and Social Revolutions* (Cambridge, Cambridge University Press)
Soboul, Albert: 1962. *Précis d'histoire de la Révolution française* (Paris, Éditions Sociales)
1964. *The Parisian Sansculottes and the French Revolution, 1793–4* (Oxford, Clarendon Press)
Sorel, Albert: 1908. *L'Europe et la Révolution française. 1, Les moeurs politiques et les traditions* (Paris, Librairie Plon)
Sorokin, Pitirim: 1925. *Social and Cultural Dynamics* (New York, American Book Co., 1937–41), 3
Staermann, E. M.: 1971. 'Progressive und reaktionäre Klassen im spätromischen Kaiserreich' (see Kossok 1971)
Starn, R.: 1971. 'Historians and "crisis"' (*Past and Present*, 52, pp. 3ff)
Stone, Lawrence: 1966. 'Theories of Revolution' (*World Politics*, 18)
1972. *The Causes of the English Revolution, 1529–1642* (London, Routledge)
Storia, 1978. *Storia del marxismo*, 1 (5 vols., Turin, Einaudi)
Sydenham M. J.: 1965. *The French Revolution* (London, Batsford)
Thompson, E. P.: 1970. 'The Moral Economy of the English Crowd in the Eighteenth Century' (*Past and Present*, 50, pp. 76–136)
Thompson, J. M.: 1944. *The French Revolution* (Oxford, Basil Blackwell)
Tilly, C.: 1969. 'Collective violence in European perspective' (see Graham and Gurr 1969)
1970. 'The changing place of collective violence' (in Melvin Richter, ed., *Essays in Theory and History. An Approach to the Social Sciences*, Cambridge, Mass., Harvard University Press)

1973. 'Does modernisation breed revolution?' (*Comparative Politics*, 5/3, pp. 425–47)
1974. 'Town and country in revolution' (see Lewis, 1974)
1975. 'Revolutions and collective violence' (in *Handbook of Political Science*, 3, *Macropolitical Theory*, ed. F. I. Greenstein and N. W. Polsby, Reading, Mass., Addison-Wesley)
1978. *From Mobilisation to Revolution* (Reading, Mass., Addison-Wesley)
Tilly, C., Tilly L., and Tilly R.: 1975. *The Rebellious Century, 1830–1930* (Cambridge, Mass., Harvard University Press)
Tocqueville, Alexis de: 1835–40. *Democracy in America* (4 vols., London, Saunders and Otley)
1861. *Memoir, Letters and Remains of Alexis de Tocqueville* (London and Cambridge, Macmillan)
Townshend, Charles: 1983. *Political Violence in Ireland* (Oxford, Clarendon Press)
Trotsky, Leon: 1936. *The History of the Russian Revolution* (London, Victor Gollancz)
1973. *1905* (Harmondsworth, Penguin Books)
Tudesq, A. J.: 1964. *Les grands notables en France, 1840–1849* (2 vols., Paris, Faculté des Lettres et Sciences Humaines de Paris)
Urrutia Montoya, Miguel: 1969. *The Development of the Colombian Labor Movement* (New Haven and London, Yale University Press)
Veliz, Claudio, ed.: 1967. *The Politics of Conformity in Latin America* (Oxford, Oxford University Press)
Vernon, Raymond: 1963. *The Dilemma of Mexico's Development* (Cambridge, Mass., Harvard University Press)
Vincent, J. R.: 1966. *The Formation of the British Liberal Party, 1857–1868* (London, Constable)
Wehler, H.-U., ed.: 1976. *200 Jahre amerikanische Revolution u. moderne Revolutionsforschung* (Gottingen, Vandenhoeck & Ruprecht)
Weiner, Myron, ed.: 1966. *Modernization: The Dynamics of Growth* (New York and London, Basic Books)
Wertheim, W. F.: 1974. *Evolution and Revolution: The Rising Waves of Emancipation* (Harmondsworth, Penguin Books)
Wolf, Eric R.: 1971. *Peasant Wars of the Twentieth Century* (London, Faber and Faber)
Womack, John R.: 1969. *Zapata and the Mexican Revolution* (London, Thames and Hudson)
Woolff, Stuart, J. ed.: 1968. *European Fascism* (London, Weidenfeld and Nicolson)
Zagorin, Perez: 1973. 'Theories of revolution in contemporary historiography', (*Pol. Science Quarterly*, 88, pp. 23ff)
1976. 'Prolegomena to the comparative history of revolution in early modern Europe' (*Comparative Studies in Society and History*, 18/2, pp. 151–74)
1982. *Rebels and Rulers, 1500–1660* (2 vols., Cambridge, Cambridge University Press)
Zeldin, Theodore: 1973. *France 1848–1945*, 1, (Oxford, Clarendon Press)

2

Revolution in antiquity

M. I. FINLEY

Revolution is one of a class of words widely employed without definition both in current speech and in professional historical and sociological writings, with a great (and even mutually) contradictory variety of meanings, and yet often (though by no means always) with sufficient intelligibility. That provides the rationale for this book. Much of it is devoted to the effort to clarify the ways in which the same word can range in meaning from, say, Copernicus's *Of the Revolutions of the Heavenly Spheres* through the Agricultural or Industrial Revolution to the American War of Independence and the Russian Revolution. The concern of this essay is narrow, namely, the use and abuse of the concept in the study of ancient (classical) history, where restriction to the political sense is traditional, so that many of the issues raised by such notions as a Scientific Revolution do not arise.

Failure to define terms and concepts is a well-known curse in historiography. But definitions do not solve problems. They are either useful or not useful (not either right or wrong, as seems to be widely thought). That is to say, a historian is free to define 'revolution' as he prefers (within limits); the question then is whether or not his choice advances our understanding of the subject on which he is discoursing. Little reflection is needed in order to reveal that at both ends of the spectrum of meanings, the term is used in a way that is not helpful. At one end, the word 'revolution' amounts to nothing more than a synonym for 'change' (or, more narrowly, for change that some people resisted, which is no more helpful). At the other end, there has developed in recent decades a view, stemming ultimately from Marx, that the term should be restricted to those moments in the history of class struggle during which a radical, violent change occurs in the class basis of the political structure. It is then easy to show that such 'revolutions' did not occur in antiquity, or at least did not occur at the times when the word 'revolution' is most commonly used – the so-called Roman Revolution, in particular – and to suggest that the word had therefore better be abandoned by ancient historians altogether.

The second of these alternatives deserves more detailed examination. It was Mommsen in his *Roman History*, originally published in 1854–6, who virtually created the label, 'the Roman Revolution', for the period from the Gracchi to Caesar. That label remained an unchallenged commonplace for a century, despite the occasional dissenting voice. Even Eduard Meyer, who thought that Mommsen's view of Caesar and of the Roman Revolution was wholly wrong-headed, did not hesitate to write that Caesar was 'a revolutionary through and through',[1] though his revolution was very different from Mommsen's, which, he said, was a mere mirror-image of 1848. Mommsen, it should be stressed, narrated what happened; he made no attempt to explain or justify his notion of a Roman revolution. Nor did Ronald Syme, whose *The Roman Revolution* (first published in 1939), has been one of the most influential books of the present century on Roman history. For him the revolutionary period began in 60 BC and ended with the reign of Augustus and the establishment of the Principate. 'The subject of the book', he writes in the opening words of his preface, 'is the transformation of state and society ... The period witnessed a violent transference of power and of property; and the Principate of Augustus should be regarded as the consolidation of the revolutionary process.' That none of this classification is self-evident seems not to have occurred to Syme: there is no attempt in the book (or in his numerous subsequent writings) to clarify or justify his terminology or his conception of revolution. The same casualness characterizes most of the many other historians of Rome who refer to the Roman Revolution in their work, but nothing would be gained by cataloguing their names.

A genuine break did not come until the centenary of the publication of Mommsen's *Roman History*, and the man who brought it about was Alfred Heuss. He more or less explicitly accepted a Marxist class-struggle definition of revolution, and then argued (1) that it was applicable to the ancient world only in the overthrow during the archaic period (in both Greece and Rome) of rule by the landed aristocracy; (2) that Mommsen did not accept (and, at least obliquely, rejected) the class-struggle concept of revolution and favoured a 'liberal' Hegelian idea; (3) that the 'Roman Revolution' used in any modern sense is therefore a misnomer (whether one dates it from the Gracchi or from Sulla or from 60 BC).[2] A lively discussion has continued for three decades, largely among German historians, complicated by the injection of a thesis of Christian Meier's that what has been called the Roman Revolution should rather be seen as a 'crisis without any alternative' (*Krise ohne Alternative*).[3]

Not everyone will find this discussion fruitful. Although a few historians have drawn the conclusion to abjure the concept of a Roman Revolution, Heuss himself decided to continue to employ the term, though stripped of its modern, Marxist connotations. That was legitimate, he said, for 'universal-historical reasons', a Toynbee-esque notion popular among German ancient historians to which I am unable to assign any meaning. Hence, in his own *Römische Geschichte* there is a chapter of nearly 150 pages entitled 'the Roman Revolution (133–30 BC)'. Others, such as Rilinger, a pupil of Meier's, have attempted a synthesis (or compromise) between the seemingly incompatible views of Heuss and Meier, which, so far as I can understand it, rests on a view of the central role of clientship in the late Republic that I find unacceptable (and indeed meaningless except as a mystique).[4]

Underneath there lies the familiar desire to impose universality on such concepts and institutions as revolution, the state, the city, at the price of a reduction which renders them useless.[5] Once it is acknowledged that the *modern* concept of revolution (and the idea itself) stems from the eighteenth century, and in particular from the French Revolution, then all 'universal-historical' attempts to bring events in the Graeco-Roman world, or generally in the pre-capitalist world, under a single rubric, 'revolution', must inevitably deprive the concept of any value for historical analysis.[6] A 'revolution' that goes on for decades or for a century, which does not bring about a massive, violent change in the social order or bring hitherto unrepresented social interests into power, which does not have an underlying faith in progress, must be qualitatively distinguished from (and not forced into a single classification with) the French or Russian Revolutions as historical phenomena.[7] So must such phenomena as the introduction by Augustus of a monarchial system in Rome. If, as is comprehensible, one prefers not to call that a revolution because the class basis of the state was untouched, it is then necessary to find an alternative label that does justice to the magnitude of the political change that occurred.

And it surely does not follow that the very notion of revolution must be avoided in ancient history: that is a wrong idea that stems from the search for global ('universal-historical') concepts. It is not even true to say that no equivalent for the term itself can be found among the ancients.[8] There are contexts in which *neoterismos* in Greek and *res novae* in Latin unequivocally mean the overthrow of a regime and are therefore properly rendered by either '*coup d'état*' or 'revolution'. In 441 BC, for example, when a war broke out between Miletus and Samos, the Milesians protested to Athens and were supported by some individual Samians 'who wished to overthrow (*neoterizo*) the regime' (Thucydides, 1.115.2). The Athenians in response sent a fleet to Samos and established a democracy there. Similarly, when in 216 BC the Samnite town of Nola in Campania was under threat from Hannibal, the local senate wished to remain loyal to Rome, according to Livy (23.14.7), but the plebs preferred a change of regime (*res novae*) and surrender to Hannibal.

Then there was the notion of a 'cycle of constitutions' (*metabole politeion*), which became an obsession with Greek political analysts from the mid-fifth century to Polybius in the mid-second century BC, and which had built into it the idea of forcible overthrow.[9] It is true, as Heuss insisted (p. 5), that the word *metabole* by itself, without 'of constitutions' has no political content, but neither does the word 'revolution' when unqualified, and even in its political sense it lacked such a content until at least the Glorious Revolution. That underscores the great divide separating modern revolutions from all previous 'revolutions'. So, more importantly, does the cyclical character, the absence in antiquity of any idea of a forward-looking, progressive change in the political or social structure. Modern revolutions, Dunn wrote, 'are either ventures in creativity or they are nothing – mere *jacqueries*'.[10] Ancient 'revolutions' were neither: they were not nothing, not mere *jacqueries*, but they were also not ventures into the future.

But the obvious and essentially banal conclusion that ancient 'revolutions' were qualitatively different from modern revolutions does not get us very far. Within whatever limits, how were kinds of 'revolutionary' change in antiquity distinguished from each other, and from other, 'non-revolutionary' change? That remains a basic question requiring an answer. In concluding the historical section of his *Constitution of Athens* written rather late in the fourth century BC, Aristotle (ch. 41) listed eleven *metabolai* that had taken place in the Athenian constitution from the earliest (legendary) times to his own day. There are difficulties with this summary account, but they need not concern us here. The essential point is that there was an oscillation between sharp changes introducing more popular controls of government and restorations of narrower political bases, whether oligarchical or 'tyrannical'. The former included the reforms of Solon in 594 BC, the Cleisthenic constitution introduced in 508 BC, following a brief civil war, the establishment of the 'Periclean' form of popular democracy under Ephialtes in 462–1 BC, and, in a different vein, the final re-establishment of the democracy in 403 BC after the overthrow of the oligarchy of the so-called Thirty Tyrants.

None of these changes radically altered the social structure or even – a point to which I shall return – the social basis of the political leadership. However, they did give political influence to new social interests, and they involved a measure of force and violence. The changes, in other words, were sharp and rapid. The elites who were responsible, furthermore, had a consciousness of purpose and a measure of ruthlessness in pursuing their objectives, and these too were necessary conditions for modern revolutions. In modern parlance, the 'revolutionary' actions under Solon, Cliesthenes and Ephialtes were qualitatively different from the 'evolution' of Athenian democracy in the generation following Ephialtes, from such steps as the steady extension of pay for office or the enlargement of the navy (which was a major contribution to the welfare of the poorer citizens). Somehow the two kinds must be distinguished. To define the distinctions away, whether by dismissing the ancient 'revolutions' because they were unlike the modern, or by a reductionism that eliminates the ancient–modern distinction, is analytically unsatisfactory.

The important question of the nature, extent and impact of popular action, of violence on the part of the excluded classes in antiquity, turns out to be very difficult. The ancient sources are regularly restricted to either bare and almost empty statements of the existence of civil conflict, though occasionally they embark on highly dramatic and obviously novelistic accounts of particular incidents that have no greater value for the historian.[11] In Argos in 370 BC, Diodorus reports (15.57–8), an oligarchic coup was secretly planned because the demagogues were stirring up the masses against the wealthy; the plotters were betrayed; the usual round of tortures and further betrayals followed, until more than 1,200 were cudgelled to death and their property confiscated; then, for no clearly stated reason, the mob turned against the demagogues and put them to death too. 'So', Diodorus concludes, 'they received the punishment fitting their crimes . . . and the *demos*, relieved of their madness, were restored to their good senses.' I do not doubt the existence of civil conflict between rich and poor in Argos at the time, but beyond that I can find nothing in the account that a historian can take hold of.

Nowhere is the situation more frustrating than in the available accounts of the three key moments in the development of Athenian democracy. It seems certain that in 594 Solon was selected (one is even tempted to write 'elected') as archon, for the express purpose of reforming the economy and the constitution. How this was done, by whom and under what precise circumstances – these are all matters open to anyone's guesses.[12] Aristotle's statement that the nobles and the people were 'in conflict for a long time' and that the latter finally 'rose' against the former (*Constitution of Athens*, 2.1, 5.1) implies that a civil war was impending (or was even under way), but he provides no further information nor does any other ancient writer. Solon then introduced his reforms. A timocratic census was introduced as the basis for officeholding, and other changes, by no means all clear today, were made in the political and judicial machinery. However, the three measures that Aristotle (*Constitution of Athens*, 9.1) called his 'most popular (*demotikotatos*)' were the prohibition of lending on the security of the person, the introduction of the right of a third party to intervene in court on behalf of anyone who had a claim, and a right of appeal to the popular courts.[13] The last is today controversial, but it is these measures that help justify the epithet 'revolutionary' for Solon in the restricted sense that I have already defined. However, troubled times continued for decades: there was a period of 'anarchy' (when officials could not be elected) and eventually Pisistratus seized power as 'tyrant'.

When the tyranny was overthrown in 510 BC, a power struggle ensued between two factions within the aristocracy, led respectively by Isagoras and Cleisthenes. The latter, we are told by Herodotus (5.66.2), turned for support to the common people, the *demos*, and 'attached them to his faction'. Isagoras brought in the Spartan king Cleomenes with a small force, Cleisthenes and his supporters (seven hundred families according to Aristotle, *Constitution of Athens*, 20.3) were expelled from Athens but were soon restored by a three-day popular uprising, and in 508–7 he made fundamental structural changes in the governmental system. All this adds up to very little in the way of information, and, as Andrewes has said, 'it is wildly unlikely that we shall acquire an earlier and better account'.[14] This is not the place in which to sort out the puzzles that still dominate the scholarly literature on Cleisthenes. The keys to his political transformation of Athens were an ingenious, artificial organization of the citizen-body into a three-tier territorial system based on *demes* (parishes) and the central governmental role assigned to the *boule*, the Council of Five Hundred, in which there was a compulsory geographical distribution of members and a restriction of membership to a maximum of two years for any citizen. Somehow Cleisthenes thus succeeded in justifying the popular support that gave him the victory over Isagoras.[15]

This little about Cleisthenes is considerable in contrast to what we know about the reforms under Ephialtes. He is not mentioned by Herodotus or Thucydides, and the only fifth-century reference to him is an unhelpful one late in the century (Antiphon, 5.68).[16] It is not even certain that Ephialtes belongs on the 'revolutionary' side of the divide, though all our ancient authorities placed him there and his assassination points in that direction as well.[17]

Nothing would be gained by proceeding to a similar consideration of individual situations in the Greek world outside Athens. The literary record is filled with incidents of violence and uprising, but they regularly come from nowhere and lead nowhere.[18] However, one generalization of importance is permissible. Apart from three or four cities, most obviously Athens, which may be classified as 'conquest-states', the Greek city-states were too tiny to be permitted the luxury of an independent policy over longer periods of time. Hence domestic and foreign policy were inextricably intertwined, and spasmodic attempts to break away from the suzerainty of a conquest-state often took on the colouring of a civil war within. However, any temptation must be resisted to draw comparisons with present-day colonial revolts that also become social revolutions (successful or not), because in antiquity emancipation movements were often led by an elite seeking a restoration of their own power within the state, not a transfer of power to new, hitherto unrepresented classes. And, after Alexander the Great, the Hellenistic monarchies made all the essential decisions (until Rome conquered them). The fate of Athens provides the perfect symbol. In 322 BC the Macedonian general Antipater imposed an oligarchical system on Athens. Eight changes of government followed in the next two generations, until all independence was finally destroyed by the Macedonians in 261 BC, and democracy with it.[19]

The long Roman story was in important respects very different, thanks above all to the inexorable expansion of Rome through conquest. The long archaic 'struggle of the orders', which lasted more than two centuries, has the appearance of a genuine class struggle, no doubt, and even Heuss allows the term 'revolution' to be used in that sense in that context. When it was over – conventionally with the passage of the lex Hortensia in 287 BC – the form of the Roman governmental system had been radically changed; the original patrician monopoly of power had been broken, to be replaced by the power of a new patrician–plebeian *nobilitas*; the law had been codified and made public. The changes had been achieved through struggle: the annalistic tradition records three occasions when the plebs 'seceded', that is to say, they refused mobilization into the army (in 494, 449 and 287), and demonstrations and riots must have been repeatedly employed short of secession. On the other hand, the success of the Roman ruling elite in withholding the substance of popular government while granting the forms is without parallel. Hence, Brunt concludes, 'the order of society was basically unchanged'.[20] That is correct, but, as we shall see in a moment, the order of society was never 'basically changed' in antiquity.

Popular discontent, often enough expressing itself in violence, did not cease after 287 BC. How could it have, since the central problems of land hunger and debt were never solved though the lower classes had been given a place in the political system? 'Cancel debts and redistribute the land' – that was the standard 'revolutionary' slogan in antiquity, and one can cite upper-class expressions of fear of such demands from one end of antiquity to the other. These fears turn out regularly to have been grossly exaggerated, apart from occasional, though sometimes very brutal, local incidents. Not even the conspiracy of Catiline in 63 BC, world-famous thanks to Cicero and Sallust, was a serious threat to Roman society or the Roman state. In a period when 'everything was held to be possible in Rome', Catiline's movement had no 'great background', little detailed planning or programme, insufficient armed support, no chance of success, and it was quickly betrayed.[21] Conceivably P. Clodius Pulcher, who as tribune in 58 BC introduced the massive free-grain distribution that remained a hall-mark of public patronage for the poor in the city of Rome for several centuries thereafter, showed signs of a revolutionary tendency (including a genuine political organization) in the interests of the urban plebs, but he was assassinated in January 52 and it is idle to speculate about how the situation might have developed had he lived on.[22] In any event, Clodius remains an isolated personality in the final decades of Republican Rome.

'Redistribution of land and cancellation of debts' was a utopian slogan, and in the end even the more rebellious Greeks and Romans accepted 'reformist' measures, such as abolition of debt-bondage, moratoria and interest maxima, and, above all, emigration abroad to so-called colonies in place of redistribution of the land at home.[23] This is not at all surprising. Where, one may ask rhetorically, was a social basis for a revolutionary economic programme to come from? It unfortunately has to be said again and again that the Roman *equites* were, in terms of their interests, not a different class from the landed aristocracy and that they never challenged the existing social order.[24] Certainly the slaves never were an answer to my rhetorical question, not even hypothetically. They were from time to time called upon for support in civil strife among the free population, but neither they nor the freemen thought of such moves as anything more than temporary tactics, without long-term implications: the role of slaves in the conspiracy of Catiline is sufficient proof.[25] Slave revolts may have been dramatic and frightening, that led by Spartacus in particular, but in the end two generalizations impose themselves: firstly, 'what is most characteristic, most striking in the history of slavery is not revolt but the absence of revolt';[26] secondly, out of the slave revolts of the late Roman Republic, the greatest in antiquity, 'there emerged no permanent struggle for freedom'.[27] Nor is there any sound reason to think that unrest or revolts on the part of the slaves (or of slaves together with peasants) contributed to the breakdown of classical society and the transition to the middle ages.[28]

We are thus left with a kind of tautology: there was no revolutionary transfer of power to a new class (or classes) because there were no new classes. Why that should have been the case would need a full discussion of the ancient economy, which I have attempted elsewhere and to which I must now refer with a brief and undefended summary.[29] The Graeco-

Roman world was from beginning to end an agrarian one. Larger holdings were worked either by slaves or by other kinds of dependent labour or were leased to tenants; most smallholders were more or less independent peasants; a hired work force was essentially restricted to seasonal labour (such as harvesting) drawn from the neighbouring peasantry. The urban sector, for all its enormous expansion from early archaic times to the peak period, between 150 BC and AD 150 in round numbers, for all the considerable profits that a small number of individuals accumulated from trade and manufacture (other than as by-products of land ownership), failed to generate new wealth, and in particular failed to create new social classes, whether entrepreneurial or labouring, that had an interest in competing for status or power with the already existing agrarian classes.

Lest there be any misunderstanding, I should say explicitly that I do not claim that trade and manufacture were unimportant. My point is rather that the non-agrarian sector of the ancient economy never approached a take-off stage. A genuine revolution requires as one pre-condition a massive desire within a large, or at least powerful, section of society for a radical change in the political structure, for the replacement of prevailing social interests controlling the levers of power by new interests. That is what I mean by a take-off stage, and it was totally absent in antiquity. That slavery and other forms of dependent labour – helots, Hellenistic *laoi*, and so on – were a major inhibiting factor seems to me to be certain, a factor that operated in both the agrarian and the urban sectors.[30]

There are revealing ideological symptoms. Modern regimes that were heading for revolutionary overthrow were faced with what Crane Brinton called 'the desertion of the intellectuals'.[31] In antiquity, in contrast, the most radical critics either looked back to a more or less mythical past or they invoked a utopian vision (Plato), or, like Diogenes the Cynic, they preached rejection of all existing values and institutions. The contrast between Diogenes and the French Encyclopedists sums it all up: Diogenes and his followers were a most comfortable opposition because they were only a pest and no more than that; in particular, their all-embracing attack stultified any form of activity, including political activity and social reform.[32] And ancient utopias were regularly static, ascetic and hierarchical, not the sort of image that could arouse popular enthusiasm in the name of progress.[33]

From time to time, continuing Roman conquest also stirred up revolts and struggles for independence among the conquered peoples. Some were massive and of considerable duration, but, with one possible exception, they, like the earlier and much smaller independence struggles in Greek city-states, lacked any revolutionary element. One of the two most important 'colonial revolts' during the Republic was led in Spain by a Roman, Sertorius, praetor in charge of the province in 83 BC, who managed to fight on until his assassination in 73 or 72. Sertorius has been the subject of much romantic historiography, but it seems clear that, as Gabba has analysed his career, the objective was a change in the Sullan orientation in *Roman* politics with the Spanish setting 'only fortuitous'.[34] Nothing is more revealing in this respect than his role in 'Romanizing' the local upper classes during his decade in Spain. Other major revolts, under King Mithridates VI of Pontus from 88 BC to his death in 69; under Florus and Sacrovir in Gaul in AD 21 and again under Vindex in 68; or under Boudicca in Britain in AD 60 need not detain us. Only the Jewish Revolt of 66–70 appears to have had exceptional elements. In so far as one can penetrate the extremely tendentious account of Josephus, the Zealot-led revolt from Rome was closely linked with an internal struggle against the Jewish ruling aristocracy. But the revolt was shattered, and on this subject, too, it is idle to speculate about what might have emerged had the course of events been a different one.

At no time and in no place in classical antiquity, in sum, was there a genuine change in the class basis of the state. There were major alterations in the nature of the state, including changes in the extent of popular participation, but the social character of the leadership remained the same, regardless of changes in personnel. The 'Roman Revolution' is the best illustration: the shift from Republic (even in its late form) to Principate cannot be underestimated – in that sense the crisis of the late Republic was not 'without any alternative' – but the base on which the Principate rested was no different from the one on which the Republic rested. That is to say that, though not a few men were killed, including members of the old ruling class, and their property confiscated (as had happened at other times, such as under Sulla), and though the ruling elite was extended outside Rome and Italy eventually to much of the empire, the elite remained a landholding one, increasingly wealthy as the years went by, massively exploiting a population that was partly servile and partly free in the legal sense. There was, in sum, an Augustan 'revolution' in the narrow but not meaningless sense of a shift from Republic to Principate, emerging from the civil war that followed the assassination of Julius Caesar, but not Syme's 'violent transference of power and of property' beginning half a century earlier, in 60 BC.

In the end, however, none of this accumulation of negatives and qualifications can remove the fundamental difference between what happened in Athens under Solon or Cleisthenes and the 'normal' oscillation between one or another form of government in Greek city-states or the difference between Solon or Cleisthenes and the Augustan 'revolution' in Rome. The critical factor was the element of popular participation in government – not a transfer of power to a new elite but the extension of a voice in the conduct of public affairs to ordinary people, to peasants, shopkeepers and artisans.[35] That was a rare step in history, not to be repeated for more than two thousand years, and it seems to me absolutely reasonable to call that step revolutionary even though certain essential modern overtones were missing. Revolutions of that type were found only in the Greek city-states of the later archaic and classical periods. The Roman pattern, in sharp contrast, was one of persistent success by the elite in aborting general popular participation by a variety of devices. One such device was to feed the Roman populace, from the tribunate of Clodius in 58 BC by a large-scale distribution of free corn. Not even Augustus could interfere with that, though he put an end permanently and completely to genuine popular participation in political life.[36]

The explanation, no simple matter, for the difference in this respect among Greek city-states or between Greece and Rome will be found, in my view, in the story of conquest in antiquity, in which size and scale must be allowed due weight. The Athenian maritime empire depended on the free poor, who provided the core of the navy, and Ephialtes and Pericles drew the appropriate political lessons. Roman conquests, by land on a scale that no Greek city-state could have imagined, rested on probably the most continuous employment of conscripted citizen-troops in Western history, with economic, social and psychological consequences of a different order from the Greek. The time even came when Rome was in the historically unparalleled position of having no genuine rivals anywhere.[37] But these are merely hints: a proper explanation would take us into a new field of discourse.[38]

NOTES

1 *Caesars Monarchie und das Principat des Pompejus* (2nd ed., Stuttgart and Berlin, 1919), p. 141.

2 See A. Heuss, 'Der Untergang der römischen Republik und das Problem der Revolution', *Historische Zeitschrift*, 182 (1956), pp. 1–28; *Theodor Mommsen und das 19. Jahrhundert* (Kiel, 1956), chap. 3; and again later, at greater length, 'Das Revolutionsproblem im Spiegel der antiken Geschichte', *Historische Zeitschrift*, 216 (1973), pp. 1–72. On the 'Revolutionspessimismus der bürgerlich-liberalen Intelligenz', see T. Schieder, 'Das Problem der Revolution im 19. Jahrhundert', *ibid.*, 170 (1950), pp. 237–71.

3 *Res publica amissa* (Wiesbaden, 1967; repr. with a long new introduction, Frankfurt, 1980). For an account of the discussion, see R. Rilinger, 'Die Interpretation des Niedergangs der römischen Republik ...', *Archiv für Kulturgeschichte*, 64 (1982), pp. 279–306; K. Bringmann, 'Das Problem

einer "Römischen Revolution"', *Geschichte in Wissenschaft und Unterricht*, 31 (1980), pp. 354–77; K. Christ, *Römische Geschichte und Wissenschaftsgeschichte* (Darmstadt, 1982), I, pp. 134–67.

4 Rilinger, *ibid.* He claims that the key explanatory role of clientship is 'widely accepted', which is hardly satisfactory; see the sharply divergent view put forward by P. A. Brunt in his forthcoming article, 'The Roman clientela: a reconsideration'.

5 I have in the past objected to such reductionism, about the state in *Politics in the Ancient World* (Cambridge, 1983), pp. 8–9, and in *The Use and Abuse of History* (rev. ed., London, 1986), pp. 113–15; about the city in 'The Ancient City ...', *Comparative Studies in Society and History*, 19 (1977), pp. 305–27, reprinted in my *Economy and Society in Ancient Greece* (London and New York, 1981), ch. 1.

6 The argument is not affected by acceptance of the view that lexically, at any rate, the modern sense of 'revolution' begins with the Glorious Revolution of 1688, as proposed by K. Griewank, *Der neuzeitliche Revolutionsbegriff* ..., 2nd ed. by I. Horn-Staiger (Frankfurt, 1969), pp. 148–50.

7 These elements are stressed by John Dunn, *Modern Revolutions* (Cambridge, 1972), which is perhaps the best introduction to the subject, though he avoids a formal definition, so that the elements I have singled out have to be hunted for in the volume: see especially pp. 2–7, 12–15, 248. Cf. R. A. Berding, 'Revolution als Prozess', in *Theorie der Geschichte*, II. *Historische Prozesse* (Munich, 1978), pp. 226–89, who writes (p. 280): 'Der emanzipatorische Impetus und der Kampf um Herrschaftspositionen sind für alle Revolutionen Konstitutiv.'

8 So, e.g., Griewank, *Der neuzeitliche Revolutionsbegriff*, p. 17.

9 The standard account is H. Ryffel, *Metabole Politeion. Der Wandel der Staatsverfassungen* (Bern, 1949). In *Politics in the Ancient World*, pp. 126–9, I suggested why the Romans showed no interest in this notion.

10 Dunn, *Modern Revolutions*, p. 2.

11 I have discussed this problem in considerable detail in *Politics*, esp. ch. 5.

12 See, above all, A. Andrewes in *Cambridge Ancient History*, 2nd ed., vol. III, 3 (1982), pp. 375–97.

13 On his economic measures, see now T. W. Gallant, 'Agricultural systems, land tenure, and the reform of Solon', *Annual of the British School at Athens*, 72 (1982), pp. 111–24.

14 A. Andrewes, 'Kleisthenes' Reform Bill', *Classical Quarterly*, 27 (1977), pp. 241–8, at p. 241. The longer account of C. Meier, *Die Entstehung des Politischen bei den Griechen* (Frankfurt, 1980), pp. 91–143, esp. pp. 113–23, suffers from an abstract conception of the objectives of the *demos* and from an unwarranted injection into the picture of a propertied middle stratum.

15 I follow very briefly the account I gave in *Politics*, pp. 44–8, where some essential bibliography is indicated. There I noted that Aristotle, in particular, was firm in his conviction of the popular support for Cleisthenes, using the word *demos* four times and also *to plethos* (the multitude) four times in the chapters (20–1) he devoted to Cleisthenes in his *Constitution of Athens*.

16 The evidence and modern views are fully discussed by C. Hignett, *A History of the Athenian Constitution* (Oxford, 1952), ch. 8, who does not disguise the desperateness of his efforts.

17 The assassination and indeed the entire tradition about Ephialtes from

Theopompus and Aristotle on become meaningless if one accepts R. Sealey's reduction of his career to a minor technical reform in the constitutional procedure: 'Ephialtes', *Classical Philology*, 59 (1964), pp. 11–22, reprinted in his *Essays in Greek Politics* (New York, n.d.), pp. 42–58.

18 I have to excuse myself for not discussing the 'revolutions' led by Kings Agis and Cleomenes in Sparta in the latter part of the third century BC. A pupil of mine, Ricardo Martinéz Lacy, will demonstrate – I use the verb advisedly – that lengthy accounts in Plutarch's *Lives* are incurably defective because they are drenched in the Spartan Lycurgus legend. For an attempt to discuss them within our context, on the assumption that the literary record can be taken at face value, see Heuss, 'Revolutionsproblem', pp. 37–46.

19 The fullest account remains that of W. S. Ferguson, *Hellenistic Athens* (London, 1911), chs. 1–4.

20 P. A. Brunt, *Social Conflicts in the Roman Republic* (London, 1971), p. 58. His ch. 3 remains the best short introduction to the struggle of the orders.

21 The phrases in inverted commas are those of C. Meier, *Caesar* (Berlin, 1982), pp. 212–3.

22 See W. Nippel, 'Die *plebs urbana* und die Rolle der Gewalt in der späten römischen Republik', in *Von Elend der Handarbeit*, ed. H. Mommsen and W. Schulze (Stuttgart, 1981), pp. 70–92; cf. J.-M. Flambard, 'Clodius, les collèges, la plèbe et les esclaves ...' *Mélanges de l'Ecole française de Rome: Antiquité*, 89 (1977), pp. 115–56. It is revealing that in the *Roman Revolution* Syme reduced Clodius to an almost non-existent figure performing trivia.

23 See my *Politics*, pp. 107–15, on all this.

24 The false image of the 'equestrian businessmen' should have been laid to rest two decades ago with the publication of P. A. Brunt, 'The equites in the late republic', in *Proceedings* of the 2nd International Conference of Economic History, Aix-en-Provence, 1962, vol. 1 (Paris and The Hague, 1965), pp. 117–49, reprinted in *The Crisis of the Roman Republic*, ed. R. Seager (Cambridge and New York, 1969), pp. 83–130; and C. Nicolet, *L'ordre équestre à l'époque républicaine* (Paris, 1966). However, it continues to reappear in the modern literature in the face of the evidence: see Finley, *The Ancient Economy* (2nd ed., London and Berkeley, 1985), pp. 193–8.

25 Of the considerable literature, it is sufficient to cite the short article by K. R. Bradley, 'Slaves and the conspiracy of Catiline', *Classical Philology*, 73 (1978), pp. 329–36.

26 J.-C. Dumont, 'Le signification de la révolte' (a review-article), *Revue des études latines*, 45 (1967), pp. 89–98, at p. 97.

27 K.-W. Welwei, 'Das Sklavenproblem als politischer Faktor in der Krise der römischen Republik', in Mommsen and Schulze, *Von Elend der Handarbeit*, pp. 50–69, at p. 51.

28 A recent attempt has been made to revive this myth: P. Dockès, *Medieval Slavery and Liberation*, trans. A. Goldhammer (London, 1982), ch. 4. However, Dockès is able to produce no evidence other than his inferences from expressions of fear of slaves and from the harsh measures taken against fugitives from what he calls the 'inner dialectic of the class struggle'.

29 *The Ancient Economy*.

30 In particular, this would explain the absence in antiquity of what modern scholarship is tending to consider to be 'key factors in the making of the

modern world', namely, 'relations between landlords and peasants, the dynamics of rural class relations': John Dunn, 'Understanding revolutions', *Ethics*, 92 (1982), pp. 299–315, at p. 307 (with bibliography).

31 C. Brinton, *The Anatomy of Revolution* (New York, 1938), ch. 2, sect. 3.

32 See 'Diogenes the Cynic', in Finley, *Aspects of Antiquity* (2nd ed., Penguin, 1977), ch. 7.

33 See 'Utopianism ancient and modern', in Finley, *The Use and Abuse of History*, ch. 11.

34 E. Gabba, *Republican Rome, the Army and the Allies*, trans. P. J. Cuff (Oxford and Berkeley, 1976), p. 124. The long ch. 3 in that volume presents the most reliable picture of Sertorius now available.

35 This is a main theme of my *Politics in the Ancient World*.

36 When I say that, I have not overlooked the continuance of elections to office for another century. If there is any truth in the allegation of Suetonius, *Augustus*, 42.4, that Augustus contemplated putting an end to free grain for the city of Rome, his abandonment of the idea shows that he thought it impossible to carry out permanently.

37 The impact of this fact on the internal history of Rome is developed by J. von Ungern-Sternberg, 'Weltreiche und Krise: Äussere Bedingungen für den Niedergang der römischen Republik', *Museum Helveticum*, 39 (1982), pp. 254–71.

38 I am grateful to my friends Peter Garnsey and Dick Whittaker for valuable suggestions.

3

*Social devolution and revolution: Ta Thung and Thai Phing**

JOSEPH NEEDHAM

As is well known, China before modern times (1911 and 1949) had no revolutions involving fundamental changes in social structure. There were profound dynastic changes, after the establishment of the first unified empire under Chhin Shih Huang Ti, and there were foreign invasions, sometimes leading to the establishment of new dynasties, covering the whole or parts of the vast Chinese *oikoumene*. Above all, there were peasant-farmer rebellions, everlastingly renewed; but always their main objective was to set up a new dynasty which should adhere more closely to the good government recommended by the sages of old. Indeed some scholars have spoken of a regular 'dynastic cycle', in which a dynasty would begin with one or more strong, just and popular rulers, after which the imperial power would more and more degenerate, until a new peasant rebellion would bring about a new and fundamental (up to a point) change. But all this did not mean that certain concepts, like rallying-cries, did not run through the whole historical scheme, surfacing century after century, and inspiring men to actions designed to restore the good government of which the sages had spoken. In this paper we shall be considering two of these: *Ta Thung*, the Great Togetherness, and *Thai Phing*, the Realm of Great Peace and Equality. Such concepts must be treated with reverence, since they represented ideals for which men were ready to fight and die century after century. In so far as the aims of peasant rebellions were so dynastic, they might be thought to agree with those cyclical conceptions of time which had been known from antiquity onwards in China; yet there was always another conception, that of social evolution in continuous time. This had ever been characteristic of Chinese

* In this chapter the system of romanization of Chinese terms is that used in the *Science and Civilisation in China* series (Cambridge, 1954ff). A conversion table can be found in vol. 5, pt 4, pp. 764–72.) The chapter originally formed part of my Henry Myers Lecture at the Royal Anthropological Institute in London 1964, which was published as *Time and Eastern Man* (1965).

philosophy, with its lists of culture-heroes and inventors, and it had also brought mankind up out of primitive savagery into a rational civilization. Whether the last Chinese Revolution (Liberation, as it is called) will prove to be a true continuation of this, it may still be a little too early to say, but at the least it must be one more stage in the long process of social evolution, one more decisive step towards the realm of freedom, towards the ideals of *Ta Thung* and *Thai Phing*.

Chinese thinkers were rather divided on the question of what had happened to human society in time, and there were two sharply contrasting attitudes. On the one hand there was the conception of a Golden Age of primitive communalism or of sage-kings from which mankind had steadily declined,[1] while on the other there was a recognition of culture-heroes as progenitors of something much greater than themselves, with an emphasis on development and evolution out of primitive savagery.[2]

The first of these views was characteristic of the ancient Taoist philosophers, and in them it was closely connected with a general opposition to proto-feudal and feudal society.[3] They harked back always to the ancient paradise of generalized tribal nobility, of cooperative primitivity, of spontaneous collectivism ('When Adam delved and Eve span, Who was then the gentleman?'), before the aenolithic differentiation of lords, priests, warriors and serfs. They were probably stimulated in this by the persistence of pre-feudal relationships among some of the tribal peoples on the fringe of Chinese society, such as those who have been known as the Miao, Chiang, Lo-lo and Chia-jung in our own time, and are only now, after more than two millennia, being integrated into Chinese society as a whole. And indeed many traces of their basic 4th-century BC opposition to feudal and feudal-bureaucratic society continued to cling to the Taoists all through Chinese history, long after their school had generated a mystical nihilism for the educated scholars and an ecclesiastical organization for the poor peasants. Their continued presence in the background of agrarian rebellions under every dynasty is alone evidence of this; they were in a perpetual opposition which only the equalitarian socialism of our own time would satisfy.[4] Of course there are many European parallels for the Taoist idea of a Golden Age – the Cronia and the Saturnalia of Rome commemorating the vanished ages of Cronos and Saturn, the repudiation of over-civilized life by the Stoics and Epicureans, the Christian doctrine of the Fall of man (perhaps deriving from the ancient Sumerian laments for lost social happiness in lordless society), the stories of the 'Isles of the Blest', and finally the eighteenth-century admiration for the Noble Savage, stimulated by the first contacts of Westerners with the real-life 'paradises' of the Pacific.[5]

By some literary accident the most famous statements of the Taoist theory of regressive devolution occur in books of other schools, the 2nd-century BC *Huai Nan Tzu*, and the 1st-century AD Confucian *Li Chi* (Record of Rites). Here we shall quote a passage from the Li Yün chapter of the latter.[6]

When the Great Tao prevailed, the whole world was one Community (*thien hsia wei kung*).[7] Men of talents and virtue were chosen [to lead the people]; their words were sincere and they cultivated harmony. Men treated the parents of others as their own, and cherished the children of others as their own. Competent provision was made for the aged until their death, work was provided for the able-bodied, and education for the young. Kindness and compassion were shown to widows, orphans, childless men and those disabled by disease, so that all were looked after. Each man had his allotted work, and every woman a home to go to. They disliked to throw valuable things away, but that did not mean that they treasured them up in private storehouses. They liked to exert their strength in labour, but that did not mean that they worked for private advantage. In this way selfish schemings were repressed and found no way to arise. Thieves, robbers and traitors did not show themselves, so the outer doors of the houses remained open and were never shut. This was the period of the Great Togetherness (Ta Thung).[8]

But now the Great Tao is disused and eclipsed. The world [the empire] has become a family inheritance. Men love only their own parents and their own children. Valuable things and labour are used only for private advantage. Powerful men, imagining that inheritance of estates has always been the rule, fortify the walls of towns and villages, and strengthen them with ditches and moats. 'Rites' and 'righteousness' are the threads upon which they hang the relations between ruler and minister, father and son, elder and younger brother, and husband and wife. In accordance with them they regulate consumption, distribute land and dwellings, raise up men of war and 'knowledge'; achieving all for their own advantage. Thus selfish schemings are constantly arising, and recourse is had to arms; thus it was that the Six Lords [Yü 'the Great', Thang, Wên, Wu, Chhêng and the Duke of Chou] obtained their distinction ... This is the period which is called the Lesser Tranquillity (Hsiao Khang).

The Mohists undoubtedly sympathized to some extent with this account of the ideal cooperative, even socialist, society which had, it was thought, existed in the remote past, but it was certainly not part of Confucian ideology at all. Nevertheless, in spite of the later universal dominance of Confucianism in Chinese life, the idea of the Ta Thung society enjoyed a certain immortality, for if it had really once existed upon the face of the earth, it might perhaps be brought into existence again.[9] Indeed, Confucianism itself, with its emphasis upon development and social evolution, contributed to this very end. And although the innumerable peasant rebellions through Chinese history rarely pushed their thinking beyond the establishment of a new and better dynasty,[10] at the same time their more visionary elements were often inclined to reverse the time-dimension of the regressive conception and turn it into a progressive one. Nineteen centuries later than the Han, in our own time, these two little words had vastly gained, not lost, in numinous, emotional and revolutionary force.[11]

There was indeed a parallel (or rather, inverse) ascending Confucian sequence, but before examining it we must take a look at another, related, conception, that of Thai Phing (the Great Peace and Equality).[12] This was another 'phrase of power', but widely varying in interpretation.[13] The Golden Age and the realizable Utopia are here not very clearly dissociable; it is hard to find definite statements in ancient texts that this was an era only in the far past which could never come back, or that it was purely something to look forward to in the future. Undoubtedly many imperial reigns were consciously trying to attain it. The term appears first in 239 BC, in the *Lü Shih Chhun Chhiu* (Master Lü's Spring and Autumn Annals), a famous compendium of natural philosophy, where it denotes a state of peace and prosperity which can be brought about magically by music in harmony with the cyclical operations of Nature.[14] During the following centuries the emphasis was sometimes upon social peace springing from the harmonious collaboration of different social classes each contented with its lot, sometimes upon a harmony of natural phenomena (which man could perhaps induce) leading to an abundance of the kindly fruits of the earth, and sometimes upon the idea of equality, with undertones of reference to that primitive classless society which might in the last day be restored. Some thought that the Great Peace had existed under the sage-kings of high antiquity, others that it was attainable by good imperial government here and now, and others again that it would come to pass at some future time. It is worth while to cite some of these different opinions.

The mysterious social magic of Master Lü appears again in the chapter on rites in the *Chhien Han Shu* (History of the Former Han Dynasty), AD 100, where it is said that the full application of the rites of the former kings will bring about the Thai Phing state.[15] This had particular reference to the seasonal ceremonies of the Ming Thang, or cosmic temple, where the emperor and his assistants carried out liturgical observances before heaven on the people's behalf. The biography of the minister Tou Ying (d. 131 BC) tells of his support for the Ming Thang and other ceremonial measures as the way in which the Great Peace could be attained,[16] and the *Huai Nan Tzu* book (120 BC) specifically connects its attainment with the ritual purity and clarity of the cosmic temple services.[17] On the other hand the biography of Tungfang Shuo (d. *c.* 80 BC) speaks of the induction of natural conditions favourable to mankind by man's own social harmony,[18] and the economic chapter of the *Chhien Han Shu* goes so far as to apply the term Thai Phing to record-harvest years.[19] One of the sections of the *Chuang Tzu* book which is probably a Han interpolation says that the highest aim, good government, Thai Phing, is to be attained not by human skill and planning, but only by following the Tao of Heaven. Now 'the Tao of Heaven is to revolve ceaselessly and not to amass virtue or things in any particular place, thus it is that all things are brought into perfection by it (*thien tao yün erh wu so chi, ku wan wu chhêng*).'[20] Here at once is the theme of Great Equality as well as Great Peace, and echoes awake throughout the Taoist writings. The 'equality of things and opinions' was the doctrine of the Chi-Hsia Academicians Phêng Meng, Thien Phien, and Shen Tao (all *fl.* 320 BC–300 BC),[21] as well as the title of a genuine chapter of the *Chuang Tzu* book (*c.* 290 BC) which contains some of Chuang Chou's clearest keys to Taoist epistemology, scientific world-outlook and democratic social thinking.[22] 'The great highway [of the Tao of justice and righteousness]', says the *Tao Tê Ching*, 'is broad and level (*ta tao shen i*)' – one of those pregnant sayings which recalls Hebrew prophecy, 'Make straight the way of the Lord', and touches the mystical poetry of road engineering in all ages and peoples, 'the valleys shall be exalted, and the mountains shall be made low.'[23] Its equalitarian meaning cannot be in doubt for the poem goes on to castigate the feudal lords for amassing wealth and oppressing the peasant-farmers: 'these are the riotous ways of brigandage, these are not the great highway'.[24]

Many ancient texts, however, speak of Thai Phing only as the Golden Age of the sage-kings of high antiquity; so Chia I in his *Hsin Shu* (*c.* 170 BC),[25] the alchemist Wu Pei talking with his patron the prince of Huai-Nan (*c.* 130 BC),[26] the chapter on rites in the *Shih Chi* (*c.* 100 BC),[27] and the *Yin Wên Tzu* book.[28] Others make it clear that in certain prosperous periods the Great Peace was considered as already having been attained. It is clear that the first emperor Chhin Shih Huang Ti was explicitly striving for it,[29] and by 210 BC claimed to have inaugurated it: an inscription set up in that year says: 'The people are pleased with the standard rules and measures, and felicitate each other on the preservation of the Great Peace.[30] So also Lu Wên-Shu (*fl.* 70 BC) considered that the reign of Han Wên Ti (179 BC to 157 BC) had been a period of Thai Phing.[31] All these different opinions can be found discussed in the *Lun Hêng* (AD 83); one chapter records its attribution to the time of the ancient sages Yao and Shun, another says that many believed it was presaged by the appearance of the phoenix and the unicorn, and in a third Wang Chhung gives his own belief that Thai Phing prosperity had occurred several times during the two Han dynasties.[32]

We come now to the incorporation of the Thai Phing concept into a temporal sequence analogous to that of the Ta Thung. It arose out of the exegesis of the *Chhun Chhiu* (Spring and Autumn Annals) by the scholars of the Han. This book was a chronicle of the feudal state of Lu between

722 BC and 481 BC, and there was a persistent tradition that Confucius himself had edited it. It has come down through the ages accompanied by commentaries in three traditions known as the *Tso Chuan*, the *Kuliang Chuan* and the *Kungyang Chuan*.[33] Master Tsochhiu's Enlargement carried the history down a little further, to 453 BC, and was compiled from ancient written and oral traditions of several states (not only Lu) between 430 BC and 250 BC, though with many later changes and additions by Confucian scholars of the Chhin and Han. Master Kuliang's Commentary and Master Kungyang's Commentary differed from this in that they were not formed partly from independent ancient historical writings, but restricted themselves to word-for-word explanations of the chronicle text.[34] The importance of this was the belief that great moral weight attached to the precise terms which Confucius had used in each given historical circumstance. During the 2nd and 1st centuries BC the scholars of the Han formed groups which specialized in the study of one or other of these traditions, indeed separate chairs were established for them in the imperial university.[35] Among those learned in the tradition of Master Kungyang was that remarkable philosopher (who made his mark in many other ways), Tung Chung-Shu (179 BC to 104 BC). Tung developed a theory of the San Shih or Three Ages, grouping the events in the *Chhun Chhiu* into a triple classification, those that Confucius himself had personally witnessed (541 BC to 480 BC), those that he heard of from oral testimony (626 BC to 542 BC), and those that he knew only through written records (722 BC to 627 BC).[36] Then in the Later Han this was converted into an ascending social evolutionary series, first applied to the Confucian redaction, and afterwards extended to a universal application. Here the key mind was Ho Hsiu (AD 129 to 182), whose work became the standard commentary on the *Kungyang Chuan*.[37] He wrote:

In the age of which he heard through transmitted records, Confucius saw [and made evident] that there was an order arising from Weakness and Disorder (Shuai Luan),[38] and so directed his mind primarily towards the general [scheme of things]. He therefore considered his own State [of Lu] as the centre, and treated the rest of the Chinese oikoumene as something outside [his scheme]. He gave detailed treatment to what was close at hand, and only then paid attention to what was further away ...

In the age of which he heard through oral testimony he saw [and made evident] that there was an order arising of Approaching Peace (Shêng Phing). He therefore considered the Chinese oikoumene as the centre, and treated the peripheral barbarian tribes as something outside [his scheme]. Thus he recorded even those assemblies outside [his own State] which failed to reach agreement, and mentioned the great officials even of small States ...

Coming to the age which he [personally] witnessed, he made evident that there was an order [arising] of Great Peace (Thai Phing). At this time the barbarian tribes became part of the feudal hierarchy, and the whole [known] world, far and near, large and small, was like one. Hence he directed his mind still more profoundly to making a detailed record [of the events of the age], and therefore exalted [acts of] love and righteousness ...

Here then we have the formal simulacrum of a process of social evolution in time, ready to be taken over into the general thought of the people as applicable to the whole of civilization.

Already before the time of Ho Hsiu, religious Taoism fermenting among the people had adopted the idea of Thai Phing in this way.[39] Much study is now being given to a corpus of ancient documents of which the chief is a book entitled *Thai Phing Ching* (Canon of the Great Peace), difficult to date because probably written at different times between the Warring States period (*c.* 4th century BC) and the end of the Later Han (AD 220).[40] Though the greater part of this is concerned with religious and superstitious practices, revelations and prophetic warnings, there are passages which link up with the revolutionary Taoism of the great national uprisings – the 'Red Eyebrows' of AD 24 led by Fan Chhung, and the 'Yellow Turbans' (AD 184 to 205) under Chang Chio.[41] It must of course be understood that the *Thai Phing Ching* and its associated texts were greatly expurgated in subsequent times by Taoists loyal to the established order.[42] But the popular religious Taoism of the Han was millenniarist and apocalyptic; the Great Peace was clearly in the future as well as the remote past. In the 'Canon' we hear of rural social solidarity, sins committed against the community and their forgiveness, an anti-technology complex, the overcoming of village feuds, and the particularly high place accorded to women. We also find a theory of cycles opposite in character to those of the Neo-Confucians which throws light upon the practices of another great Taoist rebel leader Sun Ên (d. AD 402).[43] As the sins of mankind's evil generations increase to a climax, world catastrophes, flood and pestilence sweep all away – or nearly all, for a 'holy remnant' (a 'seed people', *chung min*), saved by their Taoism, win through to find a new heaven and a new earth of great peace and equality, under the leadership of the Prince of Peace (Ta Thai-Phing Chün), of course Lao Tzu. Then everything slowly worsens again until another salvation is necessary. Thus unlike the cycles of the Neo-Confucians which rose extremely slowly and ended in a flash, those of the religious Taoists issued fresh from chaos 'wie herrlich als am ersten Tag' and then fell slowly till the day of doom. But whether or not time was thought of as boxed this way in cyclical periods, the Thai Phing ideal was now for ever inscribed upon the banners of the Chinese people in one rebellion after another. It was clearly stated to be the aim of the Ming revolutionary Chhen Chien-Hu (*c.* AD 1425); and gave of course the name to the great

Thai-Phing Thien-Kuo movement which between 1851 and 1864 nearly toppled the Manchu (Chhing) dynasty, and which is regarded in China today as the closest forerunner of the People's Republic.[44]

But this was not at all the end. One of the greatest reformers and representatives of modern Chinese thought, Khang Yu-Wei, who lived (1858 to 1927) through the period of intellectual strain when China was absorbing and digesting the new ideas which contact with the modern scientific civilization of the West had brought, drew greatly upon these age-old dreams and theories of progress. His classical studies led him to adopt positions which modern historical philology cannot now sustain,[45] but his thought was deeply influenced both by the seemingly Mohist Great Togetherness (Ta Thung) and the Taoist Great Peace and Equality (Thai Phing). Interpreting them both in the ascending evolutionary sense, he chose the former as the title of an extraordinary utopia, the *Ta Thung Shu* (Book of the Great Togetherness),[46] conceived and first drafted in 1884, partly printed in 1913, and not completely printed till 1935. It has been reprinted in Peking as recently as 1956, and an abridged English translation appeared in 1958,[47] so that Western readers now have access to a magnificent description of the future, visionary perhaps but extremely practical and scientific, which it would not be inappropriate to call Wellsian in its authority and scope, a vision which no Chinese scholar could have been expected to create if his intellectual background had been as timeless and static as Chinese thought has only too often been supposed to be. Khang Yu-Wei predicted a supra-national cooperative commonwealth with world-wide institutions, enlightened sexual and racial policies, public ownership of the means of production, and startling scientific and technological advances including the use of atomic energy. In our own time the charismatic phrases of old became the nationwide watchwords of the political parties, *Thien hsia wei kung* (Let the whole world be One Community) for the Kuomintang, and *Thien hsia ta thung* (The world shall be the Great Togetherness) for the Kungchhantang.

Enough has surely now been said to demonstrate conclusively that the culture of China manifested a very sensitive consciousness of time. The Chinese did not live in a timeless dream, fixed in meditation upon the noumenal world. On the contrary, history was for them perhaps more real and vital than for any other comparably ancient people; and whether they conceived time to contain a perennial fall from ancient perfection, or to pass on in cycles of glory and catastrophe, or to testify to a slow but inevitable evolution and progress, time for them brought real and fundamental change. They were far from being a people who 'took no account of time'.

NOTES

1 For example the great 2nd century BC medical classic *Huang Ti Nei Ching Su Wên* (ch. 14) periodizes history into ancient (*shang ku*), middle-old (*chung ku*) and recent (*tang chin*) ages, saying that there had been a gradual decline in men's resistance to diseases, so that stronger drugs and treatments were required as time went on.

2 One entire chapter of the *Huai Nan Tzu* book (*c.* 120 BC) is devoted to proving social change and progress since the most ancient times, with many references to material improvement (ch. 13, Morgan trans., pp. 143ff). The *Huai Nan Tzu* is very Taoist in many ways, but this was a viewpoint of Han Taoism rather than of that of the Warring States.

3 See *Science and Civilisation in China* (hereafter SCC), vol. 2, pp. 86ff, 99ff, 104ff, 115ff.

4 See SCC, vol. 2, p. 60.

5 See SCC, vol. 2, pp. 127ff.

6 Ch. 9, Legge trans., vol. 1, pp. 364ff, here modified from SCC, vol. 2, p. 167. Li Yün may be translated 'The mutations of social institutions'. The wording of parallel passages in the *Mo Tzu* book, chs. 11, 12, 13, 14, 15 (trans., Mei Yi-Pao, pp. 55, 59, 71, 80, 82), fix the date as fourth century BC, not first century AD. But these passages are 'progressive' rather than 'regressive' in tendency, criticizing the ancient rulerless times as an age when humanity was all 'at sixes and sevens', and placing the Ta Thung state in the future, to be brought about by the practice of universal love (*chien ai*). The actual expression Ta Thung is not used in *Mo Tzu*. A similar account to that in the *Li Chi*, but much shorter, occurs in the *Huai Nan Tzu* book (120 BC), ch. 2, where the expression Ta Chih (the Ideal Rule) is used instead of Ta Thung; cf. Morgan trans., p. 35.

7 Lit. 'for the general use', i.e., not the property of the emperor, feudal lords and patrician families.

8 This phrase, which we might equally translate the Great Community, was also used in a rather different sense by the late Warring States philosophers, namely to indicate the parallel of the microcosm (man) with the macrocosm (the universe). For an example of this see *Lü Shih Chhun Chhiu* (239 BC), ch. 62 (R. Wilhelm trans., p. 160). But the senses are not so far apart because the ancient Chinese felt that social community was 'intended by Nature' and that class differentiation and all strife was a violation of the natural order, a violation moreover, which would upset Nature and lead to natural calamities, or at least to unfavourable weather conditions, epidemics, etc. Besides, *thung* as 'with-ness' allows the translation 'Great Similarity'.

9 See the valuable paper of Hou Wai-Lu, 'Socialnye Utopii Drevnego i Srednevekovogo Kitaia' (Social utopias of ancient and mediaeval China), *Voprosy Filozofii*, 9 (1959), 75.

10 See Shih Yu-Chung, 'Some Chinese rebel ideologies', *T'oung Pao*, 44 (1956), 150.

11 On the history of the Ta Thung concept in China there is a valuable little book by Hou Wai-Lu, Chang Kai-Chih, Yang Chao and Li Hsüeh-Chin, 'Chung-Kuo Li-Tai "Ta Thung" Li Hsiang' (Kloffsüch, Peking, 1959).

12 The word *phing* has both meanings.

13 It is now under intensive study by sinologists, historians and social

philosophers. The best review of the subject in a Western language is probably that of W. Eichhorn, 'Thai-Phing und Thai-Phing Religion', *Mitt. d. Inst. f. Orientforschung*, 5 (1957), 113, seconded by T. Pokora, 'On the origins of the notions of Thai-Phing and Ta-Thung in Chinese philosophy', *Archiv. Orientalni*, 29 (1961), 448.

14 Ch. 22, Wilhelm trans., p. 56.

15 Ch. 22, Eichhorn, 'Thai-Phing', p. 116.

16 *Chhien Han Shu*, ch. 52, Eichhorn, 'Thai-Phing', p. 123.

17 Ch. 2, Eichhorn, 'Thai-Phing', p. 123.

18 *Chhien Han Shu*, ch. 65.

19 Ch. 24.

20 Ch. 13 (Thien Tao), Legge trans., vol. 1, pp. 330, 337.

21 See Fêng Yu-Lan, 'A history of Chinese philosophy' (trans. D. Bodde, Princeton Univ. Press, 1953), vol. 1, pp. 153ff. These men were all members of the Chi-Hsia academy founded by Prince Huan of Chhi, *c.* 325 BC.

22 Ch. 2 (Chi Wu Lun), Legge trans., vol. 1, pp. 176ff.

23 40: Isaiah, 3, 4. There was also a mystique of topographic levelling in Hindu and Buddhist thought, the 'alluvial' flatness left behind by world floods or catastrophes on which the Buddhas and Bodhisattvas pace. On this idea see P. Mus, 'La notion de temps réversible dans la mythologie bouddhique', *Annuaire de l'Ecole Pratique des Hautes Etudes* (*Sect. des Sciences Religieuses*), 1939, pp. 15, 33ff, 36.

24 Ch. 53, Wu trans., p. 75, Chhu trans., p. 66, Duyvendak trans., p. 117.

25 Ch. 52 (Hsiu Chêng Yü), trans., Eichhorn, 'Thai-Phing', p. 118.

26 *Chhien Han Shu*, ch. 45.

27 Ch. 23, Chavannes trans., vol. 3, p. 211.

28 Ch. 2 (Ta Tao), where Thien Phien, lecturing on the *Shu Ching* (Historical Classic), said that in the time of the (legendary) Emperor Yao, there had been Thai Phing.

29 *Shih Chi*, ch. 6, Chavannes trans., vol. 2, p. 180.

30 *Shih Chi*, ch. 6, Chavannes trans., vol. 2, p. 189.

31 *Chhien Han Shu*, ch. 51.

32 Respectively, ch. 26 (Ju Tsêng), Forke trans., vol. 1, p. 494; ch. 50 (Chiang Jui), Forke trans., vol. 1, p. 364; and ch. 57 (Hsüan Han), Forke trans., vol. 2, pp. 192ff. Wang Chhung also combated the excessive veneration of the sages and the belief in a Golden Age in his ch. 56 (Chhi Shih – that all generations are much the same), Forke trans., vol. 1, pp. 471ff. It is interesting that the phrase Thai Phing occurs in quite a number of place-names, and even more that it was used as the appellation of no less than six reign-periods. These were in the following dynasties: San Kuo (Wu) AD 256, Northern Yen AD 409, Northern Wei AD 440, Liang AD 556, Sung AD 976, and Liao AD 1021. Ta Thung was also used in reign-period names, twice, Liang AD 535 (AD 546) and Liao AD 946 (AD 947).

33 A good introductory account of this literature will be found in P. van der Loon, 'The ancient Chinese chronicles and the growth of historical ideals', art. in 'Historians of China and Japan', ed. W. G. Beasley and E. G. Pulleyblank (Oxford, 1961), p. 24. For fuller details the monograph of Wu Khang may be studied.

34 All three were supposed to derive from the oral teaching of Confucius himself.

35 This dates from 124 BC, though the governmental title of Po-Shih (doctor or

professor) had appeared already in the 3rd century BC and the principle of imperial examinations in 165 BC. When Han Wu Ti endowed 'disciples' (*ti-tzu*) as well as professors, the Imperial university may be said to have been established. By 10 BC it had as many as 3,000 students, not all, of course, 'on the foundation'. The term Thai Hsüeh, afterwards borne for centuries by the university, occurs first in a memorial by Tung Chung-Shu himself urging its establishment, though the emperor preferred the plans of Kungsun Hung for the same design.

36 See Fêng Yu-Lan, 'History of Chinese philosophy', vol. 2, p. 81.

37 *Ibid.*, vol. 2, p. 83. The passage occurs at the end of the first chapter of the *Kungyang Chuan.*

38 This phrase has an undertone of the Golden Age theory because *shuai* means decay or decadence as well as weakness and feebleness. But it is doubtful whether this was intended because an alternative form of the phrase found in many texts is Chü Luan, *chü* meaning forcible occupation or possession, the seizing of lands and goods, rebellion, etc., i.e. the correlate of weakness; in other words the state of society described in the Gospel of St Luke, 11: 21, or the 'law of the fishes' in Buddhism, unending internecine strife, 'Nature red in tooth and claw'. Cf. Hsiao Kung-Chhüan, 'Khang Yu-Wei and Confucianism', *Monumenta Serica*, 18 (1959), 96, 142.

39 If Pokora, 'On the origins' is right, the ideas of Ho Hsiu were directly derived from the popular progressive apocalyptic, possibly through the intermediation of Yü Chi (*c.* AD 120 to 200). Yü Chi was a naturalist, physician and thaumaturgist, one of the fathers of the Taoist church, and probably the author of one or more of the books which formed the material of the *Thai Phing Ching.*

40 The corpus has been newly edited with the title '*Thai Phing Ching* Ho Chiao' (Peking, 1960) by Wang Ming, who attempts to reconstitute the original text of the main work. Pokora, 'On the origins' gives a brief description of his book, and Eichhorn, 'Thai-Phing', discusses the contents of some of the documents which it includes.

41 On him see W. Eichhorn, 'Bemerkungen zum Aufstand des Chang Chio und zum Staate des Chang Lu', *Mitt. d. Inst. f. Orientforschung*, 3 (1955), 291.

42 Nevertheless it still contains eloquent passages quite in the vein of that revolutionary thinker Pao Ching-Yen who (if not a literary creation of Ko Hung's) must have flourished in the latter part of the 3rd century AD; see SCC, vol. 2, pp. 434ff.

43 On him see W. Eichhorn, 'Description of the rebellion of Sun Ên and earlier Taoist rebellions', *Mitt. d. Inst. f. Orientforschung*, 2 (1954), 325, with an appendix, 'Nachträgliche Bemerkungen zum Aufstände des Sun Ên', p. 463.

44 The standard modern work on this great but ultimately abortive revolution is by Lo Erh-Kang, 'Thai-Phing Thien-Kuo Ko-Ming Chan Chêng Shih' (A history of the revolutionary war of the heaven-ordained Kingdom of Great Peace and Equality) (Peking, 1949); and since then eight volumes of source material have been edited by Hsiang Ta *et al.*, 'Thai-Phing Thien-Kuo' (Peking, 1957). There is no satisfactory book on the subject as yet in any Western language, but three contemporary classics may be mentioned, the first by a British government interpreter, the second by a missionary, and the third by a soldier of fortune, who fought with the Thai-Phing armies. T. T. Meadows, 'The Chinese and their rebellions; viewed in connection with their

national philosophy, ethics, legislation and administration, to which is added, an Essay on civilisation and its present state in the East and West' (Bombay and London, 1856; repr. Academic Reprints, Stanford, Calif., n.d. [1953]), is a work in which the discursive background material (not in itself uninteresting) equals in amount the valuable first-hand description. W. H. Medhurst, 'Pamphlets issued by the Chinese insurgents at Nanking: to which is added a history of the Kwang-se [Kuangsi] rebellion, gathered from public documents; and a sketch of the connection between foreign missionaries and the Chinese insurrection; concluding with a critical view of several of the above pamphlets' (North China Herald, Shanghai, 1853), is naturally mainly concerned with the quasi-Christianity of the Thai-Phing revolutionaries. Lin-Le (Ling-Le, i.e. A. F.Lindley), 'Ti-Peng Tien-Kwoh; the History of the Ti-Ping revolution, including a narrative of the author's personal adventures' (London, 1866), has more about the adventures than the history, but, since the work of one who did something to counterbalance the military intervention of other foreigners (Ward, Burgevine and Gordon) on the imperialist side, it gives insights into the character of the Thai-Phing leaders otherwise unobtainable. Amongst recent publications there is the book of Chêng Chê-Hsi (J. C. Chêng), 'Chinese sources for the Thai-Phing rebellion, 1850 to 1864' (Hong Kong, 1963), but it is so lacking in commentary and explanation that it can serve only as a companion volume to other accounts. To this may be added a useful paper by Shih Yu-Chung (V. Y. C. Shih), 'The ideology of the Thai-Phing Rebellion', *Sinologica*, 3 (1951), 1; and E. P. Boardman's 'Christian influence on the ideology of the Thai-Phing Rebellion' (Madison, Wis., 1952). Lastly see also G. Taylor, 'The Thai-Phing Rebellion, its economic background and social theory', *Chinese Soc. and Polit. Sci. Rev.*, 16 (1933), 545.

45 This is a complex question which can only be touched upon here. It involves the 'Old Text' and 'New Text' controversy which divided the scholars of the Han, and no less those of the late Chhing who delved again into Han studies. This division had arisen because of the discovery, during the second century BC, of a set of versions of the classics (the *Shu Ching* or Book of History, the *Shih Ching* or Book of Odes, the *Tso Chuan* and the *Chou Li*) which differed from the texts previously accepted, and which were written in the archaic script of the early (Western) Chou. Traditionally this occurred during the destruction of the supposed house of Confucius in 135 BC when Prince Kung of Lu (Lu Kung Wang), Liu Yü, was enlarging his palace; but similar texts were also said to have been among those collected by the great bibliophile Liu Tê (d. 130 BC), the Prince of Ho-Chien (Ho Chien Wang). The terminology is rather confusing because the 'Old Texts' were those newly discovered in the Former Han, while the 'New Texts' were those which had the old authority of continuous use; one has to remember to think of them as the 'Old Script Texts' and the 'New Script Texts'. Many subsequent centuries of scholarly debate have ended in the conclusion that the story of the single discovery was a legend, and that some at least of the 'old versions' were probably forgeries, though the *Shu Ching* ones were not identical with the present 'Old Text' chapters which are known to have been compiled with ancient fragments about AD 320. From the point of view of the history of scientific thought the controversy has particular interest in that while the members of the New Text school (i.e. those who accepted the texts which had been continuously transmitted through the official teaching tradition) were textually on stronger

ground, they accepted all the superstitious pseudo-sciences of the time, and with them that empirical open-mindedness in which the sprouts of experimental science could burgeon; and, while the members of the Old Text school put their faith in false or at least dubious documents, they nevertheless tended to be rationalists, enlightened in a sense but not always so favourable to proto-scientific tentatives as the others (one thinks of alchemy, pharmacy, the study of magnetism, etc.). Among the greatest names of the Old Text school were Liu Hsin (50 BC to AD 23) and Tung Chung-Shu. By modern times, of course, the attitudes of the ancient scholars to science no longer mattered; what was at stake was the authenticity of the classics. So far as we can now tell, the differences between the 'old' and 'new' versions were numerous, though fairly minor, but the argument in the nineteenth century was that for some of the classics one no longer had the 'new' versions at all, while the 'old' ones had been produced by the Han scholars themselves. Khang Yu-Wei, for his part, led a great campaign in favour of the New Text school. He believed that the whole of the existing *Tso Chuan* and *Chou Li* had been forged by Liu Hsin himself, and that the *Kungyang Chuan* and the *Li Chi* constituted the only reliable avenue through which the true Confucius could be attained. He also believed that Confucius had been a great reformer rather than a conservative. Hence his two books, the *Hsin Hsüeh Wei Ching Khao* (Study of the forged works of the Hsin dynasty) of 1891, and his *Khung-Tzu Kai Chih Khao* (Confucius as a reformer) of 1897. Although Khang's philological beliefs are no longer tenable today, the connection between them and his faith in a Confucian blessing on the idea of social progress and evolution will now be evident. Which came first in his own development, the philological conclusions or the social philosophy, is not quite clear.

On the 'Old or New Text' controversies see Tjan Tjoe Som (Tsêng Chu-Sen), '*Po Hu T'ung*, the comprehensive discussions in the White Tiger Hall' (Leiden, 1949), vol. 1, pp. 137ff; Fêng Yu-Lan, 'A history of Chinese philosophy', vol. 2, pp. 7ff, 133ff, 673ff; Woo Kang (Wu Khang), 'Les trois théories politiques du Tch'ouen Ts'ieou [Chhun Chhiu]' Paris, 1932), pp. 186ff; C. S. Gardner, 'Chinese traditional historiography' (Harvard Press, 1938), pp. 9, 56ff. On Khang Yu-Wei's thoughts in detail see also Hsiao Kung-Chhüan, 'Khang Yu-Wei and Confucianism', 18 (1959), 96.

As for the role of Confucius himself, whether on the whole progressive or reactionary, debate continues actively among scholars both in China and the West. For a sympathetic and rather convincing statement of the former case see H. G. Creel, 'Confucius, the man and the myth' (New York, 1949; London, 1951).

46 Note that the title was taken from the *Li Chi* but the progressive content from the traditional development of the *Kungyang Chuan*, and from *Mo Tzu*.

47 By L. G. Thompson, '*Ta Thung Shu*; the One-world philosophy of Khang Yu-Wei' (London, 1958).

4

*The bourgeois revolution of 1848–9 in Central Europe**

ARNOŠT KLÍMA

News of the outbreak of revolution in Paris on 24 February 1848 and of the uprisings in Switzerland and Italy sparked a revolutionary movement throughout Central Europe. Revolutionary activity began in Baden on 27 February with a large public meeting in Mannheim; on the same day a second assembly took place in Munich, swiftly followed by similar gatherings in Stuttgart and Mainz. Appeals were made everywhere for fundamental changes to the existing political order, with similar demands being voiced not only in the various German states, but also in Austria and Bohemia. At meetings across Central Europe, people called for an end to Diets composed of the traditional Estates and for the institution of parliaments where representatives of the bourgeoisie and peasantry would sit and make decisions. Similarly, widespread demands were made for the creation of National Guards to protect the achievements of revolution against the armies of the *anciens régimes*. The revolutionaries stipulated the introduction of trial by jury to replace seigneurial courts controlled by feudal authorities, the abolition of censorship, as well as freedom of association, assembly and the press.

Representatives of the existing social and political power structures immediately perceived the seriousness of the threat to the old order. A mere four days after the Paris uprising, and a day after the Mannheim and Munich assemblies, the Prussian minister of the interior, von Bodelschwingh, instructed the civil authorities (*Oberpräsidenten*) to stand firm against the mass demonstrations. They were aiming, he said, 'to force all manner of change, following the example set in Switzerland, Italy and France.'[1]

* I understand by 'Central Europe' in 1848 the area covered by Germany, Poland, the Czech Lands (Bohemia, Moravia, Silesia), Austria, Hungary and Switzerland. I deal with the revolution in Germany, the Czech Lands, Austria and Hungary, where its impact was significant, unlike Poland and Switzerland. I discuss Northern Italy as part of the Habsburg monarchy; otherwise Italy, like Croatia, belongs to Southern Europe.

Social classes and social change

It was the dissatisfied classes who agitated these changes: the bourgeoisie, the peasantry and the proletariat. By the early nineteenth century the bourgeoisie was employing a sizeable labour force, contributing appreciably to the formation of capital, making large profits and acquiring extensive property. Under feudal conditions, however, this enhanced economic position was not matched by an appropriate political status. Further development of the economic activities of the bourgeoisie required the removal of feudal privileges and restrictions, changes that were not forthcoming as long as the bourgeoisie was excluded from political life. In the long run, nothing less than a revolutionary transformation of prevailing feudal structures would permit the unhampered development of productive forces.

The peasants, too, were desirous of social change, specifically an end to the feudal subjection which persisted in many Central European countries. Land was still considered to be the property of feudal landlords, and for its use peasants were obliged to render dues in money or in unpaid labour (*robota* in Czech and Slovak, *robot* in Magyar and German). The peasants resented this exaction of service, and wanted the right to own land themselves. Those who were feudal subjects demanded that seigneurial courts be replaced by juries, and that feudal authorities in towns and villages give way to communal self-government.

Workers, a new social class formed in the course of industrialization, also supported the changes envisaged by the bourgeoisie. They favoured the abolition of censorship, freedom of the press and assembly, the convening of a parliament, and in some cases the organization of labour and wages as well.[2] For the most part, they did not perceive entrepreneurs as their antagonists. However, during the March Revolution of 1848, they broke into factories and destroyed machines in some places, notably Meidling, Perchtoldsdorf and Schwechat (suburbs of Vienna). Their complaint was the same as that expressed by Bohemian workers during a period of similar unrest in 1844:[3] 'We have no work and no bread; the machines are to blame for this and that's why we came to smash them.'[4] Similar disturbances occurred in the Solingen region of Germany in March 1848.[5]

Reform or revolution?

The revolution of 1848–9 in Central Europe must be considered a bourgeois revolution. The bourgeoisie had a programme for transforming society and strove to see their vision realized. Some historians prefix this particular revolution with the epithet 'great',[6] and others speak of its universal significance for, despite its defeat, it marked the completion of the process of bourgeois transformation.[7] In all the revolutionary outbreaks in Central Europe during 1848 (with the exception of Hungary), the bourgeoisie took the lead. This class was divided into two camps, liberal and radical, which differed over strategy despite their shared aim of eliminating feudal fetters and creating a capitalist system. Liberals everywhere favoured a compromise with the existing power elite of princes, kings, emperor and nobles, wanting only to share power and to construct a capitalist society by parliamentary means. The radicals inclined to more dramatic measures, and in Germany, where they were generally called democrats, sought the abolition of royal powers and the formation of a republic. A more comprehensive approach was taken by radicals in Austria, Bohemia and Hungary, where they envisaged collaboration between the masses in town and country. Despite these variations all radicals were uniformly opposed to compromise in their efforts to realize bourgeois goals. Among their numbers, students and intellectuals formed a significant group, originating from families of artisans, officials and peasants, and generally representing the 'bourgeois middle' (*bürgerliche Mitte*). But people of lower social origins were also included, with workers and labourers playing an important role in the Viennese revolution.[8] On 13 March they marched from the university to the seat of the Lower Austrian Diet and delivered a petition demanding the resignation of Metternich, the chancellor of state. Clashes with troops claimed five lives, precipitating a revolutionary uprising which deposed Metternich before the day was out. The army, led by Prince Windischgrätz, was unable to control the mass movement, and within two days the Habsburg court and government had to give in to the revolutionary demands. After Metternich fell, censorship was suspended and a free press was proclaimed. A National Guard was formed and promises were exacted from the emperor (Ferdinand) that he would endorse a constitution and convene a parliament.

The Viennese revolution sent reverberations throughout Central Europe. They were felt not only in Prague, where a large public meeting had decided to present a list of demands to the emperor on 11 March, but also in Berlin, where a stormy week ending 13 March had been punctuated by mass meetings of 10,000 people in the Tiergarten (the largest park in Berlin). When news of the Viennese revolution and the fall of Metternich arrived on 15 March, the liberal bourgeoisie of the Rhenish province, led by the banker Camphausen, demanded a free press, convocation of a parliament and a unified Germany under Prussian leadership. A deputation from Cologne arrived in Berlin on 17 March to present demands to the king of Prussia, Frederick William IV, and the following day the king announced that the German Confederation, the organization of German states created in 1815, was to be reformed. Customs and censorship were to be abolished; a parliament, a constitution and a free press were promised. Events in Berlin thus ran closely parallel to those in Vienna between 13 and 15 March. But the people of Berlin went still further and demanded the withdrawal of troops from the capital, lest the army be used against them. Barricades were erected and the city became a battlefield. Approximately 230 people were killed, but the 20,000 soldiers were unable to gain control, for the court in Berlin was no more prepared than they had been in Vienna a few days earlier. Only a state of complete unreadiness could account for the failure of the Berlin and Viennese courts to contain the conflict. Frederick Wilhelm IV himself put it aptly: 'We were caught lying down'.[9] On 19 March he ordered the withdrawal of troops from Berlin, marking a significant partial victory for the revolution. Among the dead were fifty-eight journeymen, fifteen factory workers, and five apprentices, with a further thirty-three unidentified. A huge procession carried the bodies to the palace and forced the king to pay them his last respects, an act which constituted undoubted proof of the people's victory.

While the revolutionary movements in Germany, Austria, and Bohemia were unequivocally bourgeois in character, that in Hungary was marked by a number of unique features. There the initiative came not from members of the bourgeoisie but from the gentry, the segment of the nobility which sat in the Lower Chamber of the Hungarian Diet. It was there that a motion was tabled on 3 March to petition the Austrian emperor for an autonomous Hungarian government. Kossuth, the gentry's spokesman, was determined to prevent a popular uprising and ensure a position of leadership for the nobility in the changes that were under way.[10] At a sitting of the Diet in Bratislava (Pozsony in Magyar, Pressburg in German) on 14 March, he requested the addition of two demands to the petition: the introduction of a uniform system of taxation and the abolition of forced labour by offering state compensation to feudal landlords.[11]

On 15 March, after news of the successful revolution in Vienna, a deputation from the Hungarian Diet set out for Vienna to deliver the petition. When it arrived the revolution was still in full swing and the court was in a concessionary mood, so the Magyar demands were quickly approved on 17 March. On the evening of the same day Kossuth was able to announce this first Magyar victory to the people of Bratislava from the balcony of the inn 'At the Green Tree', declaring that Count Lajos Batthyány had been appointed to lead a Hungarian government. At the same time that the nobility in Bratislava were planning a self-governing Hungary within the framework of the Austrian monarchy, demands for social change were being put forward by the young radical intelligentsia in Pest, demands similar to those being submitted simultaneously in Mannheim, Vienna and Prague. They concerned the freedom of the press, the equality of all persons before the law, the abolition of feudal subjection, the introduction of communal self-government, the institution of trial by jury and the formation of a National Guard. Also called for were the release of political prisoners, the creation of a Hungarian government and the unification of Hungary with Transylvania. This group of radical intellectuals was led by writers and publicists such as Sándor Petöfi, Mór Jókai, Pál Vasvári and József Irinyi. At a public meeting in Pest on 15 March attended by about 20,000 people, they called for the establishment of a Committee of Public Safety and secured the release of the publicist Mihály Táncsics from prison. On 19 March a deputation was sent to Bratislava to deliver their demands to the Hungarian Diet. The petition was received by Kossuth, who announced that the Diet was assuming the responsibility for continuing the course of the revolution. And, indeed, after discussing the petition, the Diet enacted new laws which established a free press, a National Bank, and the indemnification of feudal landlords for the abolition of forced labour. It also passed a suffrage law based on property qualifications, thereby excluding broad sections of the population from the right to vote.[12] Count Batthyány's cabinet, composed entirely of members of the nobility, was approved on 7 April.[13]

The changes carried out in Hungary from March 1848 were clearly fundamental ones. Yet it is also clear that the Magyar nobility succeeded in taking power into its own hands by preventing radical changes and securing compensation for the concessions they granted, as in the case of land rights. Furthermore, the acquisition of new powers by the Magyar nobility gave them a ruling position throughout the whole of Hungary, where the Magyars were, after all, a minority.

News of the revolutionary successes was welcomed by the other nationalities living in Hungary – Serbs, Croats, Slovaks and Rumanians – who believed that they, too, would share in the benefits. However, the demands of representatives of the Serbs and Croats, who also arrived in Bratislava to present a petition to the Diet, were refused. Kossuth declared that the Magyars constituted the political nation of Hungary and was unmoved by pleas for national equality. The Diets of Croatia and Translyvania were consequently abolished and Magyar was proclaimed the official language. This sparked an anti-Magyar movement within Hungary, which the Viennese court employed to advantage in its efforts to suppress the revolution.

New governments were established in all the countries of Central Europe that experienced revolutionary outbreaks in 1848: Prussia, Austria and Hungary. The Viennese court was successful in so far as power was transferred from Metternich to an aristocratic member of his own cabinet, Count Kolowrat. And in Hungary, the new head of state, Count Batthyányi, was a member of the Diet's Upper House. In Prussia, however, the ministry formed on 29 April was headed by Ludolf Camphausen and David Hansemann, Cologne entrepreneurs representing the liberal bourgeoisie, which favoured a policy of compromise with the king and ruling nobility. They wanted to create a constitutional monarchy under Prussian leadership to carry out the desired structural changes. In Germany as a whole the liberal bourgeoisie was convinced – possibly looking to England as a model – that the achievements of the revolution would be reinforced by the formation of a national parliament and a central government.

In comparison with the fairly unambiguous position of the German liberal bourgeoisie, the way forward in Austria and Bohemia was much less clear. In Vienna the March revolutionaries had been content with the removal of Metternich, the abolition of censorship, the freedom of the press and the promise of a constitution. Moreover, they did not object to a member of the nobility becoming head of state, whether it was Count Kolowrat, Count Ficquelmont, or Baron Pillersdorf. Prague, however, was different and came closer to the Prussian scenario, with the Czech liberal bourgeoisie figuring prominently in all the revolutionary activities from 12 March onwards. In contrast with its counterpart in Germany, this group was led not by entrepreneurs but by members of the bourgeois intelligentsia. Some of these belonged to the 'bourgeois middle', such as Fr. L. Rieger, a graduate in law and the son of a prosperous miller, or Fr. A. Brauner, a practising lawyer. Their leading spokesman was František Palacký, who was the son of a Protestant schoolteacher and later became an eminent historian.

A further similarity with Prussia was that, although the demands presented by the Czech liberal bourgeoisie to the emperor in March 1848 aimed at social change, they were to be carried out 'in firm alliance with the whole of the Austrian state', that is, in cooperation with existing authorities.[14]

However, the liberal-bourgeois solution of structural change in harmony with the ruling classes was not the only approach envisaged in Germany and Bohemia. Segments of the bourgeoisie in both countries had advanced more radical proposals right from the outset of revolution. Democrats in Germany and radicals in Bohemia opposed any collaboration with the old order, urging instead the abolition of nobility and monarchy and the creation of a republic. German democrats spearheaded a series of uprisings in various states during 1849, and even succeeded in forming a few governments, but nowhere did they hold on to power for long and they never achieved a majority within the bourgeois camp. The situation was accurately assessed by Franz Schuselka, a leading representative of the bourgeoisie in the German National Assembly in Frankfurt and the Viennese Imperial parliament (*Reichstag*). He wrote that the majority of the population in Germany wanted reform rather than revolution, and that the Frankfurt parliament comprised mainly non-revolutionary elements.[15] The outcome in Vienna was similar. There the radical wing made determined efforts from the time of the March revolution but was ultimately unsuccessful. In Hungary, the group of radical intellectuals in Pest accepted the aristocratic leadership of Kossuth, and are therefore not comparable to the radical or liberal bourgeoisie in Germany, Austria or Bohemia.

The difference in approach between radicals and liberals explains why as early as 1848, and then for the next hundred years, the liberals were labelled 'traitors' of the revolution,[16] designated thus by those who maintained that the only way the bourgeoisie could gain genuine political power was through force. The radicals refused to accept that the liberal bourgeois solution might also achieve the structural changes they sought, maintaining that there was only one route to a capitalist society. There can be no doubt, however, that this is exactly where the programme of the German and Bohemian liberal bourgeoisie led, a fact demonstrated by the incorporation of basic civil rights into the drafted constitutions.[17] It is nevertheless clear that in 1848 *there were two visions and two revolutionary paths.*

After more than 130 years, German Marxist historiography has come to the conclusion that 'the dominance of the reformist movement in the transition from feudalism to capitalism is undeniable'.[18] Two roads were available in 1848–9 for carrying out that tradition, 'reformist and revolutionary'.[19]

The struggle for the constitution

In all of the bourgeois revolutions of 1848–9, in Germany, Austria and Bohemia, one of the fundamental demands was for a constitution, a quest which came virtually to symbolize the revolution. The constitution was to legalize not only the structural changes brought about by the revolution but was also to become the fundamental law of the new society, a legal norm that was valid for rulers and citizens alike. It was to be the legal expression of the principle that all citizens were equal before the law, demonstrating that the epoch of privileges for some and feudal subjection for others was over. It was also to demonstrate that the state, consisting of representatives elected by the people, was taking over control of the judiciary and administration from the still privileged feudal authorities. Not only the bourgeoisie, which was so resolutely advancing the constitutional cause, but also the nobility and courts were fully aware of its significance. The battle for a constitution in Germany, Austria and Bohemia consequently became the focus of the struggle between the two main contenders for power, the ruling feudal regimes and the bourgeoisie.

At the outset of the revolution the majority of the population associated the word 'constitution' with freedom, although this was interpreted in a variety of ways. In Bohemia, for example, shortly after the first big public meeting and only four days after Ferdinand promised to issue a constitution, František Palacký published an article in *Pražské noviny* (Prague News) entitled 'What is a Constitution?'. He defined it as the fundamental law that placed legislative power in the hands of the people as well as in the ruler. It also signified in his formulation the transferring of administrative power from feudal authorities to the freely elected representatives of the town and country population.

In the Central European countries shaken by revolution in March 1848, the task of drafting a constitution was started immediately. The Prussian Diet resolved on 2 April to issue a constitution, and four days later it had decided that it would contain clauses on the freedom of the press, assembly, association and the establishment of juries. Concurrently, the Hungarian Diet enacted a series of laws known as 'The Constitution of Hungary of April 1848', which set up an independent ministry designated in Clause 6 as the sole organ through which the ruler of the country was to exercise his power. This body was to consist of a prime minister and eight others responsible for departments of the interior, finance, public works and transport, agriculture, trade and industry, education and cults, justice and defence. Furthermore, a minister *a latere*, a foreign minister of sorts, was to act as a liaison between Hungary and the court. It was also decreed that the Hungarian parliament, consisting of one chamber of magnates (major nobles) and another of elected representatives, would assemble annually in Pest. Suffrage, however, was not universal and property qualifications excluded large sections of the population from taking part in elections. A further measure abolished feudal subjection, including forced labour and the payments in money or kind which went with it, while Clause 4 deprived the feudal authorities of their judicial powers. Freedom of the press and of religion were also decreed.[20]

During April the German Federal Diet (Bundestag) appointed a seventeen-member committee to outline a constitution, headed by the historian F. C. Dahlmann. By the end of the month the committee was finished but its draft was rejected on account of its monarchist character and the task was consequently transferred to the National Assemby which was inaugurated in Frankfurt on 18 May. Six days later the Assembly set up a thirty-member committee to prepare a draft to be submitted for debate and approval. The committee began on 3 July by discussing fundamental civil rights and continued its work until 20 December.

In Austria the constitution promised by the emperor was drafted by the government, but when presented on 25 April it met the same fate as that of Professor Dahlmann's committee. Although it contained articles on the freedom of the press, of assembly and of association, it was rejected outright because it proposed a bicameral parliament not unlike that designed for Hungary, which would consist of a chamber of deputies and a senate made up of members of the royal family, appointees of the emperor and one hundred and fifty representatives of the nobility. The chamber of deputies was to be elected on the basis of a suffrage law that would be devised subsequently. While legislative power was to be shared by the emperor and the parliament, executive power was to reside with the emperor alone.

This constitution met with opposition from various sectors of the Viennese population. Some were against a parliamentary system which left too much power in the hands of feudal rulers while introducing a property-based franchise which excluded many. The so-called Great Germans, who favoured the absorption of Austria into a unified Germany, opposed it because it projected Austria as an independent state. Finally, the students of Vienna university rejected the constitution on account of its limited suffrage and its inclusion of the emperor's right to appoint members of the senate. Following a large demonstration on 15 May, a march by members of the Academic Legion and National Guard was joined at the emperor's residence (*Hofburg*) by workers armed with spades and iron bars. Count Ficquelmont's government, which had been responsible for the constitution, resigned that night. Pillersdorf formed a new government and the court and emperor decided to leave Vienna for the greater calm of Innsbruck.[21]

In an effort to regain control on 23 May the new government attempted to dissolve the Academic Legion and bring forward the vacation closure of the university. The effects of these moves, however, were exactly the opposite of what was intended: one hundred and sixty barricades sprang up in Vienna, street fighting broke out, and three days later the government was forced to give way, withdrawing its troops and leaving the Legion intact. The same evening a meeting at the town hall formed a Committee of Public Safety with Dr Adolf Fischhof, the spokesman of the student movement, at its head. From then on this committee functioned alongside the government proper, giving the Austrian revolution a new and different character. The developments which culminated in this action were rooted in the struggle over the constitution, which had become both the focus and the embodiment of the battle to decide the nature of state that would replace the old order.

In both Germany and Austria, which produced the most significant of the Central European revolutions, the drafting of a constitution was the main activity of both the National Assembly and Imperial parliament, which established committees for the purpose. The decisive role in each case was played by representatives of the liberal bourgeoisie, who were concerned above all with giving a clear definition of fundamental civil rights, a task which was met with some success. Thus, at the end of September, a Czech liberal bourgeois member of the constitutional committee, Fr. L. Rieger, presented to the Imperial parliament in Vienna for further debate the section of the constitution which dealt with the civil rights. However, a few days later the October revolution broke out and interrupted the parliament's activities. The debate continued after the parliament had been transferred to the small Moravian town of Kroměříž (Kremsier in German), where the committee resumed its work, made some minor amendments and submitted its draft in December. The first reading took place on 21 December, and the second on 4 January 1849 triggered the first open conflict between the parliament and the government. It basically turned on the question whether the source of all power in a constitutional monarchy was the ruler or the people.[22] Unwilling to budge, the government and court decided not to pass the committee's constitution and to dissolve parliament before 15 March, which was the anniversary of the emperor's promise and the day appointed for the vote, and to resort to a decreed constitution. Consequently, on 7 March the army occupied Kroměříž Castle where the parliament had been holding its sessions, and a public notice announced the dissolution.

In Prussia, the second most important of the Central European states, events ran a similar course, with the king and court deciding to dissolve the parliament and issue a decreed constitution following fierce fighting in Berlin on 16 October. On 5 November the parliament was ordered to move to the small town of Brandenburg, on the Havel. When it showed an unwillingness to do so, the army occupied Berlin and dispersed it by force. Even though 227 deputies continued to debate in an inn,[23] the army's action effectively marked the end of the parliament's power, and on 5 December the king made the dissolution official and issued a decree containing the new constitution. There seems little doubt that these tactics were the prototype on which the counter-revolution in Austria was based a few months later.

The list of civil rights drafted by the committee in Vienna and then in Kroměříž, like that drafted for the whole of Germany at Frankfurt, demonstrates the revolutionary nature of the changes under way in Central Europe during this period. Asserting that 'all men have equal rights', both declared the abolition of the nobility as a separate Estate and guaranteed the freedom of the individual, of speech, press, assembly, association and religion. Clause 166 of the Frankfurt draft expressly announced the abolition of feudal subjection and Clause 167 the ending of feudal justice, police powers and all forms of feudal dues. Similarly, Clause 21 of the Kroměříž draft stated that all nations in the empire had an equal right to exist, while Clause 23 ended traditional feudal land tenure by stating that the peasant was entitled to the villein land he tilled.[24]

These formulations of civil rights drafted by the constitutional committees of the Austrian Imperial parliament and the German National Assembly indicate the far-reaching structural changes desired by the liberal bourgeoisie. Even though neither of their drafts was instituted, some of the articles were incorporated into the decreed constitutions. The economic changes that had taken place in Austria, Germany and the Czech Lands ensured that there could be no return to the *status quo ante* in any case, and that the ultimate victors would have to adapt to social changes that could not be reversed. For this reason the Prussian decreed constitution proclaimed the equality of all Prussians before the law, guaranteed the freedom of the individual and the right to emigrate, and included provisions for the freedom of press, assembly and association. In addition, Article 40 abolished feudal subjection along with the legal and administrative powers of feudal authorities.[25] Similar rights were also incorporated in the constitution issued by decree in Austria on 4 March 1849.[26]

The turmoil of Central Europe, however, was occasioned not only by the attempt to replace a feudal with a bourgeois social order, but also by the question of whether the Confederation of thirty-eight German states and towns should become a single entity. This matter was discussed by the National Assembly in Frankfurt from 18 May 1848 for almost a year, finally resulting in a constitution which was passed on 27 March 1849 by the tiny majority of 267 votes to 263.[27] According to this plan Germany was to become a constitutional monarchy, and the next day the Assembly elected Frederick William IV as emperor by a vote of 290 to 248. However, the decision was opposed by Austria, Bavaria, Württemberg, Hanover and Saxony, while the king of Prussia himself refused to accept an election by the people rather than by his fellow rulers. This opposition effectively meant the failure of one of the parliament's most fundamental tasks; Germany had both a central government and a parliament, but the former had no power, and the decisions of the latter were not accepted by the largest German states. As the implementation of the constitution was seen by many to symbolize the success of the revolution,[28] its rejection by the major German states precipitated a new outburst of revolutionary activity in the April 1849 movement, later called the 'Campaign for the Constitution of the Empire' (*Reichsverfassungkampagne*). It was strong enough to induce the king of Württemberg, on 25 April, to recognize the constitution. Unrest broke out in the Rhenish province of Prussia, and in Iserlohn in Westphalia the army had to be called in because of disturbances in which up to one hundred people died.

Far more serious outbreaks occurred in Saxony, the Palatinate and Baden. In Dresden an uprising began on 3 May 1849, headed by the deputies Tzschirner, Heubner and Todt, who wanted to force the recognition of the Frankfurt constitution. They formed a provisional government, and after fierce fighting the Prussian army was brought in on 9 May, crushing all opposition. In the Palatinate on 2 May about 12,000 people gathered in Kaiserslautern, where they sang the Marseillaise and proclaimed a republic. Fifteen days later, a provisional government was formed which immediately resolved to ally itself with the revolution in Baden.[29]

The uprising in Baden was the culmination of the German constitutional campaign. The movement was led by the Mannheim lawyer and extreme left-wing parliamentarian, Lorenz Brentano, the lawyer Max Werner and the radical republican Amand Goegg. On 13 May approximately 40,000 people attended a meeting in Offenburg and demanded the recognition of the constitution accepted at Frankfurt. Unlike elsewhere in Germany, the movement had the support of the army, and the grand duke of Baden was forced to flee to Mainz, where he appealed to Prussia for military assistance.

During this period of turmoil, the head of the central government, Heinrich von Gagern resigned on 10 May. Four days later the Prussian government recalled its deputies from the National Assembly, with Saxony and Hanover following suit. As Austria had already withdrawn its deputies the parliament was left with a skeletal body of about one hundred members who removed to Stuttgart on 20 May. On 18 May the Württemberg government ordered the closure of the meeting hall and sent in the army. The Prussian army also moved into Baden and suppressed the uprising there with unparalleled brutality, methodically shooting every tenth prisoner in the castle of Rastatt.[30] The revolution in Baden was finally defeated on 23 July, and its end effectively marked the conclusion of the revolution in Germany as a whole.

It seems clear from this narrative of events that the struggle for a constitution was a struggle for power. The representatives of the radical bourgeoisie, such as Tzschirner and Heubner in Dresden and Brentano in Mannheim, realized that enforcing the constitution entailed a complete break with the old social order, while the old feudal powers, unwilling to see any legal recognition of the social changes under way, responded with the fiercest countermeasures at their disposal.

The national question and the revolution

Throughout the chronicle of events in Central Europe of 1848–9 the problem of nationality emerges as one of the central issues of the revolution. It was one which neither the liberal nor radical bourgeoisie was able to resolve. A substantial amount of time and effort went into the attempt, but to little effect, and this failure was one of the factors contributing to the ultimately unsuccessful outcome of the revolution. Efforts in different countries produced different proposed solutions, but, since the nature of the problem varied from country to country, none of these solutions could be generally applied. If it provided no answers, however, the revolution of 1848 did at least bring the problem of nationality to the foreground, where it remained for a hundred years.

The most important of the bourgeois revolutions, in Germany, focussed on the not inconsiderable task of creating a unified state out of the thirty-eight members of the German Confederation, a body created in 1815, which included Austria as well as former members of the Holy Roman Empire such as Bohemia, Moravia and Silesia. The movement for the unification of Germany began at the very start of the revolution and, on 27 October 1848, the Frankfurt assembly endorsed it with only ninety dissenting voices. Moreover, seventy-four deputies from Austria also supported the plan, with only forty-one in favour of retaining Austria as a separate state. As the German historian Thomas Nipperdey remarked, 'There was a general view that Austria would disintegrate as a state aggregate (*Gesamtstaat*).'[31]

The German revolution's call at the outset for the creation of a unified German state strongly influenced the course of events in both Austria and the Czech Lands. Not all sections of the Austrian and Czech bourgeoisie favoured the elimination of Austria as an independent entity and its absorption into a German state. Consequently, alongside the notion of a Great Germany emerged a conception of the feudal Austrian empire transformed into a federation of equal nations under a constitutional monarchy. The latter aspiration found expression in proposals drafted by the representative of the Czech liberal bourgeoisie, František Palacký, whose governing principles were that 'freedom is only possible where all members of society have equal rights', and 'as long as nations have reason to fear for their nationhood there will be no tranquillity and peace in Austria'.[32] Between these two extremes existed also the notion of a so-called Little Germany, that is, a united German state under Prussian leadership which excluded Austria, an idea advocated by Heinrich von Gagern. This concept was in line with the views of the Czech liberal bourgeoisie and was clearly set out by Palacký in his letter of 11 April 1848 in which he declined to join, as one of six invited Austrian representatives, the preparatory 'Committee of Fifty' of the National Assembly at Frankfurt. As late as 27 March 1849 the Assembly passed as Article 1, Clause 1 of the draft constitution of a future unified Germany the statement that 'The German Empire is comprised by the territory of the existing German Confederation.'[33] The matter was shelved, however, by the defeat of the revolution, which ensured that, instead of becoming a unified state, Germany remained split into more than thirty sovereign entities until 1871.

The unification question was important not only for the various states within Germany proper, but also for Austria and for the Czech Lands, the latter region providing fifty of Austria's one hundred and twenty representatives in Frankfurt.[34] A large segment of Austrians and of the German-speaking population in the Czech Lands considered themselves German and favoured the dissolution of Austria within a unified German state, preferring the creation of a country which would become 'the first world power'.[35] In the Czech Lands, the desire for unification arose partly from the fear of the German-speaking population that the country would otherwise be dominated by the Czechs, who made up two-thirds of the population. As a deputy of the Viennese parliament and leading advocate of Great Germany, Hans Kudlich, put it: 'As soon as the role of leader slips from our hands then we, the German nationality, will be unable to exist – then we will have to seek protection with our fellow countrymen in Germany.'[36]

Not all Austrian and Bohemian Germans, however, wished to see a Great Germany. Some, most notably the Bohemian nobility, advocated the preservation of an independent Austria. Thus, Count Leo Thun, the president of the Bohemian *Gubernium*, remarked to the poet Moritz Hartmann – who represented the Litoměřice region at Frankfurt – that he didn't like the German colours of black, red and gold.[37] Prince Felix Schwarzenberg, who became prime minister in the autumn of 1848, did everything in his power to preserve a separate and independent Austria.

Czech opposition stemmed principally from the fear that they would not be able to preserve their identity in a united Germany. This concern led them to advocate the transformation of multinational Austria into a state of nations with equal rights, which was to be a constitutional monarchy rather than a feudal and absolutist one along Metternichian lines.[38]

As well as making an impact on the revolution in Austria and the Czech Lands, the German national question played a significant role in the case of the Poles of the Poznań (Posen) region. There it also became evident that the victorious bourgeoisie of the ruling nation had not succeeded in solving the nationality issue in a manner acceptable to the dependent nations. When an uprising broke out in the Poznań region in April 1848, the Poles set up their own militia and took a stand against the hegemony of feudal Prussia. Their resistance movement, however, was crushed by the Prussian bourgeois government headed by Camphausen and Hansemann and assisted by General Colomb's army, which reacted just as its feudal predecessor would have done. The Poles capitulated in May and on 27 July the Frankfurt assembly voted by 342 to 31 to annex the western part of Poznań region 'as an integral part of the German Union.'[39]

Along with Germany, Austria, the Czech Lands and the Poznań region, Hungary was also racked by conflicts over the nationality issue. After the Magyars' initial successes in Vienna, Hungary's Slavonic nations approached the Diet and later the government with the demand that their national rights be safeguarded. They were met with a refusal, over which Kossuth's victorious nobility and the young radicals of March from Pest were in perfect accord. The spokesman of the young radicals, Pál Királyi, supported the denial of Slavic rights with the statement that 'the Serbs want to establish themselves as a nation but there is only one nation in Hungary, and this consists of Magyars'.[40] A petition from the Croats elicited a similar response from the young radicals, who declared: 'We do not want to exercise control over the language spoken in your households, church services or in public. However, we want you to use the Magyar language in your dealings with the government, administrative and judiciary authorities of our fatherland. Without this, the unity of the land would be in jeopardy.'[41]

On 8 April Kossuth declared that Hungary would become a Magyar state and, refusing any negotiations over the rights of Slavic nations, announced that Magyar was to be the only official language. His unambiguous position was contained in his statement that 'if the Slavic nations of Hungary are going to demand equality of status, the issue will be settled by arms.' Kossuth and the Magyar nobility underestimated the significance that their unilateral denial of equal rights to the majority of the population would have for the revolution in Hungary, but its divisive effect was quickly grasped by diplomatic observers and the Habsburg court. As early as April 1848 the Bavarian envoy, Count Friedrich von Luxemburg, said that national separatism could prove the means of preserving the integrity of the Austrian government if it shrewdly encouraged the playing out of these disputes.[42] This was the strategy the Habsburg court in fact adopted. While the Magyar revolution refused the national aspirations of the Slavic nations, the principle of national equality in Austria was embodied in the constitution of 25 April 1848, which naturally led the Slovaks, Croats and Serbs to seek support for their cause in Vienna rather than Pest. They were joined by the Rumanians in Transylvania who formed a national committee, but their activities were halted by Magyar troops. Magyar government warrants for arresting the representatives of the Slovak national movement forced its most prominent leaders, L. Štúr, M. M. Hodža and J. M. Hurban, to leave Slovakia.

In order to build on the advantage thus gained, the Viennese court appointed General Jelačić as ban (viceroy) of Croatia. Jelačić was part of the group of Croatian politicians who supported the direct subordination of Croatia to the Viennese government. His appointment was opposed, ineffectually, by the Hungarian government and, once installed, he played an important role in helping the Viennese court to undo the revolution. When the court saw a chance to make its move against the Magyar revolution following the suppression of both the June uprising in Prague and the revolutionary movement in Italy, Jelačić was ordered to cross the Drava River and proceed into Hungary. Open intervention against the Magyar revolution began with this action, ending in its total defeat at Világos on 13 August 1849.

The court and Prince Felix Schwarzenberg's government used more than just military means to solve the national question in Hungary. The decreed constitution of 4 March 1849 proclaimed the principle of national equality in Austria, and, only a year after the outbreak of the revolution, certain nobles who counted themselves among the radicals were beginning to believe that 'it was no longer possible to ignore the national movement', and that the transformation of Hungary 'into a purely Magyar national state was no longer viable'.[43] Thus László Teleki, the diplomatic representative of the Hungarian government in Paris, recommended to Kossuth collaboration with the Serbs, Croats and Rumanians, and that 'Hungary should be transformed into a confederation of nations'.[44] Teleki's proposal (in a letter of 7 March 1849) was not heeded; on the contrary, Kossuth shortly afterwards (May 1849) ordered the Hungarian army into action against the Transylvanian Rumanians, who had withdrawn into the mountains. On 6 May Magyar units under Imre Hatvani took the mining town of Abrud, where one of the leaders of the

Rumanian revolutionary movement, Buteanu, was taken prisoner. The Rumanians won the town back after three days of fighting, but Hatvani retained Buteanu and had him executed fourteen days later.[45] The Rumanians took revenge against the local Magyar population.

Two weeks before the collapse of the Magyar revolution, the deputies of the Hungarian parliament in Szeged (where it had sought refuge after leaving Pest) approved the proposal of the prime minister, Szemere, for giving the non-Magyar nations of Hungary the right to use their own language in schools and churches. While Magyar was to remain the official language of Hungary, counties with a non-Magyar majority were to be given the right to choose the language of their official documents. However, this solution came too late to be of any use and it cannot be known whether it would have been accepted, for the surrender at Világos on 13 August 1849 marked the definite defeat of the Hungarian revolution.

The agrarian question in the revolution

One of the most imporant debates of the revolution of 1848–9 in Central Europe centred on the state of affairs in rural areas, where most of the population lived and worked. The peasants were still subjects (Untertanen) of their landlords in Austria, Hungary and the Czech Lands. In the latter region the *Robotpatent* of 1775 was still in force, requiring that each feudal subject provide labour for his landlord according to the size of his holding. This obligation could amount to two men and two teams of draught animals working three days per week, and in practice it sometimes meant a six-day week exacted from one feudal subject. In Hungary the system of forced labour was regulated by a patent of 1767.[46]

On 20 March 1848, prompted by the revolutionary events in Prague, Count R. Stadion (head of the *Gubernium* in Bohemia) urged Baron Pillersdorf (then minister of the interior in Vienna) to abolish forced labour, for unrest was brewing in the countryside.[47] On the same day representatives of the nobility met in Prague to discuss the agrarian problem. After three days they despatched a proposal for change to the emperor in Vienna, who was advised by Pillersdorf to issue a patent abolishing the *robota* within the week. This was done on 28 March 1848, and it considerably lessened tensions in the countryside.

Simultaneously, large-scale agitation against the nobility was taking place in many parts of Germany, including Hesse, Thuringia, Bavaria and Baden. Marches against the castles of Princes Hohenlohe, Neipperg, Fürstenberg and Leiningen resulted in the seizure and burning of official documents concerning feudal dues. Castles and noble homes were plundered, damaged and even burned to the ground. Thousands of peasants armed with scythes and old rifles marched through the countryside, a scene reminiscent of the German Peasant War, and the army had to be sent to control the disturbances. In Nassau the peasants demanded that allodial domains be taken over by the state and divided into lots.[48] They announced their refusal to continue paying taxes and claimed the right to hunt in the forests. The feudal obligations resented by these peasants still included, in some places, the enforcement of the traditional requirement that the best cow or horse be presented to the landlord upon the death of a subject.[49]

Similar conditions prevailed in Hungary, where the modification of feudal subjection contained in the April laws of the revolutionary government affected only part of the population and half of the arable land. Feudal subjects working on allodial estates were excluded from the reforms and their dissatisfaction erupted in disturbances during June 1848.[50] Count Batthyány's government reacted by declaring a state of martial law throughout Hungary and sending the army to subdue the villages. These acts of repression in the Hungarian countryside created a hostile attitude there towards the revolutionary government.[51]

Troops were likewise employed to quell peasant unrest during the revolution in Bavaria, Württemberg and Baden. There the liberal ministers promised the rebellious peasants that their demands would be recognized by law and, as in Austria, the promise was fulfilled. At a sitting of the Imperial parliament in Vienna on 24 July 1848, the Silesian deputy Hans Kudlich proposed the immediate abolition of feudal subjection and all the duties and obligations arising from it. The central issue for the parliament was the question of compensation to landlords. After deliberating Kudlich's motion from 8 to 31 August, the parliament decided that the landlords were to be compensated, and a law to this effect was signed by the emperor on 7 September. Through these measures the liberal bourgeoisie achieved the pacification of the coutryside, which remained calm during the revolution in Vienna in October 1848, as it did in Germany in May 1849, being effectively uninvolved in the revolutionary struggle.

The radicals, who headed the movements of October and May, did not grasp the importance of an alliance with the peasantry for a successful outcome of the bourgeois revolution. A large segment of the rural population expected the revolution to lead to the dividing up of noble estates and the allocation of lots to the landless. But in 1848 the radicals were concerned only with abolishing the more palpable remnants of feudalism – *robota*, dues, seigneurial legal and administrative powers – and the redistribution of land was not addressed. It was precisely this question, however, which could have turned a large section of the rural population into a useful ally of the radicals in the bourgeois revolution of 1848–9.

The proletariat in the revolution

Karl Marx observed as early as 1847 that when the bourgeoisie launched its power struggle against absolutism, it was already in conflict with the proletariat.[52] This clearly influenced its stand during the revolution in 1848.

A new social class of industrial workers had emerged during the period before 1848. The miserable conditions under which they lived were described by Karl Beidtel (later a deputy of the National Assembly at Frankfurt) after a journey through Lower Austria and Bohemia to investigate factories in 1847. In Bohemia he observed pale young women between the ages of twelve and twenty engaged in hard labour from 5 a.m. to 8 p.m., earning seven to eight *Kreuzer*.[53] They came from labourer and peasant families in neighbouring villages, to which they returned on Sundays, subsisting on boiled potatoes brought from their homes.[54] The working day in Austrian factories varied from twelve to sixteen hours. In 1848, dissatisfied industrial workers put forward demands for improved conditions and in both Germany and Bohemia these demands included the 'organization of labour and wages'. Workers' clubs were formed in the industrially advanced parts of Germany, and by 1849 there were about one hundred and seventy of them, with more than fifteen thousand members. Discussions in the clubs covered issues such as self-help, trade unions, sickness funds and the replacement of the police state with a socialized one. Only a small proportion of the workers were involved in these clubs, but during the revolution the majority of them were spontaneously active, directing their anger towards the factory machines. In Germany, as mentioned, this occurred in Solingen, where workers marched with red flags from factory to factory, smashing machines and destroying buildings.[55] The sixty-nine workers arrested during the suppression of this outburst were liberated from the Elberfeld prison during the revolution of May 1849.[56]

The condition of the textile workers in Bílovec, Silesia, was similar to that of workers in all industrial parts of Central Europe. Their complaint presented to the parliament in Vienna stated that, although they worked fourteen hours a day, six days a week, their wages were insufficient to maintain their families. They dressed in rags and were forced to manage on one daily meal.[57] The poverty and unemployment of the proletariat gave rise to periodic outbreaks of unrest and to general anxiety in Berlin,

Solingen, Cologne, Mannheim, Vienna, Prague and Breslau (now Wrocław in Poland). It was during his visit to the large Silesian town, at the beginning of March 1848, that the Austrian politician Franz Schuselka registered 'apprehensiveness about a communist uprising of the proletariat'.[58]

The struggle of the workers for improved conditions during 1848 culminated in a battle in Vienna in August. The violence was preceded by an announcement from Schwarzer, the minister of labour, that 20,000 public workers were to be laid off. With the further announcement on 18 August that wages were to be reduced 25 per cent, unrest began to grow. On 23 August, a group of workers marched from the Prater (now an amusement park) into the centre of Vienna in a demonstration of protest. They were met by the National Guard and during the conflict eighteen workers were killed, and more than two hundred and eighty wounded. The 'Battle of the Prater' (*Praterschlacht*) had far-reaching consequences for the revolution in Austria. On the very same day, the Committee of Safety dissolved itself, signifying its defeat in the struggle with the liberal bourgeoisie. A week later, on 30 August, Karl Marx gave a lecture at the Viennese workers' club on the working-class movement in Western Europe, in which he described the military suppression of the workers in Paris from 23 to 26 June. After the lecture, those who were present honoured the memory of the Viennese workers who had lost their lives during the previous week's fighting for improved social conditions.[59]

During the revolution of 1848 the proletariat took part in all the open confrontations: in March in Vienna and Berlin, the June uprising in Prague, the October revolution in Vienna, and the revolutionary battles in Germany during May 1849. A large number of workers, artisans and journeymen were killed, for they participated everywhere in the struggle led by the radical bourgeoisie. Marx and Engels even advised that 'the fight against the bourgeoisie should be taken up immediately after the fall of the reactionary classes in Germany'.[60] This demand proved to be unrealistic, however, and Engels wrote near the end of his life, in 1895, that 'history ... revealed that our views in those days were based on illusion'.[61]

One of the effects of the proletarian involvement in the revolution of 1848 was that it made the bourgeoisie recognize its own position in relation to the revolutionary transformation of the existing social and political framework. Support for this claim is provided by two participants in the revolution in Germany, who in fact belonged to different camps. One was Friedrich Engels, who stated that 'the bourgeoisie opted for compromise with the monarchy and nobility because of its fear of the proletariat'.[62] The other was the banker Gustav Mevissen, a liberal politician prominent in the revolution in Germany, who wrote in 1849: 'In Rhineland the Elberfeld experience will soon lead all propertied strata to support the government. They will give preference to an absolutist monarchy over a red republic.'[63]

The substantial participation of the proletariat in the revolution in various parts of Germany, Austria and the Czech Lands, reflects the fact that in these countries industrialization was considerably advanced in the first half of the nineteenth century. The same cannot be said of Hungary. According to statistics compiled in 1841 the population of Hungary was over thirteen million, and that of Austria and the Czech Lands was more than seventeen million. At the time there were 7,315 industrial enterprises within the Habsburg Monarchy, but of these only 584 were located in Hungary.[64] Hungary was basically an agrarian country in 1848–9 and, according to contemporary Hungarian historiography, the labouring population formed a class only in a weak sense. Even in the largest towns, Pest and Buda, the labouring people were journeymen and not industrial proletarians.[65]

A social movement nevertheless emerged among journeymen and workers in Hungary during the first half of 1848. In April 1848 the journeymen of the German tailors' guild in Pest demanded higher wages from the masters of the trade. When refused they responded with a strike and a pogrom against Jewish artisans and journeymen. In May the railway workers and Danube shipping workers demanded the expulsion of foreign labourers. The same demand was voiced by journeymen at a demonstration against unemployment on 8 June 1848. The low level of working-class consciousness manifested in these events was characteristic of the revolution in Hungary during 1848. The protest movement came to an end when the Hungarian government ordered a substantial quantity of varied goods for the use of the growing army, thereby revitalizing production. The entry of many young workers into military service also contributed to the reduction of unemployment. Because of all these factors, it is not possible to speak of a proletarian involvement in the revolution in Hungary, comparable to that which occurred in Germany, Austria and the Czech Lands.

Setbacks and advances

The rapid success of the bourgeois revolution in March 1848 convinced the liberal bourgeoisie in Central Europe that the revolution had been won, and that it remained only to codify the victory legally in a constitution. They acted accordingly in Prussia, Austria and the Czech Lands, paying little attention to securing their position through state power. This is manifested by the fact that the army, a fundamental component of every government, remained in the hands of the existing aristocratic command. Only in Baden did the army take the side of the revolutionaries, in May 1849. Everywhere else, those who were defeated during the March revolution of 1848 were able to make use of the army in subsequent efforts to reverse the situation; troops played a decisive role in suppressing the revolution in Prague, Milan, Vienna, Berlin, Dresden and other German towns.

Another significant lesson of the revolution, which was quickly grasped by representatives of the feudal order, was that the self-conscious national movements developing during the revolution were intolerant of the aspirations of other nationalities. The old authorities were able to turn these divisions to advantage, pitting one national movement against another.

The first open conflict of the counter-revolution took place in Prague in June 1848. Realizing the danger posed to the revolution by Prince Alfred Windischgrätz's continuing command of the army, the Czech radicals demanded his removal, and a battle ensued. The majority of German-speaking revolutionaries sided with Windischgrätz, however, and the National Assembly in Frankfurt was asked to send Bavarian and Saxon units to assist him in repressing the Bohemian movement.[66] After heavy bombardment, he secured Prague, and the revolution in Central Europe suffered its first military defeat. Windischgrätz received letters of congratulation from Germans, and was praised at a sitting of the Frankfurt parliament for crushing the Prague uprising. In his response, he made clear that it had not been a matter of conflict between nationalities, but the suppression of a revolt. Yet only one deputy in Frankfurt, J. N. Berger from Šumperk in Moravia, realized that the forces of reaction had triumphed in Prague, and that it was probably just a matter of time before Czechs and Germans would be fighting side by side against these forces.[67]

After this first victory, the court decided to take military action against the revolutionary movement in Italy as well where a similar victory was achieved by counter-revolutionary forces. The commander, Marshal Radetzky, received the same acclaim which had been showered upon Windischgrätz for his success in Prague. Johann Strauss (senior) composed a ceremonial march in honour of Radetzky which celebrates to this day the old soldier's suppression of the Italian revolution.

The Magyars apparently did not realize that with the old order restored in Bohemia and Italy, it would be their turn next. The Viennese court had been secretly negotiating with the loyal Croat Imperial officer, Jelačić, and approval was given for him to lead his army into Hungary. On 11 September, Jelačić's army crossed the Drava River and advanced into

Hungary, whereupon the Palatine of Hungary, Archduke Stephen, who represented the emperor in Pest, departed for Vienna. The court appointed General Lamberg as military commander in Hungary on 25 September, but he was lynched three days later by a mob on the bridge between Buda and Pest. After this event, Count Batthyány refused to carry on in office and his cabinet effectively disintegrated, leaving only three members: Kossuth (Finance), B. Szemere (Interior) and L. Mészáros (Defence). The Viennese government dissolved the Hungarian Diet, annulled all its enactments, gave Jelačić full powers, and prepared for the deployment of Austrian troops in Hungary. Although the Hungarians resisted, and even achieved some successes, they were overpowered by the Austrian forces and the Russian army led by General Paskevich. Their capitulation at Világos on 13 August 1849 marked the defeat of the Magyar revolution.

The army, which played such a decisive role in suppressing the revolution in Bohemia, Italy and Hungary, performed the same role in Austria. In October 1848 Windischgrätz's and Jelačić's armies, totalling 70,000 soldiers, marched against revolutionary Vienna and overcame the National Guard, led by the writer C. W. Messenhauser, in a decisive battle on the 23rd. Although revolutionaries from Brno, Linz, Salzburg and Graz came to Vienna's aid, the heroic struggle of the Viennese revolutionaries ended in defeat after 2,000 of them had been killed. That this battle signified a decisive victory for the counter-revolution in the whole of Europe was recognized by the major European leaders. The Russian tsar, Nicholas I, wrote to Prince Windischgrätz, commending him for having rendered the greatest service to Europe in suppressing the revolution in Vienna.[68] The same view was expressed by General Cavaignac, who had vanquished the Parisian proletariat in June 1848 and became president of the French Republic. The subduing of Vienna, he wrote to Windischgrätz, was a service not only to Austria and Germany, but to France and all of Europe.[69]

It is very likely that the defeat of revolutionary Vienna in October 1848 encouraged the court and army in Prussia to adopt a similar plan. With the outbreak of workers' unrest and fighting at barricades in Berlin during October, the court mounted a concerted military action against the revolutionary movement. The Prussian parliament was, as mentioned, transferred to the small town of Brandenburg on 5 November, and the army commanded by General Wrangel laid siege to Berlin. The National Guard was dissolved, the remnants of the Prussian parliament dispersed, and a Prussian constitution was decreed on 5 December. It was thus the army which again formed the main pillar of the counter-revolution. In Prussia it played the same role as it had in Bohemia, Italy, and Austria, and was to play in Saxony, the Palatinate and Baden in 1849. The victory of the Prussian army in Baden on 23 July 1849 marked the eradication of the revolution in Germany as a whole.

The counter-revolution in Austria, Bohemia, Italy and Germany, led by the courts and the nobility, was able to demolish the revolution with its own armies. In Hungary circumstances were different, for the Hungarian Diet had created its own revolutionary army there (11 July 1848), which managed to resist the forces of Windischgrätz and Jelačić, and reach the gates of Vienna in October 1848. It was only after the Viennese court appealed to the tsar for help, and a Russian army numbering 200,000 men set out for Hungary in June 1849, that the Hungarians were forced to surrender at Világos on 13 August.[70]

It can be firmly concluded that the bourgeois revolution in Central Europe in 1848–9 was defeated everywhere by counter-revolutionary forces directed by feudal courts and backed by armies. This statement is important because, after the revolution was extinguished, assertions were made about 'who was responsible' for 'the betrayal of the revolution'. The culprits were constantly sought in the bourgeois camp and the failure attributed to the liberal bourgeoisie. It was pointed out that their aims were too limited, that they were misguidedly committed to transforming the feudal order into a bourgeois system by constitutional means, and that they opposed the use of force which the radicals had urged.

In his article on 'The bourgeoisie and the counter-revolution', Karl Marx located the cause of the revolution's defeat in 'the treachery of the bourgeoisie'.[71] For him, the 'treachery' occurred at the moment when the bourgeoisie, out of fear of the proletariat, began collaborating with the representatives of the old order – the courts and the nobility – and thus in effect went over to the side of the counter-revolution. This view of Marx's resulted in the notion within Marxist historiography of the betrayal of the revolution by the bourgeoisie.[72] According to Marx and Engels, a successful revolution would have involved an appropriation of political power by the bourgeoisie alone, with which they could have carried out far-reaching changes in all areas of social life, along the lines of the French Revolution of 1789–94. The liberal bourgeoisie, however, were not attracted to this strategy, preferring to bring change by way of reforms 'exacted' from the nobility. There were thus two different conceptions of the bourgeois revolution. The course of events after the defeat of the revolution showed that the victorious counter-revolution was unable to restore pre-revolutionary conditions and was ultimately forced to concede much of what the liberal bourgeoisie had carried out. Neither the seigneurial judiciary nor the feudal administrative system could be effectively reinstated. Nor was a return to conditions of feudal subjection practicable. Instead, the courts and aristocracy had to accede to the range of temporarily suspended civil liberties for which the bourgeoisie stood: freedom of the press, assembly, association and religion.

This meant that, despite the unambiguous military and political defeat, changes were nevertheless effected which amounted to a revolutionary transformation of a feudal society into one that was decidedly bourgeois. The counter-revolution was victorious in military terms because the army, which was crucial, was on its side. But this victory was only temporary, for it was impossible to arrest the deep structural changes brought about by the development of productive forces and of the social relations of production. In the end it was these elements which triumphed in spite of the military victories of the feudal armies.

NOTES

1 K. Obermann, *Deutschland von 1815 bis 1849*, 4th ed. (Berlin, 1976), p. 263.

2 This was item XVIII in the list of demands presented by the radicals at the public assembly in Prague on 11 March 1848. See A. Klíma, *Revoluce 1848 v českých zemích* (The Revolution of 1848 in the Czech Lands) (Prague, 1974), p. 136. In the course of the revolution the demand for the 'organization of labour' was also put forward by German workers' clubs in Berlin, Cologne and Frankfurt. See T. Nipperdey, *Deutsche Geschichte 1800–1866* (Munich, 1983), pp. 620–2.

3 A. Klíma, 'Die Arbeiterunruhen in Böhmen 1844', in H. Reinalter (ed.), *Demokratische und soziale Protestbewegungen in der Zeit der Restauration und im Vormärz in Mitteleuropa* (Frankfurt-am-Main, 1985).

4 W. Häusler, *Von der Massenarmut zur Arbeiterbewegung* (Vienna, 1979), p. 151.

5 M. Henkel and R. Taubert, *Maschinenstürmer* (Frankfurt-am-Main, 1979), pp. 207–8.

6 Nipperdey, *Deutsche Geschichte*, p. 595.

7 W. Schmidt, 'Zur Rolle der Bourgeoisie in den bürgerlichen Revolutionen von 1789 und 1848', *Zeitschrift für Geschichtswissenschaft*, XXI (1973), p. 311.

8 According to Häusler, out of 933 students of the Viennese university in 1848, 47 per cent were sons of artisans and journeymen (228), low officials (128), peasants (68), workers and labourers (19). Cf. Häusler, *Von der Massenarmut*, p. 175.

9 Häusler, *Von der Massenarmut*, pp. 155–6.

10 I. Barta, 'Kampf um die bürgerliche Umgestaltung: Revolution und Freiheitskampf 1790–1849', in E. Pamlényi (ed.), *Die Geschichte Ungarin* (Budapest, 1971), pp. 299–305.

11 *Ibid.*, pp. 229–305.

12 *Ibid.*, p. 305.

13 That is, B. Szemere (Interior), L. Kossuth (Finance), I. Széchenyi (Public Works and Transport), G. Klauzál (Agriculture, Trade and Industry), J.

Eötvös (Education and Cults), F. Deák (Justice), L. Mészáros (Defence), P. Esterházy (*a latere*).

14 Klíma, *Revoluce*, p. 144.

15 F. Schuselka, *Deutsche Fahrten*, 2 vols. (Vienna, 1849), II, p. 97.

16 Cf. W. Schmidt, 'Die marxistische Geschichtswissenschaft spricht angesichts dieser Sachlage vom Verrat der Bourgeoisie an der Revolution "Schmidt", Zur Rolle der Bourgeoisie', *Zeitschrift für Geschichtswissenschaft*, XXI (1973), pp. 312–14.

17 A. Klíma, 'Karl Marx–Friedrich Engels und die Revolution von 1848 in Böhmen', *Sonderdruck des Internationalen Jahrbuchs für Geschichts- und Geographieunterricht* (Braunschweig, 1974), p. 6.

18 W. Schmidt, 'Zu den Wegen der bürgerlichen Umwälzung', *Zeitschrift für Geschichtswissenschaft*, XXVI (1978), p. 500.

19 *Ibid.*, p. 505–7.

20 E. Bernatzik, *Die Österreichischen Verfassungsgesetze* (Vienna, 1911), pp. 78–99.

21 The municipal elections in Vienna, 5 October 1848, showed what this meant in practice. In a town with a population of more than 400,000 only 8,717 people were entitled to vote. See Häusler, *Von der Massenarmut*, p. 212.

22 Bernatzik, *Die Österreichischen Verfassungsgesetze*, pp. 133–42.

23 Nipperdey, *Deutsche Geschichte*, pp. 647–50.

24 Cf. E. R. Huber, *Dokumente zur deutschen Verfassungsgeschichte* (Stuttgart, 1961), I, p. 375.

25 *Ibid.*, pp. 484–7.

26 Bernatzik, *Die Österreichischen Verfassungsgesetze*, p. 108.

27 Clause 1 of the first article stated that 'The German Empire comprises the territory of the existing German Confederation.' Cf. Häusler, *Von der Massenarmut*.

28 Ch. Klessmann, 'Zur Sozialgeschichte der Reichswerfassungkampagne von 1849', *Historische Zeitschrift*, CCXVII, p. 333.

29 *Ibid.*, p. 304.

30 Nipperdey, *Deutsche Geschichte*, p. 663.

31 *Ibid.*, pp. 656–60.

32 F. Palacký, 'O centralisaci a národnostní rovnoprávnosti v Rakousku' (Centralization and the equal rights of nationalities in Austria), *Národní noviny*, XXIII, (1849).

33 Huber, *Von der Massenarmut*, p. 375.

34 F. Prinz, 'Die Sudetendeutschen im Frankfurter Parlament', in *Zwischen Frankfurt und Prag* (Vorträge der Wissenschaftlichen Tagung des Collegium Carolinum in Frankfurt-am-Main, Munich 1963), pp. 114–15.

35 Quoted in Nipperdey, *Deutsche Geschichte*, pp. 624–30, from a speech by Vogt, a deputy on the left in the Frankfurt parliament.

36 H. Kudlich, *Rückblicke und Erinnerungen*, 3 vols. (Budweis, 1926), II, p. 219.

37 Prinz, *Die Sudetendeutschen*, p. 115.

38 A. Klíma, 'Österreich 1848 und ein einheitliches Deutschland aus böhmischer Sicht', *Österreichische Osthefte*, XXV (1983).

39 Nipperdey, *Deutsche Geschichte*, pp. 624–30.

40 G. Spira, 'The national minorities policy of the Pest revolution's Left in March 1848', *Studia Slavica Hungarica*, XVI (1970), pp. 81–90.

41 *Ibid.*

42 Prinz, *Die Sudetendeutschen*, pp. 104–5.
43 G. Spira, 'Die Nationalitätenfrage in Ungarn 1849', *Österreichische Osthefte*, XXV (1983), pp. 202–5.
44 *Ibid.*
45 *Ibid.*, p. 211.
46 J. Komlos, 'The emancipation of the Hungarian peasantry and agricultural development', in I. Volgyes (ed.), *The Peasantry of Eastern Europe*, 2 vols. (New York, 1978), II, p. 109.
47 Klíma, *Revoluce*, p. 75.
48 Nipperdey, *Deutsche Geschichte*, pp. 601–2.
49 V. Valentin, *Geschichte der deutschen Revolution 1848–1849*, 2 vols. (Cologne, 1970), I, p. 299.
50 Barta, 'Kampf', pp. 306–7; G. Spira, 'Die Linke in der ungarischen Revolution von 1848/49', in M. Kossok (ed.), *Rolle und Formen der Volksbewegung im bürgerlichen Revolutionszyklus* (Berlin, 1976), p. 198.
51 Barta, 'Kampf', p. 329.
52 'Die moralisierende Kritik und kritisierende Moral', in Marx–Engels, *Gesamt-Ausgabe* (Moscow, 1933), VI, pp. 318–19.
53 It cost 6 *Kreuzer* to buy half a kg of bread and also to pay for an evening meal. Cf. Häusler, *Von der Massenarmut*, p. 181.
54 *Ibid.*, p. 115.
55 Henkel and Taubert, *Machinenstürmer*, pp. 207–8.
56 Klessmann, *Zur Sozialgeschichte*, p. 299.
57 Häusler, *Von der Massenarmut*, pp. 327–8.
58 Schuselka, *Deutsche Fahrten*, p. 43.
59 H. Steiner, *Marx in Wien* (Vienna, 1978), p. 163.
60 *Marx–Engels Werke* (Berlin, 1959), IV, p. 493.
61 Klíma, *Karl Marx*, p. 22.
62 F. Engels, 'Karl Marx und die Rheinische Zeitung', in K. Marx–F. Engels, *Die Revolution von 1848 Auswahl aus der Neuen Rheinischen Zeitung* (Berlin, 1949), pp. 24–5.
63 Klessmann, *Zur Sozialgeschichte*, p. 299.
64 Häusler, *Von der Massenarmut*, p. 68.
65 G. Spira, 'Die Arbeiterbewegung der Monate der Revolution von 1848 in den Schwesterstädten Pest, Ofen und Altofen', *Annales Universitatis Budapestinensis de Rolando, Eötvös Nominatae Sectio Historica*, XXI (1981), pp. 83–6.
66 Klíma, *Revoluce*, p. 65.
67 Prinz, *Die Sudetendeutschen*, p. 120.
68 Klíma, *Karl Marx*, pp. 20–1.
69 Nipperdey, *Deutsche Geschichte*, p. 642.
70 Barta, 'Kampf', p. 331.
71 K. Marx, 'Die Bourgeoisie und die Konterrevolution', in *Marx–Engels Werke*, VI, pp. 101–24.
72 Schmidt, 'Zur Rolle der Bourgeoisie', pp. 312–17.

5

Socialist revolution in Central Europe, 1917–21

T. HAJDU

What is socialist revolution? And where is Central Europe? Here we have at the very beginning two questions which it is impossible to answer within the limited space of this chapter. Our task is to deal with revolutions which claimed to be socialist, though we must keep in mind that there were also socialist elements in those revolutions in this region which are generally labelled nationalist or 'bourgeois'. We should also remember that the socialist revolution in Central and Eastern Europe also had to accomplish what earlier attempts to copy the great French Revolution had failed to carry through.

'Central Europe' really existed only from the seventeenth to the nineteenth century. Prussia, Poland and the Habsburg monarchy had vast, backward, feudal agricultural areas, but the state, Church and cities were Western European; or, at least these institutions aspired to be Western European. The slowness of industrial and mercantile progress kept the region overwhelmingly agricultural; the state, balancing a weak urban population and an archaic feudalism, realized itself most naturally in an absolute monarchy based on an aggressive nobility and an army always ready to annexe any weaker neighbour. This last quality led to the creation of impossible national mixtures within state borders which were themselves changing at a time when in other parts of Europe states were being reformed on a *national* basis.

'It was symbolic that over the grave of Poland stood the three greatest figures of "enlightened absolutism" – Frederick II, Catherine the Great and Joseph II', wrote the Hungarian historian J. Szücs.[1]

After Poland had disappeared from the maps (though not from Central Europe), Turkey had given up her Balkan pashalics one after the other, and Prussia had succeeded in liberating other German lands from French and other Western influences, the political entity of Central Europe slowly faded away. Germany became, after all, part of Western Europe; Austria followed suit after her Slavic and Rumanian peoples had oriented themselves towards the new states recently liberated from the Turkish yoke. The old Carolingian borders (Elbe – Saale – Leitha – Pannonia – Istria) emerged again after a thousand years, marking the frontier between Western and the dominantly Slavic Eastern and South Eastern Europe.[2]

These political and national changes were created through war, diplomacy, and even by democratic means; but the social and economic problems they involved were not to be solved by arms and politics. About the mid-nineteenth century, when industry and accumulated wealth made Western Europe a world centre of progress yet also of class struggle, every socialist dreamed of that hotbed of revolutions stretching from England to Germany. As for the Eastern half of Europe, including Austria, democrats and socialists were sure they had only to follow the Western paths of revolution and socialism. What actually happened, however, was quite different.

After the single attempt of the Paris Commune, Western Europe went the way of class bargaining and negotiated reforms. So did Central Europe up to the end of the nineteenth century. But, during the first years of the twentieth century, its situation changed. After the success of the Christian peoples in the Balkan wars (1912–13), the Central European balance of power was so disrupted that the result was the First World War. For Western Europe the war was primarily a struggle between states and armies for the redistribution of power; but in the Eastern half of the continent, the war released from state control crucial national, class and social antagonisms. Whether these antagonisms could have been resolved without open conflict if the war had not occurred remains a question on which opinions vary according to individual sympathies. However, the war opened Pandora's box.

It is a common over-simplification to say that revolution erupted only in the defeated countries after the war. Russia was not a defeated country; Czechoslovakia and Poland were on the victorious side; and a victorious great power, Italy, lost her social balance for long years to come and was 'saved' from revolution only by Fascism.

While stating that the First World War was the soil in which the plants of revolution ripened, we ought not to forget that these plants, these antagonisms, were already maturing before the war and were not simply 'wartime products'. Although it is possible that they never would have exploded without the war, conservative and reformist thinkers hoped in vain that they would disappear after the peace treaties were signed.

The boundaries of the revolutionary region, 1917–23

Modern states have well-defined borders and writers today generally prefer to deal with their topic within the framework of a given country.

This method is not suitable for East Central Europe even in 'regular' times, much less when describing revolutions, as in every conflict between two states interested neighbours interfered. Changing borders united and divided not only nationalities, families and estates, but economic regions too. Hundreds of thousands of war prisoners and 'guest workers' took part in the Russian Revolution, thus making it a German, Hungarian, Czech, Chinese and Korean Revolution, while there were Russian prisoners in Germany and Austria–Hungary, and Poles on both sides and in both capacities.

Central European revolution has four main components: socialist, pacifist, peasant and nationalist. These were simultaneous, but not identical, and thus made the boundaries of the revolutionary region almost indefinable. Industrial workers from Hamburg to Kharkov, even as far as Baku, had a very similar problem. Unlike in Western Europe, where liberal and socialist parties were marching step by step into parliament, transforming it more and more into an exchange of democratic class compromise, in the East democracy meant a peasant majority, or, more precisely, a majority for those who could best manipulate peasant voters. There never was a really successful peasant party in Central and Eastern Europe – during the twenties the peasant could win elections, but rarely could get hold of real state power. Russian anarchists and Bolsheviks were the first to realize that they could not win power through democratic means. Austrian and Polish socialists feared peasant nationalism, and therefore made plans for supranational democratic confederations, within which peasant nationalism could be controlled and balanced by a proletarian, or urban minority. There were fiery debates in the pre-war years, without a solution being reached.

Around 1917–18, pacifist revolution had the widest boundaries, extending over the broadest region. Starting in Russia and Finland, it swept through the Baltic to the Central Powers, threatening even the Western belligerent states. As war was made by states, the pacifist revolution took place within state borders. Pacifist revolution embraced all regions of Russia, from Novaya Zemlya (Nova Zembla) to Kamchatka and Bokhara – whose inhabitants would never have dreamt of a socialist revolution – and extended to the most conservative areas of Germany and Austria, the soldiers in revolt an irresistible force which swept away states and armies, clearing the way for any previously suppressed revolutionary tendencies.

When the pacifist revolution – in Soviet and other Marxist literature usually labelled 'bourgeois-democratic' – gave way to socialist revolution in November 1917, the boundaries of the latter revolutionary area shrank: the rural areas and mid-Eastern Moslem regions turned away, and between spring and autumn 1918, the movement was restricted virtually to the central Petrograd–Moscow region, with some distant industrial centres struggling not to be swept away in the sea of peasant revolution – white (counter-revolutionary) or black (anarchist), or populist-pacifist. The German and Austro-Hungarian armies seized some of the most industrialized, i.e. revolutionary, centres from Latvia and Poland to the Donets Basin, thus securing the importation of grain, coal and revolution into their own countries. By autumn 1918, these territories had been won back again by the revolution, which spread to Germany, Austria, Hungary and the Balkans, but stopped at the borders of all neutral states, a phenomenon not perfectly understood by contemporaries who had hoped for – or feared – a Western European revolution. Until 1921, the European revolution extended from the Urals to the Rhine, though its intensity varied. But when revolution consolidated by 1920–1 it was contained within state borders new or old. From the Rhine to the East nothing reverted to pre-World War conditions. As the new state borders – permanent or not – were affirmed, revolution consolidated within them or petered out: the fluid revolutionary region of 1917–20 disintegrated.

The Pacifist revolution

The Russian tsar, Nicholas II, was dethroned by the March (or February) revolution in 1917, after two-and-a-half years of war. When I say that the March revolution was in the first place a pacifist revolution started by war-weary soldiers and ammunition workers, I do not wish to deny that it had other important aspects and aims. Its main aim, however, was peace. Lenin, who was in Switzerland at the time and therefore had no responsibility for it, wrote after he had got the first news about the Petrograd revolution: 'The new Government is unable to make peace . . . because it is bound to the capitalists of England and France by treaties and by money . . . in the first proclamation to the people this Government said not a word about the first and basic problem of the moment: what about peace?'[3]

This prophecy came true – the Lvov–Miljukov government, which was willing to fight, was followed by the Kerenski government, which was made to fight by the Entente and driven to collapse by the same. Even then, after the November revolution, the Russian commander-in-chief, General Dukhonin, was told by the French government that it would not acknowledge the new Soviet government; the French urged him to continue fighting. In a few days, the Allies revised their standpoint, and consented to Russia's ceasefire with the Central Powers, provided she would not cede territories, ammunition and POWs to the Germans. This was more sensible, but the message came too late. Dukhonin was killed by soldiers desperate for peace, and Soviet Russia made her ceasefire agreement with the Central Powers at Brest Litowsk. It was neither favourable nor dignified, but was dictated by common sense and popular pacifism.

With the Peace Treaty of Brest Litowsk in March 1918, Russia lost Poland, the Baltic and, at least temporarily, the Ukraine and Bessarabia, i.e., more or less her Central European territories. A huge chunk of territory was thereby added, or rather, returned to Central Europe, but it was a part infected with the virus of East European revolution. This East Central Europe, once one of the most revolutionary regions of Russia, spread pacifism, socialist ideas and peasant anarchy, nationalist sentiments and conflicts.

Again, pacifism came first. While the Brest Litowsk peace conference was going on, a wave of mass political strikes and anti-war demonstrations shook the Central Powers. The strikes first occurred in Vienna on 14 January 1918; then in Budapest (18 January), and after a few days Czech and German workers followed suit. The sailors of Austria–Hungary revolted on 1 February at the Cattaro naval base. The industrial workers and railwaymen of the Central Powers demonstrated their readiness for revolution, and action was postponed only at the behest of the socialist party leaders, and through an awareness amongst the participants that the army was not yet ready to join a revolution. The strikes and the revolts of some of the regiments in the following months ought to have warned the governments of the coming revolution. Teutonic discipline remained steadfast until October, and succeeded in producing tens of thousands of dead – for a lost war.

At the end of September the Bulgarian army collapsed.

> Bulgarian soldiers retreated, ceased to fight, and declared their intention of going to their homes to gather the harvest. These sturdy peasants were deaf to German expostulations. They were quite friendly to the small German forces which steadily advanced to sustain the front. The retreating battalions even spared the time to help the German cannon out of the ruts. But turn, or stand, or fight – all that was over forever![4]

The Bulgarian 'peasants wearing soldiers' uniforms', as Lenin used to characterize the Russian soldiers, proclaimed a republic and marched on Sofia, but were disarmed with German help. The Tesniak ('strict' in the sense of uncompromising) socialist party did not support the soldiers' revolt, being hostile to peasant anarchy; in 1923, they were again too radical or too dogmatic to back Stambrlijski's fight against tsarist Fascism. There was a chasm in Eastern Europe between the 'petty bourgeois anarchy' of the peasant masses, and the dogmatic Marxism of the skilled workers, who wore round hats and fob-watches on Sundays and had adopted the idea of 'the dictatorship of the proletariat' as the dictatorship of the minority (provisionally until they grew to a majority), for it seemed better than merging in the democracy of the barefoot peasant masses. In other East Central European countries the gap was not so wide, or, at least not so clearly visible, as in Balkan Bulgaria, but nevertheless it existed there as a basic problem of revolutionary democracy. For these peasant countries, democracy meant a majority of illiterates susceptible to both sorts of extremism, and thus hardly governable, unlike proletarian dictatorship, which turned out to be all too governable.

The Bulgarian Revolution was followed within a month by the Austrian, Bohemian, Hungarian and then by the German Revolutions. In these countries of the exhausted Central Powers, socialists and democrats seized the moment when the army revolted to have their organized, 'scientific' revolutions. Moderate socialists cooperated with the radical intelligentsia and bourgeoisie, to guard national interests, but also out of fear of soldier and peasant anarchy.

The Habsburg monarchy fell apart after the last lost battle on the Italian front. The national political centres – Zagreb (19 October), Fiume (23 October), Prague (28 October), Martin (30 October), Budapest (30 October) – one after another proclaimed the new nation-states; in the end Vienna too, where revolution also took place on 30 October, but the Austrian Republic was proclaimed only on 12 November. The Vienna and Budapest Revolutions preceded the November armistice by four days; the German Revolution took place two days before Germany signed the capitulation at Compiègne.

These revolutions all had a basic anti-war character – but as the war ended with them, pacifism gave place to other, more pressing problems.

The revolution of the nations

After the revolutions, the army, soldiers' soviets and officer corps exercised great influence almost everywhere where state and society were yet unshaped; in the Ukraine the Petliura army bullied and dismissed weak governments. Only with the return of peace did civilian forces and parties get the upper hand.

The collapse of Russia and Austria–Hungary gave way to the formation of new nation-states mostly during November 1918, though some new states, such as Poland, had already been forming earlier, but German occupation had deprived them of freedom of action. The peasant masses, with the help of their various churches, had, for the most part, preserved their national character through the centuries of German, Russian and Hungarian rule, and they readily accepted the new nation-states. The national churches, intelligentsia and bourgeoisie gained democratic support from the peasant masses which made up the majority of the population in all the new states, with the exception of Bohemia.

From the start of the war the Entente favoured liberating the small nations; but, in spite of several secret treaties, its ideas remained vague until the Russian Revolution. Not only the Western powers, but Slavic politicians as well were made uneasy by fears of Russian domination.[5] The Western powers remained uncertain about liquidation of the Austro–Hungarian monarchy, for they saw it as a counterweight to Russia. The Russian Revolution solved this problem: under Wilsonian influence, small national states were preferred, not only for the sake of freedom and democracy, but as a 'cordon sanitaire' against the spread of Bolshevism.

For Woodrow Wilson and for most socialists, national self-determination sounded like a proper and natural solution to state and border problems. However, the small nations' wish to dominate others was natural enough, too, no less than their unwillingness to comply with the Great Powers' wishes. To put an end to the disputes and local wars, the Great Powers – *de facto* France and Great Britain – decided the borders of East Central Europe in Paris in 1919; at that point, then, national revolution, which had made the new states, did not entirely define their borders and future.

There were some peoples to whom no place was given on the maps of the new Europe: the Ukrainians (about thirty million people) for example, and the Macedonians. The Ukrainians got limited autonomy in Soviet Russia, but nothing like they had in Poland. Some peoples, too small to get independence – Slovaks, Slovenes and Croats – were patronized by their bigger brothers. They readily joined the new Czechoslovakia and Jugoslavia, but were disappointed when they were denied autonomy. Origins and language, Western or Eastern influence in their way of life and church invisibly divided the new states, approximately along the thousand-year-old borders of Western Christianity. Knowing that their position had improved compared with what it had been in Habsburg times they accommodated themselves, but national tensions added to peasant resentment against all centralization led to problems later. Nevertheless, Jugoslavia consolidated herself within her new borders as early as the end of 1918; Czechoslovakia and Rumania by mid-1919; and Poland a year later.

The peasantry was placated through land reforms, i.e. distributing sections of the big estates. The popular vote made a socialist majority impossible; vast and clumsy peasant parties formed, oscillating between compromise and rebellion.

Should we consider the nation-states successful? Yes: since 1919, there have been no states in Europe where the *majority* is oppressed by a national minority. This was a big step forward, one that opened the way to democracy, though new problems of minorities were created. It was only later that it became obvious that some new nation-states had failed to form an economic unit which had a chance of dynamic technical progress.

Peasant revolution

The pacifist and national revolutions were almost identical to peasant revolutions. After the country's military collapse, after the 'big' revolution which had given the peasants the stimulus to pursue their own peculiar and local aims, there were waves of local peasant revolts from Russia to Hungary. Workers' and even soldiers' uprisings in Central Europe were moderate in their methods compared to the bloodshed common in Russia, Poland or Finland. But, though the peasants comprised the mass of the population, peasant revolts throughout the region were very similar.

The leaders and instigators were always soldiers returning home, well-decorated noncoms. The first step was often robbing local pubs and drinking as much as possible. The second step often consisted of robbing stores, especially when owned by Jews, Germans or other 'aliens' ('aliens' – in the Ukraine the Russians, called 'moscal'; in Galicia the Poles; in Rumanian Transylvania, the Hungarians and Armenians, etc.). They were more cautious with those who had relatives and friends in the village, fearing a vendetta. The Jews had no village friends and were frequently beaten up, but were rarely killed. The gendarmes and the local officials were more likely to be killed, mainly in ethnic neighbourhoods, especially if they had taken bribes during the war, or had misused the soldiers' brides, and so on.

The next day a soviet was elected, consisting mainly of soldiers who had returned from the front, who often imposed an extra local tax on the rich. They frequently robbed the gentry's estates – of everything from horses to Rembrandts, whatever there was to find. In some cases they took carts and 'visited' the merchants of the neighbouring town, or the railway store-rooms. They formed local guards (sometimes called Red Guards) for defence against the state and the neighbouring villages, or to rob the latter. The soviets' main concern was land redistribution, but they rarely acted without awaiting the government act to this effect. All this activity ceased after a couple of weeks, for the local soviets rarely allied with their neighbours, and lost courage when the state became stronger. But, as all this happened mainly in the first days of the new state, it made quite an impression on the policy-makers. For fear of peasant anarchy, the ruling class agreed to socialist action which was well organized and law-abiding, even if revolutionary, while the socialists grew more opportunist.

For the most part, there was no real alliance between socialist industrial workers and peasants or farm hands. Communist and other leftist socialist parties tried to organize the village poor, but the latter were interested only in land redistribution. When this took place, they lost interest because they were satisfied; if the revolution did not distribute the latifundia, they grew disenchanted and became hostile.

In Germany, Austria and in part in Poland, the peasants were against socialism from the start, mistrustful of all that came from 'Jewish' Vienna and Lemberg (Lvov) or the '*Judenregierung*' of Berlin. The only important exception was Bavaria, where Kurt Eisner gained one of the peasant unions for an ally and many hundred peasant soviets were organized. These peasant soviets gave real help to the Munich *Räteregierung*, but could not counterbalance the general conservatism of the German peasantry.[6]

Socialist revolution: Germany

The German Revolution started surprisingly red. The sailors of Kiel, Bremen and Hamburg took the initiative no less than the sailors of Kronstadt in the Russian Revolution. The radical sailors were followed by the radical socialists: the German Revolution already had a certain socialist character in the first November days. A socialist government was appointed by the executive of the Berlin workers' and soldiers' soviet at a time when in Vienna, Prague and Budapest the socialists claimed, and had, only a minority in the new, republican governments.

In actual fact, however, the prospects of German socialism were even bleaker than of Austrian or Hungarian socialism. Certainly, the German socialist parties were the strongest, with leaders of such stature as Karl Kautsky or Rosa Luxemburg, but the state and the ruling class were even stronger, though they were shattered for a few weeks under the heavy blows of military defeat and revolution. But the German state and military were harder to defeat than the Russian. Discredited by the lost war and the heavy losses, and aware of the hatred and suspicion of the victorious powers, German militarism and nationalism, always so loud, now drew back from the political stage, or at least from the more visible part of it; but there remained in the background the rock of the German state, which crushed the early attempt at a socialist revolution in January 1919. The so-called 'Spartacus revolt' which took place around 6–11 January 1919 in Berlin had a defensive character, not only because it started as a direct reaction to the departure from the government of the left-wing 'Independent' social democrats and the subsequent replacement of the Independent social-democrat Berlin police chief, Eichhorn, but mainly because the revolt's latent aim was to prevent National Assembly elections, a hopeless encounter for the new-born Communist Party, or even for the Independent socialist party.

When Rosa Luxemburg – killed by officers after the Spartacus revolt – spoke at the Communist Party founding congress at the end of December 1918 in favour of taking part in the elections, she was certainly not led by any great hopes, nor by the wish to sit in a parliament she despised, but rather by a desire to avoid a premature clash. However, on the left of the left there is always a left, and Bremen and Hamburg sailors and Dresden radicals voted Spartacus down. Historians see this majority and the independents siding with them as adventurous and over-optimistic. They surely were, but what mattered was their fear of elections and consolidation – they did not wish to give up revolutionary power voluntarily for the sake of a majority of peasant and petty-bourgeois voters. The 45 per cent for the socialists in the January 1919 elections spoke as much for as against socialism. However, the vast majority of the socialist votes were given to the moderates' party, for Scheidemann and Noske.

In Bavaria the soviets declared the *Räterepublik* soon *after* the elections, in April–May, first under independent, then under communist leadership. They did not wish to accept reality but they had to – the Bayrische *Räterepublik* existed no longer than half a month. The declaration of Soviet Bavaria was not fully democratic, and neither was her end: the occupation of Munich by the central government's troops. Munich (or Berlin or Bremen) ought not to have decided the fate of the whole of Germany (or even of Bavaria), but why was it not allowed to decide its own? At the 1920 elections the majority (i.e. moderate) socialists got only half the votes they had received the previous year; at that point, revolution was out of the question.

I do not wish to try to decide which German socialist party made the fewer blunders; I will just stick to the facts: the Communist Party certainly did not wish to admit their mistakes to themselves until the coming of Hitler made them too obvious to ignore. The Comintern, which they joined in March 1919 not without hesitation, did not make it easier for them, as the Comintern was looking to Germany as the last hope for a world revolution. The moderate socialists were better aware that the masses revolted in November more for peace than for socialism. On the other hand, some further steps towards socialist or social equality would have been as much in keeping with the party's programme as with its members' wishes. The Ebert–Groener pact of generals and social democrats in November 1918 helped to preserve the power of German militarism. What of similar importance did the generals give to Ebert in return?

For the time being, German democracy proved strong enough to repulse the Kapp-Putsch in 1920, the Hitler-Ludendorff Putsch in 1923, and the last communist attempts to gain power (1921 März-Aktion, 1923). So democracy prevailed on the surface; on the other hand, it changed very little of the traditional peasant, petty-bourgeois and philistine mentality: for that, the revolutionary period had lasted far too short a time.

Socialist revolution: Austria and Hungary

For students of mass psychology it might be illuminating to study how differently two such similar countries as Austria and Hungary reacted to their revolutions. Even the Vienna and Budapest revolutions in the last days of October 1918 were similar in their peaceful character, in the prevalence of anti-war feelings, in the new anti-Habsburg republican tone they both had, in the central part played by the Social Democratic party and the soldiers, and so on. Budapest and Vienna very much dominated the two states, suppressing all provincial opinions. The Austrian republic was declared on 12 November, the Hungarian on 16 November. The left-wing opposition abandoned the Social Democratic party and founded the communist party on 3 November in Vienna, on 24 November in Budapest. In Hungary, as in Austria, the SDP had only two members each in the new democratic governments: too few, considering their leading role both in the revolution and in maintaining order. Inside both SDPs there emerged a very strong left wing (Bauer and F. Adler in Austria, Pogány and Landler in Hungary) which remained in the party for the sake of labour unity and took a stand against the founding of the Communist Party, but demanded a radical policy and a bigger share of government power. Whether they wanted power only to strengthen democracy or for a class struggle for socialism remains a question which they clarified as little for themselves as for the revolutionary masses.

Hungary, while she gained independence after four hundred years of Habsburg rule, lost the larger part of her traditional territory, and so did Austria. While Austrian public opinion instantly, though not without pain, abandoned all hope of keeping or getting back the non-German parts of the late monarchy, no party in Hungary acquiesced to the heavy losses. There is no logical explanation for such contrasting national behaviours, except that the Austrian Germans were hoping to join Germany as compensation for their losses; but then, when the *Anschluss* was prohibited by the Paris Peace Conference, the Austrians resigned themselves to that too. The Hungarian revolutionary government of the pacifist Count M. Károlyi was compelled by public opinion to insist, at least in proclamations, on the 'territorial integrity' of historical Hungary, without, however, an army or an ally to keep the non-Magyar and mixed parts of the country from breaking away. Let us here abstain from the perpetual question posed in the Hungarian literature as to which was the better policy; suffice it to say that, though they went quite separate ways, Austria and Hungary were paid in the same coin by the Paris Peace Conference and after. What matters from our point of view is that Austria, accepting the Peace Conference resolution beforehand, could concentrate all state and political power upon inner consolidation, while the outcome of the Hungarian revolution was influenced by the hopeless attempts to hold on to Transylvania and Slovakia.

On the other hand, all revolutionary parties – except the communists – felt obliged to follow the pattern of Western democracy, that is, to hold elections as soon as possible. For all socialist parties this had the consequence that they lost their leading role in the revolution when they confronted the peasant majority at the polls. Townsfolk and army had led the revolution: the army disbanded, and Vienna gave up its domination to a hostile peasantry that was not only biassed against the revolution of the Vienna workers and Jews, but in the Tyrol and the Vorarlberg was even speculating about joining Switzerland or Germany.

In the new, republican Austrian parliament the socialists had more than 40 per cent of all the seats, a great success, but far from a majority; the conservative Catholic Christian-socialists had around 40 per cent; the remaining one-sixth of all the seats fell to the German nationalists.[7] But this non-socialist majority could not even dream of a majority government: the workers would look upon it as a counter-revolutionary attempt, and the more radically minded would surely join the small Communist Party – more dangerous for men of property than a social-democratic government. Therefore the Christian-socialist/socialist coalition had a socialist majority headed by Karl Renner, a cautious realist who was the first to give up the hopes of an *Anschluss*, and thus foresee today's Austria.

The Hungarian revolutionary government made belated and futile attempts at reconciliation with the Slovaks, Croats and the Rumanians of Transylvania. Around the New Year, when Czech troops were already marching into Pozsony (later Bratislava) and Kolozsvár (later Cluj), the conservatives lost their faith in Károlyi, whom they had earlier suspected of being a French agent, and therefore somebody able to get better terms from the victorious powers. After they discovered that he was but a patriotic pacifist and as such of no use, they turned against him, pressing him to fight, without an army, and trying at the same time, and not without success, to put the responsibility for the loss of Slovakia and Transylvania on his shoulders. And while his calls to enlist in the new army went ignored, they tried to alleviate their own sense of helplessness by putting all the blame on him.[8]

The communists and left-wing socialists were less concerned with boundary problems. Not that they were glad to see the economic unit of a prospering industry broken up. The 'Austro-Marxists', with their German orientation, were for the democratization, not for the disruption of the monarchy; as for the communists, Lenin and the Soviet government in a special message warned 'the workers, peasants and soldiers of the late Austro-Hungarian monarchy' against making an alliance with the propertied classes of their own nation, calling on them to establish 'an alliance of the workers', soldiers', and peasants' soviets of Austria–Hungary'.[9] Such aims may sound somewhat fantastic to us, but they were based on the fears of the ethnically mixed city population, partly of German and Jewish origin, anxious lest their better way of life should fall back into rural poverty – 'Balkanization'.

We have to remember that one of the numerous East European nationalities was the Jews, partly assimilated to their new homelands; the poor majority was nevertheless more sympathetic to socialism than to nationalism. Numbering about seven million, they were not among the minority groups of the area, but lived without a common territory and so without a hope of national unity. Consequently, they favoured urban supranationalism – or internationalism. Their significance was strengthened during the revolutionary period by their concentration in the big cities. In Budapest they comprised about 20 per cent of the population which also contained a great number of middle class Germans, and Slovak, Rumanian and Polish workers.

The Károlyi government, rebuked at every step for not being patriotic enough for the right, and for being too chauvinistic for the left, decided after the German and Austrian elections to go to the polls. Hoping for a majority for the coalition, they invited I. Szabó, the leader of the smallholders' party, to join the cabinet, in an effort to gain peasant votes, and get started on land distribution. On 21 February 1919 they arrested Béla Kun, leader of the Communist Party with some sixty of his followers, a step Renner would not even have dreamed of. What had proved successful in Germany – with her strong state and army, and unbroken nationalism – was a failure in Hungary. The Hungarian workers were for unity: they did not follow Kun, who was breaking this unity, but they condemned the socialist leaders who had arrested Comrade Kun. Szamuely, a friend of Bukharin, organized the underground movement; philosophers and writers helped G. Lukács to organize the propaganda. What is more, the left of the SDP turned against the policy of consolidation, and helped local soviets to seize power with impunity.

What would have happened if Hungary had gone to the polls will remain a question forever, because on 20 March 1919, Lt Colonel Vix, the head of the French military mission at Budapest, handed over a note from the Paris Peace Conference demanding that the country cede to Rumania the eastern parts of what remained from old Hungary. Next day the government resigned, as a last gesture of protest, but maybe unconsciously they felt easier after freeing themselves from the burden of the coming hard weeks. They surrendered power to the SDP which secured itself through an alliance with Kun – then still in jail.[10]

The Hungarian Soviet Republic, an enthusiastic follower of Soviet Russia, in some points differed substantially from its model. The Russian Bolsheviks first made an alliance with the 'left socialist-revolutionaries', a peasant socialist section, and therefore started with a radical land redistribution which strengthened their power very significantly. After they had broken with the socialist revolutionary party they turned to the one-party system. In Hungary there existed no peasant socialist movement of any consequence, and the Soviet government pursued a dogmatic agricultural policy, which, together with the anti-religious propaganda spread by fanatical Jewish students, alienated the peasantry from red Budapest. On the other hand, since the Hungarian communists had formed an alliance with the social democrats, their domestic and foreign policy gained in flexibility what it lacked in steadfastness, and everyday life went on quite smoothly and without much bloodshed. With the help of the moderate socialists, they maintained cordial relations with the Austrian government. The latter, while consistently refusing to form another Soviet government and thus make a red Austria–Hungary, not only helped Budapest to break the Entente-blockade, but made no objection to ammunition transport going through or from Austria, nor even to recruiting a Vienna Legion to help the Hungarian Red Army, the latter perhaps in the hope that they would thereby get rid of some Vienna communists.

These friendly relations gained the sympathy of the Austrian workers, if not of the Entente missions. But the attempts of Kun to 'organize' a Vienna revolution on 15 June failed. The proclamation of the Slovak Soviet Republic on the next day, 16 June, in the eastern parts of Slovakia invaded by the counter-attacking Hungarian Red Army did not compensate for the failure in Austria.

For the Vienna socialist leaders it was not so easy to convince their followers that Austria was not yet ripe for socialism; truly, they had first to convince themselves. The Hungarian experiment did not prove the socialization of the economy impossible even in a country less industrialized than Austria. But soon after the first steps of social transformation it demonstrated a lot of grave problems, besides the recalcitrance of the peasantry. The decisive reason for Adler and Bauer was the impossibility of integrating a socialist Austria into a capitalist Western Europe. Instead of an alliance with revolutionary Hungary, they tried to establish a social partnership inside Austria – not without success, for the moment, but later they were rejected by their partners. Kun, who had earlier severely criticized the SDP for its patriotic airs, once in power found himself preaching war – in theory for World Revolution, but in practice for the parts of Hungary annexed by Czechoslovakia and Rumania. With this bold decision he gave Paris all too good an excuse to stamp out Hungarian Bolshevism.

Socialism defeated by nationalism: Czechoslovakia and Poland

One of the most cultured and industrialized countries of the region was Bohemia. There, if anywhere, existed the possibility of rapid progress, even before it had won independence. After the partition of Poland, it seemed that Bohemia could choose only between the Austrian or the Prussian yoke. Austria seeming the lesser evil, having had a long period of economic prosperity, the Bohemian socialist movement found its place within the monarchy, where skilled Czech workmen were always welcome, and their Austro-Marxist leader, the talented Bohumír Šmeral, limited their efforts to federalization and the democratization of Austria. In Hungary, national oppression was harsher; therefore, as early as around 1905, the Slovak socialist movement maintained only formal connections with its Budapest comrades.

To be sure, the Czech people ardently wanted independence through all these years, but this seemed no more than a distant hope. Before the First World War, the Slavophilism stimulated by certain Russian circles was in line with the feelings of the people, yet some of the politicians – and their Western benefactors too – were uneasy about Russian expansion, though tsarist Russia was their ally. After the Russian Revolution, these precautions gave way to a new Entente policy of giving more definite help in the making of nation-states, even smaller ones, in the hope of their forming a reliable barrier between Germany and Bolshevik Russia. With the possibility of freedom thus closer, those demanding national unity in the Czech Social Democratic party overpowered Šmeral, who accepted his defeat and resigned, and later even went abroad so as not to be in the way of unity among the Czech socialists (the Bohemian Germans seceded).

The national victory and the Czech–Slovak union swept away 'minor' problems such as the lack of Slovak or Ruthenian autonomy. The peasantry enjoyed both freedom and the most radical agrarian reform in

Central Europe. The socialist workers' sympathies remained divided between the new democracy, where the SDP could often be an influential coalition member as in the neighbouring countries, and Soviet Russia, the more so as the aspirations of German and Hungarian nationalism were hopeless for the time being, and so the numerous German and Hungarian workers, railwaymen, postmen and the like had Bolshevism as a last resort. Šmeral, who was at heart a communist, awaited the founding of the Communist Party as long as there was a revolutionary situation, wishing to avoid an almost hopeless battle as the head of a mostly Bohemian-German CP. But his foreign comrades were impatient with him and tried to help.

First A. Muna, a POW returning with others from Russia, founded a communist party. He had some influence in Prague, Kladno, etc., was given aid by Moscow and Budapest, but remained unsuccessful: he had not the genius of Kun, and the workers of the new republic were divided by national feelings. Then the Hungarian Red Army, pressed by Czech legions while retreating before the stronger Rumanian army, made a successful counter-attack on the weaker Czech. During this campaign in May and June 1919, it occupied central and eastern Slovakia, where the Slovak Soviet Republic was proclaimed. There was no sign that this step would bring Bohemian socialism closer – on the contrary, the advancing Red Army was stopped.

One can easily say the methods of the Comintern (founded March 1919) were hasty and failed to take account of power relations. We must understand, that the Comintern planned on an international scale: a revolution in Prague or Vienna, irrespective of the power relations of the given country and possibly short-lived, would nevertheless destroy the Entente-dictated consolidation for a while – maybe to the next revolution.

The Hungarian Soviet Republic and its army were defeated on 1 August 1919; Czechoslovakia had already elected a National Assembly earlier and consolidated herself. After the revolutionary situation passed away, Šmeral founded the Communist Party of Czechoslovakia: it was a strong, left-wing party of 350,000 members throughout the twenties, sharply critical of the inborn defects of the new republic, but it made no effort to try to start a new revolution.

At the end of the war, a free, united Poland came into existence after more than a hundred years of being partitioned, oppressed, but never broken. Among the new states, Poland was the only one forced to fight a series of armed campaigns for her new borders, a situation which strengthened the always highly active Polish nationalism. The Western powers helped Poland in her fight against Ukrainian and Lithuanian nationalists, and of course, against Bolshevism.

The Polish government, constantly at war with the enemy, and beset by striking workers and economic problems, nevertheless always had a safe hold on power, thanks to national feelings, the limited agrarian and other social reforms within the country, and endless propaganda against the neighbouring powers. This safe position, however, was not so clear to contemporaries as it is for us, and the Comintern, misled by the demonstrations, strike movements and other actions of the militant Communist Party of Poland, put its hopes on Warsaw, seeing in Poland a key to the doors of Germany. Thus, when Piłsudski attacked his big neighbour and captured Kiev in May 1920, the Soviet government, after a successful counter-offensive, could not resist the vain hope of carrying revolution to Warsaw on the points of bayonets. Their defeat near Warsaw put an end not only to the Soviet offensive but also to the hopes for a European revolution. The Comintern's strategy then took a sharp turn: they understood that the Central European revolution had stopped short, and had given way to consolidation with moderate or even counter-revolutionary governments.

Central Europe consolidated

Revolutions do not last long. People get tired, the more so after a long and bloody war: the prophets of 'permanent revolution' remain alone and disarmed.

After the war with Poland, Russia signed a very bad peace with surprising quickness, and also let Rumania have Bessarabia without any formal agreement. She let the new Baltic states alone relatively soon, and kept to the borders imposed on her by the Western powers and their allies; in exchange, they let her keep all the earlier Russian territories east of Central Europe, from the Caucasus to the Arctic shore, revolutionary or not.

Central Europe emerged after the peace treaties with states, shaped partly from territories gained from Russia, partly from the remains of the Habsburg monarchy, with conservative Catholic or Protestant peasantry and more or less revolutionary towns, and, of course, with Germany, cast off by the West and punished for years with almost East European famine and humiliation.

Years of unrest and uncertainty followed for the new Central Europe. Germany could not consolidate, but neither could she go back to militaristic imperialism during the twenties: the generals themselves knew that and remained passive through the Putsch attempts of Kapp, Hitler and Ludendorff. Zinoviev, the chairman of the Comintern, made a last experiment, sending his friend Kun with a select Hungarian team to Berlin. Kun was eager to prove he could repeat March 1919, but failed: revolutions are not to be replayed over again, not even in the same place.

After the 1921 März-Aktion, the Comintern went on with its revolutionary propaganda, but warned its member-parties off any serious attempts, a condition of consolidation, if only the Western governments had been wise enough to comprehend it. As it was, Germany, Austria, Hungary, the Baltic and Finland remained hotbeds of new conflicts and were far from being able to consolidate Central Europe.

The new Slavic states and Rumania were in a better shape for progress, in spite of their social and national problems, but were neither stable nor strong enough to secure progress. They were strong enough to stifle social or national revolutions for some years, using democracy or terror combined with paternalism, but their armies and 'little Entente' disappeared when greater powers entered the stage. Thus the new Central Europe was as doomed as the old one. The new Weimar Germany, Red Vienna and independent Poland collapsed when challenged by the reborn German militarism, the little Entente disappeared as the Austro–Hungarian monarchy had disappeared before. Neither peasant nationalism, nor proletarian internationalism could resist the emerging Leviathan. Germany provoked a new entente of Big Powers, and these latter shared after their victory what once had hoped to be Central Europe.

NOTES

1 J. Szücs, 'The three historical regions of Europe', *Acta Historica* (Budapest, 1983), nos. 2–4, p. 169.
2 *Ibid.*, pp. 131–2, 177–9.
3 V. I. Lenin, *Collected Works*, vol. 23, 4th Russian edition, Moscow, Gospolitizdat, 1949. *An Outline of Theses*, 17 March 1917.
4 W. S. Churchill, *The World Crisis 1916–1918*, London, Thornton Butterworth, 1927, part 2, p. 537.
5 Th. G. Masaryk, *Die Welt Revolution*, Berlin, Erich Weiss, 1925, ch. 1.
6 F. L. Carsten, *Revolution in Central Europe*, London, Temple Smith, 1972, ch. 7.
7 Otto Bauer, *Die österreichische Revolution*, Vienna, Wiener Volksbuchhandlung, 1965, p. 139.
8 Michael Károlyi, *The Memoirs of –, Faith without Illusions*, London, Jonathan Cape, 1956, part 3.
9 *Pravda*, Moscow, 3 November 1918.
10 It is impossible to enter here into a detailed narrative of the story of the Hungarian Commune. For this see my *The Hungarian Soviet Republic*, Budapest, Akadémiai Kiadó, 1979; for a more detailed contemporary account, W. Böhm, *Im Kreuzfeuer zweier Revolutionen*, Munich, Verlag für Kulturpolitik, 1924; for the Paris Peace Conference and Hungary see Arno J. Mayer, *Politics and Diplomacy of Peacemaking – Containment and Counterrevolution at Versailles, 1918–1919*, New York, Vintage Books, 1969.

BIBLIOGRAPHICAL NOTE

A full list of important publications on the Central European Revolutions after the First World War would be larger than the text of this article itself, while to select only the most important titles seems an impossible task. I therefore mention just a few books which might make the material of my article easier to understand.

On the German Revolution F. L. Carsten gives an objective description in his *Revolution in Central Europe* (London, 1972). More sympathetic towards the revolution is David Mitchell's *1919 Red Mirage* (London, 1970). From the numerous autobiographies those of Groener, Scheidemann, and Ernst Toller are fundamental.

On the Austrian revolution the standard account is *Die österreichische Revolution*, by Otto Bauer (Vienna, 1965). *The Dissolution of the Habsburg Monarchy*, by Oscar Jászi (Chicago, 1929), gives a deep analysis of the nationality question from a democratic, but Hungarian viewpoint; the works of S. W. and Hugh Seton Watson from the viewpoint of the oppressed Slavs and Rumanians. Richard G. Plaschka, *Cattaro-Prag. Revolte und Revolution* (Graz-Köln, 1963) and Plaschka, H. Haselsteiner and A. Suppan, *Innere Front. Militärassistenz, Widerstand und Umsturz in der Donaumonarchie 1918* (Munich, 1974) give the inside story of the role of the military in the revolution. The Czechoslovak viewpoint is presented by Eduard Beneš, *Der Aufstand der Nationen* (Berlin, 1928), the separatist Slovak by Milan Hodža, *Federation in Central Europe* (London, 1942). A good insight into Šmeral's thoughts is to be found in his biography by Jan Galandauer, *Bohumír Šmeral 1880–1914* (Prague, 1981), and in B. Šmeral, *Víbor z dila*, vols. 1 and 2 (Prague, 1981), available, alas, only in Czech. Similarly, my two-volume account of the Hungarian Revolution has been published only in Hungarian: *Az 1918-as magyarországi polgári demokratikus forradalom* (Budapest, 1968), and *A Magyarországi Tanácsköztársaság* (Budapest, 1969); the essence of my writings is contained in a short English version, *The Hungarian Soviet Republic* (Budapest, 1979). A detailed social-democratic narrative by the war minister during both Hungarian Revolutions, Wilhelm Böhm, is his *Im Kreuzfeuer zweier Revolutionen* (Munich, 1924). For causes and background see O. Jászi, *Revolution and Counter-Revolution in Hungary* (London, 1924).

The connections with world politics are analysed by Arno J. Mayer, *Politics and Diplomacy of Peacemaking – Containment and Counterrevolution at Versailles, 1918–1919* (New York, 1969); also Sherman D. Spector, *Rumania at the Paris Peace Conference* (New York, 1962); and P. S. Wandycz, *France and her Eastern Allies 1919–1925* (Minneapolis, 1962). For the economic background see I. Berend and G. Ránki, *Economic Development in East-Central Europe in the 19th and 20th Centuries* (New York and London, 1974).

On the influence of the Russian Revolution over Central Europe, the standard works for the British reader are those of E. H. Carr. The first volume of I. Deutscher's Trotsky trilogy: *The Prophet Armed* (Oxford, 1954) is invaluable, if somewhat sentimental, and for the advanced reader, who can differentiate between aims and oratory, Lenin's works give the best insight.

There are valuable older works – but mainly in Russian, or even in Ukrainian – such as the memoirs of the social-democratic Ukrainian premier, Vinnitsenko or the writings of revolutionaries from Suchanow to Antonow-Ovsejenko. Some valuable essays have been translated which see the Eastern revolution through Western eyes: Gorky, Luxemburg, Balabanowa, etc. The volumes of Istoria

Grazhdanskoi Voiny (Moscow, 1936–59), vols. 1–4, are rich in facts and chronology. For today's official Soviet historiography the standard work is I. I. Mints, *Istoria Velikovo Oktiabria* (The History of the Great October) (Moscow, 1977).

6

Imperialism and revolution

VICTOR KIERNAN

'Established custom', Dr Johnson wrote after his tour of Scotland, reflecting on the Union of 1707, 'is not easily broken, till some great event shakes the whole system of things, and life seems to recommence upon new principles.' At another point in his narrative he looked further back, to the years of the Commonwealth, and thought of brute force as a mainspring of historical progress. 'What the Romans did to other nations, was in a great degree done by Cromwell to the Scots; he civilized them by conquest, and introduced by useful violence the arts of peace.'[1] We may qualify this by recalling Milton's dictum that what conquerors like the Romans brought to peoples like the Britons might be either elevating, or debasing and enslaving.[2]

There is room for much disagreement over the relative significance in history of a society's internal pulses and the influences reaching it from outside. It is a problem bearing on all world history, and in a special degree on the story of conquests and empires, the effects on one people of subjugation by another. This ubiquitous phenomenon took on a new character in modern times, in the centuries of Western ascendancy marked by the coming of capitalism and the accompanying growth of technology, thanks to which conquerors have always had – as they did not always have in earlier times – a superiority at least on the material side of life. What gains or losses have resulted for the many countries subjected to Western occupation or interference is a question all the more important because direct colonial rule has only very recently been coming to an end, and indirect control or 'neo-colonialism' is still widespread.

Western thinking has usually favoured the view that colonialism, despite much that is shameful in its record, rescued backward or stagnating societies by giving them better government, and transformed them by drawing them out of isolation into the currents of the world market and a world civilization. Marxists (European Marxists at any rate), who have given more thought than most to the subject, have often concurred in this judgement, so far as the postulate of a general lack of forward movement in the pre-colonial world outside Europe is concerned; they have been sceptical about most of the positive benefits claimed for colonial rule, and have had more to say about its predatory motives. An awkwardness is observable here in the Marxist theory of history, derived as it was from European evolution. Seeking rational explanations, it has been attracted by whatever may appear a logical interaction and unfolding of forces within a complex; yet when looking away from Europe it has felt obliged to conclude that history has been kept going, at a certain stage, or got back into motion, only by the intrusion of external forces. The symmetry of the theory is thus upset. So far as the inhabitants of Africa were concerned, the European intervention beginning in the fifteenth century was purely accidental, and therefore irrational.

It was of course no accident in terms of *Europe's* development. Broadly it may be said that Western Europe revolutionized itself, over many centuries; Eastern Europe had new ways of life thrust on it from above, by Westernizing rulers like Peter the Great, and most of Afro-Asia, still more, from outside. Even within the West, each of the great revolutions – Dutch, English, American, French – owed very much to foreign ideas and leaders with knowledge of foreign countries; more than one also to foreign armed aid. Revolutions may be, or seem, short and sharp, but social change, as Braudel says, cannot come about quickly in sudden bursts.[3] Hence genuine transformation cannot be imposed simply from above. It is almost as unlikely to come about simply from below. Mao stood for a literal faith in the self-transforming potential of the Chinese peasantry; but many struggles of earlier times had failed to demonstrate this.

A rough distinction may be drawn between *growth*, due primarily to internal evolution and ferment, and *change*, which may come about most often through external intrusion; and the deepest alterations may be supposed to have come about through a convergence of the two factors, a phenomenon extremely rare in the history of both modern and older forms of imperialism. From the penetration of one society, ripe for change, by another with some superior attainments, a third may be expected to emerge, distinct from both though inheriting much from each.

If force can be the midwife of history, as Marx termed it, a new life must be supposed already existing, struggling for birth. In Europe successive rebirths had been taking place ever since the fall of Rome; elsewhere they are much harder to descry, and Western eyes at any rate have often failed to make out any symptoms of an approach to them. Feudal-type rebellion was as common in Indian history as peasant revolt in Chinese. Yet, by the eighteenth century, Europe and Afro-Asia were existing in separate compartments; in the West time had been running faster, while the others had not even been able – or had not wanted – to make a clock. There had been no lack of novelty in Asia, partly the outcome of contacts of one region with another; shifts in styles of government, new fashions in philosophy, religious movements waxing and waning, though these were seldom more than revivalist outbreaks, turning back to the past. Of more lasting value were fresh achievements in literature and the arts. But by far the greater part of all this was confined to the upper walks of society, or the 'superstructure', and left the mode of production and its toilers untouched. Muslim rule brought various technical as well as cultural innovations into India, affecting agriculture as well as handicrafts; but it brought no basic change, economic or social. Frequently such alien dominion may have had on balance a tendency to perpetuate rather than to sweep away.

Whether such directionless eddying can continue indefinitely, if not broken in on from outside, or whether there must be some limiting point at which political or cultural variations on the ground bass of an unchanging economy must come to an end, may be arguable. Whether it is moral and psychological exhaustion rather than economic that threatens to bring a civilization to an end, or perhaps the two things combined, may also be a question. China's long inanition after a brilliant start suggests forcibly that a society has only limited potentialities of progress, sooner or later to be suffocated by an accumulation of vested interests and conservative instincts. Everywhere in Afro-Asia these grew to be strong and immobilizing. Chinese merchants and moneylenders grew rich by collaboration with the bureaucracy, and their ambition then was to gain entry to the mandarin class and bask in its prestige, very much as money-makers in early modern Europe wanted to turn themselves or their sons into landowning gentlemen. An Asian writer highly critical of the West has acknowledged the absence in the East of a functioning 'intellectual community',[4] with the ability to view critically its own society. This was an especially vital lack for, unlike developments in Europe, it was accompanied by the failure to emerge of an authentic 'bourgeoisie' – a class geared to capital accumulation and industrial production. In the East, priestcraft held dominion over men's thinking. Everywhere in the once stirring Islamic world stagnation had set in, a charmed sleep from which it had no power to rouse itself.

Even allowing for European self-complacency and prejudice, it may not be too surprising that Europeans coming in contact with Asia's elites soon felt unable to take them very seriously. Chinese mandarins were at first an exception, but as time went on and familiarity increased they came to share the contempt bestowed on all 'Celestials' of the 'Heavenly Kingdom'. 'The Chinese', a British representative in China J. F. Davis, wrote in 1840, 'have much of that childish character which distinguishes other Asiatics', the result he thought of their minds being cramped by despotic rule.[5] Asian infantility was indeed a prevalent Western impression. In the Canton trade, 'sing-songs' – musical boxes and the like – were more in demand than any other Western products; Europeans in India found high society in the Mughal empire which had been established by new invaders from Muslim Central Asia during the sixteenth century fascinated by gewgaws such as whistles or mirrors. Persians, though talented, are 'just like children', a British diplomat of this century declared.[6] Westerners reared on Descartes or Bentham had some reason for impatience with the antiquated nonsense that passed for learning or wisdom at Al Azhar, the celebrated Cairo seminary, or the Hanlin Academy in Peking whose members were the cream of Chinese scholarship.

European expansion has left behind it the problem of how much it did to transform retarded continents, or open the way at least to their renovation. Little of the sort can be credited to the Portuguese or Spanish pioneers, and not much more to the early Dutch or English who followed on their heels. Modern colonialism entered a new phase after the great events of the later eighteenth century: the Industrial Revolution and American and French Revolutions. As far away as China, Lord Macartney on his embassy in 1793–4, an unsuccessful attempt to persuade the government to open its doors to foreign trade and diplomacy, met with an 'indistinct idea' of some grand upheaval in Europe. Perhaps it was the example of 1789 that made him forecast chaos if the Chinese should revolt against their masters, the Manchus, whose ancestors had taken possession of China in the seventeenth century.[7]

In Europe itself few nations had the capacity to turn over a new leaf, and progress had to be set in motion by assaults on archaic regimes, like Napoleon's triumph over Prussia in 1806. French armies going out to emancipate Europe and staying to exploit it had some resemblance to the Europeans who were going out into Afro-Asia. Pitt was indignant at the revolutionary government's order to French generals to 'liberate' occupied territories from their rulers;[8] conservatives by the Ganges or the Yellow River must have felt that this was just what British generals were being sent out to do. By many Europeans, Karl Marx among them,[9] their doings could be viewed as bearing the promise of a new age; as a rough but necessary cure for an inveterate sleeping-sickness. Colonial rule might aspire to a radical, utilitarian, overhauling of old societies, a blend of the work of the rising bourgeoisie and of its predecessors, enlightened despots of the breed of Frederick the Great or Joseph II of Austria.

Eighteenth-century India was going through the break-up of the

Mughal empire, and on the political surface was much more in a state of mutation than most of Asia. Having lost its largely synthetic unity, the country was going through something like a 'war-lord' era, a period of power struggles that in most areas had little meaning. India unlike China was a theatre of very diverse ethnic and linguistic composition, where forces of dislocation could work themselves off in local ambitions (the prowess of the Maratha armies for example had at most a sub-national character), or in ideological currents such as the Sikh creed represented in a limited locality. Both the Maratha and the Sikh movements were hardening into old feudal moulds before the time came for them to face the European challenge. Altogether India showed very little preparedness to react to this positively.

The Far East was a distinct continent, with a character of its own (which in some respects had its closest parallel in Europe) and, despite much diversity, a common culture originating from China. It was here that Western intervention was to have its most revolutionizing effect, even though colonial occupation did not ensue except in Indo-China. In the Far East, unlike Asia further westward, foreign impact met with and released mounting internal pressures towards change. Since the seventeenth century both China and Japan had practised isolationism; but with old structures of authority and ideas ossifying, their rulers could not ban internal unrest as easily as foreign intercourse. Paradoxically India, always freely open to aliens from far and wide, proved better able to keep its old habits unaltered. There two powerful religions, Hinduism and Islam, mutually hostile, were equally vigilant guardians of established social relations. Beyond their eastern limits an eclectic mixture of Confucianism, Buddhism, and indigenous cults like the Taoist in China and the Shinto in Japan, ensured a lower intensity of religion, and a less potent damper on criticism or innovation. Ultimately it would make for a lesser barrier than in India or the Islamic world against adoption of Western modes, whether under capitalist management as in Japan or socialist as in China.

A further difference was that these kingdoms of the Far East had a kind of national sentiment scarcely known to India or Islam, though usually hitherto less outward-looking, less aggressive than Europe's. Vietnam had tenacious memories of wars of resistance against China. Korean poetry through the ages was tinged by a similar spirit.[10] In Japan the centralizing control of the Shogunate, the military-feudal regime of the dominant Tokugawa family in the seventeenth and eighteenth centuries, assisted growth of collective feeling,[11] and neo-Confucian orthodoxy was being modified by thinking of a more Japanese cast, with a Shinto admixture. Something like what Europe called 'public spirit' can be discerned in all these countries. It must have owed a debt to Confucian stress on principled concern with the affairs of this world, instead of private hope of escape to a better one.

Complexities of economic change underlay a growing restlessness. In China there had been 'centuries of prosperity and growth', including growth of population which swelled the towns and promoted inter-regional trade;[12] though it also perilously worsened land-hunger and agrarian tensions. In Japan under the Tokugawas a rice economy was giving way to a money system, partly as a consequence of the feudal lords being compelled to spend half of each year in the capital.[13] Writings on economics were one feature of the sophisticated urban life reflected in Japanese novels of the eighteenth century. Economically, however, as well as politically, the catalyst of contact with the West was needed to precipitate radical change. In China before the second half of the nineteenth century there was scarcely any sign of a 'putting-out' method of production, that forerunner of industrial capitalism in the West; Japan was closer to the goal, but the restraints of a feudal society were a heavy impediment.[14] Everywhere the *idea* of capitalism, the entrepreneurial spirit, was wanting. It had dawned first, for very complex historical reasons, in North West Europe: elsewhere, so far as may be seen, it was only from outside that it could reach the moneyed classes capable of adopting it, somewhat as the idea of socialism has not been generated within the working class but has been brought to it by middle-class theorists.

In both China and Japan from the later eighteenth century peasant revolt was endemic. In China it weakened but could not transform the fabric of the old order, until eventually it swelled into a communist-led revolution. In Japan the share of rural disturbances in rendering the Tokugawa system no longer viable is debatable. Discontent higher up in society gave the failing Shogunate most anxiety. It was fanned by cupidity for foreign trade and its profits, and for Western wares, firearms among them, and by curiosity about Western knowledge, beginning with medical science. Chinese and others have commented that Japan could take to these things readily because it had always been borrowing, and its standard culture was more Chinese than native. Transition was greatly smoothed by the availability of a Mikado, a legitimate sovereign who could be brought out of his dynasty's long seclusion at Kyoto and stage-managed by reformers. There is both resemblance and contrast between this and the action of the sepoys at Delhi in 1857 in proclaiming as their liege lord the octogenarian pensioner in the Red Fort who was the last of the Mughal emperors. In each case a people faced with Western cannon was turning back to an old monarchy for a symbol, if no more, of its independence; in the Japanese case, unlike the Indian, there were social forces capable of establishing under its auspices a new order of their own fashioning.

Confrontation with the West made it plain to an energetic wing of the *samurai*, or lower nobility, that the policy of seclusion was no longer practicable in a realm so much smaller and more vulnerable than China. This class could enter partnership with businessmen alert to the opportunities of the time, on the basis of a capitalist industrialization able to sustain up-to-date armed forces, and hence indispensable for national survival. The process could not be smooth or unruffled; the rebellion of the powerful Satsuma clan in 1877 was a quite violent affair. But it remained an internal broil among sections of an upper class divided from its inferiors by a broad gulf. No mobilizing or awakening of the masses took place. In China and Vietnam modernization was to be far slower and more painful, and in the end the masses would be brought fully into the arena. A British trade report summed up the Far East from an angle typical of undemocratic Europe: the Japanese were forging ahead because of the feudal background which gave them 'an aristocracy, and a healthy social hierarchy based on a sound subordination'.[15] China had nothing analogous to this.

What exactly had happened, in terms of the social mechanics of the 'Meiji Restoration' (Meiji was the reign-title adopted by the restored emperor) is still a matter of controversy.[16] There were to be lengthy arguments among Japanese Marxists as to whether it amounted to a 'bourgeois revolution', or seizure of power by a capitalist from a feudal class; a baffling riddle, because categories of European and non-European history have seldom coincided exactly. Industry grew up with a markedly feudal-paternal complexion: militarism or army rule was the midwife of capitalism, as in Bismarck's Germany and in a series of Third World countries later on. Capping the whole edifice was the Mikado-worship artificially worked up by the tactics well described at the time by B. H. Chamberlain.[17] Japan was travelling backward as well as forward, making far quicker material progress than British India, but morally or intellectually developing on less wholesome lines. It was to owe a significant further instalment of reform, in the agrarian and political fields, to its defeat in the Second World War and the American occupation. In Korea landlordism was partially disrupted, after the Japanese annexation in 1910, by Japanese settlers and land confiscations, and then after the Second World War dismantled in the south by American rule, in the north by communism.

In China all peasant risings had failed, for want of a genuinely new programme and leadership; the Taiping rebellion, in the mid-nineteenth century, marked the limit of what could be achieved, and its head, the self-deifying Hung Hsiu-chu'üan, degenerated before long into an imitation emperor. His ideas were partly derived from Christianity; ultimately China would get rid of its *ancien régime* with the help of other Western concepts. Within the bureaucracy no schism or mutiny took place, as it did within Japanese feudalism. Despite its dual Manchu and Chinese composition, the official class was too homogeneous, and too much insulated from reality by its antediluvian education. The landowning interests it represented had been ready when they submitted to Manchu sway, and would be ready again when the Kuomintang national party in its later years came under the reactionary despot Chiang Kai-shek and his Western patrons, to welcome foreign power against their own people. No patriotic union against the alien was possible. 'What sort of world is this?', the progressive writer Lu Hsün wrote gloomily after the abortive revolution of 1911, which achieved no more than to put an end at last to the derelict monarchy. 'The night is so long the way so long, that I had better forget or else remain silent.'[18]

Outside the Far East too there were, if not nations, a number of political entities having some national character and historical continuance, like Persia, Burma, Siam (Thailand), and in Africa the Christian state of Abyssinia and some kingdoms like Ashanti in Western Africa, a region long accustomed to European weapons. A few precariously survived, the rest were swallowed up. They failed with striking unanimity to meet the approaching menace of Europe; the internal stirrings and discords that prepared Japan for adaptation were not present, or only very inadequately. Asia's efforts to stave off encroachments by timely change spread across the continent from west to east, beginning with Turkey, and reaching Persia and India, then Burma and Siam, finally the Far East, with Vietnam the first in the field. Most effort went into attempts to improve armed forces, with foreign equipment and training; but human material to form effective officers and soldiers was often lacking, and by itself such a programme was in any case too narrow.

Nowhere was there any breakaway from old ruts of oriental government. This can be seen in two widely removed instances, the two most feverish endeavours at building an efficient war-machine, those of Mehemet Ali in Egypt and Gia Long in Vietnam. Both were new men, usurpers, conscious of changing times; the one an Albanian soldier of fortune in Turkish service, profiting by the chaotic after-effects of Bonaparte's irruption into the Near East, the other the first head (1802–20) of a new dynasty which forced its path to power through prolonged civil war. Each employed numerous Europeans, chiefly Frenchmen; each set his country to work by conscription of soldiers and labourers. In Vietnam men were dragooned, fortresses built on the principles of the famous French military engineer Vauban, warships launched. But the army was intended very largely for purposes of repression, while conscription inflamed the discontent it was meant to counteract. Egypt was caught in much the same vicious circle, even though Mehemet Ali can be said to have understood that bigger revenues required enhanced economic activity, and European markets.[19] Both countries speedily lost momentum, and before long fell under the foreign yoke, resisted in Vietnam only by the people, in Egypt by the army fighting against the will of its employers.

Among other cases may be noted Afghanistan where, after the second British invasion in 1878–80, Abd ul Rahman sought to establish unity and firm government by methods of coercion so draconic that they must often have done more harm than good, although zealously seconded by a corps of mullahs whom he took care to induct into government service. Their prominence meant that Afghanistan, even if now more cohesive, would be socially and mentally as benighted as ever. In Abyssinia the British punitive incursion of 1868 resulted in Menelik, the future emperor and repeller of Italian invasion in 1896, becoming head of a province, and it must have helped to inspire his modernizing plans.[20] But there was no political or social reconstruction to sustain them. The last Shah liked to style himself 'leader of the Iranian revolution', but squandered billions on vast and useless armaments, and put his chief trust in an organization resembling the Gestapo.

The extent to which a country was affected by the shock of complete defeat and annexation depended upon a variety of factors. Such factors included the degree of nationalism present; the relation between government and its subjects; the relation of the army to the populace and whether it was an integral part of nation or society, or – as more often – an excrescence. So many lands were under alien or semi-alien rule that the overthrow of thrones might be welcomed as the deliverance which Europeans professed to be bringing. More usually the transfer of power was watched, if ordinary villagers were conscious of it at all, with indifference, especially since the majority of the old rulers offered little or no resistance. It was so over large parts of India as British ascendancy spread.

Regular armies, or what passed for such, in most of Afro-Asia were quickly knocked out. Long-drawn resistance was likely to be of a guerrilla nature, more popular, but not on that account more pregnant with ideas of improvement. It was very apt to turn to religion for reinforcement, and religion meant defence of the past, with all its sins. Where leaders might be true innovators was in helping to forge a people out of a scattering of quarrelsome tribes, as Abd el Kader did in the 1830s and 1840s in Algeria, or the 'Mad Mullah' before and after 1900 in Somaliland. In the Caucasus the guerrilla chief Shamyl Beg, down to his final defeat in 1858, was uniting tribesmen against the Russians; he and Nicholas I were both in their way agents of revolutionary change, unwittingly aiding each other to dismantle an old order now past its time.

'Can mankind fulfil its destiny without a fundamental revolution in the social state of Asia?', Karl Marx asked,[21] and he thought he saw this under way in India. But a great deal of the past, bad as well as good, survived there. The East India Company stepped into the vacant shoes of the Mughals, taking over many of their institutions; most literally in Bengal where it took over the 'Divani' or administration of the province nominally as deputy or vassal of the fainéant Grand Mogul. Tennyson wrote a long panegyric about the British coming to inaugurate the religious freedom and toleration of which Akbar, greatest ruler of the line, could only dream. The fact that British rule was to close in a frenzy of religious passions and massacres is evidence of how far Britain's better intentions fell short of their aim, because they envisaged too little social and economic remodelling. In some important respects things were altered for the worse; in Bengal particularly, by the Permanent Settlement of 1793 which gave the land to a body of great landlords created for the purpose, with a free hand to rack-rent their tenants in Irish style. This could masquerade as an arrangement to improve agriculture, but must really have been designed to call into being a class of useful collaborators. Its outcome was a Bengal 'revolutionized', but in a deeply morbid way.

The survival of very conservative, aristocratic elements in British public life makes it less puzzling that the most advanced nation of Europe was ready to patronize the most reactionary forces in India. In its later years the British Raj was increasingly willing to make use of stragglers from the feudal past – princes and landlords – as buttresses, while it looked askance at those who were learning from the West lessons inconvenient to their superiors. The memoirs of Sir Norman Stewart, an army man posted at Madras early in this century, are one faithful expression of this dislike for the 'educated native'.[22] Colonial governments were not infrequently disposed to humour the priesthood, as the British did in India by distributing high-flown clerical as well as lay titles, or in Quebec by leaving education to the Catholic clergy and so ensuring that their French subjects would remain illiterate and give them less trouble.

Collaborators firmly moored to the past were everywhere in demand. In Morocco the French and Spaniards found few to work with them except the feudal tribal chiefs, the sort of men who provided Franco with 80,000 mercenaries and helped him to win the Civil War. In Indonesia Dutch administrators were partnered by a light-complexioned aristocracy long accustomed to prey on the darker-skinned peasantry.[23] In Africa the Germans professed themselves eager to 'strengthen the authority of the native chiefs and other natives of rank ... and to develop them into auxiliary organs of the administration'.[24] In West Africa land belonging to a tribe came to be officially vested in chiefs, who might obligingly alienate it to planters.[25] Where natives of suitable station were not forthcoming, they could be manufactured: in India landlords, in Africa chiefs or headmen. Frequently there was manipulation of the past to stabilize the present: 'British administrators set about inventing African traditions for Africans.'[26]

A regular philosophy of Indirect Rule took shape, with Oxford as one centre; Morocco under Marshal Lyautey early in this century was another. It was bolstered by arguments sometimes well-meaning, sometimes disingenuous. There was always an ambiguity between preserving native institutions and culture, and controlling the many through the few. It would mean at best a dilution of the civilizing mission, at worst its abandonment. To dream of keeping the past alive, in any meaningful sense, was futile. Tribal society disintegrated under contact with the white man and his ways, whose good and bad sides were equally fatal to it. As Leonard Barnes, one of imperialism's most trenchant critics, wrote in 1939, Western economic penetration was irresistibly breaking up the clan, or social cooperation based on kinship, which could have a 'strange fascination' for Europeans with no equivalent bond of their own, but which must give way now to class division.[27] And this would be a release from the stranglehold of the past, but a painful one, into a hazardous, uncharted new age. In a story by an African writer an old man laments the corrosion of custom, the fading of time-honoured certainties.[28] For long to come there might be nostalgic cravings for a return to them, 'projections of recovered social unity in a millennial world or in a life beyond death'.[29]

The West could admire itself at times as a revolutionizer of comatose communities; but Mark Twain's Yankee in ancient Britain, and a Yankee of Twain's own time in the Philippines, were very different personages. Still, with all its hesitations and reluctances, the title of 'Revolutionary empire' that a historian of British expansion has given it[30] was not too ill deserved, and can be shared by the Western ascendancy as a whole. A decisive break was being made in the history of Afro-Asia. Change, for the better or for the worse, owed less to conquest in itself than to the steady pressures of colonial occupation. Parts of India were under British rule for nearly two centuries, long enough to detach the comparatively few who were brought into contact with Western ideas from some outworn patterns of thought and behaviour, and to achieve a certain legitimacy. Many possessions snapped up in the riper years of imperialism came too late for this. The French were in Vietnam for barely seventy years, with scarcely any interval of tranquillity between conquest and expulsion, and even this broken in on by the shock-waves of the Great War. Administration never lost a strong military flavour; similarly French North Africa was always under the thumb of the army more than of the government at Paris. In Korea a Japanese college instructor might be seen lecturing in uniform instead of gown, with a sword by his side.

Orderly peace and quiet was always the first reform aimed at; sometimes almost the only one, but an embargo on feuding and fighting could have many repercussions, as in India when blue blood lost ground and lawyers, traders, usurers, flourished. This by itself did not ensure progress of a more far-reaching kind. In Western Europe feudalism had given way by degrees to a capitalist order; in Asia there was a risk of nothing better resulting than a broken-backed feudal society. It did at least make possible the emergence of individuals like the reforming Hindu scholar Ram Mohun Roy (1772–1833) and the enlightened Muslim Sir Syed Ahmad (1817–1898), men who genuinely believed that British rule, whatever its faults, was beneficial to India, and were desirous of learning from the West and spreading its lessons among their people. Young men bred in the climate of opinion disseminated by them were admitted by gradual stages to the higher civil service, remained loyal to the end to the British government, and in 1947 took over the running of independent India and helped to put it on the path of moderate progress.

Marx expected Western conquest to be followed by economic rehabilitation. Lenin insisted that capitalism must have time to dissolve all pre-capitalist economic features before colonies could evolve further, which they would then do on the same lines as his own country, as analysed in *The Development of Capitalism in Russia*. In reality, in economic as well as too often in political terms, imperialism showed itself more parasitic than constructive, and likelier to cripple old forms of production than to generate new ones. On the land the old bullock went on hauling the same plough. Handicrafts suffered, if not quite so fatally as was complained, from Western (in Korea from Japanese) machine competition; though this happened in independent Turkey as well as in foreign-controlled India.

Modern industry was coming in only sluggishly, even in India where conditions were least unfavourable. It was delayed by blockages on the side of both European and Asian enterprise; with the latter it was not capital that was lacking, but the true capitalist spirit. In the later years of the Raj there was lively argument within the Third International about the thesis advanced in some quarters that Britain was coming round to a policy of economic 'decolonization', and that India was being industrialized.[31] Correctly enough, the thesis ended by being discredited, and Marxists were pushed towards a radical rethinking, a conviction that imperialism prohibits capitalist development in any colony or 'neo-colonial' dependency. This belief in turn has had to be revised of late in view of the rapid industrial growth of Taiwan, South Korea, Hongkong – one of whose common features is their belonging to the Far Eastern complex.

European investment in colonies showed more inclination to follow on from old proclivities; it set up new plantations with labour forces kept in conditions not far from slavery. Often segregated in out-of-the-way hill districts, workers were largely women, and might be partly recruited, as in India, from aboriginal districts. Agriculture on these lines, and mineral extraction, were what a Boston financial journal advocated in 1901, when the United States of America was entering the colonial field; not, it stressed, 'a revolution in the habits and capacities of the people of the tropics'.[32] Crusaders had ridden into Asia to liberate holy places, not human beings; their latter-day successors were finding their holy places in tea gardens, gold mines and oil wells.

Meanwhile, in the concluding stages of empire, the newspaper, cinema, radio, along with railway-train and omnibus, were redrawing men's picture of their world, and of their own position in it, more and more quickly. Ideas or indistinct images of change were germinating; but whereas in Europe they had more or less kept pace with economic progress, in the colonial lands they were running well ahead of it, and an uneasy gap between the two was widening.

It was when a colony, or semi-colony like China or Mexico, bestirred itself to think of a recovery of freedom, that the test came of how much it had learned, how far self-examination and preparation for change, for a step forward instead of back, had gone. The character of the ruling power did much to dictate the terms of the contest, and whether it would be a trial of physical force. It was one of Marx's grounds for advocating revolution in Europe that nothing could do so much to wipe the slate clean and allow humanity to make a fresh start. Freedom won by armed struggle in colonies, it has been said, has tended to arouse 'enthusiasm for drastic social experiment', and this has served as 'a kind of mass therapy for a whole people'.[33] Fanon held that some countries might be exempt from the need,[34] but in general he was convinced of the necessity of violence: it meant 'man re-creating himself', freeing the individual 'from his inferiority complex and from his despair and inaction', and imbuing a people with a sense of collective strength.[35]

There seems however no simple answer to the question whether peaceful or armed struggle for freedom has had a more revolutionizing effect. European analogies scarcely suggest that resort to force has, by itself, much transformative virtue. Revolution with no adequate social drive may only stir up dust and leave it to drift down again. Spain came out of its five years' resistance to Napoleon rootedly reactionary; the Irish Free State for years after its start in 1922 made hardly any progress, economic or intellectual. Earlier precedents outside Europe were no more auspicious. Spanish rule in America had imparted little enlightenment to the descendants of European settlers, none to the other inhabitants. In the course of the long-drawn, murderous wars of independence, Indians and Blacks were made use of on both sides, but rarely as more than tools. Freedom won by, or as in New Zealand granted to, white settlers has always left non-white populations worse off instead of better. Mexico was exceptional in its greater involvement of Indians than elsewhere, and independence was to have a sequel in a series of revolutionary upheavals, in part risings of the largely Indian or half-Indian peasantry against feudal landlord and Church, and on occasion of the nation against foreign intervention.

North America was exceptional in other ways; its people carried over with them English institutions and axioms, and their 'revolution', which cashiered George III much as James II had been cashiered, liberalized rather than revolutionized American society, leaving the incubus of slavery untouched. At the opposite extreme was Haiti, in spite of the fighting qualities displayed in the struggle for independence from France, and the remarkable leadership of Toussaint l'Ouverture until his capture in 1802. Europe was soon able to view the black kingdom, and then republic, as proof of how a native race breaking away from the white man's leading-strings must fall back into barbarism. Always fond of drawing direful domestic parallels, conservatives predicted a collapse of civilization in Britain if Chartist or socialist workers should ever be in the saddle.

National consciousness always takes a jumble of forms. In nineteenth-century Russia it could be either Westernizing and modernizing, or Slavophil and reactionary; in Asia it wavered between similar poles. Recoil from intrusive novelty made many hide from it behind the curtain of religion, and social interests formerly upheld by traditional monarchy could turn to religion, always closely associated with it, as a bulwark now still more necessary. An intelligentsia receptive to new ideas might be in existence already or might have to come to birth in the difficult setting of a colony. India had no shortage of intellectuals, and men like Ram Mohun Roy and the idealists of Young Bengal or the Brahmo Samaj, a Hindu reforming sect, undertook the painful early work of clearing out dusty lumber-rooms. It would lead on in time to a desire for the country to be set free to go on remaking itself, without foreign meddling. But in the Bengal of the Permanent Settlement, with a bulky but to a great extent parasitic intelligentsia, progressive thinking might be muddled up with other notions. Nirad Chaudhuri recalls a prevalent and strong admiration in his native province, about 1900, for Napoleon and Bonapartism.[36] In western India social strata, mainly Brahmin, which had provided the Maratha empire with ministers and officials, were quick to adopt modern schooling, newspapers, printed books, in order to foster hopes of a revival, under their own socially conservative leadership, for Maharashtra rather than for India.

In spite of all heterogeneities, a coming together of Hindu India in a united national front was to prove possible. The longevity of the Raj permitted nationalism a gradual maturing; Britain's moderation and legalism, by comparison with most other empires, made room for a constitutional movement, deviating at most (except in August 1942) into civil disobedience. Like Europe's bourgeois-revolutionary movements, it was not initiated or led, but only encouraged or taken advantage of, by the industrial bourgeoisie, a small but growing class. Under Gandhi's management there could be a limited rallying of popular forces, chiefly urban middle-class: workers and peasants were left for the most part to their own devices, their fumbling efforts to organize and put forward their own demands. Gandhi idealized the old-time Indian village, with richer and poorer living the simple life in fancied harmony; it was a vision more democratical at least than the admiration felt by earlier romantic patriots for ancient heroes prancing on elephants.

His principle of non-violence, of *loving* the misguided foreigner away, may have had a certain moral effect, by making it hard for Britons not to see that Gandhians were better Christians than themselves. If so, it helped – the Second World War helped still more by using up Britain's strength and will for power – to make a peaceable settlement feasible. The upshot was a liberal India, where British investments could feel safe, but where reforms impressive compared with those in many other former colonies have been carried out. In addition, there have been remarkable increases in both agricultural and industrial production. On the other hand, India has not fundamentally broken with its old social order, and still faces problems seemingly insoluble within the existing framework. Indians, not only of the far left, have sometimes asked themselves whether it would have been better if British rule had provoked them into full-scale rebellion, and a more sweeping social revolution.

Muslims everywhere, disgruntled at their sudden precipitation into a new epoch, were left sullenly impervious to any new thinking. Ages of warfare between Islam and Christendom had left tenacious memories, and in many places Muslims were dislodged by European conquest from their dominant position in mixed communities. Some of their writers in India depicted Europe as a den of monsters, its history a long catalogue of horrors;[37] they saw it in fact very much as Europe saw Asia. Syed Ahmad wanted his co-religionists to wake up and open their windows, but he also wanted them to repose their trust in the British government, as their protector against the bigger and richer Hindu population. In this century the Muslim political movement, after a brief spell of alliance with the National Congress, turned away towards the mirage of an 'Islamic State', the reality of a Muslim instead of a less unprogressive Hindu ruling class.

Harshnesses inseparable from imperialism combined with the painful disruption of old habits to turn many others against not only Westerners but everything Western, good or bad. In China the Boxer Rebellion of 1900 was an explosion of such animosity, heightened by rustic superstitition. Even among the higher ranks, where religion counted less, confusion and discouragement could bring a turning back to the past; men were trying to polish up old lamps as well as to acquire new ones. Gernet notes a heightened veneration for Confucius.[38] Dostoyevsky, Tagore, in Muslim India the poet Iqbal, exalted spiritual values against Western greed and materialism. By intent or not, their message could be turned into a social red herring, with spiritual blessings to fill empty stomachs. More discriminating critics found fault with Europe's conduct without rejecting its gifts. Fukuzawa was the foremost proponent of modernism in the Meiji era, though at the same time he maintained that a true civilization for Japan must be Japanese, and denounced Western aggression. 'Wherever the Europeans touch, the land withers up, as it were; the plants and the trees stop growing.'[39]

A long train of revolts, from French Canada to Vietnam, from the Philippines to Zululand, all failed, as the Indian Mutiny and the Boxer Rebellion failed, against superior arms and discipline. Europeans were beset none the less by fears of worse things to come, a Prester John, perhaps, or a Yellow Peril. Worst of all, after the Bolshevik Revolution, was the Red Peril. At first its threat was hard to comprehend. A British general campaigning in western Persia late in the Great War saw 'revolution' as a strange, demoralizing disease, reducing men to 'a dull apathy' in which even the primitive instinct to defend hearth and home was crippled.[40] But it was not long before the spectre of communism was haunting the colonial world as well as Europe.

Marxian socialism could meet needs beyond the purview of romantic nationalism like that of Mazzini, for long in Asia an admired paladin. It was coming from Western Europe, as capitalism had come to Japan; in each case Europe was revolutionizing the outer world less by imposing its rule than by teaching others how to resist it. Sparks from the conflagration of 1917 flew far and wide, but most of them failed to catch. They failed in India, partly from lack of combustible material; it was in the Far East, outside Japan, that they had most success. Acute dilemmas arose over what classes or social forces might be best fitted to absorb Marxism and take the lead in its application, in the absence of a strong industrial working class. Cabral in Portuguese Guinea drew his most promising recruits from the petty-bourgeoisie, employees or traders with modest earnings, though he was well aware of its ambivalent outlook.[41] With Mao, Marxism learned to appeal to the peasantry as the potential battering-ram of revolution. Experience has yet to show whether this could in the long run give socialism a permanent base.

It was just after the Great War, with the 'August 4 movement', that modern Chinese nationalism came into being. It had perforce to identify itself with reform and progress; the old Confucian ideology and social order were manifestly exhausted. With enough physical strength to overthrow them, the peasantry had lacked the needful understanding; the nascent bourgeoisie had understanding but lacked strength, and was too much tied to the past by its Siamese-twin link with landownership. A small party of socialists can work deliberately to usher in a socialist society; there can scarcely be a similar sense of mission to establish capitalism, and a bourgeois party can only be strong enough to take power when capitalism is already well developed.

Hence the failure of the bourgeoisie to extend its participation under the Chiang dictatorship;[42] hence also the 'masochistic' attitude of middle-class intellectuals who welcomed the Japanese invasion on the ground that in no other way could the old China be demolished and an eventual rebirth ensured.[43] It did help indirectly, by damaging the corrupt and ineffective Kuomintang regime morally, even more than physically, and by stirring up the peasantry. Mass resistance was partly patriotic, partly or mainly long-standing agrarian discontent breaking out once more, but now under the leadership of a communist party. This had persisted in growing, in defiance of ferocious repression and an enormous death-roll;[44] in spite also of many baffled gropings amid the confusions of Chinese history and society, in search of the right road.[45]

In the final phases, whether colonies were compelled to fight for independence depended partly on geography. If they were close to the USSR, like India, fear of nationalism turning into communism, as happened in China, might make governments hesitate to go to extremes.

None of the Dutch, French, or Portuguese possessions lay anywhere near the Soviet borders. Another factor was the presence of settlers or planters; these were always a potent irritant, and had a surprising ability to veto concessions to native feeling that governments would otherwise have been willing to make. When revolt broke out in the post-1945 years it was regularly blamed on sinister communist infiltration, and this could be made the pretext for terroristic methods of repression, which might prosper for a while, or might provoke wider resistance and bring into the lead the most determined individuals, often those most indurated by Marxism.

How things turned out depended on many local circumstances, and on the leadership available. In Malaya it was the Chinese, or a Marxist-led section of them, that fought a guerrilla war; it was to the tradition-bound Malay princelings that power was eventually handed over. In Kenya the fighting was an obscure episode in the bush; after it was over power went to men who had taken no part in it, and whose only aim was to enrich themselves.[46] Indonesians waged a long struggle for freedom ending in nothing much better than the demagogic rhetoric of which Sukarno was an inexhaustible fountain, until it was cut off by the army coup, with foreign engineering, in 1965, and the massacre of some half a million real or alleged communists.

China's revolution brought inspiration after 1948 to all militant movements within earshot; above all to Vietnam, whose two or three decades of bloodshed stand in sharp contrast with India's six decades of more or less peaceful agitation. Any nation on the march had to draw on its own collective memories and ideals, though it also had to jettison a great deal of its past in order to lighten the load. Mao found in China's annals a collectivist, utopian tradition;[47] Ho Chi Minh and his party gave close attention to their national history, and made much of it in their summons to the masses.[48] Prolonged resistance to French conquest, although defeated, left inspiring memories to patriots of the next century. Vietnam was a rural society, and its literate class was close to the people; it may always have had something of the mixed feeling of the lower clergy in medieval Europe, attached to the governing interests but at times impelled to take sides with the poor. Foreign domination had a polarizing effect on this intelligentsia, part of it joining hands with the aliens, another part helping to preserve national consciousness by composing histories and patriotic poems. At a later stage some would join in the liberation movement,[49] or even go over to Marxism.

Away from the Far East, the protracted Algerian war was the salient case of freedom won by an armed rising. Algerians drew some encouragement from the example of Vietnam; but they set out from a lower cultural level, with a nationhood only recently and imperfectly conjured up by the guerrilla fighting against the French occupation. Fanon had high hopes of the transforming effects of the uprising. When it was decided to enrol women as auxiliaries, there was a striking response from them. Soldiers were ready to adopt medical and hygienic practices they had been reluctant to learn from the French.[50] Aware of the disharmonies between semi-Westernized townsmen and the more backward but more rebellious countryside, Fanon counted on battle and shared danger to bring them together as a single nation.[51]

Very much was indeed achieved. One handicap, which an Arab writer has emphasized, was the French army's determination to wipe out all elements capable of leadership,[52] though some officers liked to indulge in a bizarre theory of 'revolutionary war', or winning over the masses by blending persuasion with brutal coercion.[53] Of necessity the struggle developed too one-sidedly on military lines. In turn, partly for this reason, military activity could not rise much above the guerrilla level, whereas in Vietnam, fused with political activity, it moved on to the building of a regular army capable of fighting pitched battles. It is still not clear in what direction free Algeria is evolving, or what will be its reward for the sacrifice of a million lives. For ideas some Algerians still look, it appears, to France, others to the Middle East.

By whatever route freedom has been achieved, there are always residues of former days still to be shaken off. A society is never fully external to the individual; it can subsist only because its humbler members accept much of the mentality of their betters (the converse may also be true in some measure). The new man has to escape from himself, as well as from his environment.[54] Mao in his declining years was obsessed by fear of bourgeois cravings and illusions surviving to infect his communist utopia, the fantasies of a defeated class outliving their social base.

One important test of the thoroughness or incompleteness of change is the status of women. They played an appreciable part in freedom movements; in armed revolts they undertook, as in occupied Europe during the Second World War, many unaccustomed duties, but found little place in the leadership. They could come to the front more easily in countries like India or Ceylon, moving towards a parliamentary pattern. But male love of dominance seems tenacious in all emerging societies, not to be ended in any such summary fashion as colonial or feudal ascendancy.

For many other failings colonial rule can partly be blamed; among them, some of the senseless feuds widespread in the Third World. There was indignation in the Indian press when an outbreak of rioting in

Southall in April 1979, set off by a National Front demonstration, caused a death and numerous arrests; but a Hindu–Muslim riot in Jamshedpur a few weeks earlier had caused a hundred deaths. Many Indians accuse British rule of worsening communal relations; it would be hard to assert that it did much to improve them, or tried to do much. Clashes between peoples or states, as well as communities, were endemic in old days outside as well as within Europe. National sentiment always present, if latent, in the Far East facilitated new initiatives, but also made for pugnacity once it came to be aroused. If China can claim to have created a novel form of socialist society, Japan of capitalist, the one has been guilty of aggression against its fellow-communist neighbour Vietnam, the other of imperialism on a grand scale at the expense of fellow-Asians. There have been many symptoms lately of a rebirth of the chauvinist military spirit in Japan.

It was Lenin's hope, from before 1914, that colonial liberation movements would help to undermine capitalism in Europe, and that colonial masses and industrial working classes would press onward shoulder to shoulder. When revolution in Europe hung fire, it came to be widely believed that socialism could seize power only in backward countries.[55] More recently, euphoric dreams of salvation from the Third World, under Maoist watchwords, have receded; it may be time for Marxists to recall the Leninist principle that socialism cannot win the day anywhere before some minimum level of economic development has been reached.[56] At present capitalism is still very much with us, technically resilient if socially obsolescent and therefore unstable. As directed from Washington it has less to offer than in colonial days in the way of progressive thinking, far more in the way of material satisfactions for the few able to scramble for them. So heavily have burdens of poverty and 'unfreedom' continued to weigh on vast areas, that restless spirits have sometimes thought world peace a lesser good than collision and chaos, to shake the old fabric of things to pieces and open a door out of their prison.

Many ills are clearly connected with bad leadership, by individuals or groups among whom army bosses have had a deplorable prominence. Where freedom, or the nominal freedom of neo-colonialism, came with little exertion or sacrifice, power was likely to fall to men reared in and moulded by the colonial system. Lurid examples have been the tyrant Francisco Machia Nguema in Equatorial Guinea after it ceased to be a Spanish territory, whom it is not hard to see as an understudy of Francisco Franco, and Amin of Uganda, an erstwhile mercenary soldier serving against rebels in Kenya. Among colonies that really fought for freedom, saddest have been the fortunes of Portuguese Guinea. Its socialist founder Cabral had warned of the necessity of '*struggle against our own weaknesses* ... this battle against ourselves – no matter what difficulties the enemy may create – is the most difficult of all'.[57] He was murdered in 1973; after his brother and successor Luis was turned out by the soldiers and charged with corruption and mass killings, a visiting journalist reported that foodstuffs in the shops were scarce, whisky and expensive cars plentiful.[58]

For more than nine-tenths of a colonial population, Fanon wrote, 'independence brings no immediate change', and disillusion may be quick to set in, coupled with disgust at the affluence of a new-rich 'caste'.[59] Western rule fortified class division in Asia, and crystallized it in Africa; those at the top today do not often appear to feel more responsibility or benevolence to their subjects than Western officialdom did. Egotism is not confined to them; a jostling eagerness to get on, a restless individualism, is liable to pervade all ranks. Multitudes suffer from an itch for the possessions which they know to be abundant in happier lands, wrist-watches for instance, and which they covet also as 'status-symbols'. In the absence of economic expansion this breeds what Spaniards call *empleomanía*, hunger and thirst for government jobs of any sort, and education degenerates into a grabbing at any qualifications that can bring a salary within reach.[60] Contact with the West and its tempting wares, useful or frivolous, can frustrate socialist movements by starving them of idealism, without promoting any local capitalism.

'The people that walked in darkness have seen a great light': it was some such image that Europe cherished of the blessings bestowed by it on the outer world. At any rate it could hug the notion that the world's people had been *shown* a great light, whether they turned their eyes towards it or not. From the other side of the fence the picture has often looked very different. African and other Third World writers have complained that imperialism cut short their unfolding cultures, and replaced them with something worse; they reject 'the essential barbarism of the "civilizing" hordes'.[61] Truth must be sought not between these antithetical views, but in a complex interweaving of them. It is open to Westerners to assert that many ex-colonies have proved unfit for self-rule; and equally open to their peoples to ask why Western rulers, having come uninvited to drag them out of their yesterdays, did so little to guide them towards tomorrow.

NOTES

1 *A Journey to the Western Islands of Scotland* (1775), sections on 'Aberbrothick' and 'Inverness'.

2 *The History of Britain*, in *Prose Works*, ed. J. A. St John (London, 1848), vol. 5, pp. 197–8, 214. For a spirited defence of the ideals attributable to

modern British empire-building, reference may be made to A. P. Thornton, *The Imperial Idea and its Enemies* (London, 1959). D. K. Fieldhouse gives a scholarly survey of European expansion, with its better and worse features, in *The Colonial Empires. A Comparative Survey from the Eighteenth Century* (London, 1965). A variety of opinions will be found in *Perspectives on Imperialism and Decolonization*, ed. R. F. Holland and G. Rizvi (London, 1984). A socialist critique of the British record will be found in M. B. Brown, *After Imperialism* (revised ed., London, 1970). Marx's views are collected in the anthology *On Colonialism* (Moscow, 1960); see also articles on 'Imperialism', 'Colonialism', etc., in *A Dictionary of Marxist Thought*, ed. Tom Bottomore (Oxford, 1983). D. R. SarDesai, *British Trade and Expansion in Southeast Asia 1830–1914* (New Delhi, 1977) is a good example of how Western motives have come to be seen by many Indian and other Afro-Asian scholars.

3 Fernand Braudel, *The Perspective of the World* (1979; English ed., London, 1984), p. 61.

4 Syed Hussain Alatas, *The Myth of the Lazy Native* (London, 1977), p. 238.

5 Cited by Leila Ahmed, *Edward W. Lane* (London, 1978), p. 112.

6 Lord Hardinge, *Old Diplomacy* (London, 1947), p. 67.

7 *An Embassy to China. Lord Macartney's Journal, 1793–94*, ed. J. L. Cranmer-Byng (London, 1962), pp. 103, 239–40.

8 William Pitt (the younger), *Orations on the French War* (London, [1906]: Everyman), p. 301.

9 On the Marxist attitude see e.g. U. Melotti, *Marx and the Third World* (1972; English ed., London, 1977), pp. 114ff, 121–2, 194.

10 See P. H. Lee, *Poems from Korea* (London, 1974), p. 64, etc.

11 Yosoburo Takekoshi, *Economic Aspects of the History of the Civilization of Japan* (London, 1930), vol. 3, p. 282.

12 *Cambridge History of China*, vol. 12, part 1, ed. J. K. Fairbank (1983), pp. 19, 721–2.

13 Eijiro Honjo, 'The transition from the Tokugawa period' (*Kyoto University Economic Review*, 1932).

14 *Cambridge History of China*, vol. 12, part 1, p. 725; A. L. Sadler, *Short History of Japan* (Sydney, 1963), p. 229.

15 A. Krausse, *China in Decay* (London, 1900), p. 263.

16 The question is surveyed by G. D. Allinson in *E. H. Norman. His Life and Scholarship*, ed. R. W. Bowen (Toronto, 1984), pp. 99ff.

17 *The Invention of a New Religion* (London, 1912).

18 J. D. Spence, *The Gate of Heavenly Peace. The Chinese and their Revolution, 1895–1980* (London, 1982), p. 238.

19 R. Owen, 'Egypt and Europe', in *Studies in the Theory of Imperialism*, ed. R. Owen and B. Sutcliffe (London, 1972), pp. 198ff. This writer considers the label 'oriental despotism' unsuited to the Egyptian state of those times.

20 See H. G. Marcus, *The Life and Times of Menelik II. Ethiopia 1844–1933* (Oxford, 1975).

21 'The British rule in India' (article of 10 June 1853); reprinted in K. Marx and F. Engels, *The First Indian War of Independence 1857–1859* (Moscow, 1959), pp. 14ff.

22 See General Sir N. Stewart, *My Service Days* (London, 1908).

23 C. R. Boxer, *The Dutch Seaborne Empire 1600–1800* (1965; Harmondsworth ed, 1973), p. 213.

24 German Colonial Office, *How Natives are Treated in German and French Colonies* (Berlin, 1919), part 1, p. 7.
25 D. Fieldhouse, in *Oxford and the Idea of Commonwealth*, ed. F. Madden and D. K. Fieldhouse (London, 1982), p. 154.
26 T. Ranger, 'The invention of tradition in colonial Africa', in *The Invention of Tradition*, ed. E. Hobsbawm and T. Ranger (Cambridge, 1983), p. 212.
27 L. Barnes, *Empire or Democracy?* (London, 1939), p. 161.
28 James Ngugi, 'A meeting in the dark', in *Modern African Stories*, ed. E. A. Komey and E. Mphahlele (London, 1964); cf. Chinua Achebe's novel, *Things Fall Apart* (1958; 1962 ed., London).
29 Barnes, *Empire or Democracy?*, p. 160.
30 A. Calder, *Revolutionary Empire. The Rise of the English-Speaking Empires from the Fifteenth Century to the 1780s* (London, 1981).
31 See S. D. Gupta, *Comintern, India and the Colonial Question 1920–37* (Calcutta, 1980), ch. 4.
32 N. Etherington, *Theories of Imperialism: War, Conquest and Capital* (London, 1984), p. 17.
33 P. Calvert, 'On attaining sovereignty', in A. D. Smith, ed., *Nationalist Movements* (London, 1976), p. 145.
34 Frantz Fanon, *The Wretched of the Earth* (1961; English ed., Harmondsworth, 1967), p. 155.
35 *Ibid.*, pp. 18, 74; cf. pp. 28–9, 118, 237.
36 Nirad C. Chaudhuri, *The Autobiography of an Unknown Indian* (London, 1951), book 1, ch. 4.
37 Aziz Ahmad, *Islamic Modernism in India and Pakistan 1857–1964* (London, 1967), pp. 92–3.
38 J. Gernet, *A History of Chinese Civilization* (1972; English ed., Cambridge, 1982), p. 580.
39 Fukuzawa Yukichi, *An Outline of a Theory of Civilization*, trans. D. A. Dilworth and G. C. Hurst (Tokyo, 1973), pp. 188–9.
40 General L. C. Dunsterville, *The Adventures of Dunsterforce* (1920; London ed., 1932), pp. 4–5.
41 Amilcar Cabral, *Revolution in Guinea. An African People's Struggle* (London, 1969), pp. 88–9.
42 See M.-C. Bergère, 'The Chinese bourgeoisie, 1911–37', in *Cambridge History of China*, vol. 12, part 1.
43 Dick Wilson, *When Tigers Fight. The Story of the Sino-Japanese War, 1937–1945* (Harmondsworth, 1983), pp. 3–4.
44 See Spence, *The Gate of Heavenly Peace.*
45 See Arif Dirlik, *Revolution and History. The Origins of Marxist Historiography in China, 1919–1937* (Berkeley, 1978).
46 *Petals of Blood*, by the Kenyan novelist Ngugi wa Thiong'o (London, 1977), gives a graphic account of this.
47 M. Meisner, *Marxism Maoism and Utopianism* (University of Wisconsin, 1982), p. 214, etc.
48 Thomas Hodgkin, *Vietnam: The Revolutionary Path* (London, 1981), pp. 186ff.
49 See D. Hunt, 'Village culture and the Vietnamese revolution', in *Past and Present*, no. 94 (1982), 131ff.
50 Fanon, *The Wretched of the Earth*, pp. 51ff, 142.
51 *Ibid.*, pp. 86–9.

52 E. Hermassi, 'Impérialisme et décadence politique au Maghreb', in *Sociologie de l'impérialisme*, ed. A. Abdel-Malek (Paris, 1971), p. 137.

53 E. R. Wolf, *Peasant Wars of the Twentieth Century* (1969; London ed., 1976), pp. 242–4.

54 There is much of relevance to this in Paulo Freire, *Pedagogy of the Oppressed* (Harmondsworth, 1972). Cf. A. Memmi, *Portrait du Colonisé* (Paris, 1973).

55 Cf. Franz Marek, *Philosophy of World Revolution* (London, 1969), pp. 102–3.

56 This principle is restated in V. V. Zagladin, ed., *The World Communist Movement* (Moscow, 1973), pp. 112ff.

57 Cabral, *Revolution in Guinea*, p. 74.

58 Jill Joliffe, in the *Guardian*, 6 December 1980.

59 Fanon, *The Wretched of the Earth*, pp. 58–9, 134. Cf. V. Schwarcz, *Long Road Home. A China Journal* (Yale University, 1984), p. 44, on 'That hard, awful question that every revolutionary must ask: "What has changed, after all?"'

60 See Ronald Dore, *The Diploma Disease. Education, Qualification and Development* (London, 1976).

61 T. Hodgkin, 'Some African and Third World theories of imperialism', in Owen and Sutcliffe, *Studies*, pp. 102–3. Cf. Ad'Obe Obe, in the *Guardian*, 26 October 1984: 'The British are now seen as those who culturally "raped" Nigeria.' Judith M. Brown, *Modern India* (Oxford, 1985) argues that old India was *not* standing still, and that British rule *could not* have brought about a social transformation.

7

Socio-economic revolution in England and the origin of the modern world

ALAN MACFARLANE

In the early nineteenth century de Tocqueville contemplated the differences between France on the one hand and England and North America on the other. He came to the conclusion that he was witnessing the emergence of an unprecedented phenomenon, a new and 'modern' world compounded of democracy and individualism.[1] For an inhabitant of France, the shock of the contrast was enormous. A similar shock had jolted those eighteenth-century Scotsmen whose observations of the contrasts between England the Highland Scotland had led them into speculations which laid the foundations for economics, sociology and anthropology as we know them today. Yet the contrasts would have been magnified a hundredfold if de Tocqueville, Millar, Kames, Adam Smith and others had come not from adjacent regions, but from the great civilizations that flourished elsewhere in the world. If they had come from India, or China, for example, as yet little affected by European culture, they would have been even more struck by the extraordinary civilization which was flourishing in England and North America. Concentrating for the moment on England, what were the most outstanding features of this brave new world?

Our hypothetical oriental visitor, male or female, would have found a peculiar legal system, based on unwritten codes and precedents, known as the Common Law, combined with a separate and equally strange system known as Equity. This legal system had many unique features; for instance the use of juries, the absence of judicial torture, the concept of equality before the law. The law enshrined an obsession with property, which was conceived of as virtually private, rather than communal. These strange procedures and concepts of the law were linked to political and constitutional peculiarities. The most important of these was the idea of the sovereignty of the people and the supremacy of law. The Crown was under the law and answerable to the people in parliament; this was not an absolutist state but a limited monarchy. England was a state with representative government and a constitution, even if only a small part of the people were yet enfranchised. Political power was widely dispersed and seemed to be diffused through much of the society. There was only a small standing army, no armed police force, no huge centralized bureaucracy or court. This was far from the despotism that still existed over much of continental Europe or in much of Asia. It was a balanced constitutional system.

There were linked social peculiarities. Although very steeply ranked, with infinite gradations of status and occupation, there were no exclusive castes or orders. The fourfold orders of priests, warriors and rulers, townsmen and peasants, were blurred by numerous more important divisions. There were no legally separate orders of nobility or slaves, little differentiation between townsmen and countrydwellers, no endogamous enclosures within certain ranks. There was an unusually large and prosperous 'middling' band, lying between the very rich and the very poor. There was easy and frequent social mobility. Furthermore there was a high rate of geographical mobility. People were constantly on the move, to London and other towns, to markets and fairs, throughout the life-cycle. One set of institutions which helped both kinds of mobility was the market for paid labour. Instead of family labour providing the basis for production, most labour was purchased in the market; the institutions of servanthood, apprenticeship and wage labour were very widespread to a degree unknown elsewhere.

There were many striking features in the realm of production and economic relations. Already there was a rapidly developing use of non-human energy through steam and machinery; associated with it there was a concentration of people into new and unusually compact groupings, urbanism and factory organization. Throughout town and country there was a pervasive emphasis on monetary values, on trade, profit, accumulation. The acquisitive ethic was dominant, the division of labour was far advanced and England was truly a nation not only ruled by shopkeepers but with a generalized shopkeeper mentality. Her overseas possessions were run principally for profit, rather than for their military or political value.

There were associated features in the demographic and familial structures which would have been equally surprising to a visitor from the orient. Above all, kinship seemed very weak; people were early independent of parental power and most relied mainly on their own efforts. Even that crucial function of kinship, in dealing with accident and old age, was largely eroded for there was a highly developed and non-kinship based Poor Law. The weakness of kinship showed itself in the household structure; this was nuclear, on the whole, with few joint or extended families. The marriage system also reflected the unimportance of wider kinship. Marriages were based for the most part on personal initiative rather than parental arrangement, on a mixture of psychological and economic considerations of an unusual kind. Marriages occurred at a relatively late age and it was not seen to be absolutely necessary to marry. Only one partner at a time was allowed, divorce was almost impossible, yet remarriage after death of one partner was extensive.

An oriental visitor would probably have been saddened at the mixture of wealth and squalor, comradeship and loneliness, tolerance and aggressiveness of the civilization. Yet he would have been impressed by the demographic and economic achievement. The population was rising rapidly yet the usual positive checks of famine, war and disease were not operating. Somehow the country had escaped from the shadow of demographic crises. Wealth was conspicuously increasing, even if it was unfairly distributed, and an affluence and material ascendancy was emerging unknown elsewhere in the world. Here was a land where the fortunate and the energetic, at least, could found dynasties and where certain traditional forms of generalised 'misery' were being eradicated.

Other differences would have struck such a visitor; in religion and ritual, in art and aesthetics, in concepts of time and space, in attitudes to the natural world. Yet enough has been sketched in to make the point that for such a visitor, and for us as historians, there is something extraordinary which needs explanation. Much of what had emerged by the first half of the nineteenth century in England and North America has now permeated the world and is part of the air which many nations breathe. Time has accustomed us to it. Yet to the French, Scots and our hypothetical observer something decidedly strange seemed to have occurred in one small corner of the world. England and North America were the extreme case of many of the tendencies throughout Europe and particularly in North Western Europe. To understand how this happened is perhaps the most important of all historical questions.

For simplicity's sake we may distinguish two ways of answering this question. The first is the 'revolutionary' theory of history. 'Revolution', of course, is a misuse of the word, for it literally means a state where things come back full-circle, as in the 'revolution' of a wheel. Thus Ibn Khaldûn's cyclical view, or Edmund Leach's pendulum theories of change in Highland Burma are true 'revolutionary' theories.[2] Yet, as normally used by historians when they talk of the 'French Revolution', the 'Industrial Revolution', and so on, they mean that A has moved to B, which never existed before. There are two constituents to the concept: newness and suddenness. Although it would be possible to talk of 'revolutions' that last for thousands of years, as the 'neolithic revolution', usually the word and concept is used by modern historians to describe changes which occur over a year, decades and sometimes up to a century or so. The speed of the 'revolutions' will vary with which of Braudel's three levels of time we are dealing with. 'Geographical time' moves very slowly, over millennia; social time moves in a century or less; individual time, including political time, often moves in a year or less.[3] In this essay we are dealing mainly with the 'social' level. The element of newness, of rejection of the past, often leads to a violence in the process; it is not a rebirth, a gentle renaissance, or even a rebellion, which ultimately changes only the personnel. The rules of the game are changed, and usually many players object; hence bloody struggle. A further, added, feature of true revolutions is that they tend to be multi-stranded. That is to say, a change in one part, whether we ascribe it to the superstructure or infrastructure, will be connected to changes in other parts. For instance, a revolutionary change in demographic structures is likely to be linked to equally revolutionary changes in familial, economic, legal and other structures, since all are connected.

Given this preliminary specification of revolutionary models of change, we may ask how well they worked for the most interesting of all cases, that peculiar birth of the 'modern' world on a small island off Europe by the early nineteenth century. Those historians and philosophers who have espoused revolutionary theories in this instance have come up with a rather mixed set of answers. The major prophets of the revolutionary view, Marx and Weber, roughly dated the 'revolution' from 'feudalism' to 'capitalism', another way of labelling what we have described, as having occurred between about 1475 and 1700. One of their principal historical exponents, R. H. Tawney, therefore concentrated on the sixteenth century in England as the 'watershed' (his metaphor) between the 'medieval', 'peasant', 'pre-capitalist' world and the 'modern', 'individualist', 'capitalist' one. Hence the sixteenth century is known affectionately as 'Tawney's century'.[4] In the next generation, Tawney's successor, Christopher Hill, moved the revolution forward a century. Now the seventeenth century was the 'Century of Revolution', with many of the revolutionary developments occurring fairly suddenly in 1640.[5] More recently still there has been a move to bring the 'revolution', or at least its familistic dimensions, forward another century, into the eighteenth century, when there was invented and propagated 'affective individualism'. This was 'perhaps the most important change in *mentalité* to have occurred in the Early Modern period, indeed possibly in the last thousand years of Western history', and it was particularly linked to the rise of a particular family system from the middle of the seventeenth century, which predominated in the eighteenth.[6] The fact that there is so much uncertainty as to when the major revolution occurred, combined with a strong view that whatever did occur before the nineteenth century was a failed revolution,[7] makes us a little uneasy. Surely it should not be difficult to pin down the birth of the modern world in such a well-documented society?

Our uneasiness with this interpretation increases when we look briefly at the strands elaborated above in a little more detail. Shortage of space will force me to set boundary dates, indulge in gross simplification, and omit the supporting evidence for the assertions. Elsewhere I have tried to discuss many of the topics, briefly surveyed here, in more detail.[8] The central question is at what point, roughly, can we be certain that the features we have elaborated did not exist in the English past? Having located this 'other' world, we will be in a position to date and perhaps to search for plausible reasons for the revolutionary transformation.

We may start with law and government. The Common Law is known to have reached a mature stage of development by the end of the thirteenth century at the latest.[9] Of course the law changed, but its basic structure and principles were laid out by that time. Thus many of the peculiarities of the law, particularly in the process and in the concepts of property, were present by the thirteenth century. Likewise, the central political feature, namely that England was not an absolutist state, that the crown was responsible to parliament and under the law, was established before the time of Magna Carta in 1215. It was maintained thereafter, despite some attempts in the sixteenth and seventeenth centuries to introduce a continental-style absolutism. The related features of little central bureaucracy, no standing army, no armed police, the tradition of non-paid local administration and justice, the self-policing local community, were all very ancient. They all went back to the thirteenth century and beyond. Never did a revived Roman Law sweep away the older customs and laws, as happened on the continent.

The ancient legal and political foundations were early associated with social peculiarities. Late medieval society of the thirteenth and fourteenth centuries had a very ranked yet relatively open social structure. There was no legally privileged nobility, a great contrast with France,and there were no slaves. Serfs were 'free' men and citizens, except in relation to one person, their master. Even he had only limited rights over them. There was already a very large and prosperous middling section of townsmen, traders, artisans, yeomen, based largely on the flourishing international wool trade. There is little sign of a fourfold division of society, or of strong oppositions between townsmen (*bourgeois*) and countrymen (*paysans*). There was clearly extensive geographical mobility, again linked to the widespread and fully developed institutions of servanthood and apprenticeship. Wage labour was highly developed, with probably more than half the population working for wages rather than as family or serf labour by the fourteenth century.

Obviously there were huge technological differences between the thirteenth and nineteenth centuries. Though wind and water power were widely used, steam power and machinery were yet to come, and to this extent England in the late medieval period was different from the early nineteenth century. Yet behind the differences of technology there lay deeper similarities. Manorial account rolls and manuals, and other records show that throughout town and country the use of money was widespread. Almost everything could be represented in monetary terms and almost everything could be bought in the extensive and ubiquitous markets and fairs of Medieval England. This was a trading nation, with a highly developed market structure, thriving towns, and a keen interest among its inhabitants in profit. Land and labour were seen as commodities; there was a great emphasis both in law and in life on possession. Most services had long ago been commutted for cash and the estates were farmed for profit. The 'shopkeeper' mentality, that is the interest in accounting, in producing for exchange rather than direct consumption, the desire to make economic profits, was widespread. Whereas later the Puritans and other Protestant groups would vehemently attack usury, and the interest rates would be brought down to very low levels, in the late middle ages moneylending and mortgaging at interest were widespread and interest rates were much higher. Accounting methods, though crude in comparison to later developments and lacking double-entry book-keeping, were sophisticated enough to make it possible to keep a check on profit and loss.

The basic features of the kinship system seem to have been early laid down. The kinship terminology was in the twelfth century as it was to be in the nineteenth, a bilateral 'eskimo' system that isolated out the nuclear family. The concepts of descent were already formed into the mould that has persisted to the present. Descent was traced through both males and females, a cognatic system that we have today. The method of computing kinship was the canon-law method, based on Germanic custom. The inheritance laws were fixed in their major principles by the thirteenth century. Male primogeniture was already a distinguishing feature, with rights reserved for widows. The central principle was that inheritance was not automatic, that 'no man is the heir to a living man'. There was therefore no natural, automatic, family property, no '*restrait lignager*'; this was firmly outlined by Bracton in the early thirteenth century. Likewise the idea that property always descended and never ascended, that parents were never the automatic heirs of their own children was accepted, there was vertical rather than lateral inheritance.

The weakness of kinship in this egocentric, network-based kinship system is everywhere apparent from at least the thirteenth century. In economics, ownership, production and consumption were not based on kinship groupings. Religion did not reinforce kinship through ritual or ancestor beliefs. Political life below the level of the aristocracy was run on non-kinship lines with few indications of proper blood-feud, vendetta, mafia or clan warfare. The care of the sick, the poor, the old, had already been largely taken over by non-kinship institutions, by the parish, manor, guild and religious fraternities. The weakness of kinship showed itself in the household organization. There is no sign of a fundamentally different household structure, with a widescale presence of complex households, as far back as the documents will take us, which is the fourteenth century.

All this fits with an early developed and peculiar marriage system. We shall outline this system in a little more detail. Marriage is the crucial link between economics and biology, between the individual and society. As such, it is not only a good reflection of deeper features of the economy and society, but also the crucial determinant of demographic patterns. A 'revolution' in the socio-economic systems, for instance from a 'pre-capitalist' to 'capitalist' form in the sixteenth century to eighteenth century could hardly have occurred without a concurrent revolution in the marital system, which in turn would have altered the demographic regime. While it is not possible in a short essay like this to analyse most of the supposed revolutionary changes in any detail, it is worth looking more carefully at one institution. Because of its vital mediating position between society and economy, marriage is ideal for such an examination. We may look at the constituents of what I shall term the 'Malthusian marriage pattern'. It is so-named because it is the one that Malthus advocated in the early nineteenth century.

If we consider the major rules which constrained marriage in England in the early nineteenth century, most of them can be found in operation in the fourteenth century and often well before. Age at marriage is very difficult to estimate before parish registers and therefore there is considerable guesswork in all work on the period before the sixteenth century. Yet the relatively late age at marriage for both men and women was probably a very old characteristic in England. The late age at marriage is mentioned as a characteristic of the early Germanic peoples who brought their culture to England and there is certainly no strong evidence to show that women ever universally married at puberty, as they have done in much of the rest of the world. It has been impossible to find a revolutionary change to that 'unique west European marriage pattern' which Hajnal documented.[10] A second rule of marriage is that of single marriage, or monogamy. This is again cross-comparatively rare and is clearly a pivot of the marriage system. It is also demonstrably ancient. Again the Germanic peoples who invaded England had long been monogamous and the Christian Church, despite minor lapses, reinforced this cultural premise. A substantial change introduced by the Church, almost amounting to a 'revolution', was a growing intolerance of divorce. Yet this was a change that had occurred well before the fourteenth century. A further, informal, rule which allowed widespread remarriage after the death of a spouse was also clearly established by the thirteenth century at the latest.

The rules concerning whom one should and should not marry were probably also very early established. Jack Goody has shown that the widened rules of forbidden marriage were established in Anglo-Saxon England.[11] Of the positive, prescriptive, rules about which kin one must or should marry, there is little sign. There is thus no sign of a transformation of what Lévi-Strauss has termed 'elementary structures' of kinship into the 'complex structures' which existed in the nineteenth century.[12] Certainly, such elementary structures, if they had ever existed, were gone by the thirteenth century. To put it in another way, marriage in England was very early based on a contractual relationship, not on a status, that is kinship, tie. This was also true of another aspect of birth status, namely rank. There is little sign of endogamous groups based on blood or other criteria in the thirteenth and fourteenth centuries. The bond could patently marry the 'free' and did so, the gentry could marry the aristocracy, the trader could marry the landowner's daughter.

The customs concerning the all-important question of marriage payments and the economic negotiations at marriage are particularly well documented. England in the eighteenth and early nineteenth century exhibited a curious pattern of marital economics. The features included the payment of a 'portion' with a girl as a sort of 'dowry', which was to balance the jointure or Common Law 'dower', or the customary widowright, which she would receive from her husband. There is no sign at that date of either a full-fledged 'bridewealth' or 'dowry' system, as described for India, Africa and Southern Europe.[13] Furthermore, the relative rights of the partners in this conjugal property were of an unusual kind. They followed neither the complete merging, the 'community' of property, nor the absolute separation, the 'lineality' of possessions, both of which were found in the customs of France and Scotland. This marital-property complex was clearly very old, many elements dating back to the thirteenth century and earlier.

These formal rules and customs are consistent with the early establishment of a particular view of the purposes and nature of marriage. This was based on four central premises. The first was that marriage was ultimately of concern to the couple themselves, that it was founded on the mutual consent of bride and groom, and not on the arrangement of others. This was a widespread view in the early nineteenth century, but its curiosity is easily seen when we compare it to the majority of peasant societies which have arranged marriage. There, marriage is seen as too important a matter to be left to the personal whim of the partners. This central feature is of very ancient standing. It had been formally accepted into the Catholic view of marriage by the twelfth century and was probably based on much earlier custom.

A second feature of the attitude to marriage was equally important, namely that to marry, or not to marry, involved a choice. Hajnal has rightly seen this as the other major feature of the unique European marriage pattern, indicated by the very large proportion of females, rising to one in six on occasions, who never marry. By the eighteenth century in England there were large numbers of elderly bachelors and spinsters and it was widely accepted that marriage was optional. To the majority of societies, where marriage is seen as a 'natural', automatic, life-cycle stage, a universal experience, this would seem strange. Unfortunately the statistical sources for identifying precisely how old this feature is are again defective. All that we can say for certain is that there is plenty of evidence for non-marriage and no conclusive evidence of universal marriage in the later medieval period. This is consistent with a particular view of the married estate early adopted by the Catholic Church. Marriage was a second best; the continent, celibate, life was the highest calling, following in the steps of the bachelor Christ. Marriage was for those who failed, a remedy for lust, something for the weaker brethren. A sacrament, no doubt, but of a lower order than a life of non-marriage. This downgrading of the marital state, the making of marriage into an optional, 'cultural' event, rather than its celebration as the highest, necessary and 'natural' state as in Hindu, Muslim, or Confucian religion, is of an early and striking importance. This view was clearly well established before the thirteenth century.

A third premise was that marriage was above all to be entered into for the mutual benefits to be achieved from the husband–wife relationship, rather than as a means to produce heirs. Marriage in the nineteenth century was clearly viewed as a partnership of mind and body. The husband–wife bond superseded all others; the contractual and selected relationship which is established curiously overrode all the relations of blood, with siblings, with parents, with children. This is decidedly unusual cross-comparatively, and again it is a view of marriage that is very old in England, as well as in other parts of Christian Europe. Early on in England we see the mingling of two traditions. Though Christianity elevated the state of celibacy, on the other hand it also emphasized the conjugal bond, admonishing believers that in Paradise Adam had realized that the creation of Eve meant that 'therefore shall a man leave his father and his mother, and shall cleave unto his wife: and they shall both be one flesh'. (Genesis 2: 24). This view fitted well with the old uxoriousness of the Germanic peoples whom Tacitus described in the first century sharing their lives and cleaving closely to each other. Whatever the origins, certainly the companionate view of marriage seems to have been widely accepted by the fourteenth century. As soon as relevant documents begin, marriage seems to have been concerned more with the mutual relationship than with procreation. The absence of stress on producing children is consistent with the late age and non-universal nature of marriage and with the absence of any formal adoption procedures.

Finally there is the cultural premise that marriages are to be based on the mutual attraction of 'love'. There is considerable discussion about when 'love' marriage originated. Some place the origins in the twelfth century, some earlier, some later. What appears to be very likely from the snatches of surviving poetry, the depositions in ecclesiastical courts, from descriptions in early encyclopedias, is that by the fourteenth century at least there was a widespread acceptance of 'love' as a powerful constituent of marriage among ordinary people. Certainly, when the evidence crowds in during the sixteenth century, 'love' is widely accepted as a powerful emotion linked to marriage. There is no strong indication that this association was something suddenly invented in the fifteenth or early sixteenth centuries. Of course there were many other motives for marriage, as there were in the eighteenth and nineteenth centuries. Yet mutual liking, and preferably 'love', were widely viewed as an essential component of marriage. This distinguishing feature was not something invented as a result of Protestantism or a growing individualism of the sixteenth to eighteenth centuries.

The marital system was a mediating institution which gave rise in England to a peculiar demographic regime. A number of indications of its presence can be seen if we compare England in the seventeenth to nineteenth centuries to other parts of Europe, for instance to Sweden or France, as Wrigley has done.[14] In the mortality statistics there were two outstanding features. Firstly, England from the Black Death onwards seems to have escaped from the 'crisis' regime whereby every few generations there would be a massive rise in mortality, usually caused by a war that dislocated an already threshold-treading economy. Such warfare would lead to massive famine and disease. In England there were, of course, continued epidemics up to the seventeenth century, and there were signs of famine deaths in Cumberland up to the same period. Yet in relation to the cataclysms which the painful history of much of continental Europe, India, China, Russia and elsewhere shows up to the eighteenth century and later, the English 'crises' are relatively insignificant in the four hundred years between 1350 and 1750. A second notable feature of mortality was its relatively low perennial level. While much higher than today, as compared to many 'pre-transition' populations, we have here one of the two features of what Wrigley has termed a 'low pressure' demographic regime.[15] Infant, child and adult mortality were not as high as they are in many 'pre-transition' populations, a feature that is apparent from at least the fifteenth century.

The fertility rates were also controlled and below their theoretical maximum. This can be seen in several ways. Firstly, there was a curious absence of those spurts of population after a period of high mortality which happened in France and other 'high-pressure' regimes. In many societies, when an 'ecological niche' is freed by mortality, it is quickly filled by a new individual. Likewise, when there is an expansion of resources, this is rapidly converted into a growth in population. This is the well-known Malthusian trap. Yet England seemed to have escaped from both these phenomena from the fourteenth century onwards. After the Black Death the population did not surge back, but continued to fall for another century. During the years of economic growth between the middle of the sixteenth and eighteenth centuries, population did not rapidly rise to absorb the growing resources. This was related to the unusually controlled fertility rate. That is to say, not only was marital fertility moderate, but the overall fertility rate was well below the theoretical maximum for such a population. We now know that in the seventeenth century, when this was most evident, the lowered fertility was caused by late and selective marriage, rather than by contraception or abortion within marriage. The effect of this medium-level fertility was that it balanced the medium-level mortality; over the centuries between the fourteenth and the eighteenth, population grew very slowly indeed, allowing the country gradually to grow wealthier.

This last feature is one aspect of an even more interesting demographic peculiarity of a very long-lived kind. This was the way in which fertility somehow adjusted to economics, rather than being inflexibly linked to biological pressures. It has recently been shown by Wrigley and Schofield that there was a long-term association between fertility rates and real wages between the sixteenth and nineteenth centuries.[16] With a curious twenty-year lag, when real wages rose, so did fertility. The lag allowed a certain economic growth to occur and the association meant that population adjusted to economic forces in a beneficial way, producing the labour supply that was needed; through the fifteenth to the early eighteenth centuries, fertility was severely controlled. So powerful were the inhibiting pressures that in certain parts of England at this period the mean age at first marriage for women rose as high as thirty years; women had put off childbearing for about fifteen years after puberty and many did not marry at all. Then, where there occurred that spurt in productivity and demand for labour which we term the Industrial Revolution, the fertility rate responded. The marriage age fell and England for a century had the fastest rate of population growth in the whole of Europe. This flexible demographic system, one part of the Malthusian marriage pattern, was not a new creation of the seventeenth or eighteenth centuries, it would seem, but is evident from the fourteenth century at least. This makes it difficult to talk of the 'demographic transition' as occurring in England. To a certain extent, it had already happened before the Reformation, although the equilibrium of births and deaths established at the medium level by the seventeenth century would drop to a much lower level at the end of the nineteenth.

It is clearly necessary to add qualifications to this very brief sketch of some of the central features of English history from the fourteenth to nineteenth centuries. Some might argue that the dating of many of the traits is either too late or too early. Yet a very strong case can be made for saying that most of the central legal, political, economic, social and demographic premises that were observable in the early nineteenth century were already formed by the fourteenth century at the latest. If this is true, it is not surprising that early modern historians have been undecided as to whether the 'revolution' occurred in the sixteenth, seventeenth or eighteenth centuries. A second obvious qualification is to stress that we are here looking at the middle-level, 'social' changes, not at the deepest-level geographical time, nor at the ripple of events. Even so, we also need to bear in mind these other levels, for they are all interconnected. There were numerous political, economic and religious 'events' that had a profound influence, positive and negative, on the characteristics we have isolated. Many of these 'events' could have reshaped the whole situation which we have discussed. Cultural premises are shaped by the ripples, as much as the other way round. To stress continuity is not the same as believing in inevitability. The 'shape of Cleopatra's nose' school of history is perfectly compatible with a realization that things did, in a particular case, change less in their fundamentals than many suppose. To take one instance, the success of the Spanish Armada, bringing in its wake Roman law, Roman religion and Roman absolutism, might well have created a genuine revolution which would have broken all those continuous strands which we have elaborated. Nevertheless, as it was, the Armada was defeated, Charles I was beheaded, and, through a curious set of fluxes and chances, England remained a peculiar land which became a revolutionary force in the world not because it had undergone a revolution, but precisely because it had not. There is nothing inevitable about this, except in the distorting mirror of hindsight. We are not forced to return to a revised Whig evolutionism.

Nor need we argue that there was no change. Clearly many things did change. The oriental visitor stepping back from the early nineteenth century to the early fourteenth would have found many differences in the physical landscape, the technology, the arts and crafts, the language, the overseas dominions, the world of thought and belief. Even those features which we have looked at were constantly fluctuating, growing more complex or simple, or withering away. Nevertheless, the most accurate way to conceive of this history is not through the 'revolutionary' metaphors of sudden and catastrophic breaks which have become so fashionable during the last fifty years. While such models are no doubt helpful and appropriate for the history of many other European nations, applied to England they set up false expectations and distort the evidence.

Yet historians require ways of conceiving of change and, if we are persuaded that the revolutionary models are of only very limited use in English history, how are we to explain that very unusual world which had emerged by the early nineteenth century? An alternative approach is provided if we consult those who studied the history of England in the later nineteenth and early twentieth century. At that time a number of historians for the first time systematically investigated and began to translate the massive records of later medieval England. They were unparalleled in their command of the historical sources, which is the essential craft skill of the historian. They also had other advantages. Firstly, there was still sufficiently little published, and sufficiently little specialization in the subject, for them to be able to take a total view of English history, from Anglo-Saxon times up to their own generation. They did not suffer from that growing temporal and subject specialization which means that most historians now become 'sixteenth-century' or even 'sixteenth-century-economic' historians. This inevitable compartmentalization easily feeds into a 'revolutionary' interpretation, for it is easy to believe that everything suddenly changed either just before or just after one's period, or, even more excitingly, during it. The great historians who dominated the subject between about 1870 and 1920 could gaze on the whole of English history and were hence in a position to assess more fully whether there had been any revolutionary breaks.

A second advantage of these writers was that they still suffered under what we might now consider to be a delusion, namely that what the oriental visitor found so surprising was in fact not surprising at all. These English historians, whatever their acquaintance with the works of comparative law and anthropology, still really believed that it was the others who were peculiar. The full impact of comparative anthropology and the unsettling influence of Marx and Weber had not yet been felt. The capitalist and individualistic system of England was recognized to be different from that of the rest of Europe, yet its full curiosity at the level of world civilization was not yet really apparent. This belief was helpful for the historian. It meant that what an Englishman did was not seen as so odd that the historian was forced to assume that it could only be explained by some very violent transformation, some revolutionary break with the more usual human customs, the view to which Marx moved. The easy self-confidence of the later Victorian historians led them to be prepared to accept that what they themselves believed in might indeed have very ancient foundations, almost be 'natural'.

Thus the greatest of these historians, Stubbs and Maitland, approached English history with a long and broad vision, with an unrivalled grasp of the technicalities of the documents and the institutional world that had produced them, and no prejudice against believing that nineteenth-century England might have its roots in medieval, or even Anglo-Saxon, England. Nor were they inspired by a zeal to show that their own world was the recent product of a revolutionary change which had such shallow roots that another revolution would easily shift it. Instead, they laboured with care and high intelligence and emerged with that vision of continuity which we are now rediscovering. Of course it is not difficult to brush them aside as irrelevant and misguided. Perry Anderson, for example, asserts that 'the transition from the medieval to the early modern epochs thus corresponded in English history – despite all local legends of unbroken "continuity" – to a deep and radical reversal of many of the most characteristic traits of prior feudal development ...'[17] Legends, however, are of interest to historians, nor are they necessarily 'untrue'.

The legend told by Stubbs is indeed one of unbroken continuity. In his *Constitutional History of England* he securely laid the foundations of the English social system very early on, in Anglo-Saxon England. On this foundation, a great deal had been built by the thirteenth century. 'The great characteristic of the English constitutional system is the continuous development of representative institutions from the first elementary stage ... The nation becomes one and realizes its oneness ... It is completed under Henry II and his sons.'[18] Stubbs is of course aware that there are turmoils ahead and that political and constitutional changes of considerable importance will occur over the next six centuries. Yet he believes that the basic rules change little. 'The constitution which reached its formal and definite maturity under Edward I ... the continuity of life, and the continuity of national purpose, never fails: even the great struggle of all [*sic*], the long labour that extends from the Reformation to the Revolution [i.e., 1688), leaves the organization, the origin of which we have been tracing, unbroken in its conscious identity, stronger in the strength which it has preserved, and grown mightier through trial'.[19] There is no notion of any 'revolution' in Stubbs's work, no hint of a cataclysmic change from a 'medieval' to a 'modern' world. This was not because he was blind to changes when they did occur. He noted that the sixteenth and seventeenth centuries 'witnessed a series of changes in national life, mind, and character, in the relations of the classes, and in the balance of political forces, far greater than the English race had gone through since the Norman Conquest.'[20] These changes he listed as the Reformation, the 'transformation of the baronage of early England into the nobility of later times' and the 'recovered strength of the monarchic principle ...' Yet he did not believe that the continuity was broken.

The continuities were strongest in the middling and lower ranks in which over 99 per cent of the English population lived, 'As we descend in the scale of social rank the differences between medieval and modern life rapidly diminish', he wrote.[21] Stubbs was aware that the balance of ownership changed, yet there were always the same major groupings, the gentry, the tradesmen and artisans, the labourers, and that peculiar middling English estate known as the 'yeomanry'. Two features of the ancient yeoman tradition especially struck Stubbs, their wealth and their social mobility. He wrote that 'the wills and inventories of the well-to-do freeholder and farmer furnish similar evidence of competency; and these are an irrefrageable answer to the popular theories of the misery and discomfort of medieval middle-class life ...'. The house of the freeholder was substantially but simply furnished, his store of clothes and linen were ample, he had money in his purse and credit at the shop and at the market.[22] This is no miserable subsistence peasant, but a small capitalist farmer whose cash and credit indicates his involvement in the market economy.

The second major feature Stubbs noted is the early and easy social mobility:

> Before the close of the middle ages the rich townsmen had begun to intermarry with the Knights and gentry, and many of the noble families of the present day trace the foundations of their fortunes to a lord mayor of London or York ... it is probable that there was no period in English history at which the barrier between the knightly and mercantile class was regarded as insuperable ...[23]

This was a society of closely spaced ranks with no insuperable barriers between them from very early on.

> The city magnate formed a link between the country squire and the tradesman; and the tradesman and the yeoman were in position and in blood closely akin.

Even the villein might, by learning a craft, set his foot on the ladder of promotion ...[24]

One final feature of a 'medieval' world that looks surprisingly like that of the seventeenth and eighteenth centuries is the widespread use of wage labour and craft activity; there were, Stubbs tells us, 'whole classes of labourers and artisans, whose earnings never furnished more than the mere requisites of life ...'[25]

The same legend is told by F. W. Maitland. In his many works we look in vain for any sign of a belief that a vast and revolutionary change had occurred at some specific point in English history, dividing off 'medieval' from 'modern' England. Instead, his view that the legal and social structure of England, in its basic principles, was already laid down by the thirteenth century is shown in many passages, only a few of which we can cite here.

We are told that 'at the end of Henry III's reign our Common Law of inheritance was rapidly assuming its final form. Its main outlines were those which are still familiar to us ...'[26] By the death of Henry II (1272), 'English law is modern in its uniformity, its simplicity, its certainty ...'[27] Lawyers from the fourteenth century onwards believed that 'the great outlines of criminal law and private law seem to have been regarded as fixed for all time. In the twentieth century students of law will still for practical purposes be compelled to know a good deal about the statutes of Edward I ...'[28] This continuity, he believed, had been of great advantage to English historians, setting them off from those of continental nations where it had not occurred.

So continuous has been our English legal life during the last six centuries, that the law of the later middle ages has never been forgotten among us. It has never passed utterly outside the cognizance of our courts and our practising lawyers. We have never had to disinter and reconstruct it in that laborious and tentative manner in which German historians of the present day have disinterred and reconstructed the law of medieval Germany.[29]

This continuity is shown in the treatment of particular subjects. For instance, when analysing the forms of action at Common Law, Maitland took the period 1307–1833 as one period. He admitted that this was 'enormously long', yet wrote that 'I do not know that for our present purpose it could be well broken up into sub-periods.'[30]

The most important area of all, as Marx would have agreed, was the property law which governed relations of production. Here were the deepest continuities. This 'most salient trait' of the 'calculus of estates which even in our own day, is perhaps the most distinctive feature of English private law', Maitland thought very old. It has been a characteristic for six centuries, having taken a 'definite shape' in the second half of the thirteenth century, drawing on much older customs.[31] In his *Constitutional History of England*, which covered the period from Anglo-Saxon England up to the 1880s, Maitland made no substantial modifications to Stubbs's general vision of continuity.[32] For instance, he wrote 'take an institution that exists at the end of the Middle Ages, any that exists in 1800 – be it parliament, or privy council, or any of the courts of law – we can trace it back through a series of definite changes as far as Edward's reign ...'[33] It was because English constitutional and legal principles had been laid down so early that the history of English law which he largely wrote could amazingly end in 1272.

Maitland pointed to many respects in which thirteenth-century England was like that of the nineteenth century. There was in both an absence of patriarchal power, *patria potestas*, that subjection of children and women to the absolute power of the oldest male; there was an absence of clans or other corporate kin groups; there was no concept of familial property, of joint and communal ownership.[34] Individual possession was characteristic from very early on. The thirteenth century was already dominated by contract and not status, to use Maine's distinction; as Stubbs had also noted, there were no hereditary ranks based on blood and law, no 'castes'.[35] There was equality before the law and all had legal rights, including women, children and villeins.[36]

We may wonder whether this 'legend' of continuity, so powerfully undermining of revolutions, has been destroyed by subsequent research on those documents, many of which Maitland himself first brought to light. In the reprinting of the *History of English Law* in 1968, Milsom describes it as a 'still living authority'.[37] Nowhere in his lengthy introduction does Milsom challenge Maitland's view of the thirteenth century. Indeed Milsom concludes that 'there can be no doubt that by the end of the period covered by the book, the world was as Maitland saw it ...'[38] Maitland, writes Milsom, 'would probably wish his work to be superseded. There is little sign that this will happen soon.'[39] The world Maitland saw was 'essentially a flat world inhabited by equal neighbours. Lordship is little more than a servitude over the land of another ...'[40]

If Maitland rejects a revolutionary interpretation of English history, how does he visualize the process of time as changing? It is certainly not in a crude evolutionary pattern, through a series of organic 'stages', as advocated by a number of the evolutionary anthropologists and sociologists of the later nineteenth century. This evolutionary framework, which influenced Marx through the works of Morgan, has had a considerable influence on twentieth-century historiography. Yet, in a memorable passage, Maitland calmly shatters such necessary, single-path, evolutionism.[41] What alternative, then, can he offer? Maitland does not usually address the problem directly, but often indicates obliquely how one might use an organic-growth model, yet without any necessity for things to have occurred in a certain way. An illustration of this approach is shown in his treatment of one of the central and enduring features of English history, the system of local government. Maitland writes that

> Certainly to any one who has an eye for historic greatness it is a very marvellous institution, this Commission of the Peace, growing so steadily, elaborating itself into ever new ideas, and yet never losing its identity ... we shall hardly find any other political entity which has had so eventful and yet so perfectly continuous a life.[42]

Maitland holds here in a delicate balance both 'newness' and 'identity' over time, an institution whose history is both 'eventful' and yet 'continuous'. Such an approach allows us the flexibility to admit that by a strange paradox things can both remain the same and also change.

Such a model of change is more subtle and less crude than a revolutionary one, at least when applied to English history. No doubt it will be unattractive to those historians who agree with Butterfield that 'the chief aim of the historian is the elucidation of the unlikeness between past and present ... It is not for him to stress and magnify the similarities between one age and another ...'[43] If we are dedicated to hunt for dissimilarities, then 'revolutions' before which things were very different are what we shall hope to find, and we can safely dismiss Stubbs and Maitland as poor historians. In that case, all that has been put forward in this essay, even if true, is of no interest. It is a species of that 'so what' history to which my former teacher, Lady Rosalind Clay, used to allude. On the other hand, if we are concerned to find out how things have come to be as they are, we may well find that for certain societies the 'continuity with change' paradox is the most flexible way of looking at the past. This approach can best be stated as a contradiction, the 'Changing Same', as the jazz singer Leroy James called a song. This changing same is another way of speaking of the parable of the philospher's shoe, whose various parts were replaced bit by bit. At the end, was it the same shoe or another one? In another form, it is the metaphor used by the great historian of the Common Law, Sir Matthew Hale, when he likened the changing law to the Ship of the Argonauts. 'The ship went so long a voyage that eventually every part of it decayed and was replaced; yet [says the paradox of identity in spite of change] it remained in a meaningful sense the same ship.'[44] For English history, we would need to modify these metaphors, for the new heel, or the new planks were of a different shape and length to the ones they replaced. It was still a ship or a shoe, but the overall measurements had shifted very considerably. Put in another metaphor, an organic one, the tree had not changed from being an oak. But a small oak is very different in many respects from a large one.

One could express this model in a more modern idiom. In trying to account for the way in which behaviour is generated in a North African society, the anthropologist Pierre Bourdieu has developed the notion of *habitus*, that is the idea of a system of invisible, general, but powerful rules which guide everyday behaviour.[45] This is curiously similar to what is meant by that central English idea of 'custom', as when Bracton wrote of the *Laws and Customs of England* in the early thirteenth century. These are an assemblage of the 'way things are done', the fundamental and guiding principles, the rules of the game. If we turn Bourdieu's idea from a static one into a changing model over time, we would argue that the *habitus* of the English was very early established. How it expressed itself would vary and change, but the expressions would be in conformity to fairly basic rules which are not easily changed. One might liken these to the tides, which are unaltering. The storms and stillnesses on the surface, the individual waves, are just as important for the sailor as are the tides. Yet ultimately, the ebb and flow remains within various bounds constrained by deeper laws. No one would argue that 'revolutions' never occur, and historians should of course describe them when they do so. Yet to assume that they occur in every nation's history, and frequently, cuts short the historian's ability to respond to what the evidence tells him. It debases the historical coinage and it warps the historian's observation of the past.

Two final questions may be raised, but not satisfactorily answered in the space available. The first concerns the degree to which the non-revolutionary nature of the English past is representative or exceptional when compared to the rest of Western Europe. England was in many respects merely an extreme version of a general West European socio-economic system, and the inquiring oriental would have been almost as surprised if he had visited Italy, France or Spain, and particularly, if he had visited Holland or Denmark. On the other hand, as many travellers and observers noted, there was also something special about England. One manifestation of this was that, while there is no evidence of a real 'revolution' in England in any specific century, there are indeed grounds for calling what happened in much of continental Europe in the century after 1789 a real revolution. The legal, political, social, economic and ideological systems do seem to have undergone a rapid, interrelated and profound transformation. Of course there were continuities, but there are much stronger grounds for speaking of revolution. Thus while England, with industrialization and urbanism, went through the most rapid physical, technological and material changes, its deeper relations of production and ideology were little altered. Elsewhere, the material world altered less, but the *ancien régime* structures were toppled and a new world was born. Ironically, that 'new' world was based on the ancient models developed in England and exported to her colonies.

If it is true that a misleading paradigm of the English past has established itself in certain quarters during the first two thirds of the twentieth century, we are left with an intriguing historiographical question as to why this should have been the case. Naturally, the reasons lie at many levels. Some of these have been hinted at above: the need to make the past very different in order to make it problematic, the influence of European sociologists and particularly Marx and Weber, the self-questioning doubt induced by comparative anthropological knowledge. Other causes could be suggested, including the obvious use of the past to help predict the future. For instance, if all that exists now can be shown to be the result of a recent 'revolution', then it is easier to consider changing present institutions. What exists around us can be seen to be an artificial, almost accidental, creation. It is a part of culture, not nature. If the family system or the capitalist ethic is only a few hundred years old, it is easier to feel that it may not last long either. The vision of numerous revolutions in the recent past is essentially optimistic, utopian. The premise of continuity can conversely be attractive to those who wish to stress enduring values, who dislike profound change. Thus the fluctuations in historical interpretation tell us a great deal about the changes in political ideology in this century. Recent errors are not the result of a lack of ability among twentieth-century scholars, even if it is difficult to point to historians of the stature of Stubbs and Maitland. As historians know, theories of change, for instance the move from cyclical to linear concepts of time, from static to progressive and from evolution to revolution, are deeply influenced by changes in the environment within which historians work. While it is possible to analyse the reasons for such shifts in interpretative paradigm at the Renaissance, Enlightenment or the Evolutionary phase of the nineteenth century, it is more difficult to understand the reasons for the rise and imminent decline of what might be called 'Revolutionism'. We are still too close to the shift, some of us having even within our lives switched into and out of Revolutionism. All we can do in this short paper is to see how a useful model in other settings is inappropriate when applied to English history, distorting the evidence to fit into preconceived structures.

NOTES

All books are published in London, unless otherwise indicated.

1 Alexis de Tocqueville, *Democracy in America* (first published in 2 parts, 1835, 1840), and *L'ancien régime* (1856).

2 Ibn Khaldûn, *An Introduction to History, and Muqaddimah*, various editions; Edmund Leach, *Political Systems of Highland Burma* (1954).

3 Fernand Braudel, *The Mediterranean and the Mediterranean World in the Age of Philip II* (1976), Fontana ed., vol. 1, pp. 20–1.
4 'Tawney's century' is the title given to the first essay, by F. J. Fisher, in the *Essays in the Economic and Social History of Tudor and Stuart England* (Cambridge, 1961), ed. F. J. Fisher.
5 Christopher Hill, *The Century of Revolution 1603–1714* (Edinburgh, 1961).
6 Lawrence Stone, *The Family, Sex and Marriage in England 1500–1800* (1977), pp. 4–7; see also Edward Shorter, *The Making of the Modern Family* (1976). He even more specifically dates the change to the eighteenth century.
7 The failure of the English Revolution of the seventeenth century to change the social structure is stressed by Perry Anderson and Tom Nairn; see E. P. Thompson, 'The peculiarities of the English', in *The Socialist Register*, ed. Ralph Miliband and John Saville (1965), especially p. 314.
8 More detailed discussion of continuities in property law and social structure are contained in my *The Origins of English Individualism* (Oxford, 1978); on law, order and public administration, in my *The Justice and the Mare's Ale; Law and Disorder in Seventeenth-century England* (Oxford, 1981), and *A Guide to English Historical Records* (Cambridge, 1983). The evidence to support the remarks about marriage appear in my book *Marriage and Love in England* (Oxford, 1986).
9 An excellent outline of English Common Law history is J. H. Baker, *An Introduction to English Legal History* (1979).
10 John Hajnal, 'European marriage patterns in perspective', in *Population in History* (1965), ed. D. V. Glass and D. E. C. Eversley.
11 J. Goody, *The Development of the Family and Marriage in Europe* (Cambridge, 1983).
12 C. Lévi-Strauss, *The Elementary Structures of Kinship* (1969), p. xxiii.
13 J. Goody and S. J. Tambiah, *Bridewealth and Dowry* (Cambridge, 1973).
14 E. A. Wrigley and R. S. Schofield, 'English population history from family reconstitution: summary results 1600–1799', in *Population Studies* (1983), pp. 157–84.
15 *Ibid.*, p. 184.
16 E. A. Wrigley, 'Marriage, fertility and population growth in eighteenth-century England', in R. B. Outhwaite, (ed.), *Marriage and Society* (1981), esp. p. 183.
17 Perry Anderson, *Lineages of the Absolutist State* (1974), p. 113.
18 William Stubbs, *The Constitutional History of England, in its Origin and Development* (Oxford, 1874), 5th ed., 1891, vol. 1, pp. 584–5.
19 *Ibid.*, p. 682.
20 *Ibid.*, vol. 3, p. 3.
21 *Ibid.*, vol. 3, p. 570.
22 *Ibid.*, vol. 3, p. 573.
23 *Ibid.*, vol. 3, p. 615.
24 *Ibid.*, vol. 3, p. 626.
25 *Ibid.*, vol. 3, p. 619.
26 Sir F. Pollock and F. W. Maitland, *The History of English Law Before the Time of Edward I* (2nd ed., Cambridge, 1968), vol. 2, p. 260. Although known as Pollock and Maitland, almost all of the work was written by Maitland.
27 *Ibid.*, vol. 1, p. 225.

28 *Selected Essays of F. W. Maitland* (Cambridge, 1957), chosen and introduced by Helen Cam, p. 123.
29 Pollock and Maitland, *History*, vol. 1, p. civ.
30 F. W. Maitland, *The Forms of Action at Common Law* (Cambridge, 1968), ed. A. H. Chaytor and W. J. Whittaker, p. 43.
31 Pollock and Maitland, *History*, vol. 2, pp. 10–11.
32 F. W. Maitland, *The Constitutional History of England* (Cambridge, 1919), p. 20.
33 Maitland, *Select Essays*, p. 127.
34 Pollock and Maitland, *History*, vol. 2, pp. 438, 242ff, 13, 19, 27.
35 *Ibid.*, vol. 2, p. 233.
36 *Ibid.*, vol. 2, p. 402.
37 Pollock and Maitland, *History*, vol. 1, p. xxiii.
38 *Ibid.*, vol. 1, p. xlvii.
39 *Ibid.*, vol. 1, p. lxxiii.
40 *Ibid.*, vol. 1, p. xlvii.
41 F. W. Maitland, *Domesday Book and Beyond* (Cambridge, 1921), pp. 344–6.
42 F. W. Maitland, *Collected Papers* (Cambridge, 1911), ed. H. A. L. Fisher, vol. 1, p. 471.
43 Herbert Butterfield, *The Whig Interpretation of History* (Pelican ed., 1973), p. 17.
44 Charles Gray in the preface to Sir Matthew Hale, *The History of the Common Law of England* (Chicago Univ. reprint, 1971), p. xxxi.
45 Pierre Bourdieu, *Outline of a Theory of Practice* (Cambridge, 1977).

8

Agrarian and industrial revolutions

WILLIAM N. PARKER

'Revolution', as the word is used in economic history, commonly means a thoroughgoing change in production processes and in the social organization of labour, occurring at a faster than customary pace.[1] An agrarian or industrial revolution is an interrelated collection of innovations in technique or in organization (or in both) within these sectors of a society's economic life. Such innovations may appear almost simultaneously or they may spread gradually among a sector's individual productive units – manors, farms, households, workshops – altering their practices, equipment and internal structure. Very frequently the 'revolution' breaks units apart and re-forms the individual productive factors in new combinations to allow them to do their work in novel ways which are, by some criterion either of equity or efficiency, more effective.

No *a priori* argument can be adduced to show that change in one productive unit in a collection of producers requires or implies similar changes in others. Individual manors, farms, workshops, cottages, or commercial associations may experience their own mini-revolutions in form or technique, by changes which come to rest within their own space. On the other hand, such changes may be imitated by other units, and almost necessarily they will change the circumstances or environment in which other units function, rendering dysfunctional or sub-optimal some of their forms or activities. Then, if either competition among units or some maximizing intelligence among them is at work, changes and adjustments will be induced, and these in turn may spread the conditions for, and inducements to, change throughout the agrarian or industrial system.

At this point the question arises whether a thoroughgoing change in one aspect of agriculture or of industry must spread to other aspects of the sector's structure, and from the one sector to the other. Does change in the physical or engineering work done in a sector – i.e. in its technology – imply or require change in the human organization of its activity, in management, control, and the distribution of the product? Does change in technology or organization (or in both) in one sector conduce to parallel or reciprocal changes in the other? Does an agricultural 'revolution' require or create conditions for an industrial one, or *vice versa*? And finally, is there a link between technological and organizational revolutions in economic activities on the one hand and the intellectual, spiritual and political revolutions whose sequences have peppered the history of the West since the Renaissance? When such sequences of change have spread far and penetrated deeply enough into economic and social life, may we speak of the economy and the society, in so far as they are coherent entities of interconnected parts, as having been 'transformed'? May we say, if one makes such a choice of language, that a new mode of production, involving new social relations and new shapings of productive forces, has come into being? Such new formulations of the human and material substances and forces of life may be called both 'release' and 'repression', each of these terms implying, of course, the other.

If the entities or sub-systems composing an agriculture, an industry, an economy, a society or a mode of production are conceived as wholly dissimilar from one another, so that no tendency to competition or imitation occurs among them, or as wholly independent of one another, having no links among them, then these aggregative entities themselves are empty. Then all change is random, and it makes no sense to speak of 'revolution'. A revolution in some or all aspects of an entity or a system implies that there was a relatively less 'revolutionary' state from which the sequence of interconnected changes proceeds, and another in which, after the revolutionary energies and interconnections have exhausted themselves, it comes to rest. Revolution implies as its negative either stagnation or a slowly evolving 'dynamic equilibrium'; fast change implies a slow change, a relative stability, in which some functional interrelation among the units of a system serves to sustain and reproduce it as a whole, intact or with only gradual modification.

I

Agricultural revolutions

Revolutions, then, may affect a productive system in its social arrangements or relations, and/or in its organization of the chemicals and energies of natural productive force. In agrarian history, connection between the two has often seemed to be rather loose. The same technology of land use, crop choice, field practices, and livestock management has often been found compatible with alternative forms of control, ownership, and tenure.[2] And sometimes systems of tenure and labour organization have been able to absorb extensive technical change – shifts in crops, changes in the balance between pastoral and arable farming, even use of machinery, fertilizers and new genetic materials, without disturbing the relation of peasant within the village, of landlord to tenant on the estate, or farmers to buyers in the market. Yet thoroughgoing technical change has usually involved changes in the proportions of land to capital to labour, as well as alterations in the scale of management and supervision, and these changes have often been accompanied by changes in tenure relations and in the use of hired or family labour. On the other hand, legal and institutional change has on occasion opened the way to revision of field patterns and agricultural practice, even where not directly motivated by such prospects.

In Europe from late medieval times through the Russian Revolution, organizational rather than technical changes followed a 'revolutionary' pattern – but only after the disturbances of the fourteenth through the mid-seventeenth centuries had established the legal status of the peasantry: serfdom east of the Elbe; bodily freedom under semi-feudal tenures in the West; in England, large holdings with tenants or wage labour mixed with smaller holdings (a 'yeomanry') which declined only gradually over three hundred years. In the English case, the economic historian W. J. Ashley, as early as 1898, found a 'revolution' of enclosures of arable strips and common land for sheep raising in the period 1450–1550, in response to the growing market for wool. This occurred across a belt in the lower Midlands to East Anglia, including also Kent. These forcible enclosures[3] had formed for Marx the initial step in 'primitive accumulation', which continued by devices legal and illegal, as capitalism expanded, to the mid-nineteenth century.

Later writers on England emphasized a concentration in a 'revolutionary' period, 1750–1850. Here private and parliamentary enclosures, it was said, changed field patterns over wide areas of arable husbandry in the Midlands, the east and the south. These latter were correlated with a technological revolution, replacing open fields and triennial rotations with enclosed farms and new cropping patterns, yielding large supplies of livestock feed and so, in turn, large supplies of wool, meat, dairy products and natural fertilizer. The more intense tillage for root crops, the nitrogen fixation of the legumes, and the larger applications of manure in turn increased, or helped to sustain, per acre yields in the cereal grains. The organizational and technical revolutions were thus linked, but not – at least not after the sixteenth century – in a strict one-to-one relationship. New rotations were adopted in some open-field villages, and some enclosures of commons and even consolidation of plots occurred without disturbing the ancient patterns of rotation.[4]

On the continent, after 1750, the 'revolution' was more simply a status reform – the abolition of serfdom and feudal tenures rather than a rapid physical change in land use or allotments. Unlike in England, serfdom was abolished by 'revolutionary' decrees. Maria Theresa began the process in the Habsburg monarchy and Joseph II was able partially to carry it through before the French Revolution. In south Germany, 'enlightened' monarchs accomplished much and only in part in response to the Revolution. In Prussia little was done until, in the face of Napoleon, the von Stein and Hardenberg decrees were carried through. In Russia the loss of the Crimean War is generally credited with forcing Alexander II's hand to order the Emancipation (1861). In all these organizational reforms the abolition of feudal dependence of the peasantry and its attachment in tenant or ownership status to at least a portion of its former lands was carried out not for economic ('efficiency') reasons but out of political ('equity') considerations. If the poorer tenants were dispossessed, a further consolidation of landlordly power occurred and some wage labour estates were created. In Russia, peasant 'freedom' accelerated some consolidation and mechanization, but the village units changed little until the Stolypin reforms of 1906–11. In all these lands following the political changes, the market set about its work of accomplishing 'enclosure' and technical innovation slowly and piecemeal over the century to 1914, sometimes facilitated by the status reforms but perhaps just as often impeded by them.[5]

Technically speaking, and in a very long view, the eighteenth-century shiftover from the three-field rotation to patterns of continuous cropping, the consolidation of the medieval strips into enclosed holdings in central grain regions and the distribution of commons and woodlands were 'revolutionary'. The whole development fits the process sketched out by Ester Boserup in her notable survey of the stages of agricultural development.[6] The changes in pastoral agriculture, especially the improvements in specialization of breeds and the provision of new feed crops, were equally notable. But all this was on a time scale almost approaching that of the neolithic 'revolution'; none of it, over six centuries, compares with the post-1850 revolutions of mechanization, tractorization, and biochemical technology. In summary, then, 'revolution' defined as thoroughgoing change at an accelerated pace applies unequivocally in European agricultural history at only two points: the peasant emancipations of the nineteenth century, and the drastic technical changes since 1900 and particularly since 1940.

The British enclosures

The long-drawn-out incidence of 'enclosure' in Great Britain is hard to express in 'revolutionary' terms. The sixteenth-century enclosures mentioned above appear to have sustained a portion of Marx's point – that an 'original accumulation' of financial capital in its early stages was not a matter of impersonal market forces, but utilized conscious manipulations of force and the law by one class in a population. To Marx the 'original accumulation' giving command over labour power, and the creation of a landless labour force dependent on wages, were complementary aspects of the same acts of usurpation of peasants' rights.[7] The degradation of the poor through 'enclosures' during the decades of the Industrial Revolution was the theme of John and Barbara Hammond in *The Village Labourer*.[8] The Hammonds argued that the enclosures of the eighteenth and early nineteenth centuries ruined yeomen farmers and drove smallholders, cottagers, and holders of commons rights into an underclass of the poor, along with the cottage spinners, weavers and other skilled workers, to form the labour force in new industries. This argument was taken up by the Fabians and by the French scholar, Paul Mantoux,[9] and enters into explanations of the origin of a mobile labour force for the early factories. The view of the enclosures as a 'good thing', put forward in Lord Ernle's famous book, rested on the presumed link between them and the introduction of new cropping systems and improved livestock.[10] Principal among the revisionists were J. D. Chambers and Gordon Mingay.[11] They found that the enclosures in the areas they examined did not displace labour but rather increased rural employment, and, while squeezing out marginal village dwellers with only customary rights on the common lands, were on the whole 'fair' as among the small and large landholders in a parish. Even earlier writers emphasized as a source of factory labour not enclosures *per se*, but population growth in the countryside under the regime of rural industry and the displacement of *that* labour when rural industry declined in face of factory techniques. Recent quantitative work in local records has created an even more confused and spotty picture. Recently, Robert Allen's sample of over 1,500 villages in the south Midlands, mentioned above, has led him to suggest that enclosure on light soils did not increase productivity, or even, it would seem, facilitate technical change. Enclosure had a strong effect – it is contended – only after 1840 when, applied to heavy soils, it made organizationally possible the laying of drains.[12] This is a far cry from Marx's chapter 30 or Mingay's more optimistic assessment.

It seems plausible, one must conclude, that enclosures after 1650 did not suddenly drive large bodies of yeomen out of the villages, though evidences of impoverishment and restlessness were plain to see. They were contemporaneous with improvements in farming patterns, materials and techniques in England in the seventeenth and eighteenth centuries and on the continent in the nineteenth century. The resulting productivity gains in turn allowed European agriculture with overseas imports to feed growing populations with a declining share of the work force in agriculture. Broadly interpreted, Marx's essential point seems indisputable if one accepts his terms of reference: the development of capitalism in agriculture required the displacement of the village system of tenure and work organization, and that displacement in turn 'released productive forces' which allowed commercial farming and modern factory industry to grow within a market economy, i.e. within a capitalist framework. An agrarian revolution both in status and tenure arrangements and in techniques was needed to free labour and to provide food and materials for the Industrial Revolution at the turn of the eighteenth and throughout the nineteenth centuries. The agrarian changes did this between 1750 and 1920 largely through a slow (Boserupian) shift from medieval field patterns, practices, tools, and genetic stock to those of a continuous cropping and commercial husbandry. Market growth operated across the landscape, inducing the series of local 'revolutions' in one region after another, particularly as the system became exposed to world-wide competition. Technically speaking, these revolutions in small units and localities over 300 years produced growth in the product per unit either of the labour or of land probably no more than half as great as that which has occurred since 1900 through the absorption of the nineteenth-century mechanical inventions, through tractorization and through the genetic and chemical 'revolution' in agricultural science of the last half-century.[13] In this sense the recurrent industrial 'revolutions' of the twentieth century have been necessary to carry along those in agriculture.

II

Industrial revolution

In agriculture man works directly in cooperation with Nature, and the products supply elemental needs: food, clothing and shelter. These circumstances often seem to give agriculture a certain priority in the scale of human activities. Yet the natural element in farming, though a free gift of God, has also been an impediment. It has meant that, until recently, production processes were not readily susceptible of sudden improvement through human intervention. For the West, increases of geographical knowledge and the diffusion of new genetic materials made for discontinuities. One might speak of the 'potato revolution' of the eighteenth century, or the 'soy bean revolution' of the twentieth. But the new techniques and crops in the shift from the medieval system were not pushed out of farming by the pressure of population growth. They were pulled out by an upward draught of market opportunity, itself derived from trade, urbanization and industrial change. The mechanical changes in field and barn operations were the gift of the mechanical Industrial Revolution of the decades 1770–1850, and the rapid rises in yields since 1940 the gift of chemical and biological research, deriving only to a very small degree from farmers themselves. Even in pre-neolithic times, before settled agriculture, the gathering and use of the seeds of the wild cereal grains depended on industrial operations, cutting, crushing, grinding, and storing in pottery or wicker containers. In stimulating change, industry may be said to have priority over agriculture, and its development in both techniques and organization, whether 'evolutionary' or 'revolutionary' in character, is the dominant element, giving freer play to human imagination and contrivance than the half-natural processes of agriculture can allow. Industrial change may be impeded by an agricultural system which either in organization or in technology is resistant to change. Agriculture may change slowly, almost grudgingly, as commercial and industrial revolutions occur around it, and, having 'lagged' for a long time, may undergo political or technical 'revolutions' to 'catch up'. Its role has been on the whole a passive one, nurturing, suffering, responding to and sometimes encouraging the other movements – a traditional wife in a traditional marriage.

Still 'revolutions' in industrial operations have shared many of the characteristics of agrarian revolutions. Here, as there, form and technology have shown their separate histories; here, as there, change in one seems generally to have facilitated, and sometimes to have been a consequence of, change in the other. In both sorts of 'revolutions', the same variety has been present in internal structure, in how the revolution has been transmitted among units and establishments, in the predominant motivations that have impelled it, in the relation between form and technique, and in the mixture of the criteria of equity and efficiency by which the history may be assessed.

Do such things as industrial revolutions exist? Even more than for agricultural revolutions this question focuses attention on the case of England, Scotland and Wales, and on that of Belgium and some points in northern France: *the* Industrial Revolution of the three decades on each side of the year 1800. For Marx here, as in the case of agrarian capitalism, the fundamental revolution was the separation of the worker from his tools. This occurred, he said, from the sixteenth century on with the growth of merchants' and artisans' capital, with the funding of a public debt and the spoliation of colonial peoples. These accumulations permitted the creation of the system of 'manufacture', i.e. the division of the artisan's operations among a number of workers, labouring separately in cottages or grouped together in workshop or factory. This reorganization was for Marx the essence of the 'revolution', the replacement of the feudal mode with its artisan guilds, first by the petty producer, then by the capitalist employer with wage workers. But Marx, like Adam Smith, gives an important place to machinery, the grouping together of workers around a power-driven piece of fixed capital, the increased productivity (and surplus product) provided, the accompanying changes in the relation of factory master to worker and the altered nature of work itself.[14] Marx is nowhere clear, so far as I have been able to discover, as to where the new technologies of steam, mechanical engineering and machinery came from.[15] They appeared, one might suppose, among productive forces or potential forces, suppressed under the feudal mode and 'released' by the organizational innovations of capitalism. Having appeared, they were given full credit by Marx for creating power-driven factories, and enabling employers to use fixed capital, to increase the pace of production, lengthen the working day and extract increased surplus.

As Marx's account was made more specific or 'historical' by later English and continental scholars, it lost, perhaps inevitably, some of its Marxian flavour. The Christian socialist, Arnold Toynbee, linked the Agrarian and Industrial Revolutions of the eighteenth century together and foreshadowed many of the themes taken up by a line of scholars: the Hammonds, Mantoux, Clapham, Knowles, Beales, Ashton, Thompson, and others. Mantoux's version gave full credit to the capital accumulation in mercantile activities, and the organization by the capitalist of the 'old mode of industry', i.e. 'manufacture' and the putting-out system. Sympathy for the impoverished work force was evident; in his assessment of the short-run effects on wages and housing, Mantoux must be aligned with the 'pessimists'.[16] But he also brought two rather bourgeois figures on to the scene – the entrepreneur and the inventor. In his account the entrepreneurs seem to be something more than blind accumulators and extractors of surplus value. Their skill lies in exploiting the inventions, and he credits them with great practical sense in organizing production. Boulton and Wedgwood in his view stood out above the rest as men of culture and quality.[17] Mantoux developed, too, an account of induced invention as it occurred in the developments from Kay's flying shuttle to the spinning inventions to the power loom – a disequilibrium process by which one invention created a bottleneck at the next stage, which was broken not by factor movement in proper, neo-classical style – but by a rush of inventive activity.[18] This sensitivization of invention to economic need was a new fact about the decades 1770–1820; inventors, like entrepreneurs, acted as the shock troops of capitalist advance. Whether coming from the ranks of artisans and 'tinkerers', or with more training and skill from ingenious contrivers among educated classes, they formed a sub-society of their own. A. P. Usher's contribution to the discussion lay in a study of both the character of the inventions and the psycho-sociology of the inventors.[19] T. S. Ashton, A. E. Musson and Eric Robinson examined the social phenomenon of innovation at close range.

Now it is possible to include these themes – enterprise and invention – within Marx's argument, though they are not pursued in the historical portions of *Capital.* As capital accumulated, one may say, a surrounding culture developed, creating all sorts of personalities and talents, which were then turned to economic ends. Men, who under feudalism might have been lords or popes or warriors, became captains of industry, as Veblen later suggested. Those who might have become theologians, artists, or saints became lawyers or inventors. To enlarge the stage on which the transition to capitalism is carried out thus makes the drama richer, but it also makes its outcome more uncertain. The impression is left that the Industrial Revolution, though at the heart of nineteenth-century industrialization, was itself a historical accident. Here for the first time in human history, one must conclude, a society already far advanced in commerce and commercialized agriculture felt the capitalist impulses of its entrepreneurs released and strengthened by individualistic, rationalistic, materialistic Protestant culture which also animated an active body of thinkers and practical artisans in whom the glimmerings of science and scientific method were alive. As if by some heavenly astrological freak, the planets were all in position to disturb the tides and initiate an earthquake. Such a conclusion is troubling to anyone who continues to look deeper to seek continuity and rationality in history. To pursue it here would lead a mere economic historian to poach on the neighbouring estates in the attempt to round up the game.[20]

The same can be said for the much discussed question of the revolution's social effects, which resonated in the post-Marx/Engels literature from Toynbee on. The famous 'standard of living' argument, begun between the Hammonds and Clapham in the 1920s and carried on between R. M. Hartwell and E. J. Hobsbawm in the 1950s, has gone yet further with ever more sophisticated statistical techniques.[21] In an excellent introduction to a collection of the recent studies, J. Mokyr writes:

> Lindert and Williamson show that real wages start to rise substantially after 1819 whereas they made little real progress between 1760 and 1819. Similarly Feinstein has estimated that real private consumption per capita which had increased negligibly until the 1810's rose from £11.3 in 1811/12 to £14.6 in 1821/30 and £17.9 in 1831/40.[22]

Mokyr argues that for the fifty years before 1820, bad harvests and almost continuous wars must have depressed living standards. The speed-up in population growth, whether or not connected with the 'revolution' itself, could also have had that effect. If income distribution had become more skewed and large capital expenditures had depressed consumption, the 'revolution' could have contributed to a lower living standard for the working class. Given the small share of the affected industries (cotton and iron) in the national product, that would not have produced general stagnation or immiseration. It might however have accounted for specific and spectacular points at which workers' conditions had worsened, while the generally depressed conditions would have accounted for the inability of workers to extricate themselves from such conditions once they were in them. For the decades after 1800, Mokyr points out that the estimates of N. Crafts would reduce the earlier somewhat optimistic estimates of per capita income growth made by P. Deane and W. A. Cole, along with those of C. Feinstein, to 5 per cent capita for 1800–30, and that P. Lindert and J. Williamson find a perceptible rise in inequality from 1801/3 to 1857.

The recent studies point then to three probabilities as to the movement of living standards of industrial workers: (1) stagnation or deterioration in 1760–1810, due, however, more to war and trade dislocation than to the technical and organizational changes in the 'revolutionary' industries; (2) marked rise in 1810–30; (3) very moderate improvement over the whole period 1800–50 with an increasing inequality in income distribution. Following 1850, rises in real wages for several decades are clear and undisputed. These conclusions are not wholly consistent with the data on mortality. Wrigley and Schofield find a tiny improvement in life expectancy between 1760 and the 1830s (from 39.4 to 39.6) with little improvement thereafter to mid-century. The mid-century data also show rather high infant mortality rates.[23]

Whether or not there was an average actual deterioration over the whole eighty-year period from 1770 to 1850 in England, capital and institutions were forming which permitted the visible rises in the real wage later in the nineteenth century. Yet, whatever averages and indices may show, the horror tales of the factory system and the British urban slums made the British experience a byword among nations, an example which 'follower' areas on the continent and beyond endeavoured to avoid, and occasionally did avoid with some very limited success.

A permanent revolution?

Only sporadically since 1900 have economic historians questioned whether an Industrial Revolution in fact occurred in England in the latter decades of the eighteenth century. Biographies and industrial histories have shown the swarm of entrepreneurs and engineers. Patent and trade data and some production data have shown the rapid growth in cotton, iron and the engineering trades, and the appearance of water- and steam-powered factories. British historians adopted the idea of a revolution the more readily perhaps because, as an event of world-wide impact, it initiated the modern age *in England.* What followed was then, not unnaturally, an imitation of the British lead. David Landes in *The Unbound Prometheus* made a searching and eloquent examination of the course of events, both in Britain and on the continent and gave flesh to a model of revolution and diffusion in both the technological and the industrial spheres. Such a pattern for the history formed also the skeleton of W. W. Rostow's incursion into 'stage theory' and Alexander Gerschenkron's panoramic view of industrial change and 'relative backwardness'. Only occasionally do national-income accountants or 'real' historians – the first with a telescope, the second with a microscope – fail to find in their bodies of data the phenomenon which, to historians with unaided vision, seems so apparent. Perhaps the fair and correct way to look at the industrial changes of the 1780–1830 period in England is to call them a revolution in a few industries, and then to insist that these changes – since they spread to other industries, and to other lands – though small in themselves when they happened, were mighty in effect. The yeast does not add much to the mass of dough, but it is the essential revolutionary act for making bread.

The existence of such a discontinuity appears to be reinforced by strong theoretical considerations. Thus A. P. Usher argued the case for an Industrial Revolution and J. A. Schumpeter argued for Kondratief's long waves, from the occurrence of clusters of significant or major inventions.[24] Major inventions, Usher said, when they came, contained a striking novelty which closed a gap in engineering knowledge such that from them a series of revisions and further applications could follow. Or they furnished a new material which could be turned to many uses. The coal and iron inventions – coke smelting, iron puddling, rolling and machining – together with the steam engine formed one such cluster. The Bessemer and open-hearth processes formed another. Electricity in its first applications, and the internal combustion engine (which depended on electricity for its ignition) formed another breakthrough from which lesser inventions derived.

One robin, however, does not make a spring, and it is necessary to enlarge on Usher's idea of the 'crucial' invention to account for an Industrial Revolution.[25] A crucial or major invention in fact is the culmination of invention in several compartments of technology simultaneously and on a certain scale. For a mass of technology to develop, out of which major inventions appear, a society must contain a rather large body of inventors each going along a different route and in close communication with each other. This is particularly true in a period and in lines of invention in which the fundamental science has not been well developed. Where theory has not been worked out by careful experiments and the testing of hypotheses, invention is random, and success – intellectual or financial – comes to him who searches most widely and persists for the longest time. On a social scale, the size and variety of the activity, the closeness of communication, the sharing of a common culture create channels by which inventors give ideas to one another, derive problems from one another; the success of one becomes the raw material, the power source, the instrument for the next invention. Might we not find then on close examination that here, as in so many cases of random creation, a threshold effect is present? The analogy of an atomic pile, of a critical mass is almost inescapable. In particular, in the Industrial Revolution invention had to proceed in three separate lines simultaneously: in the improvement of iron, in the increase of motive power, and in the devices for the transmission of energy. Any one of these lines developed in isolation and ignorance of the others would have 'waste[d] its sweetness on the desert air'. Examples are the steam engine in ancient Egypt, the fine steels of the Middle East, the toys or ingenious mechanisms produced through the ages for the amusement of princes. But by 1760, both capitalism and knowledge had grown each in its several branches to a point where, in a society large enough and close enough knit, they could react on one another. This interaction is *the* novel event of the period, the first industrial revolution that set the chain in motion.

III

By 1850 a symbiosis of factory organization, wage labour and machinery was becoming prevalent in industry. There followed the industrial capitalism that Marx and Engels to a degree foresaw – an evolution which did not stop with the establishments in cotton and iron. Continuing reorganization of industrial life, at every level, has accompanied the 'permanent' technological revolution of the past two centuries. Except for the Soviet experience, the form of these parallel revolutions in technology and in industrial organization may be loosely called 'capitalistic'. Many economists like to attribute the whole development – technical, organizational, socio-political – to something called 'the market'. By binding invention tightly to 'bottlenecks' and expected returns 'the market' created a 'knowledge industry'. Through the choice of cost-minimizing locations for plants, 'the market' created great industrial districts and urban conglomerations. Through the steady pressure of competition, 'the market' achieved 'efficient' size and internal organizations of plants, firms and industries and an 'efficient mix' of private and public participation and control. Under capitalism, whatever one's assessment of its achievements, both technology and socio-economic organization have – through competitive markets – remained flexible, and continuously (in Schumpeter's phrase) 'creatively destructive'. Technology and organization have unfolded together, each producing its mini-revolutions – the one in products, processes, and materials, the other in partnerships, corporations, managerial hierarchies, networks of control, financial instruments and intermediaries, labour unions, and finally state enterprises and the interest group organizations of managerial capitalism. Socialist planning itself has been put forward not simply as just and moral, but as the only 'efficient' form of organization compatible with modern technology. Universal monopoly has been seen by some writers as an extension of the thinking that had created the factory to the society at large.[26]

One moves here beyond mere agrarian or industrial revolutions to the transitions from one great social and cultural 'epoch' to another – from feudalism to competitive capitalism to 'organized capitalism' or socialist planning and controls. The commercial 'revolution' of the Renaissance unsettled medieval agriculture and industry and began the disturbances in markets, modes of payment, and accumulation in which the 'slow' agrarian revolution participated, and the industrial changes in form and technique were initiated. Once initiated, those sequences carried on to open out a world economy to capitalist organization, markets and technology. But the Renaissance changes in economic activity formed part of a larger cultural change – a Big Bang, a gigantic cultural explosion that released Humanism in literature and art, Protestantism in religion, nationalism in politics, rationalism in philosophy, and industrialism and materialism over all.[27] For over five hundred years, these revolutions have transmitted their effects to one another, creating the conditions, the materials, the impetus for constant innovation and reformulations in all branches of European and American life, shaping and animating the human material of each successive generation to new reactions, new sensitivities, new impulses. The Renaissance spirit was one of continual, incessant, or recurrent revolution in culture, thought, politics and economic behaviour. Our uneasiness about revolution today stems from a fear that in one big revolution, this great age of continual revolution, of unceasing innovation may end, that in a last huge revolution, mankind may make a desert, and call it equilibrium. Whether that desert is also called socialism or organized capitalism seems a trivial matter to those who still live under the long shadow of the Renaissance, whether they be

Humanist or scientific in mentality, classic or romantic in taste, Christian or rationalist in religion, competitive or cooperative in economic behaviour, Marxian or Smithian in economic ideology.

NOTES

1 Revolution, according to the OED, derives from *volvere*, to turn, + 're', a prefix which combines meanings of 'back' and 'again'. It differs from 'return' or 'reverse' in conveying the idea that forward movement is continuing in the turning back; hence to turn back as in a circle is to 'revolve'. It was used as early as 1600 to mean the complete overthrow of an established government. Before 1800, however, i.e. in the age of mechanics, it retained the idea of a revolution back to an earlier form or state. Thus in Whig mythology, the 'Glorious Revolution' returned the monarchy to English principles. Even the American and French Revolutions could be considered in a similar sense. The word 'revolt' deriving from an intensified form of *revolvere*, i.e. re + *volutare*, meant a short, violent action (not necessarily successful) against the existing order or power. The nineteenth- and twentieth-century usage appears to have collapsed the two words into one, particularly in Marxist writings, where the movement from one economic formation to another is accomplished by a violent 'revolution'.

The idea of 'revolution' in the broad sense is implicit in 'stage' theories of history favoured by the older and younger writers of the German Historical School from List through Schmoller, and closely related to the romantic or 'idealistic' conception of the state and society in Hegel, A. Müller, etc. It is present in the primitive anthropology of eighteenth-century writers (Rousseau, Millar); even Adam Smith distinguishes 'barbarism' from 'civilized society', and it experienced a revival in the 1950s and 1960s among economists writing on large themes of historical development, e.g. W. W. Rostow, S. Kuznets, E. Boserup. A. P. Usher's views of 'threads' in history implied the idea of a society made of component dynamic processes – demographic, technical, political, economic, social – which in a 'stage' are held in certain equilibrium with one another. If whether through outside events or internal 'slippage' continuing over a long time, certain elements are brought to a threshold where their effect on other elements is disturbing, as, for example, in population growth relative to food supply, the equilibrium of the 'stage' is disrupted and the society experiences transition or a revolution which by *its* own internal dynamics may carry the history into the next 'stage'. Of the many stage theories, only that of Marx exhibits some effort to examine the internal structure of a stage and the internal dynamics of the transition. In my opinion, it seems to place the causes of both technological change and population growth outside the system, and so, while illuminating a wide area of social history, it not surprisingly fails to produce a fully self-contained set of 'laws of motion' for historical change.

2 An example is the susceptibility of the plantation crops – coffee, cotton, cocoa, etc. – to organization also as cash crops for peasants on smaller holdings. Even among 'plantations' a great variety of forms and internal arrangements exists. See Courtenay (1965), esp. ch. 6.

3 Ashley (1898), ch. 6. Mantoux (1961), p. 152, fn 2, speaks of Ashley's account as 'more exhaustive and more scientific' than that of Marx (*Capital*, I, ch. 27). Edwin F. Gay, the 'father' of economic history in the USA, made an estimate of only 3 to 5 per cent commons and arable enclosed in the sixteenth century (Gay, 1902–3), a conclusion which British historians continued to dispute. Since Ashley wrote, more evidence of enclosures throughout the seventeenth and early eighteenth centuries has accumulated reducing the 'revolutionary' character of the Tudor enclosures. Robert Allen (1984) has produced an estimate for enclosures in 1,568 villages distributed over six counties in the 'South Midlands' which shows three clusters of relatively heavier enclosures in 1450–1500, 1575–1675, and 1750–1825, the last accounting for half a total acreage of 2.8 million acres enclosed over five hundred years.

4 See note 11, below.

5 On the continental reforms, see Blum (1978, ch. 11). The reforms advanced by Joseph II in Hungary were caught in a counter-revolution of the nobility and effectively suppressed until 1848. The best short treatment in English, with references to the main German literature, is found in Conze (1969) for the German Federation, the eastern provinces of Prussia, the Baltic provinces of Russia, Poland, Hungary and Switzerland. See also the interesting comparative analysis in Barrington Moore (1967). E. Tuma (1965) contains a brief treatment of the French and Russian reforms in a comparative framework.

6 Boserup (1965), esp. chs. 3, 4 and 9.

7 Marx, *Capital*, I, chs. 26, 30 and throughout part 8.

8 Hammond and Hammond (1970b), chs. 1–4.

9 Mantoux (1961), part 3, ch. 3. Mantoux details the impact of the 1795 modifications of the Act of Settlement of 1662 as freeing labour from the risk of resettlement in their parish of origin. He writes, 'Insofar as man ... obeyed the economic laws of supply and demand, the mobility of labour was now complete.' In general, however, all these authors, including E. P. Thompson in his rich revival of the Hammonds' themes (Thompson, 1963), focus on the conditions of the labouring poor resulting from *all* the economic changes rather than simply on the movement of workers from the land to factory. Some acute comments on the problem of labour mobility, as on the whole agricultural development, are made in Jones (1967b).

10 Ernle (1927), pp. 248–9. Ernle, however, emphasizes the ruinous effects of enclosures of arable or commons for pasture on employment and the condition of the poor. For the latter, however, he puts much blame on the agricultural depression following the Napoleonic wars and on the old Poor Law. Pp. 298–308, 327–31.

11 See Mingay (1963a) and Chambers and Mingay (1966). The tone of their conclusions, in sharp contrast to the Hammonds', is evident in their following judicious summary: 'the effects of the enclosure were rarely great or immediate. In some instances, enclosure came as the last act to a rather long-drawn-out drama of rural change, and merely put a *finis* to the story. In others it sometimes introduced, but more often accelerated, a similar story of change. As a result of enclosure, improved farming spread more rapidly than would otherwise have been the case, larger and more efficient farms were more readily developed, and the long-run decline of the freeholder and cottager [was] hastened and made more certain' (p. 104).

12 Allen (1984).
13 The rise in wheat yields, for which the longest series are available for the EEC countries and Great Britain between 1880 and 1953–7, was about 100 per cent with another 50 per cent between 1955–9 and 1965–9 (Dewhurst *et al.*, 1961, p. 1083, and OECD, 1968, p. 52). Other cereal grains show similar trends, and these gains have surely been exceeded by the improvements in the quality and production efficiency in animal products.
14 Smith (1937), vol. 1, bk. 1, ch. 1, esp. pp. 10–12; Marx (1906), vol. 1, ch. 15, esp. pp. 430ff.
15 Cohen (1978) chs. 2 and 6, places this problem under the theoretical problem of the 'primacy of the productive forces'. Like most theoretical discussions, Marxist or neo-classical, it brings a historian no closer to an understanding of the observed historical process of technological change. Only a concrete history of science, economy and technology can do this.
16 Mantoux (1961), part 3, ch. 3, pp. 420–44.
17 *Ibid.*, part 3, ch. 2, pp.373–88.
18 *Ibid.*, part 2, ch. 1.
19 Usher (1954), ch. 4.
20 I have made a stab at this in several somewhat repetitious essays. See Parker (1984), esp. pp. 18–29, 201–2. A recent brave, but simplistic, attempt to reactivate technology as the 'single factor' inducing change in the others has led to a clear statement of the formal problem and a judicious restatement of the historian's 'solution' to it. See Gaski (1982) with the replies by Geary (1984) and Inkster (1983).
21 Mokyr (1985). Editors' introduction, sect. 6.
22 *Ibid.*
23 Mokyr (1985).
24 Usher (1954), pp. 68–70; Schumpeter (1939), vol. 2, chs 6 and 7. See especially the methodological comments on pp. 228–30.
25 See Parker (1972) where these points are developed.
26 Veblen (1921). Brady (1933, 1961).
27 Parker (1984), ch. 1.

BIBLIOGRAPHY

Allen, R. C. 1982. 'The efficiency and distributional consequences of eighteenth century enclosures', *The Economic Journal*, 92 (Dec.).

1984. 'Enclosure and productivity growth, 1450–1850', University of British Columbia, Department Papers (March).

Ashley, W. J. 1898. *An Introduction to English History and Theory*. Part 2: The end of the middle ages. 3rd ed. New York: G. P. Putnam's Sons.

Ashton, T. S. 1924. *Iron and Steel in the Industrial Revolution*. Manchester: University Press.

1964. *The Industrial Revolution 1760–1830*. New York: Oxford University Press.

1966. *An Economic History of England: The 18th Century*. London: Methuen and Co. Ltd.

Beales, H. L. 1967. *The Industrial Revolution 1750–1850*. New York: Augustus M. Kelley.

Beckett, J. V. 1984. 'The pattern of landownership in England and Wales, 1660–1880', *The Economic History Review*, second series, vol. 37 (February).

Blum, J. 1978. *The End of the Old Order in Rural Europe*. Princeton: Princeton University Press.

Boserup, E. 1965. *The Conditions of Agricultural Growth*. Chicago: Aldine Publishing Co.

Brady, R. A. 1933. *The Rationalization Movement in German Industry*. Berkeley: University of California Press.

1961. *Organization, Automation, and Society*. Berkeley: University of California Press.

Burke, P., ed. 1979. *The New Cambridge Modern History*, 13–Companion volume. Cambridge: Cambridge University Press.

Chambers, J. D. 1967. 'Enclosure and labour supply in the Industrial Revolution', in Jones, E. L. ed., *Agriculture and Economic Growth in England 1650–1815*. London: Methuen and Co. Ltd, pp. 94–127.

Chambers, J. D. and Mingay, G. E. 1966. *The Agricultural Revolution 1750–1880*. London: B. T. Batsford Ltd.

Clapham, J. H. 1930. *An Economic History of Modern Britain*, vol. 1, chs. 4, 5, 14. Cambridge: Cambridge University Press. 2nd ed. reprinted 1964.

Cohen, G. A. 1978. *Karl Marx's Theory of History – A Defence*. Princeton: Princeton University Press.

Conference on Agrarian Structures and Economic Performance. 1984. Montreal. Papers by:

Robert C. Allen, 'Enclosure and productivity growth, 1450–1850'

E. J. T. Collins, 'The "Machinery Question" in English agriculture in the nineteenth century'

G. E. Mingay, 'Agricultural productivity and rural society in eighteenth century England'

J. M. Nelson, 'England: the disappearance of the small peasantry, revisited'

F. M. L. Thompson, 'Rural society and agricultural change in nineteenth-century Britain'

Michael Turner, 'Productivity gains and social consequences of English enclosures in the eighteenth and nineteenth centuries'

Conze, W. 1969. 'The effects of nineteenth-century liberal agrarian reforms on social strucutre in Central Europe', *Vierteljahresschrift für Sozial- und Wirtschaftsgeschichte*, vol. 38 (1949). English translation in Crouzet, F., Chaloner, W. H., and Stern, W. M. eds., *Essays in European Economic History 1789–1914*. London: Edward Arnold Ltd.

Courtenay, P. P. 1965. *Plantation Agriculture*, London: G. Bell.

Dewhurst, J. F., Coppock, J. O., Yates, P. L., *et al.* 1961. *Europe's Needs and Resources*. New York: Twentieth Century Fund.

Ernle, Rt Hon. Lord (R. E. Prothero). 1927. *English Farming Past and Present*. 1983. 4th ed. London: Longmans Green.

Evans, E. J. 1983. *The Forging of the Modern State; Early Industrial Britain 1783–1870*. New York: Longman, Inc.

Flinn, M. W. 1966. *Origins of the Industrial Revolution*. London: Longman Group Ltd.

Fores, M. 1982. 'Technical change and the "technology" myth', *The Scandinavian Economic History Review*, vol. 30, no. 3.

Gaski, J. F. 1982. 'The cause of the Industrial Revolution: a brief, "single-factor" argument', *The Journal of European Economic History*, vol. 11, no. 1 (Spring), pp. 227–33.

Gay, E. F. 1902–3. 'Inclosures in England in the sixteenth century', *Quarterly Journal of Economics*, vol. 17, pp. 576–97.

Geary, F. 1984. 'The cause of the Industrial Revolution and "single-factor" arguments: an assessment', *The Journal of European Economic History*, vol. 13, no. 1 (Spring), pp. 167–73.

Gerschenkron, A. 1962. *Economic Backwardness in Historical Perspective*. New York: Frederick A. Praeger.

Hammond, J. L. and Hammond B. 1966. *The Rise of Modern Industry*, 9th ed. London: Methuen and Co. Ltd.

Hammond, J. L., and Hammond, B. 1970a. *The Skilled Labourer 1760–1832*. London: Longmans, Green and Company Ltd, 1919; reprint Harper Torchbook.

Hammond, J. L., and Hammond, B. 1970b. *The Village Labourer 1760–1832*. London: Longmans, Green and Company Ltd, 1911; reprint Harper Torchbook.

Inkster, I. 1983. 'Technology as the cause of the Industrial Revolution: some comments', *The Journal of European History*, vol. 12, no. 3 (Winter), pp. 651–7.

John, A. H. 1967. 'Agricultural productivity and economic growth in England 1700–1760 (with a postscript)', in Jones, E. L., ed., *Agriculture and Economic Growth in England, 1650–1815*. London: Methuen and Co. Ltd, pp. 172–93.

Jones, E. L. 1967a. 'Agriculture and economic growth in England 1660–1750: agricultural change', in Jones, E. L., ed., *Agriculture and Economic Growth in England 1650–1815*. London: Methuen and Co. Ltd, pp. 152–71.

1967b. 'Editor's introduction', in *Agriculture and Economic Growth in England 1650–1815*. London: Methuen and Co. Ltd, pp. 1–48.

1974. *Agriculture and the Industrial Revolution*. Oxford: Basil Blackwell.

Jones, E. L. and Woolf, S. J., eds. 1969. *Agrarian Change and Economic Development*. London: Methuen and Co. Ltd.

Kerridge, E. 1973. *The Farmers of Old England*. London: George Allen and Unwin Ltd.

Knowles, L. C. A. 1926. *The Industrial and Commercial Revolutions in Great Britain during the Nineteenth Century*, 4th ed. London: Routledge and Kegan Paul Ltd.

Kuznets, S. 1966. *Modern Economic Growth; Rate, Structure and Spread*. New Haven: Yale University Press.

Landes, D. 1969. *The Unbound Prometheus*, Cambridge: Cambridge University Press.

Lenin, V. I. 1957. *The Development of Capitalism in Russia*. London: Lawrence and Wishart Ltd.

McLellan, D., ed. 1983. *Marx: The First Hundred Years*. Oxford: Fontana Paperbacks.

McMurty, J. 1978. *The Structure of Marx's World-View*. Princeton: Princeton University Press.

Mantoux, P. 1961. *The Industrial Revolution in the Eighteenth Century*. London: Methuen and Co. Ltd (revised from first English edition, 1928).

Marx, K. 1906. *Capital – A Critique of Political Economy*. New York: The Modern Library.

1969. *Das Kapital – Kritik der politischen Okonomie*. Frankfurt: Ullstein Materialien.

Millar, J. 1806. *The Origin of the Distinction of Ranks*, 4th ed. Edinburgh: William Blackwood.

Mingay, G. E. 1963a. 'The "Agricultural Revolution" in English History: a reconsideration', *Agricultural History*, vol. 37, no. 3 (July), pp. 123–33.

1963b. *English Landed Society in the Eighteenth Century*. London: Routledge and Kegan Paul.

Mokyr, J. 1976. 'Growing-up and the Industrial Revolution in Europe', *Explorations in Economic History*, 13, pp. 371–96.

ed. 1985. *The Economics of the Industrial Revolution*. Totowa, NJ: Rowman and Allenheld.

Moore, B. Jr. 1967. *Social Origins of Dictatorship and Democracy*. London: Allen Lane.

Musson, A. E. and Robinson, E. 1969. *Science and Technology in the Industrial Revolution*. Manchester: Manchester University Press.

Organisation for Economic Co-Operation and Development. 1969. *Agricultural Statistics. 1955–1968*. Paris.

Organisation for European Economic Co-Operation. 1959. *Agricultural and Food Statistics*. Paris.

Parker, W. N. 1972. 'Technology, resources, and economic change in the West', in Youngson, A. J., ed., *Economic Development in the Long Run*. London: George Allen and Unwin Ltd, pp. 62–78.

1984. *Europe, America and the Wider World*, vol. 1, *Europe and the World Economy*. Cambridge: Cambridge University Press.

Rostow, W. W. 1960. *The Stages of Economic Growth*. Cambridge: Cambridge University Press.

Schumpeter, J. A. 1939. *Business Cycles*, vols. 1 and 2. New York: McGraw-Hill Book Company, Inc.

Sinclair, H. M. 1934. *A Preface to Economic History*. New York: Harper and Brothers Publishers.

Smith, A. 1937. *An Inquiry Into the Nature and Causes of the Wealth of Nations*. New York: The Modern Library.

Spann, O. 1930. *The History of Economics*. New York: W. W. Norton and Co.

Sweezy, P. M. 1942. *The Theory of Capitalist Development*. New York: Oxford University Press.

Thompson, E. P. 1963. *The Making of the English Working Class*. New York: Vintage Books.

Toynbee, A. 1902. *Lectures on the Industrial Revolution of the 18th Century in England*. London: Longmans, Green and Co.

Tuma, E. H. 1965. *Twenty-Six Centuries of Agrarian Reform*. Berkeley: University of California Press.

Usher, A. P. 1954. *A History of Mechanical Inventions*, 2nd ed. Cambridge, Mass: Harvard University Press.

Veblen, T. 1921. *The Engineers and the Price System*. New York: B. W. Huebsch.

Williams, J. E. 1966. 'The British standard of living, 1750–1850', *The Economic History Review*, second series, vol. 29, no. 3, (Dec.), pp. 581–9.

Williamson, J. G. 1984. 'Why was British growth so slow during the Industrial Revolution?', *Journal of Economic History*, vol. 44, no. 3 (Sept.), pp. 687–712.

9

On revolution and the printed word

ELIZABETH L. EISENSTEIN

When considering the relationship between the concept of 'revolution' and the advent of the printed word, two quite different but equally problematic topics come to mind. *First* there is the problem of how best to describe the advent of printing itself. Should we regard it as just one more step in the long evolution of the book? Or should we view it instead as a revolutionary event? If we agree on the latter course, then what sort of revolution was entailed? *Second* there are many unsolved (and, indeed, several unposed) problems concerning the effects of printing on all the other revolutions (intellectual and political) which have occurred since Gutenberg's time. It would be impossible to do justice to either of these two topics let alone to cover both in a brief essay. The following discussion, which will focus on developments in Western Europe in the age of the hand press, is intended to be suggestive rather than definitive and will touch on only a few of the many issues that seem worth further thought.

I THE PROBLEMATIC PRINTING REVOLUTION – ABRUPT RUPTURE; PROLONGED IRREVERSIBLE PROCESS

Some years ago, when Nicolas Barker gave a lecture at the Library of Congress on the advent of movable type, he titled his talk: 'The invention of printing: revolution within revolution'.[1] He thus drew attention to a prevalent semantic confusion. At least two different processes of change are now being designated by one and the same term. 'Revolution', as currently employed, may mean a decisive break with a long-enduring tradition or institution. Or it may mean a prolonged, irreversible, cumulative process with effects that become ever more pronounced the longer it goes on. These two different meanings are well illustrated by discussion of changes wrought by printing as the following comments may suggest.

In the first place, the term revolution is used, as most working historians commonly use the term, to argue against a thesis that stresses continuity and gradual change. According to a recent *Times Literary Supplement* review, the advent of movable type constituted 'a smooth acceleration of an exponential curve already taking place'.[2] Although I regard this statement as wide of the mark, it does aptly characterize the thesis adopted by many book historians. Some proponents of this thesis take a truly long view and start with the shift from roll to codex, or even earlier with the invention of the alphabet, or still earlier with the introduction of writing. Others (self-designated codicologists) tend to begin with the development of Carolingian minuscule or with the so-called twelfth-century 'book revolution'. But all point to the spread of lay literacy; the appearance of the lay 'stationer', 'libraire' or 'cartolaio'; the introduction of paper-making along with a commercial manuscript book trade in order to suggest that book publishing was carried on in the later middle ages much as it would be after printers replaced scribes.

If one is inclined, as I am, to disagree with this thesis, it is important to specify just where the disagreement lies. Too often it is assumed that one cannot assign special significance to the replacement of scribe by printer without underestimating the many prior changes which affected manuscript books. Yet surely one may fully acknowledge the importance of all the prior developments and at the same time treat them as preconditions and prerequisites of the revolution printing wrought. The point is that, during the second half of the fifteenth century, book publishing did not go on as it had done before. Major centres were relocated, shop structures were utterly transformed. One can scarcely avoid adopting a revolutionary model for what happened in Western Europe given the way printing shops sprang up in so many places in such a short time.

'Some inventions ... have taken centuries to be widely adopted and even more have taken several generations. Printing was an exception. It spread at a phenomenal speed ... and by the 1490s each of the major states had one important publishing centre and some had several.'[3] The replacement of hand-copying by printing as the chief mode of book production in Western Europe (we must underline chief to allow for the persistence of hand-copying) occurred in so many locations in such a brief interval that it simply has to be designated as a revolution even though semantic confusion may be engendered thereby.

For the term revolution is also often used – again by writers too busy to bother about theoretical models – to designate not a short-term sudden break but rather a prolonged cumulative irreversible process. This is the sense that governs references to the Industrial Revolution or to a 'demographic revolution'. This is the sense that led Raymond Williams to entitle his study of the growth of literacy, *The Long Revolution*,[4] and this sense also seems applicable to changes wrought by printing. Take for example the rate at which written materials have been accumulating since the fifteenth century. After five hundred years of printing, problems of overload have become more acute than they were a century ago, and it seems likely that they will weigh even more heavily on future generations than they do upon our own.

In this regard, the typographical revolution, which started in the fifteenth century, bears a close resemblance to the agricultural revolution which started in the eighteenth century. In both cases old problems of scarcity were solved; only to be replaced by new problems of glut. The ten farmers required to feed one townsman in the middle ages may be likened to the ten scribes required to furnish Chaucer's clerk of Oxford with the twenty books he wanted to fill his shelves.

During the millennia that intervened between the invention of writing and the introduction of printing in the West, it never took fewer than ten scribes to feed one clerk. The production, collection and circulation of books were subject to an economy of scarcity. Recovery and preservation were naturally of paramount concern. Within a century after the installation of printing shops in Western Europe, however, even while old texts reflecting problems of scarcity were becoming more available, a new economy of abundance also began to make its presence felt. A landmark in this process (which reversed earlier trends) is the bibliography compiled by Conrad Gesner and published by Christopher Froschauer in Zürich in 1545. Gesner's *Biblioteca Universalis* – his 'universal library' – excluded all vernacular publications but attempted to list all Latin, Greek and Hebrew printed works. Making use of booksellers' lists and publishers' catalogues, the author managed to track down roughly a third of actual output. Gesner's bibliography (which went through several editions and expanded with each one) was not only the first; it was also the last attempt to encompass the entire output of the Commonwealth of Learning within the confines of one work. New bibliographies issued thereafter multiplied at such a rate that bibliographies of bibliographies had to be compiled. When I was a student we were introduced to a list of bibliographies of bibliographies of bibliographies. The end of this somewhat regressive sequence is surely not yet in sight.

Mention of regress brings an additional complication to mind. Not all aspects of the 'long revolution' wrought by printing are equally irreversible and open-ended. There are signs in recent decades that some of the intellectual property rights which were a by-product of printing are beginning to be undermined. Thus commercial copy centres have begun to appear within the precincts of modern universities much as stationers' stalls did near medieval universities. In preparing assignments, teachers now have to weigh the disadvantages of infringing copyright against the advantage of making up special 'course packs'. These course packs bear some resemblance to the medieval *florilegia* which were compiled by teachers and preachers before authorship had acquired its modern form. Even while university libraries are taking on new functions as copy centres (with coins replacing writing materials), professors are beginning to acquire their own word processors which will enable them to bypass university presses and turn out justified copy in their homes. In short, we seem to be in the midst of yet another publishing revolution, one which may bring us closer to the medieval experience of everyman serving as his own scribe.

Before it acquired the modern meaning of irreversible change, the term 'revolution' had implied a circular movement associated with the rotation of the 'heavenly spheres'. Perhaps there is a certain symbolic significance in the current use of microfilm which entails a rotational movement as well as a turning from codex to roll. Even if such conjecture seems too fanciful, there is considerable evidence to suggest that, after five hundred years of printing, a cultural cycle is coming to an end. Having moved from scriptorium to printing shop, the duplication of written materials is now moving from printing shop to copy centres and to computers in the home.

Whatever the new turn of Fortune's Wheel may bring, it still seems likely that certain cultural features introduced by printing will persist. In particular, the necessity of coping with problems of overload will remain, however many copying devices may be installed. Indeed the introduction of new copiers and word processors will simply make current pressures more acute.

What has happened to the term revolution may be taken as an indication of the kinds of problems that are produced by the cumulative effects of print. For the term has itself been overloaded – made to bear the burden of three distinctively different models of change: circular movement, abrupt rupture, continuous development. Given the workings of print culture, any attempt to limit usage at this point is not only unlikely to succeed, but is also likely to be counterproductive; destined to add yet another item to the ever thickening bibliography which is filed under the problematic term. Some measure of semantic confusion appears to be inescapable. Still, whenever using the term, we ought to be as explicit as possible about which of several meanings we have in mind.

II THE PRINTED WORD AND POLITICAL REVOLUTION

Equally problematic, perhaps even more so, is the part played by printing in other revolutions experienced in the western world. In *The Printing*

Press as an Agent of Change,[5] special attention was paid to religious and scientific ramifications. Here we will turn to the political arena and consider possible connections between the advent of printing and those political upheavals which still come first to mind when the term 'revolution' is invoked. On this topic, as on many others relating to printing, guidance is hard to come by. It is true that many authorities comment on the explosion of printed materials which accompanied major upheavals. Most accounts of the seventeenth-century English Revolution, for example, pause over the sharply increased output which enabled the London bookseller, George Thomason, to collect some 22,000 separate items issued between 1640 and 1661. Students of the so-called Atlantic revolutions of the eighteenth century are similarly likely to comment on the sheer quantity of printed materials now deposited in archives.[6] The spurts of pamphleteering which marked the chief episodes of the American Revolution and accompanied the prelude to the French Revolution are still being carefully charted. The spectacular expansion of the French newspaper press (over 1,400 newspapers published in Paris alone between 1789 and 1799 are now deposited in French libraries)[7] constituted a quasi-revolution in itself. The change in quality was no less striking than the rise in quantity: 'All in all the step from the *Journal des Savants* ... to ... the *Ami du Peuple* is as big a step as any taken during the Revolution'.[8] Several recent monographs have been devoted to the structure and functioning of this revolutionary press and to the careers of revolutionary journalists. Counting and cataloguing the vast pamphlet literature has long been a minor industry. Content analysis of all printed materials (including almanacs, manifestos, engravings, and longer treatises) has of course always been the chief stock-in-trade of historians concerned with public opinion and ideological origins.

But on the more general revolutionary significance of resort to the printed word, few comments can be found. There is one instance, to be sure, where the fact of increased output is taken as a significant revolutionary syndrome:

> The revolutionary nature of the English Revolution is perhaps even more convincingly demonstrated by its words than by its deeds. The mere fact that it was such an extraordinarily wordy revolution – 22,000 pamphlets and newspapers were published between 1640 and 1661 – would by itself strongly suggest that this is something very different from the familiar protest against an unpopular government.[9]

But this sort of *aperçu* made in passing does not take us very far – save perhaps to raise the question of why a very wordy upheaval should be viewed as more revolutionary than a relatively laconic one. It appears in a volume entitled *Preconditions of Revolution in Early Modern Europe*.

The volume contains, we are told in the introduction, 'five authoritative' essays written to disclose 'the full range of conditions that generated political and social upheaval during the sixteenth and seventeenth centuries'.[10] The full range of conditions is discussed by the five essayists without yielding a single index entry on printing, printers or print.

Oddly enough, the most relevant recent studies have dealt with events that are somewhat tangential to the preconditions of any major revolution. They illuminate the part played by the printed word in both the 'Glorious Revolution' of 1688 and in English politics thereafter down through the development of 'an alternative structure of politics' under George III.[11] There is considerable evidence that English political agitation reverberated across the Channel. The Wilkite movement, in particular, probably influenced some of the French publicists such as Marat and Brissot, who were to become revolutionaries and who observed the English events at first hand. Nevertheless, political developments in Georgian England are only indirectly relevant to the revolution that broke out in Bourbon France. With regard to the latter, despite a huge literature, the unanswered questions all remain.

Just what did Lord Grenville mean when he remarked (in a parliamentary debate in 1817) that 'the press was the most powerful of agencies which produced the Revolution in France'?[12] Was Jacques Pierre Brissot simply blowing his own horn when he wrote – in a prospectus for his own forthcoming journal in 1789 – 'without journals and gazettes the American Revolution would never have occurred'?[13] Do any specific developments underlie such sweeping claims?

The claims themselves probably owed something to the long-lived association of printing with sedition – an association which was spelled out clearly in an oft-cited remark of William Berkeley, governor of the Virginia colony in the 1670s: 'I thank God there are no *free schools* nor *printing* ... *learning* has brought disobedience, heresy and sects into the world and *printing* has divulged them ...'[14]

Governor Berkeley's reference to heresy and sects reminds us that when printing was first linked with rebellion it was not so much against political as against religious authority. Early Protestants celebrated the 'divine art' as a God-given instrument which enabled Luther to succeed, where Hus had failed, in breaking with papal rule. Under Lutheran guidance defiance of popes was coupled with obedience to princes. But when the same celebratory theme was taken up later on by Puritans, it was aimed at ungodly monarchs as well as against popes. Even before the Stuart kings became targets of such attacks, Marian exiles linked the rule of Mary Tudor with that of the papal Anti-Christ while celebrating the God-given weapon that would root them both out.[15] In the course of the seventeenth-century struggle, however, the theme did acquire more radical democratic overtones: 'The Art of Printing will so spread knowledge, that the common people, knowing their own rights and liberties, will not be governed by way of oppression and so, by little and little, all Kingdomes will be like to Macaria ...'[16]

Similar connections between the diffusion of knowledge and the course of self-government were powerfully reasserted in 'the Age of the Democratic Revolution' by influential publicists such as Tom Paine:

> The opinions of men, with respect to government, are changing fast ... The revolutions of America and France have thrown a beam of light over the world ... when once the veil begins to rend, it admits not of repair.
>
> Ignorance is of a peculiar nature; once dispelled, it is impossible to reestablish it ...
>
> ... it has never yet been discovered how to make a man *unknow* his knowledge or *unthink* his thoughts.
>
> Mr Burke is laboring in vain to stop the progress of knowledge.[17]

Despite its scornful references to Burke's reliance on 'mouldy parchments' and on the 'manuscript assumed authority of the dead', *The Rights of Man* did not elaborate specifically on the part played by printing in 'rending the veil' and permanently dispelling ignorance. But Paine's closest friend and host in revolutionary Paris, Nicholas de Bonneville, did repeatedly celebrate the service to humanity rendered by the printer's art and, indeed, founded a publishing firm to serve humanity himself. The first paper the firm issued, *Le tribun du peuple*, invoked the letters of 'Junius'.[18] Probably its most important journal was *La feuille villageoise* which contained a remarkable paean to printing in an issue of 1792. Brissot's sweeping claim, cited above, fits in well with the views of his fellow members. Indeed it seems almost modest compared to claims made by other members of the *Cercle Social*:

> The importance of the press within the *Cercle Social* was no accident ... members saw the publisher as the most important, most heroic figure in history ... They saw Gutenberg's invention ... as the most important event in the history of mankind ... the printing press had virtually caused the Revolution ...[19]

Perhaps the most distinguished member of the *Cercle Social* was Condorcet who, of course, assigned printing a key position in his world historical scheme. It was fortunate, he wrote in setting the stage for his Eighth Period, that none of Gutenberg's contemporaries recognized the latent powers of the infant art; otherwise it would have been destroyed in the cradle before it had grown strong enough to fulfil its mission of unmasking priests and dethroning kings.[20]

But, although a conservative governor such as William Berkeley and a revolutionary philosopher such as Condorcet seemed to agree on the fundamentally subversive role of printing, this view has, by no means, commanded universal consent. Voltaire, for example, scoffed at the notion that printing had any real effect on the course of history. He argued that the Protestant victories owed more to the decisions made by the German princes than to all the printed treatises that the reformers penned. It was the sword not the pen which determined the fate of nations. 'From 5 to 6 thousand pamphlets have been printed in Holland against Louis XIV, none of which helped him lose the battles of Blenheim, Turin and Ramillies ...'[21]

To be sure, Voltaire had a vested interest in arguing that printed materials were innocuous and that therefore censors were wasting their time. Yet, many present-day historians, unconstrained by censorship, often take a similar stand. After all, it is argued, as a duplicating process, printing is simply a neutral instrument which could be wielded by either side in a given dispute. It was used just as effectively by Ignatius Loyola as by Martin Luther.[22] As was the case in religion, so too in politics. In the hands of royal ministers (such as Thomas Cromwell or Cardinal Richelieu), printing served the cause not of sedition but of strengthening absolutist royal claims:

> In France, the regency of Louis XIII saw the last meeting of the Estates General before 1789; it also saw the founding of the first royally sponsored newspaper in Europe. The replacement of the volatile assembly by the controlled weekly *gazette* is a concurrence symptomatic of the importance Cardinal Richelieu attached to print in his state-building objectives.[23]

The newly centralized monarchies, whether Protestant or Catholic, were determined to control the printing trades within the realm. They limited the number of licensed publishers and printers, discouraged provincial presses, and kept privileged firms under close supervision.

Yet even the most absolute monarchs found complete control of the printed word eluded their grasp. In France, the Estates General ceased to meet, but the *parlements* did not cease to issue printed remonstrances. On the contrary, 'through their remonstrances over the century they probably did more to imbue the reading public with the idea that the nation was a political entity above the king than any of the handful of writers who discussed such matters'.[24] Moreover, the weekly *Gazette*, the first royally sponsored newspaper in Europe, never did succeed in monopolizing the attention of French readers. For the realm was encircled by presses established just outside its borders: 'A fertile crescent of printing houses arched around France from Amsterdam to Avignon'.[25] From these foreign firms came French-language periodicals (such as the *Gazette de Leyde* or the *Gazette d'Avignon*) that were not royally sponsored – that were indeed edited by men who felt no special loyalty to the Bourbon king.

Special arrangements with postal officials and royal ministers, on the lookout for ways of planting stories, allowed these Francophone journals to circulate within the realm. They kept French subjects better informed on domestic as well as foreign issues than did the privileged royal *Gazette*.[26]

In absolutist theory, the king had a monopoly over the word. It was his duty to issue an *edit du silence* when public tranquillity was threatened by *la parole*. But the foreign Francophone press persisted in reprinting parliamentary remonstrances and conveying the sinister rumours as well as gory details which accompanied assassination attempts.[27]

We may agree with Voltaire that the foreign Francophone press was not responsible for Louis XIV losing the battles of the war of the Spanish Succession. But as Voltaire himself was surely fully aware, Francophone printing did play a significant role in tilting the balance against the Catholic and absolutist monarchy in the battle for men's minds. Officials charged with regulating the book trade were notoriously inconsistent and ambivalent about allowing a semi-legal traffic. Whatever happened to gray markets, moreover, black markets could never be brought fully under control. 'For a century from 1690 to 1790 the works of the most famous French writers were read in editions published outside France.'[28]

Thus, although dynastic rulers could indeed wield the new tool of printing to implement their policies, none of them achieved complete monopoly of the printed word and all had to reckon with the subversive effects of cosmopolitan trade networks that were outside their control. It was for the most part beyond the borders of well-consolidated realms that the main centres of the early modern printed book trade were located. The most far-flung networks were extended from the shelter provided by quasi-independent petty princes, town councils and the like. As long as they aimed their output at foreign markets, while enriching town coffers, master printers and merchant publishers who established firms in small principalities and city-states could count on local officials to let them have a relatively free hand. These entrepreneurs who 'voted with their feet' and set up shop beyond the reach of powerful kings and popes, were 'neutral' in the sense that they were willing to hunt with Catholic hounds and run with Protestant hares; they accepted commissions from any quarter which promised a profitable return. But this kind of neutrality had subversive implications in so far as it indicated indifference to the claims of any one religious creed or dynastic cause.

As I have argued elsewhere, such 'neutral' operations sometimes entailed covert support for advocates of heterodoxy and toleration. Indeed, printers, publishers and booksellers figure prominently in early modern subversive sects and secret societies. The important part played by the Antwerp printer Christopher Plantin in a sixteenth-century heterodox sect, the 'Family of Love', has been explored in several accounts.[29] In her recent study, *The Radical Enlightenment*, Margaret Jacob assigns a pivotal role to a libertine coterie of publishers, editors, engravers and booksellers who met in the Hague in the early eighteenth century and called themselves 'Knights of Jubilation'. The Knights' secretary, Prosper Marchand, had been a Paris publisher before his conversion to Protestantism. He served as editor, author and literary agent after leaving France for the Hague.[30] According to Jacob, Marchand and his associates were responsible for producing some of the most celebrated of those clandestine manuscripts which scandalized and titillated literary circles in *ancien régime* France.[31] They concocted some, had copies made of others and took care to publicize all by printing tantalizing items in their literary reviews.[32] Circulation of hand-copied books is sometimes regarded as being incompatible with resort to the printed word. Yet, as is shown by this example, the two could work together – to the disadvantage of censors and officials.[33]

Unlike Marchand and his associates, who exploited printed publicity quite deliberately, the Catholic officials who compiled lists of prohibited books to be placed on the Index acted unwittingly to supply Protestant publishers with free publicity. From the viewpoint of Catholic officialdom, the operations of free-wheeling merchant publishers were far from neutral and seemed designed to serve the enemies of the Roman Church. To place a title on the Index was to provide Protestant firms with a list of profit-making titles and free advertising while alerting potential Catholic purchasers to the existence of forbidden fruit.[34]

The drive to tap new markets, which differentiated the profit-seeking printer from the manuscript book dealer was not neutral with regard to censorship. It also worked against elitism and favoured democratic as well as heterodox trends. Printers reinforced opposition to theologians and priests who veiled gospel truths and sought to withhold sacred truths from the profane. Authors and translators were encouraged to write for 'ten thousand laymen' instead of 'ten able clerks'. During the Commonwealth, the London College of Physicians was accused of being papist because it resisted the use of vernaculars in medical literature.

The assault on Latin-writing professional elites did not always stop short of an assault on political elites. Indeed the two motifs were combined by both English and French revolutionaries. The Englishing of law books had been defended on patriotic grounds under the early Tudors by the versatile law printer, John Rastell. The same cause acquired political overtones in John Lilburne's *England's Birth-Right Justified* (1645) which argued that the law of the land should no longer be hidden in Latin and Old French but should be in English so that 'every Free-man may reade it as well as the lawyers'.[35]

Latin was less of an issue in pre-revolutionary France. By the mid-eighteenth century the triumph of the vernaculars had been assured. The cosmopolitan language favoured by the Republic of Letters was no longer Latin but French. In the eighteenth century, when Locke and Newton were much admired, French translators who knew English (as did Diderot) were especially likely to be in demand. But of course under the *ancien régime* cultural elitism still prevailed. Professional monopolies, privileged guilds and corporations, royal societies and academies provided innumerable targets for frustrated writers to attack: 'It may have been appropriate for a corporate society to organize its culture corporately, but such archaic organization constrained the expansive forces that might have ... supported more of the overpopulated underworld of letters'.[36] Protests against one privileged institution or another eventually merged into a general assault against privilege of every kind.

In addition to working against elitism, the printer's interest in reaching wide markets also encouraged a more respectful, even deferential, approach to the 'public' at large. From the vantage point of editors and publishers of atlases, encyclopedias and other reference works, the 'public' consisted, not of a howling mob, or a many-headed monster, but rather of potential subscribers and purchasers whose favours were to be solicited and patronage sought. Readers were invited to aid learned authors by sending in letters to editors or actual specimens and seeds.[37] As with large reference works, so too with the periodical press:

> I entreat the assistance of all those who wish well to the progress of learning and beg they will favour me ... with extracts of curious books with such original pieces and accounts of new inventions and machines and any other improvements ... as are fit to be communicated to the public. In which case I shall either mention their names or observe a religious silence as they shall desire.[38]

The citation comes from the first issue (January 1728) of *The Present State of the Republick of Letters*, an English journal which was imitating its more celebrated French precursor. In his *Nouvelles de la République des Lettres*, Pierre Bayle had been no less assiduous in soliciting the opinions of his readers.[39] Such journals not only extended lifelines to isolated subscribers (as Norman Fiering has shown in his interesting account of subscribers in the Thirteen Colonies);[40] they also conveyed a new sense of forward movement to their readership as a whole. Scattered correspondents could feel that they were actively contributing to the advancement of learning.

By means of letters to the editor and other devices, the periodical press opened up a new kind of public forum (described by Jürgen Habermas as a public 'space' or public 'sphere') which invited participation from interested readers and involved them in issues of more than local concern.[41]

> It is in the last third of the 18th century that a public opinion as such took form and indeed the very expression 'public opinion' dates in several languages from this time. It consisted in groups of people habitually interested in public events, subscribing as individuals or in clubs to newspapers and magazines ...[42]

Reading clubs and corresponding societies, membership in lending libraries, informal gatherings in bookshops created new networks of associations which had no fixed numbers of members and, in the case of informal gatherings, no membership rosters at all. One was invited to join the company of Mr Spectator and his fellow clubmen, without presenting any credentials. Unlike royal societies and provincial academies, the letters-to-editors column was open to all – to all who could read and write that is – and had access to relevant journals.

Of course such access was relatively restricted in the age of the hand-press. Mr Spectator's club, however, open to the casual reader in the coffee house, remained closed to the inhabitants of Gin Lane. Figures on literacy rates and journal circulation did not rise dramatically until after the industrialization of papermaking and printing processes. Early modern print culture encouraged vernacular translation and popularization but stopped short of mobilizing the vast majority of Europeans. 'Mass' culture was still largely oral culture before iron presses were harnessed to steam. Indeed, one might argue that the first three centuries of printing did more to increase than diminish the gap between a preliterate folk and a literate laity. Access to periodical reviews and updated reference guides encouraged readers to feel ever more superior not only to 'ignorant' and 'superstitious' forbears but also to those of their contemporaries who still relied on hearsay to keep themselves informed. Contempt for the superstitious rabble was, however, coupled with admiration for the self-made man. And it can scarcely be denied that many new opportunities for self help were extended by the printed word. By the eighteenth century, thanks to Joseph Moxon's *Mechanick Exercises* one could even teach oneself to print.[43]

The age of the hand-press was the first great age of the autodidact – and of the self-appointed tribune of the people who could address a vast public from afar:

> From his pitiful earnings as stay-maker and exciseman, Tom Paine purchased books and ... a pair of globes ... He continued his process of self-education throughout his life convinced that 'every person of learning is finally his own teacher' ... Arriving in America armed with Franklin's letter Paine speedily obtained employment with Robert Aiken, a Philadelphia printer.[44]

As the newly made editor of the *Pennsylvania Magazine*, which Aiken had started with little success, Paine turned the journal around. By March 1775 he wrote joyfully to Franklin that the number of subscribers was 'daily increasing'.[45] Political independence and increased circulation were indeed the chief leit-motifs of Paine's career. Part 2 of his *Rights of Man* had a phenomenal success, partly because its author ploughed back his royalties into furthering circulation of a cheap edition.[46] Thanks to joint subscription the work became a 'foundation-text of the English working class'.[47] The *London Corresponding Society*, which did so much to popularize Paine's work, made a point of not limiting its membership. 'That the number of our members be unlimited ... Today we might pass over such a rule as a commonplace: and yet it is one of the hinges upon which history turns. It signified the end to any notion of exclusiveness, of politics as the preserve of any hereditary *elite* or property group ...'[48]

To be sure, the *London Corresponding Society* was a most unusual corresponding society and was formed only after the French Revolution was already under way. But even in France under the *ancien régime*, opportunities to obtain books and journals were increasingly being extended to self-made men. According to François Noel Babeuf, 'his father was barely able to read and write'. He was himself 'driven by the curious mixture of confidence and insecurity which belongs to the self-made and self-taught'.[49] He could hardly aspire to join the polite literary salon in the small town of Roye where he worked. Nor was he ever admitted to full membership in the academy of Arras. But he did manage to get himself enrolled as a regular corresponding member of the provincial academy, which entitled him to receive weekly circulars and summaries of the proceedings. In the course of seeking to publish some brochures, he also made contact with a Noyon printer and bookseller who supplied him with books, pamphlets and tracts, put him in touch with Parisian journalists and introduced him to the radical underground.[50]

Political mobilization by means of the printed word was common to radical movements on both sides of the Channel. But the 'alternative structure of politics' surfaced much more abruptly and explosively in the Bourbon realm. Whereas the Wilkite agitation succeeded eventually in securing one seat in parliament for John Wilkes, the events of 1788–9 propelled into a National Assembly hundreds of men who had never held office before. Whereas 'Junius' could fill newspaper columns with savage political commentary only by hiding his real identity in order to escape prosecution, his French admirers were not only enabled to use their own names, but also obtained political power thereby. Thus Mirabeau and Sieyès were singled out as leaders of the Third Estate largely because 'in a group of men who did not yet know each other, the authorship of a famous pamphlet was enough to make a man known'.[51]

To a greater degree than is often appreciated, the events of 1788–9 themselves hinged on a seemingly inadvertent suspension of governmental controls over the printed word. On 5 July 1788 a royal council decree not only announced that there would be a future convocation of an Estates General but also invited all Frenchmen to make known their opinions on the appropriate rules to be followed:

His Majesty will always try to adopt the forms used in the past, but when they cannot be determined he wishes to supplant the silence of the ancient monuments by asking, before making any decision, the will of his subjects ...[52]

According to Georges Lefebvre, Louis XVI had not 'intended to grant freedom of the press' by this decree but was simply following a traditional procedure by inviting his subjects to express their views. The result was 'an outpouring of pamphlets that astonished contemporaries'[53] but apparently left royal ministers unperturbed, for in early September an amnesty was granted to all booksellers, peddlers, and merchants previously arrested and imprisoned for distributing tracts opposing ministerial practices. At the same time, the several Parisian societies known as 'clubs', which had been closed since August 1787, were allowed to reopen their doors.[54] According to Egret, these seemingly incautious measures were undertaken in the service of a traditional royal strategy. Intent on quelling the resistance of nobles and clergy, the Crown was turning to the Third Estate for support.[55]

What occurred thereafter was not part of any traditional strategy. Indeed it had no precedent in the annals of French statecraft and thus can be described as the point where revolution broke out.[56] It entailed a successful campaign to reverse the *parlement*'s decision (announced on 25 September 1788) that the Estates General should be constituted in accordance with the precedent of 1614. It took the form of an orchestrated protest movement aimed at securing double representation for the Third Estate. This was the first large-scale movement generated by the prolonged governmental crisis which came from no duly constituted bodies but seemed rather to emanate from the 'public' at large. 'A clamour arose from one end of the kingdom to the other'[57] on behalf of doubling the Third. What distinguished this protest movement from all previous seditions, rebellions and insurrections was that discontented groups from all parts of France reacted almost immediately to a single ruling and did so by insisting on a single demand. This was all the more remarkable considering that there was as yet no one representative body that could provide central organization for the diverse provinces of the large realm. In short, the 1788 protest movement was of particular historical significance because of the synchronization and simultaneity which it entailed. These features owed much to the use of printed materials by members of the re-established clubs. They were responsible for publishing and distributing 'the most famous pamphlets' and for establishing 'liaison with the provinces'. Their self-proclaimed goals were 'to spread simultaneity of ideas and to prepare simultaneity of aims and forces'.[58]

Not only in shaping this successful protest movement, but also in the electioneering that ensued, the leaders of the so-called 'Patriot Party' proved to be much more skilful than any of their opponents in taking full advantage of the printed word. Nor is this altogether surprising, given the composition of the party leadership, which featured men of letters alongside liberal nobles and financiers.

'What the orators of Rome and Athens were, in the midst of a people *assembled*', said Malesherbes in an address of 1775, 'men of letters are in the midst of a *dispersed* people'.[59] To be 'in the *midst* of a *dispersed* people ...' is a paradox worth pondering, for it suggests how the shift in communications changed the character of participation in public affairs. The wide distribution of identical bits of information provided an impersonal link between compatriots who were unknown to each other but who could be simultaneously mobilized on behalf of a given cause.

The long-lived contrast between the contemplative life (of the solitary philosopher) and the active life (of the orator in the market place) also became increasingly less pertinent, once solitary thinkers could make contact with crowds. Demagogues no longer required powerful lungs. If they were skilled as polemicists, they might stammer or whisper and still could be heard. Unlike Mirabeau, Abbé Sieyès had a voice that didn't carry. It was the power of his pen that made the latter chief spokesman for the Third Estate and ultimately a senator of France. This is not the place to pause over the leading roles played in the French Revolution by Brissot, Hébert, Marat, Desmoulins, St Just, Babeuf and the rest. Suffice it to note that by 1848, the staffs of two journals took over the government of France. The story of the rise of the 'Fourth Estate' to political power, however, still remains to be told.

Now the very term, 'Fourth Estate', is suggestive,[60] because it comes as afterthought – as an appendage tacked onto the traditional Three Estates: oratores, bellatores, laboratores; the Lords Spiritual; the Lords Temporal; and the Commons. It points to an occupational group which – unlike the burgher or bourgeois – did not exist in the age of scribes; an occupational group which came into existence only after the advent of printing. Those who harnessed their pens to the new power of the press were drawn from all three traditional estates. Indeed, members of the old teaching and preaching orders were more likely to become publicists than were the new merchants and manufacturers who represented the so-called rising bourgeoisie.

In 1789, the fall of the Bastille held special significance for all who were associated with this new occupational culture. Over eight hundred authors, printers, booksellers, print dealers had been incarcerated there between 1600 and 1756.[61] Its image as a dreadful symbol of royal tyranny had been built up by publicists who themselves had been '*embastillé*'. 'The métier of Aretino has always been risky', commented Grimm when Simon Nicholas Henri Linguet was thrown into the Bastille in 1780.[62] Even now, tour guides at the place de la Bastille, like many historians, dwell on the irony of expending so much effort to storm a fortress which contained so few prisoners and none of them worthy of being liberated. But to those who followed the métier of Aretino – and they were the same men who harangued the crowds assembled at the Palais Royal on the afternoon of July 12 – the aim of completely destroying the Bastille was not anomalous at all. The crowds who stormed the fortress seeking gunpowder may have seen cannon trained on crowded quarters and thought about toll-barriers and bread prices. To the pamphleteers who hailed its fall, it appeared as a symbol of a different sort of tyranny.

The meaning of its capture continued to be amplified, long after the First Republic had come to an end, by later generations of revolutionaries and by counter-revolutionaries as well. Indeed, the conspiratorial legends that have been woven around masonic lodges and the French Revolution could themselves be better understood by making more allowance for the effects of the printed word.[63] Such legends are more often propelled than dispelled by efforts that stop short with disproof. Bibliographies grow thicker and the atmosphere more charged as sceptics and true believers fail alike to convince each other.[64] The possibility that political activities were affected by the workings of the printed-book trade is a point that both parties tend to ignore and that the sceptics, at least, should be persuaded to explore. Most of them agree that pens do poison the atmosphere when they are used to accuse Protestants or Papists, Freemasons or Jacobins, Jesuits, Jews or Bolsheviks of sinister plots. If this is true, then it would seem unwise to discount the power of pens – at least when they are harnessed to the power of the press. At the very least a closer look at the changes wrought by printing would help us understand how earlier views of conspiracy – pertaining to assassination plots or to rabble rousers hired by seditious factions – gave way to the more awesome image of a vast network, controlled from secret headquarters that set men to do its bidding from afar.

NOTES

1 Nicolas Barker, 'The invention of printing: revolution within revolution', *The Quarterly Journal of the Library of Congress*, 35 (1978), pp. 64–77.
2 Robin Briggs, 'The triumph of the press', *Times Literary Supplement*, 20 April 1984, p. 435.
3 Denys Hay, Introduction, *Printing and the Mind of Man*, ed. J. W. Carter and P. H. Muir (London, 1967), p. xxii.
4 Raymond Williams, *The Long Revolution* (New York, 1966).
5 E. L. Eisenstein, *The Printing Press as an Agent of Change* (Cambridge, 1979), 2 vols. (2 vols in one, 1981).
6 J. M. Thompson, *The French Revolution* (New York, 1945), p. 14, comments on the 48,000 items collected by the indefatigable Croker which now fill five hundred shelves in the British Museum.
7 Jack R. Censer, *Prelude to Power: The Parisian Radical Press 1789–1791* (Baltimore, 1976), p. 8.
8 Crane Brinton, *A Decade of Revolution 1789–1799* (*Rise of Modern Europe*, ed. W. Langer) (New York, 1934), p. 149.
9 Lawrence Stone, 'The English Revolution', *Preconditions of Revolution in Early Modern Europe*, ed. Robert Forster and Jack P. Greene, Johns Hopkins Symposia in History (Baltimore, 1970), pp. 55–109, p. 58.
10 Introduction by editors, *Preconditions*, p. 1.
11 Lois G. Schwoerer, 'Propaganda in the revolution of 1688–89', *American Historical Review*, 82/4 (Oct. 1977), pp. 843–74. 'Press and parliament in the revolution of 1689', *The Historical Journal*, 20/3 (1977), pp. 545–67. John Brewer, *Party Ideology and Popular Politics at the Accession of George III* (Cambridge, 1976), chs. 8 and 11. See also Robert R. Rea, *The English Press in Politics 1760–1774* (Lincoln, Neb., 1963).
12 Cited by Arthur Aspinall, *Politics and the Press c. 1780–1850* (London, 1949), p. 1.
13 Prospectus for *Le patriote français*, April 1789. Cited by L. Eugène Hatin, *Bibliographie historique et critique de la presse périodique française* ... (Paris, 1866), p. 142.
14 Cited in many works. This version (taken from Hening's *Statutes*) is in *Printing and Society in Early America*, ed. William L. Joyce, David D. Hall, Richard D. Brown, and John B. Hench (Worcester, 1983), p. 140.
15 For pertinent discussion, citations and references see Eisenstein, *The Printing Press as an Agent of Change*, pp. 304–5.
16 Gabriel Plattes, 'A description of the famous kingdom of Macaria' (1641), in Charles Webster, *Samuel Hartlib and the Advancement of Learning* (Cambridge, 1970), pp. 78–90. See first and last para., p. 89.
17 Thomas Paine, *Rights of Man*, introd. by Philip S. Foner (Secaucus, NJ, 1974), p. 124.
18 Maurice Tourneux, *Bibliographie de l'histoire de Paris pendant la révolution française* (Paris, 1894), 2, ch. 8, Item 10199, p. 501.
19 Gary Kates, 'Le Cercle Social: French intellectuals in the French Revolution', unpublished Ph.D. dissertation, University of Chicago, 1978, p. 136. A long, pertinent citation given in full by Kates, from Jacques Boileau's article, 'De l'imprimerie', *Feuille villageoise*, 4 Oct. 1792, pp. 605–9, is summarized in Kates's recently published book: *The Cercle Social, the Girondins and the*

French Revolution (Princeton, 1985), p. 180. Similar praise for Gutenberg's invention is given by Abbé Sieyès in his 'Report on the liberty of the press', delivered to the Constituent Assembly on Wed. 20 Jan. 1791, *Gazette national ou Moniteur universel*, 22–3 Jan. 1790, *Réimpression de L'Ancien Moniteur* (Paris, 1860), 3, pp. 185–7.

20 Condorcet, *Esquisse d'un tableau historique des progrès de l'esprit humain*, 2nd ed. (Paris, 1866), p. 177.

21 Voltaire, 'Liberty of the press'. Excerpts from Voltaire's *Philosophical Dictionary*, trans. from French by H. I. Woolf in *The Portable Age of Reason Reader*, ed. Crane Brinton (New York, 1956), p. 274.

22 See e.g. H. O. Evennett, *The Spirit of the Counter Reformation*, ed. John Bossy (Cambridge, 1968), p. 25.

23 Joseph Klaits, *Printed Propaganda under Louis XIV* (Princeton, 1976), pp. 6–7.

24 William Doyle, *Origins of the French Revolution* (Oxford, 1980), p. 91.

25 Robert Darnton, 'Sounding the literary market in prerevolutionary France', *Eighteenth Century Studies* (special issue ed. Raymond Birn) (Summer 1984), 2/4, pp. 477–92.

26 J. Lojek, 'Gazettes internationales de langue française ...', *Modèles et moyens de la réflexion politique au XVIIIe siècle*, ed. Pierre Deyon (Lille, 1977), 1, pp. 369–81. René Moulinas, *L'imprimerie La librairie et la presse à Avignon au XVIIIe siècle (Grenoble, 1974).*

27 Pierre Rétat, ed., *L'attentat de Damiens. Discours sur l'événement au XVIIIe siècle* (Lyons, 1979), pp. 156–8.

28 Lucien Febvre and Henri-Jean Martin, *L'apparition du livre* (Paris, 1958), p. 278.

29 Alastair Hamilton, *The Family of Love* (Cambridge, 1981) and B. Rekers, *Benito Arias Montano 1527–1598* (London and Leiden, 1972) are the two most recent accounts.

30 Margaret C. Jacob, *The Radical Enlightenment: Pantheists, Freemasons and Republicans* (London, 1981). On Marchand, see also C. Berkvens-Stevelinck, *Prosper Marchand et l'histoire du livre* (Bruges, 1978). For a debate over the political radicalism and Masonic character of the 'Knights', upheld by Jacob and queried by Berkvens-Stevelinck, see *Quaerendo*, 13 (1983), pp. 50–73, 124–48; 14 (1984), pp. 63–76.

31 See Ira O. Wade, *The Clandestine Organization and Diffusion of Philosophic Ideas in France from 1700 to 1750* (Princeton, 1938) for an account of relevant manuscripts.

32 See, for example, article: 'Impostoribus', in Prosper Marchand's *Dictionnaire historique ou mémoires critiques et littéraires concernant la vie et les ouvrages de divers personnages ... dans la République des Lettres*, 2 vols. (The Hague, 1758), vol. 1, pp. 312–29.

33 Another example of how the printed word contributed to the clandestine manuscript trade is described by François Moureau, '*Les mémoires secrets* de Bachaumont, *Le courier du Bas Rhin* et les *bulletinistes* parisiens', *L'année 1768 à travers la presse traité par ordinateur*, ed. Jean Varloot and Paule Jensen (Paris, 1981), pp. 58–80.

34 Eisenstein, *Printing Press*, pp. 415–20; 442–7.

35 *Ibid.*, pp. 360–2.

36 Robert Darnton, *The Literary Underground of the Old Regime* (Cambridge,

Mass., 1982), p. 21. When Darnton asserts that the Paris 'Grub Street had no exit', he ignores the 'fertile crescent' he himself mentions elsewhere, as noted above (n. 25). Escape routes to England, Holland, Switzerland, etc., were taken by many so-called 'Grub Street' inhabitants.

37 Eisenstein, *Printing Press*, pp. 109–11, 487–8.

38 *The Present State of the Republick of Letters*, 6 vols. (London, Printed for William and John Innys at the West End of St Paul's, 1728), 1, Preface.

39 On Bayle's persistence in soliciting readers' views, see Elizabeth Labrousse, 'Les coulisses du journal de Bayle', *Pierre Bayle: le philosophe de Rotterdam*, ed. Paul Dibon (Paris, 1959), p. 105.

40 Norman S. Fiering, 'The Transatlantic Republic of Letters: a note on the circulation of learned periodicals to early eighteenth century America', *William and Mary Quarterly*, 33 (1976), pp. 642–60.

41 Jürgen Habermas, *L'espace public*, trans. Marc B. de Launay, from *Strukturwandel der Offentlichkeit*, 1962 (Paris, 1978).

42 R. R. Palmer, *The Age of the Democratic Revolution*, 2 vols., (Princeton, 1959), 1, p. 243.

43 For discussion of self-help and teach-yourself manuals, see Eisenstein, *Printing Press*, pp. 243–7. The use of Moxon is described on p. 154 in a citation from a pertinent article by Calhoun Winton, 'Richard Steele, journalist – and journalism', *Newsletters to Newspapers: Eighteenth Century Journalism*, ed. D. H. Bond and W. R. McLeod (Morgantown, West Virginia, 1977), pp. 21–30.

44 Philip Foner, Introduction to Thomas Paine, *Rights of Man*, p. 7.

45 *Ibid.*, p. 9.

46 *Ibid.*, p. 28. The incredible figure (which is often given) of 1,500,000 copies for the total circulation within the British Isles of Part 2 up to Paine's death is discussed and queried by Richard Altick, *The English Common Reader: A Social History of the Mass Reading Public 1800–1900* (Chicago, 1957), pp. 70–1. Altick, however, notes that all evidence points to a huge circulation and calls attention to the important part played in boosting figures by radical bookshops and provincial printers as well as the publicity that resulted from the government's prosecution on the charge of seditious libel.

47 Edward P. Thompson, *The Making of the English Working Class* (New York, 1963), p. 90.

48 *Ibid.*, p. 21.

49 Robert Barrie Rose, *Gracchus Babeuf* (Stanford, 1978), pp. 12, 19–21.

50 *Ibid.*, p. 44.

51 Palmer, *Age of the Democratic Revolution*, 1, p. 480.

52 Cited from Royal Council decree of 5 July 1788 by Jean Egret, *The French Prerevolution 1787–1788*, trans. W. D. Camp (Chicago, 1977), p. 180.

53 Georges Lefebvre, *The Coming of the French Revolution*, trans. R. R. Palmer (Princeton, 1947), p. 54.

54 Egret, *Prerevolution*, p. 190. It should be noted that two different ministers were involved in these events. Brienne, who was responsible for the convocation decree of 5 July, was replaced by Necker, who arranged for the release of booksellers and reappearance of the clubs.

55 *Ibid.*, p. 179.

56 For detailed discussion, see E. L. Eisenstein, 'Who intervened in 1788? A commentary on *The Coming of the French Revolution*', *American Historical Review* (Oct. 1965), 71/1, pp. 77–103.

57 Lefebvre, *Coming of the French Revolution*, p. 51.
58 Egret, *Prerevolution*, p. 193.
59 Cited from Malesherbes's acceptance speech to the French Academy (1775) in *Correspondance littéraire philosophique et politique de Grimm, Diderot, Raynal, Meister, etc.* ..., ed. Maurice Tourneux (Paris, 1879), 11, p. 36.
60 For critical discussion of the term as a self-serving, largely mythic construct, see George Boyce, 'The Fourth Estate: the Reappraisal of a Concept', *Newspaper History from the 17th Century to the Present*, ed. G. Boyce *et al.* (London, 1978), pp. 19–41. Boyce's discussion is restricted to English developments, however, and the construct may well be more pertinent to France.
61 David Pottinger, *The French Book Trade in the Ancien Régime 1500–1791* (Cambridge, Mass. 1958), p. 79.
62 Cited by Louis Trénard, 'La presse française des origines à 1788', *Histoire générale de la presse française*, ed. C. Bellanger, *et al.*, 4 vols. (Paris, 1974), 1, p. 280. On Pietro Aretino as 'father of journalism' (and of pornography and blackmail by means of print) see Eisenstein, *Printing Press*, p. 228.
63 J. M. Roberts, *The Mythology of the Secret Societies* (New York, 1972), provides a survey of the literature from a sceptical, liberal viewpoint. Some of the limits of this approach are noted in my review of Roberts's book, *American Historical Review*, 78 (October 1973), pp. 1049–50.
64 A cogent example is Norman Cohn's *Warrant for Genocide* (New York, 1966) which deals with the concocted 'Protocols of the Elders of Zion'. The work ends with useful insights but it also unwisely duplicates lurid tales and vicious cartoons which keep the old virus in circulation and may even revive some dormant strains. It was, incidentally, a satire on Napoleon III's regime as 'journalism incarnate' which provided a model for the Protocols. David Kulstein, 'Government propaganda and the press during the Second Empire', *Gazette: International Journal for Mass Communications Studies*, 10 (1964), pp. 125–44.

10

Revolution in popular culture

PETER BURKE

So far as studies of cultural history are concerned, the concept of 'revolution' has been somewhat peripheral, employed for the most part as little more than a synonym for 'watershed' or 'turning-point'. In spite – or because – of events in China in 1966, the phrase 'cultural revolution' has found little favour with historians.[1] All the same, the problems of change and continuity have been discussed in a lively and interesting way with reference to popular culture since its discovery by historians some twenty years ago. It may be useful to distinguish three approaches to the subject, three traditions of analysis which started out from very different premises, even if they have since come to merge, or at least to penetrate one another. The first of these traditions emphasizes the media through which popular culture has been transmitted; the second, the society in which it has been transmitted; and the third, the history of that transmission over the long term.

I THE MEDIA AND THE CRITICS

The twentieth century has witnessed many denunciations of popular culture, or, as it was more commonly known from the 1930s to the 1960s, 'mass culture'.[2] These denunciations, which generally came from literary critics, such as F. R. Leavis, rested on a simple view of historical development, whether or not this view was made explicit. The past was presented as a Golden Age, the age of the 'organic community' and of 'folk art'. As one critic put it, 'Folk Art grew from below', while 'Mass Culture is imposed from above'; it is 'an article for mass consumption, like chewing gum'.[3] The new 'mass art', said another, provides 'invitations to a candy-floss world' and 'sex in shiny packets', in place of the old order's 'real world of people'.[4] 'Much of what applies to the production of goods', a third critic declared, 'is true also of the mass media ... Quantity becomes more important than quality ... What is presented must be "safe", unprovocative and generally acceptable. Individual preferences are ignored, because mass-production pays best when millions of copies of a few designs are turned out rather than fewer copies of more designs.'[5]

These denunciations, of which it would be easy to multiply examples, were often perceptive, but they were (ironically enough, given their stress on the need to discriminate) themselves somewhat undiscriminating. That they did not distinguish between one journal and another, or one television programme and another was inevitable, given their assumptions about 'mass-production', a term which is partly, and dangerously metaphorical. A more weighty objection to the 'cultural critics', a convenient name for a group which includes F. R. Leavis, Richard Hoggart and Denys Thompson, is their failure to distinguish sufficiently sharply either between media or between periods.

A greater concern with the characteristics of specific media was shown by students of 'mass communications' across the Atlantic, who noted, for example, that radio was more effective in communicating than print because 'the listener gets a sense of personal access from the radio'.[6] Radio is a 'hot' medium, as the Canadian critic Marshall McLuhan liked to say, contrasting it not only with print but also with what he called the 'cool' medium of television.[7]

A still more serious criticism of the critics mentioned so far, British and American, is that they lacked a sufficiently acute sense of history. When was the Golden Age of folk art? When did the iron age of mass culture begin? Was the transition from one to the other a gradual one, or was it 'revolutionary'? Answers differed, and they were all too rarely supported by historical evidence in any detail. For McLuhan, for example, the important changes were both sudden and sharp. Television, he wrote, was 'as revolutionary a medium in America in the 1950s as radio in Europe in the 1930s', and this electric age was clearly distinct from 'the mechanical age now receding'.[8] For Richard Hoggart, concerned with the north of England rather than with McLuhan's 'global village', the important changes took place '30 or 40 years' before he wrote, beginning, in other words, about the time of his birth at the end of the First World War.[9] Other students of English culture have emphasized what has been called the 'Northcliffe Revolution', the rise of the popular press in the late nineteenth century (the *Daily Mail* was founded in 1896). Raymond Williams, on the other hand, a cultural critic with a more acute sense of history than most, has pointed out that the British popular press goes back further than 1896, indeed beyond the compulsory schooling imposed by the Education Act of 1870. According to him, this popular press began with the Sunday papers of the early nineteenth cetury, such as the *News of the World*, founded in 1843.[10] For Williams, a Marxist of a somewhat nonconforming kind, this date is no accident. He thinks in terms of a single revolution, with three main aspects ('democratic' and 'industrial' as well as cultural), although he admits that the process was spread out over a protracted period, a 'Long Revolution'.

Since the popular press in Britain goes back to the early nineteenth century, while the Sunday school, which provoked his comment, is still older, it is not difficult to appreciate Edward Thompson's complaint that modern critics of the media 'have matters out of proportion' because they 'overlook the extent and character of mass indoctrination in earlier periods'.[11] Even the criticisms of mass culture are part of a longer tradition than those who voice them generally realize. In a broad sense they go back to Plato (even if he was thinking in terms of the face-to-face community of the classical city-state); but even in a precise sense these criticisms are not exactly new. Although the term 'mass' was at the height of its vogue in the middle years of the twentieth century, the *Revolt of the Masses*, by the Spanish critic Jose Ortega y Gasset, was published in 1930, and Freud's *Mass Psychology and the Analysis of the Ego* (bowdlerized in its English translation as 'Group Psychology') in 1921. In the middle of the nineteenth century the phenomenon of mass culture had been analysed by Alexis de Tocqueville and also by Matthew Arnold, who once wrote that 'Plenty of people will try to give the masses, as they call them an intellectual food prepared and adapted in the way they think proper for the actual condition of the masses. The ordinary popular literature is an example of this way of working on the masses...'[12]

Once again we find ourselves driven back to the early nineteenth century, the age of the early Industrial Revolution. Could the rise of mass culture be the result of that revolution? The question is a reminder of one more weakness in the media-based approach, a weakness neatly exposed by the Polish sociologist Zygmunt Bauman. Bauman has drawn attention to the circularity of the common assumption that 'the media of mass communication are the parent of mass culture', while on the other hand 'mass culture is the parent of the mass comunication media'. His trenchant comment is that 'For culture to become "mass", it is not enough to set up a television station. Something must first happen to social structure. Mass culture is in a way a superstructure resting upon what we shall tentatively call "mass social structure".'[13]

II THE MARXISTS AND POPULAR CULTURE

Bauman's formulation introduces us directly to the Marxist approach to the history of popular culture. Oddly enough, the works of Marx and Engels do not. They simply did not take popular culture seriously. Marx contemptuously dismissed what he called the 'idiocy of rural life', while Engels described the attitudes of English workers before the rise of Chartism in terms so simplistic they now seem quite incredible. The workers were, he wrote, intellectually 'dead'. 'They could rarely read and still more rarely write; went regularly to church, never talked politics, never conspired, never thought, delighted in physical exercises, listened with inherited reverence when the Bible was read, and were, in their unquestioning humility, exceedingly well-disposed towards the "superior" classes.'[14] These attitudes gave way to class-consciousness, according to both Marx and Engels, when industrialization led (as it had to lead) to changes in the relation of production and made the workers into a 'proletariat', ready to take part in a political revolution. And afterwards? The question became a practical one only after 1917, and when it did, the Russian communists were divided. Some of them believed that political revolution would lead naturally to cultural revolution and that the proletariat would spontaneously develop a culture of its own, which they called *Proletkult.* Trotsky, however, argued that the proletariat, uneducated as it is, 'cannot create a culture of its own'. Culture would be brought to the people by means of education. In this respect, Trotsky sounds like almost any middle-class intellectual of the nineteenth century (even if his ideas on the kind of culture to be taken to the people were unlike most of theirs).[15]

Trotsky's argument implies that culture will not change automatically when society changes, in other words that culture is not a mere reflection of social forces, as Marx and Engels seemed on occasion to have suggested. This 'reflection' view of culture was challenged in a more direct and explicit manner by some German Marxists in the 1920s and 1930s. The Frankfurt School, notably Theodor Adorno and Max Horkheimer, argued that culture was to a considerable extent autonomous. In some ways their views resemble those of Leavis and other British critics of the media, for Adorno and Horkheimer described recent cultural history in terms of commercialization and the rise of the 'culture industry'.[16]

There is a similar emphasis on the autonomy of culture – within limits – in the work of Antonio Gramsci. He too challenged the view that ordinary people were, as he put it, mere 'receptacles' of culture. On the contrary, he argued, everyone is a philosopher, this 'spontaneous philosophy' finding its expression in language, in action ('common sense'), and in popular religion. Gramsci believed that this everyday philosophy, or popular culture, was often influenced by the ideas of intellectuals or by those of the ruling class, who often exercise a cultural 'hegemony', as he called it, over the people. However, he insisted that this hegemony was not so much imposed on as accepted by ordinary people.[17] These ideas, worked out in prison and not known very widely in Gramsci's own day, have had very great influence on the intellectual left since the end of the Second World War, and especially on students of popular culture over the last couple of decades. Their influence is not confined to Marxists. Carlo Ginzburg, for example, whose work will be discussed below, acknowledges his debt to Gramsci.

To see how the Marxist approach to culture works out in practice, a useful example to take is that of England in the nineteenth century, a privileged area so far as both the quantity and the quality of recent studies are concerned, as well as one which will bring us back to the central theme of 'revolution'. The example was set in the late 1950s and early 1960s by Raymond Williams and Edward Thompson. Neither Williams nor Thompson was content with the traditional Marxist view of culture as mere 'superstructure'. Both emphasized what they variously called 'experience', 'tradition', 'culture' or 'structures of feeling'. Williams, a historically minded critic who has made his own synthesis of Marxism with the moral–literary approach of F. R. Leavis, has studied English culture as 'a particular way of life, which expresses certain meanings and values not only in art and learning but also in institutions and ordinary behaviour', noting that the concept 'culture' was itself taken up and developed in order to make sense of the profound changes consequent on the Industrial Revolution.[18] Thompson, a historian with an unusual sensitivity to literature, has concentrated on what he calls the 'plebs' in the eighteenth century and the 'working class' in the nineteenth. His brilliant, controversial and influential account of *The Making of the English Working Class* (1963) opens with a sharp critique of earlier historical and sociological interpretations of the Industrial Revolution on the grounds that 'they tend to obscure the agency of working people, the degree to which they contribute, by conscious efforts, to the making of history'. Thompson's aim was therefore, in his own memorable phrase, 'to rescue the poor stockinger, the Luddite cropper, the "obsolete" hand-loom weaver, the "utopian" artisan, and even the deluded follower of Joanna Southcott, from the enormous condescension of posterity'.[19] He interprets the rise of working-class consciousness in the period 1792–1832 as a reaction to (and also against) economic and political pressures, but he emphasizes that this reaction was far from being an automatic one. It was shaped by what he calls a 'moral culture', a 'popular tradition'. Hence his book is concerned not only with the factory system and the repressive measures of Tory governments in the age of 'Peterloo', but also with Methodism (interpreted, in a famous controversial chapter, as a form of 'psychic exploitation'), and with the values of liberty, equality and community expressed in popular ballads, in festivals, in democratic institutions (from taverns to trade unions), and in different forms of popular protest.

Thompson's later work has gone back behind 1780, thus implying that the making of the working class was an even more protracted process than he had originally suggested. His 'Moral economy of the English crowd', for example, is a study of English food riots as moral protest, and it opens with a characteristic challenge to what he describes as the 'spasmodic view' of popular history, which reduces riots to a crude response to the stimulus of hunger.[20] Thompson has written in similar terms about charivaris, about poaching and its repression, and about anonymous threatening letters, emphasizing in each case the growing conflict between the customs of traditional village communities and the rise of capitalism.[21] Despite a famous essay on the 'poverty of theory', directed primarily against the French philosopher Louis Althusser, he has added to his conceptual baggage. Like Raymond Williams, he has moved closer to Gramsci, or at least made more explicit use of his ideas. The essay 'Patrician society, plebeian culture', which sums up the argument implicit in the more specialized studies, suggests that ruling-class control in eighteenth-century England was 'located primarily in a cultural hegemony'. The plebs were far from deferential: on the contrary, they were much given to protest, to acting out 'a theatre of threat and sedition'. However, they were not revolutionary.[22]

Neither Williams nor Thompson likes to use the phrase 'popular culture'. Williams rejects it because his view of culture is holistic, associated with a region rather than with a social group or class. Thompson rejects it for the opposite reason, not so much because it is too narrow as because it is too wide, and prefers the term 'plebeian', in the sense of proto-working class. All the same, Williams and Thompson, together with Eric Hobsbawm, who takes Europe rather than England for his province, have been the models for the many recent studies of nineteenth-century English popular culture written from a broadly Marxist perspective.[23]

This body of work, much of it sensitive and sophisticated, is now so large that it cannot be discussed here in any detail.[24] In any case, despite areas of controversy, a common vocabulary and a common framework have developed. There is, for example, general rejection of the concept 'superstructure'.[25] There is a suspicion of the 'history of leisure' approach on the grounds that it is too narrow and that popular culture should be sought in a whole way of life, including work. (All the same, less attention has been paid in Britain than in Germany to the historical conditions for the emergence of the new ideas of 'leisure' and 'free time'.)[26] There is also suspicion of the term 'social control', used by other historians to describe a movement which this group interpret as the attempt by one class, the bourgeoisie, to control another.[27]

Central to the approach of these historians – Raphael Samuel, Peter Bailey, Hugh Cunningham, Gareth Stedman Jones, Steven and Eileen Yeo, Robert Storch, and a number of others – is the idea of conflict, confrontation, or contest; a kind of cultural warfare with its offensives, counter-offensives, and struggles for territory.[28] On one side is ranged the middle class, concerned with the 'taming' of popular festivals (diagnosed as irrational and disorderly) in the name of 'discipline' and 'rational recreation', together with the police, who are presented as allies of the bourgeoisie or even as 'missionaries' of bourgeois values.[29] On the other side stand the working class, defending their traditions, resisting change, defining themselves by their opposition to the middle class.

These formulations have considerable value as a kind of historical shorthand, provided that this is what they are seen to be. They draw attention to the many specific local examples of cultural conflict, of resistance to the many attempts made by the authorities to abolish particular popular festivals and recreations (the suppression of street football in Derby in the 1840s is one example among many).[30] They make it easier to place these local struggles in a much wider context, to link them to large-scale processes of social change such as urbanization (via the competition for the use of public space), and the rise of capitalism (via the need for discipline at work and also for a regular work rhythm incompatible with the traditional pattern of holidays).

However, if the conflict model (and more especially the class-conflict model) of cultural change is to avoid the dangers of oversimplification and overdramatization, it has to take account of a whole series of distinctions.

In the first place, there are the distinctions between different groups who were trying to 'tame' the working class and their different aims. Municipal authorities concerned with public order, temperance and dissenting groups concerned with public morality, and promoters of 'rational recreation' were not necessarily the same people. Indeed, they did not always work in harmony. The 'discipline', 'conversion' and 'improvement' of the working classes were not the same ideals. Indeed, they may not always have been compatible with one another, since the encouragement of ordinary people to read and think for themselves may in the long run have rendered them less obedient to the authorities in Church, state, or factory. It is also necessary to find a place in the model for the middle-class entrepreneurs who were coming to realize the profits to be made from publishing Sunday papers or building chains of variety theatres. It would be stretching the language of warfare too far to include these entrepreneurs in the army concerned with public order or popular salvation.

In the second place, distinctions need to be drawn between different working-class reactions to the suppression of traditional recreations, or to the more general (though less visible) attempts to transform their whole culture. Resistance to suppression there certainly was, but it was not unanimous. Some members (or even some 'fractions') of the working class accepted some of the new values, such as temperance or 'respectability'. In mid-nineteenth-century Derby, for example, trade unionists denounced the traditional popular pastime of street football (while to make matters still more complicated, some members of the middle class supported it). In short, the conflict model needs to be qualified to take account of instances of what Gramsci called bourgeois 'hegemony', as opposed to coercion. However, the idea of hegemony would itself be an over-simplification if it were to be seen in rather mechanical terms as a filtering down of middle-class values which themselves remained unchanged. It might be better to follow the lead of a recent study of Edinburgh and talk of the selective appropriation of middle-class values which were reinterpreted and modified in the course of their assimilation into the working-class cultural tradition. The process is sometimes described as one of 'negotiation'.[31]

In a similar way, it has been argued that the material culture of the working class, or that of the eighteenth-century plebs, the values they expressed by their particular mode of conspicuous consumption (when they could afford it – and sometimes when they couldn't) were more in harmony with capitalism than the conflict model allows.[32] The new consumer goods, from gin to curtains, could be assimilated without too much difficulty into the working-class style of life.

This last argument raises the thorny question of the relation between popular culture and capitalism, or, more generally, between historical forces which are under human control and those which are not. It may well be the case that Thompson and his followers, in their desire to give back their human dignity to the poor stockingers and others, have underestimated the constraints and pressures on working-class culture. It is of course hard to talk about 'capitalism' without reifying or fetishizing it, turning it into a superhuman force.[33] Perhaps the Marxist 'Grand Theory' of Adorno, Horkheimer and others, discussed above, is vulnerable to this criticism. Yet the Frankfurt School's picture of the commercialization and industrialization of popular culture does contain elements missing from the new wave of Marxist studies, despite the sounder empirical basis of the latter. The next assignment is surely to investigate in more detail the relationship between those changes which can be accounted for in terms of the intentions of individuals and those which cannot, among them the shift from participatory entertainments to performances by professionals to relatively passive audiences.

Such a change of emphasis would help modify a somewhat misleading impression given by some recent studies of nineteenth-century British popular culture, the impression that the changes of that period were, if not 'revolutionary', at least rather sudden. For it has not been very difficult to show, on one side of this 'great divide', that some traditional cultural forms, such as the Lancashire wakes, were resilient enough to survive the Industrial Revolution; and on the other, as Thompson's more recent work shows, that important changes were taking place well before 1780, when *The Making of the English Working Class* begins.[34]

Again, attempts to suppress (or better, perhaps, to 'reform') traditional popular culture go back well before the nineteenth century. It has recently been shown, for example, that the critique of popular recreations by the supporters of the temperance movement in nineteenth-century Cornwall followed the lines of an earlier Methodist attack. Indeed, both movements may be said to have followed the general lines of sixteenth- and seventeenth-century attempts to reform English popular culture.[35] To understand the nineteenth-century phase of cultural change – to decide whether or not it was truly revolutionary – it is necessary to see it in perspective, the perspective of the long term.

III THE 'ANNALES SCHOOL' AND POPULAR CULTURE

The phrase 'the long term' (*la longue durée*) is, of course, one of the slogans of the French historians associated with the journal *Annales: Économies, Sociétés, Civilisations*. It is taken from an article published in 1958 by Fernand Braudel, still (in 1985) the leader of the so-called '*Annales* School'.[36] The term 'school', incidentally, should not be taken to imply a uniformity of approach – the historians associated with *Annales* differ from one another even more than contemporary Marxist historians do, and range from quantitative economic historians concerned with changes on a grand scale to ethno-historians whose world may be no larger than a village (it is a measure of the versatility of Emmanuel Le Roy Ladurie that he combines the two approaches or, more exactly, practises them alternately).

This group has a long-standing interest in the history of culture. The founders of the journal, Lucien Febvre and Marc Bloch, were rebels against the domination of history by past politics, a protest still expressed in the subtitle 'économies, sociétés, civilisations'. So far as the *civilisation* part is concerned, their distinctive approach was and remains the study of what they have called *mentalités collectives*, in other words attitudes, assumptions and feelings rather than ideas in any precise philosophical sense of that term. They were interested in the anthropological approach to 'primitive' thought by Émile Durkheim and Lucien Lévy-Bruhl, and tried to adapt it to the study of medieval and early modern Europe. Bloch's *Royal Touch* (1923) studied the beliefs surrounding the practice of touching for the 'king's evil', while Febvre's *Problem of Unbelief* (1942) discussed whether or not it was possible to be an atheist in the sixteenth century. The answer was in the negative.[37]

Although they defined the history of mentalities widely enough to include the attitudes of ordinary people, neither Bloch nor Febvre occupied himself very much with specifically popular beliefs, while Braudel has shown little interest in mentalities, to which he prefers the study of 'material culture' (*la civilisation materielle*).[38] The study which really introduced the *Annales* group to the subject was Robert Mandrou's *Popular Culture in the Seventeenth and Eighteenth Centuries*.[39]

Mandrou, a pupil of Febvre's, focused his attention on the so-called *Bibliothèque bleue*, a series of booklets produced by small publishers (in the town of Troyes, in Champagne, in particular), and distributed over much of France by itinerant peddlers. The booklets were cheap and they appear to have been bought by the better-off peasants and read aloud on winter evenings. On this assumption Mandrou analysed the contents of some four hundred and fifty of these texts as a means of reconstructing the popular mentality of the period.

This analysis led him to two main conclusions. In the first place, he argued that the function of the 'Blue Library' was to provide escapist literature, which emphasized extraordinary and supernatural events, but had little room for practical books (with the exception of a few medical texts and, to a lesser extent, almanacs). In the second place, Mandrou suggested that these little books expressed conformist values; indeed, that they represented the diffusion downwards to the peasants of cultural models created by the clergy and the nobility, and respectively expressed in lives of the saints and romances of chivalry. In other words, the French peasants of the old regime have to be imagined as excited by the exploits of Ogier the Dane, or sympathetically concerned with the persecution of St Geneviève.

At much the same time as Mandrou, Albert Soboul (a Marxist historian but one who, like his master Georges Lefebvre, was not far from the *Annales* approach) published an article on the *sans-culottes* of the French Revolution, in which he noted their apparent familiarity with the ideas of Rousseau and raised the question of the way in which these ideas could have reached them. His conclusion was that the means of diffusion was popular literature, such as almanacs and song-books.[40] Taken together, the studies of Mandrou and Soboul might suggest a neat and simple conclusion, to the effect that a revolution in popular culture accompanied the events of 1789. Ogier the Dane went out, and Rousseau came in.

However, matters were not so simple. One romance of chivalry, *The Four Sons of Aymon* was still being read aloud, by Bretons at least, in the trenches in the First World War.[41] In any case, *sans-culottes* were not peasants but craftsmen, who sometimes owned their own businesses.[42] Other qualifications and distinctions need to be made when discussing popular literature, and Mandrou has been criticized quite sharply in the last few years for failing to make them. For example, some of the items in the *Bibliothèque bleue* may not have been really 'popular', while some popular literature of the period did not appear in the *Bibliothèque bleue*. The audience of these booklets cannot be assumed to have been confined to the peasants, but can be shown to have included townspeople and even members of the upper classes (women in particular). It cannot be assumed that the readers interpreted the stories in the same ways as we do, or that they agreed with the particular moral or message they found there. To attempt to reconstruct the mentality of ordinary Frenchmen and women of this period from the contents of the *Bibliothèque bleue* is rather like discussing the attitudes of the British working class today on the basis of nothing but television programmes and tabloid newspapers, as if individuals did not make critical remarks about the programmes or tell one another that 'you can't believe what you read in the papers', a remark so common in the Yorkshire of Richard Hoggart's youth that it has some claim to be regarded as a modern proverb.[43]

Since Mandrou's book first appeared in 1964, the historians associated with *Annales* have been increasingly concerned with popular culture, which they have approached in a number of different ways. Jean Delumeau, on the fringe of the group but someone who has learned a good deal from Lucien Febvre, has concerned himself with popular Catholicism in France and Italy, and the extent to which magical, animist, and generally 'pre-Christian' attitudes survived into the age of the Counter-Reformation and even beyond.[44] Georges Duby, one of the leading medievalists in France, has interested himself in cultural diffusion down the social scale, the phenomenon described by German folklorists of the early twentieth century as *Gesunkenes Kulturgut*. However, Duby has learned from Althusser (to whom he acknowledges a debt) and others to analyse this process not as the simple diffusion of cultural models, but rather as a form of adaptation or assimilation.[45] Again, Robert Muchembled's general study of French popular culture in the early modern period attempts to combine a Durkheimian analysis of structure with a Marxian account of change, in which his major theme is the repression of popular culture by the ruling class, while the *Bibliothèque bleue* is interpreted as the opium of the people, a sort of 'tranquilliser' as the author puts it. Muchembled makes considerable play with the notion of 'acculturation', taken from social anthropology. All the same, his account of cultural conflict in the seventeenth century is curiously reminiscent of accounts of the nineteenth century given by British Marxist historians.[46]

Other French historians practise a rather more distinctive approach which derives from an intellectual movement which in fact developed under the eyes of the *Annales* group at the École des Hautes Études and at the Collège de France; in other words, structuralism. It is not easy to offer a satisfactory definition of the aims of this movement, which is no more homogeneous than Marxism or the '*Annales* School', but it is held together – however loosely – by a concern with culture as a system, in which the relation between the parts is more significant than the individual items. Like language, which provided the model in the first instance, myths, food, clothes and so on are interpreted by Claude Lévi-Strauss and his followers as systems of signs, with an emphasis on binary oppositions such as 'raw' versus 'cooked' and 'naked' versus 'dressed', and more generally between 'wild' and 'domesticated' thought, terms which replace the more traditional contrast between 'primitive' and 'civilized'.[47]

Rather different was the approach to systems of thought practised by the late Michel Foucault; indeed, Lévi-Strauss asserted that Foucault was not a structuralist at all. Actually Foucault does resemble Lévi-Strauss in his stress on the intellectual system, or on 'discourse', at the expense of individual thinkers, while differing from him by pointing to fundamental 'epistemological breaks' in the history of Western thought (around 1650, for example, and around 1800), breaks which, he argued, affected not only disciplines such as linguistics and economics, but also attitudes to insanity, poverty, crime and sex.[48]

What has all this to do with the history of popular culture? Or, indeed, with history *tout court*? A question which has been debated with some heat in France and elsewhere, with attacks on both Lévi-Strauss and Foucault as 'unhistorical', the former because he shows little interest in change, the latter because he refuses to explain it.[49] However, historians cannot afford to ignore Foucault's provocative work. His theses about breaks in the history of thought, breaks which in some ways resemble Thomas Kuhn's scientific 'revolutions', demand to be confronted and discussed.[50] Foucault also took a perverse pleasure in turning traditional views upside-down, in interpreting the rise of the modern clinic (asylum, prison, etc.), not in terms of increasing humanitarianism (as the conventional wisdom has it) but of changing forms of repression. His major works are not concerned with popular culture, at least not directly, but they do have implications for its interpretation. It would not be difficult to imagine a history of popular culture written along Foucaultian lines, in which the most effective form of repression was not Muchembled's tranquillizer, or even the rational recreation movement, but the romantic cult of the people, which involved treating them as picturesque objects.

As for the ideas, or the 'discourse' of Lévi-Strauss, it is obviously harder for a historian to come to grips with such an all-embracing system, but it could be argued that a major theory of culture is something which cultural historians cannot afford to ignore. Some French historians would add that the concepts of 'wild' and 'concrete' thought have helped them (as the ideas of 'primitive' and 'pre-logical' thought once helped Bloch and Febvre) to develop the history of mentalities; popular mentalities in particular.

It may be possible to be a little more precise. One of the best-known concepts formulated by Lévi-Strauss is that of *bricolage*; in other words, the process by which traditional or 'second-hand' elements are reconstructed to form a new cultural system, or new elements incorporated in an old system.[51] This idea has the advantage of offering historians a way of discussing cultural continuity and change without exaggerating the importance of either tradition or revolution. It is, perhaps, particularly useful for the study of popular culture (or, more generally, of 'dominated' cultures), in which it is relatively easy to see how 'foreign' elements are reinterpreted in the process of incorporation.[52] We are not so far from the idea, already discussed, of 'negotiation', as if different groups of historians are converging on the same goal by different routes.

It might also be argued, ironically enough, that *bricolage* well describes the reaction of French historians to structuralism. They are attracted not so much by the system, which seems ahistorical (if not anti-historical), as by the possibility of appropriating some elements from it and incorporating them in a more dynamic system of their own. Lévi-Strauss offers a new way of reading myths, so historians such as Jacques Le Goff and Emmanuel Le Roy Ladurie offer an interpretation of a medieval legend (that of the mermaid Melusine, for example) in Lévi-Straussian terms, before utilizing the results in a more traditional framework.[53] Roger Chartier has returned to the *Bibliothèque bleue*, which he reads in a more complex and a more structuralist manner than Mandrou did. As a result he has come to doubt the utility of the distinction between 'learned' and 'popular' culture, like the distinction between 'creation' and 'consumption', because he has found so many cultural 'exchanges' which are more exactly transformations.[54]

IV TOWARDS A SYNTHESIS?

Has there been a revolution, or have there been revolutions, in popular culture? Looking back over the last two sections, and simplifying outrageously, one might say that the reason it is difficult to give this question a straight answer is that research has been dominated by two groups: Marxists working on industrial England and *Annalistes* working on pre-industrial France, two groups separated both by their subject-matter and by the language with which they analyse it.

Of course things are more complicated than that, and becoming steadily more so. It is more difficult now than it was a generation ago to decide who is a Marxist and who follows *Annales*. Barriers between schools have crumbled and the schools themselves have fragmented. Braudel is obviously an *Annales* historian, but his pupil Le Roy Ladurie is more eclectic. If his *Peasants of Languedoc* (1966) was conceived within the *Annales* framework, *Montaillou* (1975), and *Carnival* (1979) bend the frame, if they do not burst out of it altogether.[55] Again, Christopher Hill is obviously a Marxist historian, but his pupil Keith Thomas is more eclectic. The conceptual apparatus of Thomas's 'studies in popular beliefs in Tudor and Stuart England', in other words *Religion and the Decline of Magic* (1971), has been assembled from a number of sources, including the social anthropology of the late Sir Edward Evans-Pritchard.[56]

There are many other examples of the joining of approaches which were once separated. Delio Cantimori, the historian of Italian heretics, could be described as a Marxist – in the Italian idealist manner; but his pupil Carlo Ginzburg cannot. Ginzburg's studies of popular culture, *The Night Battles* (1966) and *The Cheese and the Worms* (1976), owe something to Gramsci, but not their framework. They take something from *Annales*, yet Ginzburg rejects the 'history of mentalities'.[57] Natalie Davis, whose studies of French popular culture have been extremely influential in the USA and elsewhere, has made her own synthesis out of Marxism, *Annales* and social anthropology.[58] Aron Gurevich, a Soviet scholar who has recently produced a remarkable study of the relationship between learned culture and popular culture in the middle ages, works within a broadly Marxist framework which is informed by the semiotics developed by his countrymen Juri Lotman, Vladimir Propp and Mikhail Bakhtin, whose study of Rabelais and popular culture, written about 1940, has been an inspiration to many recent studies.[59] The ethnologists Jonas Frykman and Orvar Löfgren, authors of a historical anthropology of modern Sweden, draw on both Marxism and structuralism. Their main theme is what they call the 'cultural warfare' between the bourgeoisie and other classes, but they are also concerned with what they call the 'deep structure' of Swedish culture.[60]

These examples may be sufficient to suggest not only the current dissatisfaction with organized schools of thought, but also the international and interdisciplinary character of much recent work on popular culture. These approaches, incidentally, are no longer confined to the West. In Japan there is now a strong interest in 'people's history' (*minshushi*), while a few anthropologists find the concept of popular culture to be of analytical value in the study of the contemporary Third World. They use it to describe cultural forms which are neither traditional nor Western.[61]

After so much recent research it ought to be possible to locate one or more revolutions in popular culture. However, it must be admitted that this research has made the revolutions harder rather than easier to discern. A generation ago, it would have seemed reasonable to many scholars to point to the years around 1900 as the turning-point between 'popular' and 'mass' culture, in the West at any rate, and to speak with confidence about a revolution in communications. However, the research summarized in these pages has undermined old certainties without putting new ones in their place. One reason for this derives from the recent concern with 'micro-history', with single villages such as Montaillou or even individuals such as Ginzburg's Menocchio, at the expense of broad trends. In any case it is the *Annales* tradition to stress continuity over the long term, and even 'immobility', while Bakhtin too liked to emphasize the *bolshoye vremya*, as he called it, in other words the *really* long term.[62]

There is a serious danger of underestimating change, just as the cultural critics used to exaggerate change. My own view is that a synthesis is possible as well as necessary, and that there is no reason why we should not produce in the near future a history of popular culture (Western popular culture, at least) which would be concerned not only with its changing content but also with shifts in its structure. The relation between elites and popular culture, for example, has changed over the centuries, from participation to withdrawal and then to rediscovery.[63] The notion of cultural hegemony might well be useful in the construction of this synthesis, if only it could be more profoundly historicized than it has been so far, if we could only identify the places and times when hegemony (rather than independence or coercion) was in operation, and the conditions which gave rise to this situation.

For the purposes of this potential synthesis, the concept 'revolution' is not, I am afraid, of great utility. This political metaphor has only limited relevance to cultural history. It is misleading in two different ways. In the first place, because it implies that the major changes were consciously intended, at least by an active minority of participants (even if there were unintended consequences as well). This model of change may apply to the Chinese Cultural Revolution – it is still too early to say whether it marked a major turning-point or not – but it does not take us far in attempting to understand the history of European popular culture. Clerical and lay elites (including some of the French revolutionaries), struggled over the centuries to reform or suppress elements of popular culture (which they interpreted as 'disorder' or as 'superstition'), but without achieving any obvious breakthrough. The work had always to be done again in the next century by another group of reformers, with somewhat different aims, but similar lack of success.

The second problem that comes with the concept 'revolution' is the implication that decisive changes happen relatively suddenly, so that the post-revolutionary age can be distinguished without too much difficulty from the 'old regime'. The model seems inapplicable to Western cultural history not so much on account of long-term continuities as of the very opposite – the difficulty of locating a stable old regime, an organic community with which to contrast revolutionary changes.

The old regime was not, for example, stable in the eighteenth century, when culture (including popular culture) was increasingly affected by market forces. It was, incidentally, in the context of changes in material culture in the eighteenth century that the German historian August Schlözer made his famous remark that 'the discovery of spirits, the arrival of tobacco, sugar, coffee and tea in Europe have brought about revolutions just as great as, if not greater than, the defeat of the Invincible Armada, the Wars of the Spanish Succession, the Paris Peace, etc.'.[64] If we try to push the old regime of popular culture back into the sixteenth century, we find instability once more, for that was the period when cheap printed literature became available (in Western Europe, at least) for the first time and many ordinary people were involved in a successful movement of religious protest, the Reformation.

The pace of cultural change is far from steady, but even in the case of periods of accelerated change like the nineteenth century the term 'revolution' seems too strong. The movement was too protracted. Looking back at it, Raymond Williams saw what he described, in a phrase which has become famous, as a 'Long Revolution'. But if we are going to use the concept with any degree of precision, a long 'revolution' is a contradiction in terms.

NOTES

1 For an exception, see M. Vovelle, 'Y a-t-il eu une révolution culturelle au 18e siècle?', *Revue d'histoire moderne et contemporaine*, 22 (1975), 89–141.

2 For a useful collection of studies see *Mass Culture*, eds. B. Rosenberg and D. M. White (Glencoe, 1957).
3 D. Macdonald in *Mass Culture*, p. 60.
4 R. Hoggart, *The Uses of Literacy* (London, 1957); the quotations from the titles of chs. 4, 7 and 8.
5 *Discrimination and Popular Culture*, ed. D. Thompson (Harmondsworth, 1964), pp. 10–11.
6 P. Lazarsfeld *et al.*, *The People's Choice* (New York, 1944), p. 129.
7 M. McLuhan, *Understanding Media* (New York, 1965), p. 299.
8 McLuhan, pp. 314, 4–5.
9 Hoggart, preface. Cf. R. Williams, *The Country and the City* (London, 1973), on the way in which the great divide always seems to go back one generation before the speaker.
10 R. Williams, *The Long Revolution* (London, 1961).
11 E. P. Thompson, *The Making of the English Working Class* (London, 1963), p. 378n.
12 M. Arnold, *Culture and Anarchy* (London, 1869).
13 Z. Bauman, 'A note on mass culture' in *Sociology of Mass Communications*, ed. D. McQuail (Harmondsworth, 1972), pp. 61–2.
14 F. Engels, *The Condition of the Working Class*, quoted in R. Johnson, 'Three Problematics', in *Working-Class Culture*, ed. J. Clarke, C. Critcher and R. Johnson (London, 1979), p. 206.
15 L. Trotsky, *On Literature and Art*, quoted in A. Swingewood, *The Myth of Mass Culture* (London, 1977), p. 46.
16 T. Adorno and M. Horkheimer, *The Dialectic of Enlightenment* (1944).
17 The relevant texts from Gramsci are assembled and provided with a running commentary in *Culture, Ideology and Social Process*, ed. T. Bennett *et al.* (London, 1981), pp. 191–218.
18 Williams, *Long Revolution*, p. 57.
19 Thompson, *Making of the Working Class*, p. 12.
20 E. P. Thompson, 'The moral economy of the English crowd', *Past and Present*, 50 (1971), 76–136. He took the phrase from Andrew Ure, *The Philosophy of Manufactures* (London, 1835), but inverted it to mean 'economic morality'.
21 E. P. Thompson, 'Rough Music', *Annales: ESC*, 27 (1972), 285–310; *Whigs and Hunters* (London, 1975); 'The crime of anonymity', in *Albion's Fatal Tree*, ed. D. Hay, *et al.* (London, 1975), 255–308.
22 E. P. Thompson, *The Poverty of Theory* (London, 1978), the title essay; 'Patrician society, plebeian culture', in *Journal of Social History*, 7 (1973–4), 382–405.
23 E. J. Hobsbawm, *Primitive Rebels* (Manchester, 1959) is particularly concerned with popular culture.
24 Among the more important contributions are P. Bailey, *Leisure and Class in Victorian England* (London, 1978); H. Cunningham, *Leisure in the Industrial Revolution* (London, 1980); G. Stedman Jones, *Languages of Class* (Cambridge, 1984); *Popular Culture and Class Conflict*, ed. E. and S. Yeo (Brighton, 1981); and *Popular Culture and Custom in 19th-Century England*, ed. R. D. Storch (London, 1982). J. M. Golby and A. W. Purdue, *The Civilization of the Crowd: Popular Culture in England 1750–1900* (London, 1984), appeared too late to be discussed here.
25 A recent discussion in the introduction to Storch.

26 A recent example of the approach is J. Walvin, *Leisure and Society 1830–1950* (London, 1978). Recent critiques include G. Stedman Jones, *Languages*, ch. 2, and the Yeos, *Popular Culture*, pp. 144f. On the idea of free time, W. Nahrstedt, *Die Entstehung der Freizeit* (Göttingen, 1972), a study focused on Hamburg but with much wider implications.
27 G. Stedman Jones, *Languages*, ch. 2; the Yeos, *Popular Culture*, pp. 130f.
28 E. P. Thompson writes of the cultural 'battlefield'; Peter Bailey of the 'contest for control'; the Yeos of 'struggle', 'counter-offensive' and 'battle for territory'.
29 R. Storch, 'The policeman as domestic missionary', *Journal of Social History*, 9 (1975–6), 481–96.
30 A. Delves, 'Popular recreation and social conflict in Derby', in the Yeos, *Popular Culture*, ch. 4. For a more general study in this framework, R. W. Malcolmson, *Popular Recreations in English Society 1700–1850* (Cambridge, 1973), esp. chs. 6 and 7.
31 R. Q. Gray, *The Labour Aristocracy of Victorian Edinburgh* (Oxford, 1976), ch. 7. An influential study of contemporary popular culture in its relation to the 'hegemonic' culture is *Resistance through Rituals*, ed. S. Hall and T. Jefferson (London, 1976).
32 H. Medick, 'Plebeian culture in the transition to capitalism', in *Culture Ideology and Politics*, ed. R. Samuel and G. Stedman Jones (London, 1983), ch. 5.
33 A danger noted by the Yeos in *Popular Culture*.
34 J. K. Walton and R. Poole, 'The Lancashire wakes in the nineteenth century', in Storch, *Popular Culture*, ch. 5. For Thompson see notes 21 and 22 above; cf. Malcolmson (note 30).
35 J. Rule, 'Methodism, popular beliefs and village culture in Cornwall', in Storch, *Popular Culture*, ch. 3; cf. P. Burke, *Popular Culture in Early Modern Europe* (London, 1978), ch. 8.
36 F. Braudel, 'History and the social sciences', in *Economy and Society in Early Modern Europe*, ed. P. Burke (London, 1972), ch. 1.
37 M. Bloch, *Les rois thaumaturges*, Eng. trans. *The Royal Touch* (London, 1973); L. Febvre, *Le problème de l'incroyance au 16e siècle: la religion de Rabelais*, Eng. trans. *The Problem of Unbelief* (Cambridge, Mass., 1983). The history of this approach is sketched in P. Burke, 'Reflections on the historical revolution in France', *Review*, 1 (1978), 147–56.
38 P. Burke, '"Material Civilisation" in the work of Fernand Braudel', *Itinerario*, 5 (1981), 2, 37–43.
39 R. Mandrou, *De la culture populaire aux 17e et 18e siècles* (Paris, 1964). At this point the phrase *culture populaire* sometimes meant bringing high culture to the people. Even in 1973, when a conference on popular culture – in the English sense – was held at the University of East Anglia, the French participants only discovered the difference in usage on arrival.
40 A. Soboul, 'Classes populaires et Rousseauisme', *Annales historiques de la Révolution Française* (1964), reprinted in his *Paysans, sans-culottes, et jacobins* (Paris, 1966), 203–22.
41 P.-J. Hélias, *Le Cheval d'orgeuil* (Paris, 1975), Eng. trans., *The Horse of Pride* (London, 1978).
42 A. Soboul, *Les sans-culottes*, Eng. trans. Gwynne Lewis, *The Parisian Sans-Culottes and the French Revolution* (Oxford, 1964).

43 P. Burke, 'The "Bibliothèque bleue" in comparative perspective', *Quaderni del seicento francese*, 4 (1981), 59–66. Hoggart, *Uses*, ch. 9. Cf. R. Darnton, *The Great Cat Massacre* (New York, 1984), esp. ch. 1.

44 J. Delumeau, *Le Catholicisme entre Luther et Voltaire* (Paris, 1971), Eng. trans. Jeremy Moiser, *Catholicism from Luther to Voltaire* (London, 1977).

45 G. Duby, 'The diffusion of cultural patterns in feudal society', *Past and Present*, 39 (1968), 1–10; 'Histoire sociale et idéologies des sociétés', *Faire de l'histoire*, ed. J. Le Goff and P. Nora (Paris, 1974), vol. 1, pp. 147–68.

46 R. Muchembled, *Culture populaire et culture des élites* (Paris, 1978).

47 Of the many works of Lévi-Strauss, particularly relevant to this argument is *La pensée sauvage* (Paris, 1962), Eng. trans., *The Savage Mind* (London, 1966).

48 M. Foucault, *Histoire de la folie* (1961), Eng. trans. Richard Howard, *Madness and Civilisation* (London, 1967); *Les mots et les choses*, Eng. trans. as *The Order of Things* (London, 1973); *Surveiller et punir* (1975), English trans. *Discipline and Punish* (London, 1977); *La volonté de savoir* (1976), Eng. trans. *The History of Sexuality* (New York, 1980).

49 O. Revault d'Allones, 'Michel Foucault: les mots contre les choses', *Structuralisme et marxisme* (Paris, 1970), pp. 13–37, one of the earliest and most penetrating critiques.

50 This is not altogether coincidence. Foucault admitted a considerable debt to two French historians of science, Gaston Bachelard and Georges Canguilhem, both of them concerned with epistemological discontinuities.

51 Lévi-Strauss, *Savage mind*, ch. 1.

52 Burke, *Popular Culture*, p. 123.

53 Both interpretations appeared in *Annales*, 1971. Le Goff's is translated in his *Time, Work and Culture in the Middle Ages* (Chicago, 1980), 205–22.

54 R. Chartier, 'Intellectual history or sociocultural history? The french trajectories', in *Modern European Intellectual History*, ed. D. LaCapra and S. Kaplan (Ithaca and London, 1982), pp. 13–46.

55 E. Le Roy Ladurie, *Les paysans de Languedoc* (1966: Eng. trans. Urbane, 1974); *Montaillou village occitan* (1975); Eng. trans., *Montaillou: the Promised land of Erros* (London, 1978); *Le carnaval de Romans* (1979), Eng. trans., *Carnival* (London, 1980).

56 K. V. Thomas, *Religion and the Decline of Magic* (London, 1971).

57 C. Ginzburg, *I bendandanti* (1966), Eng. trans. *The Night Battles* (London, 1984); *Il formaggio e i vermi* (1976), Eng. trans., *Cheese and Worms* (London, 1980). The preface to the latter book includes a critique of the history of mentalities, French-style.

58 N. Z. Davis, *Society and Culture in Early Modern France* (London, 1975).

59 A. Gurevich, *Problemui sredinevekovoi narodnoi kul'turui* (Moscow, 1981). An English translation is forthcoming. M. Bakhtin, *Tvorchestvo Fransua Rable* (Moscow, 1965); Eng. trans. *Rabelais and his World* (Cambridge, Mass., 1968).

60 J. Frykman and O. Löfgren, *Den kultiverade människan* (Lund, 1979). An English translation is forthcoming.

61 C. Gluck, 'The people in history: recent trends in Japanese historiography', *Journal of Asian Studies*, 38 (1979). J. Fabian, 'Popular culture in Africa', *Africa*, 48 (1978), 315–34.

62 The comparison is made by A. J. Gurevich, 'Medieval culture and mentality according to the new French historiography', *European Journal of Sociology*, 24 (1983), 167–95.
63 A main theme of Burke, *Popular Culture*.
64 Quoted by Medick, 'Plebeian culture', p. 96. (I have emended the translation).

11

Revolution in music – music in revolution

ERNST WANGERMANN

REVOLUTION IN MUSIC

To speak about 'revolution' in connection with a topic like the history of music may appear far-fetched. But if we do so in connection with some important aspects of the history of music in the eighteenth century, we are doing no more than following the practice of some contemporary writers on musical matters. A book on the controversies aroused by Christoph Willibald Gluck with the operas he produced in Paris during the 1770s, appeared under the title *Mémoires pour servir à l'histoire de la révolution opérée dans la musique par M. le Chevalier Gluck.*[1]

There is in fact quite a lot to be said for this choice of phrase. For some of the more important eighteenth-century developments in musical form and taste can very usefully be considered as part of the social and intellectual transformation which began with what Paul Hazard has aptly called 'the crisis of the European consciousness' about 1680,[2] and which culminated in the 1780s in the French Revolution.

The writer who did most to involve the arts in that process of transformation was the Third Earl of Shaftesbury. He was not a systematic thinker, which has led some historians of thought to underrate his importance. His main achievement was to restate the constructive and positive world view of the Neo-Platonists in terms which established this view as the 'common sense' of the period. In this way, his conception of nature as the embodiment and exemplar of a harmony, which it was both an aesthetic pleasure and a moral inspiration to perceive, became a profound influence on the arts throughout the eighteenth century.

In his *Inquiry concerning Virtue*, Shaftesbury contrasted human and animal behaviour:

> In the ... Species and Creatures around us, there is found generally an exact Proportionableness, Constancy and Regularity in all their Passions and Affections; no failure in the care of the Offspring, or of the Society, to which they are

united ... The smaller Creatures, who live as it were in Citys (as Bees and Ants) continue in the same Train and Harmony of Life: Nor are they ever false to those Affections, which move them to operate towards their Publick Good.[3]

Yet, in contrast to these creatures who were all perfectly adjusted to the harmony of their natural environment, men were disastrously at odds with it:

Notwithstanding the Assistance of Religion, and the Direction of Laws, Man is often found to live in less conformity with Nature ... Marks are set on Men: Distinctions form'd: Opinions decreed, under the severest Penaltys: Antipathies instill'd, and Aversions rais'd in Men against the generality of their own Species.[4]

Stated in this way, the age-old ethical problem of human conduct presented itself in a wholly new light. The old formula of exhortation by preachers, constantly urging men to master their natural impulses and to submit to the rules enjoined by revealed religion and secular law, had not solved the problem; indeed, as Shaftesbury noted, it had often rendered men *more* barbarous and inhuman. But it was now clear why this had been so. The problem had been misconceived. For the example of the other creatures demonstrated that the challenge was to get men to *conform to* nature, not to rise above it; to get them to live as naturally as men as the animals were living as animals.[5] This is where the implication for the arts arose. Distinguishing the natural and ethical from the unnatural and unethical was not a matter of giving formal instruction, which was the business of the preacher and the moral philosopher. It was, rather, a matter of conveying to men a sense of the harmony of Nature, and thereby stimulating in them an appropriate and lasting response to their harmonious and beautiful natural environment. And that, according to Shaftesbury, was the true business of the artist.

Shaftesbury's ideas spread quickly and can be traced in the writings of both theologians and artists, in Britain and on the continent. His first German translator was the theologian Johann Joachim Spalding. He is representative of the enthusiastic response which Shaftesbury's conception of nature as man's ethical guiding light aroused among so many of his generation:

How uninteresting, how tasteless and dead do these artificial and fantastic displays of luxury and ostentation seem to me compared to the living splendour of the truly beautiful world! Compared to the joy, serenity and admiration which a flowering meadow, a rushing stream ... or the majestic vision of countless worlds afford me! Even the ... commonest creatures of nature delight me in a thousand ways ... To find and to love order, proportion, due measure and perfection everywhere – what a sublime sensation for the human spirit! I lose myself in the most intense pleasure contemplating this universal beauty, of which I try to be a part such as will in no way diminish it.[6]

Among the poets who wanted to accept the challenge which Shaftesbury put before them, the most notable was James Thomson. In a preface to the later editions of *Winter* he wrote: 'I know no subject more elevating, more amusing, more ready to awake the poetical enthusiasm, the philosophic reflection, and the moral sentiment, than the works of Nature.'[7] John Gilbert Cooper, made this point more explicitly in Shaftesburyan terms in the preface to *The Power of Harmony*:

> A constant admiration of the beauty of the creation [terminates] in the adoration of the First Cause, which naturally leads mankind cheerfully to co-operate with his grand design for the promotion of universal happiness ... This then is the design of the poem, to show that a constant attention to what is perfect and beautiful in nature will by degrees harmonize the soul to a responsive regularity and sympathetic order.[8]

The link between the beauty of Nature and God's benevolence towards man, which Cooper assumed so simply and confidently, is also the central point of Thomson's *Hymn to the Seasons*:

> Mysterious round! what skill, what force divine,
> Deep-felt in these appear! a simple train,
> Yet so delightful mixed, with such kind art,
> Such beauty and beneficence combined,
> Shade unperceived so softening into shade,
> And all so forming an harmonious whole
> That, as they still succeed, they ravish still.[9]

God, the supreme maker, had combined beauty and beneficence. The artist, by making men more aware of that beauty, could promote benevolence among them. If the fine arts could perform such an important *moral* function, it was natural that they should not be judged by exclusively *aesthetic* criteria. The effectiveness of a particular work of art, or of a particular art form, with regard to the moral function was a more important consideration. This helps to explain the high reputation in the eighteenth century enjoyed by some artists and art forms, which would be difficult to account for if purely aesthetic criteria had been applied, e.g. the pastoral Idylls of Salomon Gessner. Gessner's contemporaries thought that by his depiction of the beauty of Nature and of the simple, natural ways of the shepherds, he was effectively promoting virtue. His admirer and translator Turgot wrote that Gessner's principal object in describing all the charms of country life was 'always to make his readers feel the attractions of virtue'.[10] Though a largely neglected writer today, Gessner was in his own time the first German writer to achieve widespread popularity outside the German-speaking area.

It was in the context of the moral function ascribed to art, that music combined with poetry was accorded the supreme position among the fine arts. It was recognized of course that music could not 'imitate Nature' in the way the visual arts could. But music had a power, unrivalled by the other arts, to stir the emotions, an unrivalled power, as contemporaries put it, 'to touch the heart'. That was the decisive consideration in relation to the moral function of art. For there was an overwhelming consensus in eighteenth-century thinking about psychology that it was not man's reasoning faculty but his 'sensibility', i.e. his ability to feel compassion for the suffering of others and delight in their joy, which was the spring of all moral action. This point has been very well expressed in an article on the eighteenth-century cult of compassion: 'Rather than [in] deliberation, the measure of the good person was to be found in the instantaneity of response, the unthinking, unreasoned animal (or spiritual) act of the virtuous soul.'[11] To know one's moral duty will produce an inclination to the appropriate course of action, but will not guarantee that this course of action is actually followed. Once one's sensibility has been aroused, all hesitations impeding the appropriate course of action are overcome. Even the definition of 'sensibilité' in the *Encyclopédie*, written by the Chevalier de Jaucourt, is a statement of this psychological position:

> A tender and delicate inclination of the soul which disposes it to be moved readily ... Sensible souls may fall into errors which calculating men would never commit, simply because they are so responsive. However, they do infinitely more good ... Contemplation can make a man upright, but sensibility makes him virtuous. Sensibility is the mother of humanity and generosity. It adds to excellence, it sustains the mind; finally it convinces.[12]

Such statements show how misleading it is to dismiss the eighteenth-century cult of sensibility as a faintly ridiculous fad of a generation which happened to enjoy shedding tears. It was an expression of the moral concern of the age. And it was a clear indication to all practitioners of the fine arts how to order their priorities. They had the means at their disposal to appeal to men's sensibility, i.e. they had the power to impel them to moral action, and they must use it to the utmost. This is the position which underlies the entire aesthetic theory of Johann Georg Sulzer, the red thread which runs through all the articles of his four-volume dictionary *Allgemeine Theorie der Schönen Künste* (1772–4), through which it came to dominate European thinking on the fine arts for the rest of the century and beyond. In the keynote article, 'Schöne Künste', Sulzer himself wrote:

> We must regard the fine arts as the necessary assistants of the wisdom which cares for the welfare of men. Wisdom knows about everything that man ought to be; it points the path to perfection and to the happiness which is related to it. But it cannot give the strength to go down that often arduous path. The fine arts make the path smooth and adorn it with flowers which, by their delightful scent, irresistibly entice the wanderer to continue on his way.[13]

This 'ethico-aesthetics' which had developed from the root of Shaftesbury's conception of Nature, was a very characteristic expression of the social transformation which assumed revolutionary dimensions by the end of the eighteenth century. To make sensibility, which was at least a latent faculty of all men, the decisive moral criterion was to challenge all the surviving traditional and feudal notions as to the different moral qualities of each 'order' of society.[14] Furthermore, the moral vocation held out before the artist, made him a competitor in an area of society hitherto monopolized by the Church.

We must now consider the impact of these ideas on the actual development of musical form and taste during the eighteenth century. At many points their influence can be clearly discerned. The declining appeal of conventional Italian opera reflected the growing demand for natural simplicity in the arts, which was more likely to stir the emotions of the public than elaborate artificiality.[15] The emphasis on stirring the emotions lay behind the persistent search embarked on by both composers and performers for the best means of enhancing the emotional power of music. Both were constantly instructed by critics and in manuals to 'touch the heart' rather than merely to 'flatter the ear'.[16] The fame of Gluck after *Orfeo* (1761) and of Carl Philip Emanuel Bach was grounded in their ability to rouse the deeper emotions of their audience and to strike a note of fiery enthusiasm.[17]

The most important reflection in music of the aesthetics derived from Shaftesbury was the rise and popularity of the concert oratorio. Originally, oratorio belonged within a context of ecclesiastical observance and piety, Catholic in Italy and Austria, Protestant in northern Germany. In the course of the eighteenth century, the oratorio emancipated itself from this context, and became an integral part of secular public musical culture. The main protagonist of this development was George Frederick Handel with the oratorios he set to English texts. Handel moved in the circle of the English Shaftesburyans, who were his most enthusiastic admirers and his most consistent supporters in the controversies in which he was involved. He was introduced to the ideas of the Third Earl of Shaftesbury by no less an authority than the Fourth Earl.[18]

The link between Shaftesburyan aesthetics and Handelian oratorio is clear at every stage of the oratorio's development. It was born in the context of Cannons, the residence of the Duke of Chandos, where Handel composed *Haman and Mordechai*, the original version of the oratorio *Esther*. The duke's quickly and dubiously acquired wealth gave rise to satirical attacks suggesting that his residence had 'much more of art than nature, and much more cost than art'.[19] But such charges were indignantly rebutted by members of the Chandos circle. Thus Alexander Pope denied that his strictures on artificiality and ostentation applied to the Duke of Chandos:

> Is his Garden crowded with *Walls*? Are his Trees cut into *Figures of Men*? Do his Basins want *Water*? Are there *ten steep Slopes* of his Terras? Is he piqued about *Editions of Books*? Does he exclude all *Moderns* from his *Library*? Is the Musick of his Chappel bad, or *whimsical*, or *jiggish*? On the contrary, was it not the best composed in the Nation, and most suited to grave Subject; witness *Nicolas Haym's* and Mr Hendel's [*sic*] noble Oratories? Has it the pictures of naked Women in it? And did ever Dean Chetwood preach his Courtly Sermons there? I am sick of such fool applications.[20]

Nothing could reveal more clearly than this letter that the members of the cultural court which the duke had attracted to Cannons considered themselves to be working in the spirit of Shaftesbury and in an environment appropriate to that spirit.

From the late 1730s onwards, Handel devoted his principal effort to the composition of oratorio. This reflected the deep crisis of conventional Italian opera, which had never fully recovered from the satirical shafts of John Gay's *Beggars' Opera* (1728), and which had been inextricably involved in the unedifying quarrels of a faction-ridden court. The public response to the early oratorios was restrained, almost indifferent. The real breakthrough came only with Handel's concert season in Dublin in 1741–2. And this, too, illustrates the aesthetic context of these compositions, the Shaftesburyan link between artistic and moral endeavour.

In Dublin, just as in London, the musical academy patronized by the nobility had suffered a crisis, and by 1741 it was out of business. The musical vacuum thus created was quickly filled by a more broadly based society – some historians have referred to it as 'democratic' – the Dublin Charitable Music Society. There are some indications that this society was linked to Irish Freemasonry. It helped to finance the Dublin hospitals and to secure the release of imprisoned debtors.[21]

In 1741, the society had just completed the construction of a new music hall in Fishamble Street. It took this opportunity of asking Handel to compose a new oratorio for the benefit of the Dublin hospitals.[22] The new oratorio which Handel took with him to Dublin and which he had composed only weeks previously, was *Messiah*. It is perhaps significant that the decision to use *Messiah* for the Dublin commission was entirely Handel's own. Charles Jennens, who had compiled the text from the Anglican Prayer Book and the Scriptures, thought it would be performed in London for Handel's own benefit.[23] On 12 April 1742, the following announcement appeared in the Dublin press:

> To the benefit of three very important public Charities, there will be a grand Performance of this Oratorio [*Messiah*] on Thursday next in the forenoon ...

Many ladies and Gentlemen who are well-wishers to the Noble and Grand Charity for which this Oratorio was composed, request it as a favour that the Ladies ... will be pleased to come without Hoops, as it will greatly encrease the Charity by making Room for more company.[24]

Dublin's response to Handel's oratorios was distinctly more enthusiastic than London's response had been. Contemporaries accounted for this at least in part by reference to the association of the works with benevolence and charity. This is how John Mainwaring, Handel's first biographer, put it immediately after the composer's death:

He rightly reckoned that he could not better pave the way to his success, than by setting out with a striking instance and public act of generosity and benevolence. The first step that he made was to perform his Messiah for the benefit of the city prison. Such a design drew together not only all the lovers of Music, but all the friends of humanity. There was a peculiar propriety in this design from the subject of the Oratorio itself, and there was a particular grace in it from the situation of Handel's affairs. They were brought into a better posture by his journey to Dublin ...[25]

That 'bringing together all the lovers of music with all the friends of humanity' was the best recipe for success in this period is borne out by the subsequent reception given to *Messiah* in London. Its popularity developed slowly. But it reached a uniquely high and lasting level when its performances were associated with London's newest and greatest charity, Captain Thomas Coram's Foundlings' Hospital, to which William Hogarth also donated some of his finest work.[26] Very soon, charity concerts, among them the annual Handel Commemoration Concerts, established themselves as pivotal events in the calender of English public musical life.[27]

Some of those who listened to the early performances of *Messiah*, have recorded their reactions. From these records we can see that, through the medium of the concert oratorio, the eighteenth-century composer could fulfil to the utmost the aesthetic requirement to stir the deepest emotions of his audience. In 1752, a Dublin listener wrote to a friend in London:

If Handel's Messiah should be performed in London ... I beg it as a favour to me, that you will go early ... Take care to get a book of the oratorio some days before, that you may well digest the subject. There you will hear *glad tidings* and truly divine rejoicings at the birth of *Christ*, and feel real sorrows for his sufferings – but, oh! when those sufferings are over, what a transporting full chorus![28]

A unique record of emotional response is that of the German poet Johann Heinrich Voss, who attended the first German performance of *Messiah* in Hamburg, for which Klopstock had made a German translation. Voss described his reactions in a letter to his betrothed, Ernestine Boie, whom he later married:

Already the first accompanied recitative: Comfort ye my people, almost moved me to tears ... But nothing could touch the choruses. My heart beat almost as it does when you embrace me, and I wanted to fly through the clouds. Especially the chorus: For unto us a child is born! This has a drive which I did not think that any music could have. Imagine the greatest joy expressed in four voices, where one is continually set alight by the other, and proclaims still more vividly and joyfully the good news: a child is born to us! Then as a fugue: And the government shall lie upon his shoulders; now a few voices restrained: And his name shall be called. And then all the voices like thunder: Wonderful! The instruments echo in thunder. Louder still: Glorious! The music rises in proportion. But now, as though lightning and thunder coincided with the most powerful expression possible on this earth: Almighty God! It makes you tremble and want to prostrate yourself before his greatness. The thunder of the voices still continues with: Everlasting father! But loses itself into quiet murmur as from afar with: Prince of Peace. Then again with the voice of delight as at the beginning: For unto us a child is born ... I could have stayed for twenty-four hours without eating and drinking just listening to this chorus ... The mighty Hallelujah is so joyful and heavenly that you feel you are present at the great Sabbath in heaven. And everything from the beginning to the end was equally divine.[29]

Since oratorio was able to achieve such intensity of emotional response and since art achieved its moral function in so far as it was able to arouse an emotional response, it was natural that oratorio should come to be considered in eighteenth-century aesthetics as the highest form which music and poetry could achieve by their union. John Brown accorded it this place of honour in his *Dissertation on the Rise, Union and Power ... of Poetry and Music*:

That [the] Representation of sacred Subjects is the highest and most interesting Union of Poetry and Music, needs no elaborate Proof: It stands intimately connected with all the sublime Truths, the great and affecting Events of our Religion, which when thus exhibited by the united Powers of Poem and Song, call forth all the noblest Emotions of the human Soul; and exalt it to the highest Pitch of Elevation that our mortal Condition will admit.[30]

When Joseph Haydn returned to Vienna from his second visit to London in 1795, and composed his concert oratorios *Creation* and *The Seasons*, the response of the Vienna public was as powerful and enthusiastic as that of the Dublin and London public had been to Handel's oratorios half a century earlier.[31] The revolution in musical form and taste which we have traced to the aesthetic priorities derived from Shaftesbury's ideas, thus 'saw in' the social and political revolution of which it was one of the harbingers. We shall therefore conclude by looking at the role of music in this revolution in the light of the preceding revolution in music.

MUSIC IN REVOLUTION

From the belief that the fine arts could activate the moral inclination of the individual, it was not a very long step to the corollary that they could also have a beneficial effect on social morality and encourage public spirit and virtue. During the second half of the eighteenth century, governments were increasingly urged by writers on the arts to protect and further the arts in recognition of their potential usefulness to the state and to society. Usually the proposal was for the establishment or furtherance of academies of art. John Brown, for instance, whose views on the oratorio we have referred to, proposed the establishment of a 'Poetic and Musical Academy', which, he thought, would help to maintain a high level of social morality.[32]

The unification of the Viennese art schools in the new Akademie der Bildenden Künste under Maria Theresa (1772) was undertaken in this spirit. The men entrusted with the task had persuaded the ruler that 'the arts ... were a means to inspire patriotism among the citizens, and to encourage them to noble deeds'.[33] The major artistic enterprise sponsored by Maria Theresa in Vienna in the 1770s fully reflected this attitude. Thirty life-size statues commissioned for the 'beautification' of the park of Schönbrunn palace all represented the public virtues, attitudes and ideals which were believed to have made possible the greatness of ancient Greece and republican Rome.[34]

The same spirit inspired the artistic policy of the French government under Louis XVI. The Comte d'Angiviller, who as *directeur général des bâtiments* was a kind of 'minister of the arts', believed that the true function of art was to combat vice and preach virtue. Every year, therefore, he commissioned from the *Salon* such paintings as would recall great and noble deeds from ancient history or the history of France. The basic themes illustrated by the chosen paintings were sacrifice for the state and magnanimity of soul.[35]

One of the main elements in the Enlightenment's unbounded admiration of ancient Greece and republican Rome was the notion that in these societies the arts performed the noble function of inspiring the people with public spirit, patriotism and virtue. This image of ancient Greece can already be discerned in the poetry of James Thomson, who had discovered the 'noble simplicity' of the Doric style some years before the publication of Winckelmann's famous book:[36]

> To public virtue thus the smiling arts
> Unblemished handmaids served; the graces they
> To dress this fairest Venus.[37]

Later, writers became increasingly fascinated by the special role supposedly played in ancient Greece by the highest form of art (according to the dominant aesthetics of the period) – the union of poetry and music.

According to John Brown's *Dissertation on the Rise, Union, and Power ... of Poetry of Music* (1763), the song and the harp were the means by which the Greeks became acquainted with their laws.[38] Among those influenced by Brown's *Dissertation* was Johann Gottfried Herder. Eventually, however, Brown was overshadowed by what became the classic work on the place of music in ancient Greece, the Abbé Barthélémy's *Entretiens sur l'état de la musique grècque au quatrième siècle*, first published in 1777, and later incorporated in his monumental *Voyages du jeune Anarcharsis en Grèce*, which was published on the eve of the French Revolution in 1788. Here the concept of the original, simple and uncorrupted music of the Greeks received its classic and most influential formulation:

The first musicians excited the wonder of a barbarous people, and we expressed our admiration and pleasure in the usual hyperboles of a barbarous people. Such were the feelings of the Greeks in the Trojan war. Amphion thus animated the workmen employed in building Thebes; Orpheus tamed tigers with a few agreeable sounds from his lyre ... You have doubtless heard that a sedition in Lacedaemon was appeased by the music of Terpander; that the Athenians were induced by the songs of Solon to invade and recover the Isle of Salamis, and Arcadia likewise was civilized by music ... The rigour of their land and climate had produced a ferocity in their feelings. Accident, perhaps, taught their legislators the efficacy of music upon such habits. They applied it. Festivals, public games, processions, choruses, and dances of boys and girls were instituted; they sang to their gods; they sang their heroes, and they sang the gifts of spring, summer, autumn and winter. They were thus rendered mild, humane and benevolent ... Compare the ancient music with that which has been introduced almost in our own days. In its origin simple and natural, as it proceeded, more rich and varied, it successively animated the verses of Hesiod, Homer, Archilochus, Terpander, Simonides, and Pindar. It produced its effect in the hands of these by being the simple expression of Nature. In vocal music, this simple expression is but the intonation suited to the words and verse. Now the ancient poets, who were at once musicians, philosophers and legislators, never lost sight of this principle; they disposed their words, their melody and their rhythm accordingly, and the sense, measure and music thus all concurred in a unity of expression ... They adapted their music strictly to their subject. Did they sing of war? The Doric harmony supplied them with its force and majesty. Had they to lament the vicissitudes of life, and the falls of states, kings or heroes? The Lydian measure supplied the elegiac strain. In their sacred hymns, the Phrygian notes expressed the awe of sober feeling adapted to the occasion ... Instead of amusing itself by exciting our petty passions, [the ancient music] arouses in the bottom of our hearts the sentiments which are at once most honourable to the individual and most useful to society – courage, gratitude and devotion to the fatherland.[39]

One reason for the profound impression which Gluck's late operas made in Paris in the years 1774 to 1779 is that they conjured up before the eyes and ears of the French public precisely this image of ancient Greece and its austere, sublime music. Gluck's supporters identified his critics, the 'Piccinnists', with the adherents of the corrupted music which merely flattered the ear of the later Greeks in their decline.[40] Like the early paintings of Jacques Louis David, the late Parisian operas of Gluck were an artistic anticipation of the social aspirations, the drive and the passions to be let loose by the French Revolution. Looking back on these pre-revolutionary years, Jean Baptiste Leclerc, a member of the National Convention and the Council of Five-Hundred, wrote: 'It is not too much to say that Gluck's musical revolution must have made the government tremble. His vigorous harmonies stirred the warm hearts of the French, who were moved to lament past errors. There were signs then of a power which was to burst forth, shortly afterwards.'[41]

When the French Revolution had broken out, and means had to be found to cement the unity and fire the patriotism of a nation embarking on the adventure of self-government in a world still dominated by absolute monarchy, ancient Greece emerged from the pages of imaginary histories and from the operatic stage to be produced on the larger stage of national politics. The great *fêtes* of the Revolution, starting with the 'Festival of the Federation' on the first anniversary of the storming of the Bastille, were attempts to re-enact the popular religious festivals of ancient Greece as they had been presented to the imagination of the French public by writers like Barthélémy and composers like Gluck. In all these festivals, music played the key role. As Leclerc put it: 'The friends of liberty in their turn enlisted music's help – music which employed those manly accents to which the German composer had conditioned them'.[42]

The most important musical form evolved for these occasions was the revolutionary hymn, which was sung by various groups in the public processions, with the assembled people joining in at the appropriate time. No doubt, François-Joseph Gossec and the other composers of the music commissioned for these *fêtes* were trying to follow what they considered to be the ancient Greek model. We may assume that the contribution made by this music to the patriotic fervour which helped revolutionary France to repel and defeat the interventionist Powers was not negligible.[43]

The social transformation from the society of the *ancien régime* to that based on equality before the law, did not everywhere culminate, as it did in France, in a climactic revolutionary phase of heroic dimensions. In Denmark, for instance, the abolition of the remnants of feudalism and the emancipation of the peasants was the work of an enlightened monarch, Christian VI, and a reforming ministry under Count Bernstorf. Nevertheless, a struggle was required to overcome the resistance of the more conservative nobility which was led by the German nobles organized in the Estates of Schleswig-Holstein. As in France, therefore, the friends of liberty in Denmark 'enlisted music's help'.

The Copenhagen Opera was at this time under the direction of the

German composer Johann Peter Abraham Schulz, who had set many poems of Johann Heinrich Voss to such simple and natural melodies that they were often taken to be traditional folk songs.[44] As director of the Copenhagen Opera, Schulz drafted music into the service of the controversial reforms of Christian VI and Bernstorf. He commissioned operas on rural themes in the context of which the cause of peasant freedom and national harmony could be promoted. The most successful of these was *The Harvest Festival* by Thaarup, produced in 1795. This work celebrates the bounty of Nature and the simple morality of the peasants, very much as these are celebrated in Haydn's later oratorio *The Seasons*. The opera ends with an enthusiastic celebration of Christian as the liberator of the peasants:

> Bless our Christian,
> He ennobles even the tiller of the soil ...
> God bless Christian,
> He is devoted to freedom.
> Join in the triumphal chorus,
> Sing joyfully like us.
> God wants all men to be free,
> Christian follows him faithfully.
> Through him we are free,
> For that let us bless him.[45]

The romantic movement put an end to the taste for art in the service of a morality or of a movement based on the assumption of an orderly, harmonious and comprehensible Nature. To this day, we look askance at the moralistic literature and painting of the eighteenth century, with the possible exception of James Thomson and Jacques Louis David. The music, however, which was inspired by the eighteenth-century belief in the moral vocation of the arts, from Handel's *Messiah* to Beethoven's *Fidelio* and his Ninth Symphony, is still universally accepted as among the greatest music ever created. The eighteenth-century 'revolution in music' is still aesthetically acceptable to us today, despite the modern consensus against 'art as propaganda' or as the medium for a moral message. Whether the late eighteenth-century 'music in revolution' would still be aesthetically acceptable, it is not at present possible to say. For the music 'enlisted' by the friends of liberty in France and Denmark in the decade of revolution still awaits its modern revival. This would surely be worth attempting.

NOTES

1 Edited by G. M. Leblond (Naples, 1781; reprinted Amsterdam, 1976).
2 P. Hazard, *La crise de la conscience européenne* (Paris, 1935); English translation by J. L. May (London, 1953).

3 *An Inquiry concerning Virtue, or Merit*, ed. D. Walford (Manchester, 1977), p. 60.
4 *Ibid.*
5 E. Tuveson, 'The importance of Shaftesbury', in *A Journal of English Literary History*, 20 (1953), p. 275.
6 J. J. Spalding, *Die Bestimmung des Menschen*, Verbesserte u. vermehrte Aufl. (Leipzig, 1768), pp. 39–40.
7 J. Thomson, *Poetical Works* (Oxford Standard Authors), ed. J. Logie Robertson (London, 1908), pp. 240–1.
8 J. G. Cooper, 'The power of harmony', in A. Chalmers (ed.), *The Works of the English Poets* (London, 1810), vol. 15, p. 519. The lines are from the poetic introduction 'The Design'.
9 *Poetical Works*, p. 246.
10 *Oeuvres de M. Turgot, Ministre d'Etat*, vol. 9 (Paris, 1810), p. 159.
11 N. S. Fiering, 'Irresistible compassion: an aspect of eighteenth-century sympathy and humanitarianism', in *Journal of the History of Ideas*, 37 (1976), p. 208.
12 Quoted in *Music and Aesthetics in the Eighteenth and Early-nineteenth Centuries*, ed. P. le Huray and J. Day (London, 1979), p. 106.
13 *Allgemeine Theorie der Schönen Künste*, 2nd ed. (Leipzig, 1792–4), vol. 3, p. 78.
14 For this point, cf. G. Sauder, *Empfindsamkeit*, vol. 1 (Stuttgart, 1974), pp. 203–4.
15 Joseph Addison's well-known polemic against the conventions of Italian opera in no. 5 of the *Spectator*, 6 March 1711, is often interpreted as a case of sour grapes after the failure of the English opera *Rosamonde* for which he wrote the words. But E. Rubini, *Les philosophes et la musique* (Paris, 1983), pp. 83–4, refers to similar polemics in France (Boileau, Saint-Evremont) and Italy (Muratori) at precisely this time.
16 A lot of the material on this point has been usefully assembled by H. H. Eggebrecht, 'Das Ausdrucksprinzip im musikalischen Sturm und Drang', in *Deutsche Vierteljahresschrift f. Literaturwissenschaft u. Geistesgeschichte*, 29/3 (1955), pp. 323–49.
17 For C. P. E. Bach, P. Barford, *The Keyboard Music of C. P. E. Bach* (London, 1965), esp. pp. 5–6, 43–4; for Gluck, see G. Pestelli, *The Age of Mozart and Beethoven*, trans. E. Cross (London, 1984), pp. 75ff.
18 Handel to the Fourth Earl of Shaftesbury, 29 June 1736, in O. E. Deutsch, *Handel, a Documentary Biography* (London, 1954), p. 412.
19 J. Mainwaring, *Memoirs of the Life of the Late George Frederick Handel* (London, 1760), p. 96.
20 Alexander Pope to John Gay, 16 Dec. 1731, in *Correspondence of Alexander Pope*, vol. 3 (Oxford, 1956), p. 257. The reference is to Pope's 'Epistle to Burlington', which was thought by some to be an attack on the taste of the Duke of Chandos.
21 W. H. Grattan Flood, 'Crow Street Music Hall, Dublin, from 1730 to 1754', in *Sitzungsberichte der internationalen Musikgesellschaft*, 11 (1909/10), p. 445; and the same author's 'Fishamble Street Music Hall from 1741 to 1777', in *ibid.*, 14 (1912/13), p. 51.
22 *Ibid.*, p. 52.
23 Charles Jennens to Holdsworth, 10 July 1741, quoted by C. Hogwood, *Handel* (London, 1984), p. 167.

24 Deutsch, *Handel*, p. 545.
25 Mainwaring, *Memoirs*, p. 132.
26 R. Manson Myers, *Handel's Messiah. A Touchstone of Taste* (New York, 1948), pp. 135–45; H. Robbins Landon, *Handel and his World* (London, 1984), pp. 194–202.
27 Manson Myers, *Handel's Messiah*, pp. 188–96.
28 Benjamin Victor to William Rothery, 27 Dec. 1752, Deutsch, *Handel*, p. 729.
29 J. H. Voss to Ernestine Boie, 5 Jan. 1776, in *Briefe von J. H. Voss nebst erleuternden Beilagen*, ed. A. Voss, vol. 1, Halberstadt, 1829, pp. 295–7.
30 Quoted by H. M. Flasdieck, *John Brown (1715–1766) u. seine Dissertation on Poetry and Music, Studien zur englischen Philologie*, 68 (Halle [Saale], 1924), p. 111.
31 H. Zeman, 'Das Textbuch Gottfried van Swietens zu Joseph Haydns "Die Schöpfung"', in *Die Österreichische Literatur. Ihr Profil an der Wende vom 18. zum 19. Jahrhundert (1750–1830)*, Graz, 1979, pp. 403–5.
32 Flasdieck, *John Brown*, p. 111.
33 Unsigned memorandum to Maria Theresa, Österreichisches Staatsarchiv, Allgemeines Verwaltungsarchiv, Wien, Studienhofkommission (to 1791), F. 61.
34 E. Wangermann, 'Maria Theresa – a reforming monarchy', in *The Courts of Europe*, ed. G. Dickens (London, 1977), pp. 288, 293.
35 J. A. Leith, *The Idea of Art as Propaganda in France 1750–1799* (Toronto, 1965), pp. 77–9; R. G. Saisselin, *Taste in Eighteenth Century France* (Syracuse, 1965): 'The concept of a king as a major subject for painters gave way to that of the citizen, who, like the Romans he "imitated", was destined to play a more active role in the State.'
36 See his 'Liberty', lines 381–2, *Poetical Works*, p. 335: First, unadorned / And nobly plain, the manly Doric rose.
37 *Ibid.*, lines 365–7.
38 Flasdieck, *John Brown*, pp. 87–92.
39 In the 4th ed., Paris 1801, the passages here quoted are in vol. 3, pp. 68–83. I have used in part the original English translation (7th ed., London, 1816) to convey the contemporary flavour, but have used my own where the original is too inaccurate.
40 A. L. Ringer, 'J.-J. Barthélémy and musical utopia in revolutionary France', in *Journal of the History of Ideas*, 22 (1961), pp. 360–2; R. M. Isherwood, 'The third war of the musical enlightenment', in *Studies in Eighteenth-Century Culture*, vol. 4, ed. H. E. Pagliaro, Wisconsin, 1975, pp. 239–40.
41 Quoted in le Huray and Day, *Music and Aesthetics*, p. 241.
42 *Ibid.*
43 Cf. the vivid account of the musical side of the *fêtes* by J. Tiersot, *Les fêtes et les chants de la Révolution Française* (Paris, 1908).
44 On this see the Schulz–Voss correspondence, ed. H. Gottwaldt and G. Hahne, *Schriften des Landesinstituts f. Musikforschung Kiel*, 9 (Kassel and Basel), 1960.
45 *Das Erntefest*, German trans. by F. H. W. Frölich (Altona, 1795), pp. 18, 60, 68.

12

Revolution and the visual arts

RONALD PAULSON

My subject is the meaning and the use of the term 'revolutionary' art or a 'revolution' in art, especially as applied to painting. But to begin we must acknowledge that we are usually speaking in metaphors when we use these words, and metaphors that would not have been meaningful before the French Revolution. People may subsequently have called phenomena prior to the French Revolution revolutionary, but the participants did not. After, and indeed during, the French Revolution we find artists using the term to designate activities they considered analogous to the political phenomenon – or which they wanted to privilege by association with the honorific term. The central meaning was political.

When we turn to the practical implementation of the metaphor, we have to ask what in practice is 'revolutionary' art and/or a 'revolution' in art? Presumably any overthrow of previous practice or doctrine in art may be regarded as revolutionary.

A related issue is the *representation* of political 'revolution' in art, as in historical writing, whether from a friendly or a hostile point of view. When hostile, though patently counter-revolutionary, it may quite possibly be more 'revolutionary' as art than the orthodox pro-revolutionary art, which is trapped in a system of rhetoric that must, in order to serve its political purpose, be (or become) conservative, that is easily understood, constructed out of a lexicon of familiar images.

Trotsky makes the crucial point, that revolutionary art is a transitional art, or the art of a transitional phase between reaction and consolidation (and his formulation would apply as well to counter-revolutionary art that attacks the political revolution as it represents it): 'Revolutionary art, which inevitably reflects all the contradictions of a revolutionary social system, should not be confused with socialist art for which no basis has as yet been made. On the other hand, one must not forget that socialist art will grow out of the art of this transitional period'.[1] As revolutionary art becomes socialist art it turns from subversion and gestures of overthrow to support of politico-economic principles of the ruling elite. Revolutionary art itself is defined as an art which 'reflects all the contradictions of a revolutionary social' situation; that is, it reveals all of the tensions at a moment of cataclysmic change.

Elsewhere Trotsky expresses a stronger formulation that makes art itself a parallel and independent phenomenon, not one that merely acts as a handmaiden to political revolution. He makes revolution the model for one form of the art-process itself, supplementing the peaceful one of patiently making and matching with 'a protest against reality':

> Generally speaking, art is an expression of man's need for a harmonious and complete life, that is to say, his need for those major benefits of which a society of classes has deprived him. That is why a protest against reality, either conscious or unconscious, active or passive, optimistic or pessimistic, always forms part of a really creative piece of work. Every new tendency in art has begun with rebellion.[2]

Trotsky, however, cannot conceive of the work of art outside 'a society of classes' which has 'deprived' the artist of 'major benefits': 'true art, which is not content to play variations on ready-made models but rather insists on expressing the inner needs of man and of mankind in its time – true art is unable *not* to be revolutionary, *not* to aspire to a complete and radical reconstruction of society'.[3] He assumes that a reconstruction of the history of art must necessarily be accompanied by a reconstruction of society as well in the work of 'true art'.

Trotsky's formulation needs to be complemented by Morse Peckham's more radical proposal that great art 'offers not order but the opportunity to experience more disorder than does any other human artefact, and that artistic experience, therefore, is characterized, at least from one point of view and in one of its aspects, by disorientation . . .'.[4] Of course how we take this depends on whether we think dualistically of order/disorder or monistically of only different kinds and degrees of order; or whether we regard disorientation as a defence mechanism as powerful in its own way as order. Perhaps the work of art, as Peckham supposes, predicates a kind of psychic insulation in itself (*qua* work of art) which 'permits the individual to let down his defenses and fully expose himself to disorientation'.[5]

Both Trotsky's and Peckham's alignments of art and radical change, the one political and the other existentialist, are conditioned by the aesthetic doctrines of their times. The aesthetic privileged by the men of the French Revolution was the sublime.[6] Imagery applied to the Revolution by the hostile Burke as well as the proponent Robespierre was of extraordinary upheaval based on Nature in the form of a volcanic eruption, an avalanche, or a storm – a mixture of the accidental and the inevitable, with a very small role played by human agents. The equation of revolution and sublime assumes revolution to be uncontrollable upheaval, sweeping along its human agents; and so whenever the human agent tries to deal with it either he is swept away (or devoured) or he transforms its energy into a tyranny, if his aim is political, or into beauty, if his aim is aesthetic. In short, he de-revolutionizes the sublime.

What I am suggesting is that art, which entails closure and completion (perhaps of a lower order than the art referred to by Peckham), may be said to beautify the sublime, which is limitless and normless, and has the same effect on the revolutionary phenomenon. Analogous to the effect of the politicians, art is required to bring the primal energies under control, and so by definition of function is post-revolutionary. Thus the actors in the French Revolution were seen by many contemporaries to rehearse a plot of challenge, overthrow of authority, and finally internalization in further repression.[7] But the challenge may equally be thought of as against the revolutionary hurricane itself as the human (the Napoleonic) agent tries to control the uncontrollable.

Art enters upon the scene as the practical political accommodation which attempts to render the sublime, or the revolution *per se*, manageable. Whenever the human agent tries to simulate the sublime, whether through human heroism or stubbornness or the artist's poeticizing or painting (whether he is a Goebbels, a David, a Rivera, or a Turner), inevitably he transforms it into the beautiful. It is hard to break away from this unbridgeable dualism between sublime Nature and beautiful art, although Burke, basing his sublime on obscurity, argued that the effect is best transmitted by words which, because of their incongruence with things, can further obscure Nature. Certainly metrics, as Kant argued, enclose, define, and thus destroy the measureless sublime; and the same can be said for the line, form, and pigment of the painter.

Is there then a human mode of expression that can rupture or transcend the internalization, cyclic repetition, and repression of the revolutionary sublime? Marx's analysis of the revolutionary process in *The Eighteenth Brumaire of Louis Napoleon Bonaparte* introduces the possibility of a comic sublime.[8] Marx's own term 'tragedy', as Kant had noted, beautifies the sublime, while comedy manifests an open-ended confrontation without accommodation or mediation. Tragedy, Schiller said, relies on 'established legends or history', in other words conventional closure, while comedy depends on nothing but invention; 'by the power of its will it can tear itself out of any state of limitation'. And Marx exposes the comedy of repetition in the multiple French Revolutions and Napoleons.

Comedy involves, however, repetition and fracture of the repetitive pattern. Repetition, like internalization, is a term associated with both art and comedy – with limitation, not with the sublime: it is outside, circumscribing the sublime, and so the aspect of comedy that can be isolated as in some sense revolutionary is the Aristophanic explosion of energy, not the Plautine repetition of conventional patterns, which is already present in Aristophanes as the sealed box to be broken asunder. Plautine comic form denotes reconciliation and usually contains or domesticates the explosive energy of the young lovers and the conniving servants. It may represent a formal conservatism that is part of most comedy, at least when it is enclosed in the art form of a theatrical performance. Marx's comic sublime, for example, is limited to the awareness that represents the repetition and laughs but does not express the explosive energy that will discomfit and destroy the system of repetition. As in Georg Lukács's definition of the realistic novel as 'the deformation of the epic idea under capitalism', the question is whether the deformation is taking place in the behaviour of the ruling class we watch self-destruct or in the action of the revolutionary. The regulated comic laughter of Karl Marx is a very different phenomenon from the anarchic comedy of Groucho and Harpo. If they represent the comic sublime-in-action, Karl Marx stands for Burke's safely-distant observer of the phenomenon. Even Marx's theory of the inevitability of a revolutionary dialectic has to be distinguished from a theoretically permanent revolution, a continuing challenge-response outside any formal constraints; just as the concept of a continuing revolution must be distinguished from mere anarchy.

As the sublime process is turned into the beautiful product by art, it may be turned by comedy into the grotesque. Both comic energy and comic consciousness can be subsumed under the Hegelian grotesque, a realization of the incommensurability of the Idea and any sort of representation of it in words or images. If sublime was the honorific term of aestheticians for and against revolution from Burke to Bloom and Weiskel, Bakhtin in *Rabelais and his World* has insisted, in the context of the Russian Revolution, on the priority of the grotesque, and on its pristine purity (or unity) before a dissociation of sensibility, before a vulgarization by the forces of middle-class *Schadenfreude* into the sublime, for him a term designating the control of art.

Bakhtin's myth presupposes a theoretical stage of 'ancient pagan festivities', pre-class and pre-political social order, in which 'the serious and the comic aspects of the world and of the deity were equally sacred, equally "official"'.[9] Then follows a historical stage in which the comic forms were transferred to a non-official, a sub-culture level, where they were perforce (1) a way out of the official, (2) a commentary and criticism of the official, a standing alternative to it, and (3), as tolerated by the official, a way of channelling those subversive energies that is purgative but safe and unthreatening. At this stage from being part of a central, common ritual, these energies become carnival. This is the phase in which 'folk culture' can be discerned, but it remains a structure of separation from and reintegration into society. 'Folk humour denies, but it revives and renews at the same time', Bakhtin insists over and over. 'Bare negation is completely alien to folk culture'.[10] This stage is followed by a greater dissociation in which the sundered elements are harder to reassemble, but also further domesticated by becoming literary, that is by being enshrined in print, formalized in various ways, and cut off from the lived experience of the people who created it.

We have now reached the phase when culture has broken down into ruling-class culture and suppressed sub-culture. 'Revolution' is the reassertion of these suppressed cultural images and assumptions, which replace the dominant culture. But since the ruling and the sub-culture have always been mirror images – or at least the sub-culture had mocked by mimicry the ruling-class culture – the replacement takes us back to *what was*, that idyllic time around phase one. Here Bakhtin also returns to the primitive (pre-1789) sense of 'revolution' as a complete circle back to a point of origin.

It is important to note, first, that in Bakhtin's romanticized version of aesthetic revolution, the sub-culture is associated with comic forms, comic versions of the world and the deity. But it is equally important to note that in the case of his subject, Rabelais, Bakhtin chooses not to see the Rabelaisian grotesque as the violent assertion of the old carnival values against an entrenched scholasticism, which it was. He reviles as romantic the notion that this can be satire rather than grotesque comedy; and by doing so he cancels its sense of revolution as overthrow. By reading Rabelais as a celebrator of a proletarian Golden Age in the past, a time when dissent was possible and yet remained an organic part of society, he domesticates Pantagruel and Panurge as surely as capitalist society domesticates the sublime into an aesthetic object. This was, I presume, the case of a critic writing in the Stalinist era and necessarily choosing nostalgia over activism. But the pre-romantic grotesque, whatever its current Marxist status, was an assertion, in some degree violent, of change and transition – of the interchangeability of plants–animals–humans, or kings and beggars, which in practice may have served the ruling elite of Church and state as a safety valve, and later, when this was no longer the case, served intellectuals, including Marx, as tropes critical or destructive of accepted assumptions. The historian E. P. Thompson asks the more realistic question in his essays on 'plebeian culture' in eighteenth-century England: Is the survival of the grotesque mode in carnival a revolutionary gesture on the part of the suppressed sub-culture, or is it rather part of the theatrical interplay that keeps the sub-culture docile? – as, he would probably argue, is the closure of the most subversive comedy by its ending of conventional Komos in which everyone, the old as well as the young, is reabsorbed into society.

We have dealt so far with the aesthetic categories of the sublime, the comic, and the grotesque, and along the way have introduced another term to which we shall return, the sub-culture. But there is one further term that relates to aesthetic doctrine closely connected with politics: iconoclasm, which will bring us to the two great modern examples of revolution in which iconoclastic art has played an important role, the Mexican and the Russian.

The term iconoclasm is as historically grounded as the sublime in the eighteenth century, and with a much longer doctrinal and polemical history going back to the Reformation and much further into early Church history (and yet further back into pre-Christian controversies). The chief form taken by revolutionary art and propaganda of the French Revolution was iconoclasm. An entry in the diary of a Jacobin Club meeting lays out the process as practised in France in the 1790s, starting with the given, which is extant Christian or royal art of the *ancien régime*: 'Destroy those signs of slavery and idolatry which only serve to perpetuate ignorance and superstition. Replace them with images of Rousseau, Franklin and all the other great men, ancient and modern, which will fill the people with a noble enthusiasm for liberty.'[11] 'Destroy' is followed by 'replace': Destroy the cult of kings and saints and replace it with the cult of 'great men'. Although there was much physical destruction, the process was in general limited to the phase of replacement which took the form of re-naming: the Cathedral of Notre Dame was renamed the Temple of Reason, the Trinity was renamed Liberty, Equality, and Fraternity, and the liturgy of the Mass was rewritten or restaged as a *fête*. The old Christian calendar was replaced, the holy days and months were renamed according to the concept of 'Nature' or 'Reason'. To 'Nature' was added such 'reasonable' categories as 'Republican Rome': a kind of allegorical new-world was created by Frenchmen who renamed themselves Gracchus or Cato or renamed their squares and streets so that the Place of the Revolution was followed by the Street of the Constitution which led into the Street of Happiness.[12]

But as the Revolution progressed these Enlightenment terms of Nature, Reason, and Republican Rome were replaced – more or less as the Girondins were replaced by the Jacobins – by an iconography of the *sans-culottes*, or what I have referred to as popular sub-culture, which was summed up in practice by the substitution of Marat for Christ and of other revolutionary heroes for martyrs of the Church.

We can distinguish two forms of political iconoclasm on the French model. The first intends to replace one idol with another: the heads of Christ and his Apostles are replaced by the heads of Lenin and his Politburo. The memory of Christ fades but Lenin retains some of His (so to speak) aura. (Or, looked at in another way, the tsar, who himself has been recreated as an icon of Christ, is replaced in the Christ frame by Lenin.) This is the pragmatic iconoclasm that has to take place in a practical revolutionary situation. It could be interpreted as involving either raising Marat or Lenin with the parallel of Christ, or destroying Christ and replacing him with the contemporary national hero: and the question is whether the emphasis is on the glorification of Marat or the destruction of Christ or on the act of replacement itself. The idea of iconoclasm as replacement always poses the possibility, even likelihood, that glorification will usurp the iconoclastic aspect of the act.

There is, however, a purer iconoclasm which intends to question if not destroy *any* image, any idol (or anything it designates as an idol). The revolutionary who is also a true iconoclast seldom reaches the final phase of the revolution and stability; in fact, he cannot reach this stage of rest but must insist on the continuing, the permanent revolution.

There is an extremely reactionary tinge to French iconoclasm. After all, the artists of the French Revolution were brought up in a Roman Catholic world, and what else could they do but continue to think in terms of Catholic forms, saints, liturgy, and catechism? One superstition was replaced, at least on a popular level (for which the Jacobins claimed to speak), by another. The case in England, where there was no revolution, was very different: England entered its phase of aesthetic iconoclasm nearly three hundred years before the French, and with the sanction, indeed the encouragement of its monarch. The possibility of a thoroughgoing iconoclasm was much stronger than in France, and so by the 1790s English artists had at their call a far more powerful strategy for expressing either revolution – as in Blake's prophetic books – or counter-revolution – as in Gillray's caricatures – than the academy-oriented French artists led by David. It is not surprising that the works of Blake and Gillray are more redolent of subversion and overthrow than those of David which led logically from the celebration of the Horatii and Marat to Napoleon.

David's style was, of course, not intended to correspond to 'revolution'. The *philosophes* and artists who desired a change of the sort that became the revolution in politics and the School of David in art obviously sought equivalents to the stability of alternative values, and these – a reaction against frivolity and insecurity felt to be embodied in the Rococo style – were expressed in a style that sought clarity, order, and certainty. The neo-classical style presupposed a particular image of the political act as reaction to a flighty, contingent present, and so to secure and solid ideals of the past. The style itself was revolutionary only in the sense that at a date earlier than the political revolution it had overthrown a dominant style, and when the political revolution arrived was utilized to present an ideal 'revolutionary' ethos.

The one great revolutionary painter who emerged from the era of the French Revolution was Goya. Goya's politics were ambiguous but his paintings can be said to mark the absolute end and destruction of the European tradition of decorative wall painting as beauty, glory, and indeed 'art' – most often associated with the analogous qualities of the monarchy that commissioned them. Instead of consolidating the tradition as it was developed from Titian to Veronese to Tiepolo, or even the neo-classical style of Mengs from which he also learned, Goya dismantled the tradition and reduced its components to the barest minimum: to the detail or fragment of the great academic 'machine' and to the crudest, most sketchy and scratchy application of paint; to the lowest subject-matter and the most irrational forms (from the genre of history painting to *caprìchos* and *sueños* or nightmare); and to the denial of every sense of comfortable closure including the edges of a canvas or borderlines of an etching. This I would venture to call 'revolutionary' art, but I would of course be speaking metaphorically, perhaps subjectively, and both Trotsky and David would disagree.

As an artist Goya was revolutionary because he consciously cut himself off from the Baroque and neo-classical traditions available to artists in his time; for example, by the isolation and magnification of details to monstrous proportions he destroyed and replaced the subordination of a traditionally unified picture space. But at the same time that he was upsetting the old academic assumptions (still held to, for example, by David and even by Géricault), he was of course creating a new art idiom, perhaps even form, based on alternative principles. These principles, which he sought in the revolutionary times in which he lived, he found in the sub-culture art of the people – those superstitious, grotesque, detestable mobs that in fact carried out the revolution in Spain (however wrong the reasons and counter-revolutionary the results). For Goya's later work allows us to invoke Trotsky's view that 'The most indubitable feature of a revolution is the direct interference of the masses in historic events.' What Trotsky meant is made clearer, however, by another statement: 'Not a single progressive idea has *begun* with a "mass base", otherwise it would not have been a progressive idea. It is only *in its last stage* that the idea finds its masses' – which are always backward-looking.[13] That is, as in the Spanish Revolution, we have to distinguish between the 'progressive ideas' (terms like 'reason', 'liberty', 'equality', and so on, inherited from the French) of an intellectual elite and the reactionary notions of the 'people', which in France corresponded to the two phases of iconoclasm, replacing *ancien régime* symbols with Enlightenment constructs, and then with popular superstititions.

The question is whether an art of the people – both representing and appealing to the people we see in the great paintings of popular uprisings, the *Second* and *Third of May* – need merely represent the people interfering in historic events, fulfilling the plans of an elite or taking the initiative. In the *Second of May* Goya felt he had to elevate them by painting the very kind of Baroque composition he was repudiating in his more private works. But in the pendant, the killing of the people on the Third of May, he employed sub-culture iconography and the crude forms drawn from popular prints, not necessarily Spanish (for example Paul Revere's famous *Boston Massacre*), and low-life genres of painting, but expanded to the scale of history painting. It is not clear, however, that he drew or painted *for* the people. The people's assumptions served only as a foundation for Goya's very personal, virtually private style. For the extreme of his aesthetic revolution manifested itself in the paintings of the *Quinta del Sordo*, his private house, and in the print series of 1800 to 1820, shared with a small group of friends.

'Popular' therefore refers to the people, the masses, and the sub-culture. If we can use 'people' to cover all of these categories, we can ask if there is a revolutionary art that is an art of the people, by the people, and/or for the people? I mean *of* in the sense of not only a representation of their acts but expressive of the people, taken from their own forms; *for* in the sense of understood and absorbed by them; and *by*, actually made by them. The French Revolution drew in a limited way upon their imagery and directed at them its great *fêtes*, but these were only propaganda or bread and circuses. The important, lasting art was not of, by, or for the people, that is the *bras-nus* and *sans-culottes*, the very groups Goya drew on for sustenance. Nevertheless, the French Revolution introduced the concept of the people, and Trotsky was thinking of the French as well as the Russians when he wrote.

The one revolution with which I am familiar that has been successfully represented as both iconoclasm and as a popular phenomenon was the Mexican (1910–20). Given the fact that it was presented as a revolution of the Mexican people against foreign domination, against a small elite who even when claiming to be Mexican were of foreign descent and were cut off from the original inhabitants, the most important fact was that the artists of the revolution – who worked in the 1920s and 30s – were muralists, their art an art of and for the people in the only way this could possibly be – in public buildings and the open air.

Their reaction, as one of the muralists, Jean Charlot, has said, was against 'the twin myths of personality and art for art', and their aim was to create 'anonymous masterpieces beamed to the people at large' (which he compares with Gothic cathedrals). In the second place, the surfaces they had to paint on were 'the majestic walls of ancient palaces'.[14] Following the process of iconoclasm, the artists were appropriately 'trowelling, frescoing, desecrating these hallowed places' – or so it seemed to them – as part of the act of revolutionary painting. Finally, they were reacting not only against the tired academic painting of the Mexican elite but against the formalism of international Cubism. They sought a style that was more immediate than the one, and closer to its referent the people – less an art for art's sake – than the other.

Jose Clemente Orozco himself observed that mural art is of all art 'the more disinterested, as it cannot be converted into an object of personal gain, nor can it be concealed for the benefit of a few privileged people. It is for the people. It is for everybody.'[15] There are implications here of climatic determinants, of course, such as the warmth of Mexico, for murals to be an environmental experience; but Orozco's main point, that a mural cannot be a commodity, is related to John Berger's argument that easel painting arose with private enterprise capitalism, as a way to frame and so make personal possessions of the objects represented (whether a landscape or a nude woman).[16] These remarks pretty well sum up the usefulness of mural painting in a revolution that aims at fulfilling egalitarian principles along Marxist lines.

But the Mexican muralists were also uniquely suited to represent a popular revolution. They were able not only to destroy the extant forms – religious and cultural, hierarchical and foreign – but to connect the worker-peasants who epitomized the Mexican revolution in its propaganda aspect at least with their ancient Mexican forebears, making modern revolutionary Mexico a revival of pre-Hispanic or pre-Columbian (or what is also called pre-Latin) Mexico. The essential fiction was of a return to pre-Hispanic origins, which embodied (in the words of Carlos Pellicer) an 'organic unity between social living and art' that had long been lost but was still recoverable from primitive artifacts and remote tribes. This was felt to be an art that had been simultaneously religious, ideological, public, monumental, and civic. Even writing had been pictographic, and painting had merged with sculpture and architecture in a statement of public virtue: 'Mexico's pre-Hispanic societies spoke the great language of forms, volumes, lines, colors', which was a language of unity.[17]

The second stage of the myth, corresponding to the Fall, was the Spanish occupation which broke this unity into a dissociation of sensibility. 'Indigenous art ceased as public, state, monumental art, and was converted into furtive, inhibited, domestic art of little reach.'[18] It was replaced by European, specifically Spanish, ideals and principles which assimilated some aspects of the indigenous art to its own ends (as Christianity did Greek and Near Eastern art). The situation changed little after independence since the *criollos* assumed power and considered the Indians and *mestizos* 'foreign elements, strangers on their own soil'. By the end of the nineteenth century – in the everlasting regime of Porfirio Diaz – the official art was academic, and pre-Hispanic art survived only as a sub-culture, and so as a vocabulary ready to hand for revolutionary nationalist movements that wished to cut through the repressive official culture to something pure, original, and indigenous.

The man usually given special credit for the reaction against official Mexican art on the eve of the political revolution – and who filled the role of the subversive, consciousness-raising revolutionary artist – was Jose Guadalupe Posada. His crude and sensational prints were essentially broadsides, either cut out of zinc plates to resemble woodcuts or drawn directly on plates that were then cut away with acid, often printed on pink or red paper surrounded by crude type faces that set off the figures. They were enlivened by the *calavera* or living skeleton figures of Mexican folk culture but could also be apocalyptic in a way that would stimulate Rivera and Orozco on the larger scale of the mural.

Diego Rivera placed at the very centre of his huge Hotel del Prado mural in Mexico City (1947–8) one of Posada's female skeletons in fantastic head-dress, flanked by Posada himself in his middle class Sunday best and on the other side the young Diego, the artist of the revolution (represented as he looked at the time of Posada's innovations, his stimulation to revolutionary consciousness). The skeleton woman has one hand on Posada's arm and the other holds Diego's hand. Posada is presented as Rivera's spiritual father, with his mother (Posada's image of) Death, and between the youth Diego and the skeleton is his wife-to-be, Frida Kahlo, who holds a bitten apple. The artist, with the imagery of true and false paternity (the figure of Diaz looks frowningly down on this family group), the Christian iconography of Adam and Eve and their Fall, the conventional revolutionary imagery of youth and sexuality, places himself at the heart of an eclectic revolutionary myth.

For Rivera comes upon the scene – or saw himself as doing so – when the continental academic tradition was dominant in Mexican easel painting and the school of Daumier and the Kepplers in political cartoons.[19] Against these the crude block-print shapes of Posada offered a 'revolutionary' alternative, both in a 'people's' art and in the subversive implications of the death's heads mimicking the activities of polite society. Posada's *Dance of Death*, which levels kings and peons, draws upon the traditional Mexican carnival, the sub-culture's way of expressing itself in the eighteenth-century Spain of Goya as in the twentieth-century Mexico of Rivera. One of the prominent images is the firing squad in front of which all the victims assume heroic stances and are of the people – those earlier leaders of unsuccessful revolutions. Posada probably in fact draws on Goya's *Third of May* and his *Desastres* for these images of pre-revolutionary agitation.

And yet, despite Rivera's official history, as his own forms in all of his murals show, the original response to the revolution was not exclusively indigenous. Rather it involved the artist's usual search for equivalents wherever he could find them, especially in what he regarded as the high style. Rivera, a young artist who had assimilated all the latest Parisian styles, in 1922 returned to Mexico after ten years in Europe. The heroic phases of the revolution were already over and could be seen in retrospect. Rivera was well-schooled in the principles of Cubism, but the model both he and Orozco chose to employ in the great experimental studio for the revolutionary muralists, the National Preparatory School in Mexico City, was Italian Trecento fresco-painting in the manner of Giotto, or Quattrocento in the manner of Ambrogio Lorenzetti and Uccello. The common factors were mild climate and open-air loggias, public display, a 'primitive' art, and a religio-political purpose. The Giotto-attributed St Francis cycle in Assisi embodied all of these elements together with what still appeared to be a subversive subject, the saint who turns against the worldliness of the Church. In short, while the ethnic sub-culture – oppressed as well as national and primitive in the sense of pre-Hispanic – offered a large part of the imagery for these artists, they conveyed it (made it artistically viable) by seeing the forms of pre-Hispanic art through the mediation of Giotto, Lorenzetti, and the early-Renaissance fresco-painters on the one hand, while retaining the tight surface tensions of contemporary Cubist art on the other.[20]

The Preparatory School (an appropriate starting place because of its history as a centre of dissent) is a building with open loggias around courtyards, and also, pointing toward the later Baroque phase of the muralists, with irregularly shaped walls and ceilings in the stairways. The dominant figure in the Preparatory School was Orozco, a more sardonic, less easily satisfied painter than Rivera, who painted Giottesque panels on the stairway which secularize the religious fervour of Pietàs and Franciscan charity. But when he painted the unbroken wall of the second-floor loggia he let the panels merge into one long political comic-strip.

Beginning as a planar procession in profile, it turns at the left corner into a Baroque confrontation of capitalists and workers. Along the way there are purely symbolic decorations like the huge church poor-box being emptied into a capitalist's grasping hand.

For Orozco also derives from Posada. Basing a mural history painting on the conventions of political cartoons is not a strange strategy since the point of both is an emphasis, either heroic or monstrous, that exalts or denigrates human aspirations. Posada showed the way toward the popular imagery of political cartoons, as toward the conventions of popular parades, carnivals, and rituals. The imagery of Goya's walls in the *Quinta del Sordo* is probably in the background also, but Orozco's immediate graphic model was the cartoons of *The Masses*, with their popular implications and simple metaphoric relationships: a gigantic hand or fist coming down on helpless masses or on cringing capitalists; a huge virtuous head of Father Hidalgo or Juarez overwhelming the little wicked foreigners, or urging on the Mexican people. The forms are rendered more awesome by size and by the infusion of elements of German Expressionism, in particular the agitated brushwork, which shows up to powerful effect in the free-application of fresco painting. There are images of man-monsters made of barbed wire or humans wrapped in chains (the Emperor Maximilian wrapped in his grave-clothes, based on a photograph taken at the time of his reburial), which remind one more of William Blake than of Posada. In the Cabañas Orphanage in Guadalajara, Orozco's ceilings resemble Blake designs blown up to gigantic size. Cortez resembles Urizen with a sphinx-harpy whispering advice in his ear; the rising man of fire in the central cupola is a monstrous Orc figure; and the mechanical horses of the Apocalypse and the Urizenic face of God in the '*Bewilderment of Religions*' panels all recall the iconography of Blake's '*Bible of Hell*'. Even Orozco's colours are usually reds and grays, grays and blacks, whites and reds – perhaps symbolically fire and earth, but also the basic colours of newsprint art and of the heavy blacks surrounding Blake's figures and reappearing in German Expressionist woodcuts.

The popular political cartoon carries Orozco from the Trecento into the Baroque, to the garish foreground whores in the Belles Artes Palace mural, which resembles a huge blow-up of Toulouse-Lautrec interiors of the Moulin Rouge with red or green-tinted female faces in the foreground, out of scale with the background figures. These are, of course, images of bourgeois counter-revolutionary corruption. From the genuinely Baroque experience of the murals in Guadalajara he goes on to the Scarlet Woman, the Whore of Babylon riding on the Beast of the Apocalypse (a Mexican Jaguar) in the Sabina Ortiz Library in Jiquilpan: in the background are the

Mexican eagle and snake, but the snake is now strangling the eagle. This perverse apocalypse acknowledges that nothing is ever going to be finally right, revolution or no revolution.

Orozco shows the combat, the moment of confrontation, the never-ending conflict between bourgeoisie and proletariat – and, above all, the awareness of the discrepancy between what the Mexican Revolution intended and what it achieved. The strength of Orozco's art, and his importance for the Mexican example, lies in the unresolved quality of the continuing and faltering revolution. He is representing the phase of disillusionment which Byron and Goya represented following the decline of the French Revolution into the conquests of Napoleon. But he also represents the view of a Marat or Hébert, an anarchism that will not be satisfied with anything but a permanent revolution.

Rivera, on the other hand, tends to celebrate the triumph of Mexico's social revolution, the consummation of the process, and he is able to do so because of the continuity he recreates between the ancient Mexican past and the present. He always retains the integrity of the wall surface (which Orozco constantly violates), showing better than any of the other painters the continuity with pre-Hispanic art. He combines the peasant images of folk rituals, carnival and death, masks and banners, with the *horror vacui* of Aztec decorative painting on the one hand and its Baroque Spanish equivalent in Catholic altarpieces on the other. The huge, looming, out-of-scale carnival figures or faces become the telescopic lense, the hands and eyes of the *Man at the Crossroads* mural; which, however, operate quite differently from the huge foreground figures of Orozco. Rivera's figures, less Baroque and disorienting, serve to organize a great deal of disparate material on a single wall, to establish symbolic relationships (vs. narrative ones), and to recall the Aztec temple walls or the cutaways of Spanish mines in which the Indians slaved. His paintings all seek in various ways the strong sense of layers – of archaeological strata, of excavations, of capitalist brain centres and hidden origins deep down under the city streets. The model remains the colonial mine that fed the rich and fuelled the state.

The myth he relates begins in the insurgent phase with the rogues' gallery of oppressors – the white invaders from Quetzalcoátl to Cortez to the frock-coated Maximilian and the French–English–American capitalists who governed through Diaz. Then there is the Mexican hero who rebels and dies a martyr – priests who were unfrocked and shot by the ubiquitous firing squad (recalled in those images of Posada's) – and is followed by another and yet another martyr (one is reminded of the revolutionary myth that grew up in nineteenth-century Ireland) until at last freedom is achieved. These heroes include the Lafayette–Madero figure, the idealist of the first phase of revolution who is destroyed in the Huerta counter-revolution. Finally there are the Orc figures (to use Blake's name) of Pancho Villa or Emilio Zapata – the bandit leaders, anarchistic, truly reaching up from the bottom (as opposed the Maderos or even the Carranzas, or Obregón, who survives after all the Villas and Zapatas are dead – one of those who accomplish what the martyrs began but then, refusing to play the Cincinnatus or Washington and give up office, are assassinated by their own people).

Two facts are at the bottom of the myth: its origin in agrarian uprising and the redistribution of land to the rural masses, with the peasant heroes Zapata and Villa; and the fact of sacrifice, of freedom rising simultaneously from the land and from the blood of martyrs which 'nourished' it. These are not ancient Aztec sacrifices, which Rivera associates with Spanish oppression of the Indians, but images of natural growth and fruition, most impressively expressed in the Baroque forms of the Chapel in Chapingo which exploit not only the Romanesque vaulting of the chapel but its rounded windows, which become wombs, seed pods, and tree boles. The cross-section of Zapata and Montano dead and buried in the earth, above whose corpses rise luxuriant cornfields, embodies the myth of revolution in Mexico. The earth can be mined by slave labour and used as a brain-centre from which to control cities above, in short a huge machine-like operation; but this is a colonialist corruption of its true, natural function of genesis from which plants grow like the ones Thomas Paine described at the close of *Rights of Man*. The imagery of spring and fruition is one of assertion and reassertion, related to those counter-gestures in the political cartoons of pressing down, striking low, and bursting upward.[21]

Where did the popular mural art lead in Mexico? The Rivera aspect of the mural movement led to the façade of Juan O'Gorman's University of Mexico Library, a familiar postcard image. The Baroque of Orozco led to the dissolution of the wall, the change of architectural boundaries to correspond to visionary ones – everything focused in the contrast between static areas of wicked capitalism and surging advancing masses, or lunging male arms and female breasts. Siqueiros carried mural painting to its extreme of technical virtuosity, sending steel-breasted Amazons zooming out at the spectator and making three-dimensional the long-armed men on the front of the Humanities Building of the University. The convolutions of the walls of the Sala de Revolucion at Chapultapec Castle suggest a funhouse or a cinema lobby. Like the ceilings of La Raza Hospital, these are intended to disorient the visitor, subvert his capitalist assumptions, stimulate his revolutionary consciousness, and thrust the truth at him in the most cinematic terms. Siqueiros reminds one that the

Baroque emphases of Orozco could also owe much to the montage of Eisenstein's Russian films. The end product, however, of both the Rivera and the Siqueiros types of popular art was the Tamayo murals in the Sanborn department store along the Reforma and in the National Anthropological Museum; and the O'Gorman murals in the National History Museum in Chapultapec Castle.

One final speculation on the relationship of political and aesthetic revolution may be pertinent. The careers of the American abstract Expressionists began with the Great Depression and the public activism of the 1930s, including the assumption that painting should raise the revolutionary (or at least social) consciousness of its viewers. One lesson of that propaganda art was that the committed artist shows his outrage at the *status quo* in the marks with which he scores great expanses of flat wall. Pollock's drip paintings related in certain important ways back to the assumptions, figuration and forms he learned from the mural paintings of Orozco, with whom he worked. He presumably discarded the content, then the figuration, but retained the forms, which in Orozco's angry attack were the gestures of the artist as activist corresponding to the social gestures of the political revolutionary.

While Pollock would have claimed that by the 1940s he was thinking in purely formal terms (for which we may also read subjective) – open, to use yet another terminology, to the sway of his own body above the prone canvas – there is no way that we can subtract from those forms the political content they embodied prior to their emptying, any more than we can ignore the act of *emptying* or for that matter the powerful emotional – many would feel 'revolutionary' – charge in Pollock's most 'abstract' canvases. Pollock may have wanted to free himself from certain painterly restraints, but he did so with gestures and forms that had once carried a political meaning, and which – I think it is generally agreed – still did when their immediate end was probably formal rather than political. Not only their method but their self-affirming gestures are surely as close as we can come to the expansive energy that has been referred to as comic in the scenarios of Aristophanes, Rabelais, and the Marx Brothers. We might want to argue that these expansive forms, once attached to depictions of political revolution, were then embodied in an aesthetic revolution, and expressed it better than if Pollock had been following, say, Reginald Marsh or Diego Rivera, whose walls depicted a subject closer to Bakhtin's Edenic carnival. Pollock was subsequently (as Serge Guilbaut shows in *How New York Stole the Idea of Modern Art*) pre-empted by the bourgeois media, Time and Life, Inc., and sanitized into a product labelled American Freedom in Action Painting, to be used as a stick to beat the timid company art of the USSR.

The most obvious test case of revolutionary art was, of course, the Russian, where the concept of a revolutionary 'elite' dominates. Parallel to the small elite led by Lenin, there was an elite of avant-garde painters, and, in Kandinsky and others, innovators to whom is sometimes assigned the honour of having produced the first totally non-representational painting, which is presumably a revolutionary gesture of a sort. The issue here is the relationship between the revolutionary cadre (or elite) and the avant-garde, another sort of elite, and between the elite and the popular, the workers' uprising. For example, Lenin's overthrow and reconstitution of the traditional form of Russian government was 'revolutionary', and so was Malevich's painting of a canvas all-over white.

There was a brief period when part of the Russian avant-garde did support and help (in Robert C. Williams's words) to 'legitimize the revolution through its artistic innovation and its political propaganda'.[22] Moreover, though no one used the word 'avant-garde', many artists did associate 'artistic innovation and opposition to accepted social and political behavior', especially after the 1905 rebellion. Williams even believes that the 1905 revolt may have 'facilitated, but did not initiate, the importing of innovative elements' in Russian art. It acted as a catalyst, and some artists did try to fuse artistic innovation and revolutionary commitment in their work. But the real innovators had reached maturity around the turn of the century; the younger generation tried to merge both kinds of revolt against bourgeois society.

Suprematism and Constructivism were the two avant-garde modes that took up the successful Revolution of 1917. Both were non-objective systems based on Cubist principles, but, while the first sought an upward abstraction into theosophical spirit, the second found its abstraction in the materials of working-class culture. Both were, in terms of the art tradition, revolutionary and iconoclastic. An old order was overthrown and essential parts of what was considered 'art' were wiped out or replaced. For example, the meaning of a work of art was to be not in the representational quality of the picture but in the pictorial elements themselves and their interactions. The flatness of the picture became an important aspect of its content. And yet in these assumptions both Suprematists and Constructivists were also returning to the Russian icon, for the idealism of the first and the carpentry of the second find their equivalents in the art of Rublev.

Can the aims of these avant-garde movements be verbalized to sound like Marxist – or political-revolutionary – doctrine? There was much talk about reductivist means to express plastic values. A work based on only a compass and a ruler, devoid of all subjective elements or any idea of that bourgeois affectation 'style', aimed at expressing dynamic space and dynamic form. This was a tenet that could reasonably be shared with the ideologists of the October Revolution. Even more, the Constructivist use of materials gathered at random and not previously associated with 'high art' seems a manifestation or materialization of Trotsky's argument about the revolution and the people. Wood, metal, tar, and glass were proletarian materials used by the Constructivists not for their elitist associative and narrative values (as in, say, a Cubist collage) but for their inherent formal, textural, and colouristic possibilities – and often, as in Popova's designs, for utilitarian purposes. These were modern industrial materials associated with factory labour, with the machine age, and with dynamic movement (that word again, versus the stagnant stasis of the old regime). This synthesis of material, volume, and construction was in its dynamic sense *for* the people; as it consisted of open structures integrated with the viewer's own space, it was *of* the people; and as it emphasized the collaborative action of a group, it was *by* the people. Vladimir Tatlin and others attempted by this strategy to represent the revolutionary ideals of aesthetic materialism and utilitarianism, of artistic self-effacement and depersonalization, and thus produce an art of both the people and the revolution.[23]

Moreover, the concept of an avant-garde elite was not eliminated. As Harold Rosenberg has observed, Constructivism could imply a self-effacement of opposite kinds: either 'the utilitarian depersonalization of the factory hand' or 'the metaphysical (or mystical) self-negation of the saint or seer': 'Negation of self was also a necessary condition for an art of essences or metaphysical entities. The same abstract forms could represent either the anonymity of the conveyor belt or that of mystical revelation.'[24] Much the same could be said of Suprematism. Malevich's proposal for a cube as Lenin's mausoleum simply equated this symbol in a theosophical way (recalling Boullée in the eighteenth century) with eternity and the fourth dimension, and was in that sense an updating of the traditional Russian religious icon.[25]

The striving for the spiritual content of Marxist revolution in Suprematism and for the material in Constructivism were alternative ways, both doomed to failure because of their essential lack of contact with the 'people'. Ironically, in this case it was probably not the 'people' (if by that we mean the masses of Great Russia) who rejected this art but the petit-bourgeois civil servants of the Communist state who, like Lenin, were educated in the old, conservative, academic art forms. 'Soviet realism', according to Trotsky, 'consists in the imitation of provincial daguerreotypes of the third quarter of the last century'.[26]

It is not impossible to sympathize with Zhdanov when he laid down the party line at the All-Union Congress of 1934. He looked around him and saw a plethora of eccentric art movements, each trying to discredit the other, all apparently examples of bourgeois subjectivism, of formalism with no reference except to the art object itself. And so he discredited Constructivism along with the rest, replacing them with 'socialist realism', which was, in fact, 'a romanticism of a new kind, a revolutionary romanticism' which shows only heroes and allows the masses 'to catch a glimpse of our tomorrow' – an attempt, as rhetoric, to transform 'the human consciousness in the spirit of Socialism'.[27] In practice, painters turned back to the art of the 'wanderers', rebels of the 1860s but academicians of the 1930s, and especially to Ilya Repin who survived into the Soviet period. Repin's famous painting of Ivan the Terrible clasping the Czarevich he has just murdered (1885) shows the son slumped in the pose of a dead Christ. Walking through the Trettiakov Museum in Moscow and the Russian Museum in Leningrad, one sees that the genealogy of Russian 'socialist realism' can be traced on the one hand back to French academicism and on the other back to Russian religious icons.

This is precisely the dichotomy implied by Constructivism on a somewhat higher level of aesthetic consciousness. Thus Lenin appears as a bald Jesus-icon, and his birth is celebrated as a movable feast which every year falls on Good Friday. As a man of ideas and actions, he is a vigorously arguing Christ in the Temples or Among the Disciples.[28] The martyred worker-soldiers of the history paintings are posed in crucifixions and depositions, just as David portrayed the heroes of his revolution. The additional heritage of the avant-garde survived, for a time at least and in increasingly modified form, in posters and films. The film, the mass medium par excellence, is the best place to look for the Russians' representation of revolution – in Dovchenko's melting ice-flows and budding trees, Eisenstein's surging crowds contrasted with small groups of cigar-smoking, frock-coated capitalists enclosed in luxurious offices or clubs. The scenario of Eisenstein's *The Strike* is of oppression, revolt, suppression, but spiritual victory – the same scenario used in his retellings of the Battleship Potemkin episode and the October Revolution, but in the last followed by the release of the people by the Bolsheviks into masses that flow into and over the palaces of the *ancien régime* like the irreverent murals of Rivera and Orozco.

In so far as every revolution fails – not only the immediate failure of 1848, 1871, and 1905, but the long-run disillusionment of 1789 and 1917 – the artist who is himself 'revolutionary' (in whichever of the senses I have traced) has a subject, a retrospective view of failure and counter-revolution which may relate in interesting ways to his aesthetic experiments as well. This was still, I believe, Orozco's source of strength in the 1930s as well as Pollocks's, following the disillusionment with both America and Russia, in the 1950s.

A revolution in art can take place in times of absolute political tranquillity. We can only generalize that, in a time of disruption, art tends to be one of defences, seeking ways of putting the fear outside the range of consciousness, for the artist if not for his audience. However representational of disruption – often exaggerating and intensifying the disruption – the effect of the style is the same as that of the *fort-da* game of Freud's child, to distance and control catastrophe, loss, and uncertainty. During the time of stability and security, art has no choice but to express what is still missing. It becomes ironic and deals in discrepancies – perhaps creating discrepancies in order to resolve them. The only safe generalization is to say that great art is always *other*.

NOTES

1 'Literature and Revolution', in *Leon Trotsky on Literature and Art*, ed. Paul N. Siegel (New York, 1970), p. 60.
2 'Art and politics in our epoch', *Partisan Review*, Aug. 1938, in Siegel, *Leon Trotsky*, p. 104.
3 *Ibid.*, p. 117.
4 *Man's Rage for Chaos: Biology, Behavior and the Arts* (New York, 1967), p. 41.
5 *Ibid.*, p. 83.
6 See my *Representations of Revolution* (New Haven, 1983), ch. 3.
7 Cf. Trotsky's view of the artist rebelling prior to a revolutionary situation, when bourgeois society is 'able to control and assimilate every "rebel" movement in art and raise it to the level of official "recognition"'. But the consequence of this absorption is, as Trotsky sees, that 'a fresher revolt would surge up to attain in its turn, after a decent interval, the steps of the academy'. Then with the 'decline of bourgeois society', the absorption is no longer practicable; the conflict between artist and society is exacerbated. In both cases there is a stimulus to further and yet further departures. This view is consistent with Trotsky's advocacy of the continuing revolution, and runs counter to the art intended to represent and advertise a stable regime (see 'Art and politics in our epoch', in Siegel, *Leon Trotsky*, p. 105).
8 Gary Shapiro, 'From the sublime to the political', in *New Literary History* (Winter 1985), pp. 213–35; and my 'Versions of a human sublime', in the same issue, pp. 427–37, on which I base the following remarks.
9 *Rabelais and his World*, trans. Helene Iswolsky (Cambridge, Mass., 1965), p. 61.
10 *Ibid.*, p. 11.
11 Quoted in Albert Mathiez, *Les origines des cultes révolutionnaires* (Paris, 1904), p. 112.
12 See James H. Billington, *Fire in the Minds of Men: Origins of the Revolutionary*

Faith (New York, 1980), p. 48, n. 152.

13 Trotsky, in Siegel, *Leon Trotsky*, p. 112 (italics added).

14 Charlot, Foreword to Eva Cockcroft, John Webber, and James Cockcroft, *Towards a People's Art: The Contemporary Mural Movement* (New York, 1980).

15 Orozco, quoted in Cockcroft, Webber, and Cockcroft, *Toward a People's Art*, p. 238.

16 Berger, *Ways of Seeing* (London, 1972).

17 Carlos Pellicer, *Mural Paintings of the Mexican Revolution, 1921–1960* (Mexico City, n.d.), pp. 38–41. See also Antonio Roderiguez, *Arte murale nel Messico* (originally *Der Mensch in Flammen*, Dresden, 1967; Milan, n.d.).

18 Pellicer, *ibid.*

19 An issue of *Artes de Mexico* (18 (1971), no. 147) is devoted to 'El humorismo mexicano' and has much to say about Posada.

20 As Charlot noted, they were reacting against the formalism of Cubism and yet 'Parisian Cubism remains at the core of our murals' (Foreword to Cockcroft, Webber, and Cockcroft, p. xvii).

21 Trotsky would add to the influences I have listed the Russian Revolution itself: 'Without October, his [Rivera's] power of creative penetration into the epic of work, oppression and insurrection would never have attained such breadth and profundity. Do you wish to see with your own eyes the hidden springs of the social revolution? Look at the frescoes of Rivera. Do you wish to know what revolutionary art is like? Look at the frescoes of Rivera' (Siegel, *Leon Trotsky*, p. 110).

22 Robert C. Williams, *Artist in Revolution: Portraits of the Russian Avant-Garde, 1904–1925* (Bloomington, 1977). See also John E. Bowlt, *Russian Art and the Avant-Garde: Theory and Criticism 1902–1934* (New York, 1976).

23 See George Rickey, *Constructivism: Origins and Evolution* (New York, 1967); *The Avant-Garde in Russia 1910–30*, ed. Stephanie Barron and Maurice Tuchman (Cambridge, Mass., 1980); Christina Lodder, *Russian Constructivism* (New Haven, 1984).

24 Rosenberg, 'Metaphysical feelings in modern art', *Critical Inquiry*, 2 (1975), 224–5.

25 Constructivism was the most committed of the post-revolutionary developments. But 'while the term Constructivism was used no earlier than January 1921 in Russia and seemed to represent a genuine response to the demand for an industrial, proletarian art, it must not be forgotten that "Constructivist" design had existed in Russia well before the revolution' – without revolutionary content. Moreover, the utilitarian aspect of Constructivism, picked up by the bourgeoisie in the West and used to decorate their homes and bodies, was a weak signifier for revolution or proletarianization (John E. Bowlt, 'The old new wave', *New York Review of Books*, 16 February 1984, p. 28).

26 Trotsky, in Siegel, *Leon Trotsky*, p. 109.

27 See Bowlt, *Russian Art and the Avant-Garde*, pp. 293–4.

28 See James H. Billington, *The Icon and the Axe* (New York, 1970), pp. 36–7.

13

Revolution and technology

AKOS PAULINYI

The subject proposed by the editors was tempting. After an initial glance through the varied literature on the history of technology and culture, as well as on the philosophy of technology, I was, like W. Jonas, 'overwhelmed and bewildered by the wealth of technical revolutions',[1] but was simultaneously struck by the fact that numerous authors fundamentally rejected the idea of describing technological changes as revolutionary. There were two factors which changed my mind about making the 'revolutions' of the stirrup, fulling mill, clockwork, water wheel, steam engine and electricity – to name but a few – the focal point of my study. On the one hand, there was the limited space available. On the other hand, and more decisively, there were two perceptions gleaned from my reading. Firstly, in the majority of cases, 'revolution' is used only as a word – not as a scientific term. This means, in my opinion, that the central question, whether these 'revolutions' changed *technology as a system*, is not even put, let alone answered. Secondly, many authors deny the revolutionary character of just those technological innovations which are treated by historical handbooks in varying depth and order under the heading 'The Industrial Revolution'.

The last perception bewildered me all the more because in no book on the history or philosophy of technology is it doubted that the technological changes which took place approximately between 1760 and 1860 introduced a new era. Therefore, I have made it my primary objective to show that these changes in manufacturing techniques – which through their quality and quantity resulted in the breakthrough from 'manufacture to machino-facture'[2] do indeed constitute a technical revolution. A revolution, for the reason that these changes, the base element of which was the massive and irreversible application of machines for the forming of materials, led to the establishment of a new technological system that has been developed continuously since then and still exists.

Before we endeavour to supply proof of this assertion by comparing the basic features of the old and the new technological systems, it is first essential to define what we understand by technology, by revolution and, finally, by technical revolution.

We are dealing with technology (*Technik*) in the narrower sense of the term, one corresponding approximately with what Gottl-Ottlilienfeld called *Realtechnik* and tried to define as 'the entity of procedures and devices for actions dominating nature' ('das abgeklärte Ganze der Verfahren und Hilfsmittel des naturbeherrschenden Handelns').[3] Now, a good two generations later, we still have no definition of technology recognized by all branches of science. Over the last twenty years, however, both in the philosophy of technology and in the system theory of technology, the limitation of the term technology (*Technik*) to artifacts or the identification of technology with applied natural science has been overcome. Today, man has been brought back into the picture and, thereby, the overall divergence from the Marxist position reduced.[4]

On the basis of these results, we shall consider technology to be a system:

1 of artifacts (artificial objects) and
2 of processes, in which man (a) premeditatedly designs as well as produces these artifacts and (b) uses them to achieve a certain end (the satisfaction of a need).

Without being able to go into detail here, some of the features of technology contained in this summary should be delineated. All artifacts – from flint hand-axes to automatic lathes and from the flute to the electronic organ – were and are still the result of man's determined and purposeful actions; the realization of a 'premeditated design' through production techniques.[5] Hence, technology as the making of artifacts encompasses all areas of the production of producer and consumer goods. Technology as the application of artifacts extends far beyond this, however, and is present in the majority of areas of daily life. This necessarily means that there can be no division between man and technology and, because man is a social creature, technology cannot be independent of society and its socio-economic system. Technology is always dependent on the primarily economic needs of a society – regardless of how these needs are determined – and its development is promoted or inhibited accordingly. Further it follows necessarily also that human labour – whatever its scope or form – is an indispensable factor both in the making and in the use of artifacts for and in production.

In our considerations of whether something has happened in the course of technological development which could be described as a revolution, we shall base our interpretation on two premises. In the first place, we shall assume that, in the process of the establishment of a new socio-economic system, the word revolution characterizes the change of power, i.e., in principle, the overthrow of a ruling class and the seizure of power by the representatives of another class. Secondly, we shall take it for granted that evolution does not represent 'a rigid alternative to revolution',[6] but instead that both form a unity. In other words, we shall regard revolution as 'only' being the breakthrough, the turning-point in the development. Revolutions are prepared, accelerated or delayed by evolutionary changes in the old system over a long period of time. Such changes influence the form and course of a revolution just as much as they can help consolidate or undermine the newly established system.

Therefore, the question of revolution in the technological sphere is whether, over a certain period of time, in an existing technological system – with a structure consisting of different elements interlinked with each other and with the system – qualitative changes took place in the elements in sufficient quantity for these new elements to bring about changes in the structure and, in the last analysis, in the system itself, i.e. to have brought about a new technological system.

The system of production techniques

A question such as this, however, can neither be answered by listing or describing inventions and innovations nor by analysing their social and economic preconditions and consequences. Our aim will be to identify technical characteristics determining the technological systems in the epochs approximately before and after the middle of the eighteenth century. For this we must endeavour to analyse technology as a system.[7] In doing this, we will neglect the specific features of agricultural technology and concentrate on what we call the system of production techniques and in this on the sub-system of forming materials, i.e. on actions which result in changing the form (shape) of materials.

Initially, let us define *production techniques* as including the following technical actions:

(a) the extraction of materials and the processing of materials from the original form into a defined end form, and

(b) changing the location (the transport) of materials.

However, to fulfil all of these technical actions, *power* (energy) and *information* are required, and they must both be produced or acquired and processed, that is, transformed as well as transported, i.e. transferred. In this sense, power and information technology are as old as man: something obscured by the fact that man himself has been both the producer and converter of power, as well as the producer and transmitter of information. Only in the course of many thousands of years did these techniques take on the material form of artifacts and subsequently become independent branches of technology and industry. Nevertheless, the modern systematic scientific classification of technology seems to be a useful starting point for a historical analysis of technology and, therefore, on this basis we can define production techniques as being technical actions (techniques):

(a) for the extraction and processing of materials, energy and information, as well as,

(b) for the change of their location (their transportation).

A definition such as this does not contradict the fact that transport technology also exists outside of production techniques as a separate sub-system of technology.[8]

By the extraction of materials, we mean only the gaining of various natural materials such as clay, stone (ore), wood, bones, etc. from 'nature', i.e. from the earth, plants and animals. In raw or in processed form, i.e. after they have already been subjected to one processing stage, these materials represent the raw materials for the *processing of materials*. This is composed of a series of technical processes which, in conjunction with various technical facilities, enable the required end to be achieved. According to the principle of technology, we must firstly distinguish between two main groups in the processing of materials:

(a) *conversion of materials*, which leads to a change in the physical/chemical properties of these materials, and

(b) *forming (or shaping) of materials*, which results in materials being changed from their original form into another form essentially definable in geometric terms.

In the case of the *conversion of materials*, we are dealing with chemical and bio-chemical processes which, by means of chemical reactions, convert the original materials into materials (main and secondary products) with different chemical compositions. Basically, the conversion of material results in new materials which do not occur naturally. For example, from the thermo-chemical process of smelting using iron ore, coal and flux (mainly lime), we obtain iron as the main product and gaseous products and slag as secondary products. Material-conversion technology is dependent on material-forming techniques both for the processing of the raw materials and in the provision of the technical devices.

The aim of material-forming is the production from a given original form of another form, i.e. with a different shape, which is basically definable in geometric terms. This is the oldest type of technical action and was (and is) predominant in the overall system of production techniques.[9] Not only that, the prevailing standard of material-forming technology is decisive for the standard of production techniques as a whole because the bulk of technical artifacts for satisfying human needs is produced by means of the procedures and devices of material-forming technology.

On this basis of the present system of technology, we can reduce material-forming technology essentially to four technical processes:

1 creative forming (e.g. casting, glass blowing)
2 reforming (e.g. forging, rolling, drawing, bending)
3 separating (or cutting; e.g. turning, planing, milling, comminuting) and
4 joining (or connecting; e.g. wedging, nailing, screwing, clamping, twisting, spinning, weaving, knitting, etc.)

An important criterion in this connection is the original condition of the material. Thus, creative forming produces materials with solid bodies from 'formless' materials, i.e. liquid, pulp or powder. Reforming is concerned with changing the shape of ductile materials (for example steel and other metals, as well as today's so-called plastics). Through the separating and joining procedures, different solid materials such as stone, wood, metals, as well as animal or vegetable fibres, are processed to produce various forms, whereby, in the case of separating, the cohesion of materials is reduced or even eliminated and, in the case of joining, the cohesion of one or more materials is increased or created.

In the production process, material-forming is either carried out by only one procedure or, in the majority of cases, by several procedures with one or more increasingly differentiated and specialized means – from the simplest tool to the most complicated technical system. In distinction to material-conversion techniques where the conversion is realized through chemical reactions, all material-forming processes have a common denominator: the so-called *action pair* consisting of the *workpiece* to be processed and the *tool* for forming it.[10] The technical process for changing the form of the workpiece is carried out in pre-planned and defined relative movements between the workpiece and the tool whereby the tool acts on the workpiece. Essentially, this means a change of the mutual positions of the workpiece and the tool. For this purpose, it is necessary to provide and transmit both power and information to the action pair. Additionally, it might be necessary to change the location of the workpiece within the forming process. Thus, to a greater or lesser extent, all constituent sub-systems of production techniques are involved in every form-changing process and we can consider all means used to change the form of materials as technical systems whose individual elements perform certain functions.

What functions must be carried out in all technical systems, in order to be able to realize the necessary – i.e. the planned and defined – relative movement between the workpiece and the tool? For this purpose, the tool and the workpiece must be moved into a certain position and moved over a certain path by transmission of the power (which has been made available in one way or another). In other words, the holding (fixing) as well as the guiding and moving functions of both components of the action pair, together with the provision and transmission of energy and information, must be secured. Hence, these functions are a *conditio sine qua non* for all material-forming procedures and can be either carried out all by man alone, partly by man and partly by technical devices, or exclusively by technical devices.

Hand-tool technology and working-machine technology

Thus, the characteristic feature of technical development is the transfer of individual functions from man to technical devices and, in the case of *form-changing production processes* during the process of '*technological penetration*' (*Technisierung*)[11] lasting many thousands of years, we are basically concerned with two systems of technical action: with *hand-tool technology* and *working-machine technology*.[12] They both have several stages of development with regard to the variety, quality and degree of specialization of the technical facilities used, and are employed side by side, as well as in conjunction, for the purpose of technical actions. Neither this variety nor their coexistence should blind us to the fact that there is a principal technical difference between the two systems: in hand-tool technology, man carries out the functions of holding and guiding the tool and/or the workpiece which determine the relative movement between the workpiece and the tool. In working-machine technology, these functions must be carried out by a technical device. The result of a technical process consciously planned and determined by man is, in the first case, directly dependent upon man and, in the second case, dependent on devices designed by man.

Thus, for technologically determining the dividing line between both technologies, the most decisive criterion is how and by what means the relative movement between the workpiece and the tool is ultimately determined. Is it ultimately determined by human actions? Can we still refer to hand-tool technology when a technical device is used for one or more of the necessary functions? Let us take an example to illustrate the principle. A person wants to make a handle for a tool from a piece of wood. To achieve this objective, he employs the separating procedures for which various instruments (chipping tools such as saws, scrapers, planes, etc.) are available. The simplest stage of production is when the workpiece is held in one hand and the form-change brought about by holding and guiding the chipping tool in the other. In the second stage, the workpiece is fixed by a technical device (by wedging onto the bench or being held in a vice) so that the change in form can be carried out by holding and guiding the appropriate tools. For the third stage of 'technological penetration', in addition to the technical devices and tools of the second stage, a lathe is also employed. The workpiece (the wood) is fixed between two centres and set in rotary motion (e.g., via a treadle, crank and cord drive). The tool – a cutter fixed in a handle – is held in two hands, supported on a rest and moved against the rotating workpiece, thus achieving the form-changing chipping of the workpiece. Subsequently, after turning on the lathe, the workpiece is processed using the methods and instruments of the second stage until it has been completed. However, even if the end product were completely finished on the lathe described above, this third stage of technological penetration would remain in the field of hand-tool technology irrespective of whether the lathe was driven by a water wheel or an electric motor. Because, although this technical device carries out the functions of positioning and moving the workpiece, man is still responsible for the functions of holding and guiding the chipping tool and determining the relative movement.

Only when man transfers these functions to a mechanism, to a technical device designed to permit only the movements required for the change in the form, such as the mechanical tool holder (slide rest) on a lathe, has the decisive step been taken for converting hand-tool technology into working-machine technology.

On this basis, it is evident that the technical dividing line between hand-tool technology and working-machine technology is by no means determined by the type of energy-supply used. Naturally, without mechanical energy being provided and transmitted, it is not possible for any technical material-forming system to function. In this respect, the distinction between hand-driven and power-driven tools is fully incorrect and misleading: because the hammer wielded by a smith or the whetstone used by the reaper involve the use of mechanical power just like a forging hammer or a grinding machine. The difference lies in the sources of energy, in the mode of transformation and, naturally, in the quantity of energy required. However, a forging hammer powered by a water wheel is also just a 'mechanized' tool such as an electric hand drill, while, on the other hand, a lathe with a mechanical tool holder is a working machine irrespective of whether the power for moving the workpiece and the tool holder is supplied by man via a fiddle-bow, a treadle, crank-and-cord drive or from a steam engine or an electric motor. Hand-tool technology for material-forming can function only with a human being acting as the power source, the power transformer and transmitter. However, man can also carry out these functions when the relative movements between the workpiece and the tool are carried out with a 'lifeless' technical device, i.e. with a working machine. Only after the invention of a working machine did it become technically possible to replace man in his function of power supplier. In view of the confusion in the literature about the determining features of working-machine technology, it is important to emphasize again that the use of power engines in material-forming processes requires the existence of the working machine. However, up to a certain size, this working machine technology could and can be operated with human muscle power.[13]

To summarize so far: in the overall system of technology, it is production techniques (and within it, material-forming technology) which determine the stage of 'technological penetration'. In the technical procedures of material-forming there are two, technically different systems of technical action: hand-tool technology and working-machine technology. Since they came into being, both have been represented in the system of production techniques and both have developed quantitatively as well as qualitatively. Which of these two systems is predominant in any epoch determines the overall character of the technology.

The age of hand-tool technology

In the light of these criteria, what can we say about production techniques during the European middle ages and early modern times until approximately the middle of the eighteenth century, an age which is often described as the epoch of 'handicraft technology'[14] in the history of science and technology?

Let us begin with material-forming technology which we consider to be the factor determining the characteristics of the system. In the eighteenth century, it was also marked by the predominance of hand-tool technology. For the forming of wood – the most important material in this epoch – as well as of metals, animal and vegetable fibres, leather, glass, clay, etc., into artifacts for production or consumption, the direct action of man with a tool on the workpiece is the decisive factor in the overwhelming majority of technical actions. Or to put it in a technically more precise way: the functions determining the relative movements between the tool and the workpiece are carried out directly by man and not by technical devices used by man.

This does not mean, however, that nothing had changed in material-forming technology since the middle ages. In the first place, the increasing variety of products – a fact which can be easily deduced from the growing number of guilds – also indicates specialization in the field of hand-tools, something which was by no means simply the result of the so-called manufactory, i.e. a centralized enterprise based on the division of labour and hand-tool technology. In the second place, hand-tools were replaced by mechanized tools; for example, the hand spindle by the spinning wheel, the vertical weaving loom by the pedal loom with horizontal warp, the hand hammer by the water-powered forging hammer, etc. All of these improvements optimized hand-tool technology. They permitted the increase in output and productivity without being able to replace man as the decisive factor for carrying out the procedures of material-forming.

Besides the specialization and improvement of tools and the introduction of mechanized tools, in the middle ages and in early modern times, man also invented and put into operation a variety of technical devices which fulfil our criteria of a material-processing working machine, i.e. one which carries out the relative movements between the workpiece and the tool without direct human intervention. The earliest and most frequent examples of these machines are to be found in a specialized area of separation, namely the comminution or squeezing out of materials. As long ago as the middle ages, working machines began to supplement hand-tool technology such as grinding down grain on a solid base or in a vessel using a hand-held pestle; crushing stone (ore) with a hand-hammer; or reducing vegetable materials (fruits) and subsequently squeezing them out with bare hands or simply with the aid of a cloth. Mention can be made of at least the most widespread working machines: milling machinery for grain or for pulverizing ores; edge mills for crushing and squeezing out olives; stamp mills (stampers) for crushing ores or pulping rags in paper production, for comminuting and squeezing out oil-bearing vegetable matter; and finally screw-presses for obtaining grape juice. Some of these working machines were also used for other purposes, e.g. the fulling mill (in principle a stamp mill) for cleaning and strengthening the fabric; the screw press for smoothing fabrics and for printing. Regardless of the power technology used to set these technical devices in motion, they all have one thing in common: the relative movements between the workpiece (e.g. grains) and tool (e.g. the mill consisting of two milling stones positioned above each other) are determined by the devices designed by man and the final state of the end product (flour) is imprecisely geometrically defined (e.g. an endless quantity of particles differing in their geometric form).

However, even in the case of material-forming aiming to produce a more precise end product, the first examples of working machine technology appeared between the thirteenth and seventeenth centuries. In the field of metal reforming, rolling was introduced beside the dominant forging and, in wire production, wire drawing came to replace forging. Hand-driven rolling devices were initially used for making plates from lead, gold, silver or copper. Processing iron bars into plates with smooth rollers and then cutting them into narrow strips – primarily for nail makers – with water-wheel powered slitting mills existed in Nuremberg, Lorraine and Belgium from the sixteenth century. This process is first recorded in England in the seventeenth century.[15]

In forming by chipping, the first working machines were the saw mill, the drilling machine for wooden pipes and, later, for boring out metal. The most important advances in this field were made in the workshops of 'precision mechanics': the clockmakers, instrument makers and ornamental turners. Since the seventeenth century, machine tools – lathes made in the majority of cases from wood and non-ferrous alloys – have been used in these workshops for cutting toothed wheels, for facing plates for clockwork mechanisms and for ornamental turning. In all these devices, the tool clamped in a tool holder could only be moved, via a hand-driven mechanism, over a path determined by the fixed guides of the lathe. In solving the problem of the relative movements between the workpiece and the tool independently of human guidance, as well as of the precision of the operation, these machine tools were future-oriented in the field of metal processing but found no application outside the small-scale operations of precision mechanics.

In the textile industry, one of the quantitatively most important areas of technical action, beside the fulling mill already mentioned, the first working machine in the field of fibre processing was, the twist mill documented in Italy since the end of the thirteenth century.[16] With only three exceptions – the knitting frame, the Dutch or ribbon loom, and the gig mill – all other procedures in the production of yarn from fibres (carding, combing, spinning) and processing them into fabrics (cloths) remained the preserve of hand-tool technology.

Even though the change of location (transportation) of materials and the supply of power used for the realization of technical actions for the production of artifacts remained the domain of physical human power, medieval and early modern man introduced a great many new features in both transportation and power technology. Besides the movement of loads directly by man or beast, there was a spread in the use of wheeled transport devices – from wheelbarrows to ox- or horse-drawn carts, wagons and coaches for transporting men and materials over land. Water transport was characterized by innumerable improvements in the construction of vessels and the perfection of sails, the most important means of propulsion in shipping. For lifting liquid and solid materials – a task of major significance not only in building and mining – the range of working machines for changing the location of materials extended from the rope pulley, via the crank winch, to the swing crane and from the bucket wheel to the various technical devices for draining in ore and coal mining.

In power technology, man, the universal energy source and transformer, also produced significant innovations. Besides the treadwheel and whim (horse-gin) – energy transformers which were still dependent on the muscle power (on biological energy) of man or beast – he invented the water wheel and wind mill, a higher stage of power technology in which the energy of water and wind was transformed into mechanical energy for driving technical devices in the field of production and transportation. The provisional high point in the development of power technology after the turn of the eighteenth century came with the introduction of the first thermal power engines: Thomas Savery's steam pump and Thomas Newcomen's atmospheric steam engine.

The increasing spread of whims, water wheels and wind mills which had been in progress since the thirteenth century was undoubtedly given its first impetus by the efforts of man to replace muscle power as the driving force for the various working machines which already existed at that time (milling machinery, lifting devices). Equally, however, the existence of prime movers must have been an incentive both to employ existing working machines in larger numbers, as well as to develop new ones. However, to drive working machines by means of prime movers involves the function of 'power transportation' with some kind of transmission system that functions independently of human intervention. Solving the problem of how to transmit, as well as change the direction, speed and graduation of the mechanical energy supplied by the prime mover for the working machine was a prerequisite for using these machines, and contributed at least as much to the development of mechanical engineering as the design of mechanical clockwork.[17]

The material conversion technologies with which man produced many materials for shaping, i.e. metals, iron, glass, ceramics, etc., were also enriched by many important innovations. Without being able to go into detail here, mention should be made at least of the discovery of indirect wrought-iron manufacture (the blast-furnace; pig-iron refining) and of the so-called liquation process in silver and copper smelting. In addition, emphasis should be given again to the fact that improved processing techniques, as well as the use of prime movers, played a significant part in the further development of material-conversion technology and in the extraction of its raw materials.

If we consider production techniques during the middle ages and modern times as a system, the determining element continues to be hand-tool technology. Despite the introduction of working machines for forming and transporting materials, as well as the use of prime movers for driving them, hand-tool technology remains quantitatively preponderant in the field of material-forming processes as a whole. Without reservation, it dominated the manufacture of all technical artifacts for production. Only with hand-tool technology was it possible to make both the simplest tools and components for the most complicated machines.

Given this fact, given the proportions of hand-tool technology and working-machine technology in the overall system of production techniques, and given our interpretation of the term, 'technical revolution', it is impossible for us to accept the multitude of technical revolutions as postulated by various authors.[18] It would seem equally incorrect to imply a series of several technical revolutions stretching from the middle ages to modern times or to describe this epoch as a continuous technical revolution which supposedly began in the 'power age' of the early middle ages and continued without interruption until the present day and beyond.[19] However, it would be no less incorrect to regard this epoch as a time of standstill and technological stagnation. It was an epoch of many innovations: hand-tool technology was improved by man, the scope of its application was extended and it was used for the production of working machines and prime movers. Nevertheless, working-machine technology replaced hand-tool technology in only one sub-system of material-forming – in silk twisting – and became dominant, if at all, in the comminuting of materials and in certain fields of transport technology. On the whole, however, working-machine technology existed alongside hand-tool technology for centuries without being able to dispute the latter's leading role in production techniques.

The breakthrough to working-machine technology

Hand-tool technology lost its leading role in the system of production techniques for the first time in Great Britain during the short period from approximately 1760 to 1860. The fact that there was a qualitative change in technology during the course of the eighteenth and nineteenth centuries is generally acknowledged and, for example, is also reflected in the periodization models of technological development. Regardless of how this epoch is chronologically delineated and designated (whether it is seen as the transition from craft technology to professional or technician technology, to the technology of industrial civilization, or as transition from 'manu-facture to machino-facture'),[20] all designations refer to the technical innovations and a basic change in the technological system which occurred for the first time during the Industrial Revolution in Great Britain. Even among historians of technology, there is general agreement about the technical innovations which caused this change so long as the topic is restricted to listing the individual innovations. In other words, this unity is based on an exclusion of the problems and disintegrates as soon as the discussion moves from chronologically listing the various innovations to ranking them in order of relative importance or attempting to discern a causal chain.

There is particular disagreement about the answers to two questions:

1 Which in the 'cluster of innovations' was the most important element, the driving force which ultimately caused the change in the character of technology?
2 Taken as a whole, was this process just an evolutionary change – albeit an accelerated one – or really a technical revolution?

In the first place, it is uncontroversial to state that a whole series of innovations was realized in all sub-systems of production techniques in Great Britain between 1760 and 1860. In material-forming technology, in transport and power technology, it is easy to find a common denominator for these innovations: the introduction of machinery. In addition, there were new processes and apparatuses for the conversion of materials. With them, in addition to the use of new basic materials, it became possible to mass produce materials, such as iron, sulphuric acid, chlorine, coal gas, coal tar, etc., which were indispensable either for the production of machinery or for processing and/or finishing their raw materials and products. It is not difficult to agree with C. Babbage when he characterizes the situation reached in the 1830s as one in which 'there exists, perhaps, no single circumstance which distinguishes our country more remarkably from all others, than the vast extent and perfection to which we have carried the contrivance of tools and machines . . .'.[21]

It is certainly true that the massive application of machines is purely and simply the most important phenomenon of technological development in the Industrial Revolution. A general statement such as this will meet with general consensus. However, it does not answer the question about the driving force. Machinery as a whole is certainly correct but for the purposes of our analysis it will not suffice. Was it the massive application of working machines for forming materials or for changing the location, or prime movers which introduced and proved the driving force behind the process of change in hand-tool technology?

The sub-system of technology, in which the answer to this question must be sought, is demarcated on the one hand by our statements about the elements determining a technological system and on the other hand by the universally accepted statements about the novelty of the technology of the nineteenth century. If it is true that there was a transition from one technological system to another in the course of the eighteenth and nineteenth centuries, then the decisive changes which led from 'manufacture to machino-facture' must have taken place in those places where the old technology – the hand-tool technology – was almost completely predominant, i.e. in the sub-system of material-forming technology. There are two compelling – quantitative and logical – reasons for seeking the starting point and the driving force behind the changes in this field:

1 the sub-system of material-shaping technology contained and contains the overwhelming majority of technical actions in all technological systems and
2 the stage of development in material-forming – whether hand-tool or machine-tool technology – determines which type of power and information technology can be produced and/or put into practice.

For these reasons, we regard the starting point and the driving force as being the introduction of working-machine technology, i.e., of working machines for material-forming. However, if the introduction of working-machine technology is to be the starting point and driving force of a change in the technological system and not just a short-lived episode or one of several single occurrences in the system of hand-tool technology, then it is firstly necessary for working-machine technology to break through – not singly but in vast numbers and not briefly but permanently – into a technically and economically important sub-system of material-forming.

The starting point of this process can be seen very clearly in Great Britain with the massive application of working machines for turning fibres into yarns between the 1770s and 1790s. Without being able to go into the economic and social aspects of the question, 'Why Britain first?', and putting technical details to one side, it is nevertheless necessary at least to emphasize the most important factors.

We know that the working machines introduced in this period were not the first in the textile industry. At this time, however, working machines were developed and introduced – initially in the cotton industry – for all technical procedures both in fibre processing (opening, cleaning, carding) and in the spinning phase (drawing, roving, doubling and spinning) within a period of some twenty-five years. With only a slight lag, the new machine technology spread to the production of yarn from other fibres (wool, linen) as well as to weaving and cloth finishing. The last bastion of hand-tool technology, combing, was finally conquered by working-machine technology in the 1840s.

By this time, however, the textile industry had long been dominated by machine technology, for which entrepreneurs had found the appropriate mode of operation in the concentration of machinery, raw materials and labour force in factories. Predominantly water powered until the first decade of the nineteenth century, these factories – which were based on the division of labour and which employed production processes that were carried out in the main by working machines – had their forerunners in the medieval Italian silk-twisting mills which Thomas Lombe copied to build his factory in Derby in 1721.[22] However, this was only an island in a sea of workshops dominated by hand-tool technology. Now, beginning with Arkwright's cotton mills of the 1770s, the different branches of manufacturing taken over by working-machine technology, tended to adopt the factory as the form of industrial enterprise.

Without this last feature, the introduction of working machines for material-forming in other sub-systems of production techniques, the change in the textile industry would not have taken place. Instead, the process would have led into a *cul-de-sac*, as did the twist mills of the middle ages. This would have occurred because, at the beginning, there was naturally no way of making the working machines other than by using hand-tool technology and a high proportion of wood, the traditional construction material. However, owing to the restricted possibilities for increasing productivity and the number of workmen required, this old technical basis limited both the output of machinery, and the opportunity for introducing design improvements, as well as the replacement of wood by iron.

The use of working machines in cotton processing could become the start of an irreversible process of change in technology only when other technological sub-systems became caught up in this process, and the pillars of the new technology, the working machines and prime movers themselves, became the product of working-machine technology.[23] That this was achieved within approximately seventy years of the foundation of the first cotton mills was due to the fact that several central, closely interrelated technical problems were solved simultaneously or with only slight delays. The most important of these were:

(a) the mass production of iron and steel using coal for the material conversion (coke blast furnace, puddling process) and the transition to rolling in shaping;
(b) the development and introduction of new dimensions of working machines for forming iron and other metals by chipping (machine tools); and
(c) the energy supply to the continuously growing family of working machines on the basis of coal and the introduction of Watt's double-acting steam engine with rotary motion as the prime mover.

The impression should not be given that these central technical innovations were stimulated exclusively by the requirements of the new cotton mills. The chronological coincidence of Watt's first patent, Hargreaves's patent application for his 'Jenny', and the acceleration in the spread of coke blast furnaces should not lead to false conclusions, the most widespread of which is that the steam engine created the factories.

The stimuli which led to work on improving the steam engine and on the new methods of iron production came from quite different sources: in the first case, from the need for an efficient water pump for the mines and, in the second case, from the desire to exploit the iron and coal resources. Nevertheless, it is also true that the dramatic development of the spinning mill since the 1770s, as well as the increasing demand for prime movers and blowing engines in iron foundries represented two of the most important reasons for 'people in London, Manchester and Birmingham ... [being] ... steam mill mad' and why the entrepreneur Boulton urged the inventor J. Watt to solve the problem of the steam engine with rotary motion.[24] Without doubt, spinning mills were far less important users of cast iron and steel than other sectors (e.g. ironware production, agriculture, shipping, mining, canal construction). However, it should not be forgotten that, even at the time when spinning machines were mainly made from wood, cast iron had gradually replaced wood for the construction of transmission systems. Thus, in 1809, R. Buchanan wrote that the use of cast iron for transmission shafts, 'has now become almost universal' and emphasized that, 'for this improvement we are perhaps indebted to those who are engaged in the Cotton Manufacture. After Arkwright's invention, it became a great object with them to save time in the erection of machinery and to render it as durable as possible; for every stoppage was attended with great loss ...'[25]

In other words, the substitution of wood by iron was a possibility which promised greater profits. However, for the construction of steam engines, iron, steel and other metals were the only materials which could be used. The difficulties involved in processing the large iron parts (cylinder, piston, piston rod, stuffing box) with the old hand-tool technology and the significance of Wilkinson's cylinder-boring machine for the production of the first steam engines of James Watt is well known. But, even after the foundation of Boulton and Watt's new steam-engine factory in Soho in 1795, all other work had to be carried out using the old, hand-tool technology and they endeavoured to optimize the results by organizing the strict specialization of their skilled workmen for individual stages of the processing of various components.[26]

Production of machines by machine tools

Here and elsewhere in the metal- and wood-processing industries the solution of this problem at the turn of the nineteenth century resulted in the development of working machines and their employment for the processing of machine parts. Although the Wilkinson cylinder-boring machine was a genuine machine tool, the solution used for making the relative movement between the workpiece and the tool independently of human intervention, could not be used in other types of metal- or wood-chipping procedures.

The introduction of working-machine technology into metal and wood processing was not just any advance of the new technology into any one of the other branches of production techniques. *It was the most important step on the way to the production of machines by machines*. It took place without attracting great attention, without leaving written traces such as patents. The statement made by the Jacksonian Professor of Natural Philosophy, R. Willis, in 1851 about the planing machine, 'which made its way into the engineering world silently and unnoticed',[27] actually applies to all machine tools in metal processing. From the technical point of view, the decisive step here, as in the case of all material-forming working machines, was the transfer of the tool (and the workpiece) from the hand of the workman to a mechanism which permitted the exact guidance of the tool (and the workpiece) and thus carried out the relative movement between the workpiece and the tool without direct human intervention. This was triggered off in Britain by H. Maudslay in 1797 with the construction and application of a slide-rest for his screw-cutting lathe with a lead screw; the prototype of all subsequent self-acting lathes for industrial metal processing. With his slide-rest, Maudslay introduced an existing principle of tool holding and tool movement into the new-born mechanical engineering which could also be used for other machine tools (drilling, planing, milling, etc.). When, in the second decade of the nineteenth century, this principle was used for processing plane surfaces (i.e. for planing machines) the mechanical engineers or machine builders – a new profession in the process of separating from the millwrights – were able to produce more exactly and cheaply the most important geometric forms on plane or round surfaces made from iron and other metals or wood by means of machine tools built from iron and metal than would have been possible – if at all – using hand-tool technology. From this time onwards, it was possible to use iron and steel as the material whenever it appeared functional to do so; to realize new design solutions and optimize existing designs through improved production engineering.

This does not mean that hand-tool technology disappeared from mechanical engineering because machine tools, regardless of whether they were powered by a 'muscular Irishman'[28] or by a power engine, produced diverse components of future machines under the supervision of a workman. Until late in the twentieth century, putting them together, i.e. the assembly in functioning working machines or prime movers, remained a highly skilled craft carried out using the old hand-tool technology, a command of which was the *conditio sine qua non* for climbing upwards in the hierarchy of machine builders.

There are two basic reasons for the fact that the great significance of the introduction of the new working-machine technology in the metal- and wood-processing industries was not given sufficient emphasis or was even overlooked in economic histories and in a number of general histories of technology. In the first place, people preferred to concentrate on the most obvious and best documented products (and inventors) of the new machine technology, such as steam engines and textile machines, without asking how and with what they were produced. In the second place, apart from the cylinder-boring machine, there are no patents – sources particularly beloved of historians of technology – for the first machine tools in metal processing until the 1830s. It is noticeable that none of the first machine-tool designers such as Maudslay, Roberts, Fox or Clement took out patents on those machines where they were the furthest in advance of their competitors, i.e. their turning and planing machines, descriptions and drawings of which appeared in France and Prussia before they did in Great Britain. Clearly, the first mechanical engineers shunned the high patent fees, as well as the right of access to the patent specification, and anticipated greater benefits from employing their self-made machine tools in their own workshops, initially for the production of other types of machines for sale.

Naturally, the great significance of the slide-rest principle, 'as a substitute for manual labour and dexterity'[29] did not escape the attention of knowledgeable contemporaries. Of all those who had nothing to do with the practice or theory of engineering but who studied the technology of their time, it was Karl Marx who, on the basis of a study of the results of the London Exhibition in 1851, recognized the significance of machine tools for the development of technology as a whole. 'Large-scale industry', wrote Marx in *Capital*, 'had to take over the machine itself, its own characteristic instrument of production, and to produce machines by means of machines. It was not till it did this that it could create for itself an adequate technical foundation, and stand on its own feet.'[30]

Let us summarize the answer to the first question as to which was the most important element starting the process of change in the technological system. The dominant element of this process was the introduction of material-forming working machines which were first introduced in large numbers into the spinning sector of the textile industry,[31] the most important sub-system of technical action in Great Britain even before 1770. This new working-machine technology came about with the aid of the old hand-tool technology. However, even in the form of the Jenny or the hand-mule, it represented a new technical principle: the relative movement between the workpiece (roving) and the tools (spindles, drawing rollers) was carried out by the mechanical devices of the machine, without the intervention of the human hand. And this principle of working machines for the processing of materials gradually penetrated into other areas: in the form of rolling which gradually pushed out the forging hammer in iron making; in special machines for the mass production of spindles or rollers for spinning machines and reeds for looms; in floating dredgers for deepening river-beds; or in Whitworth's street-sweeping machine, etc.

However, the fundamental principle of the new technology can be seen most clearly in the combination of several technical devices on machine tools for shaping wood and metals by chipping. These machine tools – a term which, like the German version *Werkzeugmaschine*, was introduced first in the 1850s[32] opened the way to the production of machine parts with machines and, thereby, to the technical implementation of designs which, only a short time before, foundered on the inadequacies of the old hand-tool technology. The fact that it was H. Maudslay who turned the ingenious ideas of Bentham and Brunel for block-making machinery into functioning machines was no more a coincidence than was the fact that it was the professional machine builder, R. Roberts, who was able to employ the ideas of Cartwright, Horrocks and others to make a power loom which was technically and economically superior to the hand looms. We still know very little about the first great boom in machine building which took place roughly between the years 1800 and 1830. However, the well-documented variety of working machines for material-forming to be found in the technical literature of the 1830s, as well as the perfection of the steam engine, its use as prime mover in ships and, subsequently, in railway locomotives, are evidence that the new working-machine technology had taken a firm hold in the construction of all machines and, thereby, was capable of reproducing itself.[33]

This does not mean to say that working-machine technology dominated technical actions everywhere and without limit. This was not even the case in all technical procedures of material-forming and certainly not in the case of raw-material extraction where, despite the efforts of numerous inventors from the 1770s onwards to create an 'iron man', the old hand-tool technology was the only means of extracting ores and the most important source of energy – coal – until the closing decades of the nineteenth century. The immense difference, however, is that working-machine technology, which existed only in certain areas in the 1770s, increased quantitatively and changed qualitatively. Through the transition to mechanical spinning, it firstly took over a central sub-system of technical actions from hand-tool technology and thereafter gained more and more footholds in various sub-systems of production techniques. Although this does not mean that the old technology had been eliminated, by the 1840s it had been displaced to such an extent that working-machine technology became the determining element of the overall technological system in material-forming, as well as in the fields of power and transport technology which it required and produced.

And now to answer the question whether this process was just an evolutionary change or really a technical revolution.

Revolutionary change – a myth?

We consider this change to be a technical revolution. In the short period of approximately a hundred years, through the massive penetration of the elements of working-machine technology existing even in the old system, the system of hand-tool technology which had existed for many thousands of years was changed into a quite different one by the manifold forms of working-machine technology. In other words, we are dealing with a radical system change which took place in a comparatively short space of time and which, moreover, led to equally radical changes in the economic and social structures of society, in the way people lived and worked.

Although we could support our position with quotations which also describe these changes as 'revolutionary changes in technology',[34] or as a series of revolutions in individual branches of production,[35] it is preferable to manage without them because they are not based on an analysis of the changes in the technological system but rather on the effects of these changes on individual branches of industry. We want to turn to the arguments of the overwhelming majority of historians and philosophers of science and technology who do not deny the change in the system but its revolutionary character. Apart from the fact that many of these authors implicitly assume an irreconcilable contradiction between evolution and revolution or consider that revolution must result in destruction only,[36] the most frequent argument against a technical revolution emphasizes the continuous character of technical developments from the middle ages until the present day. Some even take up Trotsky's theory of permanent revolution by claiming that, if at all, it is only possible to speak of a 'permanent technical-industrial revolution'.[37] The following positions are typical of many writers: altogether, the industrial revolution characterizes the 'perfection of existing processing techniques and their economic exploitation on a large scale'. From a technical point of view, 'the transition from manual handicrafts to the division of labour and mechanized mass production' was 'part of a relatively continuous process of development which has its roots in earlier stages and which has continued to accelerate in cycles until the present day'. In all, the epoch between approximately 1750 and 1850 is characterized, 'neither by spontaneous new inventions nor by the technological application of scientific research but rather by systematic improvements of details and the further development of existing ideas'.[38] Another variation of such opinions – based essentially on the formulations of M. Daumas[39] – is the recent thesis held by certain British economic historians that the Industrial Revolution is neither 'the Age of Cotton [nor] of Railways or even of Steam entirely; it was an age of improvement' or 'much of the technological advance came, not from a few big inventions connoting major discontinuities, but from a mass of small-scale improvements, frequently conducted'.[40]

Now, as in the case of all commonplaces, it is certainly true that the technical changes in Great Britain between 1750 and 1850 had their forerunners, their roots and their prototypes. In no way have we tried to hide the fact that form-changing working machines, prime movers, transport machines, etc., all existed in the middle ages. The spinning machine is doubtless a further step in the creation of form-changing working machinery, and the technical principles of machine tools, as employed by Maudslay, were already to be found in the lathes of the watch and instrument makers or ornamental turners. However, an analysis of the technical principles of spinning machines shows that the central problem, namely the execution of the relative movements between the workpiece and the tool, could not be solved by 'perfecting existing processes' or by 'the development of existing ideas', or even by copying the solutions to this problem employed by other medieval working machines. The perfection of the apparatus for handspinning resulted in a better hand-spinning wheel but not in a spinning 'Jenny', water frame, etc. The perfection of the hand loom resulted in an improved hand loom, the 'Dandy loom', but not in a power loom. And it was not the case, as A. P. Usher emphasized,[41] that the 'existing principle' of the ribbon mill led directly to the power loom because, despite the principle similarity of the motions, the different scale of the latter demanded completely different technical solutions. The technical solution of the functions of the material and tool guidance in a clockmaker's lathe having a maximum travel of no more than a few centimetres was certainly an 'existing idea' for the future lathes of the machine builders. However, to convert these prototypes into machine tools fifty, one hundred or five hundred times bigger required other solutions for transmitting the forces involved and it is no coincidence that the first generation of machine tool builders did not come from the clockmakers' industry, as claimed by N. Wiener and others.[42] It was clearly easier for the millwright, smith or metal worker to introduce the clockmakers' precision into their trade than for the clockmaker to work on the millwright's scale. For these reasons, the argument favouring continuity and the perfection of existing processes is untenable unless we resort to the premise that new combinations of existing elements do not represent new inventions, i.e. that the principle of two rotating rollers – in use for a long time in metalworking – represented only the perfection of an existing process when employed for stretching and drawing fibres for spinning. Reducing technical innovations to a series of 'small-scale improvements' misses just one small point: although the improvements undoubtedly existed, these 'improvements' of the first half of the nineteenth century are perfections of the new technology of working machines: perfections of the textile machines, the machine tools, the steam engine, etc. They were concentrated on elimination of malfunctions, on increasing the speed, on improving the efficiency, etc., of the large and small inventions in the field of mechanical engineering, metallurgy, chemistry, etc.

The only remaining argument against the revolutionary character of the technological changes is that they were not 'technical applications of the result of scientific research'. This is indeed true. If the inventors and innovators had waited for this to happen, we would still be living in an age of hand-tool technology. Apart from the fact that technology is not the same as applied science, there are two confusions in this argument. In the first place, every technical action must be in accordance with scientific laws. However, this does not mean that somebody without any theoretical knowledge of these laws could not find the optimum solution to a given problem. Secondly, this breakthrough to machine technology was not promoted by scientific research. On the contrary, machine technology was based on an empirical adoption of technical knowledge and itself became a stimulus and component of scientific research.

'The process towards perfection in complicated machinery is perhaps too generally the reverse of what might be expected. When practice has shown the importance of a machine, science takes it up, investigates its principles, analyses its movements, and connects them by the assistance of mathematical precision.' Almost programmatically, the unknown author (1806) added: 'Mathematicians are seldom inventors, and workmen are rarely men of science, yet the mutual assistance of study and practice is necessary to perfect the subject which each is intent on improving.'[43]

It was a long way to this cooperation, to a time when science turned its attention to practical technical problems. At the beginning there were practical men, such as Smeaton, Watt or J. B. Neilson, the inventor of the hot blast, who acquired theoretical knowledge and were joined by scientists such as H. Davy and C. Babbage or P. Barlow and O. Gregory at the Royal Military Academy in Woolwich, who were confronted more than others with the problems of production. Nevertheless, in 1852, R. Willis, author of one of the first textbooks on applied mechanics for future engineers (1841) and an active inventor, complained about the 'unfortunate boundary wall or separation between practical and scientific men',[44] particularly in the field of mechanical engineering. However, the increasing participation of academic scientists in technology, and the endeavours of outstanding practical men such as J. Whitworth or W. Fairbairn to obtain scientific recognition were the consequence of a working-machine technology which had already become a determining element of the technological system. Because, as was emphasized by such diametrically opposed observers as J. Nasmyth and K. Marx, it was the execution of technical actions independently of human intervention by means of a working machine which opened the door to the introduction of scientific findings in the preparation of technical actions, i.e. in the design of technical constructions.[45] Thus, the revolution of technology became the powerful driving force for the development of the sciences and the emergence of practice-oriented scientific research.

The main element of the technical revolution, which we are accustomed to calling the Industrial Revolution, was the massive introduction of material-forming working machines, and it was able to change the existing technological system only because, thanks to numerous technical innovations, the barriers to the production of machines by machines had been overcome in the first thirty years of the nineteenth century. However, it was due only to the fact that energy supply and transportation, as well as raw-material extraction, had been placed on a new basis that it could become a system-determining element. If we confuse the causal links and, in common with many authors, describe the new power technology (that is, steam engine) as the driving force, we confuse at least cause and consequence because, as already emphasized, demand for energy independent of human muscle power, increases to the extent that hand-tool processes dependent on muscle power can be replaced by working-machines. This confusion of cause and consequence in the emergence of the new 'machino-facture' makes it easy to talk about other technical revolutions such as the revolutions of electricity and atomic energy. Despite the significance of these innovations which arose from the marriage of science and technology, the treatment of which lies outside the scope of this paper, we should not forget that, until the present day, the majority of technical actions in our technological system are to be found in the field of material processing and in this the principle of working-machine technology introduced massively and irreversibly in the Industrial Revolution, continues to dominate more than ever before. The emergence of electro-technology and its development was of immense significance for this working-machine technology – without which it could never have been produced. Through its development, the function of passing on information commands to the working machines, which was by and large still in the hands of man, started to be transferred from clumsy mechanical devices to electro-mechanical technical systems. This further stage of 'technological penetration', the replacement of man in passing on information to the machine by a technical system, has taken on new dimensions through electronics and micro-electronics. Nevertheless, we are still living in the age of working-machine technology which started in the second half of the eighteenth century with a technical revolution.

NOTES

1 Jonas 1975, p. 147.
2 Reuleaux 1875, p. 520; Lilley 1973, p. 187.
3 Gottl-Ottlilienfeld 1914, p. 207. In the narrower sense, *Technik* corresponds with the word 'technology' in English–American usage. The German word *Technologie* which is, unfortunately, very often translated incorrectly with 'technology' corresponds with the term 'technological science'. See Füssel 1978, pp. 28–9.
4 For the discussion about the definition of *Technik* see: Tuchel 1967, pp. 23–30; Ropohl 1979, pp. 30–46; Müller 1967; Füssel 1978, pp. 6–16.
5 Tuchel 1967, pp. 25, 31.
6 Engelberg 1965, p. 11.
7 The following system is the description of a highly simplified model formulated on the basis of the systemization of technology in the nineteenth century, e.g. Karmarsch 1888, and on the basis of current attempts to formulate a comprehensive system theory of technology, e.g. Ropohl 1979, and a general theory, e.g. Wolffgramm 1978.
8 Ropohl 1971, p. 24.
9 In the FRG in 1960, approximately 80 per cent of all companies and approximately 72 per cent of all employees were in this branch of production engineering, which accounted for approximately 60 per cent of total industrial production (DM 251 milliard) – Dolezalek 1965, p. 3.
10 To assist the action of the tool on the workpiece, so-called 'agents' can be applied to the tool or the workpiece, i.e. a formless material such as polishing paste used during polishing. For the significance of the action pair, see Wolffgramm 1978, pp. 41–53.
11 The distinction between the German term *Technisierung* (approximately: 'technological penetration' – Ropohl 1979, p. 181) and the narrower term *Mechanisierung* (mechanization) is intended to emphasize that we are not dealing with the introduction of technology, as imputed by formulations such as 'the age of technology' but rather with a process of quantitative increases in

the use of technical artifacts for the realization of technical actions. This process cannot be covered by the word mechanization. For instance, the introduction of electronic devices for control functions is technological penetration but replaces mechanization, i.e. mechanical devices.

12 In German, I developed the pair of terms *Hand-Werkzeug Technik* (hand-tool technology) and *Maschinen-Werkzeug Technik* in order to elucidate the transfer of the manipulation of the tool from man to a machine. I am very well aware that *Maschinen-Werkzeug Technik* cannot be translated literally into English because the term 'machine tool' encompasses only lathes, drilling machines, planing machines, etc., i.e. *Werkzeugmaschinen* in German. Hence, I have coined the expression, 'working-machine technology'.

13 Distinguishing between tool and machine by the type of power employed – as can be found even today in technical history and technical research ('the tool is set in motion by man's physical strength, the machine by some natural force', Singer *et al.* 1958, p. 150) – is technically absurd because even a tool can, 'be set in motion by some natural force', if it has already been transferred from the hand of man to a mechanism. And, as J. Bramah emphasized in his patent application for a planing machine, this machine 'may be worked by animal, elementary or manual force'. The fact that the type of driving force does not constitute the distinguishing feature between tool and machine was clearly recognized by Marx (1867), p. 394, cf. Paulinyi 1978, pp. 182–5.

14 Gottl-Ottlilienfeld 1914, p. 322; Ortega y Gasset 1949, p. 34; Rapp 1978, pp. 33–4, 98–9.

15 Beck 1893, pp. 945–55; Beck 1897, pp. 242–55; Stromer 1977.

16 Endrei 1974, p. 95.

17 Ropohl 1971, p. 175. Not only that: it also brought information technology into being. This might well sound exaggerated and trendy but cogged and toothed wheels, as well as the camshafts of transmission systems, realize a precisely defined functional connection between movements and can do this only because they also store information. Just like tools, they are technical creations in which man has entered and fixed the information necessary for the desired pattern of movements.

18 Carus-Wilson 1941, p. 38; Gimpel 1980; Stromer 1977; Stromer 1980.

19 Lilley 1965, p. 325; Lilley 1973, p. 190.

20 Gottl-Ottlilienfeld 1914, p. 322; Ortega y Gasset 1949, p. 34; Gehlen 1958, pp. 22–38; Lilley 1973, p. 187; Sachsse 1978, pp. 60, 85–92.

21 Babbage 1833, p. 3.

22 Poni 1972, pp. 401–2.

23 Rammert 1983, p. 50, following Marx (1867, p. 405), who was the first to point out this connection.

24 Dickinson and Jenkins 1927, pp. 55–6.

25 Buchanan 1814, p. 16.

26 Roll 1930, pp. 166–236.

27 Willis 1852, pp. 313–14.

28 Leading mechanical engineers such as H. Maudslay and R. Roberts began their careers with good machine tools which were driven by human power. See Smiles 1883, p. 180; Dickinson 1945, p. 126.

29 Nasmyth 1841, p. 398.

30 Marx 1867, p. 405. (English edition, Penguin, 1976, p. 506.)

31 Working machines in textiles in Great Britain:

	Spinning Millions of spindles	Weaving Power looms
1789	2.4	—
1810s	4.7	2,400
1830s	12.0	108,000
1850s	21.0	247,000

Compiled from Smelser, N. J., *Social Change in the Industrial Revolution* (London, 1959), pp. 114, 121, 148; Tunzelmann, G. N. von, *Steam Power and British Industrialization* (Oxford, 1978), p. 182; Ellison, T., *The Cotton Trade of Great Britain* (London, 1886), p. 325.

32 Until this time, machine tools were simply called 'tools' and then 'self-acting tools' in English. The term, machine tool, was first used by Willis (1852, pp. 311–15), and not by W. Fairbairn in 1861 as claimed by the Oxford English Dictionary, vol. 6, 1970, p. 8. In German, machine tools (*Werkzeugmaschinen*) were called *Hilfsmaschinen der Produktion* until the 1850s.

33 E.g. Barlow 1836. For the status of machine tools: Nasmyth 1841, plates.

34 Deane 1965, p. 84.

35 For example Musson 1978, pp. 61–77, firstly tries to convince the reader that the technical changes were only evolutionary and then describes the technical innovations in the chapters, 'The textile revolution', 'The revolution in coal and metals' and 'The chemical revolution'.

36 Gottl-Ottlilienfeld 1914, p. 255, emphasized that modern technology, 'professional technology', was 'profoundly evolutionary ... but not in the least revolutionary', because, 'it did not crush hand-tool technology', but instead preserved it as part of itself. With similar reasoning, i.e. that 'revolution implies a decisive break with the past, a break with their forms', Mumford 1977, p. 156, refuses to describe the so-called neolithic revolution as such.

37 Rapp 1978, p. 101.

38 Rapp 1978, pp. 100–2.

39 Daumas 1963; Daumas 1968.

40 Floud and McCloskey 1981, pp. 118, 151.

41 Usher 1954, p. 284.

42 Wiener 1952, pp. 152–3.

43 Quoted from the *Eclectic Review* by Buchanan 1814, p. 11.

44 Willis 1852, p. 297.

45 Nasmyth 1841, p. 397; Marx 1867, p. 407.

BIBLIOGRAPHY

Babbage, C. 1833. *On the Economy of Machinery and Manufactures*, 3rd ed., London, Knight.

Barlow, P. 1836. *A Treatise on the Manufactures and Machinery of Great Britain*, London, Baldwin and Cradock.

Beck, L. 1893. *Die Geschichte des Eisens*, part 2, *Das 16. und 17. Jahrhundert*, Braunschweig, Vieweg.

1897. *Die Geschichte des Eisens*, 3. Abteilung, *Das 18. Jahrhundert*, Braunschweig, Vieweg.

Bramah, J. 1803. 'Specification of the patent ... for machinery for the purpose of the producing of straight, smooth and parallel surfaces etc', *Repertory of Arts*, ss. 2, pp. 165–74.

Buchanan, R. 1814. *An Essay on the Shafts of Mills*, London, J. Taylor.

Cardwell, D. S. L. 1963. *Steam Power in the Eighteenth Century. A Case Study in the Application of Science*, London, Sheed and Ward.

1965. 'Power technologies and the advance of science 1700–1825', *Technology and Culture*, 6, pp. 188–207.

Carus-Wilson, E. M. 1941. 'An industrial revolution of the thirteenth century', *Economic History Review*, 11, pp. 39–60.

Daumas, M. 1963. 'La mythe de la révolution technique', *Revue d'histoire des sciences*, pp. 291–302.

ed. 1965. *Histoire générale des techniques*, vol. 2, *Les premières étapes du machinisme*, Paris, Presses Universitaires.

ed. 1968. *Histoire générale des techniques*, vol. 3, *L'expansion du machinisme*, Paris, Presses Universitaires.

1981. *Les grandes étapes du progrès technique*, Paris, Presses Universitaires.

Deane, P. 1965. *The First Industrial Revolution*, Cambridge, University Press.

Dickinson, H. W. 1945. 'Richard Roberts, his life and inventions', *Transactions of the Newcomen Society*, 25, pp. 123–37.

Dickinson, H. W. and Jenkins, R. 1927. *James Watt and the Steam Engine*, Oxford, Clarendon Press.

Dolezalek, C. M. 1965. 'Die industrielle Produktion in der Sicht des Ingenieurs', *Technische Rundschau*, 35, pp. 2–3.

Dolezalek, C. M. and Ropohl, G. 1967. 'Ansätze zu einer produktionswissenschaftlicher Systematik der industriellen Fertigung', *VDI Zeitschrift*, 109, pp. 636–40; 715–21.

Endrei, W. and Stromer, W. von. 1974. 'Textiltechnische und hydraulische Erfindungen in Mitteleuropa im 14./15. Jahrhundert', *Technikgeschichte*, 41, pp. 89–117.

Engelberg, E. 1965. 'Fragen der Evolution und Revolution in der Weltgeschichte', *Zeitschrift für Geschichtswissenschaft*, Sonderheft 13, pp. 9–19.

Floud, R. and McCloskey, D., eds. 1981. *The Economic History of Britain since 1700*, vol. 1, *1700–1860*, Cambridge, University Press.

Füssel, M. 1978. *Die Begriffe Technik, Technologie, technische Wissenschaften und Polytechnik*, Bad Salzdetfurth, Didaktischer Dienst Franzbecker.

Gehlen, A. 1958. *Die Seele im technischen Zeitalter*, Hamburg, Rohwolt.

Gille, B. 1978. *Histoire des techniques. Encyclopédie de la pléiade*, 41, Édition Gallimard.

Gimpel, J. 1980. *Die industrielle Revolution des Mittelalters*, Zürich, Artemis.

Gottl-Ottlilienfeld, F. von. 1914. In *Grundriss der Sozialökonomik*, part 2, *Die natürlichen und technischen Beziehungen der Wirtschaft*, Tübingen, J. C. B. Mohr, pp. 199–381.

Hausen, K. and Rürup, R., eds. 1975. *Moderne Technikgeschichte*, Cologne, Kiepenheuer and Witsch.

Jonas, W. 1975. 'Kritische Bemerkungen und Ergänzungen', in Kuczynski, J., *Vier Revolutionen der Produktivkräfte*, Berlin, Akademie Verlag, pp. 139–80.

Karmarsch, K. 1888. *Handbuch der mechanischen Technologie*, 6th ed., vol. 1, Berlin, Loewenthal.

Lilley, S. 1957. *Automation and Social Progress*, London, Lawrence and Wishart.
1965. *Men, Machines and History*, London, Lawrence and Wishart.
1973. 'Technological progress and the industrial revolution', in *The Fontana Economic History of Europe*, ed. C. M. Cipolla, vol. 3, pp. 187–254.
Ludloff, R. 1967. 'Die technische Revolution in der Geschichte', *Die Technik*, 22, pp. 421–5, 485–8, 549–51, 613–16.
Marx, K. 1867. *Das Kapital*, 3 vols., Frankfurt, Verlag Marxistische Blätter, 1976, vol. 1.
Müller, J. 1967. 'Zur marxistischen Bestimmung des Terminus "Technik". Ein Definitionsversuch', in *Rostocker Philosophische Manuskripte*, no. 5, Rostock, pp. 204–16.
Mumford, L. 1977. *Mythos der Maschine. Kultur, Technik und Macht*, Frankfurt, Fischer Taschenbuch Verlag.
Musson, A. E. 1978. *The Growth of British Industry*, New York, Holmes and Meier.
Musson, A. E., and Robinson, E. 1969. *Science and Technology in the Industrial Revolution*, Manchester, University Press.
Nasmyth, J. 1841. 'Remarks on the introduction of the slide principle in tools and machines employed in the production of machinery', in R. Buchanan, *Practical Essays on Millwork and Other Machinery*, 3rd ed., London, pp. 393–418.
Ortega y Gasset, J. 1949. *Betrachtungen über die Technik. Der Intellektuelle und der Andere*, Stuttgart, Deutsche Verlags-Anstalt.
Paulinyi, A. 1978. 'Kraftmaschine oder Arbeitsmaschine. Zum Problem der Basisinnovationen in der Industriellen Revolution', *Technikgeschichte*, 45, pp. 173–88.
Poni, C. 1972. 'Archéologie de la fabrique: la diffusion des moulins à soie "alla bolognese" dans les états vénitiens du 16e au 18e siècles', in *L'industrialisation en Europe au 19e siècle. Cartographie et typologie*, ed. P. Léon, Paris CNRS.
Rammert, W. 1983. *Soziale Dynamik der technischen Entwicklung. Beiträge zur sozialwissenschaftlicher Forschung* vol. 41, Opladen, Westdeutscher Verlag.
Rapp, F., ed. 1974. *Contributions to a Philosophy of Technology*, Dordrecht, D. Reidel Publishing Co.
1978. *Analytische Technikphilosophie*, Freiburg, Alber.
Rapp, F., Jokisch, R., and Lindner, H. 1980. *Determinanten der technischen Entwicklung*, Berlin, Technische Universität.
Reuleaux, F. 1875. *Theoretische Kinematik. Grundzüge einer Theorie des Maschinenwesens*, Braunschweig, Vieweg.
Roll, E. 1930. *An Early Experiment in Industrial Organisation: Being a History of the Firm of Boulton and Watt, 1775–1805*, London, Frank Cass reprint 1967.
Ropohl, G. 1971. *Flexible Fertigungssysteme. Zur Automatisierung der Serienfertigung*, Mainz, Krausskopf.
1979. *Eine Systemtheorie der Technik*, Munich, Carl Hanser Verlag.
Sachsse, H. 1978. *Anthropologie der Technik*, Braunschweig, Vieweg.
Singer, C. *et al.*, eds. 1956. *A History of Technology*, vol. 2, *The Mediterranean Civilization and the Middle Ages*, Oxford, Clarendon Press.
eds. 1958. *A History of Technology*, vol. 3, *From the Renaissance to the Industrial Revolution*, Oxford, Clarendon Press.

eds. 1958. *A History of Technology*, vol. 4, *The Industrial Revolution*, Oxford, Clarendon Press.

Smiles, S., ed. 1883. *James Nasmyth, Engineer. An autobiography*. London, John Murray.

Sonnemann, R. 1974. 'Mensch und Maschine, eine historische Betrachtung', *Maschinenbautechnik*, 23, pp. 442–5.

Spur, G. 1979. *Produktionstechnik im Wandel*, Munich, Carl Hanser Verlag.

Stromer, W. von. 1977. 'Innovation und Wachstum im Spätmittelalter: Die Erfindung der Drahtmühle als Stimulator', *Technikgeschichte*, 44, pp. 89–120.

1980. 'Eine "Industrielle Revolution" des Mittelalters?', in *Technik-Geschichte. Historische Beiträge und neuere Ansätze*, ed. U. Troitzsch and G. Wohlauf, Frankfurt, Suhrkamp.

Sworykin, A. A., and Osmova, N. I., etc., eds. 1967. *Geschichte der Technik*, 2nd ed., Leipzig, Fachbuchverlag.

Tuchel, K. 1967. *Herausforderung der Technik*, Bremen, Carl Schünemann Verlag.

Usher, A. P. 1954. *A History of Mechanical Inventions*, Revised ed., Harvard University Press.

Wiener, N. 1952. *Mensch und Menschmaschine*, Berlin, A. Metzner Verlag.

Willis, R. 1841. *Principles of Mechanism*, London, Parker.

1852. 'Machines and tools for working in metal, wood and other materials', in *Lectures on the Results of the Great Exhibition of 1851*, London, David Bogue, pp. 293–320.

White, L., jr. 1968. *Die mittelalterliche Technik und der Wandel der Gesellschaft*, Munich, Heinz Moos Verlag.

Wolffgramm, H. 1978. *Allgemeine Technologie*, Leipzig, Fachbuchverlag.

14

The scientific revolution: a spoke in the wheel?

ROY PORTER

– 'Kingdoms and provinces, and towns and cities, have they not their periods? and when those principles and powers, which at first cemented and put them together, have performed their several evolutions, they fall back.' – Brother Shandy, said my uncle Toby, laying down his pipe at the word evolutions – Revolutions, I meant, quoth my father, – by heaven! I meant revolutions, brother Toby – evolutions is nonsense. – 'Tis not nonsense – said my uncle Toby.

Laurence Sterne, *Tristram Shandy*

Historians write about scientific revolutions as automatically as of political, economic or social revolutions: the 'French revolution' in chemistry led by Lavoisier is almost as familiar as the political revolution which cut off his head. Indeed, the idea that science advances by revolutionary leaps has long been with us, ever since the eighteenth century in fact. For, as Bernard Cohen has shown, it was Enlightenment propagandists for science from Fontenelle and the *Encyclopédistes* to Condorcet who first began to depict the transformations in astronomy and physics wrought by Copernicus, Newton and others as revolutionary breaks with the past, creating new eras in thought.[1]

And significantly it was through being applied in this way to epochs in *science* that the term 'revolution' itself took on its present meaning. Traditionally, when used to describe political fortunes, 'revolution' had, of course, denoted change (the fall of one prince, the rise of a rival); but it was change within an essentially cyclical system in which all dynasties and empires had their rise and fall, their waxings, wanings and eclipses, for human affairs were governed by the endless 'revolutions' of Fortune's Wheel. In the traditional metaphor, in other words, it was the orbits of the planets, so gravid with astrological influence, which had defined and governed revolutions in sublunary affairs. But, from the early eighteenth century, the old equation of revolution with cycles began to yield to a secular, directional myth of human destiny. 'Revolution' kept its massiveness – a mundane event as portentous as one in the heavens, far grander than a mere revolt; but it came to signal not endless repetition but a break with the past, a fresh start, or what the Enlightenment called an 'epoch'. Hence from the *philosophes* onwards, scientific breakthroughs actually became normative for general usage, underpinning modern views of revolution as constructive and progressive, rather than as tainted by fatalism and hubris. Condorcet's faith in human perfectibility was buoyed up on hopes of scientific revolutions yet to come, programmed into the march of mind.[2]

Such a reading of science's development, not as cumulative but as punctuated by creative discontinuities, has long appealed to historians, philosophers and prophets. And scientists have endorsed it too. Back in the eighteenth century, the astronomer Bailly and the mathematician Montucla were arguing that their own disciplines had been founded upon revolutions. Indeed, as Cohen shows, Enlightenment natural philosophers actually began to cast *themselves* in the role of revolutionary heroes pitted against the scientific *ancien régime*, Lavoisier in particular announcing his own revolution in chemistry.[3] And, by the nineteenth century, scientists commonly saw their researches as no less revolutionary than the incendiary world in which they lived. Charles Darwin, for instance, judged that Charles Lyell had 'produced a revolution' through the uniformitarian vision of his *Principles of Geology* (1830–3), while forecasting that his own theory of evolution by natural selection would create 'a considerable revolution' in natural history. Savants like Darwin, who certainly held no brief for political revolution and who scorned the notion of revolutionary breaks in Nature as unscientific (like 'miracles', such 'catastrophes' pre-empted investigation), were nevertheless gripped by the drama of the revolutionariness of science.

The upshot of all this is that our dominant image of the history of science is bursting at the seams with revolutions. Browse book titles, or scan their chapter headings, and the truth of that remark strikes the eye. Revolutions, historians assume, have been so ubiquitous in science that, where they seem absent even that absence needs to be explained. Thus one of the key questions animating Joseph Needham's monumental study of *Science and Civilisation in China* is why China – for so long so scientifically advanced – never experienced a 'scientific revolution'.[4] Or, to take another example, when Butterfield pondered the mysterious lack of a seventeenth-century chemical revolution, he felt the need to label Lavoisier's new chemistry of a century later 'the postponed revolution'.[5] Yet nowadays one single chemical revolution is no longer enough. Time was, for example, when Lavoisier's demolition of phlogiston and championing of oxygen were deemed *the* 'revolution' transforming chemistry from a rag-bag of recipes into a rational system. But it is now argued that Lavoisier's own revolution itself required a prior one:[6]

> Ever since Antoine Lavoisier announced his revolution in chemistry [writes Arthur Donovan], the last two decades of the eighteenth century have been considered the well-spring of modern chemistry. But Lavoisier's revolution built upon an earlier revolution in which chemistry was reestablished as a separate and distinct science no longer subordinated to the corpuscular or mechanical conception of nature.

One may pause at the implication of revolutions 'building upon' the past in this manner.

What is more, these proliferating revolutions now come in all shapes, sizes and kinds. For instance, the advent of pure water thanks to public-health science in France, Goubert tells us, was effected by a 'quiet revolution'.[7] And so to guide us, we now have atlases provided by the philosophy of science, which itself, according to Hesse, has recently undergone a 'revolution', and where Kuhn's ultra-influential *The Structure of Scientific Revolutions* conjured up a quasi-Trotskian scenario of permanent revolution.[8] All this may be deplored as a sad devaluation of the currency, but this grumble is not unique to historians of science: inflation of 'revolution' has long been the bane of historians of all stripes.

Yet the practice of historians of science does differ in one key respect, as there is something quite singular in their use of the term. For, while making free with such localized labels as 'chemical revolution', 'Darwinian revolution', 'quantum revolution', and so forth, they also write about The Scientific Revolution, in the singular, as a unique phenomenon. It's hard to imagine an exact parallel in which other historical specialists would speak of The Political Revolution, or The Economic Revolution.

The stamp of The Scientific Revolution (that is, roughly, the totality of those transformations taking place in the early modern era) is watermarked into today's scholarship. Ever since A. Rupert Hall's *The Scientific Revolution* (1954), even the phrase itself has been turning up time and again in book titles, as in Hugh F. Kearney's *Origins of the Scientific Revolution* (1964), Vern Bullough's *The Scientific Revolution* (1970), and P. M. Harman's *The Scientific Revolution* (1983). Few challenge its validity. Even radical scholars such as Carolyn Merchant and Brian Easlea, who deny the standard eupeptic readings of The Scientific Revolution, do not question its existence.[9] And, as a consequence, it has even acquired a fetishized life of its own, so that it comes easily to write of 'the development of the Scientific Revolution in the eighteenth and nineteenth centuries', as though it were also an evolving organism.[10]

Explorers once believed in the great Southern Continent (*nondum cognita*), though they couldn't agree where it was or what it was like. The same goes for The Scientific Revolution. Look closely and, like the Cheshire cat, its features dissolve before the eyes. Take, for instance, the question of its timing. Most historians see it stretching broadly over the sixteenth and seventeenth centuries (say, from Vesalius and Copernicus through to Newton). Some, however, would abbreviate it. Thus Cohen restricts it to the seventeenth century, roughly from Kepler and Galileo to Newton (and here it might be significant that Rupert Hall has recently dubbed the sixteenth century, scientifically speaking, 'a century of confusion').[11] By contrast, Ronan confines it to an earlier era entirely, seeing it as having 'begun in the fifteenth century and carried on to the end of the sixteenth'.[12] Ronan's periodization – stopping the Revolution where others start – is eccentric, yet he isn't the only scholar who would drive The Scientific Revolution right back in time. Butterfield reckoned that The Scientific Revolution, 'popularly associated with the sixteenth and seventeenth centuries', in fact reached 'back in an unmistakable line to a period much earlier still'; and in a similar vein, Crombie has argued that, though 'from the end of the 16th century the Scientific Revolution began to gather a breathtaking speed', it should in fact be traced 'as far back as the 13th century'.[13] Doesn't the extraordinary leisureliness of this unique Scientific Revolution smack of paradox? In his 1954 survey, Rupert Hall wrote of *The Scientific Revolution 1500–1800*. This three-hundred-year revolution has been pared down by half a century in his later *The Revolution in Science 1500–1750* (1983); but compared with *Ten Days that Shook the World*, this view of the shaking of the scientific foundations risks confusing continuity with cataclysm and creating a Shandeian muddle between evolution and revolution.

Its contents as well as dating also pose interpretative problems. Most scholars argue that the astrophysical sciences form the core of the Revolution (though doubts remain, for example, whether the astronomical revolution centres on Copernicus, Kepler, Galileo, or whoever). But should the life-sciences also be included? And indeed is the *sine qua non* a question of transformations in facts and theories, in scientific method, or in man's relations to Nature? And historians remain at odds as to how The Scientific Revolution relates to total history. Some regard it as integral to other contemporary revolutions (e.g., as Bernal claimed, the Commercial and the Bourgeois Revolutions) during what Christopher Hill has called the *Century of Revolution*;[14] others, such as Rupert Hall, by contrast, have contended that scientific change was essentially independent of such socio-economic pressures.[15] Faced with these confusions, small wonder that Thackray has recently concluded that, though the notion of The Scientific Revolution remains 'a central heuristic device ... and subject of myriad textbooks and courses', it explains little: 'with each passing year it becomes more difficult to believe in the existence or coherence of a single, unique Scientific Revolution'.[16]

And, if The Scientific Revolution is 'all in doubt', what of that multitude of other putative scientific revolutions, which form, as it were, its litter? Certain champions of The Scientific Revolution have been notably unenthusiastic about these small-fry rivals. Countering Kuhn's idea that revolutions are the soul of science, Rupert Hall has reiterated 'the historical singularity of the scientific revolution of the seventeenth century'. This, he contends, laid such secure foundations for scientific rationality as thereafter to preclude further *revolutionary* breaks.[17]

But aren't we here sinking quite needlessly into a semantic bog? Shouldn't we respond to the clarion calls of the seventeenth century New Scientists, heed things not words, and just get on with our research? Yet this may be one of those occasions when it is vital to address the verbal and conceptual riddles. For one thing, our verdict on The Scientific Revolution is bound to govern our reading of the rest of science. For another, the idea of The Scientific Revolution, so often taken for granted, is in fact highly loaded.

Its tendentiousness becomes plainer if we note that, though utterly naturalized into today's historical idiom, The Scientific Revolution is actually quite a recent coining. Though specific episodes in science have been called revolutionary for over two centuries, the concept of The Scientific Revolution is less than two generations old, the phrase, it seems, having been minted by Koyré in 1939,[18] and first stamped on a book title in Rupert Hall's *The Scientific Revolution* (1954). But the idea probably passed into the Anglo-American mind chiefly through Butterfield's *The Origins of Modern Science 1300–1800* (1949), which contains the most celebrated passage ever penned about the Revolution – or rather about what Butterfield often styled the 'so-called' Scientific Revolution, as if, through the hesitation, to own the term's novelty. Here is his classic statement both of the uniqueness of The Scientific Revolution and its unparalleled contribution to Western history:[19]

> Since that revolution overturned the authority in science not only of the Middle Ages but of the ancient world – since it ended not only in the eclipse of scholastic philosophy but in the destruction of Aristotelian physics – it outshines everything since the rise of Christianity and reduces the Renaissance and Reformation to the rank of mere episodes, mere internal displacements within the system of medieval Christendom.

Comb leading nineteenth- and early twentieth-century histories of science (say from Whewell to Singer), and the formula is conspicuous by its absence. One might have supposed that the notion was current amongst Marxists. But not so. Take, for instance, Boris Hessen's provocative Marxist analysis (1931) of 'The social and economic roots of Newton's *Principia*'. This certainly sited Newton in what Hessen labelled the bourgeois and commercial revolutions of the seventeenth century.[20]

But Hessen made no reference to The Scientific Revolution. Internal evidence suggests that Bernal's Marxist account in his *Science in History* (1954) of what he termed The Scientific Revolution was heavily derivative from Butterfield. Bernal's *The Social Function of Science* (1939) makes hardly a mention of a scientific revolution.

The idea of The Scientific Revolution is not, then, part of the intellectual commons which historians have grazed time out of mind. Rather it was initially the brain-child and shibboleth of a specific cluster of scholars emerging during the 1940s, including the Russian émigré Alexandre Koyré, Butterfield, whose outline history popularized Koyré's work, Rupert Hall, who was Butterfield's pupil, and, a little later, Marie Boas [Hall]. Their scrupulous scholarship and prolific works of synthesis animated an emergent discipline, and laid down a coherent framework for future research. In their vision of the epochal nature of The Scientific Revolution – one embroidered by other scholars such as Gillispie and popularized in such works as Koestler's *The Sleepwalkers*[21] – they not only claimed that science was revolutionized in the early modern period. They also made no secret of their 'Whiggish' view that The Scientific Revolution was a good thing.[22] For it marked a triumph of mind, free and fearless, underscoring the essential link between liberty of thought and intellectual advance, a lesson not to be lost on Western democracies just freeing themselves from Hitler's and Stalin's brain-washings and from the utopian Marxism that had been the opium of the thirties intelligentsia.[23]

As analysed by these scholars, what The Scientific Revolution proved was that science was not battery farming. Great ideas could not be hatched by mechanized husbandry – Baconian data-gathering, systematic experimentation, better instrumentation, institutionalization, funding and so forth. Science had not chugged forward following Five Year Plans, but had been transformed in stupendous, unpredictable leaps of reason. Such leaps were revolutions in *thought*. And so, as Koyré, Butterfield, the Halls and their followers saw it (advancing what I shall label the 'classical interpretation'), the business of the historian of science was first to grasp the *Weltanschauungen* of entrenched science, and then show how these had been turned upside-down by the thought-revolutions of science's giants. To depict such strokes of genius, Butterfield hit upon happy metaphors such as 'picking up the other end of the stick', or 'putting on a new pair of spectacles', rather as Kuhn was later to speak of 'Gestalt-switches'. This 'classical interpretation' focussed as never before on explicating the stunning conceptual displacements involved in moving from the Ptolemaic geocentric universe to Copernicus's heliocentrism, or in Kepler's courageous imaginative leap in abandoning circular planetary orbits – *de rigueur* for centuries – and embracing elliptical ones.[24] How the bounds of the thinkable were changed by Galileo's New Science of motion, Descartes's mechanics of inertia and momentum, Boyle's corpuscular chemistry, and finally by Newton's synthesis of the laws of motion and the laws of gravity! Such triumphs – the mechanization of the world-picture, the shift from the 'closed world' to the 'infinite universe' – needed more than tireless empirical brick-laying. Copernicus's achievement did not consist in adding to Ptolemy, but in viewing old data through new spectacles. Science was revolutionized by new ways of seeing.[25]

Thus this 'classical Interpretation' paid generous tribute to creative intellect, a homage captured in an anecdote Gillispie recounts of Newton. When an admirer asked 'How do you make your discoveries?', Newton replied, 'by always thinking unto them'.[26] For these historians, science was essentially *thought* – profound, bold, logical, abstract – and thought was ultimately philosophy. As Rupert Hall put it, science is 'above all a deep intellectual enterprise whose object it is to gain some comprehension of the cosmos in terms which are in the last resort philosophical'.[27] This identification of science with philosophy has had deep consequences, not least in the academic world in the institutional marriage – not blissfully happy – between the history and the philosophy of science.[28] For if science is ultimately philosophical, it is no surprise that philosophers should claim the right to analyse past science – a tendency which, given the predominant ahistorical bent of Anglo-American philosophy, has often proved disastrous for proper historical interpretation. In particular the philosophers' itch to reconstruct the rationality of great texts has characteristically played fast-and-loose with historical contexts and meanings, and has encouraged anachronistic evaluations of rationality and irrationality in the history of science.[29]

Thus idealism has been pervasive, and its implications run even to the interpretation of detailed episodes. For instance, Koyré argued that Galileo didn't actually dirty his hands performing his kinetic experiments; or at least, if he did, he did so not with a view to making discoveries, but only after his conceptual breakthroughs, merely for the purpose of elegant demonstration.[30] Along similar lines, Marie Boas Hall reflects:[31]

> It is interesting to know that Galileo visited the arsenal at Venice or that he learned from practical men that suction pumps could raise water only thirty feet; but neither of these facts contributes as much to our understanding of Galileo's mode of thought or of his achievements or his novelty as does Koyré's analysis of purely intellectual factors.

For, she insists,

> It must not be forgotten that the scientific revolution was, in the last analysis, an intellectual revolution – a revolution in what men thought about and the way in which they did this thinking.

But *was* the real Galileo a performer not of experiments but only of thought-experiments? Or are Koyré's and Hall's portraits merely ideal-types, themselves thought-experiments about the *beau idéal* of science? Recent archival research by Stillman Drake and others suggests that Galileo did indeed perform his experiments on inclined planes as *explorations* of the phenomena of motion, and that the results of these trials may well have guided him to his theories.[32] Clearly, driving wedges between experimentation and conceptualization is fatuous, but the bias towards 'purely intellectual factors' in the 'classical interpretation' must be kept in mind.

Overall, this idealist reading of The Scientific Revolution as disembodied thought sustained a heroic, even romantic, image of the scientist, typified by Newton, 'with silent face, Voyaging through strange seas of thought alone'. For Gillispie and Koestler in particular, the scientist is dramatized as truth-seeker, dicing with the 'cruel edge of objectivity', duty-bound to confront reality regardless of psychic cost, to 'peer into a nature deprived of sympathy and all humane associations', stripped of the mythopoeic comforts of traditional cosmology. The imperative of truth demanded that the just-so stories of metaphysics and theology, with their teleology, providences and miracles, had to be swept away. The old, man-centred, anthropomorphic cosmos was now exposed as a fairy-tale, the charming correspondences of macro- and microcosm and the personification of Nature were banished and left to the poets. As Gillispie stressed, the universe as laid bare by Descartes or Hobbes was now dead, determinist, infinite, and, for Pascal, terrifying. The cosy fictions of will, value and purpose had been dissolved. With this 'disenchantment of the world', man was left a stranger, an alien. In daring to face these truths, The Scientific Revolution was thus the triumph of honesty as well as of genius, and its hero was the iconoclast, pledged to discover Nature as it really was. For some historians this was glorious. Gillispie saluted the scientist as the new Prometheus, just as more recently Ronan has celebrated the 'adventure' of his 'unprecedented voyage of conquest'.[33] For others, by contrast, new knowledge spelt a new Fall. Koestler's *Sleepwalkers* charted the new alienation of man from Nature, fact from value, head from heart, mechanism from meaning, all as new mind-forged manacles from which the West has never escaped.

Such romantic views of the agony and the ecstacy of truth-seeking were not of course new, and a noble tradition had long seen scientists as heretics, forming a dissenting academy, on the social margins. But honouring the free play of mind had clearly become a specially urgent priority against the backdrop of Fascist and Stalinist totalitarianism, whose gaggings and purges of the intelligentsia seemed to have come home to roost in Lysenkoism.[34] In the Cold War, Western scholars were glad to show how the history of science 'falsified' historical materialism's reductionist way with men and ideas. And, let it be said, the exponents of the 'classical interpretation' have been frank about drawing these political lessons of The Scientific Revolution. The Koestler of *The Sleepwalkers* (1959) was patently also the Koestler of *The God that Failed* (1950) and *Darkness at Noon* (1940), just as in his recent textbook, *Science and the Making of the Modern World*, John Marks quite openly argues that history shows that science is a desideratum which flourishes best under the kind of right-wing individualist, free-market regime proposed by F. A. Von Hayek.[35] This reading of The Scientific Revolution is thus not value-free, and should not be taken at face value. Its central assumptions – that science proceeds by heroes making 'discoveries'[36] through 'Eureka' moments, that the great scientist himself is an autonomous agent, and that science is value-free – are historically question-begging, and play a polemical part within today's politics of knowledge.

Thus the 'classical interpretation' mystified the dynamics of theory change; but a further aspect also needs scrutiny. This is the question of just what The Scientific Revolution actually revolutionized. Clearly, it is claimed – and with good reason – individual scientific disciplines were transformed: for instance, a physics of natural and unnatural movements gave way to one of forces and inertia. Equally, scientific epistemology and methodology were radically changed. Bacon, Galileo and many others made sport with time-honoured but barren preoccupations with final causes; by contrast the accent was now on material and efficient causes, and on quantities rather than qualities. Then, capping all this, The Scientific Revolution is presented as the triumph of a whole new philosophy of nature, in which, as Bernal put it,[37]

> the whole edifice of intellectual assumptions inherited from the Greeks and canonized by Islamic and Christian theologians alike was overthrown and a radically new system put in its place. A new quantitative, atomic, infinitely extended, and secular world-picture took the place of the old, qualitative, continuous, limited and religious world-picture which the Muslim and Christian schoolmen had inherited from the Greeks.

And, above all, as Hall subtitled his textbook, it amounts to 'the formation of the modern scientific attitude', which, Butterfield claimed, was a far more important watershed than the Renaissance or the Reformation. For this was, according to the 'classical interpretation', Europe's intellectual and spiritual coming of age when Western civilization grew out of traditional infantilizing mythologies and faced up (like a man) to the stark realities of Nature.[38] The Scientific Revolution thus formed the great divide between the traditional or primitive *mentalité* of the 'Ancients' and the mature rationality of the 'Moderns'. As Koestler put it, '*homo sapiens* underwent the most decisive change in his history', or, in Kearney's ringing tones, 'The Scientific Revolution created a vast gulf between traditional and modern attitudes. The past with all its virtues was gone for ever. Modernity with all its drawbacks, had been created.'[39] And such assumptions of a 'vast gulf' between the cobwebs of the medieval mind and high-powered modern thought have informed (or distorted) the interpretation of particular episodes. Take, for example, Butterfield's account of how the physiology of the heart and vascular system came to be revolutionized: 'Until the seventeenth century ... a curious mental rigidity prevented even the leading student of science from realising essential truths concerning the circulation of the blood.' Fortunately, the needle-sharp seventeenth-century mind made short work of all that. As Butterfield continued, it is only 'by watching these earlier stages of fumbling piecemeal progress, that we can gain some impression of the greatness of William Harvey, who early in the seventeenth century transformed the whole state of the question for ever by a few masterly strokes.'[41] But subsequent research has shown that Harvey's 'few masterly strokes' are the stuff of myth, not least because Harvey himself was, after all, a staunch Aristotelian. Indeed, what is the vision of The Scientific Revolution superseding tradition, myth or magic by rationality, but another myth?[42] Seventeenth-century scientists claimed to abandon words for realities, values for facts, and some historians of The Scientific Revolution have taken them at their word. But even a superficial glance at the fabric of the new science in the seventeenth century and beyond shows that it remained permeated by precisely the kinds of human values and rhetoric – the Baconian idols – it claimed to have expunged. Indeed, much of the most stimulating scholarship from the 1970s onwards has been uncovering just how important was the continuing imput into science from metaphysics, theology and human interests, long after the New Science had proclaimed its independence from these influences.[43] And it is worth remembering that the New Science's self-image of its own 'new dispensation' was clearly taken over wholesale from Biblical eschatology. Ironically the 'classical interpretation', which casts the Scientific Revolution as a watershed in the transition from primitive thought to rationality, reproduces such myths, generates new ones about progress and modernity, and runs closely parallel to the pre-history/history teleology of scientistic Marxism.[44]

Just because its historiography embodies myths, the notion of scientific revolution need not however be summarily dismissed. The question remains: is it helpful to picture the course of the history of science as revolutionary? Or might it not make better sense to stress its 'evolutionary' aspects, its continuities and accommodation to the wider socio-intellectual environment?[45] These large questions matter, not least because, with the irresistible rise of specialization, scholarship becomes myopic and fragmented, and, though philosophers continue to dogmatize, historians may be in danger of defaulting on the task of assessing the overall patterns of science.

To judge whether science has had its revolutions, we need a working idea of revolution, one compatible with common historical usage in other contexts. For my purposes, I propose that a revolution in science requires the overthrow of an entrenched orthodoxy; challenge, resistance, struggle and conquest are essentials.[46] The mere formulation of new theories doesn't constitute a revolution; neither is it a revolution if the scientific community leaps to applaud an innovation, saluting its superiority. Moreover, revolution requires not just the battering of old theories but the triumph of the new. A new order must be established, a break visible. Furthermore, revolutions presuppose both grandeur of scale and urgency of tempo. Mini-revolutions, partial revolutions, and long revolutions are terminological abuses; why dilute the word when 'change' will do stout service? Lastly, I suggest that, though it may not be indispensable that the protagonists should intend from the outset to make a revolution (revolutionaries often begin as reformers), it is vital that, at some stage, consciousness should dawn of revolution afoot. The notion of silent or unconscious revolution is next door to nonsense.

Following these guide-lines, it does seem helpful to characterize the transformations in science occurring in the seventeenth century – though not the sixteenth – as revolutionary. There is no room here, and perhaps little need, to argue this contention chapter and verse. But certain key elements are worth stressing. First, many of the protagonists clearly cast themselves as crusaders for a radically New Science, engaged in life-and-death struggles against the hidebound dogma of the schools: the very titles of Bacon's *New Atlantis*, Kepler's *New Astronomy*, and Galileo's *Two New Sciences* catch this tone of embattled innovation.[47] Bacon and Galileo amongst others were witheringly dismissive of the dead hand and dead mind of orthodoxy to a degree that finds no parallel, for instance, in Copernicus or Vesalius. Doubtless, much of this was rhetoric; doubtless, it was largely straw schoolmen who were being slain and slain again; doubtless, seventeenth-century natural philosophers tapped the scholastic legacy more than they admitted.[48] Yet the seventeenth century really saw intense struggle between rival natural philosophies, and the call for liberation from die-hard orthodoxy runs right through the century, culminating in the Ancients versus Moderns debate and the Battle of the

Books, won in science by the Moderns (according to the Enlightenment, by a knockout).

For the standard-bearers of the New Science indeed had a struggle on their hands. Traditional doctrines had been deeply entrenched in seminaries and universities, in textbooks, curricula and in the educated mind. Not least, they were protected by those watchdogs of intellectual orthodoxy, the Christian churches, notably the papacy in such episodes as the burning of Bruno and the trial of Galileo, but also by other confessions too, as witness the conservative role of Laudian Anglicanism in early Stuart England.[49] The Battle of the Books meant the burning of the books. In a radical gesture Paracelsus symbolically burnt the texts of Avicenna; and, as late as the 1680s, Oxford University was still making bonfires of Hobbes's writings. It would be foolish caricature to depict these as struggles between the forces of darkness and the children of light; yet the seventeenth century remains a cockpit of violent conflicts between rival natural philosophies, which often resolved themselves into struggles between Old and New, and which resulted – something much less true of the sixteenth century – in victory for the new.

Moreover, many sciences did undergo fundamental reorientations both in their conceptual foundations and their fine texture. A few examples will surely suffice. In astronomy, geostatic and geocentric systems still predominated in 1600; but by 1700 all members of the scientific elite espoused heliocentricity. In 1600, versions of the Aristotelian physics of finitude, local motion and the four elements still held the floor, in many cases, in newly refined and reinvigorated forms; by 1700, one mode or other of the mechanical philosophy had swept them away amongst leading scientists. Matter theory had come to hinge not on the traditional four elements and on qualities but on particles and short-range forces incorporating new laws of motion and principles of dynamics. The traditional divide between science celestial and terrestrial was challenged by Galileo, and bridged by Newton's universal gravitation. Methodologically, observation was set at a premium and so stimulated, and was in turn reinforced by, the development of new scientific instruments such as the telescope and microscope. This opened up both the macro- and microworlds, both visible and conceptual, and contributed to the general development of instrumentation which is so important a factor in modern science. Going hand in hand with this, experimentation led to a new way of doing science and a new way of promoting science's claims to 'objective truth'. Moreover, mathematical advances – pre-eminently Descartes's coordinate geometry and Newton's and Leibniz's infinitesimals – empowered science to calculate and control areas which had been impressionistic before. Such a list could be greatly extended.[50]

These changes, it must be stressed, were not just pious hopes for a great instauration;[51] they were substantial and permanent achievements which were built upon. Taken singly, it is true, the work of Kepler or Descartes, Galileo or Boyle, created as much chaos as it resolved. But collectively, their investigations amounted to a progression of fruitful reformulations of fundamentals until, with Newton above all, a synthesis was reached widely saluted as coherent, dazzling in scope and potential, ripe both for solving workaday problems (Kuhn's 'normal science') and for generating future investigations. Newton set the seal.[52]

Thus, the concepts and practice of many individual sciences – kinetics, hydraulics, optics – were transformed, and new philosophies of Nature established. Confidence in science led to the extension of mechanical models to new fields, as for example in Borelli's physiology, and boosted the prestige of natural philosophy so that it could become definitive of intellectual authority – witness the enthusiasm throughout the eighteenth century for applying Newtonianism to aesthetics, social and moral philosophy, politics and psychology. For the radical intellectuals of the Enlightenment, science's successes cast metaphysics and theology in the shade. For Locke, philosophy's job should be to serve merely as science's 'under-Labourer', sweeping aside the rubbish for science's 'masterbuilders'. For Diderot and D'Alembert, Priestley and Erasmus Darwin, science was the engine of progress.[53]

In other words, the transformations in science were revolutionary not just in techniques and concepts, but in forging an unparalleled place for science in European culture and consciousness. Above all, new conceptions of Nature and man's relation to it became dominant. The 'classical interpretation' of course acknowledged this in its claim that The Scientific Revolution rent the old veils of myth, and 'discovered' Nature as she really was: rational, regular, law-governed, mechanical. But a truer way of putting it would be to say that seventeenth-century science created and imposed its own model of Nature as a regular, mechanical order, which legitimated scientific man's intellectual and practical control of Nature. Traditional beliefs about Nature handed down via the intertwining systems of Christian theology, Humanistic philosophy and occult wisdom now seemed all too confused, difficult, anarchic, dangerous. The proliferation and ubiquity of spiritual forces, magical resonances, and providential infiltrations had confused God, man and Nature in ways that increasingly seemed scandalous and enervating to powerful intellectual currents, engaged (as Rabb has put it) in a search for stability.[54]

Seventeenth-century scientific ideologues embarked upon their task of conceptual clarification with a will. Not without fierce controversy, new formulations of the fundamentals were hammered out. The true divide between God and Nature had to be insisted upon; typically, in the mechanical philosophy, all activity was attributed to God, but a God who was increasingly distant, and Nature was reduced to a machine, inert and passive. Similarly, man and Nature were also demarcated, most extremely in Cartesian dualism in which Nature became merely extension (matter in motion) and man alone possessed consciousness. Such programmatic segregation of the divine, the natural and the human had gigantic consequences in terms of franchising man's right, through science and technological intervention, to act upon Nature. For, once Nature was thus 'disenchanted', the New Scientists increasingly claimed man's right, as Bacon put it, to 'conquer and subdue her'. If Nature were not after all alive but just an object, it could be taken to pieces, anatomized, resolved into atoms. Passive and uniform, Nature was open to experiment, or, in Bacon's grim metaphor, to be 'tortured' into revealing its truth. The dictum that science should (in Bacon's phrase) 'penetrate from Nature's antechambers to her inner closet' became axiomatic.[55]

Within these seventeenth-century reconceptualizations, God became more remote and Nature less sacrosanct. Man's right to progress (even to redeem himself) through the pursuit of knowledge of, and power over, Nature became central to influential visions of human destiny; and the conquest of Nature became a practical, noble and even godly goal. The material transformation of the West over the last three centuries would have been impossible without the technical capacity generated by seventeenth-century science; but it would also have been unthinkable without the sanction and encouragement given by the new visions of science and Nature formulated in Baconianism, Cartesianism and other parallel seventeenth-century philosophies.

Here it is important however, not to confuse causes and consequences. Much of the best scholarship of the last couple of decades has challenged the old view that science advances by individual thought revolutions, by demonstrating the huge range of intellectual traditions which helped fecundate modern science (many of them, such as magic or astrology, conventionally seen as non-scientific).[56] The new science did not spring like Pallas Athene straight from the brains of its giants; indeed it was both 'unscientific' in its origins and ideological in its functions. All this amounts to a much-needed iconoclasm. But it would be a mistake to belittle the epochal consequences of scientific change merely because the imputs of that change were 'impure'. Balance here is important. We may usefully speak of a transition from magic to science, so long as we remain alert to the magic in science and the magic of science at the close of the seventeenth century and beyond. Religion, metaphysics, and ideology continued to play key roles *within* science after Newton. The tendency to place the New Science or the Newtonian synthesis on a pedestal must be resisted, for otherwise it will become a shrine; and attempts to cut the New Science down to size must be welcomed.

Yet, when seventeenth-century science is cut down to size, what remains impressive is indeed its towering magnitude. Recent currents in the sociology of science and the 'deconstruction' of scientific knowledge have done sterling service in demythologizing 'objective knowledge' and baring science's social relations and ideological freighting.[57] Yet, if we make too much of science's *origins* in other modes of thought, we may lose sight of its extraordinary internal power, and thus render its influence and success mysterious, or intelligible only conspiratorially. Today's fears that (as Peacock's Dr Opimian put it) 'it is the ultimate destiny of science to exterminate the human race', shouldn't lead us to forget the deep attractions of the New Science to generations of Europeans disgusted by the *ancien régime* with its suffocating clerical bigotry and arid academicism. Organized science seemed active, liberal, critical, productive, enterprising. Forget this, and we will never have more than a warped understanding of what Harman has called 'the dominance of science in contemporary culture'.[58]

To call the seventeenth-century transformations of the sciences a revolution, I've been arguing, can be illuminating provided that we don't swallow whole those idealizations which see them as marking the autonomy of science and the maturity of the Western mind. Equally, we should handle critically today's jaundiced readings of the 'revolution', put forward by Morris Berman and others, as marking the birth of one-dimensional man or schizoid man, or as validating patriarchy and fuelling capitalist false consciousness. Science's role in all these was contingent not central.[59]

Thus, for example, the seventeenth-century scientific revolution was not simply a reflection of all other 'modernizing' forces. It was once argued that science marched arm-in-arm with Protestantism, especially in its 'modern' expressions, Calvinism and Puritanism; but on close investigation such correlations either break down, or prove superficial and question-begging.[60] Similarly, Christopher Hill once proposed that the mechanical philosophy was the philosophy of the mechanics.[61] But such mappings of science onto 'progressive' – or indeed reactionary – social classes prove similarly fragile. Nor do attempts to link theory-shifts directly to socio-political revolutions hold much water. Hill found it significant that William Harvey 'dethroned' the heart from its office as monarch of the body in the year parliament beheaded Charles I; but his contention proved essentially erroneous, confusing more than it clarified.[62] What such interpretations forget is that science operates in sub-cultures cushioned to various degrees from direct political pressures (for many savants the attraction of science lay precisely in its *distance* from politics). Indeed we miss one of the key and enduring features of the seventeenth-century scientific transformation unless we acknowledge that element of asymmetry.

For the seventeenth century produced two critical developments in the social siting of science. One lies in the foundation of societies exclusively devoted to natural science, initially in Italy, France and Britain, often under royal patronage but generally enjoying a measure of self-control. As Ben-David has emphasized, science was 'socialized', and thereby for the first time achieved some public presence independently of court, Church, or university. Second, science acquired a more stable international voice. In particular, the rise of scientific publishing via institutional journals such as the *Philosophical Transactions* of the Royal Society gave substance to a genuine scientific cosmopolitanism (even if national rivalry simultaneously grew more strident). Through developments such as these, a social community of science was gradually to take shape, forming an invisible college within the wider republic of letters, encouraging loyalties to science as well as to class, country or creed.[63]

These developments in turn endowed science with immense continuity as a social institution, and help explain why it has been so immune since the seventeenth century to onslaughts from counter-revolutionaries or counter-cultures. The revolutions which have been staged against the establishment of science have had remarkably little success. Events such as the Jacobin anti-elitist purge are remarkable for their rarity, brevity and failure.[64] The durability of science over the centuries has stemmed to a large degree from its success back in the seventeenth century in gaining social niches (social, political, intellectual) strategically distanced from precarious power centres such as dynasties vulnerable to overthrow, and winning a plurality of patronage sources.

Yet, if seventeenth-century science underwent organizational changes of momentous consequence, it is vital not to exaggerate the social changes it generated in the short term. Large corps of professional scientists were not suddenly called into being; science didn't capture most universities or schools, or infiltrate bureacracies on a grand scale; indeed, within the universities, the New Science spread unevenly. Neither did the New Science revolutionize craft production. Science certainly played a bit-part in mobilizing the English Industrial Revolution in the latter part of the eighteenth century, but not the lead.[65] Similarly, one must qualify the impact of seventeenth-century science upon the European mind. Paul Hazard rightly drew attention to *la crise de la conscience européenne* of the last decades of the seventeenth century, but philologists and biblical critics probably did more to precipitate that crisis than did scientists.[66] Science had some part in banishing old thought-worlds, but often it proved compatible with them, or even buttressed them. Thus, in the long run the New Science probably helped undercut beliefs in demonism, astrology, the spirit world and witchcraft, yet many enthusiasts for the New Science used it to corroborate their beliefs in witchcraft and in spirits.[67] In any case the percolation of the mechanical philosophy remained uneven. Despite all the itinerant scientific lecturers and *Newtonianism for the ladies* texts, popular culture was affected only patchily. Indeed the New Science may have contributed to driving wedges between elite and popular culture during the eighteenth century, and, in an case, it impinged little upon fields such as medical diagnosis and therapeutics, which remained stubbornly traditional.[68]

If there was, as I have argued, a seventeenth-century scientific revolution (albeit one needing revaluation), where does that leave subsequent revolutions? Some historians have claimed that such revolutions have occurred on a scale commensurable with The Scientific Revolution. Cohen notes that three have chiefly been touted (the so-called Second, Third and Fourth Scientific Revolutions). The 'second' is the advent of highly professional, institutionalized science around the turn of the nineteenth century, associated in particular with the French Revolution and Napoleonic technocracy. The 'third' constitutes the transformations of the physical sciences between the 1880s and the 1920s, involving the replacement of Newtonian physics by quantum mechanics and relativity theory as the foundations of physical science.[69] The 'fourth' is the advent of 'big science' since the Second World War, through which the interplay of science, government, technology, industry and warfare has been transformed out of all recognition.[70] Aspects of these developments are scrutinized in Mikuláš Teich's essay in this volume. But it may be said here that the claims of any such movement, before state coordination in the present century, to a scope and universality comparable to the seventeenth-century transformation, seem weak. This is hardly surprising. In the 'closed world' of early modern science, natural philosophers still commonly took all Nature as their province. The onset of the division of labour, however, as remorseless in science as elsewhere, was to make that kind of interpenetration and cross-fertilization less likely.

More plausible, therefore, is the case for later revolutions in individual scientific fields. Here the legacy of the seventeenth-century revolution was highly ambivalent. For, as Rupert Hall and others have argued, the New Philosophy of the seventeenth century did indeed lay what Burtt called 'the metaphysical foundations of modern physical science', thereby minimizing the need for further shaking of the foundations. Even so it must not be thought that post-Newtonian natural philosophy 'fell into a swoon'. Far from it; as recent research has shown, animated debate continued in areas such as matter theory and the aether. But the order of the day, within classical physics for example, was not revolution but reformation and reassessment within such common frameworks as Newtonianism. Here the 'gradualist' position, as paraphrased by Laudan, rings true:[71]

> The 'gradualists' stress the degree to which science manages to preserve most of what it has discovered. They point out that, for all the seeming 'revolutions' in optics since the early seventeenth century, we still espouse substantially the same sine law of refraction that Descartes did. They point out that, Einstein notwithstanding, contemporary mechanics still utilizes almost entirely techniques worked out by Newtonian scientists, or reasonable approximations thereto. Even Einstein, after all, regarded relativity theory not as a break with but as a modification of Newtonian physics.

Yet the seventeenth-century scientific revolution also had the opposite effect, by charging the atmosphere with revolution. Because the revolutionary labours of Galileo, Newton etc., had been glorious, revolutionariness became a touchstone that science was going well. This helps to explain the contrast between the Newton who would publicly insist that, if he saw further into Nature than others, it was because he was a dwarf standing on giants' shoulders and the Lavoisier who, a century later and capitalizing on Newton, could proclaim his own revolution in chemistry. Such ambivalences of course still persist, as is evident in the divided response to Kuhn's *Structure of Scientific Revolutions*. For, on the one hand, if science is rational, what place is there for revolutionary discontinuities? Yet, on the other hand, revolutions seem the dynamos of progress and the guarantors of personal glory.[72] These contradictory pulls come out clearly in one scientist's successive reconstructions of history. When in 1973 the geologist Anthony Hallam surveyed continental drift and plate tectonics in his *A Revolution in the Earth Sciences*, he was a convert to Kuhn's conception of normal science being punctuated by violent displacement. Ten years later (and ten years more conservative?) in his *Great Geological Controversies*, Hallam explicitly abandoned the revolutionary flightline of the history of geology, announcing his conversion instead to Lakatos's view that science shifts via the long-term competition of rival research programmes.[73]

There is no general law of scientific change; to suggest there was one would give science an 'essence' which it doesn't possess. Our criteria for plotting should be pragmatic, and, if we heed the guidelines outlined above, we find the term 'revolution' all too frequently attached to episodes which, though undoubtedly important, possess few features unique to revolution. Take, for example, in the history of medicine, what Rosenberg in an otherwise excellent article has dubbed 'the therapeutic revolution of the nineteenth century'.[74] Rosenberg shows how the time-honoured system of diagnosis and therapy based upon Greek humoralism was subjected to withering critique during the nineteenth century. This he terms a revolution. But nowhere does he show when, how, and by whom the old system was actually toppled, and what replaced it. What is depicted is not revolution but crisis. A rather similar case is the 'Copernican Revolution'. In his book of that title, Kuhn contended that Copernican astronomy, by valorizing the perfection of the circle and embracing heliocentricity, wrought a revolution. Certainly no one would deny that Copernican astronomy differed root-and-branch from the Ptolemaic. Yet Copernicus did not conquer or convert the field, and astronomy never came to be dominated by Copernicanism. Geocentrism was later revitalized by Tycho, and when geostatic astronomy finally yielded it was replaced not by Copernicus's but by Kepler's.[75]

A comparable instance of lax labelling is the claim that Charles Lyell wrought a revolution in geology. For his part, Kuhn argued that this revolution consisted in Lyell's transformation of earth knowledge from pre-scientific chaos into a scientific discipline by establishing geology's first paradigm.[76] And Wilson has claimed that Lyell worked a revolution by conquering 'catastrophism' (the view that geological change occurs through massive, sudden, convulsions, perhaps occasioned by divine intervention) with 'uniformitarianism', putting geology under the rule of universal, regularly-acting law.[77] Certainly, Lyell himself reckoned he was giving the science a fresh start, by providing it with its *Principles*; and followers such as Charles Darwin were to agree. But close scrutiny hardly bears out the revolution. *Pace* Kuhn, geology was well-established as a discipline long before Lyell. And, *pace* Wilson, it is not clear that uniformitarianism was radically more 'scientific' than approaches earlier espoused by the more sophisticated of Lyell's brethren of the hammer. Moreover, Lyell's *Principles* did not take the geological community by storm, did not convert it from catastrophism (only some had been 'catastrophists' anyway) to strict uniformitarianism. Such a view is too black and white, and, as Bartholomew has shown, very few English geologists, and hardly any continentals at all, became wholehearted Lyellians (and surely *scientific* revolutions at least must be international?).[78] Top geologists absorbed and adapted elements from a range of theories and methods. In this case, the image of revolution misdescribes what was in fact a complex dialogue of negotiation, persuasion and conviction transacted across the floor of the parliamentary debating chamber of the Geological Society of London, and on fieldwork sites throughout Europe. An international perspective shows that nineteenth-century geology remained pluralistic, and, as Laudan has stressed,[79] 'there was no geological paradigm which was either universally or uncritically accepted. A multiplicity of alternative frameworks was the rule rather than the exception.'

Yet to cite such examples is not to ditch revolution, but merely to warn against sloppy usage. Least of all should we retreat into an *evolutionary* metaphor of science's development, on some specious analogy with the dictum *natura non facit saltum*. Rather the term 'revolution' should be reserved for really fundamental transformations. These have occurred, and I shall conclude by touching upon two which display exemplary features. One is a case which has echoed throughout this essay, the chemical transformation in the late eighteenth century.[80] The chemistry of Lavoisier and such co-workers as Guyton de Morveau and Fourcuoy (collectively: the French school) was experienced by contemporaries and historians alike as revolutionary, not least the reconceptualization which abandoned phlogiston for 'oxygen' as the key to combustion. But what is crucial to the French revolution in chemistry is how Lavoisier set the science on a new footing, by stipulating a new working definition of the chemical element, by translating chemical affinities into numerical ('gravimetric') relations, and by systematically rewriting the very language of the science by analogy with Linnaean taxonomy in natural history, in such a way as to incorporate his own, often tendentious, theories (e.g. on acidity) into its very terminology.[81] Despite the opposition of eminent chemists such as Priestley and the gripes of Francophobes, Lavoisier's innovations, inscribed in his new linguistic grid, triumphed with extraordinary rapidity and completeness. In just a generation, chemistry, a science so long ashamed of its confused empiricism, achieved a remarkable degree of intellectual order.

The take-up of Darwinian evolution provides a comparable case. Of course, as many historians (most recently Peter Bowler) have stressed, it would be foolish to swallow too cataclysmic a view of Darwin's achievement.[82] Ideas of 'evolution' had long been in the air and, as Gruber has shown, Darwin's own brand of it – natural selection – didn't come to him in a flash of inspiration but only after years of mental brooding, and didn't come to him alone, but to Alfred Russel Wallace as well.[83] And, not least, the publication of *On the Origin of Species* in 1859 led to practically no naturalist being converted wholeheartedly to the fine print of Darwin's theory (indeed Darwin himself was won over to certain counter ideas of his critics).

Yet in three respects, Darwinism surely amounted to a revolution. First, its impact upon the scientific community was overwhelming. Naturalists had long been in doubt about the species question, yet before Darwin hardly any had openly subscribed to a theory of transmutation. But, forced to respond to Darwin's challenge, practically all leading naturalists publicly embraced some mechanism or other of evolutionism, many of them, like Lyell, in the teeth of deep personal and scientific conviction. Second, the scientific acceptance of descent theory triggered great changes in the perception of all facets of the living world. Its key ideas such as natural selection, the survival of the fittest, and community of descent had staggering implications for the whole range of the life and human sciences. And third, Darwinism lobbed a bomb into the sacred temple of Nature's divine order and man's place in it. Cherished beliefs were genuinely shattered (which is not to imply that new ideologies, built upon Darwinism, didn't take their place). Indeed, to a large degree, the late Victorian cliché image of science and religion locked in mortal conflict mirrored the events of the Darwinian controversy.[84]

In these brief reflections on the dynamics of the sciences, I have concentrated largely on *intellectual* transformations, and on morphology rather than causation;[85] and I have said little about the ways science may have revolutionized society (in their essays in this volume, Paulinyi and Teich explore some of these facets). I have urged that we treat with reservation the standard notion of The Scientific Revolution. Its tendency to privilege scientific thought, implying intellectual autonomy as a unique achievement and a pinnacle of psychic maturity, rightly captures science's importance, yet conjures up a mystified, ahistorical myth of its role in making the modern world. A persuasive countervailing body of research has been built up over the last two decades – I have hardly been able to touch on it here – which has, by contrast, traced the wider socio-cultural determinants of science and demonstrated that the genesis, intellectual structure and functions of the sciences are altogether more problematic. The attractive Butterfieldian notion that science is revolutionized simply by great minds putting on new thinking caps is revealed for the just-so story it is.

Yet it would be equally fatuous for today's radicals to think the task of historical understanding is complete, once we have stuck science's past under the microscope and found it not pure but 'dirty'. The danger of facile demythologizations is that they all too readily induce myopia about the wider attractions, power and role of science in shaping the modern world. Geology today has learned to be neither rigidly uniformitarian nor arbitrarily catastrophist. In a similar way, as Arthur Koestler argued twenty years ago,[86] we surely need a history of science which doesn't trap itself in false dichotomies (revolution or evolution? internal or external development?) but which shows sensitivity to science's finer shifts in tempo, its rhythms of change, and its larger historical place.

NOTES

1 I. Bernard Cohen, 'The eighteenth-century origins of the concept of scientific revolution', *Journal of the History of Ideas*, XXVII (1976) 257–88; Felix Gilbert, 'Revolution', *Dictionary of the History of Ideas*, ed. P. P. Wiener, vol. 4 (New York, 1973), 152–67.

2 See Cohen, 'Eighteenth-century origins', and his fundamental *Revolution in Science* (Cambridge, Mass., 1985). This is the connotation in the Choruses from 'The Rock':

> O perpetual revolution of configured stars,
> O perpetual recurrence of determined seasons,
> O world of spring and autum, birth and dying!
> The endless cycle of idea and action,
> Endless invention, endless experiment.

T. S. Eliot, *The Complete Poems and Plays* (London, 1969), 147.

3 Cohen, *Revolution in Science*, 229–36.

4 For a discussion see N. Sivin, 'Why the scientific revolution did not take place in China – or didn't it?', in E. Mendelsohn, ed., *Transformation and Tradition in the Sciences* (Cambridge, 1985), 531–4. Sivin argues that the question of a Chinese scientific revolution is misposed.

5 H. Butterfield, *The Origins of Modern Science 1300–1800* (London, 1949), 175.

6 A. Donovan and J. Prentess, *James Hutton's Medical Dissertation* (American Philosophical Society, Philadelphia, 1980), 16.

7 J.-P. Goubert, 'A "quiet revolution": The coming of pure water to contemporary France', *The Society for the Social History of Medicine Bulletin*, XXXV (1984), 28–9, p. 28. Goubert also writes of 'the Pasteur revolution'.

8 T. S. Kuhn, *The Structure of Scientific Revolutions* (Chicago, 1962; rev. ed., 1970); M. Hesse, *Revolutions and Reconstructions in the Philosophy of Science* (Brighton, 1980), vii.

9 C. Merchant, *The Death of Nature: Women, Ecology and the Scientific Revolution* (San Francisco, 1980); B. Easlea, *Science and Sexual Oppression* (London, 1981); *idem*, *Witch-hunting, Magic and the New Philosophy: An Introduction to Debates of the Scientific Revolution 1450–1750* (Brighton, 1980). Both deplore post seventeenth-century science's legitimization of patriarchy and capitalism.

10 J. Marks, *Science and the Making of the Western World* (London, 1984), 87.

11 I. Bernard Cohen, *The Newtonian Revolution* (Cambridge, 1981); A. R. Hall, *The Revolution in Science 1500–1750* (London, 1983), 73.

12 C. A. Ronan, *The Cambridge Illustrated History of the World's Science* (Cambridge, 1983), 269.

13 Butterfield, *Origins of Modern Science*, viii; A. C. Crombie, *Augustine to Galileo* (2 vols., London, 1961), I, 26.

14 J. D. Bernal, *Science in History* (London, 1954), 251f.

15 A. R. Hall, 'On the historical singularity of the scientific revolution of the seventeenth century', in J. Elliott and H. Koenigsberger (eds.), *The Diversity of History* (London, 1970), 199–222; *idem*, *Ballistics in the Seventeenth Century* (Cambridge, 1952).

16 Arnold Thackray, 'History of science', in P. Durbin (ed.), *A Guide to the Culture of Science, Technology and Medicine* (New York and London, 1980), 3–69, p. 28. An excellent up-to-date survey is P. Corsi, 'History of science, history of philosophy and history of theology', in P. Corsi and P. Weindling

(eds.), *Information Sources in the History of Science and Medicine* (London, 1983), 3–26.

17 Hall, 'On the historical singularity' and *Ballistics in the Seventeenth Century.*

18 A. Koyré, *Études galiléennes*, I (Paris, 1939), 6–9.

19 Butterfield, *Origins of Modern Science*, viii. It is of course interesting that the term The Scientific Revolution wasn't applied to the rise of science amongst the Greeks, arguably a far greater watershed than sixteenth- and seventeenth-century developments. This suggests that the coiners of the term were indeed preoccupied with the roots of the present. See G. Lloyd, *Early Greek Science, Thales to Aristotle* (London, 1970).

20 B. Hessen, 'The social and economic roots of Newton's *Principia*', *Science at the Crossroads* (London, 1931), 147–212. See J. Ravetz and R. S. Westfall, 'Marxism and the history of science', *Isis*, LXXII (1981), 393–405.

21 C. C. Gillispie, *The Edge of Objectivity* (Princeton, 1960); A. Koestler, *The Sleepwalkers* (Harmondsworth, 1964); for a recent instance see D. Boorstin, *The Discoverers* (London, 1984).

22 For a critique of this Whiggism see J. Agassi, *Towards an Historiography of Science, History and Theory*, monograph 2 (1963); for a defence see A. R. Hall, 'On Whiggism', *History of Science*, XXI (1983), 45–59.

23 See A. R. Hall, 'Merton revisited', *History of Science*, II (1963), 1–16; Hall writes (p. 10) 'mind determines social forms'; see also *idem*, 'The scholar and the craftsman in the scientific revolution', in M. Clagett (ed.), *Critical Problems in the History of Science* (Madison, 1959), 3–23.

24 Classic is A. Koyré, *From the Closed World to the Infinite Universe* (Baltimore, 1957).

25 Cf. Marie Boas, *Robert Boyle and Seventeenth-Century Chemistry* (Cambridge, 1958); E. J. Dijksterhuis, *The Mechanization of the World Picture* (Oxford, 1981).

26 Gillispie, *Edge of Objectivity*, 117.

27 Hall, 'Merton revisited', 14. For a good discussion see Paul Wood, 'Philosophy of science in relation to history of science', in Corsi and Weindling, *Information Sources*, 116–33.

28 There is a fine account of this tendency in Arnold Thackray, 'Science: has its present past a future?', in R. Stuewer (ed.), *Historical and Philosophical Perspectives of Science* (Minneapolis, 1970), 112–27.

29 For the debate between historians and philosophers, see P. Rattansi, 'Some evaluations of reason in sixteenth- and seventeenth-century natural philosophy', in M. Teich and R. M. Young (eds.), *Changing Perspectives in the History of Science* (London, 1973), 148–66; and in the same volume (pp. 127–47), M. Hesse, 'Reasons and evaluations in the history of science'. And for a survey see G. Basalla (ed.), *The Rise of Modern Science: Internal or External Factors?* (Lexington, Mass., 1968).

30 Koyré, *Études galiléennes.*

31 Marie Boas, *Nature and Nature's Laws* (New York, 1970), 16, 18.

32 Stillman Drake, *Galileo at Work: His Scientific Biography* (Chicago, 1978).

33 Ronan, *Cambridge Illustrated History*, 334.

34 For some approaches to Lysenkoism, myth and reality, see D. Lecourt, *Proletarian Science? The Case of Lysenko* (London, 1977).

35 Marks, *Science and the Making*, 490f.

36 The mythology of the idea of discovery is worth pondering. See J. Hendry,

'Understanding science', *History of Science*, xxi (1983), 415–24; M. Fores, 'Science and the Neolithic paradox', *History of Science*, xxi (1983), 141–83, and *idem*, 'Constructed science and the seventeenth-century revolution', *History of Science*, xxii (1984), 217–44; Cf. Boorstin's blockbusting *The Discoverers*.

37 Bernal, *Science in History*, 253.

38 See above note 9. Compare the historiography of Bachelard, who was deeply influenced by Lévy-Bruhl's notion of the rift between primitive and modern thought. See G. Bachelard, *Le nouvel esprit scientifique* (New York, 1934); M. Tiles, *Bachelard: Science and Objectivity* (Cambridge, 1984), and for a broader discussion, S. Schaffer, 'Natural philosophy', in G. S. Rousseau and Roy Porter (eds.), *The Ferment of Knowledge* (Cambridge, 1980), 55–92. For discussion of how frequently seventeenth-century scientists and their modern historians approvingly use 'macho' language to depict the penetrative power of the new hard science, see Merchant and Easlea, cited above, note 9.

39 Koestler, *The Sleepwalkers*, 549; H. Kearney, *Science and Change* (London, 1971), 235. Much of this literature looks for watersheds, 'founders', or 'fathers' of all that is admired as modernity. For critique of such father-hunting see Sylvana Tomaselli, 'The first person: Descartes, Locke and mind–body dualism', *History of Science*, xxii (1984), 185–205.

40 Butterfield, *Origins of Modern Science*, 40.

41 W. Pagel, *William Harvey's Biological Ideas* (Basel, 1967).

42 The 'classical interpretation' too has a pervasive fear of 'irrationalism'. See A. R. Hall, 'Magic, metaphysics and mysticism in the Scientific Revolution', in M. L. Bonelli and W. Shea, *Reason, Experiment and Mysticism in the Scientific Revolution* (New York, 1975), 275–81.

43 For excellent historiographical discussion see S. Shapin, 'Social uses of science', in Rousseau and Porter, *Ferment of Knowledge*, 93–142.

44 Illuminating here are F. Manuel, *Shapes of Philosophical History* (London, 1965), and C. Webster, *The Great Instauration. Science, Medicine and Reform 1628–1660* (London, 1975).

45 Cf. P. Forman, 'Weimar culture, causality and quantum theory, 1918–1927: adaptation by German physicists and mathematicians to a hostile intellectual environment', *Historical Studies in the Physical Sciences*, iii (1971), 1–116; J. Hendry, 'Weimar culture and quantum causality', *History of Science*, xviii (1980), 155–80.

46 For some wider uses see H. Arendt, *On Revolution* (London, 1963); K. Kumar (ed.), *Revolution* (London, 1971).

47 That feeling of novelty is well conveyed by the experimental natural philosopher, Henry Power, writing in 1664: 'This is the Age wherein (me-thinks) Philosophy comes in with a Spring-tide; and the Peripateticks may as well hope to stop the Current of the Tide, or (with Xerxes) to better the Ocean, as hinder the overflowing of free philosophy: Me-thinks, I see how all the old Rubbish must be thrown away, and the rotten Buildings be overthrown, and carried away with so powerful an Inundation. These are the days that must lay a new Foundation of a more magnificent Philosophy, never to be overthrown: that will Empirically and Sensibly canvass the Phaenomena of Nature, deducing the Causes of things from such Originals in Nature, as we observe are producible by Art, and the infallible demonstration of Mechanicks; and certainly, this is the way, and no other, to build a true and permanent

philosophy.' Quoted in R. F. Jones, *Ancients and Moderns* (St Louis, 1936), 195.

48 For a new view of what was new and especially of what was old in Galileo, which argues for substantial debts to Aristotle, see W. A. Wallace, *Galileo and his Sources* (Princeton, 1984).

49 Though see M. Feingold, *The Mathematician's Apprenticeship* (Cambridge, 1984).

50 E. A. Burtt, *The Metaphysical Foundations of Modern Physical Science* (London, 1924), remains impressive. For Aristotelianism see C. B. Schmitt, 'Towards a reassessment of Renaissance Aristotelianism', *History of Science*, XI (1973), 159–93. S. Shapin, 'Pump and circumstance: Robert Boyle's literary technology', *Social Studies of Science*, XIV (1984), 481–520.

51 Arguably, by contrast, the strivings of the 'hermetic philosophers' of the sixteenth and early seventeenth century failed to become codified achievements. Cf. F. Yates, *The Rosicrucian Enlightenment* (London, 1972), and, for a slightly later cadre of reformers, Webster, *The Great Instauration.*

52 Cf. Cohen, *The Newtonian Revolution*, 15.

53 For eighteenth-century Newton adoration see H. Guerlac, 'Where the statue stood: divergent loyalties to Newton in the 18th century', in E. R. Wasserman (ed.), *Aspects of the Eighteenth Century* (Baltimore, 1965), 31–4; and P. Beer (ed.), *Newton and the Enlightenment* (Oxford, 1978). The myth of Kant's 'Copernican revolution' in philosophy has now however been scotched. See Cohen, Revolution in Science, 237f.

54 T. Rabb, *The Struggle for Stability in Early Modern Europe* (New York, 1975); stimulating is I. Couliano, *Eros et magie* (Paris, 1984).

55 For further discussion see for instance Merchant, *The Death of Nature*; Easlea, *Science and Sexual Oppression*; M. Berman, *The Re-enchantment of the World* (Ithaca and London, 1981); W. Leiss, *The Domination of Nature* (New York, 1975).

56 C. Webster, *From Paracelsus to Newton* (Cambridge, 1982); for a survey see C. B. Schmitt, 'Recent trends in the study of medieval and renaissance science', in P. Corsi and P. Weindling (eds.), *Information Sources in the History of Science and Medicine* (London, 1983), 221–42.

57 See S. Shapin, 'History of science and its sociological reconstructions', *History of Science*, XX (1982), 157–211.

58 P. M. Harman, 'The scientific revolution', in P. Burke (ed.), *The New Cambridge Modern History*, XIII, *Companion Volume* (Cambridge, 1979), 248–70, p. 248. In a revealing confusion, the chapter is called 'The scientific revolution' in the contents list, and 'The scientific revolutions' in the text. For Dr Opimian see D. Garnett (ed.), *The Novels of Thomas Love Peacock* (London, 1948), 769.

59 Berman, *Re-enchantment of the World*; F. Capra, *The Turning Point* (London, 1983); D. Dickson, 'Science and political hegemony in the seventeenth century', *Radical Science Journal*, VIII (1979), 7–38.

60 For the Puritanism-and-science debate see C. Webster (ed.), *The Intellectual Revolution of the Seventeenth Century* (London, 1974).

61 C. Hill, *Intellectual Origins of the English Revolution* (London, 1965), ch. 2. Sensitive studies of the modification of scientific thought in revolutionary circumstances are J. R. Jacob, *Robert Boyle and the English Revolution* (New York, 1977), and J. A. Bennett, 'The mechanics' philosophy and the mechanical philosophy', *History of Science*, XXIV (1986), 1–28.

62 C. Hill, 'William Harvey and the idea of monarchy', and Gweneth Whitteridge, 'William Harvey: a royalist and no parliamentarian', both reprinted in C. Webster (ed.), *The Intellectual Revolution*, 180–1; 181–8.

63 J. Ben-David, *The scientist's role in society* (Englewood Cliffs, N.J., 1971); James E. McLellan III, *Science Reorganized. Scientific Societies in the Eighteenth Century* (New York, 1984). The importance of print to scientific authority should not be minimized. See Elizabeth Eisenstein, *The Printing Press as an Agent of Change*, 2 vols. in one (Cambridge, 1979), and her contribution to this volume.

64 See C. C. Gillispie, 'Science in the French Revolution', *Behavioral Science*, IV (1959), 67–101; idem, *Edge of Objectivity*, ch. 5.

65 There is a sensitive up-to-date assessment with bibliography in C. A. Russell, *Science and Social Change 1700–1900* (London, 1983).

66 P. Hazard, *La crise de la conscience européenne*, translated as *The European Mind 1680–1715* (Harmondsworth, 1964). Compare M. C. Jacob, *The Radical Enlightenment* (London, 1982).

67 See for instance K. Hutchison, 'Supernaturalism and the mechanical philosophy', *History of Science*, XXI (1983), 297–333.

68 Illuminating here is H. Lewenthal, *In the Shadow of the Enlightenment* (New York, 1976).

69 See E. Bellone, *A World on Paper* (Cambridge, Mass., 1980).

70 Classic is Derek de Solla Price, *Little Science, Big Science* (New York, 1963).

71 L. Laudan, *Progress and its Problems* (Berkeley, 1979), 139. Cf. S. Toulmin, *Human Understanding* (Oxford, 1972), 103: 'It is a caricature, for instance to depict the changeover from Newtonian to Einsteinian physics as a complete rational discontinuity. Even a cursory consideration of Einstein's influence on physics will show how little his achievement exemplifies a full-scale scientific revolution. In a highly organized science like physics, every proposed modification – however profoundly it threatens to change the conceptual structure of the subject – is discussed, argued over, reasoned about, and criticized at great length, before being accredited and incorporated into the established body of the discipline.'

72 For the Kuhnian debate and bibliography, see G. Gutting, *Paradigms and Revolutions* (Notre Dame, 1980), and I. Hacking (ed.), *Scientific Revolutions* (Oxford, 1981).

73 A. Hallam, *A Revolution in the Earth Sciences. From Continental Drift to Plate Tectonics* (Oxford, 1973); *idem*, *Great Geological Controversies* (Oxford, 1983). For discussion see Rachel Laudan, 'The recent revolution in geology and Kuhn's theory of scientific change', in Gutting, *Paradigms and Revolutions*, 284–96.

74 C. Rosenberg, 'The therapeutic revolution', in M. Vogel and C. Rosenberg (eds.), *The Therapeutic Revolution* (Philadelphia, 1979), 3–25.

75 T. S. Kuhn, *The Copernican Revolution* (Cambridge, Mass. 1957); Cf. R. Hardison, *Upon the Shoulders of Giants* (New York, 1984), 31. N. R. Hanson, 'The Copernican Disturbance and the Keplerian Revolution', *Journal of the History of Ideas*, XXII (1961), 169–84.

76 Kuhn, *Structure of Scientific Revolutions*, 10.

77 L. Wilson, *Charles Lyell, the Years to 1841. The Revolution in Geology* (New Haven, 1972), 293; *idem*, 'The intellectual background to Charles Lyell's *Principles of Geology* 1830–1833', in C. J. Schneer (ed.), *Toward a History of Geology* (Cambridge, Mass., 1969), 426–43.

78 Michael Bartholomew, 'The singularity of Lyell', *History of Science*, XVII (1979), 276–93; *idem*, 'The non-progress of non-progression: two responses to Lyell's doctrine', *The British Journal for the History of Science*, IX (1976), 166–74.

79 L. Laudan, *Progress*, 136. Laudan argues: 'It is this perennial co-existence of conflicting traditions of research which makes the focus on revolutionary epochs so misleading. These traditions are constantly evolving, their relative fortunes may shift through time, old traditions may be largely displaced by new ones, but it is generally unhelpful to focus attention on certain stages of this process as revolutionary and on others as evolutionary.'

80 For discussion see Maurice Crosland, 'Chemistry and the chemical revolution', in G. S. Rousseau and Roy Porter (eds.), *The Ferment of Knowledge* (Cambridge, 1980), 389–418.

81 W. Anderson, *Between the Library and the Laboratory* (Baltimore, 1984); and, most ambitiously, H. G. McCann, *Chemistry Transformed* (Norwood, NJ, 1978).

82 The Darwinian revolution is proclaimed in G. Himmelfarb, *The Darwinian Revolution* (New York, 1959), and M. Ruse, *The Darwinian Revolution* (Chicago, 1979). The best modern survey is P. Bowler, *Evolution. The History of an Idea* (Berkeley, 1984); see pp. 8–18.

83 H. Gruber, *Darwin on Man* (London, 1974).

84 See J. W. Draper, *History of the Conflict between Religion and Science* (New York, 1875); D. Fleming, *John William Draper and the Religion of Science* (New York, 1972); R. M. Young, 'The historiographic and ideological contexts of the nineteenth century debate on man's place in nature', in M. Teich and R. M. Young, *Changing Perspectives in the History of Science* (London, 1973), 344–438.

85 Simon Schaffer, reviewing Cohen's *Newtonian Revolution* in *History of Science*, XX (1982), 140–4, discusses how scientific ideas become revolutionized, arguing that an intellectual history approach is not sufficient. This line is further developed in his 'History of physical science', in Corsi and Weindling (eds.), *Information Sources*, 285–316.

86 Koestler, *The Sleepwalkers*, 523ff.

15

The scientific-technical revolution: an historical event in the twentieth century?

MIKULÁŠ TEICH

I

J. D. Bernal seems to have been the first to use the term Scientific-Technical Revolution (STR). He justified it in 1957 in the second edition of his *Science in History* in response to some of the critics of the first edition of the work in 1954 who

> have doubted the justice of speaking of a second scientific revolution in the twentieth century, alleging that in this case there was no break in continuity of research such as occurred between Classical times and the Renaissance, nor was there any notable slackening of the pace of advance. Now the terms revolution and continuity are inevitably relative. I have even been attacked by other critics for under-rating the continuity of Renaisssance and Medieval thought. But I feel that if we grant the term revolution in one case, we must grant it in the other. Against the revolution of the earth and the circulation of the blood, the telescope and the vacuum pump, and the upsetting of previous ideas that these implied, we may urge the discovery of the nuclear atom, relativity, and the quantum theory, as well as of the processes of bio-chemistry and the inner structure of the cell, the electron microscope, and the electronic computing machine. Add to that the sudden acceleration of all scientific activity and its application, from atom fission and television to the control of disease, and it would appear that if this is not a scientific revolution nothing is. Nevertheless, the contention that the two revolutions are not comparable may be true in another sense. The first revolution actually discovered the method of science, the second only applied it. The new revolutionary character of the twentieth century cannot be confined to science, it resides even more in the fact that only in our time has science come to dominate industry and agriculture. The revolution might perhaps more justly be called the first scientific-technical revolution ...[1]

By 1965, in the third edition of the book, Bernal claimed that the non-scientific world, especially the political segment, had come to acknowledge the epoch-making developments underlying the STR, the beginning of which he associated with the outbreak of the Second World War.[2] Indeed in Bernal's view the STR 'could be fairly seen as far back as the 'thirties'.[3] By 1969 when Bernal published the illustrated edition of the book (effectively the fourth edition) he was less sanguine about the depth of the grasp of the process: 'the scientific-technical revolution is in full swing and this is now generally recognised, but so far only in words'.[4]

By the 1960s Bernal was not alone, of course, in attributing far-reaching social effects to such discoveries as nuclear fission, space navigation, electronic computers or the genetic code. Their recognition in the West, catalysed by the launching of the first artificial satellite in the Soviet Union in 1957, resulted in organized efforts to inquire into the different aspects of the relationship of science, technology and society.[5] While this movement propelled 'science policy studies' into an identifiable discipline,[6] it also underscored the relevance of the social approach to the history of science.[7] As to its theoretical perspective, it was markedly affected by Kuhn's work[8] on the nature of normal science and scientific revolutions and the debate that it engendered.[9]

To all intents and purposes Kuhn pays no attention to socio-historical context. As the intellectual impact of his conception of normal science and scientific revolutions was wide-ranging and pervasive during the late 1960s and early 1970s, it may well be that it then helped to weaken in the West the appetite for critical analysis of the nature of the relationship between science and technology. That 'scientific revolutions' have taken place during the twentieth century has been accepted as something true.[10] But there has been far less certainty about how to conceptualize the reciprocal effects of social change and scientific and technical developments during the period. Attempts have been made to encapsulate them, as it were, in terms of two courses of events labelled, the 'Second Industrial Revolution' and 'Third Industrial Revolution'. At the back of this approach lies the view that, whereas the First Industrial Revolution centred on steam, at the heart of the Second was electric power, and the Third turns – currently – on semiconductor electronics.

Whatever the attraction, it is dubious to populate history with 'n' Industrial Revolutions on the basis of technical breakthroughs perceived to be 'revolutionary'. The problem is to cope with them as elements of wider historical processes located in time and space. This inevitably brings us to the question of the meaning of the 'First Industrial Revolution'. In both the most general and specific senses, the Industrial Revolution is about the changeover from an economy based on agriculture to one based on industry. There can be little doubt that it is in this sense that Phyllis Deane writes in her widely acclaimed book about the 'first industrial revolution' which occurred in Britain between approximately 1750 and 1850.[11] It preceded in time homologous transitions to industrial economy in other countries without being reproduced in every respect.

II

From the point of view of this essay it is of value to obtain some idea of the part played by science in the Industrial Revolution, 'the most fundamental transformation of human life in the history of the world recorded in written documents'.[12] The issue is not new and has received attention from historians of science, historians of technology and economic historians in the West, but it is no exaggeration to say that no consensus has been reached.[13]

There is no shortage of contributions to the debate adding weight to the different schools of historians who favour this or the other view of (close, intermediate, absent) relations between science and technology in the area of industrialization. In the last analysis the disagreements are traceable to conceptual reasons rather than to a lack of historical evidence.[14] There is enough of it to show that the growth of the influence of scientific knowledge on production constituted, to the extent it supplanted but did not oust empirical knowledge rooted in the experience and skill of artisan and farm (peasant) manual labour, one of the characteristic features of the Industrial Revolution.[15]

It is against this background that we consider the relations of science and technology since the beginning of the twentieth century. It is the historical experience of the atomic bomb, microelectronics or genetic engineering rather than analysis that lies behind the virtually undisputed view that, in comparison with the nineteenth century, a qualitative change in the relations between science and technology has taken place. It has found expression in a term such as 'science-based technology' which, however, does not quite do justice to the complex relationships under consideration between scientific discovery, technological development and production. It has been pointed out rightly that it implies 'an over-simplified one-way movement of ideas'.[16]

A more coherent theory of the science–production relationship began to be developed from around 1960 in the European socialist countries. It was based on the idea that the time had arrived when science was transformed into a 'direct force of production'. For example, G. Kosel in the GDR used it in 1957, as a point of departure to ask about the nature of mental labour in general and scientific research in particular, including the latter's 'productiveness'.[17] But it was not until it was incorporated into the Programme of the Communist Party of the Soviet Union, passed at its 22nd Congress in 1961, that the idea of science becoming a direct force of production began to be taken up in earnest as a theme of political and philosophical, but hardly a historical, discussion. It will be recalled that it was at the 22nd Congress that in the Soviet Union the transition to a communist society – rather rashly – was envisaged within two decades. It was to have become fact on a material and technical basis surpassing that of the United States of America, the world's most advanced capitalist state. A crucial role in this process was assigned to science which was expected to become fully a direct force of production.[18]

Now let us turn briefly to the history of the concept, and here mention has to be made of Marx's preparatory work during 1857–8, published for the first time in 1939–41 under the title *Grundrisse der Kritik der politischen Ökonomie (Rohentwurf)*. As is known or should be known, the chief aim of Marx's theoretical endeavour was to discover the laws underlying the formation and development of capital and thus to provide the key to comprehending capitalism as a historically evolved system of social production. It is in this connection that Marx encountered the problem of the role of science and technology in the development of the productive forces under capitalism.[19]

In the *Grundrisse* Marx touches on the problem, among other things, when he analyses categories such as 'labour process', 'fixed capital', 'machine', etc.

> Nature [Marx notes] builds no machines, no locomotives, railways, electric telegraphs, self-acting mules, etc. These are products of man-made industry ... They are *organs of the human brain, created by the human hand*, a power of knowledge objectified. The development of fixed capital [appearing as a machine] reveals to what degree general social knowledge has become a *direct force of production*.[20]

On following up Marx's thinking on this subject in *Capital* (1867), his major published work, we find that by then he regarded science as an intellectual potency (*geistige Potenz*) of the process of production rather than as a direct force.[21] Marx frequently refers in *Capital* to *Produktivkraft der Arbeit* in the sense of 'productivity' and writes that it is 'determined by various circumstances, among others, by the average skill of the workmen, the state of science and the degree of its practical application, the social organization of production, the extent and capabilities of the means of production and by physical conditions'.[22]

No doubt what happened was that Marx on maturer reflection concluded that a more subtle relationship between science and production had to be contemplated than the point-to-point one he had previously predicated. It has been my view for a long time that practitioners as well as theoreticians concerned currently with this issue could benefit from this approach. That is, to recognize that the relationship between science and production is a mediated one, depending on factors such as military needs, economic expectations, technological feasibility, political interests and others. Looked at in this way, scientific knowledge represents a *potential* rather than a direct force of production.[23]

III

The continuous neglect of this point, while emphasizing the linear link, has characterized the writing on the STR in the socialist countries, in particular in the USSR, GDR and Czechoslovakia where increasing attention has been paid to it since the beginning of the 1960s. Indeed, the transformation of science into a direct productive force has been identified by theoreticians and politicans there as the major driving element of the STR.

It was in Czechoslovakia, from 1965, that the most searching endeavour to investigate the STR as a social phenomenon was undertaken on an interdisciplinary basis by a group formally attached to the Institute of Philosophy of the Czechoslovak Academy of Sciences. It was headed by the philosopher Radovan Richta, whose first discussion of the problems of modern technology in wider social context appeared in 1963.[24]

Eventually the team did include sixty men and women active not only in philosophy, but in many different fields: economics, sociology, psychology, political science, history, medicine, the theory of architecture and environment, several branches of science and technology. By the spring of 1968 the material embodying the results of their collective labours was assembled and appeared in print in July of that year. What is impressive is that over fifty thousand copies of the Czech and Slovak editions were sold out immediately, demonstrating the broad and intense degree of concern in the country for the issues explored in the volume. Recognized abroad as a significant contribution to the literature on the social and human dimensions of twentieth-century scientific and technological developments, it was translated into several foreign languages. In order to acquaint the foreign reader with the climate in which the books came to be composed, a short explanatory section was added to the Introduction from which the following passage is taken:

> The work was conceived in an atmosphere of critical, radical searching and intensive discussion on the way forward for a society that has reached industrial maturity while passing through a phase of far-reaching socialist transformation. In the light of theoretical enquiries, we saw an image of all modern civilization. The choice advanced in our hypothesis emerged as a practical problem.[25]

To English-speaking readers in the 1980s, especially belonging to the younger generation, these sentences may appear rather remote and therefore, perhaps, a brief comment is in order. To say that the team was somehow consciously participating in the preparation of the events that are known as the 'Prague Spring of 1968' would be misleading. Nevertheless, its work constitutes an integral part of the latter's history (which has as yet to be written), in the sense that the analysis produced regarding the social and human impact of the twentieth-century scientific and technological developments also led to poignant critical questions and comments about the Czechoslovak social environment within which they were expected to function:

> The scientific and technological revolution brings into play a new, independent growth factor – human development on a broad front. Far more is expected of individual activity, the fullness of man's inner life, the ability to surpass oneself and to cultivate one's own capacities – and growth of the individual acquires a wider social significance. Hitherto individual socialist endeavour has tended to be put at a disadvantage, the horizons of 'reproductive life' have been hard and fast – in short, individual initiative has been curbed by a mass of directives. We now face the necessity to supplement economic instruments with socio-political and anthropological instruments that will shape the contours of human life, evoke new wants, model the structure of man's motivation, while enlarging, not interfering with, freedom of choice, in fact relying on a system of opportunities and potentialities in human development ... in the context of the scientific and technological revolution the Communist Party, as the leading force, will find it necessary to look beyond the horizon of patterns solely directed to tackling issues arising from class struggle (and the structure of political power as such); it will have to evolve a diversity of new approaches and more effective means, taking in technology, the economy, social, psychological and anthropological factors, by which to adjust conditions for socialist endeavour.[26]

The changed political climate, following the entry of military units of the Soviet Union (and Poland, Hungary, GDR and Bulgaria) on 20 August 1968 into Czechoslovakia, put paid to this promising organized approach to the historical process in which science and technology, under capitalism as well as socialism, had become paramount.

After saying this, it is necessary to stress that the theme of the STR has not disappeared from the political and philosophical agenda in Czechoslovakia. But soon a shift took place from critical analysis of the problems posed by the STR towards ideological justification of its organic connection with socialism (as a world system and movement), on the one hand, and of the essential incompatibility of the STR to function under capitalism, on the other.[27]

To those in Czechoslovakia, the Soviet Union and the GDR involved in the study of the STR, its relationship to the capitalist and socialist social systems has remained the central concern. It is at the heart of such major Czechoslovak–Soviet collaborative works as *Man Science Technology* (1973),[28] and *Socialism and Science* (1982),[29] in which the authors have been at pains to bring home to the reader all the factors that weigh heavily against the development of science and technology within the capitalist social framework and all the elements that favour it under the socialist system.

The volumes are nothing if not comprehensive. For example, *Man Science Technology* contains the following chapters: I. The scientific-technological revolution and its nature; II. The main tendencies in the scientific-technological revolution; III. Science–technology–production; IV. The scientific-technological revolution and the social systems; V. The scientific-technological revolution and the changes in the social structure of society; VI. Organization and management; VII. The shaping of life-style; VIII. The human problems and the spiritual values; IX. The influence of the scientific-technological revolution on the structure of scientific thought; X. The scientific-technological revolution and the future of humanity.

For someone looking for Marxist guidance rather than 'correct' answers reflecting the Soviet ideological position, the reading of such a book may prove heavy going. Nevertheless, if only because works of this type stimulate interest in the STR, a rather unfamiliar concept and theme in non-Marxist writings devoted to historical and social studies of twentieth-century science and technology, one should be wary of dismissing them because of their ideological framework and style. Certainly, a serious non-Marxist student in these fields cannot take exception, at a general level, to the salient proposition expressed in them that theoretical analysis of science and technology requires to take into account the whole of the socio-historical context. But he may be taken aback when he reads that the STR, associated with the major scientific and technological developments since the turn of the century, 'is inseparably linked with the social revolution which has become the banner of the 20th century'.[30]

IV

Plainly, in the socialist countries the concept of the STR has been developed in the framework of the 'stages of development' theory as a component of the revolutionary transformation of capitalism into socialism. What attracts attention is that this conceptualization of scientific-technological and social relationship in the twentieth century has virtually been ignored in the capitalist world.[31] Here for all the expansion of the social history of science and science policy fields since the 1960s the capitalist and socialist contexts of science as such have not received the attention which they deserve.[32]

Now it would be presumptuous to pretend to know all the reasons for this state of indifference. Doubtless the notion that capitalism, in contrast to socialism, appeared to work well must have been one reason during the 1960s. It implicitly underlay the then unfolding inquiries into the effects of scientific and technological change on society, in general, and on its economic and other aspects in particular.[33]

This attitude was clearly reflected in E. G. Mesthene's *How Technology*

Will Shape the Future which first appeared as an article in *Science* (1968) and subsequently as a reprint in the series growing out of the Harvard Program on Technology and Society.[34] As Mesthene was its director, this study, though brief, offers a representative avenue to non-Marxist thinking about technological impact on society at the time.

In fact, from the outset Mesthene made explicit two points. One, that he was concerned with the American and West European, that is capitalist, societies respectively. The other, that he rejected the opinion regarding technology as 'univocally determinative of culture and social structure' which he unsupportedly associated with the Marxist tradition. He instead adopted the view that new technologies made for changes in social organization, 'with a very high probability' ('probabilistic determinism').

As to Mesthene's notion of 'changes in social organization', it would seem he related them to effects on 'our principal institutions: industry, government, universities'. Previously these operated separately, he wrote, but with the technological winds of change blowing strongly, entwining tendencies developed:

> The economic affluence that is generated by modern industrial technology accelerates such institutional mixing-up by blurring the heretofore relatively clear distinction between the private and public sectors of society ... In our society, affluence is a precondition of such an emphasis.[35]

Taken by and large, to Mesthene the future looked very rosy indeed: never more than when he discussed the implications of technological change for employment:

> Few serious students of the subject believe any longer that the progress of mechanization and automation in industry must lead to an irreversible increase in the level of *involuntary* unemployment in the society, whether in the form of unavailability of employment, or of an extension of the period of formal schooling. These developments may occur, either voluntarily, because people choose to take some of their increased productivity in the form of leisure, or as a result of inadequate education, poor social management, or failure to ameliorate our race problem. But reduction of the overall level of employment is not a necessary consequence of new industrial technology.[36]

While not envisaging mass unemployment, nonetheless, Mesthene did grant that advancing technology 'displaces some jobs by rendering them more efficiently performed by machines than by people'. As a result he anticipated, among others, that more than one career per lifetime will be the norm. Though Mesthene evidently played down the extent of the problem, he identified it as one that had come to stay and which had to be attended to. It was up to society to find appropriate ways and means.

> These may range from financial and organizational innovations for diverting resources to neglected public needs to social policies which no longer treat human

labor as a market commodity. Whatever the form of solution, however, the problem is more than a 'transitional' one. It represents a qualitative and permanent alteration in the nature of human society consequent to perception of the ubiquity of change.[37]

Having followed Mesthene so far we come to the last and least satisfactory section of his study. Mesthene was quite aware that the issue under discussion was not merely a question of theoretical understanding but also of political practice. This he related to decision-making by government whose role, as a result of technological changes, he saw enhanced.[38] What Mesthene did not discuss was the ways of achieving governmental decisions nor the social basis of the power underlying them. If he had done so he could not have escaped the problem of whether his demand for ceasing to treat human labour as a market commodity could have been met by the American and West European contemporary society he specifically had been concerned with.

Be that as it may, within a few years, in the 1970s, the American economy running into serious problems demonstrated Mesthene's by no means isolated misjudgement of its secure structure. Reviewing the situation, thoughtful defenders of US capitalism noted that something was wrong with it without being able to specify what it was. For example, in a book examining contemporary American economic problems from a historical perspective of two hundred years it was stated:

Clearly, Americans today enjoy a material standard of living which is far above that of 1929. Yet, despite our great affluence, our sophisticated technology, and all the lessons we have (we hope) learned since 1929 – despite all this, Americans as they enter the 1980s seem insecure about their future – just as they were in 1930.

The fact that, after fifty years of progress, economic security remains an elusive goal is both frustrating and perplexing. Indeed, in some respects the present situation is even more frustrating than that of the 1930s. The forces that produce economic insecurity today seem to be more subtle than those that produced anxiety during the depression ... For most of us, the malaise itself is something of an enigma.[39]

As the confidence of the 1960s in the all-round and wholesome role of scientific-technological advance began to be shaken, Congress itself wished to find out how its potentialities could be utilized and realized effectively. Not least because of the unprecedented costs of research and development: federal expenditure rose from \$1.2 billion in 1950 to \$33.5 billion in 1980; \$29.5 billion was the estimated comparable sum disbursed by the private sector in the same year.[40]

In 1976 Congress made provisions for the first and in 1980 the second 'Five Year Outlook for Science and Technology'. Occupied in contributing to the latter, the American Association for the Advancement of Science convened in November 1980 a workshop (attended by thirty-five people) organized around the domestic theme, 'Applying science and technology to public purposes', and in December 1980 a workshop (attended by thirty-four people) devoted to the international theme, 'Toward personal change: science, technology and international security'. Participants came from universities, government agencies, industrial firms and non-profit-making organizations and included demographers, computer and information scientists, geologists, economists, microbiologists, agronomists and experts from a number of other fields. They discussed such topical issues as the challenge of scientific advance and technological change to values and institutions; management attitudes and practices; information and communications technology; applied molecular genetics; risks and hazards emanating from scientific-technical advance; science, technology and international security; science and technology in the developing countries; U.S. agriculture and the world food situation; trends and prospects in world population; international security implications of material and energy resource depletion; science and national defence. The issues were brought into focus and solidly presented in eleven papers. What these did not do was to indicate a way that American capitalism was to cope politically and institutionally with the social and economic problems deriving from scientific and technological developments. In a 'synthesis essay' the author called attention to the dilemma as follows:

> Finally, an underlying theme of the papers, and the conference where they were discussed, is that scientific and technological advance has posed deep, perhaps unanswerable, challenges to our established political values, institutions and processes. This last theme is perhaps the most disquieting because few have any clear vision about how to restore existing institutions to a satisfactory level of performance. But diagnosis must precede prescription, and recognition of the problem is thus a constructive step forward.[41]

Among politicians, economists, scientists, technologists and others concerned with these matters, whatever their political and ideological differences, there is or can be common ground on the following. The chain of scientific and technological developments in this century has provided mankind with the means, in the context of nuclear and space warfare, to destroy itself completely. Alternatively, it has provided impetus for states, irrespective of their social systems, to look for non-military solutions to international problems. How this unparalleled situation has come about should be of interest to historians, not least to historians of science and technology.[42]

Such a quest goes beyond the exploratory scope of this essay. Even so, it is apparent, against the background of history, that the chain of scientific and technological developments set in motion since the turn of the century has come to occupy a momentously 'socializing' influence. Transcending its common connotations (economic, educational), here socialization is taken to encompass the contradictory movements of human society to come fully into its own. It is in the context of the historically unprecedented socializing role of science and technology that it seems apt to call the chain of scientific and technological developments in the twentieth century the Scientific-Technological Revolution.

NOTES

1 J. D. Bernal, *Science in History*, 2nd ed. (London, 1957), p. 960. In this essay the terms 'Scientific-Technical Revolution' and 'Scientific-Technological Revolution' are interchangeable.

2 J. D. Bernal, *Science in History*, 3rd ed. (London, 1965), p. xv.

3 *Ibid.*, p. xvi. In this connection it is of interest to read what Bernal wrote in 1938: 'To see the function of science as a whole it is necessary to look at it against the widest possible background of history. Our attention to immediate historical events has, up till very recently, blinded us to the understanding of its major transformations. Mankind is, after all, a late emergence on the scene of terrestrial evolution, and the earth itself is a late by-product of cosmic forces. Up till now human life has only undergone three major changes: the foundation first of society and then of civilization, both of which occurred before the dawn of recorded history, and that scientific transformation of society which is now taking place and for which we have as yet no name.' Cf. J. D. Bernal, *The Social Function of Science*, 3rd reprint (London, 1942), p. 408. See also J. D. Bernal, 'The Social Function of Science', *The Modern Quarterly* 1 (1938), 15–22 (p. 15).

4 J. D. Bernal, *Science in History*, illustrated ed., 4 vols. (London, 1969), 1, p. 15.

5 In this essay 'science' relates to *the* human activity, evolved historically, for the purpose of the systematic practical examination of Nature along qualitative and quantitative lines and the production of correlative theoretical knowledge about it. As to the meaning of 'technology' adopted here, it coincides with the view expressed by A. Paulinyi in chapter 13.

6 For a brief informative treatment see J. J. Salomon, 'Science policy studies and the development of science policy', in I. Spiegel-Rösing and D. de Solla Price (eds.), *Science, Technology and Society: A Cross-Disciplinary Perspective* (London and Beverly Hills, 1977), pp. 43–70.

7 For sequence of developments (problems, approaches, inter-disciplinarity) in the history of science and technology after the Second World War up to around 1970, it is possible to consult M. Clagett (ed.), *Critical Problems in the History of Science* (Madison, 1959), A. C. Crombie (ed.), *Scientific Change* (Oxford, 1963), and M. Teich and R. Young (eds.), *Changing Perspectives in the History of Science* (London, 1973). See also the useful study by R. MacLeod, 'Changing Perspectives in the Social History of Science', in Spiegel-Rösing and de Solla Price, *Science, Technology and Society*, pp. 149–95.

8 T. S. Kuhn, *The Structure of Scientific Revolutions*, 1st and 2nd eds. (Chicago, 1962, 1970).

9 This is revealed, for example, by B. Barnes in the 'Introduction' to *Sociology of Science* (Harmondsworth, 1972) which he edited: '... great prominence is ... given to the work of Thomas Kuhn which provides insight into stability and change in the culture of science, and is currently being used by sociologists in this field to construct an entirely new theoretical approach to it. Kuhn's description of science (which this writer regards as a landmark in the process of understanding science as it is, rather than as it "ought" to be) points the way to a new and deeper appreciation of its internal processes' (p. 11).

10 Cf. 'The scientific revolution in nuclear physics and in such fields as genetics ... seems certain to have a more radical effect on our political institutions than did the industrial revolution' (Don K. Price, *The Scientific Estate* (Oxford, London, New York, 1965), p. 15.

11 P. Deane, *The First Industrial Revolution* (Cambridge, 1965), p. 2.

12 E. J. Hobsbawm, *Industry and Empire* (Harmondsworth, 1969), p. 13.

13 This clearly emerges from the Proceedings of the Burndy Library Conference (1973) on *The Interaction of Science and Technology in the Industrial Age*, edited by N. Reingold and A. Molella and published in *Technology and Culture*, 17 (1976), 619–742.

14 Cf. 'I think I hear in [the] plea for more detailed case studies the implicit hope that some sort of new resolution of our conceptual problem will automatically emerge. This seems to me not to be a well-grounded hope. Just as there is no pure, dispassionate science or technology, there is no pure, dispassionate history either.' A. Thackray, *Ibid.*, 672.

15 Phyllis Deane gives great prominence to the 'widespread and systematic application of modern science and empirical knowledge to the process of production for the market', which tops her list of seven distinguishable related changes underlying 'the first industrial revolution'. See Deane, *The First*, p. 1.

16 See C. Freeman, *The Economics of Industrial Innovation*, 2nd ed. (London, 1982), p. 16. Freeman writes that 'science-related technology' is usually preferable. But this term is not without problems either since it can be applied to earlier connections between science, technology and production. For example, the combination of 'science-related technology' of steam-engines, artificial refrigeration and pure yeast cultivation contributed decisively to the completion of industrialization of brewing in Germany after 1880. This is dealt with in detail in my book *Bier, Wissenschaft und Wirtschaft in Deutschland 1800–1914* which is in preparation. See also M. Teich, 'Fermentation theory and practice: the beginnings of pure yeast cultivation and English brewing 1883–1913', *History of Technology*, 8 (1983), 117–33.

17 G. Kosel, *Produktivkraft Wissenschaft* (Berlin, 1957).

18 See *Kommunist*, no. 16 (1961), 61.

19 For a perceptive study see N. Rosenberg, 'Marx as a student of technology', *Monthly Review*, 28 (1976), 56–77. Reprinted in L. Levidow and B. Young (eds.), *Science, Technology and the Labour Process: Marxist Studies*, 1 (London, 1981), pp. 8–27, and N. Rosenberg, *Inside the Black Box: Technology and Economics* (Cambridge, 1982), pp. 34–51.

20 K. Marx, *Grundrisse: Foundations of the Critique of Political Economy (Rough Draft)*, translated with a Foreword by M. Nicolaus (Harmondsworth, 1973), p. 706 (slightly modified); cf. *Grundrisse der Kritik der politischen Ökonomie (Rohentwurf)* (Berlin, 1953), p. 594. My italics and interpolations.

21 K. Marx, *Capital* (London, 1938), 1, p. 355; *Das Kapital* (Berlin, 1947), 1, p. 379.
22 Marx, *Capital*, p. 7.
23 M. Teich, 'Does science function as a direct productive force?' Paper no. 16, Conference on Man and Society in the Scientific-Technological Revolution, Marianské Lázně, 1–6 April 1968 (Prague, 1968).
24 R. Richta, *Člověk a technika v revoluci našich dnů* (Man and Technology in the Revolution of Our Time) (Prague, 1963).
25 R. Richta and a research team, *Civilization at the Crossroads: Social and Human Implications of the Scientific and Technological Revolution*, trans. M. Šlingová, 3rd expanded ed. (Prague, 1969), p. 21.
26 *Ibid.*, pp. 284–6: 'reproduction life' altered to 'reproductive life' (printing error).
27 Cf. J. Filipec and R. Richta, *Vědeckotechnická revoluce a socialismus* (The Scientific-Technological Revolution and Socialism) (Prague, 1972).
28 Originally published in Moscow and Prague in Russian, Czech and English. I rely on the German version ed. M. Buhr and G. Kröber, *Mensch Wissenschaft Technik* (Cologne, 1977). The Russian version was reviewed by S. Lieberstein, *Technology and Culture*, 16 (1975), 691–3.
29 S. R. Mikulinski and R. Richta (eds.), *Socialism and Science* (Prague, 1983). The Czech version appeared in 1982.
30 See 'Theses of the USSR Academy of Sciences' Institute of World Economy and International Relations', in *The Scientific-Technological Revolution and the Contradictions of Capitalism* (Moscow, 1982), p. 24.
31 The literature is indeed meagre. E. P. Hoffman has written on the topic: 'Contemporary Soviet theories of scientific-technological and social change', *Social Studies of Sciences*, 9 (1979), 101–13. The STR as such is discussed (in particular in relation to the electronics industry, the role of government and the unions) in I. Benson and J. Lloyd, *New Technology and Industrial Change: The Impact of the Scientific-Technical Revolution on Labour and Industry* (London and New York, 1983). For a critical perspective on the STR as a product of 'scientistic Marxism', see B. Young, 'Is nature a labour process?', L. Levidow and B. Young (eds.), *Science, Technology and the Labour Process: Marxist Studies*, 2 (London, 1985), pp. 206–32 (p. 209).
32 In this connection it is instructive to consult the volume *George Sarton Centennial* (Ghent, 1984). It contains extended abstracts of the bulk of the papers presented at the Sarton Centennial meeting (14–17 November 1984) that was organized by three bodies: Communication and Cognition, the European Association for the Study of Science and Technology and the Society for Social Studies of Science. It does seem that out of about 490 only one contribution, dealing with the use of science and technology (nuclear weapons), explicitly took account of social relations specific to capitalist and socialist systems: R. Dittmann and M. Ogden, 'Theories to explain the phenomena of nuclear escalation', pp. 415–19.
33 The Harvard University Program of Technology and Society was established in 1964 by a grant from the International Business Machines Corporation. The science policy research unit at the University of Sussex was established in 1966.
34 E. G. Mesthene, *How Technology Will Shape the Future*, Harvard University Program on Technology and Society, reprint no. 5 (n.d.).

35 *Ibid.*, p. 13.
36 *Ibid.*, p. 14.
37 *Ibid.*, p. 15.
38 *Ibid.*, p. 18.
39 R. L. Ransom, *Coping with Capitalism: The Economic Transformation of the United States 1776–1980* (Englewood Cliffs, 1981), pp. 146–7.
40 R. A. Rettig, 'Applying science and technology to public purposes: a synthesis' in A. H. Teich and R. Thornton (eds.), *Science, Technology and the Issues of the Eighties: Policy Outlook* (American Association for the Advancement of Science, 1982), p. 8.
41 *Ibid.*, p. 9. Cf. 'To capture the outcome of the workshop deliberations, an additional paper – a "synthesis essay" – was commissioned for each workshop ... The synthesis essays were conceived as papers that, ideally, would be viewed by the authors of the workshop papers and by the workshop participants as incorporating and fairly representing their papers and deliberations. At the same time, the synthesis authors were expected to draw upon their own knowledge and expertise to provide overall structure, organization and thematic unity that would go well beyond simple reportage.' *Ibid.*, p. xiii.
42 This essay contains an elaboration as well as a revision of views I held when I began to be interested in the subject in the early 1960s. The interest was a by-product of my coordination of the activities of a team working on the history of technology in Czechoslovakia. (See F. Graus, *Jahrbücher für Geschichte Osteuropas*, 24 (1976), 612–14; M. Teich, *Annals of Science*, 34 (1977), 210–12.) It resulted in the publication of 'K některým otázkám historického vývoje vědecko-technické revoluce' (The scientific-technical revolution: problems of historical development), *Sborník pro dějiny přírodních věd a techniky*, 10 (1965), 7–31. For a German version see 'Zu einigen Fragen der historischen Entwicklung der wissenschaftlich-technischen Revolution, *Jahrbuch für Wirtschaftsgeschichte*, part 2 (1966), 34–62. I also dealt with the theme in 'Some historical problems of the scientific-technical revolution', Paper no. 10, Conference on Men and Society in the Scientific-Technological Revolution, Marianské Lázně, 1–6 April 1968 (Prague, 1968) and briefly in 'Science and technology in the 20th century' in F. C. Lane (ed.), *Fourth International Conference of Economic History Bloomington 1968* (Paris, 1973), pp. 244–6.

Index

Abd ul Rahman, 129
Abrud, 89
Abyssinia, 129
Adler, F., 111, 115
Adorno, Theodor, 209
Afghanistan, 129
Afro-Asia: and imperialism, 122–4, 125–33, 136–41; *see also* India
agriculture, 4, 81, 167, 172–3, 179, 276, 318; agrarian question, 90; biochemical technology, 170; capitalism in, 172; commercialised, 175; enclosure(s), 169, 170–2; fertilizer(s), 169; land, 84, 107–8, 113, 169; landlord(s), 75, 77, 90–1, 169; mechanisation, 170; peasant unrest, 14, 62–3, 106, 126–8; reforms, 23, 75, 90–2, 106–9, 115–16, 168, 170; and revolution, 168, 170; tenants, 169–70; tractorisation, 170
Ahmad, Sir Syed, 132, 136
Alexander II, Tsar, 170
Algeria, 24, 138–9
'aliens': in Central Europe, 105, 108
Allen, Robert, 171
Althusser, Louis, 211, 216
American Revolution, *see* USA
Amin, Idi, 140
ancien régimes, 74, 163, 198, 236, 245, 248, 158; Chinese, 128; scientific, 291, 304
Andrewes, A., 52
Angiviller, Comte d', 234
'*Annales* School', 214–17, 219, 220
Anschluss, 111, 112
Antipater, 53
Aretino, P., 201
aristocracy: and British colonialism, 130; Greek, 52; *see also* nobility
Aristophanes, 243, 255
Aristotle, 50, 51–2
Arkwright, Sir Richard, 275–6
armies, 35, 105, 106, 114, 116, 140; conscript, 13, 128–9; in counter-revolution, 95–6, 138; guards, 74, 76, 78, 93, 98, 108; guerilla, 6, 14, 129–30, 138–9; Roman plebs 'seceded', 53
arts, 4, 226–30; and patriotism, 234–7; visual 240–4, avant-garde, 256–9, iconclasm, 245–7, 248–55, sub-cultures, 244–5; *see also* music
Ashley, W. J., 169
Asia, *see* Afro–Asia
assembly, freedom of, 74–5, 84, 98
association, freedom of, 74–5, 84, 98
Athens, 49–53, 56, 57
atomic bomb, 319
atomic energy, 283
Austria, 170; 1848–9 revolution, 74, 76, 77, 79–83 *passim*, 94, industrial unrest, 92, independence, 86–7, 1918 revolution, 105–6, 107, republic, 106, 111–12, socialism, 114–15; *see also* Vienna
automation, 324

Babbage, C., 273
Babeuf, Francois Noel, 198
Bach, Carl Philip Emanuel, 230
Bacon, Francis, Baron Verulam, 300, 303
Baden: 1848–9 revolution, 85–6, 91, 95, 97
Bailly, Jean Sylvain, 291
Bakhtin, Mikhail, 219, 220, 243–4, 255; *Rabelais and his World*, 243
Balzac, Honoré de, 33
Barker, Nicholas, 186
Barlow, P., 282
Barnes, Leonard, 131

Baroque, 247–8, 252–4
Barthélémy, Abbé J.-J., 235
Bartholomew, Michael, 308
Batthyány, Count Lajos, 77–9 *passim*, 91, 96
Bauer, O., 111, 114
Bauman, Zygmunt, 208
Bavaria, 90, 91, 109; Räterepublik, 110
Bayle, Pierre, 196
Beethoven, Ludwig van, 237
Beidtel, Karl, 92
Ben-David, J., 305
Bengal, 130, 135
Bentham, S., 279
Berger, J. N., 95
Berger, John, 249
Berkeley, William, 191
Berlin: 1848–9 revolution, 76–7, 83, 93, 95; Spartacus revolt, 109–10
Berman, Morris, 304
Bernal, J. D., 298, 317–18
Bernstorf, Count, 236–7
Bessarabia, 117
Bibliothèque bleue, 215–16, 217, 218
Bílovec, 92
Black Death, 154–5
Blake, William, 246, 252
Bloch, Marc, 214, 215, 218
Boas, Marie, (Hall), 295, 296
Bohemia: 1848–9 revolution, 74, 76, 77, 79–80, 81, 90, 94, 95, independence, 87–8, industrial unrest, 92; 1918 revolution, 106; *see also* Czechoslovakia; Prague
Boie, Ernestine, 232
Bolivia: 1952 revolution, 23, 24
Bolshevik: 6, 19, 23; revolution, 136
Bolshevism, Bolsheviks, 103, 107, 115–16, 258; *see also* communism
Bonneville, Nicholas de, 192
books: burning, 301; *see also* printing and the press
Boserup, E., 170, 172
Boulton, Matthew, 17, 174, 276
Boumedienne, Colonel H., 24
Bourdieu, Pierre, 163
bourgeois: democracy, 28; liberalism, 25–6, 79
bourgeois revolution, 17, 30–1, 75, 91; and compromise, 23; defeat of, 97; Japan, 127; model, 26; and nationalism, 86–90; seventeenth century, 294
bourgeois social order (system), 84, 97, 256
bourgeoisie, 74–6, 79–80, 86–7, 93–4, 97–8, 106, 220, 253; China, 123, 137; India, 135; and literacy, 201; revolution, 22, 76, 83, 92, 97, *see also* Europe
Bowler, Peter, 309
Boxer rebellion, 136
Boyle, Robert, 296, 302
Bracton, Henry de, 163
Brahe, Tycho, 308
Brahmo Samaj, 135
Brandenberg, 83
Bratislava, 112; Diet, 77–8
Braudel, Fernand, 122, 148, 214, 215, 219
Bremen: sailors, 109, 110
Brentano, Lorenz, 85–6
Breslau, 93
Brest Litowsk, Treaty of, 105
Bretons, 216
bricolage, 218
Brinton, C. C., 6, 55
Brissot, J. P., 192
Brown, John, 233, 234–5
Brunel, I. K., 279
Brunt, P. A., 53
Buchanan, R., 276
Buda, 94
Budapest: 1918 revolution, 105–6, 111, 113
Bukharin, N. I., 113
Bulgaria: 1918 revolution, 105–6
Burke, Edmund 241–3
Burtt, E. A., 306
Buteanu, 90
Butterfield, H., 162, 293–5 *passim*, 298, 299
Byron, Lord G. G. N., 253

Cabral, Amilcar, 137, 140–1
Caesar, Julius, 48, 56
Camphausen, Ludolf, 76, 79, 88
Cannons, 230
Cantimori, Delio, 219
capital, 169, 175–6; agrarian, 172–3; artisan, 173; financial 171; fixed, 174, 320; formation, 75; merchant, 173; technology, 175
capitalism, 10, 76, 80, 132, 137, 140, 146, 150, 158, 172–3, 175, 212–13, 243, 249, 320, 325; in agriculture, 172; Asia, 126–7; Chinese, 123; industrial, 178; and knowledge, 178; managerial, 179; early modern marriage, 151; organised, 179; science (and technology) under 322–3
capitalist, 10, 104, 253; employer, 174; Japan, 127
Carlist Wars, 5, 28
Catiline conspiracy, 53–4
Cattaro revolt, 105

Caucasus, 130
Cavaignac, General L. E., 96
censorship, 194, 201, 301; abolition of, 74–6, 79
Cercle sociale, 192
Chamberlain, B. H., 127
Chambers, J. D., 171
Chandos, James Brydges, 1st Duke of, 230–1
Chang Chio, 67
Charlot, Jean, 249
Chartier, Roger, 218
Chartism, 134, 209
Chaudhuri, N. C., 135
chemistry, 309
Chhen Chien-Hu, 67
Chhien Han Shuy, 64
Chhin Shih Huang Ti, 61, 65
Chhun Chhiu, 65–6
Chia I, 65
Chiang Kai-shek, 128
Chile, 8
China, 3, 6, 17, 122, 124–8; cultural revolution, 32; lack of scientific revolution 32; nationalism, 136, 137; post Mao, 30; revolution, 5, 22, 26, 29, 30, 31, 138, 140; social devolution, 62–8; Western influence, 124
Christ, 245–6, 258
Christian VI, King, 236
Christian–Socialism(-ists), 113, 174
Christianity, 102, 294, 298, 301
Chuang Tzu, 64–5
Church and faith, 106, 125, 129, 130; and marriage, 152, 153–4; and New Science, 301–3; role of printing, 191, 195
city-states, 52, 57
civil rights, 80, 82, 83–4, 98
civil war: ancient Greece, 51, 53; Irish, 24
Clapham, J. H., 175
class: analysis in revolution, 14, 27, 76; ancient China, 64; antiquity, 53–4, 56; British, 146, 159; and colonialism, 141; and literacy, 197; early modern, 149; transformation, 84, 131
Clay, Lady Rosalind, 162
Cleisthenes, 50–1, 52, 53, 56
Cleomenes, 52
Clodius, 54, 57
Cluj, 112
Cohen, Bernard, 290–2 *passim*, 306
Cole, W. A., 176
Colomb, General, 88
Colombia, 20, 22,
colonialism, 3, 128–9, 137, 138, 139; and change, 121, 124, 131; 'civilizing mission', 131, 141; and Greek rebellions, 53; Indo-China, 125; and media, 133; resistance to, 129; Roman, 54–6
Common Law, 145, 149, 160, 162
communism/communist, 110–11, 113–18 *passim*, 136, 209; China, 137; Comintern, 110, 116, 117; Party, *also* CP, 109–10, 116–17, 319, 322; society, 320; threat, 138; uprising, 93
Compiègne, 106
Condorcet, M., Marquis de, 192, 291
Confucianism, 63–4, 66, 125, 136, 137
conquest-state, 52–3, 57
constitution: Athenian, 50; Austria, 82; demands of 1848, 80, 83; in English history, 158; Greek 'cycle of', 50; Hungarian, 81, 89; Prussian, 81, 83
constitutional monarchy: Britain, 145–6; Germany 1848, 83–4, 88
Constructivism, 256–8
Cooper, John Gilbert, 228
Copenhagen Opera, 236
Copernicanism, 308
Copernicus, N., 296, 300
Coram's Hospital, 232
Cornwall: temperance movement, 214
Counter-Reformation 216
counter-revolution, 9, 11, 12, 24, 84, 95–8, 305; 1848, 95; and army, 96; Austria, 86; and printing, 193; strategists of, 12
Crafts, N., 176
Crimean War, 170
Cristero civil war, 24
Croatia: nationalism, 78, 88; 1918 revolution, 107, 112
Crombie, A. C., 293
Cuba, 6; revolution and Bay of Pigs, 24, 26, 29, 31
Cubism/cubists, 249, 251, 256–7
culture, popular, 215–18, 219–21; '*Annales* School', 214–17, 219, 220; Marxist, 208–14; and media, 206–8; oral, 197
Cumberland: famine, 154
Czech Lands, *see* Bohemia
Czechoslovakia: consolidation, 107, 116; scientific-technical revolution, 321–2; territories, 115

Dahlmann, F. C., 82
Darwinism, 291, 309–10
Daqumas, M., 281
David, Jacques Louis, 236, 237, 242, 246–7, 258

Davies, Natalie, 219
Davis, J. P., 123
Deane, Phyllis, 176, 318
Debray, R., 6
Delumeau, Jean, 216
democracy, 17, 57, 103, 106, 108, 111, 118, 145; Athenian, 49, 51; and language, 196; 'Periclean', 50
democratic republic, 28
demography, 147, 154–5, 176; Central Europe, 94; and change, 126; and revolution, 32
Denmark: cultural revolution, 236–7
devolution, social, 62–8; and evolution, 61–2, 63–4, 66–7
Diodorus, 51
Diogenes, 55
Dominican Republic, 12
Drake, Stillman, 297
Drava River, 89, 95
Dresden: 1848–9 revolution, 85, 95
Dublin: music audiences, 231–2
Duby, Georges, 216
Dukhonin, General, 104
Dunn, John, 50
Durkheim, Émile, 215

East India Company, 130
Ebert, F., 110
Ecuador, 10
Edinburgh: social study, 213
Egret, J., 199
Egypt, 128–9
Einstein, Albert, 307
Eisenstein, S. M., 255, 258
Eisner, Kurt, 109
Elberfeld prison, 92, 94
electoral representation, 27, 78, 81
electricity, 177, 261, 283
electronic computers, 317–18
electronics, 284, 318
Encyclopedists, 55
energy (power), 178, 263, 265–7, 271, 283; atomic, 283; electric, 318; human muscle, 268, 270–1, 277, 283; steam, 318; *see also* electricity, steam, technology
Engels, Friedrich, 93, 97, 175, 178, 208–9
engineering, 278; genetic, 319; mechanical, 271, 277, 282; production, 277
England, 27, 79; enclosures, 169, 170–2; revolution and printing, 190, 191; socio-economic revolution, 145–8, 157–64; laws, 149, 160–2, social structures, 149–56; *see also* imperialism; Industrial Revolution
Enlightenment, 17, 245, 248, 290–1, 301–2
Ephialtes, 50–1, 52, 57
Ernle, Rt Hon. Lord, 171
Europe: Asia compared, 122–4
Europe, Central: bourgeois revolution, 74–89, 95–8, constitution, 80–6, nationalism, 78, 86–90, working class, 92–4; scientific-technical revolution, 321–3; socialism, 101–4, 109–15, consolidation, 117–18, nationalism, 106–8, 115–17, pacificism, 103, 104–6; *see also* agriculture; *individual countries*
Evans-Pritchard, Sir Edward, 219
evolution, 10, 291; and historiography, 161; social, 51, 61; versus revolution, 300, 309
Expressionism, 252, 255

Fabians, 171
factories, *see* industry
Fan Chhung, 67
Fanon, F., 133, 139, 141
Far East, 125
farms/farmers/farming, 169, 171–3; cottagers, 171; manors, 167; smallholders, 171; yeomen, 171
Fascism, 18, 102; totalitarianism, 297
Febvre, Lucien, 214, 215, 218
Ferdinand I, Emperor of Austria, 76, 81
Feinstein, C., 176
feudalism, 9, 75–6, 80–1, 84, 95, 97–8, 101, 130, 174, 179, 236; Asian, 126, 132; Central Europe, 86, 90–1
Ficquelmont, Count, 70, 82
Fiering, Norman, 196
films, 133, 258
Finland, 177
Fischhof, Adolf, 82
Foucault, Michel, 217–18
France, 145; in Algeria, 139; French Revolution, 2, 4–6, 11, 13, 17, 24, 26, 30, 33–5 *passim*, 49, 124, 190, 191, 198–201, arts, 234–6, 240–2, 245–7; role of printing, 190, 198–201; *see also* Paris
Franco, F., 130
Frankfurt: Assembly, 80, 82, 84, 86, 87, 95: School, 209, 213
Frederick William IV, King, 77, 84
freemasonry, 201, 231
French Revolution, *see* France
Freud, Sigmund, 208, 259
Fronde revolt, 16
Frykman, Jonas, 219
Fukuzawa Yukichi, 136

Gabba, E., 56
Gagern, Heinrich von, 85–6, 87
Galileo, 296–7, 300–2, 307
Galtung, J., 8
Gandhi, M. K., 135
Gay, John, 231
Gazette, 193–4
genetic code, 318
genetic engineering, 319
geology, 308–9
Géricault, Théodore, 247
German Democratic Republic: scientific-technical revolution, 321, 322
Germans: in Central Europe, 108, 111, 113
Germany: 1848–9 revolution, 74–5, 76–7, 79, 90–1, constitution, 80–2, 83–6, industrial unrest, 92; militarism, 118; 1918 revolution, 106, 109–10; *see also* Berlin, Prussia
Gerschenkron, Alexander, 177
Gesner, Conrad, 188
Gessner, Salomon, 228
Gia Long, 128
Gillispie, C. C., 295, 297
Ginsburg, Carlo, 210, 219
Glorious Revolution, 50
Gluck, Christoph Willibald, 226, 230, 235–6
Goegg, Amand, 85
Gossec, François-Joseph, 236
Gottl-Ottlilienfeld, F. von, 262
Goubert, J.-P., 292
government, 29, 78, 81; popular participation, 57, 103, 106–8
Goya, F. J. de, 247, 251, 252, 253
Gramsci, Antonio, 11, 27, 209, 211, 213, 219
Greece, ancient, 234–5, 236; *see also* Athens
Griewank, K., 9, 34
Gruber, H., 309
guerrilla war, 6, 14, 129–30, 138–9
Guilbaut, Serge, 255
Guinea, 137, 140–1
Gurevich, Aron, 219

Habermas, Jürgen, 196
Haiti, 134
Hale, Sir Matthew, 162
Hall, A. Rupert, 292–6 *passim*, 298, 306
Hallam, Anthony, 307
Hamburg: sailors, 109, 110
Hammond, John and Barbara, 171, 175
Han Dynasty, 63, 64, 66–7
Han Wên Ti, 65
Handel, George Frederick, 230–1; *Messiah*, 231–2, 237
handicrafts, 268, 280
Hansemann, David, 79, 88
Hargreaves, James, 275
Harman, P. M., 304
Hartmann, Moritz, 87
Hartwell, R. M., 175
Harvey, William, 299, 304
Hatvani, Imre, 89–90
Haydn, Joseph, 233, 237
Hayek, F. A. von, 298
Hazard, Paul, 226, 305
Herder, Johann Gottfried, 235
Herodotus, 52
Hesse, M., 292
Hesse, 90
Hessen, Boris, 294–5
Heuss, Alfred, 48–9, 50, 53
Hill, Christopher, 148, 219, 293, 304
historians, 2, 8; academic, 157; on revolution, 13, 29, 30, 32–3, 47–8, 156–8, 161; of Roman Revolution, 48; of science, 292
historical change, 8, 10; Chinese concept, 68; continuity, 8, 156, 158–9; English, 158–9; European versus Afro-Asia, 122; and evolution, 161; organic growth model, 162
historical materialism, 299
historiography, 80, 94, 157, 160, 161; Butterfield on, 162; Confucian, 66; and ideology, 164, 175; of revolution, 5–7, 20, 49; of science, 291, 293, 299, 310
history, 1–2, 293; agency in, 12; and change, 138, 157, 160, 296–7; invention of tradition, 131, 295, 299
Hitler, A., 295; Putsch, 111
Ho Chi Minh, 138
Ho Hsiu, 66–7
Hobsbawm, E. J., 2, 175, 211
Hodža, M. M., 89
Hogarth, William, 232
Hoggart, Richard, 207
Horkheimer, Max, 209
Huai Nan Tzu, 63, 64
Hung Hsiu-Ch'üan, 128
Hungary, 170; 1848–9 revolution, 76, 79–80, 81, 90, 91, 97, Magyar movement, 77–8, 88–90, 95–6, working population, 94; 1918 revolution, 105, 106, government, 113–15, territories, 111, 114–16; republic, 111, 113, 114; *see also* Budapest
Hurban, J. M., 89

iconoclasm, 245–6, 248–9
imperialism, 121–2; Afro-Asia, 122–4, 125–33, 136–41; India, 124–6, 131–3 *passim*, 134–6; and nationalism, 133–9
India: and imperialism, 124–6, 131–3 *passim*, 134–6; rioting, 139–40
individualism, 145, 148, 158
Indonesia, 130–1, 138
industrial enterprise: factory, 75, 171–4, 176–8, 212, 274–6; manufactory, 269; mill, 275
Industrial Revolution, 2, 124, 156, 171–6, 177–8, 187, 208, 210, 271, 273, 283, 305, 318, 319
industrialisation, 8–9, 75, 94, 146, 175, 209, 213, 219; and agriculture, 172–3; Asian 132
industry 4, 81, 102, 113, 167, 179, 318; automation in, 324; canal construction, 276; cotton, 176–8, 274; engineering, 177; entrepreneur(s), 79, 174, 177, 212–13, 274, 276; iron, 176–8, 275; mechanisation in, 324; mining, 276; putting-out, 174; rural, 171; shipping, 276; textile, 270, 274–5, 278
innovation(s): artistic, 250, 256; financial, 324; organisational, 324; and revolution, 300; technological (technical), 167, 170, 261, 263, 272–3, 283
Innsbruck, 82
intelligentsia, 55, 79, 106, 134–6, 295, 297
inventions/inventors, 172, 275–9, 281–2; and revolutionary change, 174–5, 177–8, 187
Iran, 18, 19, 35, 129
Ireland, 6, 24; Irish Free State, 134
Isagoras, 52
Iserlohn, 85
Islam, 123–5, 136, 298
Italy: and Abyssinia,, 129; 1848–9 revolution, 74, 89, 95; *see also* Rome

Jacob, Margaret, 195
Jacobinism, 5, 305
Jacobins, 13, 33, 245–6
Japan, 220: Meiji, 34, 127, 136; militarism, 140; social change, 125–7
Jaucourt, Chevalier de, 229
Jelačić, General Josef, 89, 95, 96, 97
Jennens, Charles, 231
Jewish Revolt, 56
Jews: in Central Europe, 94, 108, 109, 112–14 *passim*
Johnson, C., 19
Joseph II, Emperor, 101, 170
Josephus, 56
Jugoslavia: consolidation, 107
'Junius', 192, 198

Kandinsky, V., 256
Kant, I., 242
Kapp Putsch, 111, 117
Károlyi, Count M., 111, 112, 113
Kautsky, Karl, 109
Kearney, H., 299
Kenya, 138
Kepler, Johann, 300, 302, 308
Khang Yu-Wei, 68
Kiev, 117
kinship, 146, 150
Királyi, Pál, 88
Klopstock, F. G., 232
Koestler, Arthur, 295, 297–9 *passim*
Kolowrat, Count, 79
Korea, 132: social change, 125, 127
Kosel, G., 319
Kossuth, Louis, 77–8, 80, 88, 89, 96
Koyré, Alexandre, 294–6 *passim*
Kroměříž: parliament, 83, 84
Kronstadt: sailors, 109
Kudlich, Hans, 87, 91
Kuhn, T. S., 217, 292, 294, 295, 302, 307, 308, 318
Kuliang, Master, 66
Kun, Bela, 113–15 *passim*, 117
Kungchhantang, 68
Kungyang, Master, 66
Kuomintang, 68, 128, 137

labour, 146, 172, 262, 320; antiquity, 55; division of, 269, 273, 280; early modern, 150, 169–70; forced, 77–8, 81, 90; manual, 278, 319; as a market commodity, 325; mental, 319; organisation of, 75, 92, 167–8; unpaid, 95; wage, 178
labour force, 171, 274
labourers, 76, 92
Ladurie, Emmanuel LeRoy, 214, 219
Lamberg, General, 96
land reform, 23, 53–4, 75, 90–2
Landes, David, 177
Lao Tzu, 67
Latin America, 10, 22
Laudan, L., 307, 309
Lavoisier, Antoine-Laurent, 291–2, 307, 309
law, 52–3, 145
Leavis, F. R., 206–7, 209, 210
Lecler, Jean Baptiste, 236

Lefebvre, George, 199, 215
leisure, 212–14
Lemberg, 109
Len Hêng, 65
Lenin, V. I., 9, 12, 13, 15, 18–20, 25, 104, 113, 132, 140, 246, 256–8
Lévi-Strauss, Claude, 152, 217, 218
Lévy-Bruhl, Lucien, 215
lex Hortensia, 53
liberalism, 17; and representative government, 28; and revolution, 27, 76, 94, 97, 135; 'traitors' of 1848, 80
Li Chi, 63
Lilburne, John, 195
Lindert, P., 176
literacy, 4, 187; and change, 200; and elitism, 197; *The Long Revolution* by Raymond Williams, 187
living standard(s), 175–6, 325
Löfgren, Orvar, 219
Lombe, Thomas, 275
London: music audiences, 231, 232
London College of Physicians, 195
London Corresponding Society, 198
Lotman, Juri, 219
Lu Hsün, 128
Lü Shih Chhun Chhiu, 64
Lu Wên-Shu, 65
Ludendorff Putsch, 117
Lukás, George, 113, 243
Luxemburg, 109, 110
Luxemburg, Count Friedrich von, 89
Lyautey, Marshal, H., 131
Lyell, Charles, 291, 308, 310
Lysenkoism, 298

Macartney, George, Lord, 124
Macedonia, 107
machines/machinery, 75, 92, 174, 178, 273–7, 281–2, 320; *see also* working machines
machino-facture, 261, 272, 274, 283
McLuhan, Marshall, 207
Magyar movement, 77–8, 88–90, 95–6
Mainwaring, John, 232
Maitland, F. W., 158, 160–2
Malaya, 138
Malesherbes, C. G. de L. de, 200
Malevich, C., 256, 257
Malthusian marriage, 151, 156
Malthusian trap 155
Manchus, 68, 124, 128
Mandrou, Robert, 215–16
Mannheim, 78
Mantoux, Paul, 171, 174
manu-facture/manufacture, 173–4, 261, 272–4
Mao Tse-Tsung, 6, 122, 137–9 *passim*
Marat, J. P., 245–6, 253
Marchand, Prosper, 195
Maria Theresa, Empress, 170, 234
market (economy), 172, 178–9; forces and change, 172, 178–9, 188; and printing, 196
Marks, John, 298
marriage, 147, 151–4, 156
Marx, Karl, 1, 9, 10, 11, 16, 92, 93, 97, 122, 124, 130, 132, 133, 148, 158, 161, 164, 169, 171–4 *passim*, 178, 208–9, 242–3, 283; *The Eighteenth Brumaire of Louis Napoleon Bonaparte*, 242; *Grundrisse*, 320; *Kapital*, 175, 278, 320
Marxism, 1, 2, 7, 9, 15–18 *passim*, 80, 105, 121–2, 127, 136–8, 217, 219; and class analysis, 14, 22, 47–8, 97; and popular culture, 208–14; scientific, 294–5, 299
Marxist(s), 11, 17, 121, 133; Japanese, 127; theory of history, 122; writing, 7, 294
März-Action, 111, 117
mass culture, *see* culture, popular
mass mobilisation, 9, 34, 137; versus political activists, 35
materialism, 141, 179, 257
materials: comminution of, 269; conversion of, 264, 273, 275; extraction of, 263–4, 271, 279, 283; forming (shaping) of, 264–5, 269; processing of, 264, 269; squeezing 'out of', 269; transport of, 263, 270
Maudslay, H., 277, 279, 281
medicine, 139, 306, 308
Mehemet Ali, 128–9
Meier, Christian, 48–9
Menelik II, Emperor, 129
Messenhauser, C. W., 96
Mesthene, E. G., 323–5
Mészáros, L., 96
Metternich, Prince, 76, 79, 88
Mevissen, Gustav, 93
Mexico: Indians, 134; Revolution, 6, 8, 13, 18, 22–6 *passim*, 30–2, 33, 134, arts, 248–55
Meyer, Eduard, 48
micro-electronics, 284, 319
micro-history, 220
Milan: 1848–9 revolution, 95
Ming Thang, 64
Mingay, Gordon, 171
Mirabeau, H. G. R., Comte de, 198

mode of production, 160, 168; Asian, 123, 126; British, 146
Mohism, 63, 68
Mokyr, J., 175
Mommsen, Theodor, 48
monarchy, 49, 53, 145, 149
Montucla, Jean Étienne, 291
Moore, B., 7
Morocco, 18, 130, 131
mortality, 32, 154–6, 176
Moxon, Joseph, 197
Muchembled, Robert, 216–17
Mughals, 124–6, 130
Muna, A., 116
Munich, 110: Räteregierung, 109
music, 4; moral function of, 226–37 *passim*; opera, 235–7; oratorio, 230–4, 237
Muslims, 135–6
Musson, A. E., 175

Napoleon, 5, 30, 124, 128, 246, 253
Nassau, duchy of, 91
nationalism, 3, 17, 34, 78, 86–90, 95, 106–8, 115–17, 133–9, 140
Needham, Joseph, 291
neo-Confucianism, 67
Newcomen, Thomas, 271
newspapers, 133, 190, 207–8
Newton, Sir Isaac, 294, 296, 302, 307
Newtonianism, 302, 304, 306–7
Nguema, F. M., 140
Nicholas I, Tsar, 96–7, 130
Nicholas II, Tsar, 104
Nipperdey, Thomas, 86
nobility, 77–9, 81–2, 84, 87–8, 90, 93, 236
'Northcliffe Revolution', 207
nuclear fission, 317–18

October Revolution, 12, 83, 93
O'Gorman, Juan, 254, 255
Orozco, Jose Clemente, 249, 251–3, 254, 255, 258–9
Ortega y Gasset, Jose, 208

Paine, Tom, 192, 197–8, 254
painters/painting, 240, 248–59 *passim*
Palacký, František, 79, 81, 87
pamphlets, 190
Paris: Commune, 102; 1848–9 revolution, 74; Peace Conference, 111, 112, 114
Paskevich, General I. F., 96
Paul I, Tsar, 10
Paulinyi, Akos, 310
peasant(s)/peasantry, 74–6, 84, 91–2, 103, 105–15, 118, 137, 169–70, 237; culture, 215–16; *see also* agriculture
Peckham, Morse, 241–2
Pellicer, Carlos, 249
Pennsylvania Magazine, 198
periodicals, 196–7; scientific, 305
Pest, 81, 94: deputation, 78, 88
Phêng Meng, 65
Pillersdorf, Baron, 79, 82, 90
Piłsudski, J., 117
Pisistratus, 52
Pitt, William (the younger), 142
Plantin, Christopher, 195
plebs, 210–11, 213; plebeian culture, 244
poets/poetry, 228, 233
Poland: 1848–9 revolution, independence, 88; 1918 revolution, consolidation, 116–17
Polanyi, K., 8
political activists: and change, 35; and printing, 190, 198
political constitutions, 30–1, 80–6
politics: and revolutions, 31–2, 50; and science, 305
Pollock, Jackson, 255, 259
Poor Law, 146–7
Pope, Alexander, 230
popular cultural forms: almanacs, 215–16; ballads, 210; carnival, 244, 253; charivaris, 211; festivals, 210, 212, 236; *fêtes*, 236, 245, 248; song-books, 216; street football, 313; temperance movement, 214; variety theatres, 216; wakes, 214; *see also Bibliothèque bleue*
Posada, Jose Guadalupe, 250–1, 252
power(s), 76, 102, 111, 113, 116–17; class, 263; feudal, 86; labour, 171; landlordly, 170; motive, *see* energy (power); political, 74, 80, 112, 322; social, 74, 325; state, 112; world, 87
Poznán, 88
Prague: 1848–9 revolution, 75, 76, 78, 89, 93, 95
'Prater, Battle of the', 93
printing and the press, 186–9, 197; freedom, 75–9 *passim*, 82, 84, 98; political output, 189–98, French Revolution, 190, 198–201; vernacular, 195–6
production: force(s) of, 168, 174, 319–21; of machines by machines, 277–8, 283; processes, 275; relations of, 10, 98, 160, 167–8, 209, in antiquity, 53, in publishing, 188; techniques, 263–5, 268, 271, 274, 277, 279
productive forces, 10, 98, 172

productivity, 171, 174, 319–20, 324
progress, 1; and revolution, 291; and science, 302, 307
proletariat, 75; dictatorship of the, 105; in revolution, 92–4, 96; *see also* workers
Propp, Vladimir, 219
Prussia, 170: 1848–9 revolution, 74, 76–7, 79, 83–4, 96

Rabb, T., 302
Rabelais, F., 244, 255
Radetsky, Marshal J. J., 95
radical bourgeoisie, 86, 93
radical revolutionaries, 76, 78, 80, 91
radio, 133, 207
railway workers, 94
Rastatt castle, 85
Rastell, John, 195
reform, 75, 80, 115, 117, 170; antiquity, 51–2, 54; and revolution, 300
Reformation, 159, 221, 245, 294, 298
relativity theory, 306, 317
religion, 81, 98, 136, 179–80, 227, 303; Catholicism, 216; Christian, 180, 250; Church, 212, 230, 244–5, 251; colonialism, 129–30; Methodism, 210; Protestantism, 179; and science, 304; and 'Westernisation', 125
Renaissance, 168, 179–80, 294, 299, 317
Renner, Karl, 112, 113
Repin, Ilya, 258
representational government: and revolutions, 29, 78, 81
Republican Rome, 54, 56
Revere, P., 248
revolution, 5–12; in antiquity, 47–50, 53–7, democracy, 51–3; bourgeois-liberal, 22–3, 26–30, 74–89, 95–8; cause and effect, 15–20, 21–4; long-term, 24–5, 30, 33–4, 187–8, 200, 214, 221; post-liberal, 30–2; and situation, 12–14, 16–20; socialist, 101–4, 109–15; time concepts, 6, 9–10, 32–3, 34–5, 63–6, 68, 147–8, 161–3; *see also* agriculture, Industrial Revolution, technology, *individual countries*
revolution, scientific, 4, 292–9, 306–10; and New Science, 299–306; technical, 317–24, socialization, 325–7
Richta, Padovan, 321
Rieger, Fr. L., 83
Rilinger, R., 49
Rivera, Diego, 242, 250–1, 253–4, 255, 258
Roberts, R., 279
Robinson, E., 175
Robotpatent, 75, 90
Rome, 234; Revolution, 47–9, 53–4, 56
Ronan, C. A., 293
Rosenberg, C., 308
Rosenberg, Harold, 257
Rostow, W. W., 177
Rousseau, J. J., 215, 216, 245
Roy, Ram Mohun, 132, 134
Rublev, A., 256
Rumania: 1848–9 revolution, nationalism, 78; 1918 revolution, consolidation, 107, territories, 114–17 *passim*
Russia, Russian Revolution, *see* USSR
Ruthenia, 115

sailors, 14, 105, 109, 110
Saint-Just, L. A. de, 29
sans-culottes, 215–16, 245, 248
Satsuma rebellion, 127
Savery, Thomas, 271
Scheidemann, P., 110
Schiller, J. C. F. von, 242
Schlözer, August, 221
Schofield, R. S., 155, 176
Schulz, Johann Peter Abraham, 236–7
Schumpeter, J. A., 177, 179
Schuselka, Franz, 80, 93
Schwarzenberg, Prince Felix, 87, 89
science, 175, 178, 290 *passim*; agriculture(-al), 172, 317; applied, 282–3; and government, 306; and medicine, 308; New, 299–301, 304; and objectivity/truth, 297; physical, 301; and politics, 305; relationship with production, 319–21; relationship with technology, 283, 318–19; research, 173, 281–2, 319, costs of, 325–6; sociology of, 304; technology and society, 321–7; (and technology) under capitalism, 322–3; under socialism, 322–3
scientific revolution, 4, 292
Scientific Revolution, The, 292–3
scientific societies, 305
Scotland, 10, 145, 147
Serbia: 1848–9 revolution, nationalism, 78, 89
Sertorius, 56
Shaftesbury, Anthony Ashley Cooper, 3rd Earl of, 226–7, 229, 230–1
Shen Tao, 65
Shih Chi, 65
shipping workers, 94
Sieyès, Abbé, 198
Siqueiros, D. A., 254–5

Skocpol, T., 6, 7, 19, 21
slavery, 9, 54–5, 56–7, 245
Slovakia: 1848–9 revolution, nationalism, 78, 89; 1918 revolution, 107, territories, 112; *see also* Czechoslovakia
Slovenia, 107
Šmeral, Bohumir, 115, 116
Soboul, Albert, 215–16
social democracy/democrats, 114, 115; independent, 109–10
Social Democratic Party (also SDP), 111, 113–16
social dysfunction, 10
social equilibrium, 8
social evolution: China, 61–2; Confucianism, 63, 67; of science, 305
social relations, 3, 98; antiquity, 50; British, 146; early modern, 149
social revolution, 10, 11, 12, 94; lack in India, 135
social scientists 5, 7, 158
socialism/socialists, 102–3, 106, 108–15, 137, 140; ideal in China, 63; ideas, 105; party(ies), 105, 109–10, 112; science (and technology) under, 179, 322–3
socialist art, 240
socialist realism, 258
Socialist Revolutionary Party, 114
societies: scientific, 305; secret, 194–5
Solingen, 75, 92
Solon, 50, 51–2, 56
Spain: Carlist Wars, 28; Civil War, 130; 1820 revolution, 25; reactionaries, 134
Spalding, Johann Joachim, 227
Spartacus, 54
Spartacus revolt, 109–10
Spectator Club, 197
Stadion, Count R., 90
Stalin, J., 33
Stalinism, 1, 6; totalitarianism, 295, 297
state: and class in antiquity, 49, 56; power, 21, 29, 57, 81; and science, 306; and social change, 79; structural changes, 84
steam, 3, 146, 197, 261, 275–6, 278–9, 282–3, 318
vom Stein and Hardenberg decrees, 170
Stephen, Archduke, 96
Stewart, Sir Norman, 130
Stolypin reforms, 170
Strauss, Johann (the elder), 95
structuralism, 1, 217–18, 219
Stubbs, William, 158–62 *passim*
Štúr, L., 89
suffrage, 78, 81, 82
Sukarno, A., 138
Sulzer, Johann George, 229
Sun Ên, 67
Switzerland: 1848–9 revolution, 74
Syme, Ronald, 48, 56
Szabo, I., 113
Szamuely, T., 113
Szeged, 90
Szemere, B., 90, 96
Szücs, J., 101

Ta Thung, 61–2, 63–4
Ta Thung Shu, 68
Tacitus, 154
tailors' guild (Pest), 94
Taiping rebellion, 127
Táncsics, Mihály, 78
Taoism, 62–3, 65, 125; religious, 67; revolutionary, 67
Tatlin, Vladimir, 257
Tawney, R. H., 148
technological penetration, 266–8, 284
technological system(s), 3, 261–3, 267–8, 272, 278, 280, 283
technology, 3, 172; classification of, 264; craft, 272; hand-tool, 266–75, 277–80, 282; information, 263, 274; innovations, 167; material-conversion 264, 271; material-forming, 264–5, 267–9, 271–5; power, 269–71, 273–4, 283; professional, 272; technician, 272; transport(-ation), 263–4, 270, 272–3, 280; working-machine, 266–72, 274–5, 277–80, 283–4
Teich, Mikuláš, 306, 310
Teleki, László, 89
television, 207–8
temperance, 214
textile industry, 274–5, 278–9
Thaarup's *Harvest Festival*, 237
Thackray, Arnold, 293
Thai Phing, 61–2, 64–5
Thai Phing Ching, 67
Thai-Phing Thien-Kuo movement, 68
Thien Phien, 65
Thomas, Keith, 219
Thomason, George, 190
Thompson, E. P., 208, 210–11, 213–14, 244
Thomson, James, 228, 234, 237
Thun, Count Leo, 87
Thuringia, 90
Tilly, C., 7
Tocqueville, Alexis de, 12, 28, 145, 208
Tokugawas, 125–6
tools, 265–70, 273, 275, 277–9, 281
totalitarianism, 295, 297
Tou Ying, 64

MCAT® High-Yield Problem-Solving Guide

Edited by Alexander Stone Macnow, MD

Published by Kaplan Publishing, a division of Kaplan, Inc.
395 Hudson Street
New York, NY 10014

Printed in the United States of America

10 9 8 7

Item Number: MM5055E

The *Kaplan MCAT Review* Team

Alexander Stone Macnow, MD
Editor-in-Chief

Tyra Hall-Pogar, PhD
Editor

Bela Starkman, PhD
Editor

Laura L. Ambler
Kaplan MCAT Faculty

Uneeb Qureshi
Kaplan MCAT Faculty

Alisha Maureen Crowley
Kaplan MCAT Faculty

Derek Rusnak, MA
Kaplan MCAT Faculty

Kelly Kyker-Snowman, MS
Kaplan MCAT Faculty

Kristen L. Russell, ME
Kaplan MCAT Faculty

Jason R. Pfleiger
Kaplan MCAT Faculty

Pamela Willingham, MSW
Kaplan MCAT Faculty

MCAT faculty reviewers Elmar R. Aliyev; James Burns; Jonathan Cornfield; Nikolai Dorofeev, MD; Raef Ali Fadel; Samer T. Ismail; Elizabeth A. Kudlaty; John P. Mahon; Matthew A. Meier; Nainika Nanda; Caroline Nkemdilim Opene; Kaitlyn E. Prenger; Nicholas M. White; Allison Ann Wilkes, MS; and Tony Yu

Thanks to Kim Bowers; Tim Eich; Owen Farcy; Dan Frey; Robin Garmise; Rita Garthaffner; Joanna Graham; Adam Grey; Allison Harm; Beth Hoffberg; Aaron Lemon-Strauss; Keith Lubeley; Diane McGarvey; Petros Minasi; John Polstein; Deeangelee Pooran-Kublall, MD, MPH; Rochelle Rothstein, MD; Larry Rudman; Sylvia Tidwell Scheuring; Carly Schnur; Karin Tucker; Lee Weiss; and the countless others who made this project possible.

About the MCAT

The structure of the four sections of the MCAT is shown below.

Chemical and Physical Foundations of Biological Systems	
Time	95 minutes
Format	• 59 questions • 10 passages • 44 questions are passage-based, and 15 are discrete (stand-alone) questions • Score between 118 and 132
What It Tests	• Biochemistry: 25% • Biology: 5% • General Chemistry: 30% • Organic Chemistry: 15% • Physics: 25%
Critical Analysis and Reasoning Skills (CARS)	
Time	90 minutes
Format	• 53 questions • 9 passages • All questions are passage-based. There are no discrete (stand-alone) questions. • Score between 118 and 132
What It Tests	Disciplines: • Humanities: 50% • Social Sciences: 50% Skills: • *Foundations of Comprehension*: 30% • *Reasoning Within the Text*: 30% • *Reasoning Beyond the Text*: 40%
Biological and Biochemical Foundations of Living Systems	
Time	95 minutes
Format	• 59 questions • 10 passages • 44 questions are passage-based, and 15 are discrete (stand-alone) questions • Score between 118 and 132
What It Tests	• Biochemistry: 25% • Biology: 65% • General Chemistry: 5% • Organic Chemistry: 5%

Psychological, Social, and Biological Foundations of Behavior	
Time	95 minutes
Format	• 59 questions • 10 passages • 44 questions are passage-based, and 15 are discrete (stand-alone) questions • Score between 118 and 132
What It Tests	• Biology: 5% • Psychology: 65% • Sociology: 30%
Total	
Testing Time	375 minutes (6 hours, 15 minutes)
Questions	230
Score	472 to 528

The MCAT also tests four *Scientific Inquiry and Reasoning Skills* (SIRS):

1. Knowledge of Scientific Concepts and Principles (35% of questions)
2. Scientific Reasoning and Problem-Solving (45% of questions)
3. Reasoning About the Design and Execution of Research (10% of questions)
4. Data-Based and Statistical Reasoning (10% of questions)

The MCAT is a computer-based test (CBT) and is offered at Prometric centers during almost every month of the year. There are optional breaks between each section, and there is a lunch break between the second and third section of the exam.

Register online for the MCAT at www.aamc.org/mcat.

For further questions, contact the MCAT team at the Association of American Medical Colleges:

MCAT Resource Center
Association of American Medical Colleges

(202) 828-0690
www.aamc.org/mcat
mcat@aamc.org

How This Book Was Created

The *High-Yield Problem-Solving Guide* (HYPSG) project began in November 2012 shortly after the release of the *Preview Guide for the MCAT 2015 Exam*, 2nd edition. Through thorough analysis by our staff psychometricians, we were able to analyze the relative yield of the different topics on the MCAT and began constructing tables of contents for the books of the *Kaplan MCAT Review* series to which the HYPSG is related.

Writing of the books began in April 2013. A dedicated staff of 19 writers, 7 editors, and 32 proofreaders worked over 5000 combined hours to produce these books. The format of the books was heavily influenced by weekly meetings with Kaplan's learning science team.

This book was submitted for publication in June 2014. For any updates after this date, please visit www.kaplanmcat.com.

Each question in this book has been vetted through at least six rounds of review. To that end, the information presented in these books is true and accurate to the best of our knowledge. Still, your feedback helps us improve our prep materials. Please notify us of any inaccuracies or errors in the books by sending an email to KaplanMCATfeedback@kaplan.com.

Using This Book

The *High-Yield Problem-Solving Guide*, along with the other seven books in your student kit, is the cornerstone of your prep for the MCAT. This book offers the content review, strategies, and practice that make Kaplan the #1 choice for MCAT prep. After all, twice as many doctors prepared with Kaplan for the MCAT than with any other course.

This book is designed to help you practice problem-solving by applying your content knowledge and critical thinking skills to a wide variety of practice questions. Each question aligns with one of the chapters of the *Kaplan MCAT Review* series and is presented in the worked example format in which the answer is determined through a number of logical steps. Your approach to a given question may vary from the ones presented in this book—and that's okay! The solutions presented in this book represent just one possible way that MCAT experts determine the correct answer to the question. Look for opportunities to improve your speed and efficiency with these questions, and apply what you learn in this book to your own MCAT practice. Please understand that strategy review—no matter how thorough—is not sufficient preparation for the MCAT! The MCAT tests not only your problem-solving skills but also your science knowledge, critical reading, and reasoning skills. Do not assume that simply memorizing the contents of this book will earn you high scores on Test Day; to maximize your scores, you must also improve your reading and test-taking skills through MCAT-style questions and practice tests.

RELATED QUESTIONS

At the end of each example, you'll find three related practice questions. These may be similar to the worked example presented, or may focus on different but related applications of the material. Most of these questions focus on the second of the *Scientific Inquiry and Reasoning Skills* (Scientific Reasoning and Problem-Solving), although there are occasional questions that fall into the first SIRS (Knowledge of Scientific Concepts and Principles).

SIDEBARS

The following is a guide to the three types of sidebars you'll find in the *High-Yield Problem-Solving Guide*:

- **Key Concepts**: These sidebars draw attention to the most important subtopics presented in the worked example and its related questions. If you understand nothing else, make sure you grasp the Key Concepts for any given subject.
- **Takeaways**: These sidebars draw attention to the most important takeaways in a given topic, and they sometimes offer synopses or overviews of complex information.
- **Things to Watch Out For**: These sidebars either highlight pitfalls and common mistakes students make with a given topic, or describe common applications of the topic on the MCAT. Think of these as words of warning—warning you what you might see on Test Day, and warning you what mistakes you should be careful to avoid.

In the end, this is your book, so write in the margins, draw diagrams, highlight the key points—do whatever is necessary to help you get that higher score. We look forward to working with you as you achieve your dreams and become the doctor you deserve to be!

Contents

The *Kaplan MCAT Review* Team iii
About the MCAT v
How This Book Was Created vii
Using This Book viii

Chapter 1: Behavioral Sciences **1**
Regions of the Brain 2
Vision 4
Associative Learning 8
Language 10
Theories of Emotion 12
Formation of Identity 14
Bipolar and Depressive Disorders 16
Social Processes 20
Verbal and Nonverbal Communication 22
Attribution Theory 24
Demographics 26
Disparities in Health and Healthcare 28
Solutions to Related Questions 30

Chapter 2: Biochemistry **37**
Elements of Peptide Structure 38
Lineweaver–Burk Plots 40
Isoelectric Focusing 44
Isomerism in Carbohydrates 48
Lipid Saponification 50
DNA Replication 52
Operons 56
Membrane Traffic 58
Glycolysis 60
Electron Transport Chain and Oxidative Phosphorylation 62
β-Oxidation 64
Hormonal Regulation of Metabolism 66
Solutions to Related Questions 68

Chapter 3: Biology 77
Prokaryotic Genetics . . . 78
Menstrual Cycle . . . 82
Stages of Embryogenesis . . . 86
Action Potential . . . 88
Endocrine Organs . . . 90
The Respiratory System . . . 92
Oxyhemoglobin Dissociation Curve . . . 94
Immune Function . . . 98
The Digestive System . . . 100
Kidney Function . . . 102
Muscle Contraction . . . 104
Hardy–Weinberg Equilibrium . . . 106
Solutions to Related Questions . . . 108

Chapter 4: General Chemistry 115
Atomic Mass and Weight . . . 116
Periodic Trends . . . 118
VSEPR Theory and Geometry . . . 122
Stoichiometry . . . 126
Rate Laws . . . 130
Reaction Energy Profiles . . . 134
Hess's Law . . . 138
The Ideal Gas Law . . . 140
Molar Solubility . . . 142
Titrations . . . 146
Balancing Oxidation–Reduction Reactions . . . 150
Electrochemical Cells . . . 152
Solutions to Related Questions . . . 155

Chapter 5: Organic Chemistry 165
Nomenclature . . . 166
Stereoisomers . . . 170
Hybridized Orbitals . . . 172
Nucleophilicity Trends . . . 174
Reactions of Alcohols . . . 178

Identifying the Structure of an Unknown Oxy Compound 182
Enolate Chemistry 186
Nucleophilic Acyl Substitution Reactions 190
Properties of Carboxylic Acid Derivatives 194
Phosphorus-Containing Compounds 196
Spectroscopy 200
Extraction 204
Solutions to Related Questions 206

Chapter 6: Physics and Math 213

Inclined Plane 214
Projectile Motion and Air Resistance 218
Thermodynamics 220
Fluid Dynamics 228
Electrostatics 232
Resistor Circuits 234
Doppler Effect 238
Snell's Law 242
Nuclear Reactions 246
Dimensional Analysis 250
Study Design 254
Graphical Analysis 256
Solutions to Related Questions 260

1

Behavioral Sciences

Key Concepts

Behavioral Sciences Chapter 1
Forebrain
Hindbrain
Midbrain
Hypothalamus
Thalamus

Regions of the Brain

The story of Phineas Gage, who experienced significant personality changes after being impaled with a railroad spike, laid the foundation for associating the frontal lobe with personality. The forebrain is also associated with emotion and memory. What areas of the brain may be affected if one or multiple lesions are found in the forebrain, and what cognitive or life functions would be lost? Could an individual survive the loss of this area of the brain?

1 Determine the parts of the forebrain.

The first part of the question requires you to know the parts of the forebrain, which include the cerebral cortex, basal ganglia, limbic system, thalamus, and hypothalamus.

2 Determine what the parts of the forebrain do.

In order to identify what functions an individual would lose, you must first identify the normal functions of each brain area:

- **Cerebral cortex:** The outer covering of the cerebral hemispheres. It is divided into four lobes, each of which serves specific functions:
  - **Frontal lobe:** Executive function, impulse control, long-term planning (prefrontal cortex), motor function (primary motor cortex), speech production (Broca's area)
  - **Parietal lobe:** Sensation of touch, pressure, temperature, and pain (somatosensory cortex); spatial processing, orientation, and manipulation
  - **Occipital lobe:** Visual processing
  - **Temporal lobe:** Sound processing (auditory cortex), speech perception (Wernicke's area), memory, and emotion (limbic system)
- **Basal ganglia:** Coordinate muscle movements as they receive information from the cortex and relay this information to the brain and the spinal cord. The basal ganglia smoothen movements and help maintain postural stability.
- **Limbic system:** Comprises a group of interconnected structures looping around the central portion of the brain and is primarily associated with emotion and memory:
  - **Septal nuclei:** Involved with feelings of pleasure, pleasure-seeking behavior, and addiction
  - **Amygdala:** Controls fear and aggression

    - **Hippocampus:** Consolidates memories and communicates with other parts of the limbic system through an extension called the fornix
- **Thalamus:** Serves as an important sensory relay station for incoming sensory information, including all senses except for smell. After receiving incoming sensory impulses, the thalamus sorts them and then transmits them to the appropriate projection areas in the cerebral cortex.
- **Hypothalamus:** A key player in emotional experience during high-arousal states, aggressive behavior, and sexual behavior. It also controls many endocrine functions as well as the autonomic nervous system. The hypothalamus serves many homeostatic functions, and its receptors regulate metabolism, temperature, and water balance.

Takeaways

The brain is organized by the evolutionary order of its development, so the complexity of its functions generally increases as you move up the organ. Notice that the brain structures associated with basic survival are located at the base of the brain and that these are the first areas to develop.

3 Assess whether survival would be possible.

It is widely believed that an individual would survive with loss of forebrain functions, although there may be dramatic changes in quality of life, ability to take care of oneself, and mood. Individuals with significant forebrain damage may require medication to regulate mood and endocrine functions. The midbrain and hindbrain are generally believed to be required for survival. The midbrain controls the reception of sensory and motor information, whereas the hindbrain controls balance, motor coordination, breathing, and general arousal processes, such as sleeping and waking. While the functions of the forebrain are critical for interacting with others and with the world, they are not absolutely necessary for survival.

Things to Watch Out For

It is easy to confuse the terminology of the brain. While the frontal lobe is part of the forebrain, the forebrain also includes many other structures. While the brainstem is the hindmost part of the brain, not all parts of the brainstem are in the hindbrain (the midbrain is separate from the rest of the brainstem). Further, the MCAT will not always group brain areas anatomically but may categorize according to the functions of various brain regions.

Related Questions

1. What are the parts of the hindbrain and the meaningful functions these areas serve?
2. What are the three parts of the hypothalamus and what functions does each part serve?
3. What parts of the brain make up the cerebrum? How is the cerebrum associated with Parkinson's disease and schizophrenia?

Key Concepts

Behavioral Sciences Chapter 2

The eye
Visual transduction
Visual processing
Central nervous system pathways

Vision

Multiple sclerosis (MS) is a common demyelinating disorder that affects the white matter of the central nervous system. The visual pathways are commonly affected; optic neuritis, which is inflammation of the optic nerve, is one of the most common presentations. Less commonly, MS may cause lesions of an entire section of the visual pathway, leading to visual field defects. What would be the visual field defect in an individual who lost function of the right optic nerve? Of the fibers crossing in the optic chiasm? Of the right optic tract? Of the right occipital lobe?

1 Determine what fibers are carried in the right optic nerve.

The right optic nerve collects the axons of neurons leaving the retina of the right eye. The nasal visual field (toward the nose) projects to the temporal retina (toward the side of the head). Similarly, the temporal visual field projects to the nasal retina. Together, all of these fibers form the right optic nerve.

If the entire right optic nerve were lesioned in MS, then all of information from the right eye would be lost. In medicine, this may be represented as shown:

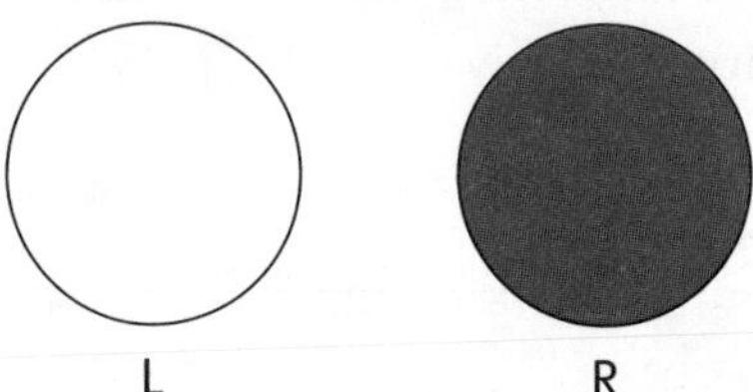

When reading visual fields, imagine that you are looking out at the world through the two circles; in this example, nothing is visible through the right eye.

2 Determine what fibers cross in the optic chiasm.

In the optic chiasm, the nasal fibers cross while the temporal fibers pass directly through to the ipsilateral (on the same side) optic tract. Remember that the nasal fibers carry information from the temporal visual field. Therefore, a lesion of the fibers crossing in the optic chiasm would knock out nasal fibers from both eyes and cause a loss of the temporal visual field from both eyes. This is called bitemporal hemianopsia, and can be represented as shown:

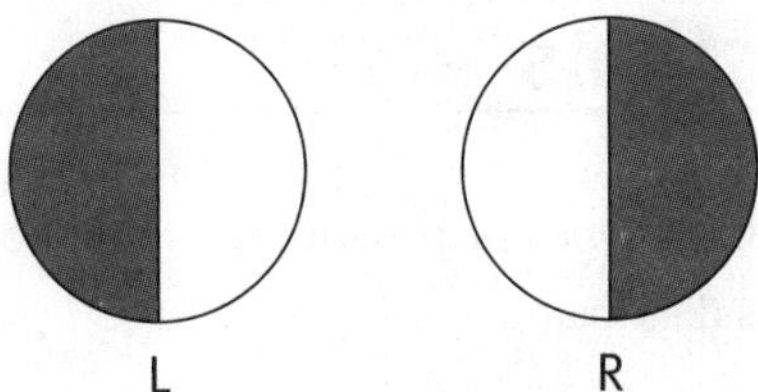

3 Determine what fibers are carried in the right optic tract.

Because of the crossing in the optic chiasm, the right optic tract carries the nasal fibers from the left eye and the temporal fibers from the right eye. These correspond to the temporal visual field from the left eye and the nasal visual field from the right eye, respectively—which is the left visual field of each eye. A complete lesion of the right optic tract would therefore cause a loss of the left visual field from both eyes. This is called homonymous hemianopsia and can be represented as shown:

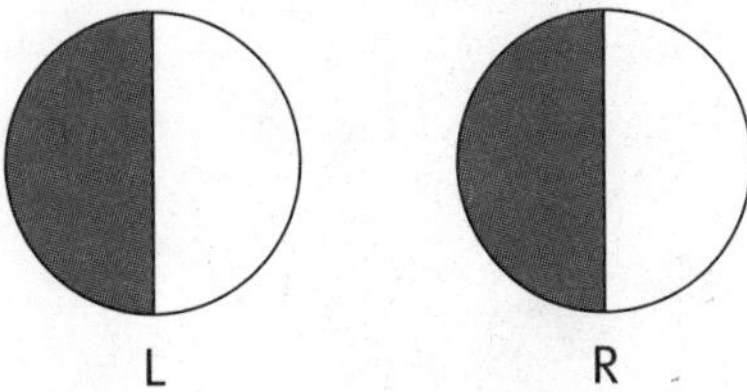

4 Determine what fibers are carried in the right occipital lobe.

The optic tracts project directly to their respective occipital lobes. Therefore, damage to the right occipital lobe will cause loss of the left visual field. Interestingly, occipital lobe lesions (which occur commonly during a stroke) are often marked by macular sparing, or survival of the central visual field in each eye, and can be represented as shown:

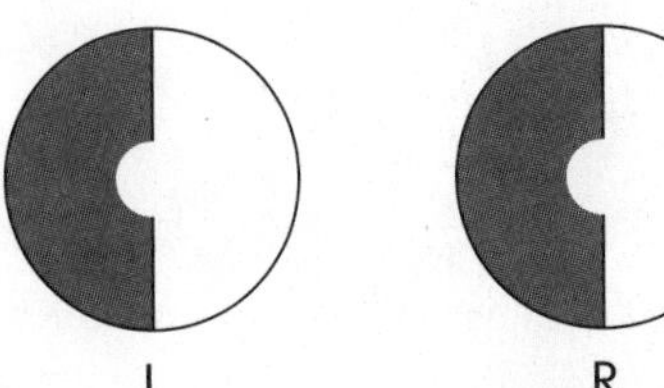

This is due to differences in circulation to the different parts of the occipital lobe, which is outside the scope of the MCAT.

Takeaways

An optic nerve carries all the information from the associated eye. The optic chiasm contains crossing nasal fibers (the temporal visual field) from each eye. An optic tract carries all the information from the opposite visual field.

Things to Watch Out For

It is very easy to misread a question about the visual system—does the answer refer to a part of the visual pathway or to a part of the visual field? Wrong answers often simply mix up *left* and *right* or *nasal* and *temporal*.

Related Questions

1. What are the two main types of photoreceptors in the retina? How are these photoreceptor types distributed?
2. What is feature detection theory?
3. What is parallel processing?

High-Yield Problem-Solving Guide questions continue on the next page. ▶ ▶ ▶

Key Concepts

Behavioral Sciences Chapter 3

Operant conditioning
Reinforcement
Punishment
Schedules of reinforcement

Associative Learning

> A pigeon is placed in a cage with two buttons: blue and green. The blue button releases a food pellet after a random period of time if it has been pressed at least once since a food pellet was last provided, but it also inflicts an electrical shock on the pigeon each time it is pressed. The green button, when pressed, temporarily shuts off the blue button's shock mechanism until a food pellet is released. Assume that the pigeon can be taught to use these buttons. In keeping with the role of each button as an operant conditioner, what is the expected frequency at which each button will be pressed?

1 Determine the types of reinforcement and punishment described.

The blue button has two consequences. One, the electrical shock, is used as a positive punishment because it adds an unpleasant stimulus that is meant to deter behavior. Remember that *positive* refers to the addition of a stimulus (the shock) and *punishment* refers to the intended outcome (to decrease behavior). The other outcome—the food pellet—is a positive reinforcer because it provides a desirable result for the bird. Remember that *reinforcement* refers to the intended outcome (to increase behavior).

The green button, on the other hand, removes an unpleasant stimulus, making it a negative reinforcer. Remember that *negative* refers to the removal of a stimulus (the shock). Because the green button prevents the shock from occurring, pressing it is also an example of avoidance learning.

2 Determine the schedules of reinforcement described.

The blue button functions under two schedules as described. Because the shock occurs each time the button is pressed, it is on a fixed-ratio schedule. The food pellet is produced after an amount of time that is unpredictable, which can be described as a variable-interval schedule. The green button provides the same result each time it is pressed, even if subsequent presses within an interval are superfluous, so it too is on a constant fixed-ratio schedule.

3 Describe the frequency of the button presses in terms of their reinforcement schedules.

Because the question asks us to assume that the pigeon can be taught how both buttons work, we can expect that the pigeon will be able to use the buttons to always avoid being shocked. Because the food reward for the blue button is on a variable-interval schedule, we expect the frequency of button presses to be relatively low but constant. A button on a fixed-ratio schedule would normally be pressed more frequently than on a variable-interval schedule, but in the scenario described, the green button only affects the consequences of the blue button. We would therefore expect the green button to be pressed only as needed: once per interval immediately after the food reward from the previous interval.

Takeaways

There are many terms that can be used to describe an operant conditioning scenario; it's important to break down described scenarios carefully to determine what is being added or taken away (positive *vs.* negative) and what effect that will have on the target behaviors (reinforcement *vs.* punishment).

Things to Watch Out For

When presented with an operant conditioning question, be careful not to confuse negative reinforcement with punishment. Reinforcers always increase the likelihood of a behavior, and punishments always decrease the likelihood of a behavior.

Related Questions

1. Emily wishes to stop her cat from knocking items off of a shelf, but doesn't believe in punishment. How can she use operant conditioning to decrease this behavior without punishing the cat?
2. A fetish is a nonsexual behavior or object that becomes sexualized and is often able to provide sexual satisfaction on its own. How might the principles of associative learning help to explain fetish development?
3. Ted's favorite restaurant plays the same music each day during lunch. He realizes that whenever he hears one of the songs, he feels hungry. Describe the classical conditioning stimuli and responses in this scenario. What will happen if he stops going to the restaurant?

Key Concepts

Behavioral Sciences Chapter 4

Aphasia
Language development
Language acquisition
Central nervous system pathways

Language

A 73-year-old male patient has recently had a stroke. While he appears to be recovering and is able to follow verbal instructions, he has lost the ability to speak. What language disorder has this patient likely developed? What part of the patient's brain has likely been damaged to cause this disorder?

1 Determine the scope of possible language disorders in this patient.

Because the patient has had a stroke, he most likely has developed aphasia—a disturbance in the ability to comprehend or formulate language resulting from dysfunction in a specific brain region. Three major forms of aphasia are Broca's aphasia, Wernicke's aphasia, and conduction aphasia.

2 Recall the characteristic symptoms of the different types of aphasia.

When one assesses aphasia, the three most important characteristics to look for are speech comprehension, speech production, and the ability to repeat verbal information.

Speech comprehension is primarily the responsibility of the temporal lobe; more specifically, Wernicke's area on the superior temporal gyrus is involved in interpreting the content of speech. Other regions of the temporal lobe are important for interpreting other auditory stimuli, such as incident sound and music.

Speech production is primarily the responsibility of the frontal lobe; more specifically, Broca's area on the inferior frontal gyrus is involved in the coordination of the muscles of the larynx, pharynx, palate, tongue, and lips that allow for the production of speech.

The ability to repeat verbal information is the combined responsibility of Wernicke's area, Broca's area, and the arcuate fasciculus—a band of white matter that connects the two areas. While all three areas must be intact to permit repetition of speech, an isolated loss of the ability to repeat verbal information (conduction aphasia) may result from isolated damage to the arcuate fasciculus.

Identify the patient's aphasia symptoms.

This patient has intact speech comprehension, as evidenced by his ability to follow verbal commands, but has difficulty with speech production. We do not have enough information to assess his ability to repeat verbal information; however, even if a clinician tested for repetition ability, the results would be obscured by the difficulty with speech production.

4 Match the patient's symptoms to the correct form of aphasia.

The inability to produce speech, combined with intact speech comprehension, is characteristic of Broca's aphasia. Broca's aphasia results from damage to Broca's area; this is a very common lesion in strokes because it falls in the vascular distribution of the middle cerebral artery—the most frequently affected vessel in a stroke.

It is possible that this patient also suffered damage to the nearby arcuate fasciculus, but we do not have enough information to draw this conclusion. We have strong evidence for Broca's aphasia, which would mask the symptoms of conduction aphasia.

Takeaways

Broca's aphasia includes intact speech comprehension but reduced or absent speech production; Wernicke's aphasia includes intact speech production but reduced or absent speech comprehension; conduction aphasia includes intact speech production and comprehension but the loss of the ability to repeat verbal information.

Things to Watch Out For

Many cases of aphasia can incorporate attributes of the different diagnoses described in this question; major damage to both the frontal and temporal lobes could lead to loss of both speech production and speech comprehension, for example.

Related Questions

1. What is the typical timeline for language development in children?
2. What is the nativist theory of language acquisition?
3. What is the learning theory of language acquisition?

Key Concepts

Behavioral Sciences Chapter 5

James–Lange theory of emotion
Cannon–Bard theory of emotion
Schachter–Singer theory of emotion
Universal emotions

Theories of Emotion

A car cuts you off as you're driving down a highway at 60 miles per hour. As a result, you feel angry. You also notice that your heart rate is elevated, your mouth feels dry, and your skin feels hot. How does the James–Lange theory of emotion account for the anger you feel as a result of the actions of the other driver?

1 Recall the James–Lange theory.

The James–Lange theory of emotion states, in brief, that a stimulus results first in physiological arousal, which leads to a secondary response in which the emotion is labeled. Thus, when a emotional stimulus is sensed, the first result is physiological arousal, which activates the sympathetic nervous system. When the peripheral organs receive this sympathetic input and respond, this response is subsequently labeled as an emotion by the brain. This theory implies that without the feedback from the visceral organs, an emotion could not be experienced.

2 Determine the relevant factors in the question that apply to the theory.

In this question, the stimulus is getting cut off by another driver while traveling at a high speed. Physiological arousal is indicated by increased heart rate, dry mouth, and increased skin temperature—the sympathetic nervous system innervates the heart and speeds up its rhythm, increases the viscosity (and decreases the flow) of saliva from the salivary glands, and increases bloodflow to the locomotor muscles and skin. The secondary response here is the conscious perception of an emotion: anger.

Takeaways

The James–Lange theory of emotion states that an emotion is the result of physiological arousal caused by a stimulus, which is then labeled by the brain as an emotion.

Things to Watch Out For

Make sure you understand the subtle differences between the James–Lange, Cannon–Bard, and Schachter–Singer theories of emotion—all three play a part in our current understanding of how emotions arise. Also remember that the spinal cord is not the only pathway for feedback from the visceral organs—the vagus nerve, which feeds directly into the medulla oblongata, performs this function as well.

3 Correlate the relevant factors from the question to the theory.

The emotion of anger you experience in this situation is initiated by your perception of the driver who cuts you off. This stimulus leads to your physiological arousal in the form of changes in heart rate, salivary flow, and skin temperature. These sensations are then labeled as anger by your brain.

Related Questions

1. What is the sequence of events in the Cannon–Bard theory of emotion?
2. What is the sequence of events in the Schachter–Singer theory of emotion?
3. What did Darwin have to say about emotions? How did Ekman further develop Darwin's ideas?

Key Concepts

Behavioral Sciences Chapter 6

Kohlberg's theory of moral reasoning development
Psychosexual development
Psychosocial development
Locus of control

Formation of Identity

Lois and Marvin debate the passing of a law that would require businesses to pay all of their employees a minimum wage that is tied to the annual rate of inflation. Lois claims that such a law is necessary because it helps to combat poverty, thereby preventing crime and civil unrest. Marvin maintains that the law is unjust because businesses have a right to operate in a way that maximizes their profits and allows them to stay in business. According to Lawrence Kohlberg, which phase and stage of moral development is each person exhibiting? Are these stages of moral reasoning expected in adults?

1 Describe the reasoning of each person.

Note that Kohlberg's theory does not focus on the ultimate decision of each individual (whether the law is good or bad, necessary or unnecessary, just or unjust), but rather the route by which one arrives at this decision. Lois's reasoning is based on the effects the law would have on society. Because her argument hinges on the prevention of crime and civil unrest, one could characterize her method of reasoning as being focused on maintaining social order.

Marvin's argument, on the other hand, is derived from the rights of an individual or entity. While his conclusion focuses on larger-scale issues (the justice of the law), his argument focuses on individual rights.

2 Match the reasoning to a phase.

Lois's reasoning focuses on societal concerns and understanding and accepting social rules. This puts her thought process squarely into conventional morality. Each of Kohlberg's phases is divided into two stages. Here, Lois's reasoning is mostly focused on societal concerns and maintaining social order, which puts her thinking into Kohlberg's stage four (often called *law and order*).

Marvin's reasoning is based on abstract principles such as justice and individual rights, meaning that it fits within the postconventional phase. More specifically, individual rights are a hallmark of stage five of Kohlberg's theory of moral reasoning (often called *social contract*).

 Determine whether these stages are expected in adults.

Kohlberg's theory does not expect that all individuals will reach stage six of moral reasoning (*universal human ethics*). Stages one and two (*obedience* and *self-interest*) constitute preconventional thought, which is common in preadolescents. Stages three and four (*conformity* and *law and order*) constitute conventional thought, which is common in adolescents and adults. Not all adults reach stages five and six (*social contract* and *universal human ethics*), which constitute postconventional thought. Therefore, Lois and Marvin are both using moral reasoning patterns expected in adults.

Takeaways

Keep in mind that the conclusion of an argument is irrelevant to determining the stage of moral reasoning. Lois and Marvin could have come to opposite conclusions and still have fallen in the same stages of moral reasoning.

Things to Watch Out For

While the differences between phases of moral reasoning are fairly clear-cut, the differences between the numbered stages can be subtle. Make sure to be able to describe the six stages clearly, and carefully examine the content of the arguments made in any moral reasoning question.

Related Questions

1. A three-year-old child has begun to explore her surroundings and is learning that she is able to control the world around her. She brushes her own teeth, dresses herself, and has begun to develop personal interests. According to Erikson's stages of psychosocial development, what is the next conflict this child will face?
2. Two college roommates are constantly at odds because one is extremely messy and the other is obsessively tidy. According to Freudian analysis, how can the differences between these roommates be explained in terms of psychosexual fixation?
3. A child of busy parents is often left on his own to play and learn. According to Vygotsky, what effect would the consistent absence of a more knowledgeable other have on the child's locus of control and self-efficacy?

Key Concepts

Behavioral Sciences Chapter 7

Manic episodes
Depressive episodes
Bipolar I and II disorders
Major depressive disorder

Bipolar and Depressive Disorders

A 46-year-old woman is brought by her husband to the emergency room after she was found on the roof of her home, yelling incomprehensible statements at the sky. Her husband says that, over the last two weeks, she has been staying up late at night, shopping for expensive clothes that she cannot afford, and sleeping only two to three hours per night. She cannot stop talking and moves rapidly from one topic to another. When asked how she feels, she exclaims, *I'm fantastic!* Last month, she was diagnosed with depression and started on a medication for her symptoms. What diagnosis is she most likely to have?

1 Characterize the mood.

The symptoms described here are consistent with mania. Bipolar and depressive disorders were historically classified under the same umbrella of mood disorders in the previous version of the *Diagnostic and Statistical Manual of Mental Disorders* (DSM), the DSM-IV-TR. In the DSM-5, these two types of disorders have been split into separate diagnostic categories. They still share some characteristics, however, so it is useful to think of them together.

Bipolar disorders—at least their manic components—are characterized by elevated, expansive, or irritable mood. In other words, these individuals feel on top of the world or feel irritable. Depressive disorders are characterized by sadness, lack of interest, or apathy. The patient in this example clearly has an elevated mood, as evidenced by her feeling *fantastic!*

Determine whether the manic symptoms constitute a manic episode.

According to the DSM-5, a manic episode must include an elevated, expansive, or irritable mood as described earlier and must last for at least one week (although the duration does not matter if the episode is severe enough to warrant hospitalization). The patient must also have at least three of the following symptoms (four if the mood is only irritable):

- Easily **D**istracted
- Decreased need for sleep (**I**nsomnia)
- Increased self-esteem or **G**randiosity
- **F**light of ideas or racing thoughts

- Increased goal-directed activity or motor **A**gitation
- Increased talkativeness or pressured **S**peech
- Involvement in high-risk behavior (**T**houghtlessness)

These symptoms must cause significant impairment, require hospitalization, or be accompanied by psychosis. The mnemonic **DIGFAST** is a simple way of remembering these symptoms.

The patient in the question meets criteria for a manic episode. These symptoms have been ongoing for two weeks, she has decreased need for sleep, flight of ideas, increased goal-directed activity (purchasing clothes online), and increased talkativeness. The symptom of yelling at the sky implies psychosis, but we at least know that the symptoms are significantly impairing her home life—enough for her husband to bring her into the hospital.

3 Rule out nonpsychiatric diagnoses.

Many diagnoses in the DSM-5, including bipolar and depressive disorders, have the disclaimer that they must not be caused by substance use or an underlying illness. In this scenario, we have no indication that there is an underlying nonpsychiatric explanation for the patient's symptoms.

4 Match the symptoms to a diagnosis.

The presence of a manic episode alone is enough to make the diagnosis of bipolar I disorder; however, the patient's history of depression strengthens this diagnosis because most patients with bipolar I disorder cycle between manic and depressive episodes.

This patient was originally diagnosed with major depressive disorder. This diagnosis requires at least one major depressive episode but cannot include manic episodes. Therefore, this patient's diagnosis is more accurately reflected by bipolar I disorder than major depressive disorder.

Bipolar II disorder has similar symptoms but includes hypomanic episodes instead of manic episodes.

Takeaways

Manic episodes are at least one week of elevated, expansive, or irritable mood with at least three of these symptoms: distractibility, insomnia, increased self-esteem or grandiosity, flight of ideas or racing thoughts, increased goal-directed or agitated motor activity, increased talkativeness or pressured speech, and high-risk behavior. They cannot be accounted for by a drug or underlying disorder.

Things to Watch Out For

As with many diagnoses in the DSM-5, a patient must fit the criteria of a disorder to be diagnosed with that disorder. Other related disorders, such as bipolar II disorder and major depressive disorder, have some shared symptomatology but do not meet the criteria for bipolar I disorder.

Related Questions

1. What is a depressive episode? What diagnoses may include a depressive episode?
2. What is a hypomanic episode? What diagnoses may include a hypomanic episode?
3. This patient's bipolar I disorder was not recognized until she started medication for a major depressive episode. Why is this commonly the case?

High-Yield Problem-Solving Guide questions continue on the next page. ▶ ▶ ▶

Key Concepts

Behavioral Sciences Chapter 8

Social processes
Bystander effect
Deindividuation
Peer pressure
Social facilitation

Social Processes

At a fundraising event, a room full of people are socializing and eating hors d'oeuvres. The approximately 300 people in the room, who vary in age from 21 to 50, have all participated in fundraisers together previously. An individual in the room becomes unsteady and falls while walking toward the bathroom. Initially, no one reacts or rushes to aid the fallen person. What social phenomenon describes this scenario? Evaluate the following scenarios in terms of likelihood of response and response time: If the event had fewer attendees, what outcome would be expected? If the attendees were complete strangers, what outcome would be expected? If the attendees had prior knowledge that the fallen person suffered from a heart condition, what outcome would be expected?

1 Determine what social phenomenon is described in the text.

This scenario is an example of the bystander effect, a social phenomenon that occurs in social groups wherein individuals do not help a victim when others are present.

2 Evaluate the effect of an event with fewer attendees.

It has been shown that the number of individuals in the room (or comparable environment) is inversely related to the likelihood and timeliness of response to the victim. If fewer attendees were present, we would expect it to be more likely that an individual would come to the aid of the victim. We would also expect that the response time would be faster with fewer people present.

3 Evaluate the effect of the attendees being strangers.

The question states that the 300 individuals have interacted previously at fundraising events. Research has shown that increased cohesiveness of the group and closeness with the victim can partially mitigate the bystander effect. Groups of people who are better acquainted are more likely to uphold social responsibilities and come to the aid of the victim. If the group were made up of strangers, we could expect that the likelihood of response would be lower and response time would be slower.

Evaluate the effect of prior knowledge of the victim having a heart condition.

It has been shown that the degree of emergency or danger to the victim influences the response of the group. If individuals in the group were aware that the fallen person had a heart condition, it would increase the degree of danger perceived by those individuals, as the person might not have simply lost his or her balance, but might be experiencing a complication related to his or her heart condition—perhaps even an arrhythmia or heart attack. This would increase the likelihood of a response and decrease the observed response time.

Related Questions

1. Children were observed on Halloween while trick-or-treating. Candy was left on the porch of a home with a note saying *Please take only one piece of candy*. It was observed that children trick-or-treating alone or with one friend or sibling were very likely to take only one piece of candy, but that children in groups were dramatically more likely to take handfuls of candy. What social process is at play, and what influence does the nature of the holiday have on the observed results?
2. An Olympic weightlifter is preparing for a competition and records his clean-and-jerk weights over a period of three months during his independent training sessions. He sees increases in his lifts as he progresses toward the competition, but plateaus in the final month. At the competition, he reaches a personal record, adding seven kilograms to his lift. What social process best describes the improved performance at the competition?
3. Max is a high school student who has typically shown mediocre performance. He transfers to a new school and befriends a group of high-achieving students. Max's grades in his first semester are much above his previous grades. What social process describes these results?

Takeaways

The bystander effect describes the observed phenomenon that being in a group makes individuals less likely to come to the aid of a victim. The number of individuals in the group is inversely related to likelihood and timeliness of response. The effect is also influenced by cohesiveness of the group and the perceived danger of the situation.

Things to Watch Out For

Make sure you realize that the inverse relationship means that the more people there are in the group, the less likely it is that any one individual will respond, and that if an individual responds, the response time will generally be slower.

Key Concepts

Behavioral Sciences Chapter 9

Verbal communication
Nonverbal communication
Impression management strategies
Authentic self
Tactical self

Verbal and Nonverbal Communication

Tom is on the interview trail for medical school. He wears a tailored black suit and a pin from his premedical honor society to every interview and makes references to the influential physician–scientists with whom he's done research. At one particular school, he arrives slightly late to the interview. *Pardon me for being late*, he says. *I couldn't find where to park.* What are some of the impression management strategies Tom is using during this interview day?

1 Define impression management.

Impression management refers to a person's attempts to influence how others perceive him or her. This is accomplished through the regulation or controlling of information in social interactions. There are a number of impression management strategies that are used in specific social situations.

2 Determine what elements constitute impression management strategies.

There are two main elements of impression management in this story. First, Tom is wearing particular clothes—a tailored black suit and the pin from his premedical honor society—and creating a positive image by associating himself with influential physician–scientists. Second, he is providing a socially acceptable excuse for why he arrived late at an interview. Whether the excuse is actually true has some bearing on the label we can give to this impression management strategy.

3 Determine the strategy being used when Tom wears certain clothes and refers to specific professional associations.

The strategy of using props, appearance, emotional expression, or associations with others to create a positive image is called managing appearances. This impression management strategy usually requires a balance between presenting the authentic self—who Tom actually is—and the tactical self—who he markets himself to be when he adheres to others' expectations of him. While managing appearances can play a role in any social situation, we commonly think of its application in settings where an individual wishes to establish authority or to appear knowledgeable and trustworthy, especially in cases where a power dynamic exists.

4 Determine the strategy being used when Tom mentions that he could not find parking.

We are not given enough information to know whether Tom's claim that he could not find parking is true. Regardless, Tom is trying to make questionable behavior (being late for a medical school interview) acceptable through an excuse. This strategy is called aligning actions, and it is most commonly used when someone fails to live up to a particular expectation, such as being on time for an interview, scoring poorly on an exam, or missing a deadline.

Aligning actions is often associated with an external locus of control, in which someone considers personal successes or failures to be the result of factors outside of his or her control. Aligning actions also encourages others to make situational attributions about an individual's behavior, inferring that the causes of the behavior are features of the surroundings, rather than personal beliefs, attitudes, or personality characteristics.

Takeaways

Aligning actions is related to excuse-making and rationalization of questionable behavior. It may be associated with an external locus of control and may be used to encourage others to make situational—rather than dispositional—attributions.

Things to Watch Out For

Impression management techniques can overlap, and one may use multiple impression management techniques in the same social situation. Be prepared for questions that ask about mixing these strategies.

Related Questions

1. How does nonverbal communication add to a conversation?
2. What is alter-casting?
3. What is ingratiation?

Key Concepts

Behavioral Sciences Chapter 10

Attributions
Correspondent inference theory
Fundamental attribution error
Attributional bias

Attribution Theory

You are walking through a crowded lecture hall with a stack of books and your laptop in your arms. The next thing you know you are on the ground with your books sprawled around you and a cracked laptop after tripping over a classmate's leg. You immediately get up and yell at the person in the seat next to where you fell: *Why did you trip me? Are you trying to kill me and break my laptop?* What type of attribution have you made? What explains why you reached this conclusion? What is another type of attribution that you could have made?

1 Determine the causes for attribution and what type is made in the example.

Attribution theory explains the tendency for individuals to infer the causes of other people's behavior. There are two main categories of attributions: dispositional and situational. Dispositional, or internal, attributions are related to the features or characteristics of the person whose behavior is considered, including his or her beliefs, attitudes, and personality characteristics. Situational, or external, attributions are external and based on the features of the surrounding environment, such as threats, money, social norms, and peer pressure. In this case, when you immediately assumed the classmate was trying to trip you, you attributed the behavior to intentional malice of the person, believing that he or she tripped you on purpose out of rudeness, mean-spiritedness, or spite. This is a dispositional attribution.

Takeaways

We have a tendency to blame others. When inferring causes of others' behavior, we tend to make dispositional—rather than situational—attributions. When rationalizing our own mistakes or shortcomings, we tend to assume an external—rather than internal—locus of control.

2 Explain the tendency to make this type of attribution.

When examining the causes of others' behavior, there is a general bias toward making dispositional rather than situational attributions, which is known as the fundamental attribution error. In this case, the assumption was that the person deliberately meant to trip you. The fundamental attribution error is more common in negative contexts and when dealing with others whom we do not know well.

Things to Watch Out For

Think about attribution theory and fundamental attribution error any time you see one person analyzing another person's behavior. Be on the lookout for assumptions that lead to dispositional attributions.

3 Consider alternative attributions and associated examples.

If you had not made the fundamental attribution error, you might have considered other external reasons for your fall by making situational attributions. You could have attributed your falling not to the person intentionally tripping you, but rather to a failure to see you when stretching his or her legs, to the person's attempt to get out of the way of another person, or to your own distraction in the crowded lecture hall, which caused you not to see the person who accidentally tripped you.

Related Questions

1. What theory describes the tendency to make dispositional attributions for behavior we see as intentional?
2. When Itai wins his event at a track meet, he says it is because he trained hard and performed his best. When he loses the following week, he says it is because he had a poor lane position and the ground was soft from the rain. What describes his views of success and failure?
3. Kristin is usually at the top of the class and gets As on all of her tests. You are surprised to hear that she got a D on her latest math test. What cue are you likely to use to explain her usual behavior? What type of attribution are you likely to make for this low math test score?

Key Concepts

Behavioral Sciences Chapter 11

Demographic structure
Fertility
Migration
Mortality
Urbanization

Demographics

A hypothetical town currently has 1000 people. Of the 1000 people, 480 are women and 520 are men; 170 individuals self-describe as white, 280 as black, 230 as Asian, and 320 as Hispanic. The crude mortality rate is 15 for every 1000 persons per year. In one year, 45 children are born, 200 Hispanic individuals leave the town, and 150 Asian individuals enter the town. How has the population changed in terms of size and racial demographics? Which factors contributed to population growth or decline?

1 Determine which details contribute to population size.

Population size is affected by reproduction, death, and net migration rates. The mortality rate for the town is 15 for every 1000 persons per year and the birth rate is 45 for every 1000 persons per year. The difference in the two provides the rate of natural increase. Net migration rate is the difference between immigration into and emigration from an area. In total, 150 people immigrate into this town and 200 people emigrate from it.

2 Evaluate the relative rates and determine whether the population size is expected to rise or decline.

Because the birth rate is higher than the death rate, the population is expected to naturally increase. The rate of natural increase is the difference between these two, or:

$$\frac{45 \text{ births}}{1000 \frac{\text{persons}}{\text{year}}} - \frac{15 \text{ deaths}}{1000 \frac{\text{persons}}{\text{year}}} = \frac{+30 \text{ persons}}{1000 \frac{\text{persons}}{\text{year}}}$$

In addition, the net migration rate is the difference between the immigration and emigration rates, or:

$$\frac{150 \text{ immigrants}}{1000 \frac{\text{persons}}{\text{year}}} - \frac{200 \text{ emigrants}}{1000 \frac{\text{persons}}{\text{year}}} = \frac{-50 \text{ persons}}{1000 \frac{\text{persons}}{\text{year}}}$$

Adding these two rates together gives us the overall population growth rate:

$$\frac{30 \text{ persons}}{1000 \frac{\text{persons}}{\text{year}}} + \frac{-50 \text{ persons}}{1000 \frac{\text{persons}}{\text{year}}} = \frac{-20 \text{ persons}}{1000 \frac{\text{persons}}{\text{year}}}$$

Thus, this population is shrinking at a rate of 20 persons per 1000 persons per year, or 2%.

Determine how the demographics of the population have changed.

The population was initially 17 percent white, 28 percent black, 23 percent Asian, and 32 percent Hispanic. The birth and death rates per racial demographic are not given; do not assume that these rates will be uniform across the population. While we cannot derive predictions about the changes in demographics from these rates, we can predict some qualitative changes from the migration statistics.

The percentage of Asians increased dramatically over the year, growing from 230 to 380 due to immigration. If we assume that all deaths were in this group, we know that the minimum population of Asians is 380 – 15 = 365 individuals. If we assume that all births were in this group, we know that the maximum population of Asians is 380 + 45 = 425 individuals. We can confidently say that this group will be the largest demographic in the population.

The Hispanic population, which was previously the largest, will decrease to between 105 and 165 individuals (320 – 200 = 120; 120 – 15 = 105; 120 + 45 = 165). Depending on the changes in the white population, either the Hispanic or the white population is now the smallest demographic in the population.

Takeaways

There are three main ways for a population to grow: have more babies, have fewer deaths, or have more people move into the population than out of it. There are three main ways for a population to shrink: have fewer babies, have more deaths, or have more people move out of the population than into it.

Things to Watch Out For

Be careful with the sign convention in demographics. To determine the overall rate of change in the population, subtract the mortality rate from the birth rate and then add the result to the net migration rate.

Related Questions

1. India has seen a large population growth in the past 50 years; however, the growth of Mumbai is significantly higher than in outlying areas. What migration phenomenon best explains this trend?
2. The recent U.S. trend to outsource work to other countries is an example of what social shift?
3. Russia has a rate of natural increase of –4.93. What does this mean in terms of birth and death rates?

Key Concepts

Behavioral Sciences Chapter 12

Race inequities in health
Gender inequities in health
Class inequities in health
Race, gender, and class inequities in healthcare

Disparities in Health and Healthcare

Researchers studied four groups: high-income females, high-income males, low-income females, and low-income males. Which group is expected to have the best health profile? How do they differ? How do access and usage of healthcare services differ among these groups?

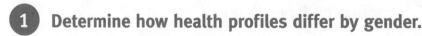

1 Determine how health profiles differ by gender.

Statistics show that females have better health profiles than males. Life expectancy for women is higher than for men. Death rates due to heart disease, cancer, chronic respiratory disease, and diabetes are higher for men. Men are also more likely to die from accidents, homicide, and suicide. While men have higher mortality rates, women tend to have higher morbidity rates.

2 Determine how health profiles differ by class.

Low-income groups have far worse health profiles than high-income groups. Low-income groups are more likely to have poor health and to die younger. They are more likely to have life-shortening diseases and to die from homicide or suicide. In addition, infant mortality rates are higher for low-income groups.

3 Determine which group is expected to have the best health profile.

According to gender and income status, the high-income female group is expected to have the best health profile.

4 Determine how usage and availability of healthcare differs among different genders and classes.

We have identified that women have better health profiles than men. Women are also more likely to utilize healthcare services. They are more likely to be insured and to have routine visits to primary care doctors, and they have a higher frequency of physician visits per year. However, women experience more difficulty with access and delays in healthcare services. Low-income groups have poorer healthcare

Takeaways

It is important to be familiar with both health and healthcare trends with respect to race, gender, and class. It is more useful to be aware of the trends than to memorize specific statistics.

Things to Watch Out For

While females are more likely than men to seek out healthcare services, they often experience longer delays or more difficulty in receiving care than men.

profiles and poorer access to and utilization of healthcare services. The high-income female and high-income male groups have better access to healthcare and higher usage than both low-income groups. Females of both groups will utilize healthcare more often than their male counterparts.

Related Questions

1. How do the health profiles of white Americans, African-Americans, and Asian-Americans compare?
2. A low-income female from a small town goes to her local urgent care center. She knows all of the nurses and doctors because of the size of the town. A high-income male from out of town has more severe symptoms and has been at the urgent care center for five hours when the woman arrives, but is seen after her. What is the most likely cause for the discrepancy in care?
3. Rachel is a 35-year-old female with a body mass index of 21.3 from a low-income group. Stephanie is a 35-year-old female with a body mass index of 34.5 from a high-income group. Rachel visits her primary doctor for routine checkups more frequently and reports high satisfaction with care. Stephanie is less likely to visit the doctor and has changed primary care providers three times in the past five years. What best explains this discrepancy?

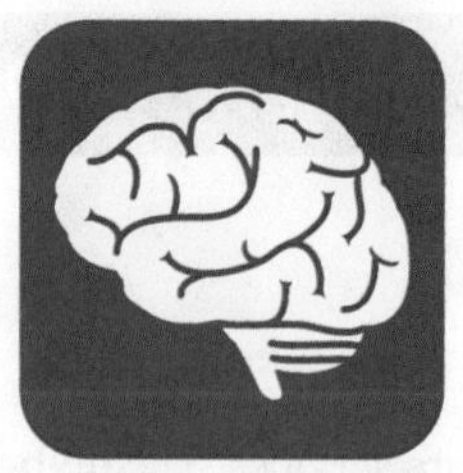

Solutions to Related Questions

1. Regions of the Brain

1. The hindbrain is located where the brain meets the spinal cord and includes the medulla oblongata, the pons, the cerebellum, and the reticular formation. The medulla oblongata is responsible for regulating vital functions such as breathing, heart rate, blood pressure, and digestion. The pons contains sensory and motor pathways between the cortex and the medulla. The cerebellum is at the top of the hindbrain and helps maintain posture, balance, and coordination of body movements. Damage to this area causes clumsiness, slurred speech, and loss of balance; note that these are similar to the impairments caused by alcohol, which largely affects the cerebellum. The reticular formation controls general arousal processes and alertness.

2. The hypothalamus is subdivided into three areas: lateral, ventromedial, and anterior. The lateral hypothalamus is referred to as the hunger center and contains special receptors thought to detect when the body needs more food or fluids. The ventromedial hypothalamus is identified as the satiety center and provides signals to stop eating. The anterior hypothalamus regulates sexual behavior, sleep, and body temperature.

3. The cerebrum is composed of the basal ganglia, limbic system, and cerebral cortex; it can also be divided between left and right hemispheres. The basal ganglia coordinate muscle movements as they receive information from the cortex and relay this information to the brain and spinal cord. The basal ganglia include the extrapyramidal motor system, which gathers information about body position and carries this information to the brain and spinal cord, helping to smoothen movements and steady posture. Damage to this area is associated with Parkinson's disease, which is characterized by jerky movements and uncontrolled resting tremors, among other symptoms. The basal ganglia are also believed to play a role in schizophrenia. Within the cerebrum are ventricles filled with cerebrospinal fluid that ultimately flows into the central canal in the middle of the spinal cord. Research has linked abnormally enlarged ventricles with symptoms often seen in schizophrenia, including social withdrawal, flat affect, and catatonic states. The functions of the limbic system and cerebral cortex are detailed in Step 2 of the main question.

2. Vision

1. The duplicity theory of vision states that the retina contains two types of photoreceptors: cones and rods. Cones come in three types and are used for color vision and to perceive fine details. Cones are most effective in bright light (daylight or artificial light). In reduced illumination, rods function best and allow perception only of an achromatic, lower-resolution image. Rods allow for night vision, when cones cannot function. Overall, there are many more rods than cones; however, the fovea at the center of the retina contains only cones. As one moves further away from the fovea, the proportion of rods increases and the proportion of cones decreases. Therefore, visual acuity is best in the fovea, and the fovea is most sensitive in normal daylight vision.

2. Feature detection theory states that we interpret objects by assessing specific characteristics, such as lines, shapes, or specific kinds of motion to identify something of importance *vs.* something of little value. Fishing is a good example of feature detection applied to animals: the person fishing attempts to mimic the features of something recognizable to the fish as food. Some cell types involved in feature detection are cones (for color), parvocellular cells (for shape and boundary detection), and magnocellular cells (for motion).

3. Parallel processing is the psychological counterpart to feature detection theory and refers to our analysis of different attributes of an object through separate pathways before integrating them. Parallel processing requires the interpretation of color, motion, shape, and depth as separate entities, which are then combined to create a cohesive view of the world.

3. Associative Learning

1. At first, this may seem like a paradox—decreasing behavior is the goal of punishment, after all. However, Emily can decrease the frequency of the negative behavior by reinforcing incompatible behaviors. For example, she might provide treats when the cat stays down off of the shelf or pet the cat when it is in a different room.

2. In terms of associative learning, a fetish is an example of a conditioned reinforcer. The fetish object has become paired with sexual gratification such that fixation on it and its use provide satisfaction without a specific sexual context. Once paired, the experienced gratification becomes a reward (positive reinforcer) that increases the use of the fetish object.

3. Ted has been conditioned to associate the songs played in the restaurant with the smell or taste of the food served there. The food is the unconditioned stimulus, the music is the conditioned stimulus, and the feeling of hunger is both the unconditioned and conditioned response. If Ted stops going to the restaurant, extinction of the conditioned response—a decreased feeling of hunger when hearing this music—should follow.

4. Language

1. Babies usually begin to babble in the first year of life; babbling peaks between 9 and 12 months. From 12 to 18 months, infants add about one word per month to their vocabularies. Around 18 months, there is an "explosion of language" in which the infant learns dozens of words and begins to use inflection and gestures to indicate different meanings for the same word. From 18 to 20 months, the infant also begins to use two-word sentences. From two to three years, a child beings to form three-word (or longer) sentences. By age five, children have largely mastered the rules of language.

2. According to the nativist (biological) theory of language acquisition, humans have an innate capacity for language. This capacity is sometimes referred to as the language acquisition device, a theoretical pathway in the brain that allows infants to absorb and process language rules. It is thought that this device is triggered by exposure to language. Thus, the nativist theory posits that children must be exposed to language during a critical period between the age of two and puberty in order to fully develop their linguistic abilities.

3. The learning (behaviorist) theory states that language acquisition is accomplished through operant conditioning. Caregivers repeat and reinforce the sounds that mimic their own spoken language. Thus, over time, the infant perceives that certain

sounds are highly valued and are reliably reinforced, while others have little value and are not reinforced, with the result of shaping the child's acquisition of language.

5. Theories of Emotion

1. The Cannon–Bard theory, in contrast to the James–Lange theory of emotion, states that neither the physiological arousal nor the corresponding visceral stimulation for a particular emotion is distinct enough for the brain to label that emotion. Instead, this theory states that sensory information is received and sent to both the cortex and the sympathetic nervous system simultaneously by the thalamus. In other words, the physiological and cognitive components of emotion occur simultaneously (rather than in sequence) and result in the behavioral component of emotion.

2. According to the Schachter–Singer theory of emotion, both arousal and the labeling of arousal on the basis of environmental cues must take place in order for an emotion to be experienced. The subjective experience of emotion arises from the interaction between changes in physiological arousal and the cognitive interpretation of that arousal. In the absence of any clear emotion-provoking stimuli, the interpretation of physiological arousal depends on what is happening in the environment. In other words, physiological arousal could be labeled as anger, fear, or happiness, depending on environmental cues.

3. Darwin believed that emotions are products of evolution and that as a result, emotions and their corresponding expressions are universal. Because all humans evolved the same set of facial muscles, these muscles would show the same expression when communicating an emotion, regardless of differences in society or culture. Paul Ekman identified seven universal emotions: happiness, sadness, contempt, surprise, fear, disgust, and anger. Also, his research showed that each of these universal emotions comes with a specific set of facial cues, regardless of culture or society.

6. Formation of Identity

1. As described, this child has successfully resolved the conflict of autonomy *vs.* shame and doubt. When resolved favorably, an individual feels able to exert control over the world and to exercise choice as well as self-restraint. The next conflict should be initiative *vs.* guilt, which normally occurs between ages 3 and 6. If resolved favorably, the child will feel a sense of purpose, can initiate activities, and can enjoy accomplishment.

2. Extreme tidiness and messiness, according to Freud, are two sides of the same coin: both indicate fixation in the anal stage of psychosexual development, which normally occurs between one and three years of age. The difference lies in which part of the unconscious is stronger. The tidy roommate's superego influences his behavior, whereas the messy roommate's id influences his behavior. Remember that the superego is focused on perfectionism, while the id is focused on satisfying primal, inborn urges.

3. Lacking a more knowledgeable other, this child would likely have difficulty accomplishing tasks that are within his zone of proximal development. This refers to tasks that a child cannot do on his or her own but can accomplish with the assistance of this more knowledgeable other. Consistent failure to learn new tasks could lead to a feeling of ineffectiveness and helplessness, thereby likely causing low self-efficacy. This could, in turn, lead to a persistent external locus of control, or a feeling that one's successes and failures are due to circumstance, rather than personal characteristics and actions.

7. Bipolar and Depressive Disorders

1. Depressive episodes last at least two weeks and include at least five of the following: feeling down or **sad**, changes in **S**leep patterns, loss of **I**nterest, feelings of **G**uilt, loss of **E**nergy, difficulty **C**oncentrating, changes in weight or **A**ppetite, **P**sychomotor retardation or agitation (feeling or seeming slowed down or agitated), and recurrent thoughts of death or **S**uicide. These can be remembered with the mnemonic **sadness + SIG E. CAPS**. As with manic episodes, depressive episodes must not be accounted for by an underlying disorder. Major depressive disorder, bipolar I disorder, and bipolar II disorder may all include major depressive episodes.

2. Hypomanic episodes are less severe than manic episodes. While the diagnosis of a hypomanic episode also requires three symptoms of a manic episode (four if the mood is irritable only), they do not cause significant impairment to everyday life, cannot have psychotic symptoms, and need not last as long (at least four days). Bipolar II disorder is characterized by hypomanic episodes with or without depressive episodes.

3. Manic symptoms and depressive symptoms are, to an extent, at opposite ends of the same mood spectrum. Patients who actually have bipolar I disorder or bipolar II disorder may first present with a depressive episode. Without any history of mania (at the time), the person may be diagnosed with major depressive disorder. However, treatments of depression are aimed at activating the person and increasing energy and mood. In a patient who has an underlying bipolar disorder, the activation caused by the medication can actually lead to a manic episode, unmasking the bipolar disorder.

8. Social Processes

1. The process seen with these trick-or-treating children is deindividuation. When in groups, individuals are more likely to behave in ways that they would not if they were alone. The group setting increases the anonymity of the behavior and can result in behavior that is inconsistent with a person's typical behavior. During Halloween, children are dressed up in costumes, which increases anonymity, making them even more likely to behave in atypical ways.

2. Social facilitation is at play in this example. Individuals are more likely to exhibit enhanced performance in the presence of others—especially if they already feel a high sense of self-efficacy with the task at hand. The lifter completes his training sessions independently, but during competition, judges observe him and there may be a cheering crowd. Being watched enhances his ability to perform, resulting in a new personal record.

3. Peer pressure refers to social influence placed on an individual by a group of peers or others one perceives as equals. While peer pressure is often seen as a negative influence, it can also be positive. In Max's case, the fact that his new group of friends are high-achieving students places pressure on him to perform at the level of his peers. His desire to be socially accepted by his peer group results in behavior to meet the norm—in this case, higher grades in school.

9. Verbal and Nonverbal Communication

1. Nonverbal cues serve several functions in communication, but their primary purpose is often to express emotions. Ekman's seven universal emotions are a classic example of these emotion-disclosing facial expressions that do not differ across cultures. Nonverbal communication can also be used to convey attitudes; for example, smiling at someone while maintaining eye contact conveys *I like you*. One can communicate personality traits through nonverbal communication as well; for example, someone who is outgoing may use bold, broad hand gestures, an energetic tone of voice, and voice inflection to add to verbal communication. Nonverbal cues may be culture specific: maintenance of eye contact, an acceptable amount of personal space, and the meanings of different postures or hand signals can vary between groups. In these cases, successful communication is often contingent on knowledge of cultural symbols and display rules.

2. Alter-casting is the imposition of an identity onto another person. In this impression management strategy, one assigns a role to another person. This is often done subtly by implying that a desirable quality is associated with a given behavior. Examples include a friend saying *A real friend would...* or Kaplan saying *As a good MCAT student...* in our books.

3. Ingratiation is the use of flattery or conforming to expectations to win someone over. In this impression management strategy, one may blindly agree with another person, may compliment another person before asking for a favor, or may simply try to live up to "good boy, good girl" imagery.

10. Attribution Theory

1. Correspondent inference theory describes the tendency to make dispositional attributions when behavior is seen as motivated or intentional as opposed to accidental. We tend to assume that unexpected actions are representative of an individual's personality or motives; thus, in cases when an individual unexpectedly performs a behavior that helps or hurts us, we assume that this is reflective of the person (dispositional attribution) rather than of circumstance (situational attribution).

2. Self-serving attributional bias is the tendency to attribute successes to dispositional factors and failures to situational factors. Itai sees his success as a result of hard work and personal achievement. On the other hand, he sees his failure as a result not of his own actions, but rather of lane position and track conditions. We could also say that successes are explained with an internal locus of control, whereas failures are explained with an external locus of control. It is noteworthy that in some cases of depression, self-serving attributional bias becomes reversed: the individual attributes success to situational factors (*I got lucky this time*) and failure to personal factors (*It was all my fault*).

3. When making attributions, we consider a person's behavior over time. Because Kristin has always gotten As, we expect her to continue to get As. These are consistency cues, which refer to having consistent behavior over time, as well as distinctiveness cues, which refer to having similar behavior in similar situations. On the latest test, Kristin got a D, which is not consistent with her past behavior. In this case, we are likely to attribute the behavior to situational as opposed to dispositional factors because we have familiarity with Kristin's "normal" behavior.

11. Demographics

1. While birth and death rates likely play a role in the disproportionate growth of Mumbai in comparison to outlying areas of the city, urbanization is also likely one of the main drivers of population growth. Urbanization is the migration of large groups of people to densely populated urban areas, creating cities. In fact, analysis of the outlying areas may demonstrate that these towns are actually decreasing in size as large portions of their populations move into the city for economic or social opportunities.

2. Outsourcing is an example of globalization. Globalization is defined as the increase in internationally connected systems and integration, with the tapping of foreign labor markets and increased availability of goods and services.

3. The rate of natural increase is the crude birth rate minus the crude death rate. Having a negative rate of natural increase translates to the death rate being higher than the birth rate in a population. This means that, assuming no immigration or emigration, the population will shrink at a rate of 4.93 percent per year.

12. Disparities in Health and Healthcare

1. Asian-Americans have the best health profiles of the group, followed by white Americans. African-Americans have the worst health profiles of the three. Specifically, Asian-Americans have lower mortality rates associated with cancer, heart disease, and diabetes and lower infant mortality rates than other populations. African-Americans, on the other hand, have higher mortality rates linked to cancer, heart disease, diabetes, drug and alcohol use, and HIV/AIDS and higher infant mortality rates than other populations.

2. It has been shown that preferential treatment often arises from in-group associations. The female in this story is part of the in-group because she knows everyone in the town—most importantly, the doctors and nurses who will be involved in her healthcare. The male, on the other hand, is part of an out-group, and thus, despite having more severe symptoms and spending a longer time in the waiting room or triage, still waits longer to receive healthcare services.

3. While it is expected that high-income females are more likely to visit the doctor and have better access to healthcare, obesity is potentially a factor in this case. Stephanie's body mass index puts her in the obese range (over 30). Obesity bias is an identified issue in healthcare. Obese patients are more likely to change doctors, and they report lower levels of trust in their primary care physicians. Doctors are also less likely to recommend effective weight-loss programs to obese patients, sometimes on the basis of the flawed assumption that obese patients lack the willpower to effectively lose weight. Obese patients are also less likely to be offered quality preventative care and screenings.

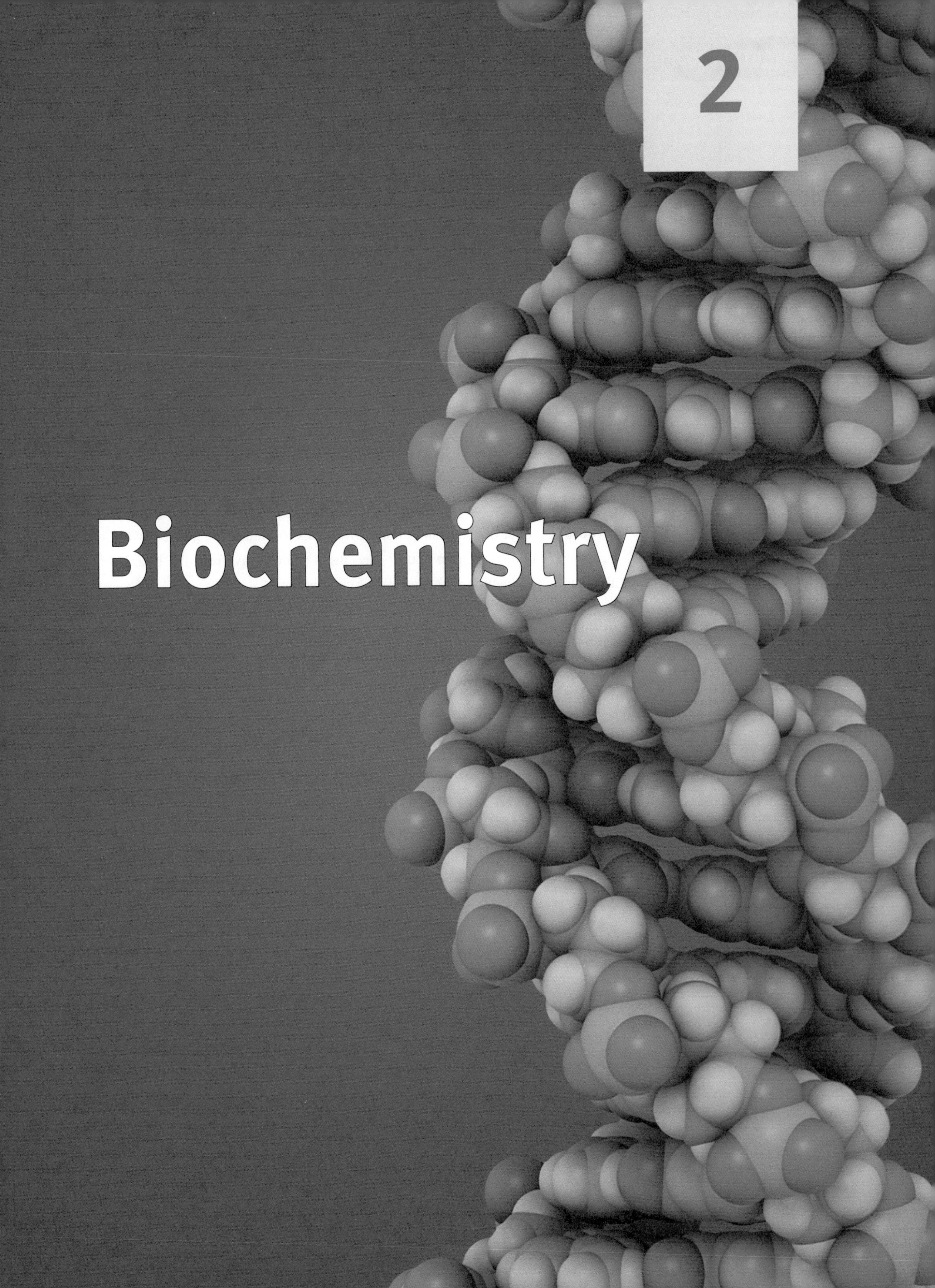

2

Biochemistry

Key Concepts

Biochemistry Chapter 1

Peptide structure
α-Helices
β-Pleated sheets
Proteases

Elements of Peptide Structure

Creutzfeldt–Jakob disease is a neurodegenerative disorder caused by a prion protein. This prion protein induces a change in secondary protein structure from α-helices to β-pleated sheets. What are possible biochemical consequences of this change in secondary protein structure?

1 Identify the characteristics of α-helices and β-pleated sheets.

α-Helices are rodlike structures in which the peptide chain coils clockwise about a central axis. The helix is stabilized by intramolecular hydrogen bonding that occurs between carboxyl oxygens and amino hydrogens located four residues away from each other. Typically, amino acid side chains point away from the helix's core, allowing for interaction with the cellular environment.

In β-pleated sheets, the peptide chains form rows that are held together by intramolecular hydrogen bonding that occurs between the carboxyl oxygen on one peptide chain and the amino hydrogen on another. Pleating maximizes hydrogen bonding in the structure.

2 Determine how structure affects function.

The structural properties of a peptide affect its function. After analyzing the structure of the protein, determine how each feature may affect the chemical properties of the protein. α-Helical structure involves extension of hydrophilic side chains away from the core of the protein toward the aqueous environment of the cell. β-Pleated sheets are less likely to assume this sort of confirmation; however, one side of the β-pleated sheet may contain hydrophobic side chains, while the other may be hydrophilic.

If we wanted to determine how structure affects protein degradation, we would need to compare the ease with which enzymes could access the amide bonds in each conformation. α-Helices are strandlike structures, while β-pleated sheets are more flat. An α-helix is more easily degraded because its peptide bonds are more accessible to *peptidases*—enzymes that cleave peptide bonds. On the other hand, β-pleated sheets are more stable and expose far fewer residues to the cellular environment.

 Predict how changing a protein from an α-helix to a β-pleated sheet may affect the organism.

Prions convert proteins from a more soluble, easily degraded α-helical conformation to a less soluble, more difficult to degrade β-pleated sheet conformation. Insoluble proteins that cannot be degraded will eventually build up and form plaques, which can lead to loss of cell function and ultimately cell death. As cells die, aberrant proteins may be left behind, resulting in pockets of protein within tissues, and complete loss of function of cells, tissues, and even whole organs.

Takeaways

α-Helices create proteins that are more strandlike, more soluble, and easier to degrade. β-Pleated sheets create proteins that are flatter, less soluble, and more stable (harder to degrade).

Things to Watch Out For

Many questions on the MCAT integrate knowledge from multiple science areas. While the focus in this question was on the biochemistry of prion diseases, other questions could focus on the fact that they can be genetically inherited or can be spread as an infectious disease.

Related Questions

1. A point mutation changes a cysteine residue to an alanine residue. How might this affect protein structure?
2. A protein is treated with a 6 *M* solution of hydrochloric acid. What levels of protein structure are most likely disrupted by treatment with this solution?
3. A point mutation causes a single leucine residue to be substituted for an isoleucine residue in the transmembrane section of a G protein-coupled receptor. How might this change affect overall protein structure and function?

Key Concepts

Biochemistry Chapter 2

Enzyme activity

K_m

v_{max}

Competitive inhibitors

Lineweaver–Burk plots

Lineweaver–Burk Plots

A Lineweaver–Burk plot of *HMG-CoA reductase*, the rate-limiting enzyme of cholesterol synthesis, is shown below. Statins, such as atorvastatin (Lipitor), simvastatin (Zocor), and rosuvastatin (Crestor), are routinely used to treat patients with high cholesterol because they are competitive inhibitors of HMG-CoA reductase. How would use of a statin affect the Lineweaver–Burk plot?

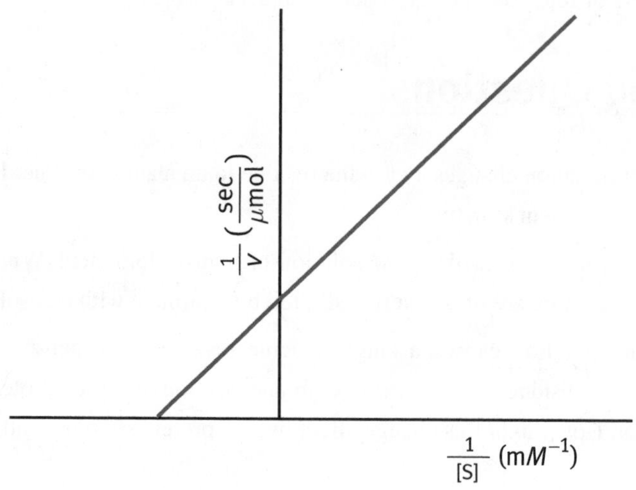

1 Analyze the axes and intercepts of the plot.

The first step for any question involving a graph on Test Day is to analyze the axes. Lineweaver–Burk plots measure reaction rate as a function of the concentration of substrate available to bind to the enzyme. In this case, the *y*-axis represents the reciprocal of the velocity or reaction rate, $\frac{1}{v}$, and the *x*-axis represents the reciprocal of substrate concentration, $\frac{1}{[S]}$. This is why Lineweaver–Burk plots are sometimes called double reciprocal plots.

The *y*-intercept is the reciprocal of the enzyme velocity when $\frac{1}{[S]} = 0$. If $\frac{1}{[S]} = 0$, then $[S] = \infty$. The enzyme velocity when [S] is infinitely large is termed the maximal velocity, v_{max}; therefore, the *y*-intercept corresponds to $\frac{1}{v_{max}}$. The *x*-intercept in a Lineweaver–Burk plot corresponds to $-\frac{1}{K_m}$. While this information can be extrapolated from the plot data on Test Day, it is easier and faster to memorize these intercepts.

2 Determine the effect of a competitive inhibitor on v_{max}.

Competitive inhibitors compete with the substrate for binding to the active site of an enzyme. The presence of these inhibitors results in fewer active sites being available to act on the substrate, resulting in decreased enzyme activity. Competitive inhibition can be overcome by increasing the substrate concentration. Excess substrate can outcompete the competitive inhibitor, allowing the enzyme to regain v_{max}. Therefore, while it may take more substrate to reach v_{max}, the value of v_{max} itself does not change.

3 Determine the effect of a competitive inhibitor on K_m.

The Michaelis constant, K_m, is defined as the substrate concentration at which enzyme velocity equals half of v_{max} or $\frac{v_{max}}{2}$. In competitive inhibition, v_{max} is unchanged, while K_m is increased. As described in the previous step, increasing the substrate concentration allows the substrate to outcompete the inhibitor and the enzyme can regain the same maximal velocity. However, because a higher concentration of substrate is necessary to reach the same v_{max}, the K_m of the enzyme will also increase. K_m can be thought of as a measure of the affinity between an enzyme and its substrate; a higher K_m indicates decreased affinity between an enzyme and its substrate, as would be expected in the presence of a competitive inhibitor.

Takeaways

Competitive inhibitors occupy the active site of an enzyme, but the binding of the inhibitor can be reversed if the substrate concentration is high enough. Competitive inhibition does not change v_{max}, but does increase K_m (the substrate concentration needed to achieve half-maximal velocity).

4 Predict the graphical changes in the Lineweaver–Burk plot.

In the presence of a competitive inhibitor, v_{max} is unchanged. The y-intercept of the Lineweaver–Burk plot corresponds to $\frac{1}{v_{max}}$, so there is no change expected in the y-intercept.

In the presence of a competitive inhibitor, K_m increases. The x-intercept of the Lineweaver–Burk plot corresponds to $-\frac{1}{K_m}$; therefore, an increase in K_m indicates a decrease in the magnitude of $-\frac{1}{K_m}$, resulting in the x-intercept moving closer to the origin. This can be seen in the diagram below that compares the Lineweaver–Burk plot of an enzyme in the absence of inhibitor with an enzyme in the presence of inhibitor:

Things to Watch Out For

K_m can be easily misinterpreted. Because it is the concentration at which half-maximal velocity is reached, an increase in K_m can indicate an inefficient enzyme, the presence of an inhibitor, or a decrease in the affinity of the enzyme for its substrate.

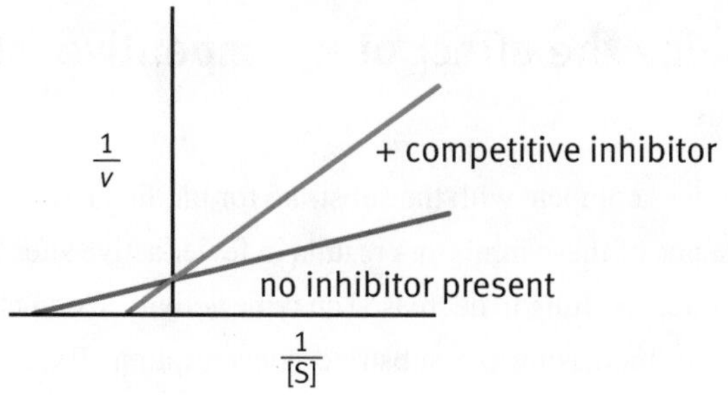

Related Questions

1. How would the Lineweaver–Burk plot change in the presence of a noncompetitive inhibitor?
2. How would the Lineweaver–Burk plot change in the presence of an uncompetitive inhibitor?
3. If the information in the HMG-CoA reductase experiment had been represented as a Michaelis–Menten plot instead of a Lineweaver–Burk plot, what changes would be observed in the presence of a competitive inhibitor?

High-Yield Problem-Solving Guide questions continue on the next page. ▶ ▶ ▶

Key Concepts

Biochemistry Chapter 3

Isoelectric focusing
Determining isoelectric point
Electrolytic cells
Amino acids

Isoelectric Focusing

A biochemist is trying to separate glycine, glutamic acid, and lysine given the following information:

	$pK_{a,COOH\ group}$	$pK_{a,NH_3^+\ group}$	$pK_{a,R\ group}$
Glycine	2.34	9.60	—
Glutamic acid	2.19	9.67	4.25
Lysine	2.18	8.95	10.53

The three points below indicate where the three amino acids stopped migrating in the gel. Which point corresponds to each amino acid?

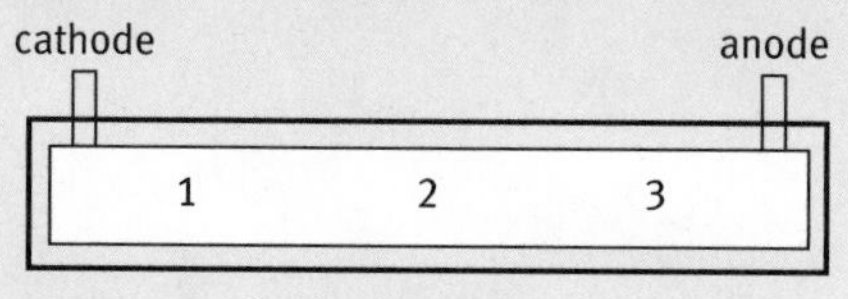

1 Identify if it is an isoelectric focusing problem.

Whenever a question gives you the pK_a of the substance being purified, think ion-exchange chromatography or isoelectric focusing. In the above question, we can be certain that isoelectric focusing is used because the separatory apparatus has a cathode and an anode and because we're told that each amino acid will eventually stop migrating through the gel.

2 Determine the isoelectric points of the samples.

To find the pI for an amino acid, identify the deprotonation reaction that converts the amino acid with a +1 overall charge into a zwitterion with 0 overall charge; also, identify the deprotonation reaction that converts the zwitterion into a form with a –1 overall charge. The pI for the amino acid is the average of the pK_a values for these two reactions.

For glycine, the sequence of deprotonation reactions is the following:

$$NH_3^+-\underset{H}{\overset{R}{C}}-COOH \underset{}{\overset{pK_{a1}=2.34}{\rightleftharpoons}} NH_3^+-\underset{H}{\overset{R}{C}}-COO^- \overset{pK_{a2}=9.60}{\rightleftharpoons} NH_2-\underset{H}{\overset{R}{C}}-COO^-$$

The pK_a values for the reactions leading to and from the zwitterionic form of glycine are p$K_{a,\text{COOH group}}$ and p$K_{a,NH_3^+\text{ group}}$ in the table given in the question. Hence, the pI for glycine is the average of these two pK_a values:

$$pI_{glycine} = \frac{2.34 + 9.60}{2} = 5.97$$

For glutamic acid, the sequence of deprotonation reactions is the following:

$$NH_3^+-\underset{H}{\overset{RH}{C}}-COOH \overset{pK_{a1}=2.19}{\rightleftharpoons} NH_3^+-\underset{H}{\overset{RH}{C}}-COO^- \overset{pK_{a2}=4.25}{\rightleftharpoons} NH_3^+-\underset{H}{\overset{R^-}{C}}-COO^- \overset{pK_{a3}=9.67}{\rightleftharpoons} NH_2-\underset{H}{\overset{R^-}{C}}-COO^-$$

Glutamic acid has an acidic side chain, so there is an extra reaction corresponding to its deprotonation. The pK_a values for the reactions leading to and from the zwitterionic form of glutamic acid are p$K_{a,\text{COOH group}}$ and p$K_{a,\text{R group}}$ in the table given in the question. Hence, the pI for glutamic acid is the average of these two pK_a values:

$$pI_{glutamic\ acid} = \frac{2.19 + 4.25}{2} = 3.22$$

For lysine, the sequence of deprotonation reactions is the following:

$$NH_3^+-\underset{H}{\overset{RH^+}{C}}-COOH \overset{pK_{a1}=2.18}{\rightleftharpoons} NH_3^+-\underset{H}{\overset{RH^+}{C}}-COO^- \overset{pK_{a2}=8.95}{\rightleftharpoons} NH_2-\underset{H}{\overset{RH^+}{C}}-COO^- \overset{pK_{a3}=10.53}{\rightleftharpoons} NH_2-\underset{H}{\overset{R}{C}}-COO^-$$

Lysine has a basic side chain, so there is an extra reaction corresponding to its deprotonation. The pK_a values for the reactions leading to and from the zwitterionic form of lysine are p$K_{a,NH_3^+\text{ group}}$ and p$K_{a,\text{R group}}$ in the table given in the question. Hence, the pI for lysine is the average of these two pK_a values:

$$pI_{lysinne} = \frac{8.95 + 10.53}{2} = 9.74$$

3 Determine the relative pH gradient of the gel.

Electrophoresis is always run in an electrolytic cell. Recall that electrolytic cells require an outside source of energy. The negative terminal is connected to the cathode, and the positive end is connected to the anode. This means that the anode (acidic end of the gel) will attract negative anions and the cathode (basic end of the gel) will attract positive cations.

By extension, we know that zone 1 is at a higher pH than zone 2, which is at a higher pH than zone 3.

Takeaways

To solve isoelectric focusing questions, determine the pI of the samples being separated. Then, determine the orientation of the pH gradient in the gel. As a rule of thumb, **a**nions are attracted to the **a**node, which is in the **a**cidic part of the gel.

Things to Watch Out For

Be careful with problems that ask you to separate proteins. Remember that the pI of a protein cannot be determined simply by averaging the pI values of the individual amino acids. If the isoelectric point of a protein is not given, then another method must be used to separate the proteins.

 Determine where the samples will migrate.

Amino acids will migrate toward their pI. At the pI, the amino acid will have zero net charge because it will be in its zwitterionic form and it will stop migrating. In this question, lysine will migrate to region 1, glycine will migrate to region 2, and glutamic acid will migrate to region 3.

Related Questions

1. If a polypeptide with a pI of 6.7 is subjected to electrophoresis at pH 5, will the segment move toward the anode or cathode?
2. Why does an amino acid stop migrating when it reaches the part of the gel with a pH equal to its pI?
3. If the pH gradient of the gel were reversed relative to the electrodes, what would happen during the separation of these amino acids?

High-Yield Problem-Solving Guide questions continue on the next page. ▶ ▶ ▶

Key Concepts

Biochemistry Chapter 4

Fischer projections
Carbohydrate structure
Carbohydrate terminology
Stereoisomers
Chiral centers

Isomerism in Carbohydrates

What is the relationship between the two structures presented below?

CHO
H—OH
H—OH
H—OH
CH_2OH

CHO
HO—H
H—OH
H—OH
CH_2OH

1 Describe structural similarities.

Start by carefully analyzing each carbohydrate molecule, taking note of similarities between the structures. Both structures are aldoses that contain five carbon atoms and are therefore termed aldopentoses. The highest-numbered chiral carbon (located farthest from the carbonyl group) contains a hydroxyl group (–OH) pointing to the right in the Fischer projection, making the configuration D for both sugars. Remember that while D- and L-isomers of the same sugar are enantiomers, this nomenclature is relative to the stereochemistry of the highest-numbered chiral carbon in glyceraldehyde, and has no automatic correlation to the direction of rotation of plane-polarized light.

2 Determine structural differences.

The only difference between the structures is the configuration of C-2. In the first structure, the –OH group points to the right, giving this carbon an (*R*) configuration, while the –OH group points to the left in the second structure, giving this carbon an (*S*) configuration.

3 Choose the appropriate terminology to describe this difference between the sugar molecules.

When describing the isomerism of sugars, there are a few words we could use to describe differences between stereoisomers. We already discussed enantiomerism in Step 1; enantiomers differ in configuration at all chiral carbons and are nonsuperimposable mirror images of each other. These two sugars are not enantiomers because they differ at only one of their three chiral carbons.

Isomers that differ at some—but not all—chiral centers are considered diastereomers. While this term would be an appropriate choice to describe the differences between these sugars, the MCAT tends to choose the most specific term possible to describe isomers. Epimers are diastereomers that differ at exactly one chiral carbon and can be named based on this carbon; these two molecules could be called C-2 epimers of each other.

Finally, anomers are a subtype of epimers in which the chiral center that differs between the two sugars is the anomeric carbon (the chiral center that is created by ring closure of the sugar, in which one of the hydroxyl groups attacks the carbonyl carbon in a nucleophilic addition reaction). These molecules cannot be considered anomers of each other because they are in their straight-chain forms.

Thus, these molecules are epimers, a subtype of diastereomers. These structures are D-ribose (on the left) and D-arabinose (on the right).

Takeaways

Carbohydrate isomerism utilizes unique terminology. On Test Day, you must be familiar with the specific vocabulary associated with carbohydrates (aldose, ketose, furanose, pyranose, epimer, anomer, and so on).

Things to Watch Out For

Take the time to identify the distinguishing characteristics of each sugar structure. Checking the relative (*not* absolute) configurations of each chiral carbon can prevent you from missing important details.

Related Questions

1. Mutarotation is the interconversion between the α- and β-cyclic forms of a sugar. In solution, the α and β forms are in equilibrium. What is the term that describes the relationship between these two sugars?
2. Cellulose is created from β-D-glucopyranose, while glycogen is created from α-D-glucopyranose. Human digestive enzymes cannot break down cellulose while glycogen is readily degraded to release glucose. What accounts for this difference?
3. Identify the pairs of epimers and their relationships in the set of molecules below:

CH_2OH
C=O
HO—H
H—OH
H—OH
CH_2OH

D-fructose

CHO
H—OH
HO—H
H—OH
H—OH
CH_2OH

D-glucose

CHO
H—OH
HO—H
HO—H
H—OH
CH_2OH

D-galactose

CHO
HO—H
HO—H
H—OH
H—OH
CH_2OH

D-mannose

Key Concepts

Biochemistry Chapter 5

Saponification
Triacylglycerols
Enzymatic cleavage
Anions and cations

Lipid Saponification

Inflammation of the pancreas, or pancreatitis, occurs due to premature activation of digestive enzymes in the pancreas. Hypocalcemia, or lowered blood calcium concentration, may result from lipase hydrolysis of triacylglycerols in areas surrounding the pancreas. What is the most likely mechanism by which this hypocalcemia occurs?

 Simplify the question.

Some questions on Test Day may appear very complex, and it may even seem that there is not enough information provided. However, simplifying and rewording the question may turn a difficult-appearing question into a much simpler one. The question stem states that *lipase* cleaves triacylglycerols, resulting in a lowered calcium concentration in the blood. A simpler form of this question might be: *What are the products of triacylglycerol hydrolysis and why do these products lower blood calcium?*

 Determine the products of triacylglycerol hydrolysis by lipase.

Enzyme names are one of the many areas of biochemistry in which nomenclature is helpful. Enzymes are generally named after their substrates or main functions. In this case, the name *lipase* implies that the substrate is fat (*lip–*); *–ase* is a suffix identifying the entity as an enzyme.

Human *pancreatic lipase* digests triacylglycerols to form two free fatty acid molecules and one molecule of 2-monoacylglycerol. Like the pancreatic proteases (*trypsin*, *chymotrypsin*, and *carboxypeptidases* A and *B*), pancreatic lipase is secreted as a zymogen—a proenzyme that must be activated to carry out its function. This is mostly a protective function; digestive enzymes cannot differentiate between self and nonself, thus pancreatic lipase is only activated once it reaches the duodenum, preventing autodigestion of the pancreas. Not all of these details are absolutely necessary to answer the question. The most important thing to note about lipase is its main function: that it causes the release of free fatty acids from dietary triacylglycerols.

3 Identify what product is capable of binding to calcium.

Calcium is a Group IIA (Group 2) alkaline earth metal; as such, it normally exists in compounds or as a +2 cation. If calcium is being pulled from the bloodstream, it is most likely forming an ionic bond with one of the products of saponification. Therefore, let's determine if one of the products is negatively charged.

Water is required in the hydrolysis of triacylglycerols by pancreatic lipase. The water can protonate the hydroxyl groups of glycerol once the free fatty acids are released, as well as the hydroxyl group within the carboxyl moiety of the free fatty acid itself. However, this reaction takes place within the alkaline environment of the pancreas (pH $\approx$ 8.5), which normally releases bicarbonate to neutralize the acidic chyme dumped into the duodenum by the stomach. Thus, this reaction does not take place in an environment that favors the protonation of these compounds. The stronger acid between glycerol and the free fatty acids will be more easily deprotonated, and will exist in a negatively charged form.

Fatty acids contain a carboxylic acid group, the pK_a of which is usually around 4. Glycerol contains alcohols, the pK_a values of which are usually around 17. While it is not necessary to have memorized the various pK_a values of the different functional groups, you should recognize that a carboxylic acid is generally much more acidic than an alcohol.

Therefore, we would expect that most of the free fatty acid molecules would exist in a negatively charged state. Calcium ions are positively charged and will react with fatty acids to form a chalky white substance. This is an example of saponification, which is essentially the hydrolysis of triacylglycerols followed by binding of a cation to the free fatty acids.

Takeaways

Saponification does not always involve sodium hydroxide, although NaOH and KOH are frequently used for this reaction. Saponification is a general term for soap-making, in which an amphipathic carboxylate group is bound to cations after hydrolyzing a lipid ester to form a polyol and free fatty acids.

Things to Watch Out For

Many questions are interdisciplinary and require diverse knowledge in multiple areas. In this particular example, it is necessary to understand biochemistry (lipid structure), biology (the digestive system), general chemistry (group trends), and organic chemistry (functional groups' p*Ka* values). Expect that the MCAT will ask some questions asking you to bring together multiple content areas.

Related Questions

1. Common household soap is produced by reacting a fat or oil with a base to form sodium or potassium salts of long-chain fatty acids. When used in hard water, which contains high concentrations of mineral salts, a precipitate may form that is difficult to remove. What is this precipitate, and what other conditions might reduce the effectiveness of soap?
2. Adipocere, or grave wax, will form on a dead body buried in cold, humid, and low-oxygen conditions. What is likely to account for the formation of adipocere?
3. What would result following treatment of a triacylglycerol with a strong acid rather than a base? Could this result in saponification?

Key Concepts

Biochemistry Chapter 6

Semiconservative replication
DNA
DNA replication
Polymerase chain reaction

DNA Replication

The following molecule of DNA is replicated using two cycles of PCR in the presence of ^{15}N-labeled guanine. What percentage of the DNA strands will contain the labeled guanine in both strands (sense and antisense strands)?

5′—CATACTGATCATCTAGCGTATGCGT—3′

3′—GTATGACTAGTAGATCGCATACGCA—5′

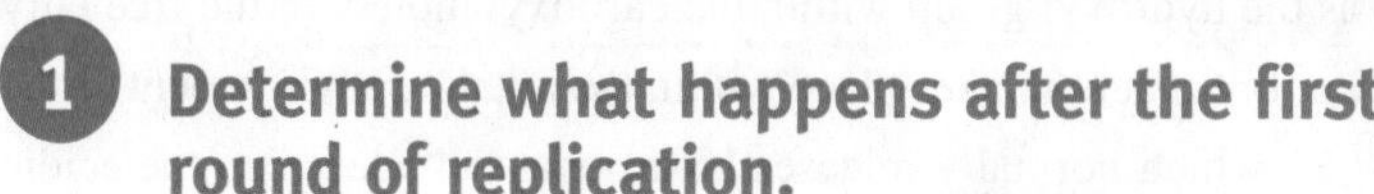

1 Determine what happens after the first round of replication.

DNA replication is semiconservative, which means that for each of the two original strands of DNA, one new strand of DNA is synthesized as its complement.

Our templates for this first round of replication are these strands:

5′—CATACTGATCATCTAGCGTATGCGT—3′

3′—GTATGACTAGTAGATCGCATACGCA—5′

Neither of these original strands contains the labeled guanine. Hence, the first round of replication gives us these two DNA molecules:

5′—CATACTGATCATCTAGCGTATGCGT—3′

3′—GTATGACTAGTAGATCGCATACGCA—5′

and

5′—CATACTGATCATCTAGCGTATGCGT—3′

3′—GTATGACTAGTAGATCGCATACGCA—5′

where G represents ^{15}N-labeled guanine.

The original strand with the 5′ to 3′ polarity at the site of replication will be the lagging strand because nucleotides can only be added in the 5′ to 3′ direction. *Primase* lays down a short RNA primer to which *DNA polymerase* can bind; as the replication fork moves down the DNA molecule, more single-stranded DNA is exposed and additional primers are laid down to fill in the opened space. Thus, the lagging strand is synthesized in short fragments (called Okazaki fragments). The RNA primers are subsequently replaced with DNA before *ligase* joins the short fragments together. This process allows the lagging strand's production to follow the replication fork. This is not a concern for the leading strand, which can synthesize a continuous strand of DNA after one primer is laid down.

2 Determine what happens after the second round of replication.

Our templates for the second round of replication are as follows:

5′—CATACTGATCATCTAGCGTATGCGT—3′

3′—GTATGACTAGTAGATCGCATACGCA—5′

and

5′—CATACTGATCATCTAGCGTATGCGT—3′

3′—GTATGACTAGTAGATCGCATACGCA—5′

Hence, the second round of replication gives us these four DNA molecules:

5′—CATACTGATCATCTAGCGTATGCGT—3′

3′—GTATGACTAGTAGATCGCATACGCA—5′

and

5′—CATACTGATCATCTAGCGTATGCGT—3′

3′—GTATGACTAGTAGATCGCATACGCA—5′

and

5′—CATACTGATCATCTAGCGTATGCGT—3′

3′—GTATGACTAGTAGATCGCATACGCA—5′

and

5′—CATACTGATCATCTAGCGTATGCGT—3′

3′—GTATGACTAGTAGATCGCATACGCA—5′

where G again represents ^{15}N-labeled guanine.

In the second round of replication, the strands resulting from the first round of replication are used as templates to create new DNA strands.

Determine the percentage of DNA molecules that only have ^{15}N-labeled guanine.

After two rounds of replication, two double-stranded DNA molecules have both strands labeled with the ^{15}N-labeled guanine, whereas the other two double strands of DNA still maintain one original strand. Thus, of the double-stranded DNA molecules, 50 percent will have both strands with the ^{15}N-labeled guanine.

Takeaways

DNA replication is semiconservative. The newly synthesized strand of DNA will be identical to the old complementary strand, provided that there are no mutations.

Things to Watch Out For

Be careful in noting the polarity of the strands. Remember that DNA is always synthesized in the 5′ to 3′ direction.

Related Questions

1. Polymerase chain reaction, or PCR, may be performed to amplify small samples of DNA for analysis. In PCR, a sample is denatured with heat, replicated, and then cooled to reanneal the strands. The strands undergo this process several times to rapidly increase the amount of sample available for biochemical testing. The DNA polymerase used for this process is *not* generally human DNA polymerase, but that of *T. aquaticus*, a bacterium. Why is human DNA polymerase NOT used for PCR?
2. Which strand is more prone to mutations, the leading strand or the lagging strand?
3. A molecule of DNA is replicated using three cycles of PCR in the presence of ^{15}N-labeled adenine. How many of the newly formed DNA molecules will contain at least one unlabeled strand?

High-Yield Problem-Solving Guide questions continue on the next page. ▶ ▶ ▶

Key Concepts

Biochemistry Chapter 7

Operons
Gene expression in prokaryotes
Inducible systems
Repressible systems

Operons

> Prokaryotes often use operons to control gene expression. The *lac* operon, present in prokaryotes, has been studied extensively. In the presence of lactose and the absence of glucose, how are the appropriate genes induced? What happens when lactose levels fall and glucose levels rise?

Identify the role of the *lac* operon.

Operons are functional units found in bacterial chromosomes and include structural genes that can code for cellular proteins such as enzymes. In addition, a typical operon also contains a promoter, an operator region, and a regulatory gene. The promoter is the site at which *RNA polymerase* binds. The operator serves as the binding site for the repressor protein encoded by the regulatory gene. All of the genes within the operon are controlled by this unique mechanism. When the repressor binds to the operator region, the polymerase is blocked and transcription does not occur.

The *lac* operon is a prototypical inducible system. The genes in the *lac* operon regulate enzymes needed to break down lactose in prokaryotes. Gene transcription is a significant energy cost for an organism. In order to prevent wasteful use of energy, inducible systems allow for the transcription of genes only when they are beneficial in the current environment. The *lac* operon, in particular, allows for transcription of genes essential to the digestion of lactose when glucose is not present.

2 Recall the function of the *lac* operon.

As mentioned above, the *lac* operon is an inducible system that encodes genes used in the digestion of lactose. The repressor protein is normally bound to the operator region, preventing transcription. When the disaccharide lactose enters the cell, it binds to the repressor. This binding is considered a form of allosteric regulation. The binding of lactose causes a conformational change, resulting in dissociation of the repressor from the operator DNA sequence, making those genes available for transcription. However, this is not the end of the story—there has to be something that attracts RNA polymerase to the site to transcribe those genes.

 Determine the process by which these genes are transcribed.

Once the repressor has been unbound from the operator region, the normal process of gene transcription can occur. However, it is important to recognize that transcription of the genes for lactose digestion require both the presence of lactose *and* the absence of glucose.

If the promoter sequence varies from the consensus sequence, then RNA polymerase will not bind tightly without help. The solution to this problem is the catabolite activator protein (CAP), which is present when glucose levels are low. In the absence of glucose, *adenylate cyclase* is also active and produces cAMP. CAP binds cAMP, and this complex binds to the CAP-binding site located just before the promoter region. Once bound, the complex helps recruit RNA polymerase, which can then start transcribing the genes for lactose digestion.

It is not necessary to know all of these details to answer this question; the important point to note is that the transcription of the genes for lactose digestion requires not only that lactose is *present*, but also that glucose is *absent*.

Takeaways

Operons are complex systems used to control gene transcription. Inducible systems allow for the transcription of genes as needed for survival.

 Predict what happens when lactose levels fall and glucose levels rise.

As lactose levels fall, lactose will dissociate from the repressor, which then binds to the operator region. The presence or absence of glucose also affects the intracellular concentration of cyclic AMP (cAMP) because catabolites of glucose will inhibit adenylate cyclase and inhibit the production of cAMP. Without cAMP, the cell cannot transcribe the genes needed to metabolize lactose, even when lactose is present. This results in the preferential use of glucose. Both of these conditions help to decrease the production of the enzymes required for lactose digestion.

Things to Watch Out For

Avoid making the question more complicated than it is. While we covered additional details about the *lac* operon in this explanation, the key point is that operons have multiple parts that each serves a specific function. Operons are complex, but can be broken down into simpler pieces.

Related Questions

1. What happens to the *lac* operon in the presence of both lactose and glucose?
2. What is the difference between an inducible system and a repressible system?
3. The *trp* operon governs the synthesis of tryptophan by prokaryotes. In a tryptophan-poor medium, what is the process by which the genes for tryptophan synthesis can be turned on?

Key Concepts

Biochemistry Chapter 8

Tonicity

Concentration gradients

Sodium–potassium pump

Osmosis

Membrane Traffic

The sodium–potassium pump is an ATPase that pumps 3 Na^+ out of the cell and 2 K^+ into the cell for each ATP hydrolyzed. Cells can use the pump to help maintain cell volume. What would most likely happen to the rate of ATP consumption if a cell were moved to a hypertonic environment?

Determine the relationship between the two solutions to predict the flow of water.

When an environment is described as hypertonic, it means that the environment is more concentrated than the cell is. Note that you can also express this condition by stating that the cell is hypotonic to the environment. A hypotonic solution is one that is less concentrated than the solution to which it is being compared:

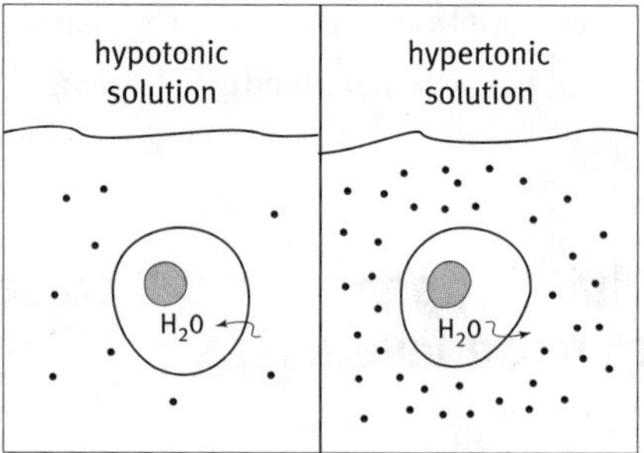

The cell is being moved into a hypertonic environment, which means that the environment is more concentrated with solutes than the interior of the cell is. Water will naturally flow from the hypotonic environment to the hypertonic environment across a semipermeable membrane; thus, we can predict that water will flow out of the cell.

Given the flow of water, determine how the cell might regulate the sodium–potassium pump to maintain homeostasis.

Without any compensation, water will flow out of the cell, decreasing cell volume. The sodium–potassium pump moves two potassium ions into the cell as it moves three sodium ions out of the cell. The net effect of the pump is to decrease cell solute concentration by one ion per ATP hydrolyzed. Therefore, to counter the efflux of water from the cell, the sodium–potassium pump can be downregulated. This would decrease the number of ions leaving the cell; because water follows dissolved solutes, less water would leave the cell accordingly:

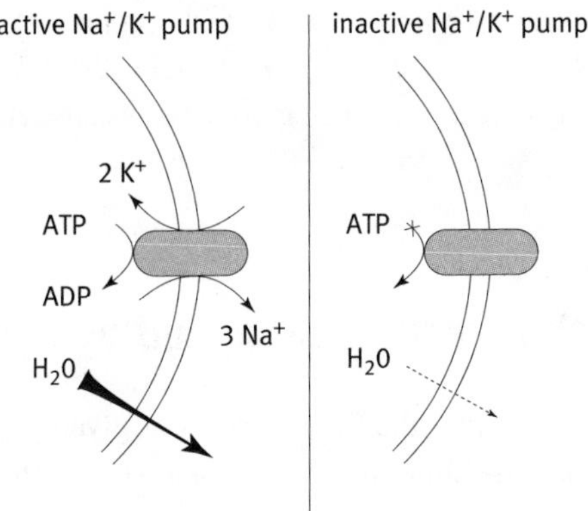

Thus, when brought into a hypertonic environment, we would expect that the cell would decrease the rate of ATP consumption to maintain a constant volume. If the cell were brought into a hypotonic environment, the opposite trend would be observed.

Related Questions

1. Antidiuretic hormone (ADH) directly increases the ability of the blood to reabsorb water from the nephron. If an individual's blood becomes hypotonic with respect to the filtrate, would ADH secretion increase or decrease?
2. The reabsorption of water from the filtrate increases as the concentration of the interstitial fluid increases. Using the terms *hypertonic* and *hypo-osmotic*, describe the relationship between the interstitial fluid and the filtrate as well as the relationship between the filtrate and the interstitial fluid.
3. Alcohol and caffeine block the activity of ADH, a hormone that increases the ability of the blood to reabsorb water from the filtrate. An individual drinks a large cup of coffee in the morning and, when he goes to the restroom, finds that his urine is nearly colorless. Was the urine produced hypotonic, isotonic, or hypertonic to the blood?

Takeaways

Questions that involve osmosis are usually combined with other biology topics (particularly renal physiology), general chemistry topics (colligative properties), or biochemistry topics (membrane transporters) to necessitate multistep solutions. The key is to have a solid understanding of what the terms hypertonic and hypotonic mean and to be able to apply them to situations correctly.

Things to Watch Out For

Some students presume that the scenario presented will eventually return to equilibrium and may predict that ATP consumption will decrease and then increase again. However, the question stem does not guarantee a return to equilibrium. Be wary of trying to read too much into the question.

Key Concepts

Biochemistry Chapter 9

Glycolysis
Substrate-level phosphorylation
Red blood cells
ATP

Glycolysis

> Pyruvate kinase deficiency is a partial enzyme defect that often results in anemia caused by a decrease in the integrity of red blood cells. What is the purpose of this enzyme and why does a deficiency in its activity cause anemia?

 Identify the reaction catalyzed by pyruvate kinase.

Pyruvate kinase (PK) catalyzes the final reaction of glycolysis. While the focus in this question is on PK, remember that the other high-yield glycolytic enzymes to remember for Test Day are *hexokinase/glucokinase*, *phosphofructokinase-1* and *-2*, *glyceraldehyde-3-phosphate dehydrogenase*, and *3-phosphoglycerate kinase*.

Pyruvate kinase is a notable enzyme for three reasons. First, it catalyzes the formation of pyruvate from phosphoenolpyruvate (PEP) during the final reaction of glycolysis. Second, this reaction is one of the substrate-level phosphorylation steps during glycolysis, generating ATP from ADP and an inorganic phosphate. Because glucose is split into two three-carbon molecules during glycolysis, the conversion of PEP to pyruvate occurs twice for every glucose molecule and results in 2 ATP. Finally, this reaction catalyzed by pyruvate kinase is one of the irreversible reactions of glycolysis. Thus, pyruvate kinase cannot be used to generate PEP from pyruvate—this conversion requires *pyruvate carboxylase* and *phosphoenolpyruvate carboxykinase* (PEPCK) during gluconeogenesis.

 Determine the effect of the inability to form pyruvate.

If an individual has a partial enzyme defect of pyruvate kinase, then significantly less pyruvate will be generated during glycolysis. Pyruvate kinase deficiency is the only common partial enzyme defect of glycolysis and is caused by a mutation in the *PKLR* gene. A variety of mutations in this gene can all cause reduced function of the pyruvate kinase enzyme. The *PKLR* gene produces an isoform of pyruvate kinase in various body tissues—most notably, the liver and red blood cells. Logically, these cells with reduced pyruvate kinase activity produce less pyruvate. In addition, because one of the substrate-level phosphorylation steps is lost, the net production of ATP per molecule of glucose drops from two to zero. In most cell types, this would mean that glucose could not be processed, but there would be little impact on the β-oxidation of fatty acids and other energy-producing pathways.

Consider why the lack of pyruvate kinase would be so detrimental to red blood cells in particular.

The question tells us that a person with pyruvate kinase deficiency often has anemia due to a decrease in the integrity of red blood cells. Why might this be? Mature erythrocytes lack mitochondria and rely solely on glycolysis for ATP production. In the absence of pyruvate kinase, red blood cells have little energy available for necessary processes such as membrane maintenance, leading to changes in cell shape. Ultimately, these misshapen cells are phagocytized by macrophages in the spleen. This premature destruction of red blood cells results in a shortage of red blood cells, or anemia. This anemia is exacerbated by the fact that some red blood cells may lyse within the vasculature because they cannot use the sodium–potassium pump to maintain cell volume effectively. Chronic hemolytic anemia also results in splenomegaly, or an enlarged spleen, excess iron in the bloodstream, and reduced oxygen transport.

Takeaways

Pyruvate kinase is an essential enzyme for red blood cells in particular. Biochemical pathways do not occur in isolation; each aberration in a pathway may have far-reaching consequences for the organism as a whole.

Things to Watch Out For

Many students, upon seeing this question, will recognize the red blood cell will have difficulty making pyruvate; however, it is important to go one step further to determine the real reason why this is uniquely such a problem for the red blood cell.

Related Questions

1. Which step(s) in glycolysis require an *input* of ATP?
2. Which step(s) in glycolysis *produce* ATP?
3. Which step(s) in glycolysis catalyze the reduction of NAD^+?

Key Concepts

Biochemistry Chapter 10

Electron transport chain
Oxidative phosphorylation
Respiratory complexes
Mitochondrial membranes

Electron Transport Chain and Oxidative Phosphorylation

> Cyanide is a deadly poison that binds irreversibly to cytochrome *a*/a_3. What are the most likely immediate consequences of this disturbance?

1 Identify where in the electron transport chain cytochrome *a*/a_3 is located.

The electron transport chain consists of a set of four complexes distributed within the inner mitochondrial membrane that are sequentially reduced and oxidized by the passage of electrons. In this question, knowledge of the order of the complexes is helpful. In complex I, electrons are transferred from NADH to coenzyme Q. This is not a direct transfer as flavin mononucleotide (FMN) and an iron–sulfur cluster are used as intermediates. In complex II, electrons are transferred from succinate to coenzyme Q, using FAD and an iron–sulfur cluster as intermediates. In complex III, electrons are transferred from coenzyme Q to cytochrome *c*. Finally, in complex IV, electrons are transferred from cytochrome *c* to oxygen, using cytochrome *a*/a_3—the target of cyanide—as an intermediate.

2 Recall the function of the electron transport chain.

Energy-rich molecules, such as glucose or fatty acids, are metabolized in a series of oxidation reactions that donate electrons to coenzymes, including nicotinamide adenine dinucleotide (NAD^+) and flavin adenine dinucleotide (FAD). In their reduced forms, NADH and $FADH_2$ each donate electron pairs to the specialized carriers in the electron transport chain. While shuttling electrons to oxygen, the electron transport chain generates a proton gradient by pumping protons from the mitochondrial matrix to the intermembrane space, across the inner mitochondrial membrane. More specifically, complexes I, III, and IV are all involved in creating this proton-motive force, a concentration gradient that is subsequently used to power ATP synthase. As protons flow down the concentration gradient back into the mitochondrial matrix, energy is released; this energy is used to phosphorylate ADP with an inorganic phosphate (P_i), producing ATP.

 Determine the effects of cyanide.

Now that we have identified the location of cytochrome a/a_3 within the electron transport chain and described the overall function of the chain—in particular, the generation of the proton-motive force—we can predict the toxic effects of cyanide in the mitochondrion. Cytochrome a/a_3 is the only electron carrier that contains a heme iron with a free ligand that can react with oxygen. The cyanide anion inhibits cytochrome a/a_3 by binding to the iron moiety, essentially blocking the transport of electrons from cytochrome *c* to oxygen. This disruption means that electrons cannot be passed to oxygen, the final electron acceptor of the chain. Thus, oxygen will not be reduced to water. It is important to note that electron transport is tightly coupled to oxidative phosphorylation through the proton-motive force, so this site-specific inhibition of the electron transport chain will also prevent ATP synthesis. Halting the electron transport chain will eventually result in a buildup of NADH, an important regulator of a number of metabolic enzymes. A buildup of NADH would inhibit *citrate synthase*, *isocitrate dehydrogenase*, and the *α-ketoglutarate dehydrogenase complex* in the citric acid cycle. In an effort to continue glycolysis, lactate would be formed in order to regenerate NAD^+.

Takeaways

It is not sufficient to memorize the electron transport chain. Fundamental understanding of the electron transport chain and how a toxin may change its function is necessary to answer questions like these on Test Day.

Things to Watch Out For

The electron transport chain is nothing more than a series of oxidation–reduction reactions in which each complex has a higher reduction potential than the one that preceded it. This allows for a flow of electrons down the chain. Remember that oxidation is a loss of electrons, and reduction is a gain.

Related Questions

1. Certain compounds, such as 2,3-dinitrophenol, serve to uncouple the proton gradient and ATP production. Besides a decrease in ATP production, what other effects would be likely to occur if an individual was administered one of these uncoupling agents?
2. If a toxin were administered that inhibited the electron transport chain at complex I, would the amount of ATP produced be more or less than if cyanide were administered?
3. What is one possible explanation why $FADH_2$ produces less ATP than NADH?

Key Concepts

Biochemistry Chapter 11

β-Oxidation

Electron carriers

ATP

NADH

$FADH_2$

β-Oxidation

How many NADH and $FADH_2$ will be formed by the oxidation of one molecule of palmitate (16:0) to form acetyl-CoA?

 Determine how many acetyl-CoAs will be made from one molecule of palmitate.

Palmitate is one of the most common saturated fatty acids found in humans—*saturated* meaning that the fatty acid does not contain multiple-order bonds. Palmitate also contains an even number of carbons and thus can be metabolized completely to acetyl-CoA. (If a fatty acid with an odd number of carbons is oxidized, a three-carbon propionyl-CoA will also be produced.) The β-oxidation of a fatty acid occurs by successively removing two-carbon fragments from the carboxyl end of the fatty acyl-CoA molecule. These two-carbon units are acetyl-CoA molecules. Thus, dividing the total number of carbons in the chain by two will give the number of acetyl-CoA molecules produced from one palmitate molecule. That is, $16 \div 2 = 8$ units of acetyl-CoA will be released from one molecule of palmitoyl-CoA.

 Recall the number of NADH and $FADH_2$ molecules produced in each oxidation step.

The energy yield from the β-oxidation pathway is high, which explains why fatty acids are considered a desirable energy source. Each cycle in the β-oxidation pathway results in the removal of two-carbon molecules of acetyl-CoA and consists of a sequence of four reactions. In the first reaction, the fatty acid is oxidized to form a double bond. This oxidation step is coupled to the reduction of a molecule of flavin adenine dinucleotide (FAD) to its energy-carrying form, $FADH_2$. The second reaction features hydration of this double bond, forming a hydroxyl group. Third, the hydroxyl group is oxidized to form a carbonyl; this reaction is coupled to the reduction of nicotinamide adenine dinucleotide (NAD^+) to its energy-carrying form, NADH. Finally, the fatty acid is cleaved into a shorter acyl-CoA and acetyl-CoA. Thus, for each cycle of β-oxidation, one molecule of NADH and one molecule of $FADH_2$ are generated.

3 Determine how many rounds of oxidation must occur to split palmitate into 8 acetyl-CoA molecules.

The steps that lead to the release of acetyl-CoA are repeated in an even number fatty-acid chain $\frac{n}{2} - 1$ times, where n is the number of carbons in the chain. Note that the final thiolytic cleavage will result in two acetyl groups; only one molecule of NADH and one molecule of $FADH_2$ are produced during the generation of *both* of the final acetyl-CoA molecules. Palmitate consists of 16 carbons and yields 8 molecules of acetyl-CoA. Thus, there are $\frac{16}{2} - 1 = 7$ rounds of oxidation during the metabolism of palmitate. The image below illustrates these cleavage steps, where a vertical line indicates each oxidation step:

4 Calculate the yield of NADH and $FADH_2$.

Because there will be seven oxidations, and each oxidation yields one molecule each of NADH and $FADH_2$, then seven molecules of NADH and seven molecules of $FADH_2$ will result from the oxidation of palmitate.

Takeaways

Calculations of yields should be carried out methodically. If you are unsure of how many oxidations will occur by simply glancing at the description of the molecule, given here as (16:0), then draw it out to ensure a correct answer.

Things to Watch Out For

Remember that oxidation and reduction reactions are always paired with one another. Therefore, if there are two oxidation steps during a round of β-oxidation, then two molecules must be reduced in the process. In this case, one molecule each of NADH and $FADH_2$ are produced via the reduction of their oxidized forms.

Related Questions

1. β-Oxidation of a fatty acid yields nine molecules of NADH and nine molecules of $FADH_2$. How many carbons were initially present in the fatty acid, assuming it was saturated?
2. How many molecules of ATP would be generated by the complete oxidation of one molecule of palmitate (16:0)?
3. How many molecules of ATP would be generated by the complete oxidation of one molecule of arachidic acid (20:0)?

Key Concepts

Biochemistry Chapter 12

Postprandial (absorptive or well-fed) state
Postabsorptive (fasting) state
Insulin
Glucagon

Hormonal Regulation of Metabolism

Shortly after ingesting a high-carbohydrate meal, hormones are released that stimulate the body to utilize and store this fuel. What is the most significant of these hormones? What are the effects of this hormone on its target tissues?

 Identify the hormone released in response to carbohydrates.

Insulin secretion by the β-cells of the islets of Langerhans in the pancreas occurs when the cells sense a rise in blood glucose concentration. This rise in blood glucose concentration, which takes place after a carbohydrate-rich meal, is the trigger for insulin release from the pancreas. Together, the GLUT 2 glucose transporter and the glycolytic enzyme *glucokinase* act as a glucose sensor, detecting the relative concentration of glucose and releasing insulin appropriately.

 Determine the target tissues and effects of insulin.

If insulin is released in response to the high blood glucose concentrations that occur during the postprandial state, then it makes sense that the functions of insulin can be grouped into two themes: utilization of fuel and storing of fuel energy in more compact forms for later use.

The three main target tissues for insulin are liver, muscle, and adipose tissues. In the liver, insulin inhibits gluconeogenesis, which decreases *de novo* production of glucose. Insulin also stimulates *glucokinase* and *glycogen synthase*—and inhibits *glucose-6-phosphatase* and *glycogen phosphorylase*, thereby initiating storage of excess glucose as glycogen. In muscle and adipose tissue, insulin increases the uptake of glucose into the cell by increasing the number of GLUT 4 transporters found in the cell membrane. This decreases blood glucose levels by increasing the uptake of glucose by these tissues. In adipose tissue, insulin also promotes the conversion of excess glucose into fatty acids and triacylglycerols. In muscle, insulin also promotes protein synthesis. Interestingly, the brain, renal tubules, intestinal mucosa, red blood cells, and β-cells are not sensitive to insulin. Thus, circulating glucose is oxidized to CO_2 and water in these tissues (or to pyruvate in red blood cells) during both the well-fed and postabsorptive states.

 Determine the effects of increased blood glucose and insulin on other pathways.

When blood glucose concentration and insulin levels are elevated, certain pathways are inhibited to prevent futile cycling. For example, regulatory enzymes in glycogenolysis and gluconeogenesis (like glucose-6-phosphatase and glycogen phosphorylase, mentioned earlier), are inhibited by insulin. This prevents the production or release of extra glucose when glucose concentrations are already relatively high. In addition, ketone body formation will also be inhibited (unless insulin is completely absent, as is the case in an individual with type 1 diabetes mellitus). Protein breakdown in muscle will also be inhibited and insulin can stimulate the uptake of amino acids and protein synthesis in muscle cells.

Takeaways

Hormonal regulation of metabolism is a commonly tested topic. Insulin, glucagon, and blood glucose levels all play a large role in regulation of various metabolic pathways.

Things to Watch Out For

While the MCAT can certainly test particular details of a given pathway, it behooves you to understand the main purpose of a given pathway to predict its regulation. Given that insulin is released when blood glucose concentrations are high, it only makes sense that insulin would be an activator of glycogen production (glycogenesis) and an inhibitor of glycogen breakdown (glycogenolysis).

Related Questions

1. Identify the hormonal changes that occur during the postabsorptive state.
2. An insulinoma is a tumor that secretes high levels of insulin. What would be likely symptoms of this condition?
3. A glucagonoma is a tumor that secretes high levels of glucagon. What would be likely symptoms of this condition?

Solutions to Related Questions

1: Elements of Peptide Structure

1. Cysteine residues contain sulfhydryl groups that form disulfide bonds, a type of tertiary structure. Disulfide bonds can also stabilize local secondary and other tertiary structures as well. In addition, disulfide bonds help form a hydrophobic core within proteins, facilitating hydrophobic interactions. A change in a single cysteine residue may interrupt a key disulfide bridge, resulting in the inability of a protein to maintain its secondary and tertiary structures or its hydrophobic core. Ultimately, this may also disrupt quaternary structure by changing interactions between multiple peptides. Thus, this single change can cause disruption of protein structure and function.

2. 6 *M* HCl is concentrated solution of a strong acid. In fact, the pH of this solution is approximately –0.78. For comparison, gastric acid has a pH of 2 and a concentration of approximately 0.01 *M* HCl. Treatment of a protein with a strong acid will result in denaturation of the protein, or loss of elements of secondary, tertiary, and quaternary structure. Concentrated strong acid may also permit hydrolysis of the peptide bond, interrupting primary structure.

3. This question combines concepts from both amino acid structure and peptide function. A G protein-coupled receptor contains a transmembrane domain that consists mainly of hydrophobic residues. Because this mutation is not in the binding site of the receptor, it is unlikely to affect substrate binding. The specific mutation described substitutes one hydrophobic amino acid for another, which should cause minimal changes in the secondary and tertiary structures of the protein. Therefore, this mutation is unlikely to affect the structure or function of the peptide.

2: Lineweaver–Burk Plots

1. A noncompetitive inhibitor binds to an allosteric site, rather than the active site. Binding of the inhibitor to an allosteric site changes the conformation of the active site, leading to a decrease in the efficiency of enzyme catalysis, which results in a decrease in v_{max}. However, K_m will not change due to noncompetitive inhibition because any copies of the enzyme still in the active conformation can bind the substrate with the same affinity. Therefore, compared to the line without inhibitor, the line with a noncompetitive inhibitor will have the same *x*-intercept, but a higher *y*-intercept. This is shown in the diagram below:

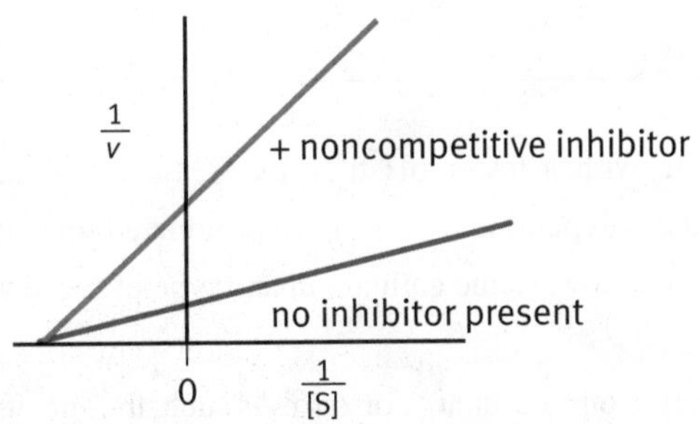

2. An uncompetitive inhibitor binds to an allosteric site, but only when the substrate is already bound to the enzyme. This results in an increased affinity for substrate bound to enzyme and decreased dissociation of the enzyme–substrate complex. Therefore, uncompetitive inhibition results in a decrease in both v_{max} and K_m. Compared to the line without an inhibitor, the line with an uncompetitive inhibitor will have a more negative *x*-intercept and higher *y*-intercept—a shift upwards and to the left, which is shown in the diagram below:

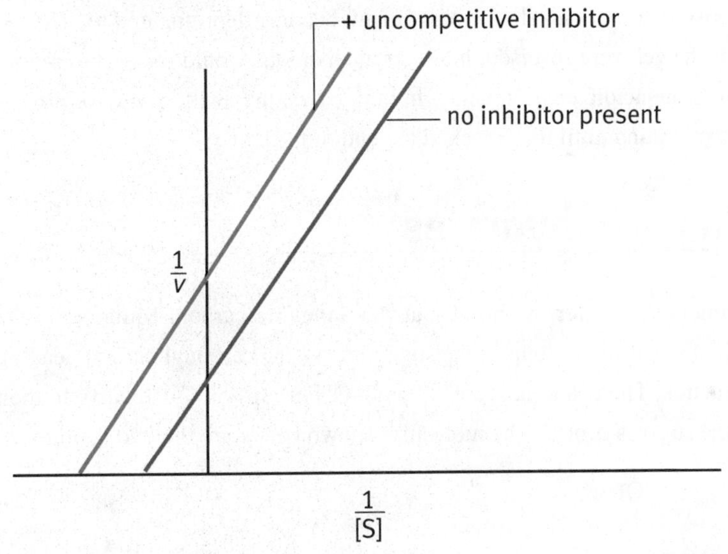

3. Michaelis–Menten plots contain the same information as Lineweaver–Burk plots, but have different axes. The *y*-axis in a Michaelis–Menten plot is reaction rate or velocity, *v*, and the *x*-axis is substrate concentration, [S]. Monomeric enzymes will result in a hyperbolic shape in the graph, reaching a plateau at v_{max}. A competitive inhibitor will not affect v_{max}; however, the curve will be stretched to the right because K_m increases, as shown in the diagram below:

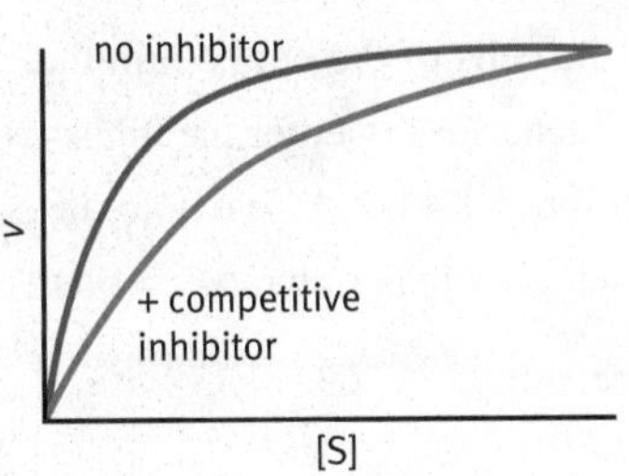

3: Isoelectric Focusing

1. If a polypeptide is in an environment with a lower pH than its pI, then this implies that it is in a relatively acidic environment compared to its pI and the polypeptide will be more protonated than at its pI. This means that it will take on a positive charge. Cations always migrate toward the cathode in any type of electrochemical cell.

2. When an amino acid reaches its pI, it takes on a net charge of zero. As such, the species overall no longer has an electrostatic force acting on it $\left(\mathbf{F}_e = \frac{kQq}{r^2}\right)$. Even if we considered the force on each charge within the zwitterion separately, we could say that the species is in translational equilibrium: the negatively charged carboxylate group (or deprotonated R group) is attracted to the anode and the positively charged amino group (or protonated R group) is attracted to the cathode.

3. If the pH gradient were reversed, then the samples would run off of the gel. A negatively charged sample would migrate toward the anode. In a standard isoelectric focusing setup, this would mean that the sample would move into a more acidic environment, pick up protons to achieve an overall charge of zero, and then stop moving. The opposite would occur for cations, which would move to a more alkaline environment, become deprotonated to achieve an overall charge of zero, and then stop moving. If the gel were reversed, however, then anions would move into more alkaline environments and cations would move into more acidic environments. In both cases, the zwitterionic form would not be achieved and the samples would continue migrating until they reached the end of the cell.

4: Isomerism in Carbohydrates

1. Anomers are cyclic epimers that differ in chirality at the anomeric carbon. Mutarotation occurs about the anomeric carbon, which arises when a hydroxyl group in the sugar attacks the carbonyl carbon, leading to ring closure through a nucleophilic addition reaction. The position of the –H and –OH groups on C-1 relative to the free $-CH_2OH$ group in the sugar dictates whether the sugar is α or β. The molecules shown below are the two anomers of D-glucose.

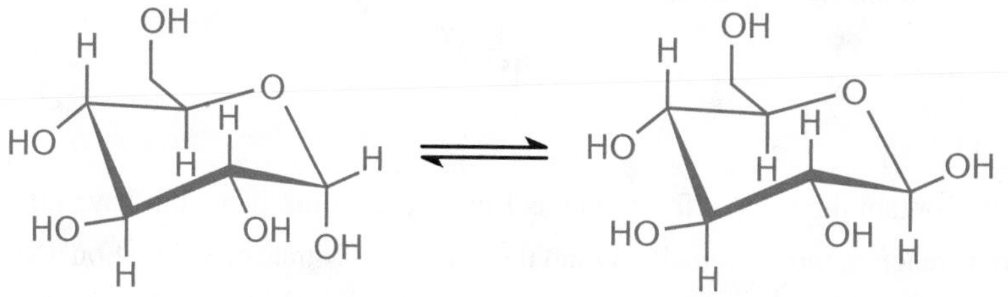

α-D-glucopyranose ⇌ β-D-glucopyranose

2. Cellulose, or dietary fiber, cannot be digested by humans and acts as a bulking agent in feces. Monosaccharides can traverse the walls of the intestine to enter the cells of the epithelium that lines the digestive tract. Polysaccharides must be enzymatically broken down into monosaccharides to enter the digestive tract. Cellulose is a large polysaccharide and humans lack the enzymes required to break the β-1,4 bonds that hold the compound together. This is reflective of enzyme specificity of the active site: human enzymes can break down α-1,4 bonds, but not β-1,4 bonds.

3. Epimers are sugar diastereomers that differ in configuration at exactly one chiral carbon. The first structure, fructose, contains a carbonyl group at C-2. None of the other structures contain a carbonyl on C-2, so fructose has no epimers in this group. Next, compare D-glucose and D-galactose. These two sugars differ only at C-4; therefore, D-glucose and D-galactose are C-4 epimers. Next, a comparison of D-glucose and D-mannose reveals inverted configuration at C-2, making them C-2 epimers. Finally, comparison of D-galactose and D-mannose reveals inverted configuration at C-2 and C-4, which means that these molecules are diastereomers of each other, but not epimers.

5: Lipid Saponification

1. Soap is a carboxylate salt of a fatty acid ionically bonded to a cation. Soap consists of two parts: a hydrophilic, negatively charged carboxylate group with a high affinity for water, and a nonpolar, hydrophobic alkyl tail that interacts with organic materials, such as soil and grease. The buildup is likely composed of fatty acids that are bonded to other cations that reduce its solubility in water, such as calcium (like the example with pancreatitis) or magnesium. In addition to hard water decreasing the solubility of soap, water that is acidic can reduce the effectiveness of soap. Acidic solutions contain large quantities of protons and will rapidly protonate the negatively charged carboxylate groups of the fatty acids. This reduces the hydrophilicity of these groups, reducing the effectiveness and solubility of soap.

2. The question stem states that adipocere or grave wax occurs in a cold, humid, low-oxygen environment. Bodies quickly begin decomposing after death as bacteria begin to digest the corpse. A low-oxygen environment favors anaerobic bacterial species. These anaerobes carry out saponification of fatty tissues in the body, leading to the formation of a chalky substance in and around fatty tissues.

3. Treating a triacylglycerol molecule with an acid instead of a base could still result in hydrolysis of the ester bonds; however, the carboxylate ions would undergo rapid protonation to form carboxylic acids, resulting in diminished interactions between the polar heads and water. This would decrease the solubility of the resulting carboxylic acids relative to the carboxylate anions. These compounds could not be considered soap. Soap, by definition, is composed of carboxylate salts—not carboxylic acids.

6: DNA Replication

1. Human DNA polymerase is not used for PCR because of the heating and cooling processes involved. PCR requires enough heat to be transferred to the DNA molecules to cause them to denature and separate into two single strands. This amount of thermal energy would also likely denature human DNA polymerase, rendering it unable to carry out replication. The genus name of *T. aquaticus*, *Thermus*, is reflective of the fact that this bacterium's DNA polymerase is active at very high temperatures and is able to carry out replication even under the harsh conditions required in PCR.

2. The lagging strand is significantly more likely to acquire mutations than the leading strand. The lagging strand is synthesized in a discontinuous manner as Okazaki fragments, which must subsequently be coupled together by DNA ligase. This means that the lagging strand contains many more RNA primers, which must be removed and substituted for by DNA. This stop-and-start synthesis pattern and the fact that the lagging strand requires more postreplicatory modifications means that the lagging strand is more prone to mutations.

3. While the ^{15}N-labeled guanine question given in this chapter showed each of the daughter strands individually, there is another way to approach this question. Each of the two original unlabeled strands will end up in only one of the resulting DNA molecules; thus, only two of the eight resulting DNA molecules will contain an unlabeled strand.

7: Operons

1. Glucose is the preferred fuel for most organisms. As such, even in the presence of lactose, there is no need to process this disaccharide if glucose is plentiful. When there is glucose present, adenylate cyclase is inactive, which means that cAMP is not available to bind to CAP. Without the cAMP–CAP complex, RNA polymerase cannot bind strongly to the DNA. By extension, transcription of the genes for lactose digestion will not occur.

2. Inducible genes require the presence of a compound known as an inducer. In other words, the genes of the operon are only transcribed in the presence of a particular substrate—in the example in the question, this substrate is lactose. Repressible systems are repressed in the presence of a specific substrate and allow for certain genes to be turned off under particular conditions. Repressible systems are examples of negative feedback, in which the presence of the product of a pathway suppresses the pathway itself. This mechanism helps prevent wasteful energy use by the cell.

3. The *trp* operon is a repressible system. In the absence of the amino acid tryptophan, the repressor is unable to bind to the regulator sequence. Because there is no repressor, the genes required for tryptophan synthesis are available for transcription. In repressible systems, the default setting for the gene is *on*. When tryptophan is present, it binds to the repressor and the tryptophan–repressor complex binds to the operator region, halting transcription of the genes required for tryptophan synthesis.

8: Membrane Traffic

1. If an individual's blood becomes hypotonic with respect to the filtrate, then the body would aim to increase free water excretion to regain homeostasis. This means that the kidney would decrease the amount of water reabsorbed from the filtrate into the blood. This could be accomplished by decreasing the secretion of ADH, which would promote the loss of more water in the urine, increasing the blood concentration.

2. If the concentration of the interstitial fluid is higher than that of the filtrate, then the interstitial fluid is hypertonic (or hyperosmotic) relative to the filtrate. The filtrate, then, is hypotonic (or hypo-osmotic) to the interstitial fluid.

3. If the activity of ADH is blocked, then it is unable to carry out its function—concentrating the urine by promoting the reabsorption of water from the filtrate into the interstitial fluid. Thus, after drinking coffee, an individual would excrete larger volumes of water. The fact that the urine is clear is indicative of its low concentration. When water cannot be reabsorbed from the collecting duct, the urine will be less concentrated (hypotonic) relative to the blood.

9: Glycolysis

1. ATP is consumed during two steps in glycolysis. The first is the conversion of glucose to glucose 6-phosphate by hexokinase or glucokinase. The second ATP-requiring step occurs during the conversion of fructose 6-phosphate to fructose 1,6-bisphosphate by phosphofructokinase-1 (PFK-1). Both of these steps involve the phosphorylation of sugars; ATP provides the phosphate required for these reactions.

2. ATP is produced through substrate-level phosphorylation in two different reactions. The first occurs during the conversion of 1,3-bisphophoglycerate to 3-phosphoglycerate by phosphoglycerate kinase. The second is the conversion of phosphoenolpyruvate to pyruvate by pyruvate kinase. Notice that each of these steps involves the removal of a phosphate from an intermediate of glycolysis. It is important to remember that 2 ATP are produced in each of these reactions for every glucose that enters glycolysis. This is because fructose 1,6-bisphosphate is cleaved into dihydroxyacetone phosphate and glyceraldehyde 3-phosphate.

3. The conversion of glyceraldehyde 3-phosphate to 1,3-bisphosphoglycerate by glyceraldehyde-3-phosphate dehydrogenase results in the reduction of NAD^+ to NADH. Like the substrate-level phosphorylation reactions described previously, 2 NADH are generated for every glucose that enters glycolysis. NADH can then feed into the electron transport chain to be used in oxidative phosphorylation.

10: Electron Transport Chain and Oxidative Phosphorylation

1. Uncoupling often occurs because the inner mitochondrial membrane has been made "leaky" by increasing its permeability. This dissipates the proton gradient, reducing the amount of ATP produced. In a futile attempt to restore the proton gradient and regain the necessary level of ATP production, more NADH is oxidized and more oxygen is consumed as the electron transport chain increases its activity. Many of the reactions in respiration release heat. Thus, use of 2,3-dinitrophenol can result in (potentially fatal) hyperthermia.

2. The amount of ATP produced if the electron transport chain were inhibited at complex I is, perhaps counterintuitively, greater than if the chain were inhibited at complex IV (such as by cyanide). Complex I is responsible for the oxidation of NADH and the pumping of some protons into the intermembrane space. While inhibition of complex I would stop this electron carrier from feeding electrons into the chain, $FADH_2$ could still provide electrons because it transfers them to Complex II, after the point of inhibition. This would still allow creation of a proton-motive force using Complexes III and IV, with no buildup of electrons at the end of the chain. Thus, ATP could still be produced from $FADH_2$, even if it cannot be made from NADH.

3. As described previously, $FADH_2$ donates electrons to the electron transport chain at Complex II, while NADH donates electrons at Complex I. Assuming no inhibition occurs, protons are pumped into the intermembrane space, thereby increasing the proton-motive force. The proton-motive force is directly proportional to the energy stored in the concentration gradient; therefore, the larger the proton-motive force is, the more energy available for generating ATP.

11: β-Oxidation

1. In order to yield nine molecules of NADH and nine molecules of $FADH_2$, there must be nine rounds of oxidation. Using the same equation given in this question to determine the number of cycles (or mathematical deduction), the number of carbons can be found:

$$\frac{n}{2} - 1 = 9$$
$$n = 20$$

Thus, the original fatty acid must contain 20 carbons. This is arachidic acid (20:0).

2. β-Oxidation of palmitate would yield 7 NADH and 7 $FADH_2$, as described in the question. Each NADH can generate 2.5 ATP, whereas each $FADH_2$ can result in 1.5 ATP. Thus, there are $7 \times 2.5 + 7 \times 1.5 = 28$ ATP generated from the molecules of NADH and $FADH_2$. In addition, each molecule of acetyl-CoA can generate 3 NADH, 1 $FADH_2$, and 1 molecule of GTP (which is easily converted to ATP) during the citric acid cycle, resulting in an additional $3 \times 2.5 + 1 \times 1.5 + 1 = 10$ ATP per acetyl-CoA. β-Oxidation of palmitate yields 8 acetyl-CoA molecules, which results in 80 molecules of ATP. Therefore, in total, $28 + 80 = 108$ molecules of ATP will be created by complete oxidation of one molecule of palmitate. However, one molecule of ATP was required at the beginning to activate palmitate to palmitoyl-CoA. Therefore, the final yield is $108 - 1 = 107$ ATP.

3. First, the number of oxidation cycles, acetyl-CoA molecules, and NADH and $FADH_2$ molecules produced must be determined. Using the same logic as in the previous questions, β-oxidation of arachidic acid will result in nine NADH (22.5 ATP) and nine $FADH_2$ (13.5 ATP), for a total of 36 ATP. Because there are 20 carbons in arachidic acid, 10 acetyl-CoA molecules will result. Each acetyl-CoA molecule will yield 10 ATP, resulting in 100 ATP. The total quantity of ATP produced from complete oxidation of arachidic acid is 136 ATP. However, one molecule of ATP as required for activation of arachidic acid, making the total yield 135 ATP.

12: Hormonal Regulation of Metabolism

1. The postabsorptive (fasting) state occurs when blood glucose concentrations start to drop following a meal. Glucagon and epinephrine levels rise. In the liver, glycogen is broken down and the resulting glucose is released into the bloodstream. Gluconeogensis is also upregulated in response to glucagon, but this response is much slower. Amino acids are released from skeletal muscle, and free fatty acids are released from adipose tissue in response to increased epinephrine and decreased blood glucose. Amino acids and free fatty acids are taken up by the liver, where the amino acids provide the carbon skeletons and the oxidation of fatty acids provides the ATP required for gluconeogenesis. Concomitantly, pathways such as glycogenesis and lipid synthesis are inhibited.

2. An insulinoma releases excess insulin. This excess release of insulin results in low blood glucose levels (hypoglycemia). Because the brain cannot function properly at low blood glucose concentrations, altered mental status may occur. In addition, low blood glucose levels affect the nervous system, which can result in headache, fatigue, double vision, and blurring of vision. It is also important to note that as blood glucose levels fall, epinephrine is released, which can lead to tremors, palpitations, sweating, hunger, anxiety, and nausea.

3. A glucagonoma releases excess glucagon, causing elevated blood glucose levels (hyperglycemia). Normally, insulin has a suppressive effect on the secretion of glucagon. The marked increase in glucagon will cause breakdown of triacylglycerols in adipose tissue, resulting in the release of into the bloodstream, which can ultimately result in weight loss. Patients with this condition often present with diabetes mellitus because of lipids the body's inability to manage blood glucose levels, despite a compensatory increase in insulin secretion.

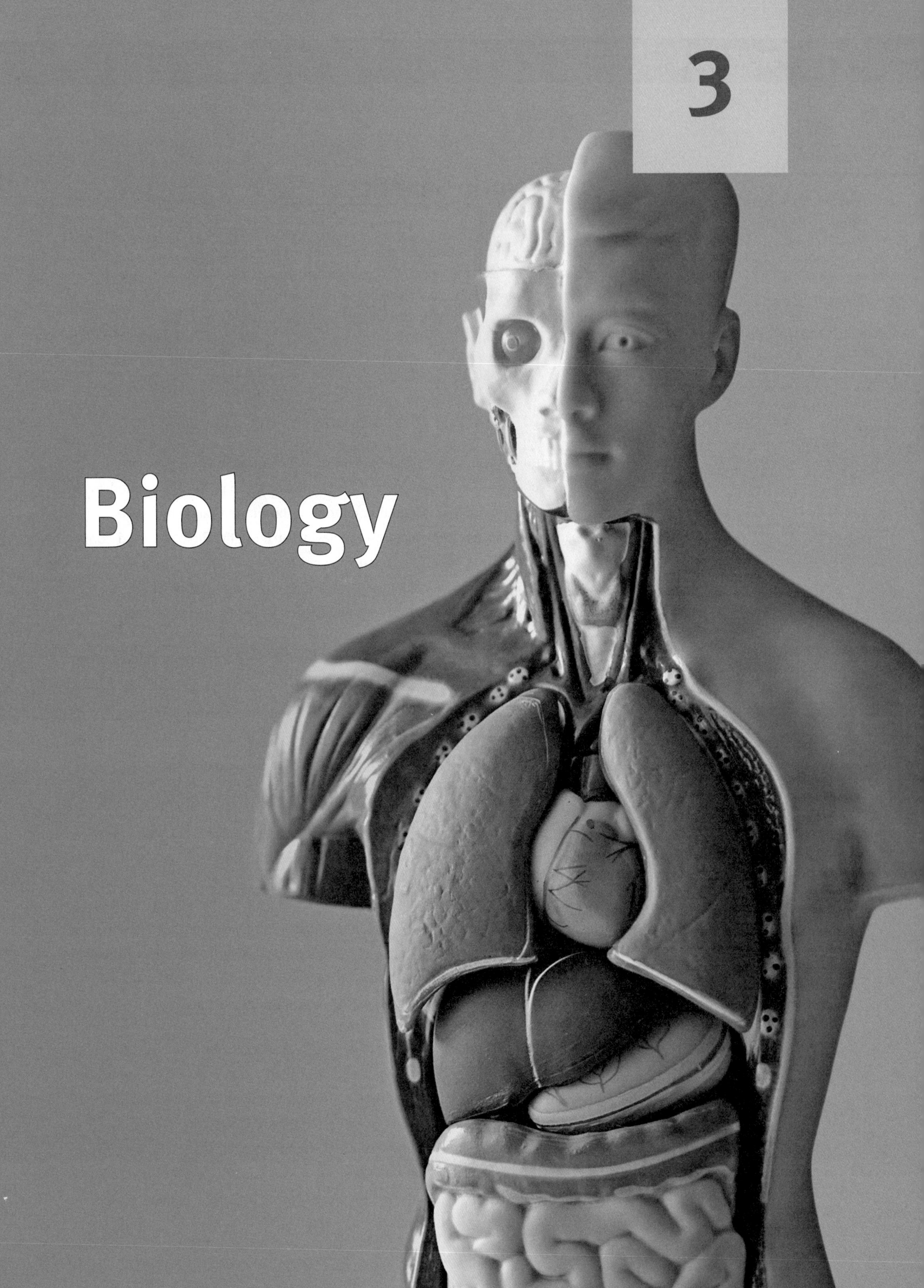

3

Biology

Key Concepts
Biology Chapter 1
Prokaryotic genetics
Antibiotic resistance
Transformation
Conjugation
Transduction

Prokaryotic Genetics

Bacterial genetic recombination can result in enhanced resistance to antibiotics. What bacterial genetic recombination process(es) is/are most likely to quickly convert entire bacterial colonies from being sensitive to a given antibiotic to being resistant to that antibiotic?

 Formulate a plan for answering the question.

This question is asking for identification of various methods used by bacteria for genetic recombination, and which of these processes may be most suited to the widespread acquisition of genes that confer antibiotic resistance in a colony. This indicates that this question requires two levels of thought. First, we need content knowledge regarding bacterial genetic recombination. Then, we must think critically about these processes with an eye toward recognizing what processes are most favorable for the rapid and widespread acquisition of antibiotic resistance.

Note that while there are two prokaryotic kingdoms—Archaea and Bacteria—our focus in this question is on bacteria, specifically.

 Recall and define each bacterial genetic recombination process.

Overall, there are three main methods of exchanging genetic information between prokaryotic cells: transformation, conjugation, and transduction.

Transformation occurs when a prokaryote picks up a piece of foreign DNA from the environment and integrates this DNA into its genome. Once integrated, this foreign DNA will be replicated in all subsequent rounds of binary fission and will thus be passed on to all daughter cells of this prokaryote. Transformation is a particularly common method of genetic recombination in gram-negative bacilli.

Conjugation is a prokaryotic form of sexual reproduction in which a conjugation bridge is formed between two cells. One cell, called a donor male (+), forms a sex pilus that can attach to a recipient female (–) cell. Once the sex pilus has fused with the recipient cell, genetic material can be passed through the conjugation bridge. This transfer is unidirectional, from the donor male to the recipient female. To form the sex pilus, a cell requires a sex factor, the best studied of which is the fertility (F) factor. During conjugation, a plasmid may be passed through the conjugation bridge; the

F factor is commonly transferred, turning the recipient female into a donor male cell as well. Other times, the donor male can attempt to donate its entire genome to the recipient female.

Finally, transduction is the transfer of genetic material from one prokaryote to another using a bacteriophage as an intermediate. This is an accidental method of genetic recombination because it arises from improper packaging of genetic material during the formation of new virions within a bacterium. First, a bacteriophage infects a bacterium, and its genetic material is replicated as new virions are assembled within the cell. As these viral genomes are packaged into capsids, small segments of bacterial DNA may accidentally be trapped within the capsid. The bacterium ultimately lyses, releasing these virions. When the virion carrying bacterial genetic information infects another bacterium, the transfer is completed; the second bacterium receives genetic material from the first via the bacteriophage vector.

Determine which of these processes is most favorable for the transferral of antibiotic resistance.

Which of these methods can transfer genetic material for antibiotic resistance? In short: all of them. Each process can transfer genetic material that codes for antibiotic resistance mechanisms. However, two of these processes are fairly random: transformation and transduction. Transformation requires the bacterium to encounter the genetic material for antibiotic resistance in its environment. While it is entirely possible for this to occur for individual bacteria, it is unlikely to convert an entire established bacterial colony from being antibiotic sensitive to being antibiotic resistant. Similarly, transduction requires the accidental removal of bacterial genetic information followed by packaging into phages. While this may convert individual bacteria from being antibiotic sensitive to being antibiotic resistant, it is unlikely to convert an entire colony.

Conjugation, on the other hand, is a deliberate and specific transferal of genetic material from one bacterium to another. Further, in many cases of conjugation, the recipient cell acquires the necessary sex factor to carry out conjugation with other cells; that is, the recipient is converted into a donor. This would allow rapid, exponential spread of genetic material between bacterial organisms. If the sex factor were located on the same plasmid as an antibiotic resistance gene, then this would allow the rapid conversion of an entire preexisting colony from being antibiotic sensitive to being antibiotic resistant.

Takeaways

Antibiotic resistance may be acquired through any of the three major prokaryotic genetic recombination processes, but the rate and ubiquity of the acquisition varies between the three processes. Transformation and transduction both occur on the individual level, whereas conjugation can convert entire colonies.

Things to Watch Out For

The wording of this question is important—it implies that the bacterial colonies acquiring antibiotic resistance in this question already exist. Transformation and transduction could result in whole colonies with antibiotic resistance—but these colonies would have to be descended from an individual cell that underwent recombination.

Related Questions

1. A pharmaceutical company would like to induce the production of a target protein by a particular strain of *E. coli*. What would be the required characteristics of the plasmid in order to create large colonies of *E. coli* that produce the target protein?
2. A researcher discovers that a type of bacteriophage removes the exact same sequence of DNA from each bacterium infected. What does this information likely indicate about the bacteriophage's ability to feed into either the lytic or lysogenic cycle?
3. It is noted by a researcher that a certain colony of bacteria has developed an extremely high rate of recombination, acquiring multiple phenotypic changes in a very short period of time. What mechanism related to conjugation would most likely explain this finding?

High-Yield Problem-Solving Guide questions continue on the next page. ▶ ▶ ▶

Menstrual Cycle

Key Concepts

Biology Chapter 2

Menstrual cycle
FSH
LH
Estrogen
Progesterone
Positive and negative feedback

During the follicular phase of the menstrual cycle, a dominant follicle is produced that secretes estrogen. If this follicle produces normal amounts of estrogen during the early days of its maturity but declines in estrogen production by day 10 of the menstrual cycle, what would be the result?

Visualize the menstrual cycle, focusing on the follicular phase.

During the follicular phase, the hypothalamus secretes gonadotropin-releasing hormone (GnRH), which acts on the anterior pituitary to promote the release of follicle-stimulating hormone (FSH). FSH acts on the ovary and promotes the development of several ovarian follicles. The mature follicle begins secreting estrogen. Together, the hypothalamus, anterior pituitary, and ovary form one of the many endocrine axes (often called the hypothalamic–pituitary–ovarian or HPO axis):

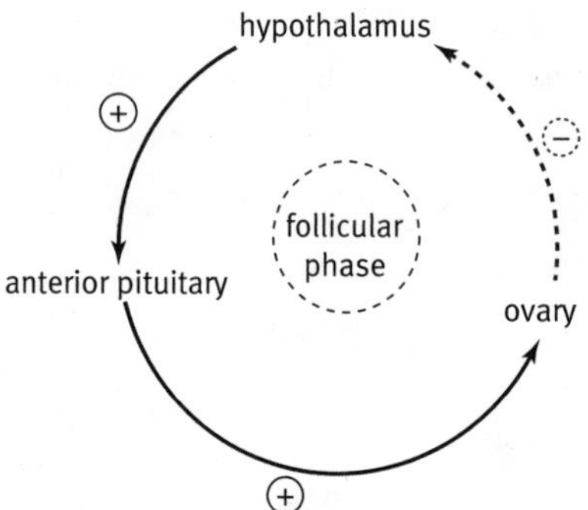

Determine the normal role of estrogen up until day 10.

Estrogen has both positive and negative feedback effects in the menstrual cycle. Early in the follicular phase, estrogen acts on the uterus, causing vascularization of the endometrium. It also acts in a negative feedback loop to inhibit the release of FSH from the anterior pituitary in order to prevent the development of multiple eggs:

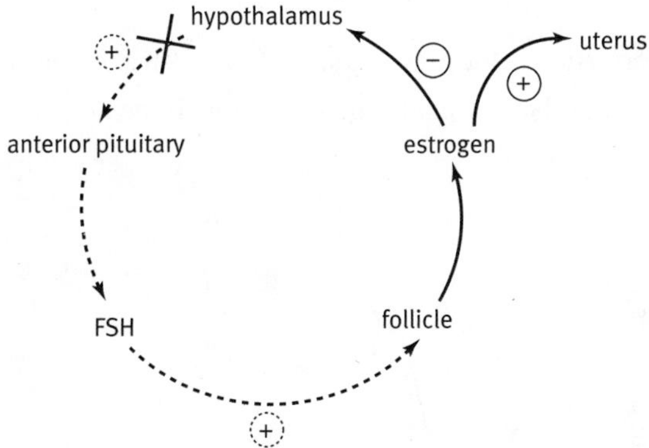

Because the question stem states that early levels of estrogen are normal, vascularization of the uterus and inhibition of FSH will both occur normally.

3 Determine the normal role of estrogen after day 10.

The question also states that estrogen levels decline after day 10. Start by considering the normal role of estrogen after this point. Estrogen levels increase rapidly around day 12 of the cycle, and this burst of estrogen surpasses a threshold to begin having a positive feedback effect on the secretion of FSH and luteinizing hormone (LH). This results in the LH surge. The LH surge is responsible for ovulation, or the release of an egg:

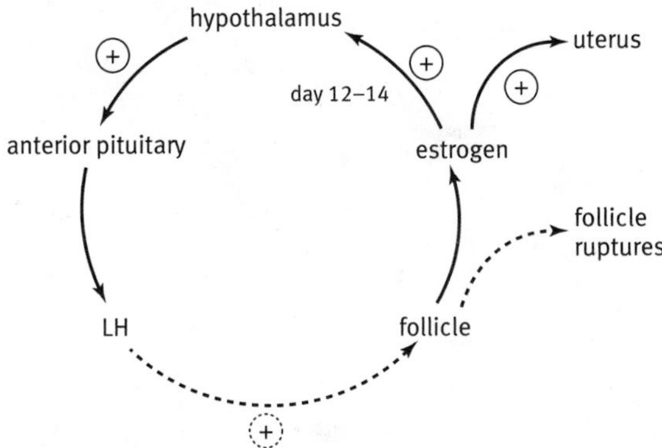

Takeaways

It is important to have a good understanding of the normal way that systems such as the menstrual cycle function. Using that knowledge, different variables, such as disease or dysfunction, can be applied to the system, and the results of that dysfunction can be found in a methodical way.

Things to Watch Out For

Estrogen has both negative and positive feedback effects on FSH and LH at different times in the menstrual cycle. Remember that estrogen levels fall dramatically after the LH surge but rise again during the luteal phase. During this phase, however, both estrogen and progesterone are now produced by the corpus luteum, and both have a negative feedback effect.

4 Examine the consequences of a decrease in estrogen after day 10.

Based on the information in the previous step, if estrogen levels decrease after day 10 rather than increase as they normally should, there will be no ovulation:

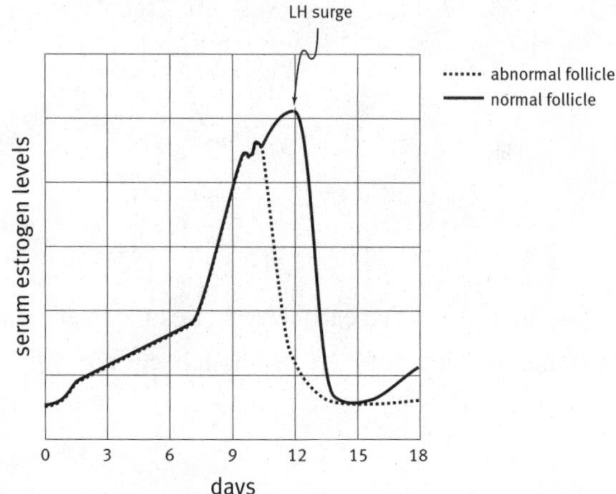

Related Questions

1. At what point in the follicular phase is FSH inhibited?
2. How do the levels of progesterone change during the menstrual cycle? What is the function of progesterone?
3. How could ovulation be prevented during the menstrual cycle through biochemical means?

High-Yield Problem-Solving Guide questions continue on the next page. ▶ ▶ ▶

Key Concepts

Biology Chapter 3

Neurulation
Gastrulation
Implantation
Cleavage

Stages of Embryogenesis

> Hirschsprung's disease is a congenital disorder that occurs when neural crest cells fail to complete their migration to the digestive tract. That is, the neural crest cells that should migrate the farthest under normal circumstances never reach their final location. How might this affect function?

1 Recall the functions of neural crest cells.

Neural crest cells arise from the tips of the neural folds. As the neural folds fuse in the midline, they form the neural tube; the neural crest cells are displaced from the tube and migrate to various sites in the body. These cells differentiate into the peripheral nervous system (including the sensory ganglia, autonomic ganglia, adrenal medulla, and Schwann cells), as well as specific cell types in other tissues (such as calcitonin-producing cells of the thyroid, melanocytes in the skin, and others).

2 Identify the pattern of neural crest cell migration.

Neural crest cells migrate outward from the tip of each neural fold. They enter the walls of the digestive tract in a cranial-to-caudal fashion, meaning that they innervate the portions of the tract closest to the mouth first, and the portions of the tract closest to the anus last.

3 Determine the effect of a lack of neural crest cells on function in the digestive tract.

In Hirschsprung's disease, the neural crest cells destined for the distal portions of the digestive tract never reach their location, and thus cannot form the parts of the enteric nervous system that would normally exist in these parts of the gut tube. Hirschsprung's disease can affect a variable length of the gut tube starting from the anus and including some length of the large intestine.

Because the neural crest cells ultimately form both sensory and autonomic ganglia, both of these modalities would be lost. This means that there would be reduced sympathetic and parasympathetic responses in the digestive tract (slowed or absent peristalsis, reduced secretion) as well as a loss of visceral sensation, making it difficult for a person with this diagnosis to sense when he or she needs to defecate.

Takeaways

Neural crest cells originate from the tips of the neural folds and migrate to form a diverse group of tissues, including the peripheral nervous system, calcitonin-producing cells of the thyroid, melanocytes, and others.

Things to Watch Out For

Neural crest cells migrate into the wall of the digestive system in a cranial-to-caudal (mouth-to-anus) fashion. Note that this is the opposite direction as the formation of the gut tube itself, which grows from anus to mouth in deuterostomes, such as humans.

Related Questions

1. Gestational trophoblastic neoplasms include choriocarcinoma, a highly invasive cancer that has often widely metastasized by the time of diagnosis. Why might choriocarcinoma have a propensity to invade and metastasize?
2. A mutation occurs in the mesoderm very early in gastrulation. This mutation is then propagated through many cell divisions. What organ systems are likely to be affected by such a mutation?
3. A zygote undergoes indeterminate cleavage to form two separate zygotes. What is a possible outcome of this division?

Key Concepts

Biology Chapter 4

Action potentials
Depolarization
Refractory periods
Nervous stimuli

Action Potential

A neuron's action potential is depicted below. If during the action potential a stimulus was applied at the time point indicated by the arrow, what would be the result?

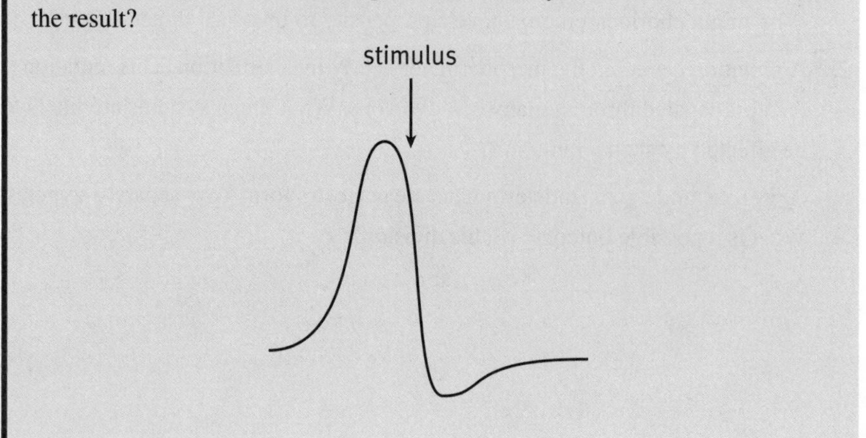

1 Identify the parts of the action potential.

The action potential can be broken down into four portions:

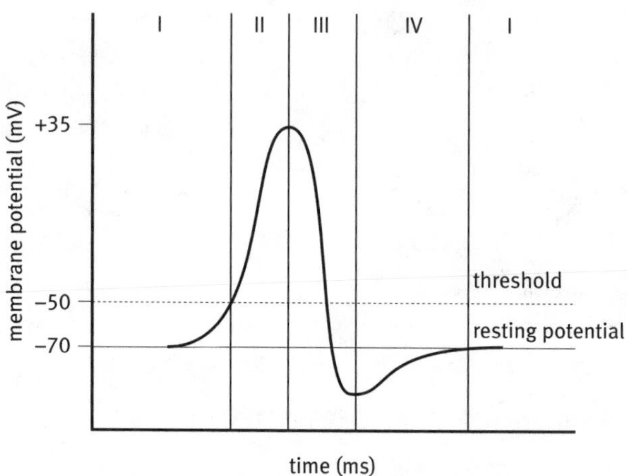

- **Region I:** The cell is at rest and all gates are closed.
- **Region II:** Depolarization—The sodium channels open and sodium flows into the cell, moving the membrane toward the sodium equilibrium potential.
- **Region III:** Repolarization—The sodium channels inactivate and potassium channels open, moving the cell closer to the potassium equilibrium potential.

- **Region IV:** Hyperpolarization—The sodium channels are deinactivated but closed and the potassium channels are closed. The cell is ready to undergo another action potential, but the distance to the threshold is greater so it is harder to stimulate the cell. This is known as the relative refractory period.

2 Review the characteristics of the action potential.

Action potentials propagate by the spread of charge to adjacent segments of membrane. They are considered *all-or-nothing* phenomena because once threshold is reached, an action potential will continue through the same stereotyped pattern of electrical potential changes, regardless of the identity or magnitude of the initiating stimulus. During the depolarization and repolarization phases of the action potential (regions II and III), no other action potential can be elicited, no matter how large the stimulus. This is known as the absolute refractory period.

Takeaways

While the potassium channels involved in the action potential can be open or closed, the sodium channels have three possibilities: open, closed, or inactivated. Inactivation occurs at positive potentials and the channel must be brought down below threshold to be deinactivated. Note that when the channel is deinactivated, it is still closed, not open; the membrane potential will have to be brought to threshold again for this channel to be opened.

3 Evaluate the region in which the new stimulus is being applied.

The new stimulus is applied during repolarization. This is part of the absolute refractory period, a time during which no new action potentials can be elicited—no matter how strong the stimulus. Therefore, the new stimulus will *not* produce a new action potential. Instead, the action potential will continue through the rest of its electrical potential changes unchanged.

Things to Watch Out For

This question is an example of one with which many students have difficulty: the "nothing changes" question. It may seem anticlimactic that the answer to this question is that the action potential continues unaltered, but the MCAT sometimes includes scenarios where a new piece of information has no effect. This can be seen in *any* section—including CARS.

Related Questions

1. At what point during the action potential is sodium closest to its electrochemical equilibrium?
2. How does a neuron encode the magnitude of a stimulus?
3. How could an action potential be inhibited?

Key Concepts

Biology Chapter 5

Anterior pituitary
Hypothalamus
Thyroid
Negative feedback

Endocrine Organs

Thyroid function is often measured by blood levels of thyroid-stimulating hormone. Why is this an effective measure of thyroid function?

 Identify the function of thyroid-stimulating hormone.

Thyroid-stimulating hormone, or TSH, triggers the uptake of iodine by the thyroid and the production and secretion of triiodothyronine (T_3) and thyroxine (T_4) from the gland. These thyroid hormones regulate the basal metabolic rate of the body by making energy production more or less efficient, as well as altering the utilization of glucose and fatty acids. Increased amounts of T_3 and T_4 will lead to increased cellular respiration. This leads to a greater amount of protein and fatty acid turnover by speeding up both synthesis and degradation of these compounds.

 Recall the axis in which TSH plays a role.

Many of the endocrine pathways start with the hypothalamus signaling to the pituitary. This establishes a number of axes, the relevant one here being the hypothalamic–pituitary–thyroid or HPT axis. The hypothalamus secretes thyroid-releasing hormone, or TRH. TRH travels through the hypophyseal portal system directly to the anterior thyroid, which releases TSH in response. TSH then acts on the thyroid to stimulate the release of thyroid hormones, which can act on target tissues.

 Recall how the pathway is regulated.

In addition to acting on target tissues, the thyroid hormones also act as inhibitors of the hypothalamus and anterior pituitary. When levels of T_3 and T_4 are adequate, they suppress synthesis and secretion of TRH and TSH. This paradigm, known as negative feedback, is common throughout the body, and is likely to show up in some form on Test Day.

 Draw a conclusion.

TSH levels give an indication of the cause of thyroid dysfunction. If an individual presents with symptoms of hyperthyroidism, simply taking a measure of the concentrations of thyroid hormones is insufficient to determine the cause of the symptoms. Is the problem in the thyroid itself, leading to excessive secretion of thyroid hormones despite a lack of signaling from the endocrine tissues in the brain? Is the problem in the central nervous system, leading to excessive secretion through the release of high levels of TSH? This can only be determined by measuring an accurate level of TRH or TSH. TRH is hard to measure because it is in high concentrations within the hypophyseal portal system, but not in the systemic circulation. TSH, however, can easily be measured from a peripheral blood sample.

If an individual has hyperthyroid symptoms, a high level of TSH in the blood would indicate that the problem originates within the brain (or that TSH is being secreted from a tumor somewhere in the body). The high levels of TSH cause the thyroid gland to produce more thyroid hormones, leading to the symptoms. On the other hand, if an individual has hyperthyroid symptoms with a low level of TSH, this would indicate that the problem is at the level of the thyroid (or that thyroid hormones are being secreted from a tumor somewhere in the body). These thyroid hormones cause negative feedback on the hypothalamus and anterior pituitary, leading to a low level of TSH (and TRH, if one measured its concentration in the hypophyseal portal system).

If an individual has hypothyroid symptoms, the same delineation could be made by measuring TSH. A low level of TSH with hypothyroid symptoms implies that the problem is at the level of the hypothalamus or anterior pituitary, whereas a high level of TSH with hypothyroid symptoms implies that the problem is at the level of the thyroid.

Takeaways

Negative feedback systems are common throughout the endocrine system. Many of these systems can be organized into axes, including the hypothalamic–pituitary–adrenal, hypothalamic–pituiary–thyroid, and hypothalamic–pituitary–ovarian, –testicular, or –gonadal axes.

Things to Watch Out For

Proper diagnosis of an endocrinopathy usually requires measurement of at least two different hormones or analysis of at least two different organs. This allows determination of the site of the problem. In this question, a high concentration of thyroid hormone could be due to a problem in the brain or the thyroid; measurement of TSH would distinguish between these two sites of pathology.

Related Questions

1. A pituitary tumor compresses the stalk and causes a cessation of ACTH secretion. What effects would this lack of ACTH secretion have?
2. The posterior pituitary gland is also known as the neurohypophysis. Based on the relationship to other brain structures, why does this name make sense?
3. The pancreas is said to have both exocrine and endocrine functions. What is the difference between an exocrine and an endocrine organ?

Key Concepts

Biology Chapter 6

The respiratory system
Alveoli
Gas exchange
Dead space

The Respiratory System

The volume of the lungs that does not participate in gas exchange is considered physiological dead space. There are two types of dead space that are seen at rest: anatomical and alveolar. Anatomical dead space includes the conducting areas, such as the mouth and trachea, where oxygen enters the respiratory system but does not contact alveoli. Alveolar dead space is the area in the alveoli that does contact air but lacks sufficient circulation to participate in gas exchange. How can physiological dead space be reduced?

1 Examine each type of dead space separately.

Anatomical dead space refers to the air that remains in the conducting pathways—the mouth and trachea—with every breath. Because the size and length of the mouth and trachea are set and relatively unchangeable for a given individual, it is unlikely that physiological dead space can be decreased much through changes in the anatomical dead space.

Alveolar dead space consists of alveoli that contact air but do not participate in gas exchange. Because the alveoli are normal, they are capable of participating in gas exchange under the right conditions; therefore, alveolar dead space can be reduced.

2 Review the method of gas exchange at the tissues and in the lungs.

In the normal lung, oxygen will diffuse from alveolar air into the pulmonary capillaries. When the partial pressure of O_2 in the alveolar air and capillary blood equilibrate, the diffusion stops. Normally, this occurs before the blood in the pulmonary capillary exits the lungs and is considered perfusion-limited gas exchange. This O_2 is bound to hemoglobin and is taken and released to the tissues. CO_2 is produced by the tissues and diffuses into capillary blood, where it is carried to the lungs primarily as HCO_3^-. At the lungs, the reaction is reversed and CO_2 is exhaled:

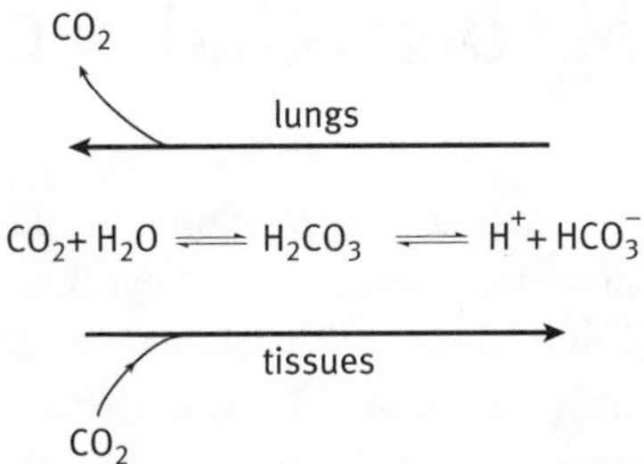

Determine why some alveoli do not participate in gas exchange.

There is not sufficient bloodflow through the capillaries of these dead space alveoli to induce them to participate in gas exchange. There must be bloodflow to a given alveolus for gas exchange to occur in that alveolus.

Determine how to increase bloodflow through the lungs.

If pulmonary bloodflow were increased, then more alveoli would be perfused with blood and would therefore participate in gas exchange. Increasing pulmonary bloodflow would require increasing the output of the right ventricle. Cardiac output increases during exercise because there is an increased heart rate and increased venous return due to skeletal muscle activity. Therefore, exercise would increase the amount of pulmonary bloodflow. This increased flow of blood through the lungs would recruit more alveoli for gas exchange and, therefore, reduce alveolar and physiological dead space.

Pulmonary bloodflow could also be increased through the administration of vasodilators, which open the blood vessels, lowering vascular resistance and increasing flow. Certain vasodilators are particularly active in the lungs.

Takeaways

The respiratory system is intimately linked to the circulatory system. Oxygen is delivered to tissues, and CO_2 is removed from tissues and ultimately removed from the body through exchange from the pulmonary capillaries into the alveolar space.

Things to Watch Out For

Under resting conditions, alveolar oxygen equilibrates with the blood in the pulmonary capillaries. This is considered a perfusion-limited exchange. Under conditions of exercise, the partial pressures of oxygen do not necessarily equilibrate along the length of the pulmonary capillary and a partial pressure gradient is maintained even at the venous end of the capillary.

Related Questions

1. What is the result if bloodflow to the left lung is completely blocked by a pulmonary embolus?
2. If an area of the lung is not ventilated due to an obstruction of the airways, what is the partial pressure of oxygen (P_aO_2) in the pulmonary capillaries of that area?
3. At what point will the diffusion of oxygen from the alveolus to the capillary stop?

Key Concepts

Biology Chapter 7

Oxyhemoglobin dissociation curve
Carbon monoxide
Hemoglobin
Left and right shifts

Oxyhemoglobin Dissociation Curve

Carbon monoxide (CO) binding to hemoglobin occurs in competition with oxygen (O_2) binding to hemoglobin; hemoglobin's affinity for CO is over 200 times its affinity for O_2. However, the binding of CO at one site increases the affinity for O_2 at the remaining sites. Draw the oxyhemoglobin dissociation curve for CO poisoning, measuring hemoglobin oxygen content (in units of % hemoglobin saturation) on the vertical axis.

1 Visualize the normal oxyhemoglobin dissociation curve.

The oxyhemoglobin dissociation curve shows the percent saturation of hemoglobin as a function of the partial pressure of oxygen (PO_2). At a PO_2 of 100 mmHg (the partial pressure of oxygen in the lungs), hemoglobin saturation is 100 percent, which means that four oxygen molecules are bound to nearly every hemoglobin molecule. At a PO_2 of 40 mmHg (the partial pressure of oxygen in resting tissues), hemoglobin is 80 percent saturated. At a PO_2 of 20 mmHg (the partial pressure of oxygen in exercising tissues), hemoglobin is 30 percent saturated with oxygen molecules. Oxygen binds cooperatively to hemoglobin, meaning that the binding of the first oxygen molecule facilitates the binding of the next, and so on. This results in a sigmoidal, or S-shaped, curve:

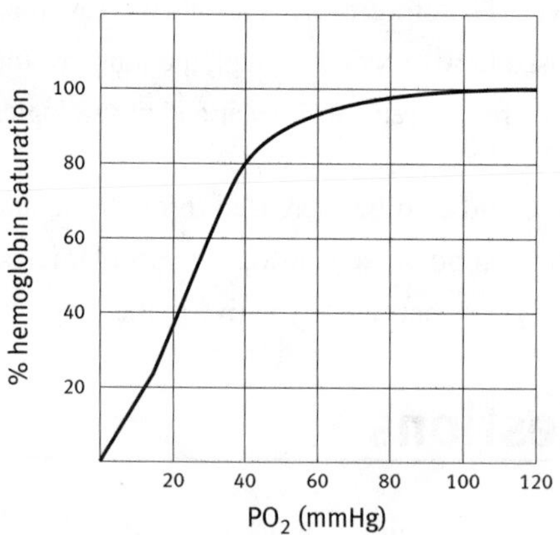

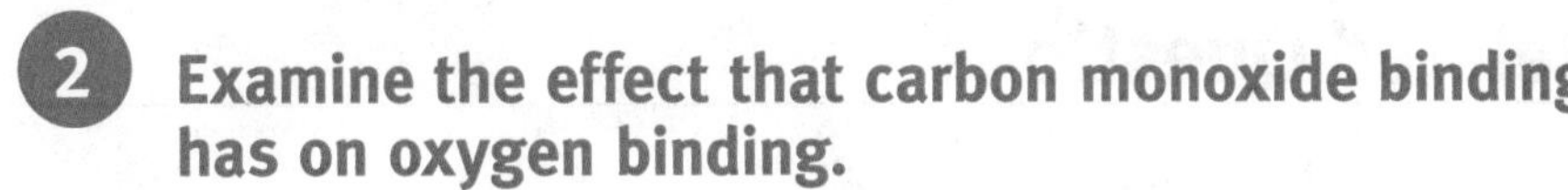

2 Examine the effect that carbon monoxide binding has on oxygen binding.

The question stem states that CO competes with O_2 when binding hemoglobin. Because hemoglobin's affinity for CO is 200 times greater than O_2, hemoglobin will preferentially bind CO first. This will decrease the amount of O_2 that can bind to hemoglobin and, therefore, decrease the amount of O_2 that is in the blood.

3 Determine the effect that carbon monoxide binding will have on the oxyhemoglobin dissociation curve.

The question stem also states that the binding of CO increases hemoglobin's affinity for O_2 at the remaining sites. Any physiological factor that increases the affinity of hemoglobin for oxygen (such as decreased PCO_2, increased pH, or decreased temperature) has the effect of shifting the curve to the left. Any physiological factor that decreases the affinity of hemoglobin for oxygen (such as increased PCO_2, decreased pH, or increased temperature) has the effect of shifting the curve to the right. The right shift is known as the Bohr effect. However, in this case, the affinity of hemoglobin for oxygen is increased, and so there will be a left shift in the oxyhemoglobin dissociation curve. It is this left shift that makes CO poisoning so deadly; with CO bound to hemoglobin, the O_2 molecules are bound so tightly that they cannot be offloaded at the tissues, and tissue hypoxia occurs:

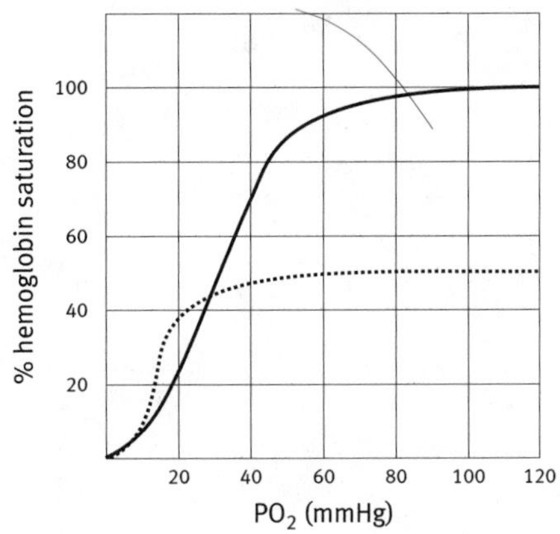

Takeaways

Be familiar with the concepts of PO_2 and PCO_2, what factors change their values, and how they are represented graphically.

Things to Watch Out For

Right shifts in the dissociation curve (Bohr effect) are more commonly seen, but be prepared for the factors that can cause the curve to shift to the left, including decreased PCO_2, increased pH, decreased temperature, fetal hemoglobin, and certain pathological states—such as carbon monoxide poisoning.

Related Questions

1. How would exercise affect the oxyhemoglobin dissociation curve?
2. What type of compensatory reactions would a high PCO_2 cause?
3. What would the oxyhemoglobin dissociation curve look like in a patient with metabolic alkalosis?

High-Yield Problem-Solving Guide questions continue on the next page. ▶ ▶ ▶

Key Concepts
Biology Chapter 8
Immunoglobulins
Active immunity
Passive immunity
Innate immunity
Adaptive immunity

Immune Function

X-linked severe combined immunodeficiency (SCID) occurs due to a mutation in a protein necessary for the receptors for interleukins IL-2, IL-4, IL-7, IL-9, and IL-15. This results in the absence or near absence of T-cells and natural killer (NK) cells. B-cells are present but are nonfunctioning in these individuals. Why, despite their presence, are B-cells nonfunctional in those with SCID?

1 Summarize and simplify the question.

The question stem states that severe combined immunodeficiency (SCID) results when there is a mutation in a protein required for the receptors for various interleukins. This results in a lack of T-cells and natural killer (NK) cells. B-cells are still present but are nonfunctional. Given this information, this question is really asking about how a receptor mutation will cause a lack of some cell types (T-cells and NK cells), while producing nonfunctional B-cells.

2 Identify the normal purpose of interleukins.

Interleukins are the language of communication in the immune system. Interleukins direct the proliferation and maturation of lymphocytes including T-cells and B-cells. In addition, portions of the innate immune system are also coordinated by interactions with interleukins. Interleukins are known to activate macrophages, NK cells, and B-cells.

3 Determine how a mutation in an interleukin receptor may affect immune system signaling.

Communication between cells often requires interactions between some soluble molecule and a receptor. Lack of a functioning receptor often has the same effect as a lack of the effector molecule.

The question stem states that there is a mutation in a protein required for interleukin receptors. This mutation affects the function of multiple interleukins. The dysfunction of this interleukin receptor results in defective immune system signaling. If the immune system cannot signal between cells properly, then numerous processes may be affected. Interleukins are part of the system that induces proliferation of T-cells and NK cells. In addition, without effective interleukin signaling, T-cells that are produced may not be able to migrate to the thymus for maturation. A lack of mature T-cells will result in the inability of T-cells to signal to B-cells. If there is no signaling to B-cells, then plasma and memory cells will not form, and antibody production will not occur. Therefore, there will be little to no humoral protection against antigens in these individuals.

Takeaways

Because of the interdependencies of the immune system, dysfunction of one arm of the immune system may cause dysfunction of other arms of the immune system. In this example, a lack of functional T-cells leads to a lack of functional B-cells.

4 Using the information discussed, propose a hypothesis.

To summarize the information previously considered, lack of a functioning interleukin receptor results in a near complete loss of function of the adaptive immune system. T-cells and NK cells do not mature, and B-cells are not able to function. If the same protein is involved in multiple receptor types, then mutations of this protein will affect multiple interleukin receptors. The resulting phenotype is a nonfunctioning adaptive immune system. T-cells and NK cells are unable to proliferate, and signaling to B-cells is severely limited.

Things to Watch Out For

Many of the questions focusing on the immune system on the MCAT focus on the crosstalk of this system. Most important among these forms of communication are those between the innate and adaptive immune systems and those between T- and B-cells.

Related Questions

1. During pregnancy, some immunoglobulins are transferred across the placenta. After birth, breast milk also contains antibodies that provide the infant with reduced susceptibility to infection. What is a potential disadvantage of this type of immunity?
2. Allergic reactions, such as seasonal allergies, rely on the cross-linking of immunoglobulins that are already on the surface on mast cells. Why does the first exposure to an allergen rarely result in an immune response?
3. Respiratory droplets, created during sneezing or coughing, can carry bacteria and viruses. What type of immunity is represented by the cilia of the respiratory passages that carry these viruses toward the oropharynx to be swallowed or expelled?

Key Concepts

Biology Chapter 9

Digestive enzymes
Pancreatic enzymes
Pancreas
Duodenum
Gastric acid

The Digestive System

During the gastric phase of digestion, the presence of food in the stomach, particularly amino acids and peptides, causes G cells to secrete gastrin, which in turn stimulates parietal cells. Gastrin secretion is normally inhibited once acidic chyme, with a pH less than 3, reaches the duodenum. What would occur if a tumor secreted excess gastrin in an unregulated fashion?

1 Determine the role of gastrin in the stomach.

According to the question stem, gastrin stimulates parietal cells when food is present in the stomach. Parietal cells secrete hydrochloric acid, and therefore gastrin is a physiological agonist of HCl secretion. Once the chyme reaches a certain acidity ($pH < 3$) and moves into the small intestine, gastrin secretion is inhibited and therefore HCl secretion is decreased.

2 Determine the role of hydrochloric acid in the stomach.

In the stomach, HCl is necessary for the proper function of *pepsin* because low pH promotes activation of *pepsinogen* to pepsin; this enzyme is also most active in the pH range of 1–3.

3 Examine what occurs when acidic chyme reaches the small intestine.

Once the chyme moves into the small intestine, the pH needs to be increased to reach the optimal pH for pancreatic proteases and lipases (around 8.5). Therefore, gastrin release is inhibited, and the pancreas is stimulated to secrete bicarbonate into the duodenum to neutralize the acid. The pancreas also releases hydrolytic enzymes, such as *amylase*, *trypsinogen*, *chymotrypsinogen*, *carboxypeptidases A* and *B*, and pancreatic lipase.

4 Examine the effect of a gastrin-secreting tumor.

A gastrin-secreting tumor will secrete gastrin at all times and will not be inhibited by normal feedback mechanisms, such as the presence of chyme in the small intestine.

This gastrin will continually stimulate parietal cells to produce HCl. This excess of acid will move with the chyme into the small intestine. Normal amounts of bicarbonate will be released; however, this is not enough to neutralize such an excess of HCl.

This condition—caused by a gastrin-secreting tumor—is called *Zollinger–Ellison syndrome*. The tumor is usually located in the pancreatic islets of Langerhans.

5 Determine the effects of an acidic environment in the small intestine.

Pancreatic enzymes require a more alkaline environment than gastric enzymes for optimal activity. If the environment in the small intestine is too acidic, then pancreatic enzymes will be unable to function normally. While proteins and carbohydrates are partially digested before they reach the small intestine, fats have very little digestion until they reach the duodenum. If *pancreatic lipase* is unable to function due to an excessively acidic environment, it will not be able to digest lipids. This will result in the malabsorption of lipids, which leads to excretion of fats in the feces, also known as *steatorrhea*. The excess acid can also cause gastric and duodenal ulcers, in which the mucosal lining is worn away and acid can damage the underlying epithelial cells.

Takeaways

The effects of excess acid on the digestive system include the direct effects of acid on the tissues (gastric and duodenal ulcers) as well as biochemical effects on the digestive enzymes (denaturation and decreased activity).

Things to Watch Out For

An acidic duodenal pH will affect the function of all of the pancreatic enzymes, but some protein absorption can still occur because proteins are partially digested in the stomach. Carbohydrate digestion does not rely heavily on pancreatic secretions; absorption of some carbohydrates can still occur because they begin digestion in the mouth and continue to be broken down by disaccharidases in the intestinal brush border.

Related Questions

1. A patient with a peptic ulcer takes a large dose of antacid. This would primarily reduce the activity of which digestive enzyme?
2. Pancreatic ductal cells secrete bicarbonate, which is moved into the intestinal lumen. What would be the physiological results if these ductal cells were destroyed by an autoimmune disorder?
3. Pancreatitis is a disease that prevents the pancreas from being able to produce adequate amounts of lipase. What will be the physiological result of this component of the disease?

Key Concepts

Biology Chapter 10

Plasma osmolarity
Filtrate osmolarity
Antidiuretic hormone
Aldosterone
Water reabsorption

Kidney Function

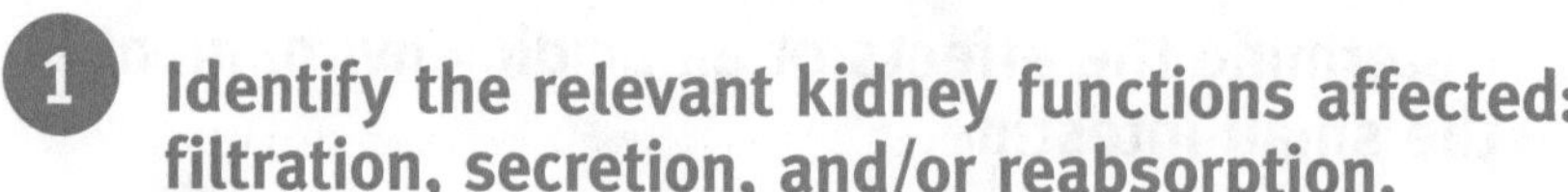

A student discovers that drinking diet caffeinated soda results in a significant increase in urine volume and frequency. What are the physiological factors driving this phenomenon?

1 Identify the relevant kidney functions affected: filtration, secretion, and/or reabsorption.

Excessive urine output means that there is a failure to reabsorb water from the nephron. Thus, the problem is at the level of reabsorption.

Renal failure relating to filtration usually results in irregular plasma osmolarity (for example, the urea concentration may be too high, or the albumin concentration may be too low). Secretion plays a critical role in maintaining blood pH, potassium concentrations in blood, and nitrogenous waste concentrations in the filtrate. Reabsorption also affects filtrate concentration, as essential substances such as glucose, amino acids, vitamins, and salts are returned to the blood.

2 Identify the roles of plasma osmolarity and antidiuretic hormone.

Caffeine (as well as alcohol) inhibits either the secretion or activity of antidiuretic hormone (ADH or vasopressin), thus decreasing water reabsorption from the collecting duct.

ADH works directly on the collecting duct by increasing its permeability to water; thus, a decrease in ADH levels will lead to a decrease in water reabsorption. ADH secretion is normally triggered by a sustained increase in plasma osmolarity. The reabsorption of water from the filtrate into the blood dilutes the blood, lowering the plasma osmolarity. Thus, if ADH is not released or cannot activate its receptor, water will not be reabsorbed and the plasma osmolarity will remain high. If the water remains in the urine, it increases urinary volume and frequency.

Identify the roles of blood pressure, renin, and aldosterone.

Ingestion of a large volume of soda increases arterial pressure, leading to a decrease in renin and aldosterone secretion and, therefore, a decrease in water reabsorption.

Recall that renin is released in response to low blood pressure in the kidneys. Renin activates angiotensinogen to angiotensin I, which is converted to angiotensin II by angiotensin-converting enzyme in the lungs. Angiotensin II promotes secretion of aldosterone from the adrenal cortex. Recall that aldosterone increases sodium reabsorption in the distal convoluted tubule and collecting duct, and because water follows sodium from the filtrate into the blood, aldosterone also increases water reabsorption.

If renin and aldosterone secretion is reduced, then sodium and water will not be reabsorbed in the distal convoluted tubule and collecting duct, and are excreted in the urine. The increase in water increases urinary volume and frequency.

Identify the role of filtrate osmolarity.

An abnormally high filtrate osmolarity will decrease the osmotic gradient between the tubule and the interstitial fluid, causing a drop in water reabsorption.

Diet sodas substitute aspartame for sugar, but unlike glucose, the aspartame cannot be reabsorbed back into the blood from the nephron—hence the high filtrate osmolarity. Even if you did not know that aspartame cannot be reabsorbed from the nephron, it is imperative to recognize the role that filtrate osmolarity can play in water reabsorption. Recall that in diabetes mellitus, a similar mechanism is at play: due to the high glucose concentration, not all of the sugar can be reabsorbed from the nephron, leading to an abnormally high filtrate concentration, less water reabsorption, and ultimately the excretion of a larger volume of urine that also contains glucose.

Takeaways

Questions related to the nephron appear in varying contexts. The key is to isolate the relevant component of kidney function being tested (filtration, secretion, and/or reabsorption) and then to tease apart which particular components of that function (such as filtrate osmolarity or hormonal control) are being affected.

Things to Watch Out For

Under most circumstances, the kidney produces urine that is hypertonic to the blood, but in the situation described here, the urine produced is likely to be hypotonic to the blood. Alcohol consumption produces similar physiological effects. However, frequent urination does not always mean that the urine is hypotonic to the blood. Patients who excrete protein in their urine (filtration failure) have low blood osmolarities, and thus have a low level of water reabsorption. Therefore, the urine produced may still be hypertonic to the blood.

Related Questions

1. A patient has been found to have insufficient levels of antidiuretic hormone. What symptoms would this individual have?
2. Diabetics who fail to take insulin experience dehydration. What are the physiological factors driving this phenomenon?
3. A patient with renal failure has nephrons that lack the ability to actively secrete or reabsorb any substances. What functions might the kidney still be able to perform?

Key Concepts

Biology Chapter 11

Muscle contraction
Parathyroid hormone
Calcium homeostasis
The sarcomere
Cardiac muscle

Muscle Contraction

What process during muscle contraction is likely to be affected by a deficiency of parathyroid hormone?

1 Identify the function of parathyroid hormone.

Parathyroid hormone (PTH) is involved in calcium homeostasis. Release of parathyroid hormone results in an increased calcium concentration in the blood. Specifically, PTH decreases excretion of calcium by the kidneys, increases absorption of calcium in the gut (via vitamin D), and increases bone resorption, thereby freeing up calcium. PTH is subject to feedback inhibition—as levels of plasma calcium rise, PTH secretion is decreased.

PTH also affects phosphorus homeostasis by resorbing phosphate from bone and reducing reabsorption of phosphate in the kidney (thus promoting its excretion in the urine). PTH also promotes the activation of vitamin D, which is required for the absorption of calcium and phosphate in the gut. For this question, we will focus primarily on the role of PTH in calcium homeostasis.

2 Predict the effect of a deficiency of parathyroid hormone.

If parathyroid hormone is not released, then all of these mechanisms will be down-regulated. Calcium excretion in the kidneys will be decreased, less calcium would be absorbed from the gut, and bone resorption would decrease. This could lead to hypocalcemia, or low concentrations of calcium in the blood.

3 Recall the role of calcium in muscle contraction.

During muscle contraction, depolarization of the muscle cells results in the opening of calcium channels in the sarcolemma. Calcium then binds to troponin, causing a conformational change in tropomyosin, which exposes the myosin-binding sites on actin.

Identify the process affected by low calcium levels.

If prolonged enough, low calcium levels in the blood can lead to low calcium levels within the sarcoplasmic reticulum of muscle cells. When stimulated, these muscle cells will have a smaller efflux of calcium from the sarcoplasmic reticulum, which will affect the binding of calcium to troponin.

Under normal circumstances, it is the binding of calcium to troponin that causes a conformational change in tropomyosin, exposing the myosin-binding sites on actin and permitting cross-bridge formation for muscle contraction. Therefore, a decreased calcium concentration in the muscle cell will lead to less cross-bridge formation and a weaker muscle contraction. Because each muscle fiber contains numerous molecules of troponin, this may also result in an inability to recruit all of the muscle fibers in an organized, efficient fashion.

Takeaways

The intracellular environment of the muscle cell can be impacted by its extracellular environment. Prolonged changes in blood concentrations of various electrolytes can impact the internal environment of muscle (and other) cells, leading to changes in their physiology.

Things to Watch Out For

This question was very specific. You may know that one of the symptoms of hypocalcemia is tetany, but that phenomenon is related to changes in permeability of neurons, rather than muscle contraction itself. When a question is very specific, provide a specific answer related to the theme of the question stem.

Related Questions

1. An autoimmune disease produces antibodies against the acetylcholine receptor at the neuromuscular junction. Which step in muscle contraction is likely to be affected most directly by this disease?
2. Which division of the sarcomere does not change in size during muscle contraction?
3. A student is attempting to identify types of muscle tissue by microscopic examination. A sample contains cells with one or two nuclei and intercalated discs between the cells. The overall appearance is striated. What muscle type is likely included in this sample?

Key Concepts

Biology Chapter 12

Hardy–Weinberg equilibrium

$p^2 + 2pq + q^2 = 1$

Allele frequencies

Genotype frequencies

Hardy–Weinberg Equilibrium

Gigantism is coded for by a recessive allele. The dominant allele for the same gene codes for the normal phenotype. In an isolated geographic area, 9 people out of a sample of 10,000 were found to have gigantism, whereas the rest had normal phenotypes. Assuming Hardy–Weinberg equilibrium, calculate the frequency of the recessive and dominant alleles as well as the number of heterozygotes in the population.

1 Solve for the frequency of the recessive allele.

Because gigantism will only emerge with a homozygous recessive genotype, it will be represented as gg. In the Hardy–Weinberg equation, the recessive genotype frequency is depicted as q^2. By taking the square root of q^2, we get the frequency of the recessive gigantism allele, q, which is 0.03:

$$\text{gigantism} = \text{homozygous recessive} = \text{gg} = q^2$$

$$q^2 = \frac{9}{10{,}000} = 0.0009$$

$$q = 0.03$$

recessive allele frequency = 3%

2 Solve for the frequency of the dominant allele.

The frequency of the dominant allele, p, plus the frequency of the recessive allele, q, equals 1. To solve for the frequency of the dominant allele, simply subtract the recessive allele frequency from 1:

$$p + q = 1$$

$$p = 1 - q$$

$$= 1 - 0.03$$

$$= 0.97$$

dominant allele frequency = 97%

Solve for the number of heterozygotes.

To find the number of heterozygotes, we need to recall which part of the Hardy–Weinberg equation corresponds to the frequency of heterozygotes in the population. This is the expression $2pq$:

$$2pq = \text{frequency of heterozygotes}$$

$$\text{Gg} = 2pq = 2 \times 0.97 \times 0.03$$

$$= 0.058\ (5.8\%)$$

To find the size of the heterozygous population, multiply the frequency by the total size of the population:

$$0.058 \times 10{,}000 = 580 \text{ people}$$

Related Questions

1. Suppose a similar survey was done in another area. This time, 90 people with gigantism were found from a survey of 200,000 people. Calculate the same parameters with the new survey.
2. An allele f occurs with a frequency of 0.8 in a wolfpack population. Determine the frequencies of the genotypes FF, Ff, and ff.
3. If the frequency of homozygous recessive individuals for a certain autosomal recessive disease is 16 percent, determine the percentage of phenotypically normal individuals.

Takeaways

Remember both Hardy–Weinberg equations: $p + q = 1$ and $p^2 + 2pq + q^2 = 1$. p is the frequency of the dominant allele; q is the frequency of the recessive allele. p^2 is the frequency of the homozygous dominant genotype, $2pq$ is the frequency of the heterozygous genotype, and q^2 is the frequency of the homozygous recessive genotype.

Things to Watch Out For

There are five circumstances in which the Hardy–Weinberg equations may fail to apply. These are: mutations, migration, genetic drift, nonrandom mating, and natural selection. The Hardy–Weinberg equations refer to populations that are stable and *not* evolving.

Solutions to Related Questions

1. Prokaryotic Genetics

1. In this question, we must think about the characteristics required to induce the transcription of the DNA encoded on the plasmid. First, in order for bacteria to transcribe the genetic sequence, an appropriate promoter must be present. In addition, the genetic material to be transcribed must be close enough to the promoter to facilitate effective transcription. In order to ensure efficient conversion of all of the bacteria in a colony to bacteria able to produce this protein, the plasmid should also encode a sex factor so that the plasmid can be efficiently transferred between cells.

2. The fact that the same bacterial genetic sequence is transferred each time this bacteriophage infects a bacterium implies that the process of transduction is not random in this case. This is likely the case if the phage genome integrates into the bacterial genome and, when the phage genome is later released from the bacterial genome, it takes a small segment of bacterial DNA with it. This implies that the bacteriophage must enter the lysogenic cycle. To replicate and subsequently infect other bacteria, the bacteriophage will also have to reenter the lytic cycle at some point.

3. Sometimes, the sex factor becomes incorporated into the bacterial genome. This information is generally carried on a plasmid, but, by the process of transformation, it may become part of the bacterial genome itself. When this occurs, the entire genome will be replicated and the bacterium will attempt to transfer the entire genome during conjugation. The conjugation bridge is usually not stable enough to permit transfer of the entire bacterial genome, but sizable portions of it are often still transferred. This results in high frequency recombination. Cells that have undergone this particular change are known as Hfr or high frequency of recombination cells.

2. Menstrual Cycle

1. FSH is inhibited early in the follicular phase to prevent the development of multiple follicles. While some FSH is necessary for the development of a follicle at all, the body prevents the formation of many follicles by negative feedback of estrogen on the hypothalamus and anterior pituitary. Later in the follicular phase, FSH levels rise in parallel with LH levels as estrogen's feedback mechanism switches from negative feedback to positive feedback.

2. Progesterone levels are very low during the follicular phase of the menstrual cycle, and do not begin to rise until the luteal phase. The corpus luteum, which does not exist until the secondary oocyte has been released from the ovary, secretes progesterone to develop and maintain the endometrium. Thus, progesterone levels rise during the luteal phase. It is the drop in the level of progesterone that ultimately stimulates menses, which—by definition—begins on day 0 of the cycle.

3. Ovulation can be prevented biochemically by manipulating the hormones involved in the menstrual cycle. Birth control pills, or oral contraceptive pills (OCPs), keep estrogen and progesterone levels elevated so that FSH and LH are constantly inhibited. Because of this inhibition, a follicle does not develop and the LH surge does not occur, thereby preventing ovulation.

3. Stages of Embryogenesis

1. Trophoblasts are the cells that form the placenta. In formation of the placenta, these cells must invade the endometrium to create the interface between the mother and the developing embryo. This means that this cell type is particularly inclined toward rapid division and invasion of foreign tissues. Thus, if a malignancy develops, the ability of this cell to invade blood vessels and spread (metastasize) is often more pronounced than with other cell types.

2. The mesoderm is the middle germ layer within the gastrula. The mesoderm gives rise to the musculoskeletal system, the circulatory system, much of the excretory system, the gonads, the muscular and connective tissue layers of the digestive and respiratory systems, and the adrenal cortex. Thus, a mutation that occurs early in the process of development will have far-reaching consequences, affecting each of these organ systems.

3. Indeterminate cleavage means that the cells are still capable of developing into any cell type, and could even develop into entire organisms. If a zygote undergoes indeterminate cleavage, and the cells actually separate from each other, then twinning may occur. Because these twins arose from the same zygote, they would be considered monozygotic or identical twins. Depending on when during development the organisms split from each other, the resulting twins could be dichorionic/diamniotic, monochorionic/diamniotic, or monochorionic/monoamniotic.

4. Action Potential

1. The opening of the sodium channel brings the membrane potential closer to sodium's electrochemical equilibrium potential. The longer the channel is open, the closer the membrane potential will get to this equilibrium potential. Therefore, sodium is closest to its electrochemical equilibrium right before the sodium channels are inactivated. This corresponds to the highest point of the action potential in the graph—the point right between regions II and III, around +35 mV (the actual equilibrium potential for sodium is close to +60 mV).

2. An action potential is an all-or-nothing response, so the speed and magnitude of an individual action potential cannot be altered. Rather, the magnitude of a stimulus is encoded by the frequency of action potential firing. A lower-magnitude stimulus elicits a lower firing frequency; a higher-magnitude stimulus elicits a higher firing frequency.

3. When a membrane is hyperpolarized, it is further from the threshold potential and would require a larger stimulus to create an action potential. Therefore, hyperpolarizing a membrane would be a way to inhibit an action potential. Action potentials are also inhibited during the absolute refractory period, which occurs during the action potential itself. Finally, blockage or inactivation of the sodium channel will prevent the depolarization phase of the action potential, thereby inhibiting the rest of the action potential from occurring.

5. Endocrine Organs

1. ACTH, or adrenocorticotropic hormone, is one of the tropic hormones released by the anterior pituitary. The hypothalamus releases corticotropin-releasing factor (CRF), which triggers the release of ACTH from the anterior pituitary. Then, ACTH stimulates cortisol secretion from the adrenal cortex. Cortisol is one of the hormones that aids in wakefulness as well as aiding in the maintenance of blood pressure. Lack of cortisol is likely to result in fatigue and low blood pressure.

2. The posterior pituitary is best thought of as an extension of the hypothalamus. The bodies of the nerves of the posterior pituitary are actually located in the hypothalamus, which sends axons down the length of the pituitary stalk into the region of the posterior pituitary. The two main hormones released from the posterior pituitary, antidiuretic hormone (ADH or vasopressin) and oxytocin, are made in the hypothalamus and stored in the nerve terminals of the posterior pituitary. Thus, *neurohypophysis* is an appropriate name for the posterior pituitary as this organ is simply an extension of certain hypothalamic neurons.

3. An exocrine organ is one that secretes its products into ducts, which empty onto an epithelial surface. Examples of exocrine organs include lacrimal glands, sweat glands, salivary glands, mammary glands, and the digestive portions of the pancreas. Endocrine organs secrete hormones into the bloodstream, where the hormones travel to distant target tissues. Examples of endocrine organs include the hypothalamus, pituitary gland, thyroid, parathyroid glands, pancreas, adrenal glands, and gonads.

6. Respiratory System

1. If respiration is occurring normally but there is no bloodflow to the left lung, then there is no gas exchange occurring in the left lung. If no oxygen is being diffused from the air into the blood and no CO_2 is being released, then the P_AO_2 of the alveoli will equal the PO_2 of inspired air, around 100 mmHg O_2.

2. If there is an airway obstruction but bloodflow to the lung is normal, then there is no gas exchange. The blood that flows into the lung will have the same PO_2 and PCO_2 as systemic venous blood. Because no gas exchange occurs, this value will remain the same for blood that exits the lung and throughout the pulmonary capillaries in that area. P_VO_2 is approximately 40 mmHg and P_VCO_2 is approximately 47 mmHg.

3. When the P_AO_2 of inspired air equals the P_aO_2 of capillary blood, then diffusion of oxygen from the alveolus to the capillary will stop. Note that in physiology, *A* stands for alveolar, whereas *a* stands for arterial.

7. Oxyhemoglobin Dissociation Curve

1. Exercise will lead to an increase in body temperature as well as an increase in CO_2 production by the tissues. Through the bicarbonate buffer system, the excess CO_2 generates protons, lowering the pH. The pH may be further lowered if anaerobic metabolism is occurring, generating lactic acid. These factors cause the Bohr effect—a shift in the oxyhemoglobin dissociation curve to the right.

2. A high PCO_2 will lead to an increase in ventilation rate. This allows the body to exhale additional carbon dioxide, bringing the body back to a normal PCO_2. In prolonged cases of hypercarbia (high concentrations of carbon dioxide in the blood), the kidney may begin excreting additional acid, shifting the bicarbonate buffer system to lower the concentration of carbon dioxide in the blood.

3. In metabolic alkalosis, blood pH will be increased due to the loss of H^+ ions (or production of bicarbonate ions). Increased pH shifts the oxygen dissociation curve to the left, increasing the affinity of hemoglobin for oxygen.

8. Immune Function

1. Infants can receive antibodies from their mothers across the placenta and through breast milk. This type of immunization is known as passive immunity. The infant receives IgG antibodies while *in utero*, and then receives IgA antibodies while breast-feeding. This provides some protection from immunity while the child is very young. However, this form of immunity is not permanent and wanes rapidly when exposure to these antibodies ceases. The only way to maintain ongoing protection against a particular antigen is through the creation of memory cells. Without memory cells, the infant will be susceptible to the antigen as soon as the passive immunity wanes. Thus, the primary disadvantage of this type of immunity is that it is not permanent.

2. The question stem states that the immunoglobulins required for an allergic reaction are already attached to mast cells. This means that the immunoglobulins must already be present in the body. During the first exposure, the immunoglobulins required for allergic reactions have not yet been synthesized. During the creation of immunoglobulins, the first ones created are of the IgM class. After exposure to the antigen, isotype switching occurs, which allows for the production of IgE—the main form of antibody involved in allergic reactions. It is these IgE molecules on mast cells that must cross-link in order to cause degranulation of the mast cell and the release of the inflammatory mediators that cause an allergic reaction. Thus, the reason that the first exposure does not result in an allergic reaction is that IgE is formed *after* and *in response to* this first exposure.

3. Cilia, along with mucus, line the respiratory tract. The mucus is able to entrap an offending substance, and the cilia are able to move this mucus up to the oropharynx, where it can be swallowed or expelled. Because this type of immunity is not specific to a particular antigen, it is known as innate immunity.

9. The Digestive System

1. A large dose of antacid would increase the pH of the stomach and therefore inactivate pepsin. The optimum pH for pepsin is between 1 and 3; pepsin is denatured and inactivated at pH values greater than 5.

2. If the ductal cells were destroyed and the pancreas could not secrete bicarbonate, the acidic chyme that moves into the duodenum would not be neutralized and pancreatic lipase would not be able to function. This would result in the malabsorption of lipids and steatorrhea (fatty stools). This may also leave the duodenum susceptible to ulceration.

3. Inadequate amounts of pancreatic lipase will lead to steatorrhea. If lipids are not broken down by lipase, they cannot be absorbed by the small intestine and will be excreted in the feces. Steatorrhea is often described as the formation of greasy or oily stool, which is often foul-smelling due to partial breakdown by gut bacteria. These stools often float because of their high concentration of fat.

10. Kidney Function

1. If a patient has insufficient levels of antidiuretic hormone (ADH or vasopressin), he or she would suffer symptoms of diabetes insipidus, a disease characterized by ADH deficiency or lack of response by the kidneys to ADH secretion. These symptoms include excess urine production because of the inability to reabsorb water in the collecting ducts, extreme thirst due to fluid loss, and a hyperosmolar blood plasma concentration.

2. The reason why diabetics who fail to take insulin experience dehydration is linked to their excess blood glucose. Having a higher concentration of glucose in the blood means that there will be more glucose filtered into the urine—more than can be reabsorbed in the proximal convoluted tubule. With this system overloaded, glucose continues to pass through the nephron and pulls water with it. The more water that is pulled into the nephron, the more will get excreted in the urine, thus causing dehydration.

3. Just because this patient's nephrons have lost the ability to actively secrete or reabsorb substances does not mean that they cannot passively move substances. Therefore, the passive flow of ions and water will still occur. The kidney may also be able to filter blood effectively, permitting the passage of water, ions, and dissolved biomolecules while retaining cells and proteins in the vasculature. The kidney may also be able to carry out its nonurinary functions as well, such as vitamin D activation and production of erythropoietin.

11. Muscle Contraction

1. This condition, called *myasthenia gravis*, renders acetylcholine receptors nonfunctional. Acetylcholine is the neurotransmitter used at the neuromuscular junction; thus, if acetylcholine is unable to bind, then the muscle cell will not be depolarized. If depolarization does not occur, then the sarcoplasmic reticulum will not open, and calcium release will not occur. Myasthenia gravis is characterized by muscle weakness, especially after repeated stimulation of the same skeletal muscle tissue.

2. The sarcomere is divided into segments (bands or zones) depending on the filaments within that segment. The Z-lines define the boundaries of each sarcomere, and the M-line defines its middle. Because a sarcomere shortens during contraction, the Z-lines and M-lines must become closer to each other. The I-band consists only of thin filaments, whereas the H-zone consists only of thick filaments. During contraction, the thin filaments slide along the thick filaments, resulting in smaller I-bands and H-zones. The A-band contains the entire length of the thick filaments. This band remains constant in size during contraction; the actin and myosin filaments slide over one another but do not change length themselves.

3. There are two types of striated muscle: cardiac and skeletal muscle. Skeletal muscle has numerous nuclei, whereas cardiac muscle contains one or two nuclei per cell. In addition, intercalated discs contain many gap junctions that allow for rapid conduction of charge between adjacent cardiac muscle cells. Therefore, it is cardiac muscle that is described in the question stem.

12. Hardy–Weinberg Equilibrium

1. If a similar survey found 90 people with gigantism out of 200,000 people, then the frequency of the recessive allele is $\sqrt{\frac{90}{200,000}} = \sqrt{\frac{9}{20,000}} = \sqrt{\frac{4.5}{10,000}} \approx \frac{2.1}{100} = 0.021$. The frequency of the dominant allele is $1 - 0.021 = 0.979$. The number of heterozygotes in the population is $(2 \times 0.979 \times 0.021) \times 200,000 \approx 2 \times 1 \times 21 \times 200 = 8400$ people (actual = 8305).

2. If allele f occurs with a frequency of 0.8, then allele F occurs with a frequency of 0.2. Thus, the frequency of FF = $0.2 \times 0.2 = 0.04$ (4%), the frequency of Ff = $2 \times 0.2 \times 0.8 = 0.32$ (32%), and the frequency of ff = $0.8 \times 0.8 = 0.64$ (64%).

3. If the frequency of homozygous recessive individuals is 0.16 (16%), then $1 - 0.16 = 0.84$ (84%) of individuals are phenotypically normal, assuming that the phenotype coded for by the dominant allele is "normal."

4

General Chemistry

Key Concepts

General Chemistry Chapter 1

Atomic mass
Atomic weight
Mass number
Isotopes

Atomic Mass and Weight

Following an experiment, an unknown element has several isotopes with the following abundances:

$^{64}X = 48.89\%, 63.929$ amu
$^{66}X = 27.81\%, 65.926$ amu
$^{67}X = 4.11\%, 66.927$ amu
$^{68}X = 18.57\%, 67.925$ amu
$^{70}X = 0.62\%, 69.925$ amu

What is the atomic weight of the unknown element? What is the element's identity? How many protons, neutrons, and electrons does $^{70}X^{+}$ have?

1 Determine the atomic weight of the element.

The atomic weight is the weighted average of the different atomic masses. To find a weighted average, we start by multiplying the atomic mass of each isotope by its relative abundance, given as a decimal. In this example, we are precise with the calculations, but on Test Day, you would want to round these values to simplify the arithmetic and arrive at the answer more quickly:

$$63.929 \text{ amu} \times 0.4889 = 31.2549 \text{ amu}$$
$$65.926 \text{ amu} \times 0.2781 = 18.3340 \text{ amu}$$
$$66.927 \text{ amu} \times 0.0411 = 2.7507 \text{ amu}$$
$$67.925 \text{ amu} \times 0.1857 = 12.6137 \text{ amu}$$
$$69.925 \text{ amu} \times 0.0062 = 0.4335 \text{ amu}$$

Now, add together the values. Unlike average calculations in arithmetic, we have already taken into account the relative abundances and therefore do not need to divide by n, the number of samples:

$$31.2549 + 18.3340 + 2.7507 + 12.6137 + 0.4335 = 65.3868 \text{ amu}$$

Thus, the atomic weight of this element is $65.3868\ \frac{\text{amu}}{\text{atom}}$; its molar mass would be $65.3868\ \frac{\text{g}}{\text{mol}}$.

2 To determine the unknown element, look in the Periodic Table and find the element with the atomic weight closest to your estimated value.

By definition, the weighted average of the atomic masses is the atomic weight. This is the value listed in the Periodic Table for that element's weight. The value we calculated, 65.3868 $\frac{\text{amu}}{\text{atom}}$, is closest to the atomic weight of zinc (Zn), which is listed in our Periodic Table as 65.4 $\frac{\text{amu}}{\text{atom}}$.

3 Determine the number of protons, neutrons, and electrons in a zinc-70 +1 cation.

Looking at the Periodic Table, the atomic number of zinc is 30. The atomic number, *Z*, represents the number of protons in an element and actually defines the element's identity; that is, all atoms of zinc contain 30 protons.

The mass number, *A*, represents the number of protons plus the number of neutrons in a given atom. The various isotopes of zinc in this question have the same number of protons, but vary in their numbers of neutrons. For zinc-70, there are 70 – 30 = 40 neutrons.

There are equal numbers of protons and electrons in a neutral atom. In the zinc-70 cation, there will be one fewer electron, giving the atom a charge of +1. Therefore, there are 30 – 1 = 29 electrons in the zinc-70 +1 cation.

Takeaways

The atomic number is the number of protons in an element; if the element is neutral, it is also the number of electrons. The mass number is the number of protons and neutrons combined. The atomic weight is reported on the Periodic Table and is the weighted average of the atomic masses of each isotope.

Things to Watch Out For

One of the biggest traps with math-heavy general chemistry questions is trying to make calculations precise. On the MCAT, answer choices are usually far enough apart that you can round and still get sufficiently close to identify the right answer. Avoid holding onto four decimal places, as we did here, because it will greatly increase the amount of time it takes to answer the question.

Related Questions

1. Which has a larger number of molecules—a mole of carbon dioxide, or a mole of water? Which one has a larger mass?
2. The atomic weight of silicon is 28.086 amu. If the isotopes in a sample are silicon-23, 24, 25, 26, and 29, which isotope is the most abundant?
3. A nuclear detector finds 80 atoms of oxygen-16 (15.999 amu), 60 atoms of oxygen-14 (13.999 amu), and 60 atoms of oxygen-18 (17.999 amu). What is the molar mass of this sample?

Key Concepts

General Chemistry Chapter 2

Periodic trends
Ionization energy
Atomic radius
Electron affinity
Electronegativity

Periodic Trends

Arrange the following elements in ascending order in terms of the following periodic properties: (a) electronegativity, (b) ionization energy, and (c) atomic radius.

Rb, Fr, Mg, Ca, P, Fe, Sb, O, Cl, F

 Assess the trends.

This first step just requires us to think about how periodic trends work. For all trends, there is a general direction of increasing value. Electronegativity and first ionization energy increase as one moves up and to the right in the Periodic Table (with some exceptions). Atomic radius, on the other hand, decreases in value in that direction.

 Order the elements from bottom left to top right.

We'll use electronegativity as our trend of choice while ordering these elements. Begin with the least electronegative element, francium (Fr), and the most electronegative element, fluorine (F), at the ends of the spectrum:

Fr < __ < __ < __ < __ < __ < __ < __ < __ < F

Let's compare oxygen (O) and chlorine (Cl), which are next to F. To determine which is more electronegative, consider the hypochlorite ion (ClO^-). The hypochlorite ion has a charge of –1. Recall that chlorine typically attains a charge of –1 in compounds, and oxygen typically attains a charge of –2, to complete their respective octet configurations. This cannot be the case in ClO^- because adding these oxidation states gives us –1 + (–2) = –3, when the ion's charge is –1.

Oxygen and chlorine do not have the same electronegativity, so there must be a polar covalent bond between them. If chlorine were more electronegative, then it would take on charge of –1. To maintain the overall –1 charge of the ion, oxygen's charge would have to be 0. This cannot be the case—a polar covalent bond requires that one side be slightly positive and the other slightly negative. However, if oxygen were more electronegative, then it would take on a charge of –2. To maintain the ion's overall –1 charge, chlorine's charge would have to be +1. This makes sense—there is a polar covalent bond between the two atoms, giving oxygen a slightly negative (–2) charge and chlorine a slightly positive (+1) charge. Therefore, oxygen must be more electronegative, and we can put these two elements into the list:

Fr < __ < __ < __ < __ < __ < __ < Cl < O < F

The next closest atoms to the top right corner of the Periodic Table are phosphorus (P) and antimony (Sb). Phosphorus is closer to F, O, and Cl than antimony and is more electronegative:

Fr < __ < __ < __ < __ < Sb < P < Cl < O < F

Iron (Fe) is a transition metal and is the next closest to the top right corner, so it comes next:

Fr < __ < __ < __ < Fe < Sb < P < Cl < O < F

Finally, the remaining metals can be ranked based on their proximity to Fr. Rubidium (Rb) is just two periods above Fr so it will be just slightly more electronegative than Fr. Calcium (Ca) is the next highest, and finally magnesium (Mg). Thus, the trend for electronegativity is:

Fr < Rb < Ca < Mg < Fe < Sb < P < Cl < O < F

Recognize that ionization energy should roughly parallel the order for electronegativity. For reference, the electronegativities and ionization energies of these elements are tabulated below:

Element	Fr	Rb	Ca	Mg	Fe	Sb	P	Cl	O	F
Electronegativity (Pauling Scale)	0.7	0.82	1.00	1.31	1.83	2.05	2.19	3.16	3.44	3.98
Ionization Energy $\left(\frac{kJ}{mol}\right)$	380	403	590	738	763	834	1012	1251	1314	1681

3 Reverse the trend to get the ranking for atomic radius.

Unlike electronegativity and first ionization energy, which increase as one moves up and to the right on the Periodic Table, atomic radius *decreases* as one moves up and to the right.

Thus if,

Fr < Rb < Ca < Mg < Fe < Sb < P < Cl < O < F

is the order of increasing electronegativity and first ionization energy, the reverse order is the one in which the atomic radii increase:

F < O < Cl < P < Sb < Fe < Mg < Ca < Rb < Fr

Note that there are different definitions for atomic radius; most scientists use empirical or calculated atomic radii to make predictions about periodic trends.

Takeaways

Electronegativity, ionization energy, and electron affinity generally increase as one moves up and to the right in the Periodic Table. Atomic radius generally decreases in the same direction.

Things to Watch Out For

Remember that these are only trends, and are not absolute. There are many exceptions to the periodic trends, especially in the transition metals. Usually, if the MCAT asks for analysis of a particular periodic trend, the question will involve elements that follow that trend as expected.

Related Questions

1. Rank the following elements or ions from smallest to largest radius: B^{3+}, C, Be, O^{2-}
2. Which element—phosphorus or selenium—would you expect to have a higher ionization energy?
3. The first ionization energy of an element is 549.5 $\frac{kJ}{mol}$, its second ionization energy is 1064.2 $\frac{kJ}{mol}$, and its third ionization energy is 4138 $\frac{kJ}{mol}$. To which group does this element most likely belong?

High-Yield Problem-Solving Guide questions continue on the next page. ▶ ▶ ▶

Key Concepts

General Chemistry Chapter 3

VSEPR theory
Coordinate covalent bonds
Covalent bond notation
Geometry and polarity

VSEPR Theory and Geometry

A student attempts to form an amminated vanadium complex using a concentrated aqueous ammonia solution. During the reaction, the solvated vanadium ions undergo a side-reaction to produce the hydrated coordination complex $[V(H_2O)_6]^{4+}$. Assuming the complex ion structure is solely based on the ligands and central ion, what is the geometry of this complex?

The student attempts to decompose this complex with heat to reform solid vanadium. The complex changes color but does not yield pure vanadium. The student performs thermochemical analysis and determines the reaction to be:

$$[V(H_2O)_6]^{4+} \rightarrow [VO(H_2O)_5]^{2+} + 2\ H^+$$

What is the geometry of the decomposed complex ion?

During the decomposition process, the student notices that the aqueous ammonia remaining in solution forms ammonium cations. Crystallizing the solution and measuring the bond angles using X-ray diffraction spectrometry, the student notices that there is a mixture of compounds with bond angles of 104.5°, 107°, and 109.5°. What molecules do these bond angles likely belong to?

Count the number of bonds and lone pairs in the first vanadium complex.

As written, the complex is composed of six ligands and a central metal ion. The metal ion does not have lone pairs, so it must organize six groups of electrons around itself. This can be represented with the shorthand AX_6, which corresponds to octahedral geometry:

Note that even though the water molecules have lone pairs, we can ignore them because they will not alter the structure around the central cation.

2 Determine the number of bonds and lone pairs in the second vanadium complex.

The decomposed molecule has one fewer aqua ligand, but now has an oxygen atom. Oxygen will create a double bond with the vanadium to complete its octet, while the other five water molecules will serve as ligands around the central vanadium cation. Thus, vanadium still must organize six groups of electrons around itself (AX_6). The geometry remains octahedral:

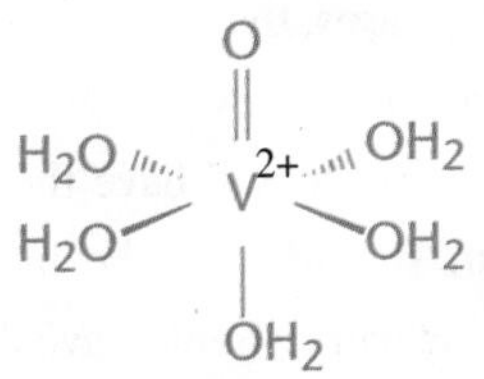

O
||
H_2O ''''... V^{2+} ...'''' OH_2
H_2O — — OH_2
|
OH_2

Note that this would be a slightly distorted octahedral geometry because the V=O double bond creates slightly more repulsion than the single bonds with the aqua ligands.

3 Determine the compounds remaining in solution.

We are told that the ammonia in solution forms ammonium cations. The solution is aqueous and thus also contains water molecules. Therefore, there are three molecules: water, ammonia, and ammonium:

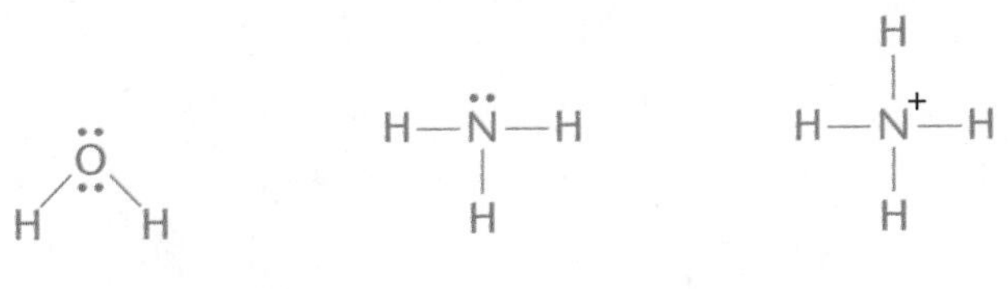

H_2O (H—Ö—H, two lone pairs)   H—N̈—H with H below NH_4^+ (H—N⁺—H with H above and below)

4 Analyze the structures for their molecular and electronic geometries.

Count the number of bonds and lone pairs in each molecule to identify their geometries. All three of these molecules have four groups around the central atom, which means that they all have tetrahedral electronic geometries. The angles that we are given, however, refer to molecular geometries. Remember that molecular geometry considers only the positions of the various nuclei, and not of the lone pairs. Water

Takeaways

As the number of lone pairs increases around a central atom, the bond angles in the molecular geometry decrease in magnitude. Multiple bonds can also cause slight distortions in geometry.

Things to Watch Out For

Lone pairs will affect molecular geometry. If lone pairs are not explicitly mentioned for a molecule, you must determine whether lone pairs exist by analyzing the Lewis structure.

has two bonds and two lone pairs, and therefore takes on bent molecular geometry. Ammonia has three bonds and one lone pair, and therefore takes on trigonal pyramidal molecular geometry. Ammonium has four bonds and no lone pairs, and therefore takes on tetrahedral molecular geometry.

5 Determine which compound has each of the bond angles based on their numbers of lone pairs.

As the number of lone pairs increases, the bond angle decreases because lone pairs can sit closer to the central nucleus and exert a greater degree of repulsion. Therefore, water, with its two lone pairs, should have the smallest bond angle (104.5°). Ammonia, with one lone pair, should have the intermediate bond angle (107°). Finally, ammonium, with no lone pairs, should have the largest bond angle (109.5°).

Related Questions

1. Why is the geometry of aluminum chloride different from that of phosphorus tribromide?
2. Why is the maximum bond angle between adjacent groups in a bent molecule greater than that of an octahedral molecule?
3. Why is the geometry of the sulfate anion the same as that of a sulfuric acid molecule?

High-Yield Problem-Solving Guide questions continue on the next page. ▶ ▶ ▶

Key Concepts

General Chemistry Chapter 4

Gram equivalent weight

The mole

Molar mass

Balancing equations

Stoichiometry

During the course of the disproportionation reaction

$$H_2PO_4^- \rightleftharpoons HPO_4^{2-} + H_3PO_4$$

how many grams and molecules of phosphoric acid could be created from 242.5 grams of dihydrogen phosphate? If this amount of phosphoric acid were dissolved in enough water to create one liter of solution, what would the normality of this solution be (with respect to protons)?

1 Balance the formula.

The given formula is unbalanced. To balance it, we simply need to double the number of dihydrogen phosphate molecules:

$$2\,H_2PO_4^- \rightleftharpoons HPO_4^{2-} + H_3PO_4$$

2 Convert the given units to moles.

Stoichiometry is nothing more than an extended application of dimensional analysis. There are four major conversion factors that can be used to convert from the given units to moles (or vice-versa):

- **Molar mass**, **molecular weight**, or **formula weight** (from the Periodic Table): convert from mass (in grams or amu) to moles
- **Avogadro's number** ($6.02 \times 10^{23}\ \text{mol}^{-1}$): converts from a number of particles to moles
- **Molarity**, **molality**, **normality**, or other **measures of concentration**: convert from volume or mass of solution to moles
- **Ideal gases at STP** ($22.4\ \frac{\text{L}}{\text{mol}}$): converts from volume of gas to moles

In this question, we are given a mass (242.5 g), which must be converted to moles. To do this, we need to know the molar mass of dihydrogen phosphate, which can be determined using the Periodic Table. The molar mass is $2 \times 1\ \frac{\text{g}}{\text{mol}} + 1 \times 31\ \frac{\text{g}}{\text{mol}} + 4 \times 16\ \frac{\text{g}}{\text{mol}} = 97\ \frac{\text{g}}{\text{mol}}$.

Now, dividing the given mass by the molar mass gives us the number of moles:

$$\frac{242.5\ \text{g}}{97\ \frac{\text{g}}{\text{mol}}} = 2.5\ \text{mol}$$

 Multiply by the mole ratio.

The next step requires us to use the balanced chemical equation to shift from calculations for dihydrogen phosphate to calculations for phosphoric acid. The mole ratio is simply the stoichiometric coefficient of the desired compound (phosphoric acid) divided by the stoichiometric coefficient of the compound we are given information about (dihydrogen phosphate):

$$2.5 \text{ mol } H_2PO_4^- \times \left[\frac{1 \text{ mol } H_3PO_4}{2 \text{ mol } H_2PO_4^-}\right] = 1.25 \text{ mol } H_3PO_4$$

In other words, reacting 2.5 moles of dihydrogen phosphate will result in 1.25 moles of phosphoric acid.

 Convert from moles to the desired units in the answer choice.

We are asked for two different units: mass and number of molecules. Starting with mass, we use the molar mass to convert from moles to grams:

$$1.25 \text{ mol } H_3PO_4 \times \left[\frac{98 \text{ g } H_3PO_4}{1 \text{ mol } H_3PO_4}\right] = 122.5 \text{ g } H_3PO_4$$

This first example points out the utility of setting up all of the conversion factors before multiplying. Consider if Steps 2 through 4 were done in one large multiplication problem:

$$242.5 \text{ g } H_2PO_4^- \times \left[\frac{1 \text{ mol } H_2PO_4^-}{97 \text{ g } H_2PO_4^-}\right]\left[\frac{1 \text{ mol } H_3PO_4}{2 \text{ mol } H_2PO_4^-}\right]\left[\frac{98 \text{ g } H_3PO_4}{1 \text{ mol } H_3PO_4}\right] \approx \frac{240}{2} = 120 \text{ g } H_3PO_4$$

Even with rounding, the answer obtained is still very close to the actual answer.

For the number of molecules, we use Avogadro's number:

$$1.25 \text{ mol } H_3PO_4 \times \left[\frac{6.02 \times 10^{23} \text{ molecules}}{1 \text{ mol } H_3PO_4}\right] = 7.53 \times 10^{23} \text{ molecules}$$

 Determine the normality of a one liter solution containing 1.25 moles of phosphoric acid.

The normality is the molarity of a given molecule multiplied by the number of equivalents of interest given off by one mole of the molecule. For this question, the equivalent of interest is protons. Thus, we simply need to multiply the molarity of the solution by the number of protons that can be given off by phosphoric acid.

Takeaways

Stoichiometry is an extended version of dimensional analysis that can be answered with a consistent three-step method:

1. Convert from the given units to moles
2. Use the mole ratio
3. Convert from moles to the desired units in the answer choices

Things to Watch Out For

Stoichiometry problems can take up a lot of time if you do each step individually. Writing out all of the conversion factors before doing the math may work to your advantage, as the MCAT tends to use numbers that cancel out "nicely."

The molarity is equal to the moles of solute divided by liters of solution:

$$\frac{1.25 \text{ mol } H_3PO_4}{1 \text{ L}} = 1.25\, M\ H_3PO_4$$

Because phosphoric acid can give off three protons, the normality is:

$$1.25\, M\ H_3PO_4 \times 3 = 3.75\, N\ H_3PO_4$$

Related Questions

1. In the formation of water from diatomic hydrogen and oxygen gases, how many grams and molecules of water are produced when 26 g of hydrogen gas react in the presence of excess oxygen?
2. If butane is combusted in the presence of excess oxygen, resulting in the production of 179.2 L CO_2 at STP, what mass of butane was present at the beginning of the reaction?
3. If 44.8 L of heptane react with 1.204×10^{24} molecules of oxygen in a combustion reaction, how many grams of water are produced?

High-Yield Problem-Solving Guide questions continue on the next page. ▶ ▶ ▶

Key Concepts

General Chemistry Chapter 5

Reaction kinetics

Reaction mechanisms

Rate laws

Rate tables

Rate Laws

Consider the nitration reaction of benzene:

$$C_6H_6 + HNO_2 \longrightarrow C_6H_5NO_2$$

The rate data below were collected with the nitration of benzene carried out at 298 K. From this information, determine the rate law for this reaction.

Trial	$[C_6H_6]$ (M)	$[HNO_2]$ (M)	Initial Rate $\left(\frac{M}{s}\right)$
1	1.01×10^{-3}	2.00×10^{-2}	5.96×10^{-6}
2	4.05×10^{-3}	2.00×10^{-2}	5.96×10^{-6}
3	3.02×10^{-3}	6.01×10^{-2}	5.40×10^{-5}

1 Write down the general form of the rate law.

The general form of the rate law includes a rate constant, k, multiplied by the concentrations of each of the reactants raised to a certain power:

$$\text{rate} = k[C_6H_6]^x[HNO_2]^y$$

2 Determine the order of the reaction with respect to benzene.

Choose two trials in which the concentration of benzene changes while the concentration of nitrous acid remains constant. When we do this, we can set up a proportionality between the rate and the concentration of benzene:

$$\text{rate} = k[C_6H_6]^x[HNO_2]^y$$

If k and $[HNO_2]$ are constant, then:

$$\text{rate} \propto [C_6H_6]^x$$

Let's use trials 1 and 2. Here, the concentration of benzene quadruples while the concentration of nitrous acid remains constant. The rate does not change. Putting this information into the proportionality, we get:

$$\frac{\text{rate}_2}{\text{rate}_1} = \left[\frac{[C_6H_6]_2}{[C_6H_6]_1}\right]^x$$

$$1 = 4^x$$

$$x = 0$$

Thus, the reaction is zero-order with respect to benzene.

3 Determine the order of the reaction with respect to nitrous acid.

The fact that the reaction is zero-order with respect to benzene is great news because it means that the rate law must be:

$$\text{rate} = k[HNO_2]^y$$

We can ignore the concentration of benzene in our calculations because its concentration will have no effect on the rate. So, let's compare trials 1 and 3 to determine the order with respect to nitrous acid. From trial 1 to trial 3, the concentration of nitrous acid tripled, and the rate went up by a factor of 9. Plugging this in, we get:

$$\frac{\text{rate}_3}{\text{rate}_1} = \left[\frac{[HNO_2]_3}{[HNO_2]_1}\right]^y$$

$$9 = 3^y$$

$$y = 2$$

Thus, the reaction is second-order with respect to nitrous acid.

4 Write down the rate law with the correct orders.

Taking this information together, the rate law must be:

$$\text{rate} = k[C_6H_6]^0[HNO_2]^2 = k[HNO_2]^2$$

Takeaways

To determine the order with respect to a particular reactant, use the equation: change in rate = (proportional change in concentration)^x, where x = the order with respect to that reactant.

Things to Watch Out For

Make sure that you select two trials where one reactant's concentration changes but all other concentrations are constant. If there are no two trials where one of the reactants changes, create a new trial using the information you've gleaned about the reaction orders with respect to the *other* reactants.

Related Questions

1. What is the value of the rate constant k for the nitration of benzene? What are its units?

2. Given the data below, determine the rate law for the reaction of pyridine with methyl iodide. Find the rate constant k for this reaction and its units.

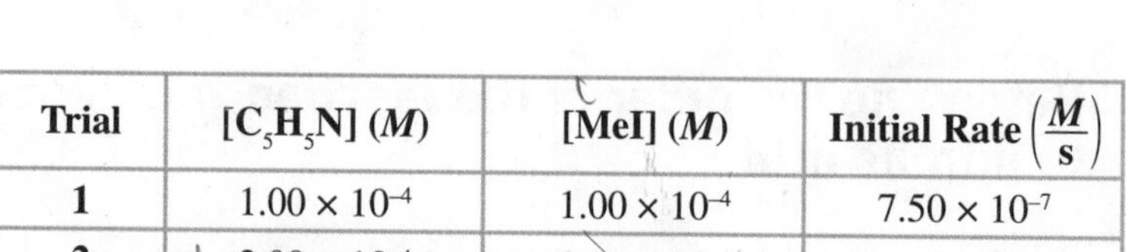

Trial	$[C_5H_5N]$ (M)	[MeI] (M)	Initial Rate $\left(\frac{M}{s}\right)$
1	1.00×10^{-4}	1.00×10^{-4}	7.50×10^{-7}
2	2.00×10^{-4}	2.00×10^{-4}	3.00×10^{-6}
3	2.00×10^{-4}	4.00×10^{-4}	6.00×10^{-6}

3. Cerium(IV) is a common inorganic oxidant. Determine the rate law for the following reaction and compute the value of the rate constant k along with its units:

$$Ce^{4+} + Fe^{2+} \rightarrow Ce^{3+} + Fe^{3+}$$

Trial	$[Ce^{4+}]$ (M)	$[Fe^{2+}]$ (M)	Initial Rate $\left(\frac{M}{s}\right)$
1	1.10×10^{-5}	1.80×10^{-5}	2.00×10^{-7}
2	1.10×10^{-5}	2.80×10^{-5}	3.10×10^{-7}
3	3.40×10^{-5}	2.80×10^{-5}	9.50×10^{-7}

High-Yield Problem-Solving Guide questions continue on the next page. ▶ ▶ ▶

Key Concepts

General Chemistry Chapter 6

Thermodynamics

Kinetics

Reaction energy profiles

Gibbs free energy

Reaction Energy Profiles

When chalcone (**A**) is subjected to reductive conditions with sodium borohydride, two products can result. The two products are the so-called 1,2-reduction product (**B**), in which the carbonyl is reduced, and the 1,4-reduction product (**C**), in which the conjugated alkene is reduced.

C "1,4-reduction" ← $NaBH_4$ — **A** — $NaBH_4$ → **B** "1,2-reduction"

The reaction profiles leading to each reduction product at 298 K are both shown in the plot below:

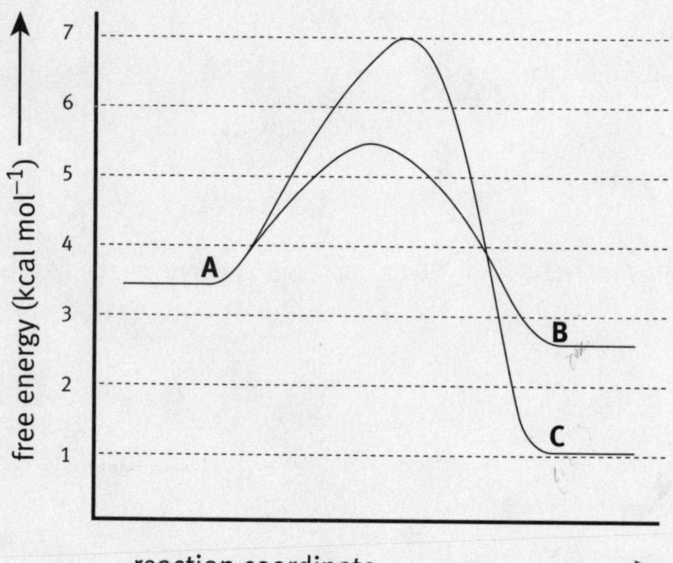

Based on the plot above, answer the following questions:

1. Which product is more thermodynamically stable? Which one forms faster?
2. Assume that **A** is in equilibrium with **C**. What will the ratio of **C** to **A** be at equilibrium?
3. How could the rate of the reaction of **A** to **C** be made closer to the rate of the reaction of **A** to **B**?
4. Which product would be favored if **A** were subjected to high temperatures for a long time? If **A** were subjected to low temperatures for only a brief period of time? Explain why for each situation.

$\left(\text{Note: } R = 1.99 \frac{\text{cal}}{\text{mol} \cdot \text{K}}\right)$

1 Look at the energy differences between the starting material and the products, as well as the differences between the starting material and the transition state leading to each product.

Notice that the energy of **C** is lower than that of **B**. Therefore, it is the more thermodynamically stable product.

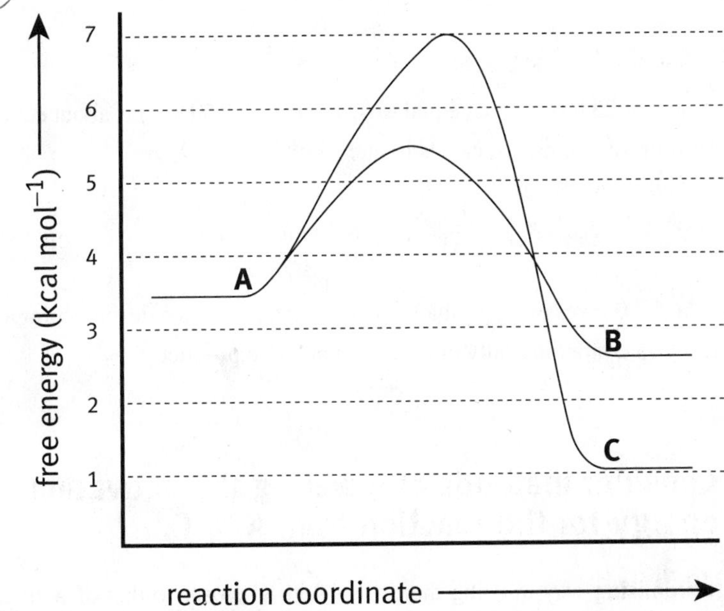

The rate of formation of each product is determined by the difference in energy between the starting material **A** and the top of the hump leading to each product. Because this difference is lower for the formation of **B**, it forms faster.

2 Note that the difference in energy between the starting material and the products determines the ratio of products (C) to reactants (A) at equilibrium.

The relevant equation relating the change in free energy to the concentrations of reactants and products at equilibrium is:

$$\Delta G° = -RT \ln K_{eq}$$

We can rearrange it to solve for K_{eq}:

$$\ln K_{eq} = \frac{-\Delta G^\circ}{RT}$$

$$K_{eq} = e^{\frac{-\Delta G^\circ}{RT}}$$

Note from the diagram that $\Delta G^\circ \approx 1000 - 3500 = -2500 \frac{\text{cal}}{\text{mol}}$. We are told that $R = 1.99 \frac{\text{cal}}{\text{mol} \cdot \text{K}}$ and that $T = 298$ K. Plugging into the equation, we get:

$$K_{eq} \approx e^{\frac{2500 \frac{\text{cal}}{\text{mol}}}{(2 \frac{\text{cal}}{\text{mol} \cdot \text{K}})(300\ \text{K})}} = e^{\frac{25}{6}}$$

Let's assume that 25 ÷ 6 is about equal to 4, and that e (2.718…) is about equal to 3. With these simplifications, we can estimate:

$$K_{eq} = \frac{[\text{C}]}{[\text{A}]} \approx 3^4 = 81 \text{ (actual} = 68)$$

Note that $\Delta G^\circ < 0$ gives more product than reactant, as one would expect for a spontaneous reaction containing only one reactant and one product.

3 Consider methods of lowering the activation energy for the reaction from A to C.

The most promising way to bring the rate of **A** to **C** closer to that of **A** to **B** is to lower the activation energy of the **A** to **C** reaction. This could be accomplished by adding a catalyst for the **A** to **C** reaction. Remember: a catalyst speeds up the reaction but is not consumed in the process.

Takeaways

The goal of a reaction profile is to give information about energy *differences*. Make sure to identify the important differences and their significances, as in this problem.

Things to Watch Out For

Be careful to take note of the units of energy on the *y*-axis if there are any necessary computations. The *y*-axis could be given in joules, calories, or Calories (kilocalories).

Consider the effects of temperature on the reactions.

At high temperatures for a long time, **A** has sufficient energy to keep reacting over and over again to form **B** and **C**, which can then react back to reform **A**. Over time, the lowest energy (thermodynamic) product, **C**, would predominate because it is the most stable.

Between the two products, **B** will form much faster than **C** because its activation energy (the height of the hump) is lower. At low temperatures, there may not be sufficient energy for **B** to revert back to **A**, or for **A** to convert to **C**. Therefore, the faster-forming (kinetic) product, **B**, will predominate.

Related Questions

1. What would be the ratio of **B** to **A** at equilibrium?
2. If a catalyst were added to the reaction of **A** going to **C**, as in Step 3 earlier, would the energies of **A** and **C** be changed as a result? Why or why not?
3. There are actually intermediates involved in the reactions producing both **B** and **C**, which are shown below. Sketch how each reaction profile would look, including the involvement of these intermediates. Be sure to indicate which intermediate is relatively more stable.

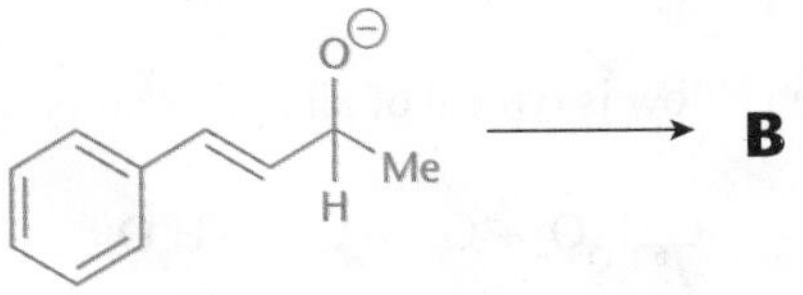

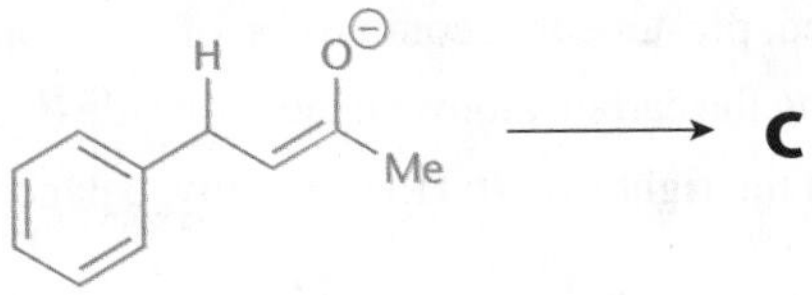

O⊖ H Me → **B**

H O⊖ Me → **C**

Key Concepts

General Chemistry Chapter 7

Hess's law

$\Delta H^\circ_{rxn} = \sum \Delta H^\circ_{f,products} - \sum \Delta H^\circ_{f,reactants}$

Heat of formation

Combustion

Hess's Law

> The standard heat of combustion of glucose ($C_6H_{12}O_6$) is –2537.3 $\frac{kJ}{mol}$. If the ΔH°_f of CO_2 (*g*) is –393.5 $\frac{kJ}{mol}$ and the ΔH°_f of H_2O (*g*) is –241.8 $\frac{kJ}{mol}$, then what is the ΔH°_f of glucose?

1 Write a balanced equation for this reaction.

The unbalanced reaction below is typical of all hydrocarbon combustion reactions:

$$C_6H_{12}O_6 + O_2 \rightarrow CO_2 + H_2O$$

(Unless otherwise noted, presume that combustion of a carbohydrate is with oxygen gas.) Begin by balancing the carbon atoms on the right side (6 CO_2), and then balance the hydrogen atoms on the right side (6 H_2O). Finally, balance the oxygen atoms on the left side (6 O_2):

$$C_6H_{12}O_6 + 6\ O_2 \rightarrow 6\ CO_2 + 6\ H_2O$$

2 Apply Hess's law.

To start, let's define a few terms. The standard heat of formation, ΔH°_f, is the amount of thermal energy required to synthesize a compound from its elements in their standard states (the phase in which the element exists at room temperature, 298 K). The heat of reaction, ΔH°_{rxn}, is the amount of thermal energy required to convert the reactants to the products of a reaction. Hess's law states that the difference between the heats of formation of the products and the heats of formation of the reactants is equal to the heat of the reaction:

$$\Delta H^\circ_{rxn} = \sum \Delta H^\circ_{f,products} - \sum \Delta H^\circ_{f,reactants}$$

In this question, we are given the heats of formation for carbon dioxide gas and water vapor, as well as the heat of reaction. What about the standard heat of formation of oxygen? Because oxygen is already in its standard state (a diatomic gas), its standard heat of formation is zero.

With that information, we can plug into Hess's law:

$$\Delta H^\circ_{\text{rxn}} = \sum \Delta H^\circ_{\text{f,products}} - \sum \Delta H^\circ_{\text{f,reactants}}$$

$$-2537.3\,\frac{\text{kJ}}{\text{mol}} = \left[6\times\left(-393.5\,\frac{\text{kJ}}{\text{mol}}\right) + 6\times\left(-241.8\,\frac{\text{kJ}}{\text{mol}}\right)\right] - \left[\Delta H^\circ_{\text{f,glucose}} + 6\times\left(0\,\frac{\text{kJ}}{\text{mol}}\right)\right]$$

$$\Delta H^\circ_{\text{f,glucose}} = [6\times(-393.5) + 6\times(-241.8)] - (-2537.3)$$

$$\approx 6\times(-400) + 6\times(-250) + 2500$$

$$= -2400 - 1500 + 2500 = -1400\,\frac{\text{kJ}}{\text{mol}}\left(\text{actual} = -1274.5\,\frac{\text{kJ}}{\text{mol}}\right)$$

A negative standard heat of formation means that heat is released to form the compound, whereas a positive standard heat of formation means that heat is required to form the compound. Therefore, forming one mole of glucose from solid carbon, diatomic hydrogen gas, and diatomic oxygen gas releases 1274.5 kilojoules of heat.

Takeaways

Always determine the balanced equation for the reaction before you begin to apply Hess's law. Recall that enthalpy is a state function, so regardless of the path one takes to get from the reactants to the products, the change in enthalpy will be the same.

Things to Watch Out For

At least one of the wrong answer choices for thermochemistry questions will be the result of carelessness with signs. Carefully organized scratchwork will help you avoid this problem, but perhaps more important is the ability to round judiciously. Only experience (practice) will breed such wisdom.

ΔHf ethane

Related Questions

1. Given the ΔH°_f of carbon dioxide and water, what other piece(s) of information would you need to have to calculate the $\Delta H^\circ_{\text{comb}}$ of ethane?
2. If the ΔH°_f of acetylene is 226.6 $\frac{\text{kJ}}{\text{mol}}$, what is the $\Delta H^\circ_{\text{comb}}$ of acetylene?
3. If the ΔH°_f of NaBr (*s*) is –359.9 $\frac{\text{kJ}}{\text{mol}}$, what is the sum of each $\Delta H^\circ_{\text{rxn}}$ of the following series of reactions?

$$\text{Na}(s) \rightarrow \text{Na}(g) \rightarrow \text{Na}^+(g)$$

$$\tfrac{1}{2}\text{Br}_2(g) \rightarrow \text{Br}(g) \rightarrow \text{Br}^-(g)$$

$$\text{Na}^+(g) + \text{Br}^-(g) \rightarrow \text{NaBr}(s)$$

The Ideal Gas Law

0.503 m^3 of oxygen gas (density = 1.43 $\frac{kg}{m^3}$) is pumped into a rigid 600 mL container. Once inside, the pressure is measured to be 300 atm. What is the temperature of the gas, assuming ideal behavior? $\left(\text{Note: } R = 8.314 \frac{J}{mol \cdot K}\right)$

1 Determine the number of moles of gas.

Let's start with the given volume and density and determine the mass of oxygen gas present:

$$0.503\ m^3\ O_2 \times 1.43 \frac{kg}{m^3} \approx 0.72\ kg\ O_2 = 720\ g\ O_2$$

When dealing with gas laws, always carefully hold on to units to make sure the math works out correctly. Now that we have a given mass of oxygen gas, we can determine the number of moles present:

$$720\ g\ O_2 \times \left[\frac{1\ mol\ O_2}{32\ g\ O_2}\right] = 22.5\ mol\ O_2$$

2 Convert the remaining variables' units to match those of the given ideal gas constant.

The MCAT frequently makes a simple mathematical problem more challenging by using alternative units and testing your ability to use conversion factors. Here, our pressure will have to be converted to kilopascals:

$$300\ atm \times \left[\frac{101.325\ kPa}{1\ atm}\right] \approx 3 \times 10^4\ kPa$$

Similarly, our volume will have to be converted to liters:

$$600\ mL \times \left[\frac{1\ L}{1000\ mL}\right] = 0.6\ L$$

3 Plug the variables into the ideal gas law.

Now that we have the pressure, volume, number of moles of gas, and ideal gas constant in the same units, we can plug into the ideal gas law equation:

Key Concepts

General Chemistry Chapter 8

The ideal gas law
Conversion factors
Pressure
Volume
Temperature
Density

Takeaways

Use scientific notation to avoid long multiplication and division problems that eat up time on Test Day. This is especially useful if all of the answer choices vary by powers of ten; you can often omit the coefficient and just focus on the relevant exponents to predict the correct answer choice.

$$PV = nRT \rightarrow T = \frac{PV}{nR}$$

$$T = \frac{(3 \times 10^4\ \text{kPa})(0.6\ \text{L})}{(2.25 \times 10^1\ \text{mol})\left(8.314\ \frac{\text{J}}{\text{mol} \bullet \text{K}}\right)}$$

$$\approx \frac{1.8 \times 10^4}{1.8 \times 10^2} = 10^2\ \text{K} = 100\ \text{K}\ (\text{actual} = 97.6\ \text{K})$$

Things to Watch Out For

Always hold on to units for MCAT calculations, especially when SI and non-SI units are mixed in a question. It is important to make sure that the units cancel correctly to confirm that you have arrived at the correct answer; if the units don't work, the answer cannot be right!

Related Questions

1. A 22.4 liter vessel contains nitrogen gas at STP. What mass of nitrogen is in the vessel? $\left(\text{Note: R} = 8.314\ \frac{\text{J}}{\text{mol} \bullet \text{K}}\right)$
2. Humans breathe out a tidal volume of about 0.5 liters of gas at 1.0 atm and 37°C. How many moles of gas are present? (Note: Assume that only carbon dioxide is present in the exhaled gas and that $\text{R} = 0.0821\ \frac{\text{L} \bullet \text{atm}}{\text{mol} \bullet \text{K}}$)
3. What is the volume of 2 mol of chlorine gas pressurized to 4000 mmHg at 700°C? $\left(\text{Note: R} = 62.4\ \frac{\text{L} \bullet \text{mmHg}}{\text{mol} \bullet \text{K}}\right)$

Key Concepts

General Chemistry Chapter 9

pH
Molar solubility
Common ion effect
Le Châtelier's principle
K_{sp}

Molar Solubility

The molar solubility of iron(III) hydroxide in pure water at 25°C is 9.94×10^{-10} *M*. How would the substance's molar solubility change if placed in an aqueous solution with a pH of 10.0 at 25°C?

1 Identify the balanced equation for the dissociation reaction.

The generic dissociation reaction may be expressed as follows:

$$A_xB_y\,(s) \rightleftharpoons x\,A^+\,(aq) + y\,B^-\,(aq)$$

For iron(III) hydroxide, the reaction expression is:

$$Fe(OH)_3\,(s) \rightleftharpoons Fe^{3+}\,(aq) + 3\,OH^-\,(aq)$$

This step allows us to see how many moles of ions are dissolved into the solution per mole of solid dissolved.

2 Find the K_{sp} expression for the dissociation reaction.

K_{sp} is an equilibrium constant, just like any other *K*, and it is given the special name *solubility product* because it is related to the dissolution of a salt into solution. The expression for any *K* is simply the concentration of each product raised to its stoichiometric coefficient over the concentration of each reactant raised to its stoichiometric coefficient; only gases and aqueous species are included. Remember that the values of all *K*s vary only with temperature.

For iron(III) hydroxide, the K_{sp} expression is:

$$K_{sp} = [Fe^{3+}][OH^-]^3$$

3 Determine the K_{sp} from the molar solubility.

When solid iron(III) hydroxide is placed into water, some of the salt will dissolve. Based on the balanced chemical equation, if *x* moles of iron(III) hydroxide dissolve, then *x* moles of iron(III) and 3*x* moles of hydroxide ions will be dissolved into solution:

$$x\,Fe(OH)_3 \rightleftharpoons x\,Fe^{3+} + 3x\,OH^-$$

The molar solubility is the amount of salt that dissolves to create a saturated solution. If we say that the value of x in this equation is the molar solubility, this implies that—at saturation—there will be x molar Fe^{3+} and $3x$ molar hydroxide ions. From this information, we can determine the K_{sp}:

$$K_{sp} = [Fe^{3+}][OH^-]^3 = (x)(3x)^3 = 27x^4$$

The molar solubility, x, is given as 9.94×10^{-10}. Plugging in, we can find the value of K_{sp}:

$$27 \times (9.94 \times 10^{-10})^4 \approx 27 \times (10^{-9})^4 = 27 \times 10^{-36} = 2.7 \times 10^{-35}$$

4 Determine the molar solubility in the solution with a pH of 10.0.

If the pH is 10.0, then the pOH of this solution is 14 – 10 = 4. This means that the hydroxide ion concentration is 10^{-4}. If x moles of iron(III) hydroxide dissolve, then x moles of iron(III) and $3x$ moles of hydroxide ions will still be dissolved into solution—the difference here is that the hydroxide ion concentration starts at 10^{-4}, not 0. Therefore, the concentration of hydroxide ions at saturation will not be $3x$, but rather $3x + 10^{-4}$. We can include this in the K_{sp} expression:

$$K_{sp} = [Fe^{3+}][OH^-]^3$$
$$2.7 \times 10^{-35} = (x)(3x + 10^{-4})^3$$

On the MCAT, the value of x will almost always be sufficiently small to be considered negligible if we are adding or subtracting x (or, in this case, $3x$):

$$2.7 \times 10^{-35} \approx (x)(10^{-4})^3 = x(10^{-12})$$
$$x \approx 2.7 \times 10^{-23}\ M$$

5 Compare the molar solubilities in water and in a solution with a pH of 10.0.

For the solution with a pH of 10.0, the molar solubility is on the order of 10^{-23} *M*, which represents a significant decrease from its molar solubility in water (around 10^{-9} *M*). This is due to the common ion effect. If we consider this from the perspective of Le Châtelier's principle, we could point out that the addition of more OH^- will shift the reaction to the left; thus, less iron(III) hydroxide will dissociate.

Takeaways

The value of K_{sp} does not change when a common ion is present; it is a constant that is dependent on temperature only. The molar solubility of the salt, however, does change if a common ion is present.

Things to Watch Out For

Be careful when applying Le Châtelier's principle in cases of precipitation and solvation. For a solution at equilibrium (that is, a saturated solution), adding more solid will not shift the equilibrium to the right. More solid does not dissociate to raise the ion concentrations; it just precipitates to the bottom.

Related Questions

1. Given a substance's K_{sp}, how could you solve for its molar solubility in pure water? What if a common ion were also present in solution?
2. Given a table listing substances and their solubility constants, how could you determine which substance was most soluble in pure water?
3. Given that the sulfate ion can react with acid to form hydrogen sulfate, how would the molar solubility of sulfate salts be affected by varying a solution's pH?

High-Yield Problem-Solving Guide questions continue on the next page. ▶ ▶ ▶

Key Concepts

General Chemistry Chapter 10

Titrations
Acids and bases
Equivalence points
Half-equivalence points
pH

Titrations

Hydrazoic acid, HN_3, is a highly toxic compound that can cause death in minutes if inhaled in a concentrated form. 100 mL of a 0.2 *M* aqueous solution of HN_3 ($pK_a = 4.72$) is to be titrated with a 0.5 *M* solution of NaOH. What is the pH of the HN_3 solution before any NaOH is added? How much of the NaOH solution will be needed to reach the equivalence point? What is the pH at this point? How much of the NaOH solution will be needed to reach the half-equivalence point? What is the pH at this point?

1 Determine the concentration of H_3O^+ in the hydrazoic acid solution before the titration.

To determine the pH, we need to know the concentration of hydrogen ions in solution. This can be determined from the concentration of dissociated hydrazoic acid, which is the main contributor of hydrogen ions to the solution (there will be a small contribution from the water itself, which autoionizes to produce 10^{-7} *M* H_3O^+). To determine the hydrogen ion concentration from hydrazoic acid, we will follow the three-step method that can be applied to all *K* questions:

1. Write out the balanced expression for the reaction
2. Write the expression for *K*
3. Plug in the values from the question stem or data table

Here, the balanced expression is that for the dissociation of hydrazoic acid in solution:

$$H_2O\ (l) + HN_3\ (aq) \rightleftharpoons H_3O^+\ (aq) + N_3^-\ (aq)$$

The *K* expression is the acid dissociation constant, K_a, which would be written as:

$$K_a = \frac{[H_3O^+][N_3^-]}{[HN_3]}$$

Before any hydrazoic acid has dissociated, its concentration in solution is 0.2 *M* according to the question stem. At this point, the concentrations of H_3O^+ and N_3^- are negligible. If *x* moles of hydrazoic acid dissociate to reach equilibrium, then the concentration of hydrazoic acid at equilibrium is $0.2 - x$, and the concentrations of H_3O^+ and N_3^- are each *x*:

$$K_a = \frac{x^2}{0.2 - x}$$

Remember that the value of x on the MCAT is usually small enough to be considered negligible when added or subtracted. This simplifies our calculations quite a bit:

$$K_a = \frac{x^2}{0.2} = 5x^2$$

We were not given the value of K_a, but we were given pK_a. Remember that "p" is shorthand for –log, so raising 10 to the power of –pKa will give us the K_a:

$$K_a = 10^{-4.72} \approx 10^{-5}$$

Bringing this all together, we can solve for the concentration of H_3O^+:

$$K_a \approx 10^{-5} = 5x^2$$
$$x^2 = 2 \times 10^{-6}$$
$$x = 1.4 \times 10^{-3} = [H_3O^+]$$

2 Find the pH of the hydrazoic acid solution based on the concentration of H_3O^+.

Remember that for a solution with a hydronium ion concentration written in the form $n \times 10^{-m}$, the pH can be approximated as $m - 0.n$, where $0.n$ represents moving the decimal place of the coefficient one position to the left. Therefore, the pH of a solution with a hydronium ion concentration of 1.4×10^{-3} is roughly $3 - 0.14 = 2.86$ (actual = 2.71).

3 Find how much NaOH is needed to reach the equivalence point and the pH at this point.

The equivalence point occurs when the quantity in moles of acid present is equal to the moles of base added. First, calculate the number of moles of hydrazoic acid that we started with:

$$0.1 \text{ L} \times 0.2\ M = 0.02 \text{ mol } HN_3$$

That means we need to know how much of the NaOH solution is required to obtain 0.02 mol NaOH:

$$\frac{0.02 \text{ mol}}{0.5\ M} = 0.04 \text{ L NaOH solution}$$

At the equivalence point, all of the HN_3 has been consumed, leaving N_3^- behind. N_3^- is a Brønsted–Lowry base; as such, it will determine the pH at this point. To figure out the pH, we will need to use the K_b of N_3^-, which can be determined from the K_a of hydrazoic acid and the water dissociation constant:

$$K_{a,\text{acid}} \times K_{b,\text{conjugate base}} = K_w$$

The K_b of N_3^- is therefore:

$$\frac{K_w}{K_a} \approx \frac{10^{-14}}{10^{-5}} = 10^{-9}$$

Now we can proceed with the same three-step method. First, we determine the balanced reaction:

$$N_3^- (aq) + H_2O (l) \rightleftharpoons HN_3 (aq) + OH^- (aq)$$

Then, the K expression:

$$K_b = \frac{[HN_3][OH^-]}{[N_3^-]}$$

Finally, we put in the relevant values. The concentrations of hydrazoic acid and OH^- are negligible without the reaction of N_3^-, but what is the initial concentration of N_3^- itself? While we would like to say that it's the 0.2 M concentration that hydrazoic acid had at the beginning of the titration, the volume has increased. This dilutes the N_3^-, making its concentration a bit lower:

$$[N_3^-] = \frac{0.02 \text{ mol}}{0.1 \text{ L} + 0.04 \text{ L}} \approx 0.15 \, M$$

Putting the relevant values into the K_b expression, we can solve for $[OH^-]$:

$$10^{-9} = \frac{[x][x]}{[0.15 - x]} \approx \frac{x^2}{0.15}$$

$$x^2 = 0.15 \times 10^{-9} \approx 10^{-10}$$

$$x = [OH^-] \approx 10^{-5}$$

If $[OH^-]$ is close to 10^{-5}, then the pOH is close to 5. This makes the pH close to 9 (actual = 8.94). Remember to ask yourself whether or not this result makes sense. Here, because we have a basic species (N_3^-), the pH should be above 7, which it is.

 Find how much NaOH is needed to reach the half-equivalence point and the pH at this point.

Takeaways

Make sure to practice this three-step method to make quick work of questions involving equilibrium constants on Test Day. You are likely to see six main types of equilibrium constants: K_{eq}, K_{sp}, K_f, K_a, K_b, and K_w.

The half-equivalence point will occur when half of the hydrazoic acid has been neutralized. We can simply divide the volume of NaOH needed for the equivalence point by two, which means that 20 mL of the NaOH solution are needed to reach the half-equivalence point.

We could go through the whole three-step method to determine the pH at the half-equivalence point, or we could use a little common sense to avoid computation. At the half-equivalence point, half of the HN_3 has been consumed and converted to N_3^-. Therefore, the HN_3 and N_3^- concentrations are equal:

$$K_a = \frac{[H_3O^+]\cancel{[N_3^-]}}{\cancel{[HN_3]}} = [H_3O^+]$$

Taking the negative logarithm of both sides, we get pH = pK_a = 4.72.

Things to Watch Out For

Be careful in choosing whether to use K_a or K_b to determine the pH. Make this decision based on whether the dominant species in solution is acidic or basic, respectively.

Related Questions

1. What is the pH after the equivalence point has been exceeded by 5 mL of the NaOH solution in this titration?
2. What would be the pH if the same amount of NaOH solution necessary to get to the half-equivalence point in this titration were diluted into enough pure water to form one liter of solution?
3. If the pK_a of acetic acid is 4.76, then what is the pK_b of acetate?

Key Concepts

General Chemistry Chapter 11

Oxidation

Reduction

Balancing electrochemical half-reactions

Conservation of charge

Balancing Oxidation–Reduction Reactions

Balance the following reaction, which takes place in basic solution:

$$ZrO(OH)_2\ (s) + SO_3^{2-}\ (aq) \rightleftharpoons Zr\ (s) + SO_4^{2-}\ (aq)$$

1 Separate the two half-reactions.

$$ZrO(OH)_2 \rightleftharpoons Zr$$
$$SO_3^{2-} \rightleftharpoons SO_4^{2-}$$

Break the reactions up by looking at atoms *other* than hydrogen and oxygen.

2 Balance the atoms of each half-reaction.

First, balance all of the atoms except H and O. Next, in a basic solution, use OH^- and H_2O to balance the O and H atoms (in an acidic solution, use H_2O and H^+):

$$H_2O + ZrO(OH)_2 \rightleftharpoons Zr + 4\ OH^-$$
$$2\ OH^- + SO_3^{2-} \rightleftharpoons SO_4^{2-} + H_2O$$

3 Balance the charges of each half-reaction.

Add electrons as necessary to one side of each reaction so that the charges are equal on both sides. The top equation has a total charge of –4 on the right from the 4 hydroxide ions, so 4 electrons need to be added to the left side of the equation. In the bottom equation, there is a total charge of –4 on the left (–2 from the two hydroxide ions and –2 from the sulfite anion) and –2 on the right (from the sulfate anion):

$$4\ e^- + H_2O + ZrO(OH)_2 \rightleftharpoons Zr + 4\ OH^-$$
$$2\ OH^- + SO_3^{2-} \rightleftharpoons SO_4^{2-} + H_2O + 2\ e^-$$

During this step, be careful to account for all charges, including the charges contributed by molecules other than H^+ and OH^-.

4 Multiply each reaction by the necessary integer to ensure that equal numbers of electrons are present in each reaction.

Here, the lowest common multiple between the four electrons in the top reaction and the two in the bottom is four electrons, so we must multiply everything in the bottom reaction by two:

$$4\,e^- + H_2O + ZrO(OH)_2 \rightleftharpoons Zr + 4\,OH^-$$
$$4\,OH^- + 2\,SO_3^{2-} \rightleftharpoons 2\,SO_4^{2-} + 2\,H_2O + 4\,e^-$$

Takeaways

Don't fall into the trap of simply balancing mass in these reactions. If oxidation and reduction are occurring, one must go through this procedure to balance the reaction accurately.

5 Add the half-reactions, canceling out terms that appear on both sides of the reaction arrow.

$$ZrO(OH)_2 + 2\,SO_3^{2-} \rightleftharpoons Zr + 2\,SO_4^{2-} + H_2O$$

Things to Watch Out For

These kinds of problems can be extremely tedious. Questions that ask you to balance complicated oxidation–reduction reactions are best saved until the end of the section if you have time left over.

6 Confirm that mass and charge are balanced.

There is a –2 net charge on each side of the reaction equation, and the atoms are stoichiometrically balanced. This last step is extremely important. If mass and charge aren't balanced, then we have made an error in one of the previous steps.

Related Questions

1. Which atom is being oxidized in the original equation? Which is being reduced? Identify the oxidizing and reducing agents.
2. A disproportionation reaction is one in which the same species is both oxidized and reduced during the course of the reaction. One such reaction is shown below. Balance the reaction, assuming that it takes place in acidic solution:

   $$PbSO_4\,(s) \rightarrow Pb\,(s) + PbO_2\,(s) + SO_4^{2-}\,(aq)$$

3. Dentists may use zinc amalgams to make temporary crowns for their patients. It is absolutely vital that they keep the zinc amalgam dry. The reaction of zinc metal with water is shown below:

   $$Zn\,(s) + H_2O\,(l) \rightarrow Zn^{2+}\,(aq) + H_2\,(g)$$

   Balance this reaction, assuming that it takes place in basic solution. Why is it so important to keep the amalgam dry?

Key Concepts

General Chemistry Chapter 12

Oxidation–reduction reactions
Electrochemical cells
Stoichiometry
Electromotive force
$\Delta G = -nFE^\circ_{cell}$

Electrochemical Cells

A galvanic cell is to be constructed using $MnO_4^- \mid Mn^{2+}$ ($E^\circ_{red} = +1.49$ V) and $Zn^{2+} \mid Zn$ ($E^\circ_{red} = -0.76$ V) half-reactions in acidic solution. Assume that all potentials given are measured against the standard hydrogen electrode at 298 K and that all reagents are present in 1 *M* concentrations. What is the maximum possible work output of this cell per mole of reactant if it is used to run an electric motor for one hour at room temperature (298 K)? During this amount of time, how much Zn metal would be necessary to run the cell, given a current of 5 A?

 1 Determine which half-reaction is occurring at the anode and which is occurring at the cathode of the cell.

Compare the standard reduction potentials for both reactions. The standard reduction potential is a measure of how much a particular material "wants" to be reduced. The permanganate reduction potential is greater than that of zinc, so it would "prefer" to be reduced, and zinc would "prefer" to be oxidized. This is a galvanic cell, which houses a spontaneous chemical reaction. Therefore, the zinc will be oxidized at the anode, and the manganese will be reduced at the cathode.

 2 Write a balanced reaction for the cell.

This can be done using the ion–electron method shown in the previous *Balancing Oxidation–Reduction Reactions* question:

$$1. \begin{cases} MnO_4^- \rightarrow Mn^{2+} \\ Zn \rightarrow Zn^{2+} \end{cases}$$

$$2. \begin{cases} 8\,H^+ + MnO_4^- \rightarrow Mn^{2+} + 4\,H_2O \\ Zn \rightarrow Zn^{2+} \end{cases}$$

$$3. \begin{cases} 8\,H^+ + MnO_4^- + 5\,e^- \rightarrow Mn^{2+} + 4\,H_2O \\ Zn \rightarrow Zn^{2+} + 2\,e^- \end{cases}$$

$$4. \begin{cases} 16\,H^+ + 2\,MnO_4^- + 10\,e^- \rightarrow 2\,Mn^{2+} + 8\,H_2O \\ 5\,Zn \rightarrow 5\,Zn^{2+} + 10\,e^- \end{cases}$$

$$5.\ 16\,H^+ + 2\,MnO_4^- + 5\,Zn \rightarrow 2\,Mn^{2+} + 8\,H_2O + 5\,Zn^{2+}$$

Calculate the standard potential for the cell.

Use the equation $E^\circ_{\text{cell}} = E^\circ_{\text{red,cathode}} - E^\circ_{\text{red,anode}}$:

$$E^\circ_{\text{cell}} = +1.49 - (-0.76) = 2.25 \text{ V}$$

The standard potential for the cell is positive, confirming that this is a galvanic (voltaic) cell—once the electrodes are hooked up and immersed in the designated solutions, current will start to flow spontaneously.

Compute ΔG° for the cell.

Use the equation $\Delta G^\circ = -nFE^\circ_{\text{cell}}$:

$$\Delta G^\circ = (-10 \text{ mol } e^-)\left(10^5 \frac{\text{C}}{\text{mol } e^-}\right)(2.25 \text{ V}) = -2.25 \times 10^6 \frac{\text{J}}{\text{mol}}$$

$$(\text{actual} = 2.17 \times 10^3 \frac{\text{kJ}}{\text{mol}})$$

The upper limit on the amount of work a reaction can perform is the same thing as ΔG°. Here, the maximum work output per mole of reactant is $2.17 \times 10^3 \frac{\text{kJ}}{\text{mol}}$.

5 Use the Faraday constant to determine the number of moles of electrons transferred and to determine the amount of zinc necessary to run the cell for one hour.

Remember that current is charge passing though a point per unit of time, and that the Faraday constant indicates how many coulombs of charge make up one mole of electrons. We can use the current and time to determine the amount of charge transferred; we can use the Faraday constant to determine how many electrons are in that amount of charge:

$$\begin{aligned} n &= \frac{It}{\text{F}} \\ &= \frac{(5 \text{ A})(3600 \text{ s})}{10^5 \frac{\text{C}}{\text{mol } e^-}} \\ &= 0.18 \text{ mol } e^- \end{aligned}$$

Each atom of zinc releases two electrons during oxidation, so 0.09 moles of zinc are necessary to liberate 0.18 moles of electrons. We can then determine the necessary mass of zinc from its molar mass:

$$0.09 \text{ mol Zn} \times 65.4 \frac{\text{g}}{\text{mol}} \approx 6 \text{ g Zn (actual} = 6.10 \text{ g)}$$

Takeaways

Double-check your work when you balance the cell equations to make sure that you haven't made any arithmetic errors. One small addition or subtraction mistake can have drastic consequences.

Things to Watch Out For

In a galvanic (voltaic) cell, the species with the higher reduction potential will be reduced. In an electrolytic cell, the species with the higher reduction potential will be oxidized.

Related Questions

1. How could one alter the cell setup to reverse the direction of current flow?
2. What would happen to the electromotive force produced by this cell if the amount of zinc present were doubled?
3. Compute the minimum mass of potassium permanganate ($KMnO_4$) necessary to run the cell for the same amount of time as specified above.

Solutions to Related Questions

1. Atomic Mass and Weight

1. A mole of any substance has a quantity of molecules equal to Avogadro's number ($N_A = 6.02 \times 10^{23}\ \text{mol}^{-1}$). Therefore, while one mole of each substance has the same number of molecules, their masses will be different. Water has a molar mass of $2 \times 1 \frac{\text{g}}{\text{mol}} + 16 \frac{\text{g}}{\text{mol}} = 18 \frac{\text{g}}{\text{mol}}$, whereas carbon dioxide has a molar mass of $12 \frac{\text{g}}{\text{mol}} + 2 \times 16 \frac{\text{g}}{\text{mol}} = 44 \frac{\text{g}}{\text{mol}}$.

2. Given an atomic weight, it is not always possible to tell which isotope is most abundant; for example, bromine has two abundant isotopes: bromine-79 and bromine-81. The atomic weight sits between these two, at 79.9. Bromine-80, which is the closest to this value, is *not* the most abundant isotope. In this case, however, we can tell that silicon-29 must be the most common isotope. For the atomic weight to be 28.086, there must be enough silicon-29 to balance out the other isotopes, which are all less than 28.

3. This question is no different than the one given for zinc; here, let's use rounding to simplify the calculations. There are 200 total atoms, 40% of which are oxygen-16, and 30% of which are oxygen-14 and oxygen-18, respectively. If we multiply the atomic masses by their relative abundances and then add those results together, we get the atomic weight: $0.4 \times 16 \frac{\text{amu}}{\text{atom}} + 0.3 \times 14 \frac{\text{amu}}{\text{atom}} + 0.3 \times 18 \frac{\text{amu}}{\text{atom}} = 6.4 + 4.2 + 5.4 = 16 \frac{\text{amu}}{\text{atom}}$. The question asks for the molar mass, which is the mass of one mole of a substance in grams. This has the same value as the atomic weight, but different units. The molar mass of oxygen is $16 \frac{\text{g}}{\text{mol}}$. Note that we could have actually bypassed all of these calculations—the value reported in the Periodic Table *is* the atomic weight for an element.

2. Periodic Trends

1. In the neutral state, we would expect atomic radii to increase as we move from the upper right corner of the Periodic Table to the lower left: O < C < B < Be. When an atom gains electrons, its size increases significantly; in fact, we would predict that the divalent oxygen anion would be the largest. The opposite is true for cations; we would expect that boron, having lost three electrons, would be the smallest species. Therefore, we could rank these species from smallest to largest as follows:

$$B^{3+} < C < Be < O^{2-}$$

2. Both phosphorus and selenium are equidistant from the upper right corner of the Periodic Table. However, the element with the higher effective nuclear charge (Z_{eff}) will have the higher ionization energy. Selenium has more electrons that shield valence electrons from the nucleus, reducing its Z_{eff}. Therefore, we would expect phosphorus to have a higher first ionization energy than selenium.

3. The second ionization energy of an element will always be higher than the first ionization energy, and the third ionization energy will always be higher still. Thus, this trend is expected. However, note that the increase from second to third ionization energy is much higher than the increase from first to second ionization energy. This implies that it requires some energy to remove one electron from the element, more energy to remove a second electron, and then much, much more energy to remove a third. In other words, this element seems to gain some stability after losing two electrons that is greatly disturbed by removing a third. Elements in Group IIA (Group 2) best fit this description; specifically, these are the ionization energies for strontium (Sr).

3. VSEPR Theory and Geometry

1. The formula for aluminum trichloride is $AlCl_3$, and that for phosphorus tribromide is PBr_3. Based solely on the number of bonds, we might expect that both will have trigonal planar geometry. We must analyze the Lewis structure to determine if there are lone pairs. Aluminum is in Group IIIA (Group 13), so it has three valence electrons. Because it has already formed three single bonds, it has no electrons left to form a lone pair and will have the expected trigonal planar geometry. Phosphorus is in Group VA (Group 15), so it has five valence electrons. Because it has formed three single bonds, it must have one lone pair remaining; it therefore has trigonal pyramidal geometry. These two molecules vary in geometry because phosphorus has a lone pair, while aluminum does not.

2. A molecule with octahedral geometry has six groups organized around a central atom. In order to maximize the distance between any two groups, four of the groups occupy a square plane around the atom, and two are axial (up and down). This makes the maximum angle between two adjacent groups 90°. In a bent molecule, there are four groups (two of which are lone pairs). With fewer groups to arrange in three-dimensional space, each group can spread farther away from the others to minimize the amount of repulsion between adjacent groups. In bent molecules, this angle is around 104.5°. In other words, the angle is larger in a bent molecule than an octahedral molecule because fewer groups are sharing the same space.

3. The sulfate anion (SO_4^{2-}) has a tetrahedral structure because it has four groups arranged around a central atom (AX_4 geometry). The negative charges do not influence its overall geometry because the electrons are delocalized due to resonance. Thus, the charge is distributed around the whole molecule. Sulfuric acid (H_2SO_4) has two hydroxyl groups and two S=O bonds. While there are slight deviations in the angles between sulfate and sulfuric acid, the fact that both molecules arrange four groups around the central sulfur atom means that the geometry is tetrahedral for both.

4. Stoichiometry

1. Water is formed from hydrogen and oxygen gases through the reaction $2\ H_2 + O_2 \rightarrow 2\ H_2O$. 26 g of hydrogen gas corresponds to 13 moles of H_2 (molar mass = $2\ \frac{g}{mol}$), which will produce 13 moles of water. 13 moles of water can then be converted to the various desired units to obtain 234 g H_2O (molar mass = $18\ \frac{g}{mol}$) and 7.83×10^{24} molecules H_2O (using Avogadro's number). Note that the phrase *excess oxygen* implies that no limiting reagent calculation is required.

2. Let's start by balancing the reaction for the combustion of butane. The balanced reaction is:

$$2\,C_4H_{10} + 13\,O_2 \rightarrow 8\,CO_2 + 10\,H_2O$$

For this calculation, we are given the units of liters of gas at STP, which can be converted to moles using the equivalence factor $22.4\,\frac{L}{mol}$. Then, we'll use the mole ratio from the balanced equation above. Finally, we'll convert to a mass of butane using its molar mass ($4 \times 12\,\frac{g}{mol} + 10 \times 1\,\frac{g}{mol} = 58\,\frac{g}{mol}$). The calculations are:

$$179.2\text{ L }CO_2 \times \left[\frac{1\text{ mol }CO_2}{22.4\text{ L }CO_2}\right]\left[\frac{2\text{ mol }C_4H_{10}}{8\text{ mol }CO_2}\right]\left[\frac{58\text{ g }C_4H_{10}}{1\text{ mol }C_4H_{10}}\right]$$

$$\approx \frac{180 \times 2 \times 60}{20 \times 8} = 9 \times 15 = 135\text{ g }C_4H_{10}\text{ (actual} = 116\text{ g)}$$

3. This question is similar to those from before, but also introduces a limiting reagent. Start by balancing the equation. The balanced equation for the combustion of heptane is:

$$C_7H_{16} + 11\,O_2 \rightarrow 7\,CO_2 + 8\,H_2O$$

To determine the limiting reagent, convert each of the units given to moles: 44.8 L of heptane represents 2 moles of heptane; 1.204×10^{24} molecules of oxygen represents 2 moles of oxygen. Now, think logically. To react to completion, 2 moles of heptane would require 22 moles of oxygen based on the balanced chemical equation. Because we have only 2 moles of oxygen, this must be the limiting reagent. Now, we proceed as with any other stoichiometry calculation, using the 2 moles of oxygen as our given:

$$2\text{ mol }O_2\left[\frac{8\text{ mol }H_2O}{11\text{ mol }O_2}\right]\left[\frac{18\text{ g }H_2O}{1\text{ mol }H_2O}\right]$$

$$= \frac{288}{11} \approx \frac{286}{11} = 26\text{ g }H_2O\text{ (actual} = 26.2\text{ g)}$$

5. Rate Laws

1. The value of the rate constant can be determined by plugging the values from any of the trials into the rate law:

$$\begin{aligned} \text{rate} &= k[HNO_2]^2 \\ 5.96 \times 10^{-6} &= k[2.00 \times 10^{-2}]^2 \\ 5.96 \times 10^{-6} &= k[4.00 \times 10^{-4}] \\ 1.49 \times 10^{-2} &= k \end{aligned}$$

Its units can be determined by considering the other units in the rate law. The rate is measured in $\frac{M}{s}$, whereas $[HNO_2]$ is measured in M. Thus, the units of k must be $\frac{1}{M \bullet s}$.

2. If we compare trials 2 and 3, we can quickly determine that doubling the concentration of MeI while holding the concentration of pyridine constant resulted in a doubling of the rate. This means the exponent on MeI must be 1 ($2^1 = 2$). Determining the rate with respect to pyridine is a bit more challenging. Let's invent another trial based on what we know about MeI. If we hold the concentration of pyridine constant while *halving* the concentration of MeI, the rate should get cut in half:

Trial	$[C_5H_5N]$ (M)	[MeI] (M)	Initial Rate $\left(\frac{M}{\text{s}}\right)$
1	1.00×10^{-4}	1.00×10^{-4}	7.50×10^{-7}
2	2.00×10^{-4}	2.00×10^{-4}	3.00×10^{-6}
2a	2.00×10^{-4}	1.00×10^{-4}	1.50×10^{-6}
3	2.00×10^{-4}	4.00×10^{-4}	6.00×10^{-6}

Now we can compare trials 1 and 2a. The concentration of pyridine doubles while the concentration of MeI remains constant. The rate also doubles. Therefore, the exponent on pyridine must also be 1 ($2^1 = 2$). The rate law is rate = $k[C_5H_5N][\text{MeI}]$. The rate constant could be calculated from trial 1:

$$\begin{aligned}\text{rate} &= k[C_5H_5N][\text{MeI}]\\ 7.5\times10^{-7}\,\frac{M}{\text{s}} &= k[1.00\times10^{-4}\,M][1.00\times10^{-4}\,M]\\ 75\,M^{-1}\,\text{s}^{-1} &= k\end{aligned}$$

3. The same steps can be used here, even though the numbers do not work quite "cleanly." Between trials 1 and 2, the concentration of cerium(IV) is constant while the concentration of iron(II) gets multiplied by just a bit more than 1.5. The rate also gets multiplied by just a bit more than 1.5. Therefore, the order with respect to iron(II) is 1 ($1.55^1 = 1.55$). Comparing trials 2 and 3, the concentration of cerium(IV) is multiplied by a bit more than 3, while the concentration of iron(II) is constant. The rate also gets multiplied by a bit more than 3. Therefore, the order with respect to cerium(IV) is also 1 ($3.1^1 = 3.1$). The rate law for the reaction of cerium(IV) and iron(II) is therefore rate = $k[Ce^{4+}][Fe^{2+}]$. The rate constant can be determined using trial 1:

$$\begin{aligned}\text{rate} &= k[Ce^{4+}][Fe^{2+}]\\ 2.00\times10^{-7}\,\frac{M}{\text{s}} &= k[1.10\times10^{-5}\,M][1.80\times10^{-5}\,M]\\ 2.00\times10^{-7}\,\frac{M}{\text{s}} &\approx k[2\times10^{-10}\,M^2]\\ 10^3\,M^{-1}\,\text{s}^{-1} &\approx k\ (\text{actual} = 1.01\times10^3\,M^{-1}\,\text{s}^{-1})\end{aligned}$$

6. Reaction Energy Profiles

1. The ratio of **B** to **A** at equilibrium can be determined using the equation $\Delta G° = -RT \ln K_{eq}$:

$$K_{eq} = \frac{[\mathbf{B}]}{[\mathbf{A}]} = e^{\frac{-\Delta G°}{RT}} = e^{\frac{900\,\frac{\text{cal}}{\text{mol}}}{(2\,\frac{\text{cal}}{\text{mol}\cdot\text{K}})(300\text{ K})}} \approx e^{1.5} \approx \text{between 3 and 9 (actual} = 4.56)$$

2. If a catalyst were added to the reaction of **A** forming **C**, the energies of **A** and **C** would not be changed. A catalyst only lowers the activation energy by lowering the energy of the transition state, and does not affect the energies of the reactants or products.

3. The complete reaction profiles for the reactions producing **B** and **C** from **A** are shown below. The intermediate leading to **C** is relatively more stable because the electrons in the double bond and in the lone pair on the oxygen atom can be delocalized. This can be seen in the plot from its lower energy.

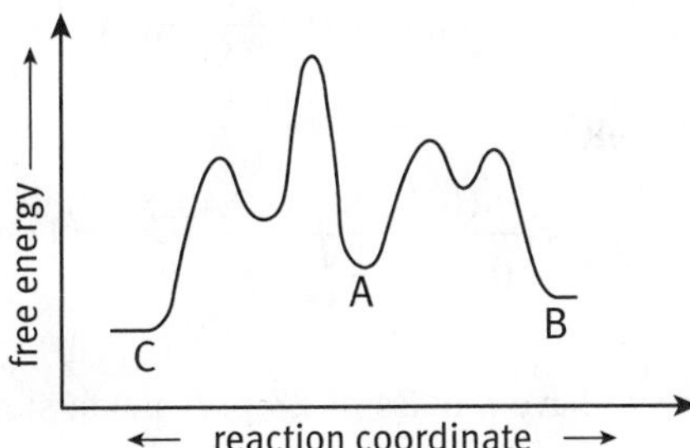

7. Hess's Law

1. An ideal hydrocarbon combustion reaction has two reactants (the hydrocarbon and oxygen) and two products (carbon dioxide and water). To determine the heat of reaction—which is combustion in this case—we will need the heats of formation for all of the reactants and products. We know that the heat of formation of diatomic oxygen gas is zero, so if we are given the heats of formation for carbon dioxide and water, we also need to know the heat of formation of ethane to determine the heat of combustion.

2. First, we must balance the chemical equation for the combustion of acetylene:

$$C_2H_2 + \frac{5}{2}O_2 \rightarrow 2\,CO_2 + H_2O$$

Note that the fractional stoichiometric coefficient in front of oxygen is not a concern because we'll be multiplying that coefficient by the heat of formation of oxygen gas, which is zero. We can apply Hess's law to answer this question. The heats of formation of all of the reactants and products are given, so we can solve for the heat of combustion:

$$\begin{aligned}
\Delta H^\circ_{rxn} &= \sum \Delta H^\circ_{f,products} - \sum \Delta H^\circ_{f,reactants} \\
\Delta H^\circ_{comb} &= \left[2\times\left(-393.5\,\frac{kJ}{mol}\right)+1\times\left(-241.8\,\frac{kJ}{mol}\right)\right]-\left[1\times\left(226.6\,\frac{kJ}{mol}\right)+\frac{5}{2}\times\left(0\,\frac{kJ}{mol}\right)\right] \\
&\approx 2\times(-400)-250-225 \\
&= -800-475 = -1275\,\frac{kJ}{mol}\left(\text{actual} = -1255.4\,\frac{kJ}{mol}\right)
\end{aligned}$$

3. Enthalpy is a state function; therefore, the path taken to get from the reactants to the products does not matter in determining the enthalpy change. If we add these five reactions together, the net reaction is:

$$Na\,(s) + \frac{1}{2}Br_2\,(g) \rightarrow NaBr\,(s)$$

This is equivalent to synthesizing sodium bromide from its elements in their standard states, which is, by definition, the standard heat of formation. Thus, the sum of the heats of reaction for these five reactions is $-359.9\,\frac{kJ}{mol}$.

8. The Ideal Gas Law

1. Recall that nitrogen is a diatomic gas (molar mass = 28 $\frac{g}{mol}$), and that STP has conditions of 273 K and 1 atm (101.3 kPa). The given volume is 22.4 L and the ideal gas constant is 8.314 $\frac{J}{mol \cdot K}$. Let's set up the ideal gas law equation again:

$$PV = nRT$$

$$n = \frac{PV}{RT} = \frac{(101.3\ \text{kPa})(22.4\ \text{L})}{(8.314\ \frac{\text{J}}{\text{mol} \cdot \text{K}})(273\ \text{K})} = 1\ \text{mol}$$

One mole of diatomic nitrogen gas should have a mass of 28 g. A much simpler way of solving this question would require remembering the ideal gas conversion factor—1 mole of any ideal gas at STP occupies a volume of 22.4 liters, the volume given in the question.

2. We'll use the ideal gas law equation to solve this question, but first, make sure that all of the units match those of the ideal gas constant. We are given temperature in degrees Celsius. Remember to add 273 to this value to get the temperature in kelvins: 37°C + 273 = 310 K. Now we can plug into the ideal gas law equation:

$$PV = nRT$$

$$n = \frac{PV}{RT} = \frac{(1\ \text{atm})(0.5\ \text{L})}{(0.0821\ \frac{\text{L} \cdot \text{atm}}{\text{mol} \cdot \text{K}})(310\ \text{K})} \approx \frac{0.5}{25} = 0.02\ \text{mol}$$

3. We can use the ideal gas constant equation again, but must convert the units of degrees Celsius to kelvins: 700°C + 273 = 973 K. Now we can plug into the ideal gas law equation:

$$PV = nRT$$

$$V = \frac{nRT}{P} = \frac{(2\ \text{mol})\left(62.4\ \frac{\text{L} \cdot \text{mmHg}}{\text{mol} \cdot \text{K}}\right)(973\ \text{K})}{(4000\ \text{mmHg})} \approx \frac{2 \times 60 \times 1000}{4000} = 30\ \text{L (actual} = 30.4\ \text{L)}$$

9. Molar Solubility

1. One can always use the same three-step method to determine molar solubility from K_{sp} or K_{sp} from molar solubility:

   1. Write out the balanced expression for the dissociation reaction

   2. Write the expression for K_{sp}

   3. Plug in the values from the question stem or data table

   If there is no common ion effect, this three-step method can be abbreviated by remembering three shortcuts. For a compound of general formula MX, $K_{sp} = x^2$, where x is the molar solubility; for a compound of general formula MX_2, $K_{sp} = 4x^3$; and for a compound of general formula MX_3, $K_{sp} = 27x^4$. When a common ion is present, these shortcuts cannot be used, and the three-step method listed above must be used instead.

2. Given a list of solubility constants, to find the substance most soluble in pure water, you would need to find the substance with the highest molar solubility. Because all of the compounds are being dissolved in pure water, the three shortcuts listed above can be used to speed up this process. Additionally, it makes most sense to compare the compounds with a particular general formula to one another, and then to compare the most soluble of the three groups. That is, of all the compounds with the general formula *MX*, the one with the highest K_{sp} is the most soluble. The same is true when comparing all of the compounds with the general formula MX_2 and those with the general formula MX_3. Finding the molar solubility of only these three salts and comparing them will allow you to find the most soluble salt as quickly as possible.

3. Decreasing the pH will cause greater dissolution of the sulfate salt because there will be more H^+ available to react with sulfate; this removes products from the dissociation reaction, driving the equilibrium toward the right. Increasing pH will have the opposite effect, driving the equilibrium to the left and disfavoring the dissolution of the sulfate salt.

10. Titrations

1. Adding an extra 5 mL of 0.5 *M* NaOH means that we've added another 2.5×10^{-3} mol OH^- to the solution. This is in 145 mL of solution, which represents a concentration of approximately 0.02 *M*. The amount of dilution to the N_3^- is negligible, so we can calculate the expected pH using the K_b for N_3^-:

$$K_b = \frac{[HN_3][OH^-]}{[N_3^-]}$$

$$10^{-9} = \frac{[x][0.02 + x]}{[0.15 - x]} \approx \frac{x}{8}$$

$$x = 8 \times 10^{-9}$$

$$[OH^-] \approx 0.02 + x \approx 0.02$$

Because the calculated value of *x* is so small, it is actually negligible in comparison with the 0.02 *M* OH^- in solution. If $[OH^-]$ is approximately 2×10^{-2} *M*, then pOH is approximately $2 - 0.2 \approx 1.8$, and pH is approximately $14 - 1.8 = 12.2$ (actual = 12.23).

2. If 20 mL of 0.5 *M* NaOH were diluted with pure water to form one liter of solution, the concentration of hydroxide ions would be approximately $0.5\ M \times \frac{20}{1000} = 0.01\ M$. The pOH would be 2, and the pH would be 12.

3. The K_a of an acid multiplied by the K_b of its conjugate base is 10^{-14}:

$$K_{a,acid} \times K_{b,conjugate\ base} = K_w$$

Taking the negative logarithm of both sides, we get:

$$pK_{a,acid} + pK_{b,conjugate\ base} = 14$$

Therefore, the pK_b of acetate is $14 - 4.76 = 9.24$.

11. Balancing Oxidation–Reduction Reactions

1. When present, transition metals are often the oxidized and reduced species in an oxidation–reduction reaction. After transition metals, elements further down in the p-block are relatively common as well. Therefore, let's start by identifying the oxidation states of zirconium and sulfur in this reaction. Zirconium starts with a +4 charge. Each of the hydroxide groups in $ZrO(OH)_2$ has a –1 charge, and oxygen usually has a –2 charge; so zirconium must have a +4 charge for the compound to be neutral overall. As a solid, zirconium has an oxidation state of 0. Therefore, zirconium has gained electrons and has been reduced—it is also the oxidizing agent. Sulfur, on the other hand, started with a +4 charge (each of the three oxygens has a –2 charge, and the overall charge of the molecule is –2) and ends with a +6 charge. Therefore, sulfur has lost electrons and has been oxidized—it is also the reducing agent.

2. We'll balance this oxidation–reduction reaction using the same method as the question. Note that no multiplication is needed in Step 4:

$$1. \begin{cases} PbSO_4 \rightarrow Pb + SO_4^{2-} \\ PbSO_4 \rightarrow PbO_2 + SO_4^{2-} \end{cases}$$

$$2. \begin{cases} PbSO_4 \rightarrow Pb + SO_4^{2-} \\ 2\,H_2O + PbSO_4 \rightarrow PbO_2 + SO_4^{2-} + 4\,H^+ \end{cases}$$

$$3. \begin{cases} PbSO_4 + 2\,e^- \rightarrow Pb + SO_4^{2-} \\ 2\,H_2O + PbSO_4 \rightarrow PbO_2 + SO_4^{2-} + 4\,H^+ + 2\,e^- \end{cases}$$

$$4. \begin{cases} PbSO_4 + 2\,e^- \rightarrow Pb + SO_4^{2-} \\ 2\,H_2O + PbSO_4 \rightarrow PbO_2 + SO_4^{2-} + 4\,H^+ + 2\,e^- \end{cases}$$

$$5.\ 2\,PbSO_4 + 2\,H_2O \rightarrow Pb + PbO_2 + 2\,SO_4^{2-} + 4\,H^+$$

3. We'll balance this oxidation–reduction reaction using the same method as the question. Again, no multiplication is needed in Step 4:

$$1. \begin{cases} Zn \rightarrow Zn^{2+} \\ H_2O \rightarrow H_2 \end{cases}$$

$$2. \begin{cases} Zn \rightarrow Zn^{2+} \\ 2\,H_2O \rightarrow H_2 + 2\,OH^- \end{cases}$$

$$3. \begin{cases} Zn \rightarrow Zn^{2+} + 2\,e^- \\ 2\,H_2O + 2\,e^- \rightarrow H_2 + 2\,OH^- \end{cases}$$

$$4. \begin{cases} Zn \rightarrow Zn^{2+} + 2\,e^- \\ 2\,H_2O + 2\,e^- \rightarrow H_2 + 2\,OH^- \end{cases}$$

$$5.\ Zn + 2\,H_2O \rightarrow Zn^{2+} + H_2 + 2\,OH^-$$

The amalgam must be kept dry because upon reacting with water in basic solution, hydrogen gas is generated. The expansion of the gas could potentially cause the crown or tooth to crack.

12. Electrochemical Cells

1. To reverse the direction of the current, one would have to place a battery of greater than 2.25 V in the circuit (with the positive terminal connected to the cathode of the galvanic cell setup). This would override the electromotive force of the cell, causing the current to flow the opposite direction.

2. The amount of zinc present would have no effect on the electromotive force of the cell (assuming that at least some zinc is present). The electromotive force is calculated as the difference in reduction potential between the cathode and the anode, and does not depend on the amount of zinc present.

3. Keeping in mind that 0.18 moles of electrons are transferred during the course of one hour, we can skip to determining how many moles of $KMnO_4$ are necessary to accept these electrons. Because each molecule of permanganate can accept five electrons, only about 0.03 moles of $KMnO_4$ are needed. We can then use the molar mass to determine the mass needed:

$$0.03 \text{ mol } KMnO_4 \times 158 \frac{\text{g}}{\text{mol}} \approx 4.8 \text{ g } KMnO_4 \text{ (actual = 5.90 g)}$$

5

Organic Chemistry

Key Concepts

Organic Chemistry Chapter 1

Nomenclature

Functional group priority

Nomenclature

What is the IUPAC name for the following compound?

O O
OEt
OMe

1 Identify the longest carbon chain containing the highest-order functional group.

In this case, the highest-priority functional group is the ester. Therefore, we will name everything attached to the ester as a substituent, including the cyclohexyl ring on the left. The longest continuous chain containing the ester is three carbons long.

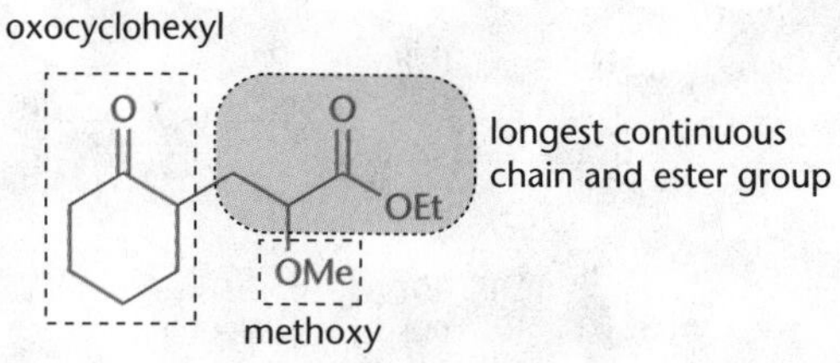

2 Number the chain.

As mentioned in Step 1, the longest continuous chain containing the ester is three carbons long. Carbon 1 will be the carbonyl carbon because the ester is the highest-priority functional group. Because the ester has three carbons, this will be a *propanoate* ester.

O O
3
2
1 OEt
OMe

3 Name the substituents.

The first substituent is the ethyl group on the ester, which we will identify by placing the word *ethyl* in front of the ester name. Next, there is a methyl group attached to an oxygen, which will be named as a *methoxy–* group. Finally, there is a cyclohexane containing a ketone, the naming of which will be discussed in the next step.

4 Assign a number to each substituent.

The ethyl group is the esterifying group and is not assigned a number, but rather is listed as an adjective before the rest of the molecule's name.

The methoxy group is on carbon 2.

How do we handle the ring attached to carbon 3? If there were nothing attached to the ring, we would simply name the ring as a *cyclohexyl* substituent. However, there is a ketone in the ring. Recall that when aldehydes or ketones are named as substituents, they are named with the prefix *oxo–*. The numbering works, as shown, by assigning the number 1 to the carbon attached to the parent carbon chain. Therefore, the ketone on the ring will be at carbon 2. We'll name the whole ring as a *(2-oxocyclohexyl)–* substituent and put it in parentheses to indicate that it follows a numbering system *within* a substituent.

O O 3 2 1 OEt 4 6 OMe 5

5 Complete the name.

The name of our compound will be ethyl 2-methoxy-3-(2-oxocyclohexyl) propanoate.

Takeaways

The key to the nomenclature problems is to be as systematic as possible. Don't try to do everything at once, or you risk confusing yourself.

Things to Watch Out For

Don't forget to include parentheses if a substituent is further substituted so that you don't confuse the two numbering systems.

Related Questions

1. How would the name be altered if the alkyl group attached to the ester oxygen contained substituents?

2. Upon reduction with sodium borohydride, followed by dilute acid workup, the molecule below gave two products in unequal yield. Draw them and provide the correct IUPAC name for each.

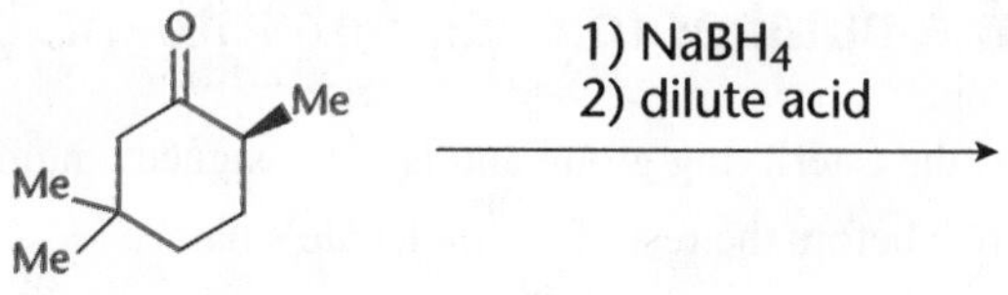

O, Me, Me, Me — 1) $NaBH_4$ 2) dilute acid

3. What are the two possible products of the reaction shown below? Draw and provide IUPAC names for both.

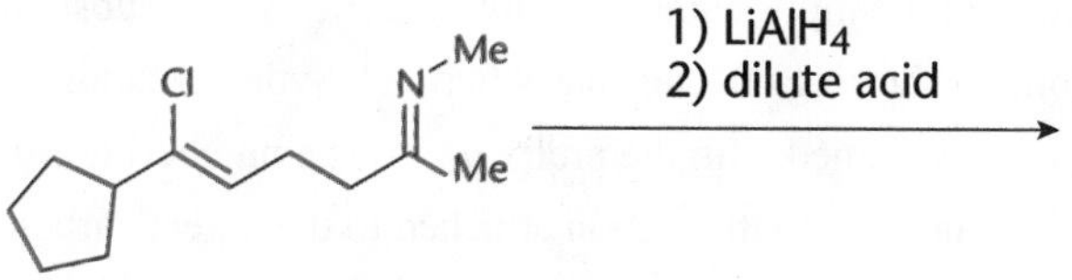

Cl, N, Me, Me — 1) $LiAlH_4$ 2) dilute acid

High-Yield Problem-Solving Guide questions continue on the next page. ▶ ▶ ▶

Key Concepts

Organic Chemistry Chapter 2

Stereochemistry

Fischer projections

Oxidation–reduction reactions

meso compounds

Stereoisomers

A student wanted to prepare chiral polyols by taking sugars and reacting them with sodium borohydride. She took D-xylose, shown below, and treated it with sodium borohydride, followed by a dilute aqueous acid workup. On purifying and isolating the product, she found that it did not rotate plane-polarized light. What was the structure of the product, and why didn't it rotate light?

OH OH O / H / OH OH

1 Convert the molecule from a Natta projection to a Fischer projection.

Natta (wedge-and-dash) projections are frequently used in organic chemistry, but are more challenging to use for absolute configuration determinations than Fischer projections. This is especially true when the highest-priority group for Cahn–Ingold–Prelog nomenclature (–OH, in this case) is in the "back." Converting to a Fischer projection may enable you to see stereochemical relationships more clearly. Note that the center carbon atom is drawn in reverse because the rules of Fischer projections require that the horizontal bonds always project forward, not backward.

OH OH O (R) (S) (R) H OH OH → CHO; (R) H—OH; (S) HO—H; (R) H—OH; CH_2OH

2 Draw the product of the initial reaction.

Sodium borohydride is a reducing agent and will reduce the aldehyde to a primary alcohol.

CHO; H—OH; HO—H; H—OH; CH_2OH —1) $NaBH_4$ 2) dilute acid→ CH_2OH; H—OH; HO—H; H—OH; CH_2OH

3 Look for planes of symmetry in the product.

There are two major ways that optical activity could be lost in a previously optically active solution: the formation of a racemic mixture, or the generation of an achiral compound. In the latter case, the molecule could have zero chiral centers or could be a *meso* compound—one that has stereocenters but also contains a plane of symmetry. It is easiest to check for a *meso* compound because all we need to do is identify a plane of symmetry. To check for a racemic mixture, we would have to assign (*R*) and (*S*) designations to every chiral carbon in the molecules. In this case, there is a plane of symmetry in the product running through C-3:

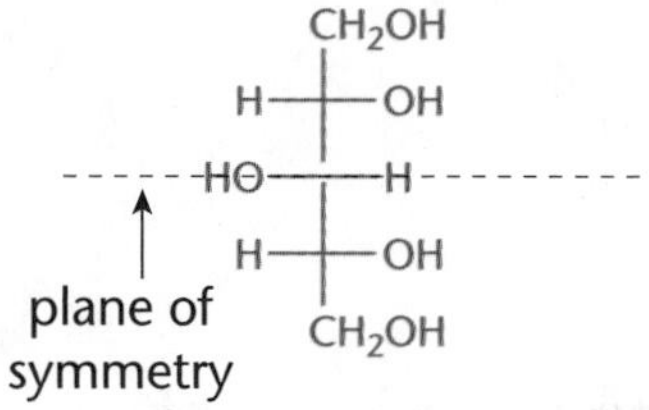

CH_2OH
H—|—OH
HO—|—H (plane of symmetry)
H—|—OH
CH_2OH

Takeaways

Any time optical activity is lost in a reaction, either a racemic mixture or an achiral compound has been formed.

Things to Watch Out For

With molecules that contain multiple stereocenters, consider drawing them as Fischer projections to be able to spot planes of symmetry or assign (*R*) and (*S*) nomenclature easily.

Related Questions

1. The specific rotation of a certain D-carbohydrate is +140°. What is the specific rotation of its L-isomer? What would be the observed rotation in a solution containing 1 *M* of each isomer?
2. Which of these three D-aldopentoses (shown below) would result in achiral polyols when subjected to borohydride reduction?

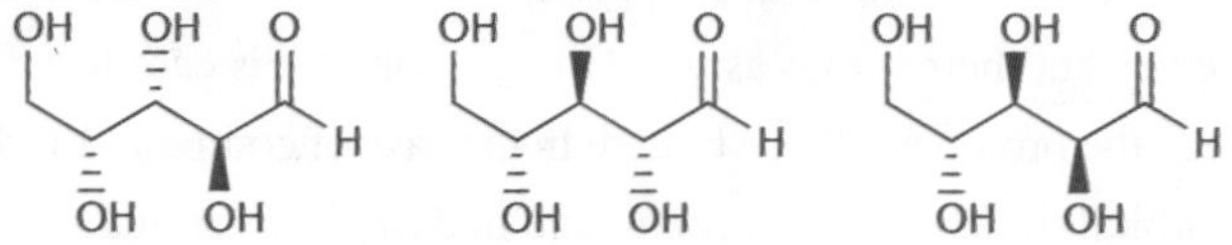

OH OH O ... H / OH OH — OH OH O ... H / OH OH — OH OH O ... H / OH OH

3. A *meso* compound contains chiral centers but is overall achiral. Is the reverse true? That is, can a molecule that does *not* contain chiral centers be overall *chiral*?

Key Concepts

Organic Chemistry Chapter 3

Hybridized orbitals
Covalent bonding
s- and *p*-orbitals
pK_a
Bond dissociation energy

Hybridized Orbitals

Orbital hybridization affects more than just the shape of molecules. In fact, *sp* hybrid orbitals can have quite different properties than sp^3 orbitals, even on atoms of the same element. The compounds below differ only in the hybridization of the carbon atom highlighted. First, arrange them in order of increasing pK_a for the highlighted protons. Then, arrange them by increasing bond dissociation energy between the two carbons.

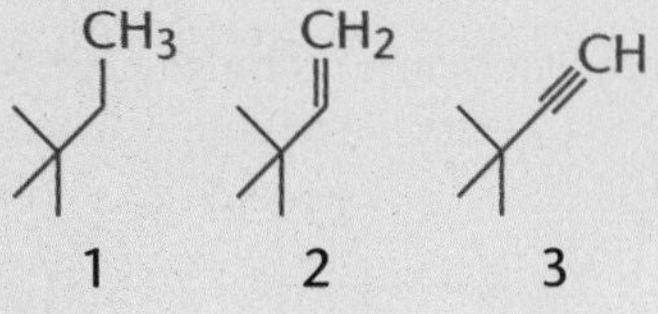

CH_3 CH_2 CH

1 2 3

1 Order the compounds by pK_a.

The K_a (acid dissociation constant) of a molecule measures its acidity; the higher the K_a, the more acidic the compound. The term "p" is shorthand for –log, so pK_a = –log K_a. This mathematical relationship means that the *lower* the pK_a, the more acidic the compound. In each of these three compounds, the proton to be lost differs only by the hybridization of the carbon to which it is attached. The C–H bond in compound **1** is sp^3-hybridized, the C–H bond in **2** is sp^2-hybridized, and the C–H bond in **3** is *sp*-hybridized.

To understand the acidity trend in this group, we need to consider not only the neutral molecules but their anions as well. Each anion in this case has a lone pair of electrons where the proton was once bound. In the case of compound **1**, the electrons are in an sp^3 orbital; in **2**, an sp^2 orbital; and in **3**, in an *sp* orbital.

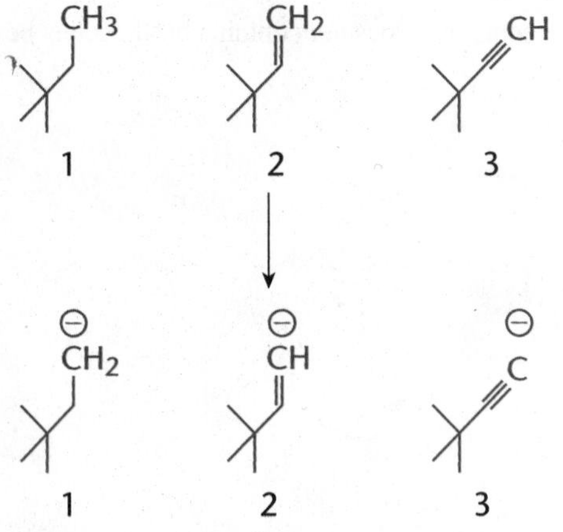

CH_3 CH_2 CH

1 2 3

↓

⊖ ⊖ ⊖

CH_2 CH C

1 2 3

It's useful to say that these lone pairs are in different hybrid orbitals, but how does that actually affect the relative stabilities of their anions? The anions' stabilities are dependent on the energies of the two electrons in the lone pair; these energies are in turn based on the energies of the orbitals in which they are located. Each of these orbitals is a hybrid of *s*- and *p*-orbitals. Remember that *s*-orbitals are much lower in energy than their *p* counterparts, and hybrid orbitals have energies that are weighted averages of their constituent orbitals. Therefore, the anion with the most *s* character should be the most stable, and the anion with the most *p* character should be the least stable. The order of anion stability is:

$$\mathbf{1 < 2 < 3}$$

This isn't the whole picture, though. We were asked to arrange the compounds in order of increasing pK_a, not anion stability—and the less stable the anion is, the less acidic its conjugate acid will be. The less acidic the conjugate acid, the higher the pK_a. Putting it all together, the molecules can be arranged in order of increasing pK_a:

$$\mathbf{3 < 2 < 1}$$

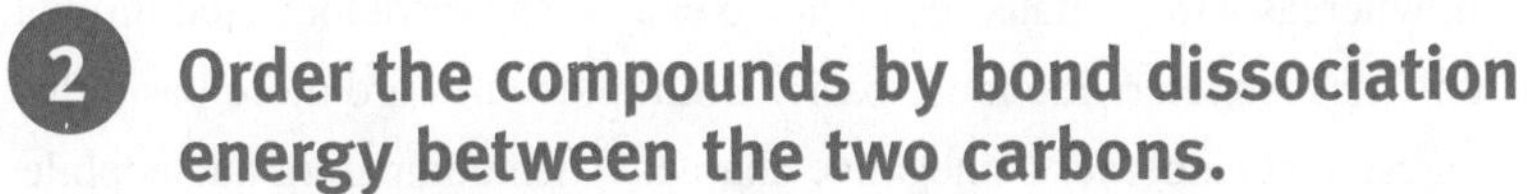

2 Order the compounds by bond dissociation energy between the two carbons.

Bond dissociation energy is the energy required to break a bond, leaving one electron with each fragment, which forms two radicals. It is the standard measure of bond strength in organic chemistry. In general, bond strength and bond energy are related: as bond strength increases, so does bond dissociation energy. Also, the shorter the bond, the stronger it is. For instance, triple bonds are stronger and shorter than double bonds between the same atoms; these, in turn, are shorter and stronger than single bonds. Thus, the C≡C bond in the *sp*-hybridized compound (**3**) should be the shortest and strongest. The weakest will be the one between two sp^3-hybridized carbons (**1**). Thus, the order should be:

$$\mathbf{1 < 2 < 3}$$

Takeaways

Stronger bonds are shorter bonds: triple bonds are the strongest and shortest, while single bonds are the longest and weakest.

Things to Watch Out For

pK_a (acid strength) is determined not only by the acid itself but also by the conjugate base that is formed upon the loss of a proton.

Related Questions

1. Which will lose a hydrogen more easily, a compound with a higher or lower pK_b?
2. What is the hybridization of the carbon atom in carbon dioxide?
3. What is the highest bond order in 5-hydroxy-2,6-dimethyl-3-heptanone?

Key Concepts

Organic Chemistry Chapter 4

Acids and bases
Nucleophilicity
Polar solvents
Protic solvents

Nucleophilicity Trends

Rank the following compounds in order of increasing nucleophilicity toward the same electrophile in a polar protic solvent:

CH_3OH Et_3N $H_3CCO_2^{\ominus}$ Et_3P $CH_3O^{\ominus}$

1 Separate out nucleophiles with the same attacking atom and rank them first.

Let's look at the oxygen-containing nucleophiles first. Here, the methoxide anion is more basic than the acetate anion $\left(CH_3CO_2^-\right)$, which in turn is more basic than methanol. With the methoxide anion, the lone pair on oxygen is "stuck" on the oxygen atom, whereas with acetate, the negative charge can be delocalized through resonance; this makes methoxide more basic. Both molecules are more basic than methanol because methanol lacks a negative charge. When comparing nucleophiles with the same attacking atom, nucleophilicity parallels basicity. Therefore, the methoxide anion will be the most nucleophilic of the three oxygen-containing molecules.

2 Look next for nucleophiles where the attacking atom is in the same group.

Because phosphorus is directly below nitrogen in the Periodic Table, triethylphosphine is more nucleophilic than triethylamine. This is where the nature of the solvent makes a big difference. The more basic molecules are better hydrogen bond acceptors, which means that they will be surrounded by the polar protic solvent molecules and therefore less available to attack the electrophile. The differences in basicity are less pronounced when comparing attacking atoms that are the same or are in the same *period*; this effect is only notable when the attacking atoms are in the same *group*.

Comparing the basicity of triethylphosphine and triethylamine is a bit more complicated than the previous molecules. The key to determining their relative basicities is remembering that in triethylphosphine, the lone pair on phosphorus is contained in an sp^3-hybridized orbital that is made up of one $3s$ and three $3p$ orbitals. Contrast this with triethylamine, where the nitrogen lone pair is in an sp^3-hybridized orbital composed of one 2*s* and three 2*p* orbitals. The hybridized orbitals on phosphorus are composed of larger atomic orbitals, and as such are larger than the hybridized orbitals on nitrogen.

This, in turn, means that the electrons in the phosphorus lone pair are more stable because they have a larger volume of space in which to move around. If the phosphorus lone pair is more stable, then it is less basic (less likely to reach out and grab a proton). Therefore, triethylphosphine is a better nucleophile in a polar protic solvent than triethylamine. Again, this phenomenon is only relevant when the attacking atoms of two nucleophiles are in the same group.

If the solvent were polar aprotic, then the trend would be exactly the opposite. Here, the hydrogen bonding effect is removed, so the molecules with the most localized charge density—the most basic—will also be the most nucleophilic.

3 Look for relationships between nucleophiles in the same period.

Now the question is between the two groups we have ordered separately. Which one is more nucleophilic? In most cases, this question is answered by realizing that for different nucleophiles where the attacking atoms are in the same period, nucleophilicity roughly parallels basicity. Nitrogen is less electronegative than oxygen. The less electronegative an atom, the less pull it will have on its attached electrons, making those electrons more available to act as a basic pair. Therefore, nitrogen is more basic than oxygen, and thus triethylamine is more nucleophilic than the oxygen-containing compounds. In summary, the compounds can be ranked by nucleophilicity toward the same electrophile in a polar protic solvent:

$$CH_3OH < CH_3CO_2^- < CH_3O^- < Et_3N < Et_3P$$

This trend is borne out experimentally. The relative reactivities of each nucleophile toward CH_3I in CH_3OH are as follows:

Nucleophile	Relative Rate
$CH_3CO_2^-$	1
CH_3OH	20,000
CH_3O^-	1,900,000
Et_3N	4,600,000
Et_3P	520,000,000

Takeaways

Sort out differences in nucleophilicity two or three molecules at a time. Don't try to order all the molecules at once or you risk confusing yourself.

Things to Watch Out For

Remember that basicity sometimes *parallels* nucleophilicity (comparing nucleophiles with the same attacking ion, in the same period, or in polar aprotic solvents) but sometimes opposes it (comparing nucleophiles in the same group in a polar protic solvent).

Related Questions

1. Place the following molecules in order of increasing nucleophilicity: pyridine (benzene with one of the carbons in the ring replaced by a nitrogen), triethylamine, acetonitrile (CH_3CN), and 4-dimethylaminopyridine (DMAP). (Note that the solvent doesn't impact nucleophilicity here because the same atom is nucleophilic in all four compounds.) Which of the two nitrogens in DMAP is more nucleophilic, and why?
2. How would the nucleophilicity of fluoride, chloride, bromide, and iodide rank in an S_N2 reaction with methyl iodide in methanol? In dimethyl sulfoxide (DMSO)?
3. How would you order the nucleophilicity of the following molecules in methanol: Et_3N, Ph_3P, Et_3P, Ph_3N, and Et_3As? Provide a rationale for your ordering.

High-Yield Problem-Solving Guide questions continue on the next page. ▶ ▶ ▶

Key Concepts

Organic Chemistry Chapter 5

Isomers
Important reactions of alcohols
Protecting groups
Tosylates

Reactions of Alcohols

Determine the identities of products 3 and 4. What is the relationship between the two products?

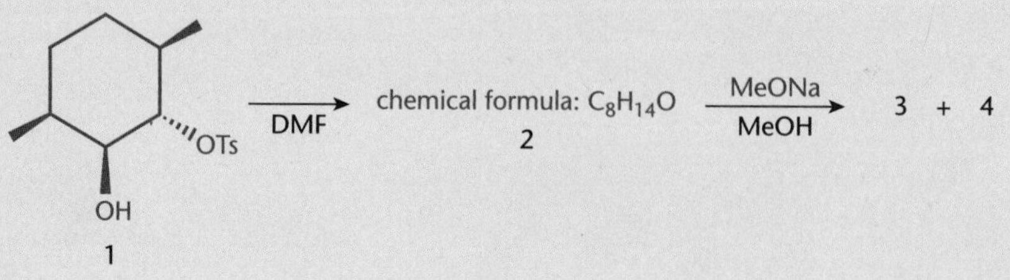

1 $\xrightarrow{\text{DMF}}$ chemical formula: $C_8H_{14}O$ (2) $\xrightarrow[\text{MeOH}]{\text{MeONa}}$ 3 + 4

1 Identify the intermediate, 2.

Before **3** and **4** can be identified, the structure of **2** must be found. Interestingly, no reagents are given in this reaction aside from the solvent (DMF), so we will have to look more closely at the starting reactant. The molecule we are given has two reactive groups that immediately stand out: –OTs, a tosylate group, and –OH, a hydroxyl group. Tosylate is a very good leaving group; the hydroxyl substituent is a poor leaving group and a good (but not great) nucleophile.

Because we have a leaving group but no strong base or nucleophile, the reaction is likely to proceed through an S_N1 mechanism (or E1, although elimination reactions are not tested directly on the MCAT). The first step is the loss of the leaving group, leaving a carbocation intermediate, as shown below:

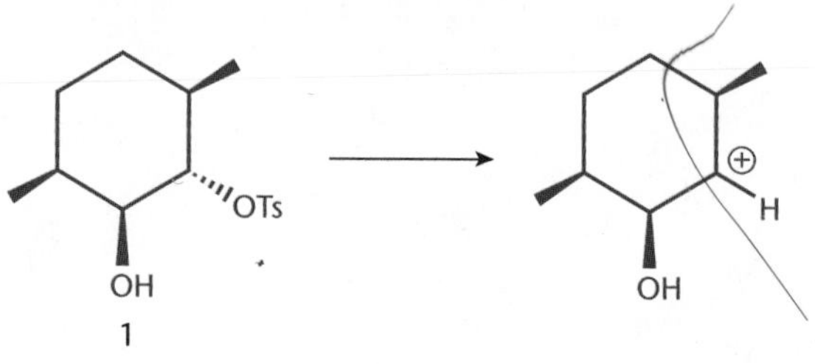

This carbocation intermediate has the formula $C_8H_{15}O$—that's just one hydrogen more than what we're given for intermediate **2**. What's the next step? Next, the nucleophilic hydroxyl group can attack the carbocation. This still leaves us with an intermediate containing an extra hydrogen, which the tosylate group can remove, giving us the structure of intermediate **2**.

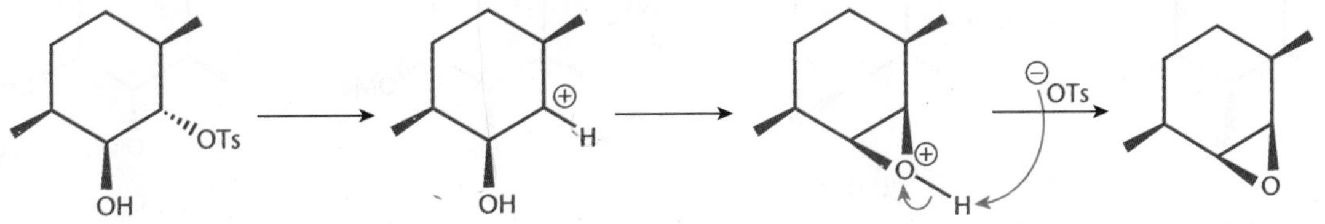

OTs
OH
1
H
OH
OTs
O
H
O
2

2 Using the structure of 2, identify products 3 and 4.

Starting with the structure that we figured out for **2**, we can work through the next set of reagents and determine products **3** and **4**. Our intermediate, **2**, only has one particularly reactive group, the epoxide. While epoxides are not on the official MCAT content lists, it makes sense that the oxygens they contain make good leaving groups. In **2**, the three-membered oxygen-containing ring has a high degree of angle strain, which can be relieved by opening the ring.

Epoxides can open under acidic or basic conditions, but don't do much else. Looking at the reactants, we have sodium methoxide in methanol. Methoxide is both a good base and a good nucleophile. In this case, the less reactive methanol will act as the solvent.

Methoxide can attack at either of two positions, performing our predicted ring-opening reaction:

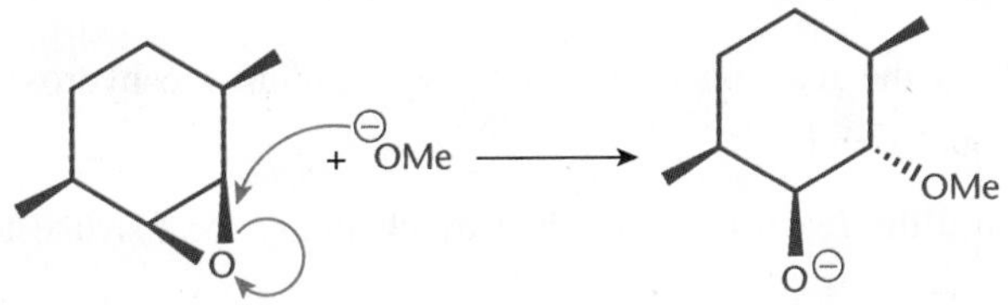

O
+ OMe
OMe
O
2

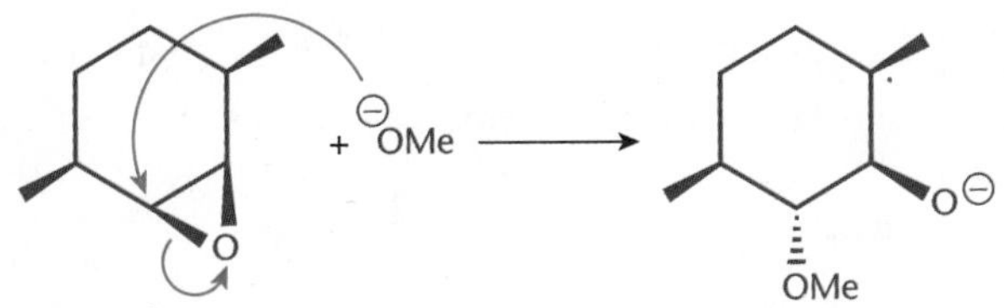

O
+ OMe
O
OMe
2

Protonating these molecules gives us our final products, **3** and **4**. The overall reaction is shown below:

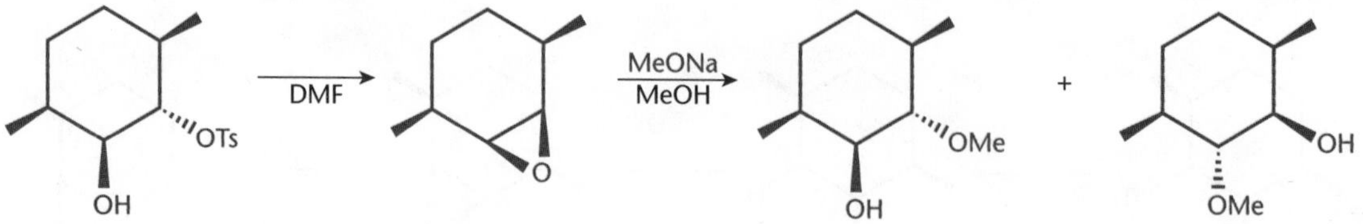

3 Find the relationship between 3 and 4.

Because **3** and **4** share a molecular formula, they are isomers of one another. These molecules have the same connectivity, so they are stereoisomers—not configurational isomers:

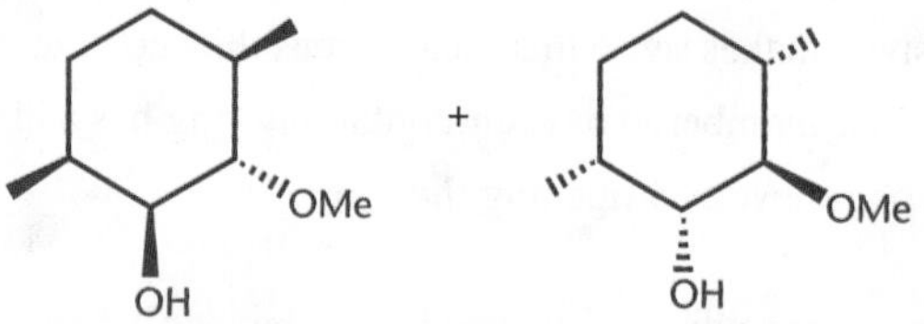

While the connectivity is the same, the stereochemistry is different. These two molecules are nonsuperimposable mirror images, and are therefore enantiomers.

Takeaways

Reactivity in the presence of a good leaving group depends on the quality of the nucleophile. Identifying the quality of a leaving group and the strength of the nucleophile will help determine what happens during the reaction.

Things to Watch Out For

Be sure to keep in mind the stereochemistry of a given reaction; backside attack and planar intermediates both indicate specific changes to stereochemistry. Know how to distinguish between different types of isomers.

Related Questions

1. How would the reaction be affected by changing the hydroxyl group to a stronger nucleophile?
2. How would the reaction be affected by changing the tosylate to a hydroxyl group?
3. Is it possible to favor one product over the other in this reaction?

High-Yield Problem-Solving Guide questions continue on the next page. ▶ ▶ ▶

Key Concepts

Organic Chemistry Chapter 6

Reaction mechanisms

Oxidation–reduction reactions

Aldehydes and ketones

Oxygen-containing functional groups

Carbonyl chemistry

Identifying the Structure of an Unknown Oxy Compound

A student carried out the following series of transformations in the lab:

(*S*)-3-methylcyclohexanol $\xrightarrow{\text{PCC}}$ **A** ($C_7H_{12}O$) $\xrightarrow{\text{cat. } H_2SO_4,\ PhCH_2NH_2}$ **B** + **C** ($C_{14}H_{19}N$)

B + **C** $\xrightarrow{\text{1) } LiAlH_4 \text{ 2) dilute acid}}$ **D** + **E** ($C_{14}H_{21}N$)

Upon **A**'s reaction with catalytic acid and benzylamine, the student obtained a mixture of two products, **B** and **C**. The mixture of **B** and **C** was subjected to lithium aluminum hydride. Following a dilute acid workup and chromatographic separation, two more products, **D** and **E**, were obtained in unequal yield.

Identify the structures of compounds **A** through **E**, given their molecular formulas.

1 React the alcohol with PCC.

The first step of this process is to take the secondary alcohol and subject it to pyridinium chlorochromate (PCC) oxidation, which results in a ketone:

3-methylcyclohexanol (OH, Me) $\xrightarrow{\text{PCC}}$ 3-methylcyclohexanone (O, Me), $C_7H_{12}O$

2 Subject the ketone to an acid catalyst and benzylamine.

You should suspect that some sort of nucleophilic addition is going to take place. Recall that a ketone that reacts with a primary amine gives an imine:

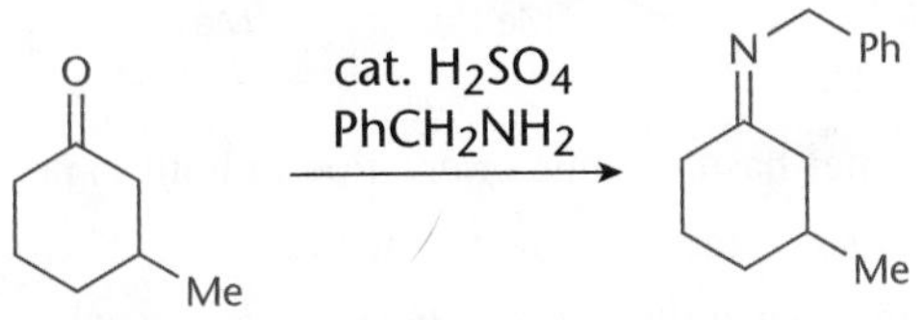

O Me cat. H_2SO_4 $PhCH_2NH_2$ N Ph Me

$C_7H_{12}O$ $C_{14}H_{19}N$

3 Determine the other product of this reaction.

Remember that any time there is an immovable bond (like a double bond), there exists the possibility of having *cis–trans* isomers. The immovable bond doesn't have to be a carbon–carbon double bond; it can also be between different constituent atoms, like the imine here. Thus, the other product must be the other geometric isomer:

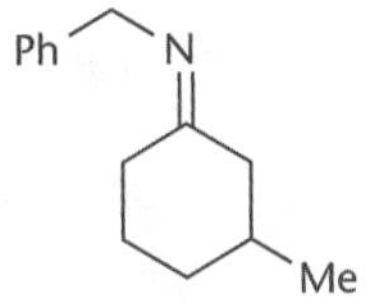

Ph N Me

4 React the imines with $LiAlH_4$.

Reacting each of the imines with lithium aluminum hydride ($LiAlH_4$ or LAH) will result in an amine. Note that you should be able to identify $LiAlH_4$ as a reducing agent because it contains a large number of hydrides (H^-) attached to a metal (aluminum):

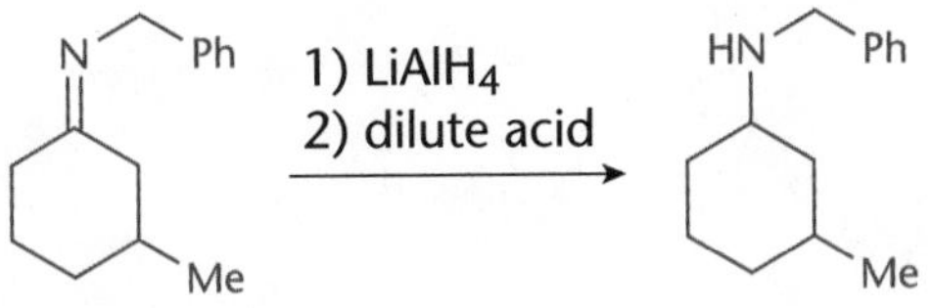

N Ph Me 1) $LiAlH_4$ 2) dilute acid HN Ph Me

$C_{14}H_{19}N$ $C_{14}H_{21}N$

Once reduced, the carbon atom from the imine can assume one of two different stereochemistries, resulting in two possible products:

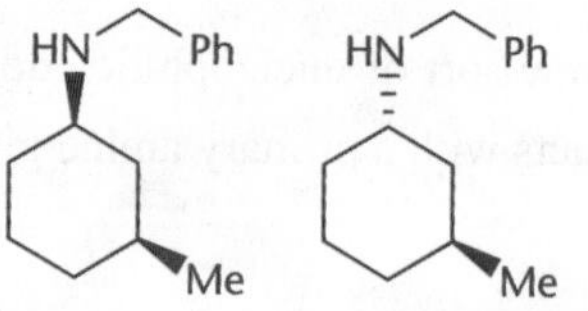

The methyl stereocenter has the same orientation in both molecules because it has remained unchanged since the beginning of the reaction. Therefore, the difference in stereochemistry must be at the nitrogen-bearing carbon atom.

Takeaways

The key to these types of problems is identifying the chemical nature of the reagents and then identifying how they would react with the starting materials for each step. Look for nucleophiles and electrophiles, oxidizing and reducing agents, and acids and bases.

Things to Watch Out For

If the molecular formulas are supplied, be sure to check your structure against the given molecular formula. Practice this skill to avoid losing a sizable amount of time in checking on Test Day.

Related Questions

1. How many stereoisomers exist for product **E** (whether or not they were obtained in this particular reaction)?
2. The final amine products were mixed, in equal amounts, with an achiral solvent. The solution was placed in a polarimeter and found to rotate plane-polarized light. Why is this finding not surprising?
3. In addition to compounds that contain double bonds, what other class of compounds can have *cis–trans* isomers?

High-Yield Problem-Solving Guide questions continue on the next page. ▶ ▶ ▶

Key Concepts

Organic Chemistry Chapter 7

Enolate chemistry

Aldehydes and ketones

α-Hydrogen acidity

Keto–enol tautomerization

Enolate Chemistry

Enolate chemistry has blossomed in the last few decades, becoming one of the most powerful tools in organic synthesis. In reactions involving enolates, small structural differences in reactants can result in vastly different products. Take, for instance, the reaction of cyclohexanone, a common synthetic precursor, with methyl vinyl ketone; what are the products of this reaction?

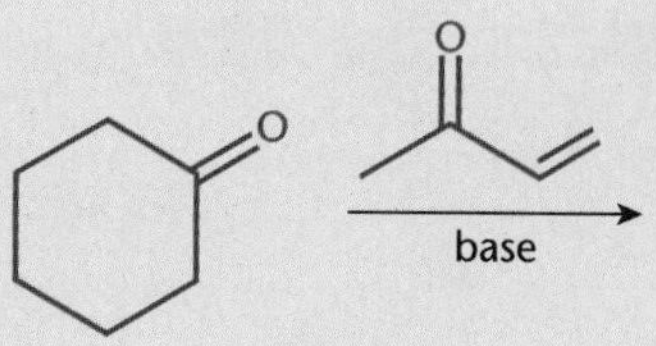

O
O
base

1 Form the enolate.

Whether you recognize the reaction of cyclohexanone and methyl vinyl ketone as what is called a Robinson annulation, you should recognize that the use of ketones under basic conditions means we'll be doing enolate chemistry. Whenever you see a base and an aldehyde or ketone, look for the most acidic proton and deprotonate. In this case, the most acidic protons are on the cyclohexanone. Deprotonating one of the α-carbons results in the cyclohexyl enolate:

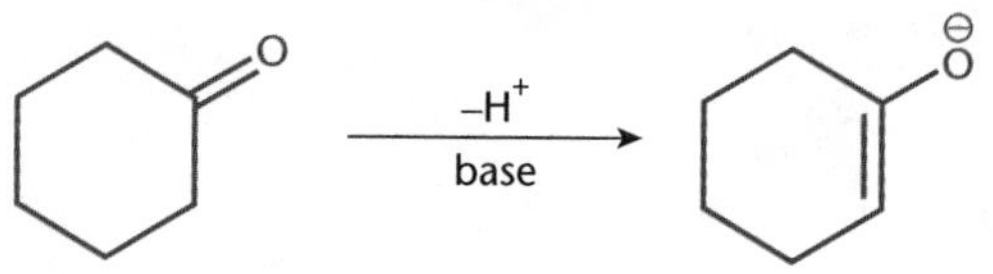

O
$-H^+$
base
$O^{\ominus}$

2 React the enolate with an electrophile.

Enolates are nucleophilic species. Therefore, the next step will require an electrophile. The only electrophile present in this reaction is the methyl vinyl ketone. It would be reasonable to assume that the enolate will attack the methyl vinyl ketone at the carbonyl carbon, its most electrophilic region, as shown below:

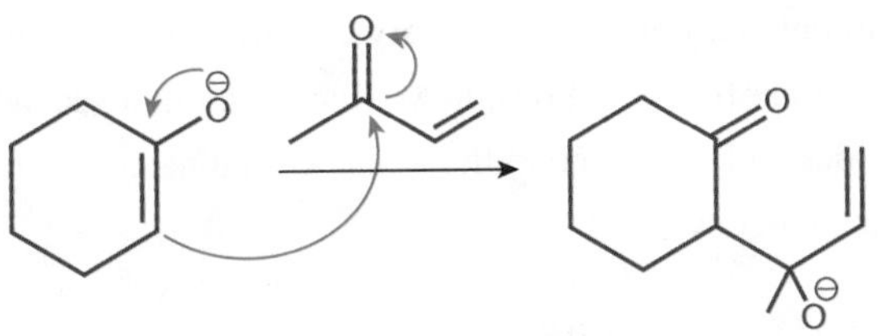

However, this requires a very crowded transition state to form. Instead, the enolate could attack C-4 on the methyl vinyl ketone because the primary carbon is significantly easier to reach. Indeed, this is what happens, resulting in the enolate shown below:

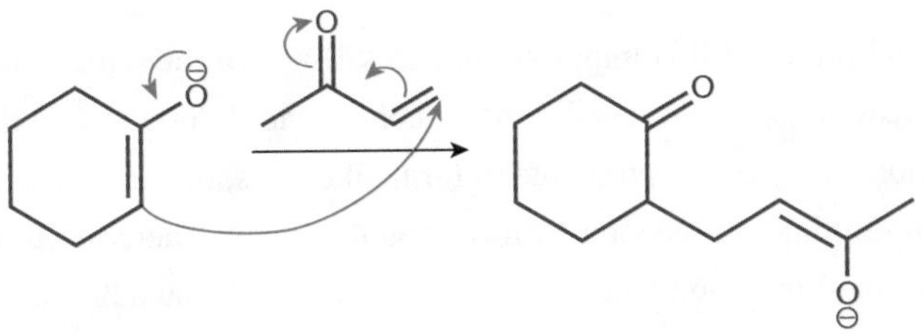

3 React the second enolate with an electrophile.

Again, we're left with an enolate and a carbonyl. In theory, we could have the enolate attack the carbonyl immediately. However, this results in the rather unfavorable formation of a four-membered ring. The cyclization is significantly slower than the isomerization of the enolate, shown below.

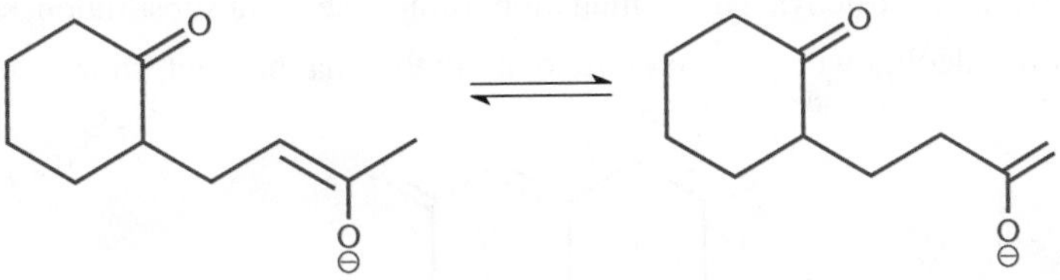

This isomerization is important because the newly formed primary enolate can attack the carbonyl carbon and form a six-membered ring—much more favored than the formation of a four-membered ring. It should be noted that the isomerization is a multistep acid–base reaction, involving protonation of one α-carbon, followed by deprotonation of the other.

Attack of the carbonyl carbon by the primary enolate is shown below. This results in alkoxide and ketone functionalities, as well as creating a second ring structure. Generally, alkoxides under basic conditions can be protonated; the result in this case is the alcohol shown below:

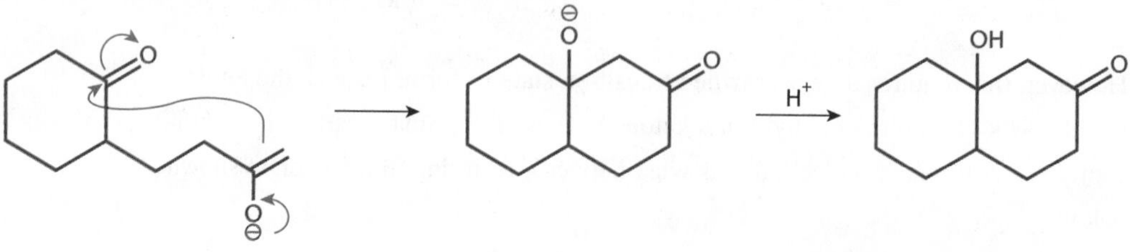

Is this our final product? It is important to check if any of the remaining functional groups will react under basic conditions. Alcohols can do one of two things under basic conditions: they can deprotonate to form alkoxides, or they can act as leaving groups in an elimination reaction to form double bonds. There are three possible isomers from an elimination reaction of our last product, shown below:

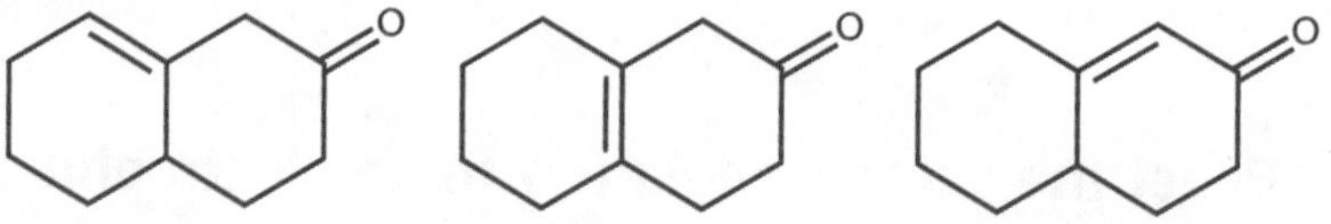

Takeaways

Enolates can allow the formation of cyclic products in molecules that contain both a carbonyl and the enolate functionality.

Things to Watch Out For

Keep track of nucleophiles and electrophiles to understand how the reaction will progress. Make sure you've reached the end of the mechanism and that nothing else will react!

At first, one might assume that the tetrasubstituted double bond (the middle structure) would be preferentially formed because more-substituted double bonds tend to be more stable than less-substituted ones. However, the rightmost compound, while having only three substituents on the double bond, also puts the double bond in conjugation with the carbonyl. This conjugation trumps the extra substitution, so elimination of the alcohol will result preferentially in the final product, shown below:

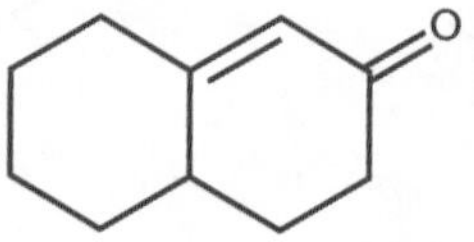

Related Questions

1. Cyclohexanone does not have a proton present on its oxygen atom. How does the first step of this reaction mechanism proceed?
2. What does it mean for a molecule to be conjugated? Why does conjugation increase the stability of a molecule?
3. When 2,2,6,6-tetramethylcyclohexanone reacts with 4,4-dimethylhexanal, which molecule serves as the nucleophile? Which molecule serves as the electrophile?

Key Concepts

Organic Chemistry Chapter 8

Nucleophilic acyl substitution reactions
Carbonyl chemistry
Carboxylic acids
Carboxylic acid derivatives

Nucleophilic Acyl Substitution Reactions

Carboxylic acid derivatives are found in a vast array of organic molecules. Luckily, these can often be prepared from a few common intermediates. Take, for instance, the following reactions with methyl pivalate. Each of these produces a unique product. What are the products of each of these reactions?

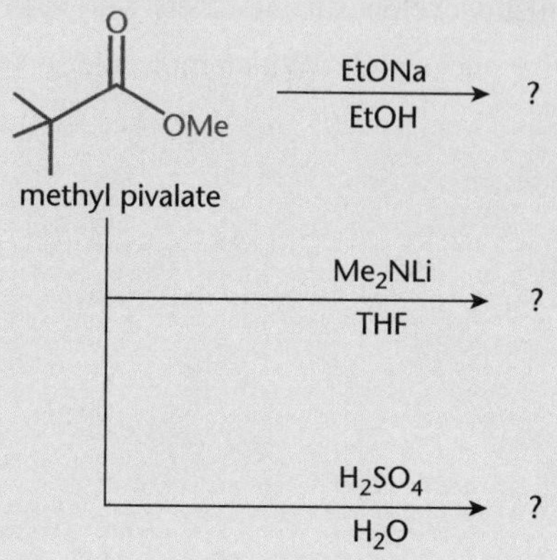

methyl pivalate: EtONa, EtOH → ?; Me_2NLi, THF → ?; H_2SO_4, H_2O → ?

1 Complete the reaction of an ester with an alkoxide (transesterification).

In the first reaction, the ethoxide anion is a strong nucleophile and the carbonyl carbon in the pivalate is a good electrophile. The likely first step is an attack on the carbonyl carbon by ethoxide, as shown below:

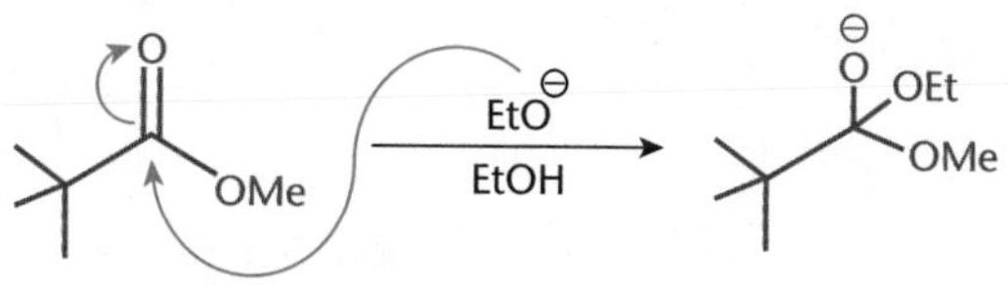

OMe; $EtO^{\ominus}$, EtOH → $O^{\ominus}$, OEt, OMe

The first intermediate after the nucleophilic attack is a tetrahedral alkoxide. The lone pair of electrons on the oxygen can push back down and reform the carbonyl if there is a good leaving group. In this case, both ethoxide and methoxide are reasonable leaving groups under basic conditions. Displacing ethoxide would simply return the original compound; to get a new product, the methoxide must leave, as shown in the following mechanism, to give us an ethyl ester as the final product:

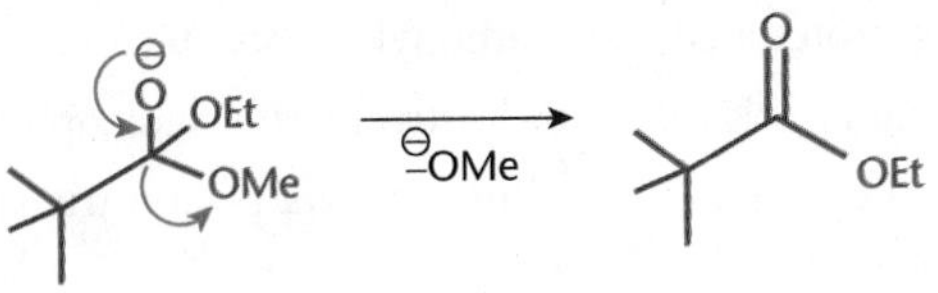

2 Complete the reaction of an ester with an amine (amide formation).

Unsurprisingly, when one treats an ester with a nitrogen-containing anion as opposed to an alkoxide, the overall reactivity is similar; this process forms an amide. The nitrogen-containing anion is extremely nucleophilic, much like the alkoxide anion. In fact, the electron pushing is identical, as shown below:

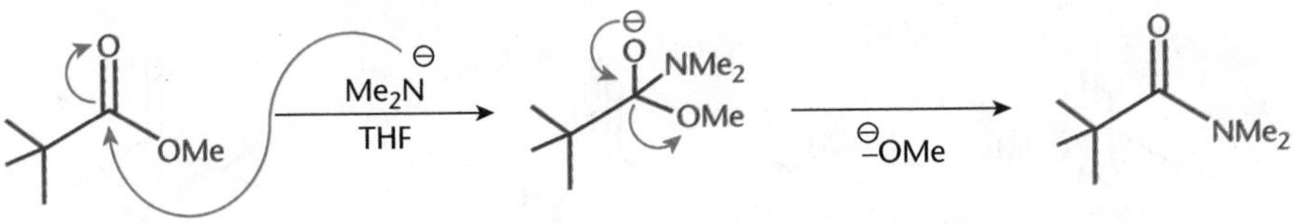

In this case, the reaction is driven by the inherent stability of the final product. Amides, such as the final product shown, are relatively robust and nonreactive compounds.

3 Complete the reaction of an ester with water (hydrolysis).

Whenever the conditions for a reaction call for a strong acid (or base) and water, your first thought should be hydrolysis. When esters are treated with a strongly acidic aqueous solution, they rapidly undergo hydrolysis to form the analogous carboxylic acid. As usual, the first step in acidic media is protonation of the most basic part of the molecule. In this case, it is the carbonyl oxygen:

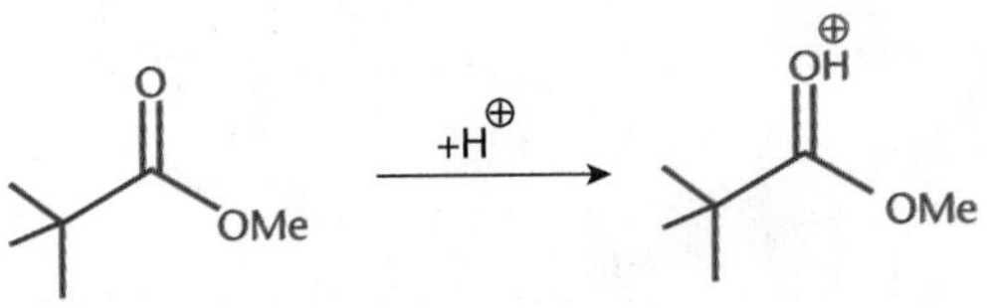

Once the oxygen is protonated, the carbonyl carbon becomes significantly more electrophilic, allowing attack from the relatively non-nucleophilic water. Note that the initially produced cation is in equilibrium, via proton transfer, with the cation on the right:

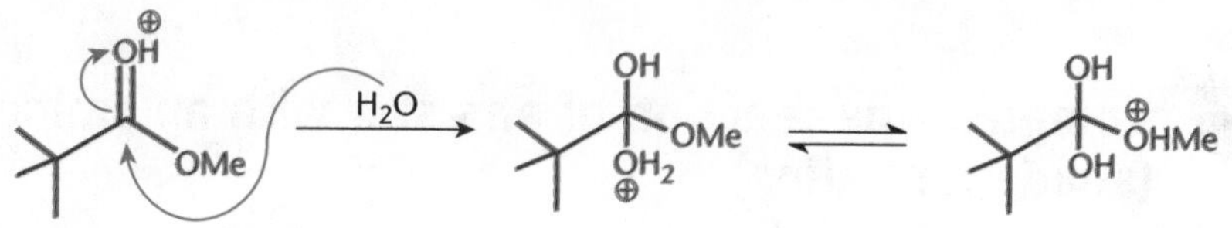

H_2O

The rightmost cation contains an excellent leaving group: methanol. If methanol leaves, one of the remaining oxygens can push one of its lone pairs to reform a protonated carbonyl. This cation can then be deprotonated to give the final product, a neutral carboxylic acid:

–MeOH

$-H^{\oplus}$

Takeaways

No matter the reaction, identifying nucleophiles, electrophiles, and leaving groups will help you figure out how the reaction will progress.

Things to Watch Out For

Remember if you see an acidic aqueous workup to keep an eye out for the possibility of hydrolysis—particularly in esters.

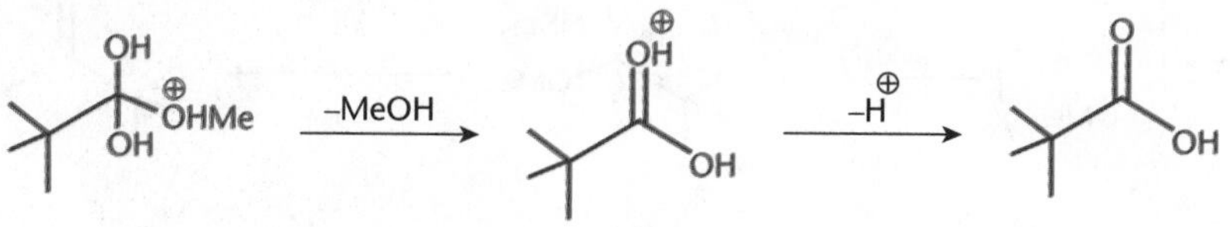

Related Questions

1. Which is a better leaving group, methanol or ethanol?
2. What is a lactone? What reactant(s) would be required to make a lactone through a nucleophilic acyl substitution mechanism?
3. What is a lactam? What reactant(s) would be required to make a lactam through a nucleophilic acyl substitution mechanism?

High-Yield Problem-Solving Guide questions continue on the next page. ▶ ▶ ▶

Key Concepts

Organic Chemistry Chapter 9

Anhydrides
Esters
Amides
Leaving group ability
Steric hindrance

Properties of Carboxylic Acid Derivatives

In an ideal reaction, there is exactly one nucleophile present that can react with exactly one electrophile. In practice, though, there are often multiple nucleophiles (and electrophiles) that compete with one another. Rank the carbonyl carbons in the following compounds in order of increasing electrophilicity toward a single nucleophile in a single polar protic solvent.

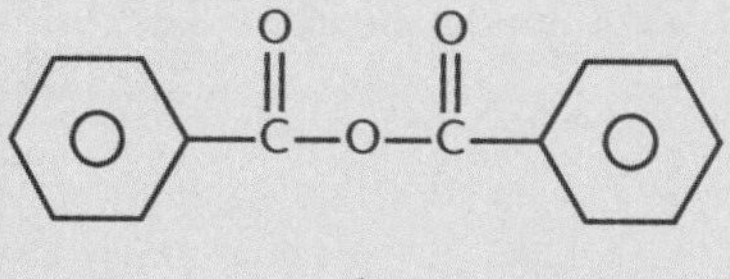

1 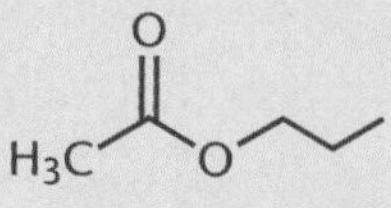 2 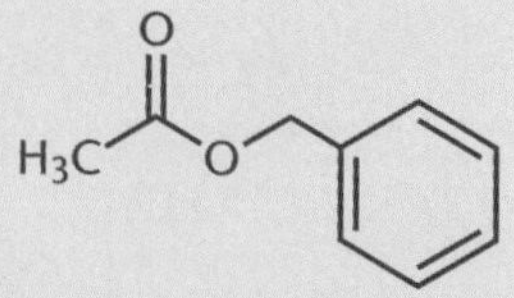 3

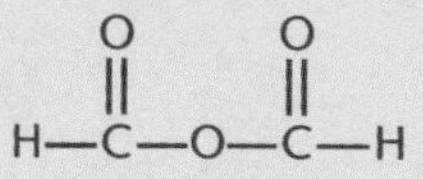

4 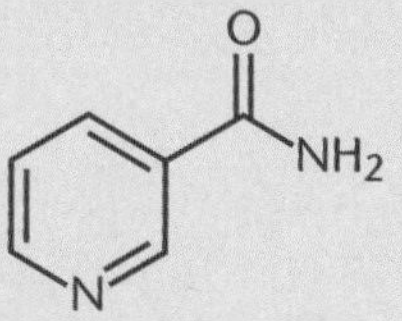 5

1 Order the reactivities of the molecules by the identity of the acyl derivative.

In the compounds listed above, there are three types of carbonyl functional groups: amides, esters, and anhydrides. These functional groups can be ranked by electrophilicity, which is based on the stability of their leaving groups. Anhydrides (**1** and **4**) are the most reactive (that is, most electrophilic) because their leaving groups are carboxylic acids, which can delocalize the lone pair left behind after heterolysis through resonance. Esters (**2** and **3**) are the next most reactive, while amides (**5**) are the least reactive. This is because the leaving group of an ester is an alkoxide ion or alcohol, which is less nucleophilic than the nitrogen-containing anion or amine leaving group of an amide. Leaving groups should be unreactive, so stronger nucleophiles generally make poorer leaving groups.

2 Account for steric hindrance.

Next, we can rank within these groups. The more steric hindrance an electrophile presents to a nucleophile, the less reactive that molecule will be. Of the two anhydrides, **1** has significantly more steric hindrance, caused by its bulky phenyl groups, and is therefore less reactive than **4**, which has hydrogen atoms instead. Of the esters, the additional phenyl group on **3** means it will not react as readily as the less sterically hindered **2**.

3 Order according to these rules.

With these rules in mind, we can order our compounds. The sterically hindered, least reactive amide **5** will be the least electrophilic; the unhindered and most reactive anhydride **4** will be the most electrophilic. **1**, **2**, and **3** fall in the middle. It is important to keep in mind that reactivity based on functional group may be counterbalanced by steric hindrance. In this case, although it is an anhydride, **1** will be significantly impeded by sterics, and will therefore be less reactive than the esters. On the MCAT, you would not be expected to know the relative contribution of each of these trends, but could be tested on any of them in isolation. This gives us our final order:

$$5 < 1 < 3 < 2 < 4$$

Takeaways

Ordering carboxylic acid derivatives by reactivity depends not only on the identity of the functional group (which is indicative of the resulting leaving group), but also on the characteristics of the substituents; sterics are important to keep in mind when analyzing reactivity.

Things to Watch Out For

Remember that on Test Day you can refer to the Periodic Table; periodic trends, like electronegativity, can help you figure out relative electrophilicity or nucleophilicity.

Related Questions

1. Why is it important that the peptide bonds in proteins, which are a special form of amide bonds, are relatively stable?
2. Which would you expect to be more reactive toward a given nucleophile, an aldehyde or a comparable ketone? Why?
3. Which carboxylic acid derivatives can participate in hydrogen bonding with themselves?

Key Concepts

Organic Chemistry Chapter 10

Phosphorus-containing compounds

pK_a

Polyprotic acids

Acid–base reactions

Zwitterions

Phosphorus-Containing Compounds

Physiologically, phosphoric acid may be found as a neutral compound or as a mono-, di-, or trivalent anion. Accordingly, it has three pK_a values: 2.15, 7.20, and 12.35. What are the relative concentrations of phosphoric acid and its ions at physiological pH (around 7.4)? If a pure sample of phosphoric acid were dissolved in *n*-butanol, would there be a reaction? If so, what would the products be?

1 Determine the most abundant forms of phosphoric acid from the pK_a values.

The question gives us three pK_a values: 2.15, 7.20, and 12.35. Remember, the concentration of an acid and its conjugate base are equal when pH = pK_a. For example, $[H_3PO_4] = [H_2PO_4^-]$ at pH = 2.15. As the pH increases above 2.15, the concentration of H_3PO_4 will decrease as the concentration of $H_2PO_4^-$ increases. A pH of 7.4 is sufficiently far from 2.15 that there is essentially no H_3PO_4 present at all. Similarly, PO_4^{3-} is also present in negligible quantities at pH 7.4 because pK_{a3} is so high (12.35).

The two intermediate forms, $H_2PO_4^-$ and HPO_4^{2-}, predominate at physiological pH because this pH is close to pK_{a2} for phosphoric acid (7.20). We could predict that because 7.4 is slightly more basic than 7.20, there will be a slightly higher concentration of HPO_4^{2-}, the conjugate base, than $H_2PO_4^-$ at this pH. Indeed, we can determine the relative concentrations from the Henderson–Hasselbalch equation:

$$\text{pH} = \text{p}K_a + \log\frac{[HPO_4^{2-}]}{[H_2PO_4^-]}$$

$$7.4 = 7.20 + \log\frac{[HPO_4^{2-}]}{[H_2PO_4^-]}$$

$$0.2 = \log\frac{[HPO_4^{2-}]}{[H_2PO_4^-]}$$

$$10^{0.2} = \frac{[HPO_4^{2-}]}{[H_2PO_4^-]} \approx 1.58$$

In summary, the relative concentrations of the various conjugates can be expressed as a ratio (H_3PO_4:$H_2PO_4^-$:HPO_4^{2-}:PO_4^{3-}):

~0:1:1.58:~0

2 Determine the possible reaction(s) of phosphoric acid with *n*-butanol.

This part of the question is asking whether phosphoric acid can react with alcohols. The answer to this question is undoubtedly *yes*, but what is the reaction? Any time an acid is present, we should look for a group to protonate—in this case, the hydroxyl group on *n*-butanol is the best candidate.

Alternatively, phosphoric acid can be viewed as the hydrolyzed form of an organic phosphate. It is reasonable to think that this reaction might be reversible, creating mono-, di-, or tri-*n*-butyl phosphates. Let's examine these two reactions to determine what products can result.

3 Consider the reaction that occurs when phosphoric acid protonates *n*-butanol.

As described in Step 2, phosphoric acid could protonate the hydroxyl group of the alcohol. When this happens, the hydroxyl group (which is now a water molecule) becomes a good leaving group, forming a carbocation. While elimination reactions are not tested directly on the MCAT, it is reasonable to predict that the molecule will seek to stabilize or reduce the positive charge; formation of a double bond through an elimination reaction would be one way to accomplish this goal:

OH $\xrightarrow{+H^{\oplus}}$ $\overset{\oplus}{O}H_2$ $\xrightarrow{-H_2O}$ ⊕ H $\xrightarrow{:B}$

4 Consider the reaction that occurs when *n*-butanol attacks phosphoric acid.

Another potential mechanism is the formation of a phosphate ester, which could occur if the butanol attacked the phosphate group. Elimination of a hydroxyl group as water could then follow.

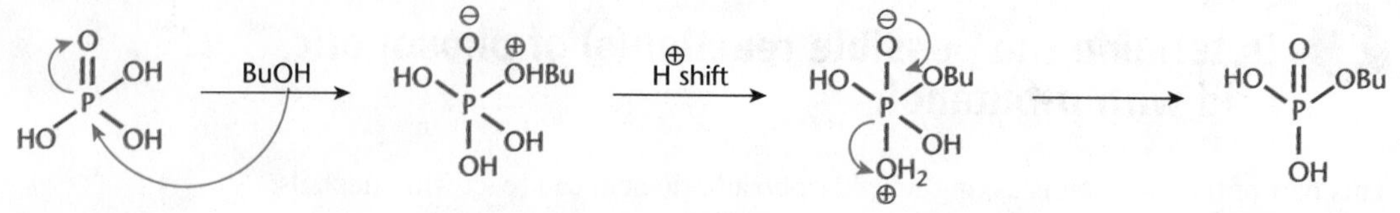

Note the similarity between this reaction and nucleophilic acyl substitution (specifically, esterification). Given the two additional hydroxyl groups on the phosphorus, one could imagine two more iterations of this mechanism to produce the di- and tributyl esters.

Takeaways

The different forms of phosphoric acid have different pK_a values; phosphoric acid commonly reacts by protonating a leaving group to improve that group's ability to leave.

Things to Watch Out For

When comparing two plausible reactions, consider the relative nucleophilicity, electrophilicity, and leaving group abilities of the reacting compounds.

Related Questions

1. Which class of biomolecules *always* contain phosphorus? Which ones *sometimes* contain phosphorus?
2. One way to increase blood pH is to increase the excretion of *titratable acid* (protonated phosphates) from the kidney. Urine is usually slightly more acidic than physiological pH. What would happen to the relative concentrations of the different forms of phosphoric acid at this slightly lower pH?
3. $H_2PO_4^-$ is a Brønsted–Lowry acid because it can give up a proton. Would $H_2PO_4^-$ react in the same fashion with butanol as H_3PO_4 did?

High-Yield Problem-Solving Guide questions continue on the next page. ▶ ▶ ▶

Key Concepts

Organic Chemistry Chapter 11

IR spectroscopy
^{1}H–NMR spectroscopy
Equivalent hydrogens
Splitting

Spectroscopy

An unknown compound was discovered in an old, unused laboratory. Its molecular formula was determined to be $C_6H_9NO_2$ by high-resolution mass spectrometry. The following IR stretches were recorded: 3300 (sharp), 2890 (medium), 2220, 1740 (sharp), 1220, 984, 700, and 650 cm^{-1}.

The ^{1}H–NMR spectrum of the compound is as follows:

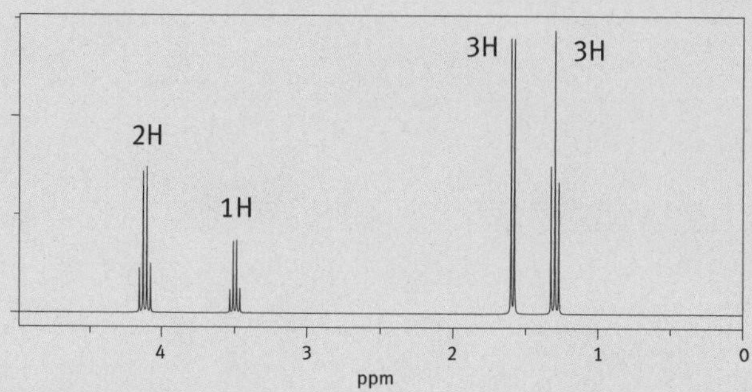

Given this information, determine the structure of the unknown compound.

1 Look at the IR stretches to determine what functional groups are present.

Here, the most important signal is the sharp peak at 1740 cm^{-1}, which indicates the presence of a carbonyl. A carbonyl indicates that there must be one of the following functional groups in our molecule: aldehyde, ketone, carboxylic acid, anhydride, ester, or amide. It can't be an aldehyde because there are no aldehyde signals in the NMR (a single proton around 9–10), and it can't be a carboxylic acid because there is no hydroxyl group stretch in the IR (a broad absorption around 2800–3200). Nor can it be an anhydride because there are not enough oxygen atoms in the molecular formula—anhydrides require at least three. Because the stretch is close to 1750, it is most likely to be an ester. This is also supported by the ^{1}H–NMR data, as discussed below.

2 Look at the ^{1}H–NMR data to determine the structure of the esterifying group.

The signal for the esterifying group should be the furthest downfield (to the left) in the ^{1}H–NMR spectrum because it is attached to the most electronegative element in the molecule. The peak farthest to the left is composed of two hydrogens, which are split into four peaks. Keeping in mind the $n + 1$ rule, this implies that there are two hydrogens on the carbon closest to the ester oxygen, and three hydrogens on the next one. This is supported by the three hydrogens split into a triplet around 1.3 ppm. Thus, we know the molecule must contain the following structure:

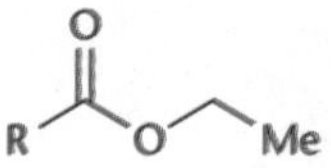

R–C(=O)–O–CH₂–Me

3 Use the molecular formula to discern the presence of unsaturation in the parent chain.

So far, we have determined that there is an ester with an ethyl esterifying group. This accounts for three carbon atoms (the carbonyl carbon and two in the esterifying group), two oxygen atoms, and five hydrogen atoms. Subtracting these from the molecular formula, $C_6H_9NO_2$, we are left with three carbon atoms, four hydrogen atoms, and a nitrogen atom. Immediately, we should recognize that there must be at least one multiple bond in the molecule because there are not enough hydrogens to create an alkyl chain. There are three possibilities for the parent chain to get the right numbers: a carbon–carbon triple bond, a carbon–nitrogen triple bond, or two carbon–carbon double bonds.

4 Use the ^{1}H–NMR data to determine which option for unsaturation is the correct one.

We can immediately eliminate the two carbon–carbon double bonds as an option because this would mean that at least one carbon is *sp*^{2}-hybridized; *sp*^{2}-hybridized carbons absorb in the range of 4.6–6, and there are no peaks in this range. Between the carbon–carbon triple bond and the carbon–nitrogen triple bond, then, we can determine that it must be the latter. If there was a carbon–carbon triple bond, the nitrogen would have two hydrogens on it to form an amine, and there are no peaks remaining that consist of only two hydrogens. Therefore, this compound must contain a nitrile.

Takeaways

With these combined structure problems, make sure to utilize all of the data at your disposal. The process is very much like taking the pieces of a jigsaw puzzle and putting them together.

Things to Watch Out For

Be sure to avoid overinterpreting the IR data. Many peaks can correspond to multiple functional groups or are inconclusive. ¹H–NMR data, on the other hand, is a wealth of information that, when interpreted carefully, can provide nearly all the information to figure out a molecule's structure.

 Determine the backbone of the parent chain.

If we account for all of the atoms in the ester and nitrile functionalities, we are left with two carbons and four hydrogens. There can only be two possibilities, structurally:

Note that the protons in the structure on the left would have to give rise to two triplets because each is adjacent to a carbon with two protons. However, the only signals we haven't accounted for in the NMR are a doublet integrating for three protons and a quartet integrating for one. These signals exactly match the structure on the right, so that must be the unknown.

Related Questions

1. Why is it unlikely that the compound in the original question is cyclic?
2. If the molecule were a methyl ketone rather than an ester (that is, replacing the ethoxy group with a methyl group), where would you expect that the carbonyl IR stretch would appear? Why?
3. In the compound described in the previous question, where would the signal for the methyl ketone protons show up in the ¹H–NMR spectrum, relative to the signal for the protons adjacent to the oxygen in the ester?

High-Yield Problem-Solving Guide questions continue on the next page. ▶ ▶ ▶

Key Concepts

Organic Chemistry Chapter 12

Extraction (liquid–liquid separation)
Acid–base properties
Separation and purification schemes
Polarity

Extraction

A student wishes to separate methyl phenyl ketone, aniline ($C_6H_5NH_2$), and phenol from a solution. To perform the separation, the solution is dissolved in 500 mL H_2O and 500 mL dichloromethane. The solution is then washed with water three times, and the aqueous layer (**A**) is extracted. The remaining solution is then washed with 20% aqueous Na_2CO_3 three times, and the aqueous layer (**B**) is collected. The remaining organic layer is finally washed with 10% aqueous HCl three times and the aqueous layer (**C**) is once again collected, leaving behind the organic layer (**D**). What are the contents of samples **A**, **B**, **C**, and **D**?

1 Determine the differences between the molecules being separated.

Methyl phenyl ketone, aniline, and phenol are all organic compounds. However, aniline is a weak base (it contains an amine group) whereas phenol is a weak acid (it contains a hydroxyl group). Methyl phenyl ketone is the most hydrophobic of the three compounds because it doesn't possess any functional groups capable of making hydrogen bonds.

2 Determine into which phase each of the compounds will dissolve after the first set of washings.

All three compounds are uncharged organic compounds and will dissolve in the organic layer, dichloromethane. Thus, the first set of washings will not aid in separating any of the three compounds, and sample **A** will contain only water and water-soluble impurities.

3 Determine into which phase each of the compounds will dissolve after the second set of washings.

When the sample is washed with Na_2CO_3—a base—phenol will be deprotonated to yield phenoxide (the conjugate base of phenol). Because this molecule is charged, it will move into the aqueous layer. After the washing, the deprotonated phenol will move into the aqueous phase (**B**), while methyl phenyl ketone and aniline will remain in the organic layer. In general, washing a mixture with a base is an effective way to move acidic compounds from the organic layer into the aqueous layer.

4 Determine into which phase each of the compounds will dissolve after the third set of washings.

At this point, the only remaining compounds in the organic layer are methyl phenyl ketone and aniline. When the sample is washed with HCl—a strong acid—aniline will be protonated to yield anilinium (the conjugate acid of aniline). After the washing, the protonated compound will move into the aqueous phase (**C**), while methyl phenyl ketone will remain in the organic layer (**D**). In general, washing a mixture with an acid is an effective way to move basic compounds from the organic layer into the aqueous layer.

Takeaways

In an extraction problem, each compound will either be dissolved in the aqueous layer or the organic layer. However, if a compound is acidic or basic, it is possible to transpose it to the aqueous layer by using basic or acidic washes, respectively.

Things to Watch Out For

Don't assume that the organic phase will be on top—this depends on the densities of the two phases. For example, dichloromethane $\left(1.3 \frac{g}{mL}\right)$ is denser than water $\left(1.0 \frac{g}{mL}\right)$; dichloromethane will sink to the bottom of the separatory funnel, with the water floating on top.

Related Questions

1. What would be an appropriate extraction procedure to separate a mixture of phenol and benzoic acid dissolved in ether?
2. In order to extract *p*-nitrophenol from phenol in an ether solution, a student washes the organic layer with 10 mL of a 5% aqueous solution of NaOH. After the washing, what will be left in the organic layer?
3. Why does the student perform three sets of washings in each step of the extraction?

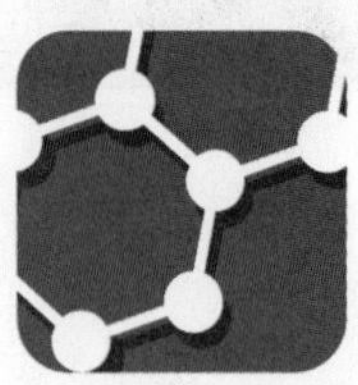

Solutions to Related Questions

1. Nomenclature

1. The alkyl group on the ester oxygen is called the esterifying group. It is named as a separate word before the rest of the compound name. This word should be viewed as an adjective describing the ester; the compound we named was the *ethyl* ester. Therefore, if the ethyl (alkyl) group of ethyl 2-methoxy-3-(2-oxocyclohexyl)propanoate contained substituents, the word *ethyl* would be replaced with whatever group was attached to the ester oxygen, using the suffix *–yl*.

2. Sodium borohydride ($NaBH_4$) is a reducing agent; as such, it will reduce the ketone in this molecule to a secondary alcohol. The two products of the reduction reaction would be (1*R*,2*S*)-2,5,5-trimethylcyclohexanol and (1*S*,2*S*)-2,5,5-trimethylcyclohexanol, which are shown below:

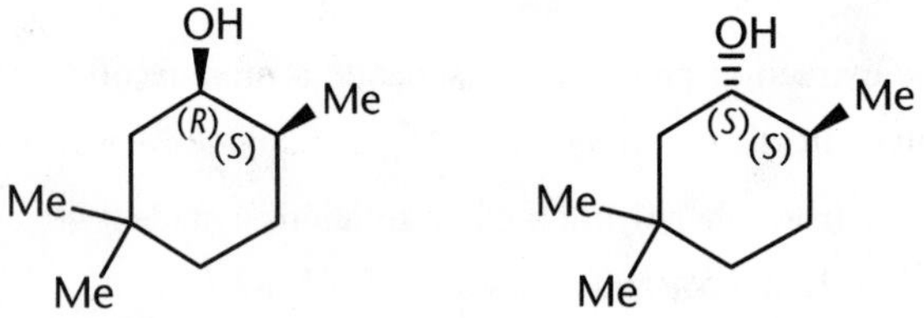

3. Lithium aluminum hydride ($LiAlH_4$) is an even stronger reducing agent than sodium borohydride and will reduce the imine in the molecule to a secondary amine. It is not strong enough to reduce the alkene to an alkane, however. The two products of the indicated reaction would be (*S*,*Z*)-6-chloro-6-cyclopentyl-*N*-methylhex-5-en-2-amine and (*R*,*Z*)-6-chloro-6-cyclopentyl-*N*-methylhex-5-en-2-amine, which are shown below:

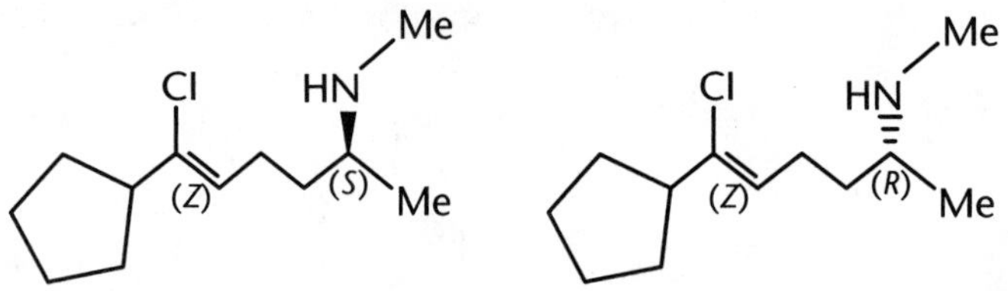

2. Stereoisomers

1. The D- and L-isomers of a compound are enantiomers of each other, which means that they have opposite stereochemistry at all chiral carbons and no internal plane of symmetry. As such, they are nonsuperimposable mirror images. Enantiomers always have opposite specific rotation, so the specific rotation of the L-isomer must be –140°. Racemic mixtures contain equal concentrations of both enantiomers. The specific rotations from the two enantiomers cancel each other, resulting in an optically inactive solution (0° rotation).

2. Only the middle compound would give rise to an achiral polyol upon reduction. The other two would not contain a plane of symmetry.

3. For the purposes of the MCAT, it is not possible to have a chiral compound that does not contain chiral centers. Chiral compounds not only need to contain chiral centers, but must also have the right geometry, such that the chiral centers do not cancel each other out (as occurs in a *meso* compound). There are rare examples of complex polyaromatic compounds and certain allenes that do show chirality despite a lack of chiral centers, but such compounds are outside the scope of the MCAT.

3. Hybridized Orbitals

1. The lower the pK_a of a compound, the more acidic it is. Similarly, the lower the pK_b, the more basic it is. Compounds with low pK_b values are stronger bases. As such, they are not good proton donors (Brønsted–Lowry acids), preferring to accept protons (Brønsted–Lowry bases). Therefore, the higher the pK_b, the more acidic (less basic) the compound.

2. Carbon dioxide contains two double bonds. This requires two unhybridized *p*-orbitals—one to participate in each of the π bonds. Therefore, the hybridization of the carbon must be *sp*. Be careful not to fall into the trap of assuming that the presence of double bonds automatically means sp^2 hybridization. Indeed, because there are only two areas of electron density in carbon dioxide, the carbon must be *sp*-hybridized.

3. Careful reading of this compound's name indicates that there is only one double bond in the molecule, implied by the suffix *–one*. If we draw out the structure of 5-hydroxy-2,6-dimethyl-3-heptanone, it confirms that the highest bond order is 2 (double bond):

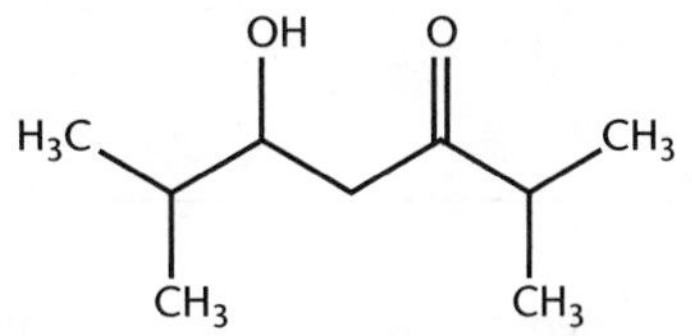

OH O
H_3C CH_3
CH_3 CH_3

4. Nucleophilicity Trends

1. Because all of the nucleophiles contain the same attacking atom (nitrogen), nucleophilicity will parallel basicity, irrespective of the solvent used. Here, resonance delocalization and hybridization each play a role.

First, we will compare pyridine, triethylamine, and acetonitrile, as they each have only one nitrogen atom with one isolated lone pair. It may appear that the lone pair on the pyridine nitrogen may be resonance-stabilized, but in fact that lone pair does not engage in the aromatic ring delocalization. The nitrogen in acetonitrile is *sp*-hybridized, the nitrogen in pyridine is sp^2-hybridized, and the nitrogen in triethylamine is sp^3-hybridized. In a similar manner to the carbon atoms discussed in the *Hybridized Orbitals* question, the *sp*-hybridized lone pair will be the most stable (least basic), while the least stable (most basic) is the pair on triethylamine. The basicity order for these three compounds is acetonitrile < pyridine < triethylamine.

Now we must consider DMAP. The heterocyclic nitrogen (the nitrogen in the ring) is similar to pyridine, while the other nitrogen looks similar to that of triethylamine. However, while the lone pair of the ring-bound nitrogen is not delocalized (similar to pyridine), the lone pair of the tertiary nitrogen does form resonance structures with the ring. This resonance delocalization makes those electrons much less basic, and so the heterocyclic nitrogen is the one that acts as the base. Now we must decide whether DMAP is more or less basic than pyridine. When DMAP gains a proton, the positive charge is stabilized via resonance with the amino substituent, making DMAP more likely to gain a proton than pyridine, thereby making it more basic (and nucleophilic).

The final order is acetonitrile < pyridine < DMAP < triethylamine.

2. Methanol is a polar protic solvent, so we should be careful when considering how nucleophilicity and basicity relate. The halogens are all in the same group, so the stronger the base, the *weaker* the nucleophile in a polar protic solvent. To assess the basicity of the halogens, consider the strength of their conjugate acids, HF, HCl, HBr, and HI. The strongest acid (HI) has the weakest conjugate base, and the weakest acid (HF) has the strongest conjugate base. Therefore, the nucleophilicity for the halogens in a polar protic solvent like methanol is $I^- > Br^- > Cl^- > F^-$.

   DMSO is a polar aprotic solvent. Nucleophilicity always parallels basicity in polar aprotic solvents, so the nucleophilicity trend in DMSO is $F^- > Cl^- > Br^- > I^-$.

3. The order of increasing nucleophilicity in methanol is $Ph_3N < Et_3N < Ph_3P < Et_3P < Et_3As$. Triphenylamine and triphenylphosphine are less nucleophilic than triethylamine and triethylphosphine, respectively, because in the phenyl analogs, the lone pair can be delocalized into the three phenyl rings, making it less reactive and less nucleophilic. As for comparing the nitrogen, phosphorus, and arsenic compounds, the amine is more basic than the phosphine, which is more basic than the arsine. Because these are all in the same group and the solvent (methanol) is protic, the nucleophilicity is backwards from basicity, making arsenic the most nucleophilic of the group.

5. Reactions of Alcohols

1. Changing the hydroxyl group to a stronger nucleophile would change the mechanism by which it proceeds to S_N2 (or E2). S_N2 reactions proceed via a one-step (concerted) mechanism. While S_N1 and S_N2 reactions often have pronounced differences in stereochemistry, in this case the stereochemistry would be the same. This is because the nucleophile in the first step will have to attack from above the ring, resulting in an epoxide (or other three-membered ring intermediate) sticking out of the plane of the page, regardless of the nucleophilic substitution mechanism used. Thus, while the mechanism would be different with a stronger nucleophile, the products would be the same.

2. Changing the tosylate group to a hydroxyl would leave us without a good leaving group. While this reaction could still occur under acidic conditions (because acid would protonate they hydroxyl groups, making them better leaving groups), it would no longer occur under the conditions given.

3. In this case, it is not possible to favor one product over the other without changing the reactant molecule. The two compounds are almost identical in stability, meaning that both will form in approximately equal amounts. If the reactant molecule could be altered by changing one of the methyl substituents, or by adding another substituent to the ring, this could sterically impede the ring-opening nucleophile and favor one product over the other.

6. Identifying the Structure of an Unknown Oxy Compound

1. Product **E** is one of four possible stereoisomers. While **D** and **E** are diastereomers of each other, each also has an enantiomer that has opposite absolute configurations at both the nitrogen-bearing carbon and the methyl group on C-3. Looking just at the stereocenters, we could describe these compounds as: (1*R*,3*R*), (1*R*,3*S*), (1*S*,3*R*), and (1*S*,3*S*).

2. The products in this reaction are diastereomers of each other. While a racemic mixture (equimolar concentrations of two enantiomers) should have no optical activity, this is because enantiomers always have specific rotations with equal magnitude but opposite sign—canceling each other in solution. Diastereomers do not have the same predictable relationship; knowing the specific rotation of one diastereomer gives no indication of the specific rotation of another. Therefore, we would not expect the specific rotations of the two diastereomers to cancel, and a solution containing equimolar concentrations of two diastereomers *should* have optical activity.

3. *Cis–trans* isomers differ by the positions of groups around an immovable bond. This can refer to a double bond (C=C, C=N, C=O), but can also refer to the bonds in a cyclic molecule. Cycloalkanes can also have *cis–trans* isomers.

7. Enolate Chemistry

1. The most acidic atoms in cyclohexanone are the α-carbons, which readily give up a proton in the presence of a base. This results in the formation of a secondary carbanion, which can push its lone pair to form a double bond with the carbonyl carbon. This converts the carbonyl to the enolate intermediate.

2. Conjugation refers to alternating single and multiple bonds, which necessarily means that there are unhybridized *p*-orbitals aligned with each other. This allows delocalization of π electrons throughout those *p*-orbitals, resulting in a cloud of electron density above and below the plane of the molecule. Delocalization of these electrons stabilizes a molecule because electrons are able to spread out over a larger volume of space, decreasing their energy. Conjugated molecules can stabilize charges, as well, by delocalizing them throughout the π-electron clouds.

3. 2,2,6,6-Tetramethylcyclohexanone does not have any α-hydrogens because both α-carbons are quaternary carbons, as shown below:

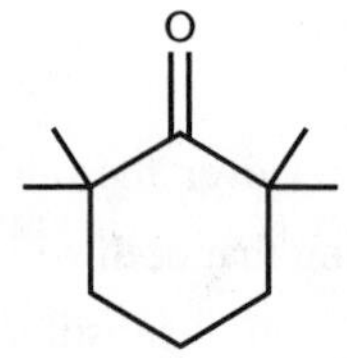

4,4-Dimethylhexanal, on the other hand, has α-hydrogens on its α-carbon because the α-carbon is secondary, as shown below:

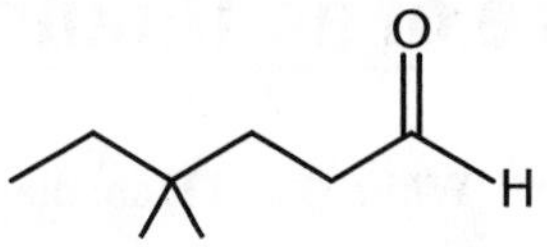

Because 2,2,6,6-tetramethylcyclohexanone does not contain any α-hydrogens, it cannot be deprotonated at the α-carbon to form forming the nucleophilic enolate. Thus, it must act as the electrophile. 4,4-Dimethylhexanal will form the enolate and will serve as the nucleophile in this reaction.

8. Nucleophilic Acyl Substitution Reactions

1. Methanol is generally a better leaving group than ethanol. Alkyl chains are electron-donating and therefore destabilize the negative charge that remains on the alkoxide oxygen after heterolysis. (They also destabilize the lone pairs that remain on the hydroxyl oxygen, under acidic conditions). This effect is less pronounced for the shorter alkyl chain of methanol than for the longer alkyl chain of ethanol.

2. Lactones are cyclic esters. They can be synthesized by intramolecular attack in a molecule that contains both a hydroxyl group and a carboxylic acid. The nucleophilic hydroxyl group attacks the carbonyl carbon, as shown below:

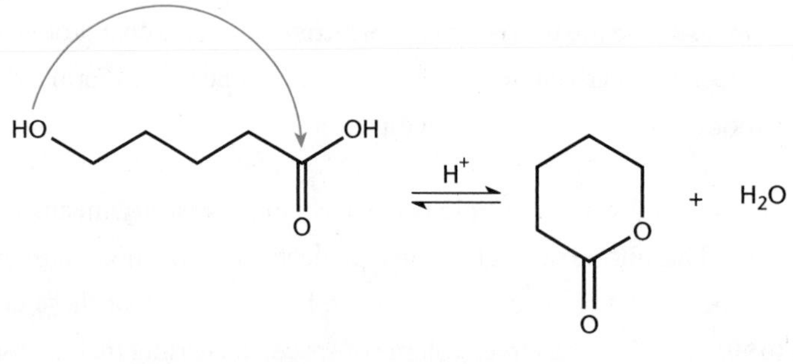

3. Lactams are cyclic amides. They can be synthesized by intramolecular attack in a molecule that contains both an amine and a carboxylic acid, in a similar mechanism to lactone formation. An example of a lactam is shown below:

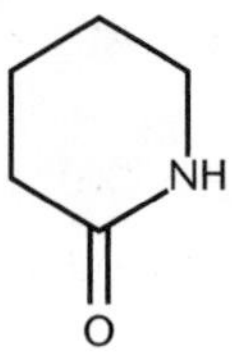

9. Properties of Carboxylic Acid Derivatives

1. Peptide bonds join amino acids together in proteins. Many proteins in the body serve a structural role or must withstand tension, both of which require that the integrity of the amino acid sequence be maintained. The body is also an aqueous environment. Under normal conditions, water does not react with an amide to form a carboxylic acid and an amine (hydrolysis). Amide bonds are stable and relatively nonreactive; were they more reactive than carboxylic acids, life as we know it would not exist.

2. Aldehydes are always terminal groups and, as such, have less steric hindrance than comparable ketones, which are always internal in a compound. By extension, an aldehyde will be more reactive toward a nucleophile.

3. Hydrogen bonding occurs in molecules containing a hydrogen bound to a very electronegative atom (N, O, or F). Amides may have hydrogens on the amide nitrogen, and can therefore hydrogen bond. Carboxylic acids can also hydrogen bond because they have a hydrogen on the acyl oxygen. Under normal circumstances, neither anhydrides nor esters can hydrogen bond.

10. Phosphorus-Containing Compounds

1. Out of the four major classes of biomolecules (carbohydrates, lipids, proteins, and nucleic acids), only nucleic acids *require* phosphorus. It is a component of adenosine triphosphate (ATP), which is used for energy storage, and also of organic phosphates, like the nucleotides that make up RNA and DNA. On the other hand, phosphate groups can be found attached to at least *some* lipids, proteins, and carbohydrates (for example, the phospholipids in the cell membrane).

2. As the pH drops slightly from physiological pH, the concentration of $H_2PO_4^-$ will increase and the concentration of HPO_4^{2-} will decrease; lower pH means more protons are available in solution, so the protonated form will become more favorable. At a pH of 7.20 (pK_{a2} of phosphoric acid), the concentrations of these two species will be equal. At a pH of 7, the ratio between the two species will be reversed from the ratio at 7.4. That is, $H_2PO_4^-:HPO_4^{2-} = 1.58:1$. Note that the concentrations of phosphoric acid and phosphate anion will remain essentially zero; the pH is still far away from their corresponding pK_a values.

3. $H_2PO_4^-$ is not nearly as strong of an acid as H_3PO_4—pK_{a2} is over five pH scale values higher than pK_{a1}! As a much weaker acid, $H_2PO_4^-$ cannot protonate the alcohol to any significant extent, so the dehydration reaction will not occur.

11. Spectroscopy

1. There are only six carbon atoms in the molecular formula, which means that any rings present would have to be small. Small rings have a high degree of angle strain (especially if there are double or triple bonds in the ring), which would make having one or multiple rings in the unknown very unlikely.

2. If the molecule were a methyl ketone rather than an ester, the carbonyl IR stretch would be closer to 1700 cm^{-1}. The resonance donation of the ester alkoxide makes the C=O bond more unstable and therefore higher in energy.

3. The methyl ketone protons would be further upfield in the ^{1}H–NMR spectrum (closer to 2 ppm than 4 ppm). This is because the alkyl group in the ketone is less electron-withdrawing than the highly electronegative oxygen in the ester.

12. Extraction

1. To separate a mixture of benzoic acid and phenol dissolved in ether, it would be best to take advantage of their relative acidities. Benzoic acid is a stronger acid than phenol, so a weak base ($NaHCO_3$, for example) can be used to deprotonate benzoic acid and move it into the aqueous phase, while leaving phenol in the organic phase.

2. After washing the mixture with 5% NaOH, *p*-nitrophenol and phenol will both be deprotonated by the strong base and will move into the aqueous phase. Nothing will be left in the organic layer except for the ether solvent and water-insoluble impurities.

3. Each compound has a given solubility in water, which may be exceeded if it has a high concentration in the organic solvent. Further, not all of the desired product necessarily comes into contact with the water during the first extraction and may remain dissolved in the organic solvent. In general, it is more effective to perform multiple small washes, as done by this student, than to try to extract all of a desired product in one step with a larger amount of solvent.

6

Physics and Math

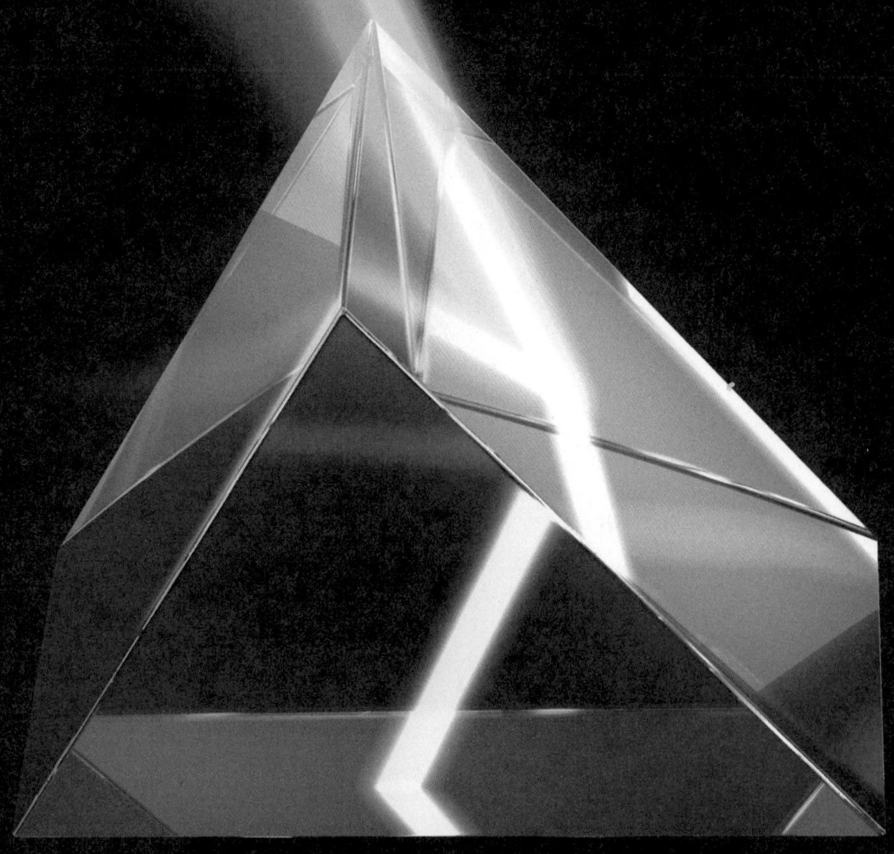

Key Concepts

Physics and Math Chapter 1

Newton's laws

Friction

Kinematics

Newtonian mechanics

Inclined Plane

A block with a mass of 2 kg is sliding down a plane that is inclined at 30° to the horizontal. The coefficient of kinetic friction between the block and the plane is 0.3. Starting from rest, how far does the block travel in 2 seconds?

1 Draw a free body diagram of the forces present.

There are three forces acting on the block: the force of gravity ($\mathbf{F}_g$, the magnitude of which is mg), which always acts straight down; kinetic friction (labeled $\mathbf{f}_k$), which always acts opposite the direction of motion; and the normal force (labeled **N**), which is always perpendicular to the plane:

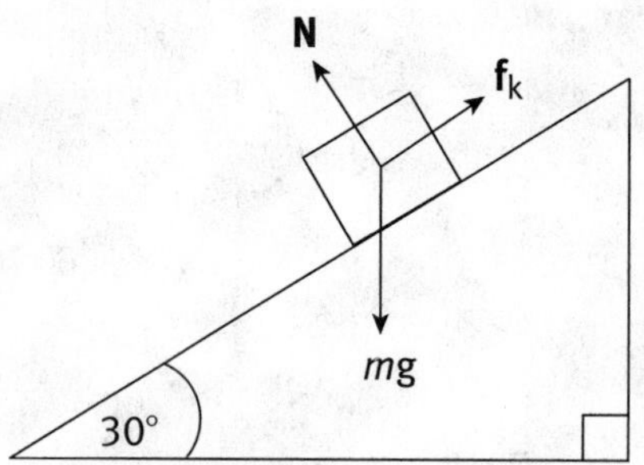

2 Break the weight into parallel and perpendicular components.

Orient the axes in this question to be parallel and perpendicular to the plane; this will make calculations much easier because we can solve for the acceleration in the parallel direction. **N** points in the positive perpendicular direction, and $\mathbf{f}_k$ points in the negative parallel direction. The weight, $\mathbf{F}_g$, must be broken into components along these axes:

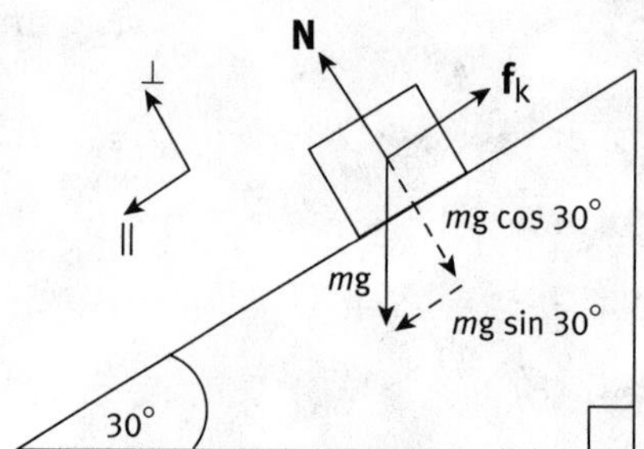

The parallel component of the gravitational force, $\mathbf{F}_{g,\parallel}$, is equal to $mg \sin \theta$. The perpendicular component of the gravitational force, $\mathbf{F}_{g,\perp}$, is equal to $mg \cos \theta$.

3 Write the sum of the forces in each direction.

The sum of the forces in a given direction is always equal to $m\mathbf{a}$ according to Newton's second law:

$$\mathbf{F}_{\text{net},\parallel} = m\mathbf{a}_{\parallel} = mg \sin 30° - \mathbf{f}_{k}$$

$$\mathbf{F}_{\text{net},\perp} = m\mathbf{a}_{\perp} = \mathbf{N} - mg \cos 30°$$

4 Solve for the normal force.

We know that the block is not accelerating in the perpendicular direction because it is not sinking into the plane or coming off of the plane; thus, we can set $\mathbf{a}_{\perp} = 0$ and solve for **N**:

$$\mathbf{a}_{\perp} = 0$$

$$\mathbf{N} - mg \cos 30° = 0 \rightarrow \mathbf{N} = mg \cos 30°$$

5 Solve for the acceleration of the block.

The force of friction depends on the magnitude of the normal force, N, and the coefficient of kinetic friction, μ_k. Plug in the expression for normal force from Step 4 to determine the frictional force:

$$f_k = \mu_k N = \mu_k mg \cos 30°$$

Then, plug this expression for frictional force into the forces in the parallel direction expression from Step 3 to determine the acceleration:

$$m\mathbf{a}_{\parallel} = mg \sin 30° - \mathbf{f}_{k}$$

$$m\mathbf{a}_{\parallel} = mg \sin 30° - \mu_k mg \cos 30°$$

$$\mathbf{a}_{\parallel} = g(\sin 30° - \mu_k \cos 30°)$$

$$\approx \left(10\,\frac{\text{m}}{\text{s}^2}\right)\left(\frac{1}{2} - 0.3 \times 0.866\right)$$

$$\approx \left(10\,\frac{\text{m}}{\text{s}^2}\right)\left(\frac{1}{2} - 0.27\right) = 10 \times 0.23 = 2.3\,\frac{\text{m}}{\text{s}^2}\left(\text{actual} = 2.40\,\frac{\text{m}}{\text{s}^2}\right)$$

Note that the mass cancels out completely.

6 Use a kinematics formula to calculate the displacement.

We are given an acceleration, an initial velocity (starting from rest), and a time. Thus, we can determine the displacement:

$$\Delta \mathbf{x} = \mathbf{v}_0 t + \frac{\mathbf{a}t^2}{2}$$

$$= 0 + \frac{\left(2.4\,\frac{\text{m}}{\text{s}^2}\right)(2\,\text{s})^2}{2} = 4.8\,\text{m}$$

Takeaways

In every force problem, the process is the same: draw a free body diagram, write Newton's second law expressions for each dimension, and then solve.

In most single-entity problems, the mass will cancel out of the equation. Notice that this problem would be much simpler if the ramp were frictionless.

Things to Watch Out For

The geometry can become confusing on Test Day, so it is helpful to memorize that the component of the gravitational force along the plane is $mg \sin \theta$, where θ is the angle of the ramp relative to the horizontal.

Related Questions

1. A block of mass 5 kg is placed on an inclined plane at 45° to the horizontal. What is the minimum coefficient of static friction so that the block remains at rest?
2. A block is given an initial velocity of 2 $\frac{\text{m}}{\text{s}}$ up a frictionless plane inclined at 60° to the horizontal. What is the highest point above the original height reached by the block?
3. What is the velocity of a 10 kg block sliding down a frictionless inclined plane at 30° to the horizontal 5 seconds after it is released from rest?

High-Yield Problem-Solving Guide questions continue on the next page. ▶ ▶ ▶

Key Concepts

Physics and Math Chapter 2

Conservation of energy
Kinetic energy
Potential energy
Nonconservative forces
Kinematics

Projectile Motion and Air Resistance

An arrow with a mass of 80 g is fired at an angle of 30° to the horizontal. It strikes a target located 5 m above the firing point and impacts the target traveling at a speed of $20\frac{\text{m}}{\text{s}}$. If 10 percent of the initial energy of the arrow is lost to air resistance, what was the initial speed of the arrow?

1 Write an expression for the final energy of the arrow.

The total energy of the arrow is its potential energy plus its kinetic energy. The potential energy of the arrow is *mgh*. For simplicity, make the height at the firing point the datum ($h = 0$) so that the final height is 5 m. Remember that finding a numerical value at this point is not necessary. Writing a variable expression will save you time because some term (usually the mass) may cancel out in a later step. Thus, the final energy is:

$$E_f = K_f + U_f = \frac{1}{2}mv_f^2 + mgh_f$$

2 Write an expression for the initial energy of the arrow.

As stated in Step 1, the initial height is assigned the value of zero, so the potential energy at this point is also zero:

$$E_i = K_i + U_i = \frac{1}{2}mv_i^2 + mgh_i = \frac{1}{2}mv_i^2$$

3 Relate the change in energy to the energy lost to air resistance.

The conservation of energy equation tells us that all of the energy of a system must be accounted for. Whatever energy is lost between the beginning and the end must have been due to air resistance:

$$\begin{aligned} W_{\text{nonconservative}} &= E_i - E_f \\ &= \frac{1}{2}mv_i^2 - \left(\frac{1}{2}mv_f^2 + mgh_f\right) \end{aligned}$$

4 Relate the energy lost to the initial energy.

The question states that 10 percent of the initial energy is lost. Thus, the energy lost is the initial energy times 0.1:

$$W_{\text{nonconservative}} = 0.1 \times E_i = 0.1\left(\frac{1}{2} \times mv_i^2\right)$$

5 Solve for the initial speed.

$$W_{\text{nonconservative}} = \frac{1}{2}mv_i^2 - \left(\frac{1}{2}mv_f^2 + mgh_f\right)$$

$$0.1 \times v_i^2 = v_i^2 - \left(v_f^2 + 2gh_f\right)$$

$$0.9 \times v_i^2 = v_f^2 + 2gh_f$$

$$v_i = \sqrt{\frac{v_f^2 + 2gh_f}{0.9}} \approx \sqrt{\frac{\left(20\ \frac{\text{m}}{\text{s}}\right)^2 + 2 \times 10\ \frac{\text{m}}{\text{s}^2} \times 5\,\text{m}}{0.9}}$$

$$= \sqrt{\frac{400 + 100}{0.9}} \approx \sqrt{529} = 23\ \frac{\text{m}}{\text{s}}\left(\text{actual} = 23.5\ \frac{\text{m}}{\text{s}}\right)$$

Takeaways

Note that the angle and the mass were never used in the calculation. This will often be the case when using the conservation of energy equation to solve problems. These problems can be worded in many different ways, but the problem-solving process is the same for all of them:

1. Write an expression for the initial energy and an expression for the final energy.
2. If there is friction, air resistance, or viscous drag, the difference between final and initial energy is the energy lost due to these forces.
3. If there is no friction, air resistance, or viscous drag, the energy lost is zero, so set the two expressions equal to each other.
4. Solve for the quantity of interest.

Keep a realistic view of these problems to check your answers for math errors. Note that the initial speed is faster than the final speed, which we expect because the target is higher than the firing point and some energy is lost due to air resistance.

Related Questions

1. A rock is dropped from the top of a 100 m tall building and lands while traveling at a speed of 30 $\frac{\text{m}}{\text{s}}$. How much energy was lost due to air resistance?
2. Two different objects are dropped from rest off of a 50 m tall cliff. One lands going 30 percent faster than the other. The two objects have the same mass. How much more kinetic energy does one object have at the landing than the other?
3. A projectile is fired vertically at a speed of 30.0 $\frac{\text{m}}{\text{s}}$. It reaches a maximum height of 44.1 m. What fraction of its initial energy has been lost to air resistance at this point?

Things to Watch Out For

The mention of lost energy in the question stem should tip you off that you need to use the conservation of energy equation. In general, unless you are asked for an acceleration or time value, the energy approach is easier and faster than the kinematics and Newton's laws approach for these questions.

Key Concepts

Physics and Math Chapter 3

State functions

Thermodynamic processes

Heat

Work

Internal energy

Thermodynamics

A theoretical ideal engine, known as a Carnot engine, uses the thermodynamic properties of a closed gas piston system. The cycle involves two isothermal steps—one of expansion and one of compression—as well as an expansive and a compressive adiabatic step. This four-step system is shown in a pressure–volume diagram below:

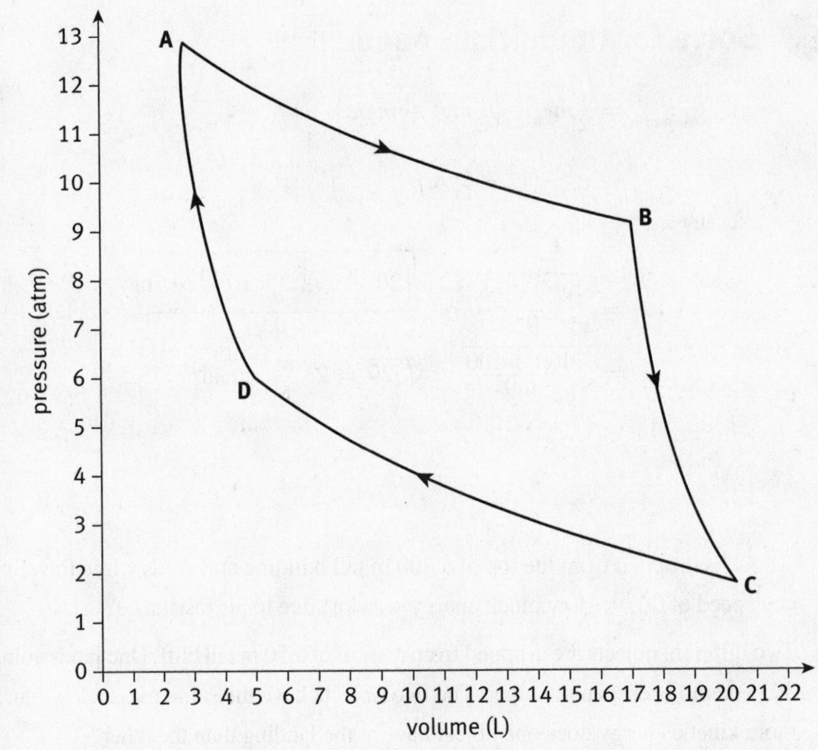

What is the total heat, work, and internal energy change over the course of a single cycle beginning at point **A** and moving through points **B**, **C**, and **D**?

 Identify the types of processes involved and their properties.

First, we must identify the individual steps as well as the entire process as known thermodynamic functions. Both isothermal and adiabatic processes appear hyperbolic on a pressure–volume graph, but adiabatic processes are steeper than isothermal ones. The path from **A** to **B** is not very steep and thus is an isothermal process; because the volume increases, it is an expansion. The path from **B** to **C** is steeper and is an adiabatic expansion. The cycle then proceeds through an isothermal compression and an adiabatic compression to return to **A**.

In addition to the four steps of this process, we must note that it is a closed system as stated in the question stem; thus, only energy may be exchanged between the system and the environment. It is also a closed cycle, which means that the internal energy at the start and finish must be the same.

2 Set up any known mathematical relationships.

For thermodynamic relationships, we have certain known quantities. The first law of thermodynamics can be stated as $\Delta U = Q - W$, where ΔU is the change in internal energy, Q is the heat entering the system, and W is the work done by the system.

For the closed cycle from **A** to **B** to **C** to **D** and back to **A**, $\Delta U = 0 = Q - W$; thus, $Q = W$. We need only determine one quantity to determine the second as well. For the isothermal processes between **A** and **B** and between **C** and **D**, the same relationship is true. Because temperature remains constant, internal energy also remains constant and $\Delta U = 0 = Q - W$; thus, $Q = W$.

For the adiabatic processes between **B** and **C** and between **D** and **A**, there is no heat exchange with the environment. The first law can simplify to $\Delta U = 0 - W$; thus, $\Delta U = -W$.

Finally, we know that work can be calculated from the area under the curve in a pressure–volume graph; thus, we can obtain work from the graph by approximating the area using trapezoids.

3 Determine the work from each process and the total work.

Work is determined graphically as the area under a pressure–volume curve. For Test Day, it is useful to approximate the area under the curve using trapezoids. The area of a trapezoid is given by:

$$A_{\text{trapezoid}} = \left(\frac{b_1 + b_2}{2}\right)h$$

Keep in mind that the bases b_1 and b_2 are vertical in this graph and the height h is the distance along the x-axis. For the isothermal expansion from **A** to **B**, the calculation of the area under the curve is modeled here:

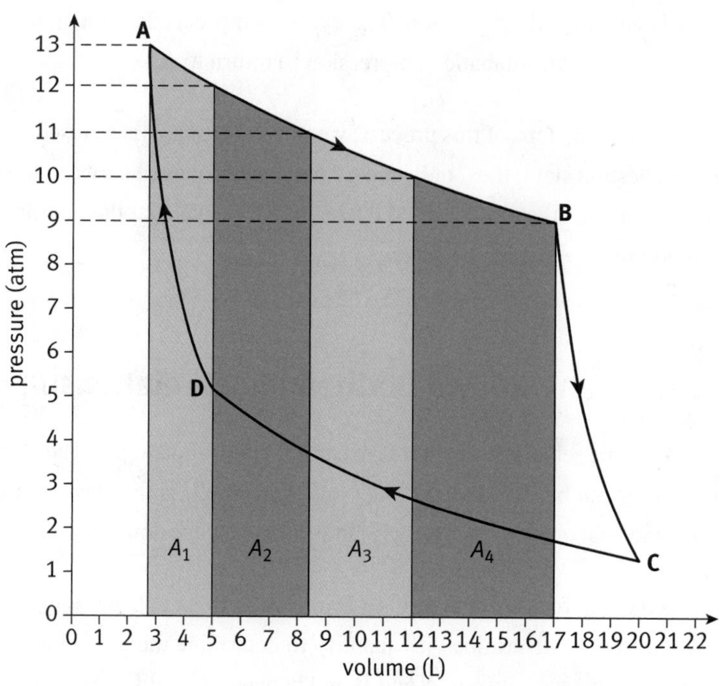

Work is done by the gas as it expands. This is considered positive work. Heat is also added to the gas. To calculate the area, take the average of the bases and multiply by the height:

$$A_1 = \frac{13\,\text{atm} + 12\,\text{atm}}{2}(5 - 2.5\,\text{L}) = 31.25\,\text{L} \bullet \text{atm}$$

$$A_2 = \frac{12\,\text{atm} + 11\,\text{atm}}{2}(8.5 - 5\,\text{L}) = 40.25\,\text{L} \bullet \text{atm}$$

$$A_3 = \frac{11\,\text{atm} + 10\,\text{atm}}{2}(12 - 8.5\,\text{L}) = 36.75\,\text{L} \bullet \text{atm}$$

$$A_4 = \frac{10\,\text{atm} + 9\,\text{atm}}{2}(17 - 12\,\text{L}) = 47.5\,\text{L} \bullet \text{atm}$$

The total area is $A_1 + A_2 + A_3 + A_4 = 31.25 + 40.25 + 36.75 + 47.5 = 155.75$ L • atm.

This is an unusual unit for work, and even more unusual for heat. It makes sense to convert this answer to joules. Using the conversion factor 1 atm = 101,325 Pa, we can obtain the work in joules:

$$1 \text{ atm} \approx 10^5 \text{ Pa}$$

$$1 \text{ L} \bullet \text{atm} = 10^5 \text{ L} \bullet \text{Pa}$$

$$= 10^5 \text{ L} \bullet \text{Pa} \times \left[\frac{1000 \text{ mL}}{1 \text{ L}}\right] \times \left[\frac{1 \text{ cm}^3}{1 \text{ mL}}\right] \times \left[\frac{1 \text{ m}}{100 \text{ cm}}\right]^3 \times \left[\frac{1 \frac{\text{N}}{\text{m}^2}}{1 \text{ Pa}}\right]$$

$$= \frac{10^5 \times 10^3}{10^6} = 100 \text{ J}$$

Thus, 155.75 L • atm ≈ 15.5 kJ (actual = 15.8 kJ).

This process must be repeated for the path from **B** to **C**. The same method is used for the path from **C** to **D** and from **D** to **A**, but the values calculated are negative because the gas is undergoing compression. The total work is the sum of the work for these four paths:

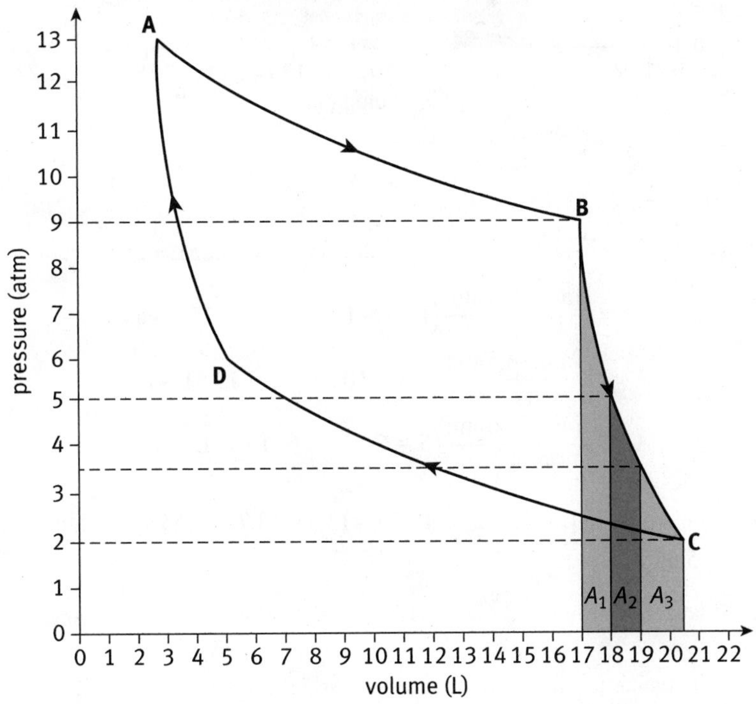

$$A_1 = \frac{9 \text{ atm} + 5 \text{ atm}}{2}(18 - 17 \text{ L}) = 7 \text{ L} \bullet \text{atm}$$

$$A_2 = \frac{5 \text{ atm} + 3.5 \text{ atm}}{2}(19 - 18 \text{ L}) = 4.25 \text{ L} \bullet \text{atm}$$

$$A_3 = \frac{3.5 \text{ atm} + 2 \text{ atm}}{2}(20.5 - 19 \text{ L}) = 4.125 \text{ L} \bullet \text{atm}$$

The total area for **B** to **C** is 7 + 4.25 + 4.125 = 15.375 L • atm ≈ 1.5 kJ (actual = 1.56 kJ).

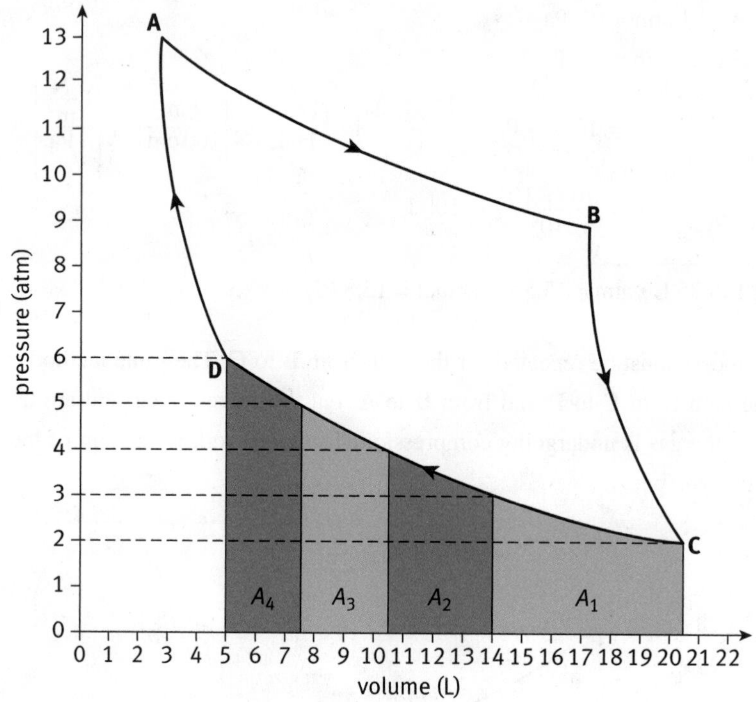

$$A_1 = \frac{2\,\text{atm} + 3\,\text{atm}}{2}(14 - 20.5\,\text{L}) = -16.25\,\text{L} \bullet \text{atm}$$

$$A_2 = \frac{3\,\text{atm} + 4\,\text{atm}}{2}(10.5 - 14\,\text{L}) = -12.25\,\text{L} \bullet \text{atm}$$

$$A_3 = \frac{4\,\text{atm} + 5\,\text{atm}}{2}(7.5 - 10.5\,\text{L}) = -13.5\,\text{L} \bullet \text{atm}$$

$$A_4 = \frac{5\,\text{atm} + 6\,\text{atm}}{2}(5 - 7.5\,\text{L}) = -13.75\,\text{L} \bullet \text{atm}$$

The total area for **C** to **D** is –16.25 – 12.25 – 13.5 – 13.75 = –55.75 L • atm ≈ –5.6 kJ (actual = –5.65 kJ).

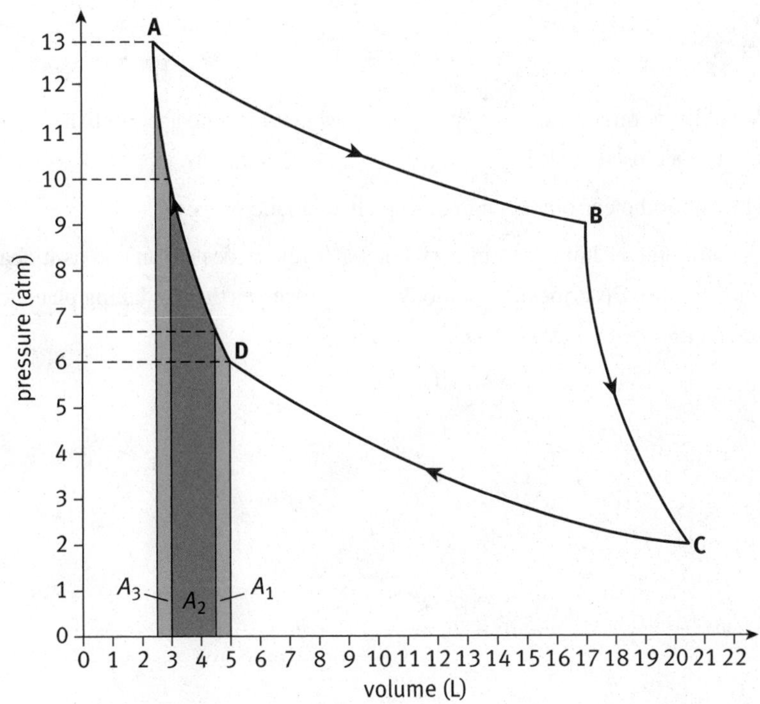

$$A_1 = \frac{6\,\text{atm} + 6.5\,\text{atm}}{2}(4.5 - 5\,\text{L}) = -3.125\,\text{L} \bullet \text{atm}$$

$$A_2 = \frac{6.5\,\text{atm} + 10\,\text{atm}}{2}(3 - 4.5\,\text{L}) = -12.375\,\text{L} \bullet \text{atm}$$

$$A_3 = \frac{10\,\text{atm} + 13\,\text{atm}}{2}(2.5 - 3\,\text{L}) = -5.75\,\text{L} \bullet \text{atm}$$

The total area for **D** to **A** is –3.125 – 12.375 – 5.75 = –21.25 L • atm ≈ –2.1 kJ (actual = –2.15 kJ).

The total work throughout the cycle is the sum of the work for each portion of the cycle:

$$15.8 + 1.56 - 5.65 - 2.15 = 9.54\text{ kJ}$$

Insert work into the earlier relationships to determine heat.

As established earlier, for a closed-loop process, $\Delta U = 0 = Q - W$; thus, $Q = W$. If the system has performed 9.54 kJ of work, then it has also absorbed 9.54 kJ of heat during the process.

Takeaways

Sign conventions play a significant role in thermodynamic problems. $Q > 0$ means that the system absorbs heat (endothermic), whereas $Q < 0$ means that the system gives off heat (exothermic). $W > 0$ means that the system performs work (expansion), whereas $W < 0$ means that work is done on the system (compression). $\Delta U > 0$ means the temperature increases, whereas $\Delta U < 0$ means the temperature decreases.

Things to Watch Out For

Isothermal processes are often mistaken for adiabatic processes and vice-versa. Remember that in an isothermal process, heat is exchanged for work, so heat must enter or leave the system to maintain a constant temperature.

Related Questions

1. What is the minimum number of processes that must be accomplished in order to have a closed cycle?
2. How does the entropy change during an adiabatic process?
3. A thermometer immersed in very hot water undergoes expansion as it changes temperature. Describe the thermodynamic processes that are taking place within the thermometer and the water.

High-Yield Problem-Solving Guide questions continue on the next page. ▶ ▶ ▶

Key Concepts

Physics and Math Chapter 4

Pressure
Density
Bernoulli's equation
Continuity equation

Fluid Dynamics

A water storage tank is located 300 m away from a water outlet, as shown in the diagram below:

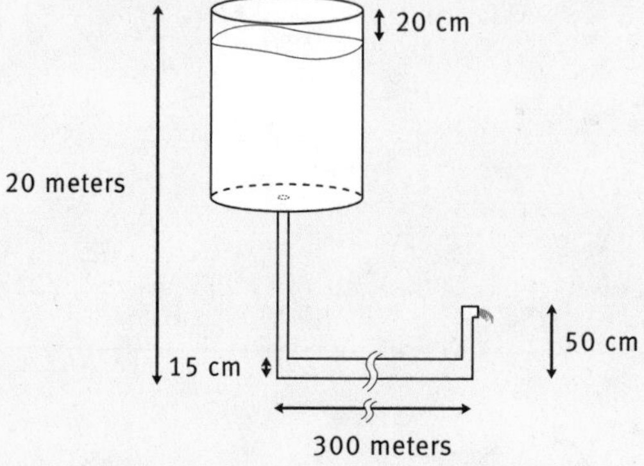

The empty space in the water tank is held at a pressure of 3 atm. The storage tank has a diameter of 5 m, and the outlet has a diameter of 1 cm. What is the speed of the water exiting the outlet? (Note: 1 atm = 101.325 kPa; $\rho_{water} = 1000\frac{kg}{m^3}$)

1 Write an expression using Bernoulli's equation.

Bernoulli's equation is a statement of the conservation of energy for fluids. It has three terms—one for pressure (a form of stored energy), one analogous to kinetic energy, and one analogous to gravitational potential energy:

$$P_1 + \frac{1}{2}\rho v_1^2 + \rho g h_1 = P_2 + \frac{1}{2}\rho v_2^2 + \rho g h_2$$

Write the expression for Bernoulli's principle at the two points of interest, just as you would write the total energy of a mechanical system at two points. For this problem, the two points are the top of the water level in the storage tank and the outlet.

2 Use the continuity equation.

In almost all applications of Bernoulli's equation, you will need to eliminate some of the terms in order to solve the problem. A common one here is speed. The continuity equation relates linear flow speed to area:

$$A_1 v_1 = A_2 v_2$$

This shows that the product of the cross-sectional area and linear flow speed is a constant. Given that the diameter of the water tank is 5 m and of the spout is 1 cm, the linear flow speed at the surface is near zero. Think about it like this: as this vessel drains, the surface will drop at a nearly negligible speed compared to the speed of the fluid leaving the spout. This simplifies the equation:

$$P_1 + \rho g h_1 = P_2 + \frac{1}{2}\rho v_2^2 + \rho g h_2$$

3 Plug in the given information, and solve.

The pressure inside the tank is 3 atm. Convert this to pascals, the SI unit for pressure:

$$P_1 = 3\,\text{atm}\left[\frac{101\,\text{kPa}}{1\,\text{atm}}\right] = 3.03 \times 10^5\ \text{Pa}$$

$$P_2 = 1.01 \times 10^5\ \text{Pa}$$

The pressure at the outlet is 1 atm (101,325 Pa) because the outlet is exposed to outside air.

Now we have all the necessary variables:

$$h_1 = 20 - 0.2 = 19.8\ \text{m}$$

$$h_2 = 50\ \text{cm} = 0.5\ \text{m}$$

$$\rho = 1000\ \frac{\text{kg}}{\text{m}^3}$$

Plug into Bernoulli's equation:

$$P_1 + \rho g h_1 = P_2 + \frac{1}{2}\rho v_2^2 + \rho g h_2$$

$$3.03 \times 10^5\ \text{Pa} + \left(1000\ \frac{\text{kg}}{\text{m}^3}\right)\left(10\ \frac{\text{m}}{\text{s}^2}\right)(19.8\ \text{m}) = 1.01 \times 10^5\ \text{Pa} + \frac{1}{2}\left(1000\ \frac{\text{kg}}{\text{m}^3}\right)v_2^2 + \left(1000\ \frac{\text{kg}}{\text{m}^3}\right)\left(10\ \frac{\text{m}}{\text{s}^2}\right)(0.5\ \text{m})$$

$$3.03 \times 10^5 + 1.98 \times 10^5 = 1.01 \times 10^5 + 0.05 \times 10^5 + 500v_2^2$$

$$3.95 \times 10^5 = 500v_2^2$$

$$790 = v_2^2$$

$$v_2 \approx 28$$

Takeaways

Bernoulli's equation looks complicated, but it is really just a statement of the conservation of energy. The process is the same for every problem:

1. Write Bernoulli's equation at the two points of interest.
2. Eliminate any variables if possible (often via the continuity equation).
3. Solve for the unknown quantity.

Things to Watch Out For

A common use of Bernoulli's equation is with no change in height, so that $P + \frac{1}{2}\rho v^2 = \text{constant}$. In this situation, a decrease in pressure is associated with an increase in velocity. This is known as the Bernoulli effect and is responsible for balls curving in flight, windows exploding during hurricanes, and (partially) for airplane wings experiencing lift.

Related Questions

1. The pressure at one point in a horizontal pipe is triple the pressure at another point. How do the linear flow speeds compare at these two points?
2. A tapered pipe has two points labeled. At point A, the radius is twice that at point B. The pipe is horizontal and is subjected to a fluid pressure of 1.6 atm. What is the ratio of linear flow speeds these two points in the pipe?
3. A water storage tank is open to air on the top and has a height of 1 m. If the tank is completely full and a hole is made at the center of the wall of the tank, how fast will the water exit the tank?

High-Yield Problem-Solving Guide questions continue on the next page. ▶ ▶ ▶

Key Concepts

Physics and Math Chapter 5

Work

Electrostatics

Electrical potential energy

Charge distributions

Electrostatics

Three charges are lined up along the x-axis at 1 mm intervals. Charge 1 has a charge of $+1\ \mu C$. Charge 2 has a charge of $-2\ \mu C$. Charge 3 has a charge of $+4\ \mu C$. How much work was required to assemble this distribution of charges, assuming that the charges were initially very far apart? $\left(\text{Note: } k = 9 \times 10^9\ \frac{N \cdot m^2}{C^2}\right)$

1 Find the work required to place Charge 1.

The work done to move a charge equals the magnitude of the charge times the change in electrical potential. The work done to place Charge 1 is zero because there is no change in electrical potential:

$$W = \Delta U = q\Delta V = 0$$

As a matter of convention, the work to place the first charge is always zero.

2 Find the work required to place Charge 2.

The same formula is used in this step as in Step 1. Here, Charge 2 has an initial electrical potential of zero because it is very far away from Charge 1. The final electrical potential is given by the formula $V = \frac{kQ}{r}$ where Q is the stationary charge and r is the distance between the charges.

$$W = \Delta U = q\Delta V = \frac{kQq}{r}$$

$$W = \frac{\left(9 \times 10^9\ \frac{N \cdot m^2}{C^2}\right)(1 \times 10^{-6}\ C)(-2 \times 10^{-6}\ C)}{1 \times 10^{-3}\ m}$$

$$= -18\ J$$

3 Find the work required to place Charge 3.

Just like in Step 2, the work to place Charge 3 equals the magnitude of Charge 3 times the change in the electrical potential. Once again, the initial electrical potential is 0. The final potential is the potential due to Charge 1 plus the potential due to Charge 2. Be careful, because the distances must be from Charge 1 to Charge 3 (call this r_1) and from Charge 2 to Charge 3 (call this r_2), respectively:

$$W = \Delta U = q\Delta V_1 + q\Delta V_2 = \frac{kQ_1q}{r_1} + \frac{kQ_2q}{r_2} = kq\left(\frac{Q_1}{r_1} + \frac{Q_2}{r_2}\right)$$

$$W = \left(9 \times 10^9 \, \frac{\text{N} \bullet \text{m}^2}{\text{C}^2}\right)\left(4 \times 10^{-6}\,\text{C}\right)\left(\frac{1 \times 10^{-6}\,\text{C}}{2 \times 10^{-3}\,\text{m}} + \frac{-2 \times 10^{-6}\,\text{C}}{1 \times 10^{-3}\,\text{m}}\right)$$

$$= 36 \times 10^3\left(-1.5 \times 10^{-3}\right) = -54\text{ J}$$

Takeaways

To find the work required to assemble a distribution of charges, find the work required to place each charge individually, and then add them together. The work to place the first charge is always zero.

4 Add the work from Steps 1, 2, and 3.

Add the work from Steps 1, 2, and 3 to find the net work. The net work is negative, meaning that the potential energy of the system has been lowered:

$$W_{\text{net}} = 0 - 18 - 54 = -72\text{ J}$$

Things to Watch Out For

It is common to make errors with the sign convention on these types of problems. Keep this in mind when checking your work: like charges increase in potential energy as they are brought closer to each other; unlike charges decrease in potential energy as they are brought closer to each other.

Related Questions

1. A +1 μC charge sits 1 cm from a −2 μC charge. How much work is done in tripling the distance between these charges?
2. How much work is done in assembling a square-shaped charge distribution with a side length of 1 μm if all of the charges have a charge of 5 nC?
3. Charges 1, 2, and 3 are lined up, in that order, at 1 mm intervals along the y-axis. Charge 1 has a charge of +4 μC. Charge 2 has a charge of −2 μC. Charge 3 has a charge of −3 μC. What is the change in potential energy of the system if Charge 1 is removed?

Key Concepts

Physics and Math Chapter 6

Ohm's law

Resistors in series

Resistors in parallel

Voltage sources

Resistor Circuits

What is the current through R_1 in the circuit shown below?

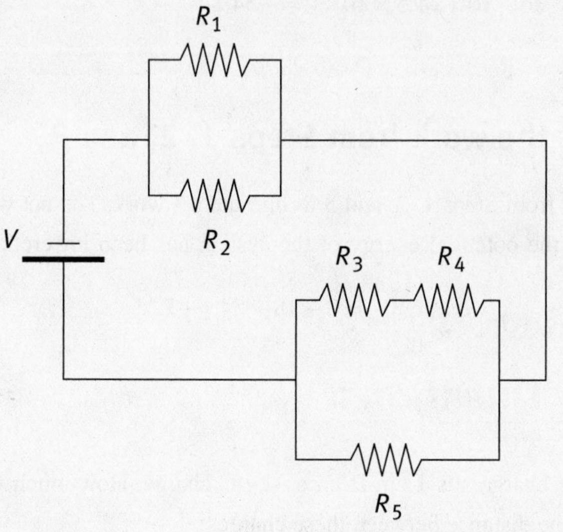

(Note: $R_1 = 30\ \Omega$; $R_2 = 6\ \Omega$; $R_3 = 20\ \Omega$; $R_4 = 10\ \Omega$; $R_5 = 30\ \Omega$; V = 30 V)

1 Find the equivalent resistance of the network.

The first part of this problem is to find the equivalent resistance of the entire circuit. This will take several steps. Begin by combining R_1 and R_2 using the equation for the equivalent resistance of two parallel resistors:

$$\frac{1}{R_{\text{eq1}}} = \frac{1}{R_1} + \frac{1}{R_2} = \frac{1}{30\ \Omega} + \frac{1}{6\ \Omega} = \frac{1}{30} + \frac{5}{30} = \frac{6}{30} = \frac{1}{5}$$

$$R_{\text{eq1}} = 5\ \Omega$$

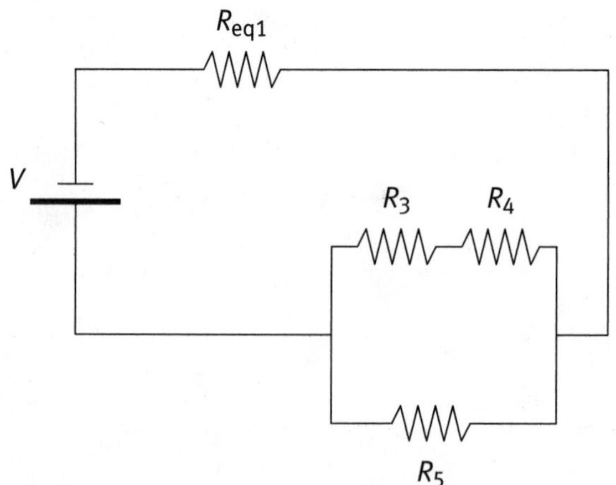

Now, combine R_3 and R_4, which are in series:

$$R_{eq2} = R_3 + R_4 = 20\,\Omega + 10\,\Omega$$

$$R_{eq2} = 30\,\Omega$$

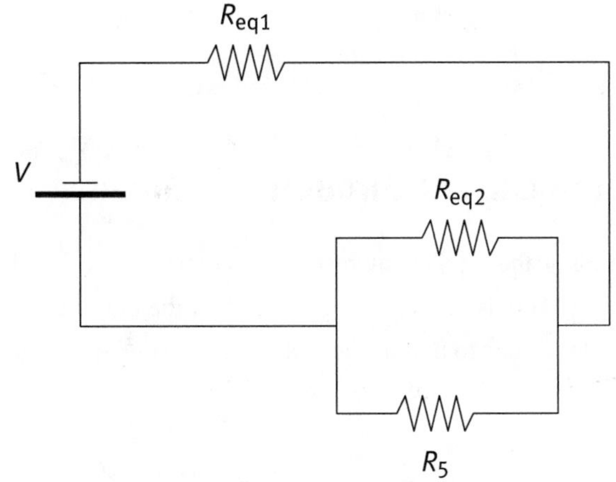

Now, combine the equivalent resistance R_{eq2} with R_5. These resistors are in parallel:

$$\frac{1}{R_{eq3}} = \frac{1}{R_{eq2}} + \frac{1}{R_5} = \frac{1}{30\,\Omega} + \frac{1}{30\,\Omega} = \frac{2}{30}$$

$$R_{eq3} = 15\,\Omega$$

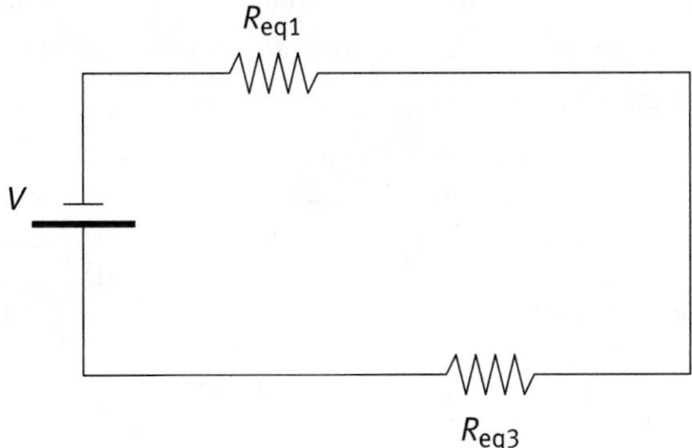

Finally combine R_{eq1} and R_{eq3}. These resistors are in series:

$$R_{eq4} = R_{eq1} + R_{eq3} = 5\,\Omega + 15\,\Omega$$

$$R_{eq4} = 20\,\Omega$$

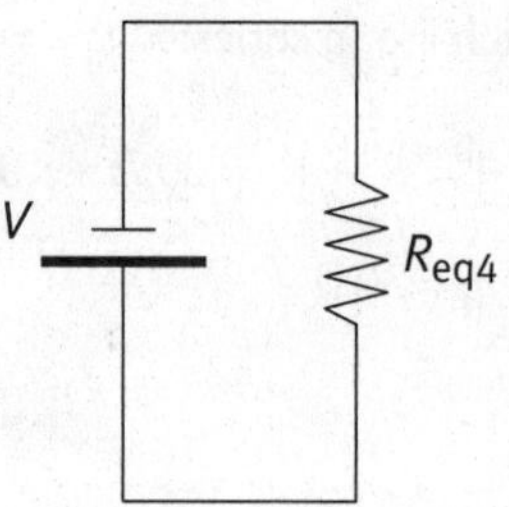

2 Find the current through the circuit.

The point of finding the equivalent resistance is so that we can find the current through the circuit. This is also often referred to as the current through or leaving the battery. Use Ohm's law to find the current from the source voltage and equivalent resistance:

$$V = IR \rightarrow I = \frac{V}{R} = \frac{30\text{ V}}{20\ \Omega} = 1.5\text{ A}$$

3 Expand the circuit.

Now expand the circuit back out and apply what we know about resistors in series and parallel to find the current and voltage through individual resistors. All resistors in series must have the same current, so we know that the current from Step 2 must equal the current through R_{eq1} and R_{eq3}:

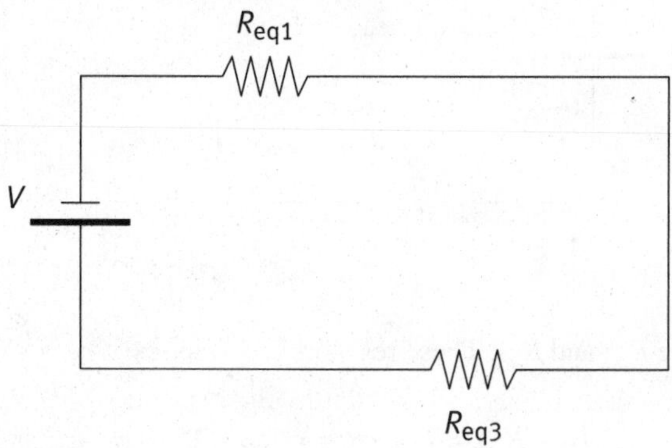

Use Ohm's law to find the voltage across R_{eq1}:

$$\begin{aligned} V_{eq1} &= I_{eq1}R_{eq1} \\ &= (1.5\ \text{A})(5\ \Omega) \\ &= 7.5\ \text{V} \end{aligned}$$

Because R_{eq1} is a parallel combination of R_1 and R_2, we know that R_1 and R_2 must have the same voltage as R_{eq1}. Any two (or more) circuit components in parallel must have the same voltage as the others:

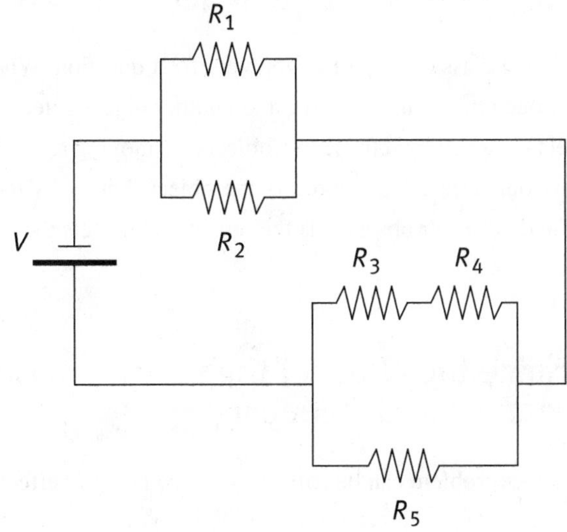

Use the voltage and resistance of R_1 to find the current through R_1:

$$\begin{aligned} V_1 = I_1R_1 \rightarrow I_1 &= \frac{V_1}{R_1} \\ &= \frac{7.5\ \text{V}}{30\ \Omega} = 0.25\ \text{A} \end{aligned}$$

Takeaways

There is a standard process for solving these types of resistor problems:

1. Find the equivalent resistance by combining series and parallel resistors.
2. Find the current through the circuit.
3. Expand the circuit back out, step by step.
4. Apply knowledge of series and parallel resistors to find the quantity of interest.

Things to Watch Out For

The arithmetic for calculating the equivalent resistance in parallel can be confusing. Another version of the formula is $R_p = \frac{R_1R_2}{R_1 + R_2}$. Note, however, that this only works for two resistors and cannot be easily expanded to account for three resistors.

Related Questions

1. In the circuit shown in the original question, what is the voltage across R_4?
2. Four resistors are attached in parallel to a voltage supply of 9 V. If the resistances of the resistors are $10\ \Omega$, $20\ \Omega$, $30\ \Omega$, and $40\ \Omega$, what is the current through the battery?
3. There are six resistors in a circuit. R_1, R_2, R_3, R_4, and R_5 are all in parallel with each other, and they are all in series with R_6. If the current leaving the battery is 10 A and each of the resistors has a resistance of $1\ \Omega$ except for R_6, which is unknown, what is the resistance of R_6 if $V = 20$ V?

Key Concepts

Physics and Math Chapter 7

Doppler effect

Wavelength

Frequency

Speed

Doppler Effect

> Two cars, Car A and Car B, are moving toward each other, with each car traveling at 50 $\frac{\text{m}}{\text{s}}$ when Car B starts to beep its 475 Hz horn. Assuming that the speed of sound is 343 $\frac{\text{m}}{\text{s}}$, what is the wavelength of the horn as perceived by the driver of Car A?

1 Identify this as a Doppler effect problem and determine the source and detector of the wave.

This problem has the classic setup of a Doppler effect question. Whenever you see a setup in which one object emits a wave and another object detects it, think about the Doppler effect—especially if those two objects are moving relative to each other. First, let's define our terms. The source is the object that emits the sound wave; this is Car B. The detector or observer is the object that detects the wave; this is the person in Car A.

2 Determine the effect of the velocity of the detector on the perceived frequency.

Every Doppler effect problem can be solved using the Doppler effect equation:

$$f' = f\frac{(v \pm v_D)}{(v \mp v_S)}$$

where f' is the observed frequency, f is the emitted frequency, v is the speed of sound in the medium, v_D is the speed of the detector, and v_S is the speed of the source. The most complicated aspects of using the Doppler effect equation are remembering where to place the variables and the sign convention. While we present the logic for the sign convention throughout this explanation, a mnemonic can be used: if memorized in this form, the top sign should be used when the detector or source is moving *toward* the other object, whereas the bottom sign should be used when the detector or source is moving *away* from the other object.

Let's start with the detector (the person in Car A). The detector is moving toward the source; therefore, the observed frequency, f', will be greater than if the detector were stationary. The numerator of the Doppler effect equation represents the motion of the detector; the fact that the detector is moving toward the source implies that a plus sign should be used in the numerator. Remember: the top sign in the numerator (plus) should be used when the detector is moving toward the source:

$$f' = f\frac{(v + v_D)}{(v \mp v_S)}$$

3 Determine the effect of the velocity of the source on the perceived frequency.

Now, let's consider the source (the horn on Car B). The source is moving toward the detector; therefore, the observed frequency, f', will be greater than if the source were stationary. The denominator of the Doppler effect equation represents to motion of the source; the fact that the source is moving toward the detector implies that a minus sign should be used in the denominator. Remember: the top sign in the denominator (minus) should be used when the source is moving toward the detector:

$$f' = f\frac{(v + v_D)}{(v - v_S)}$$

4 Plug the values into the Doppler effect equation.

We are given the following values:

$$f = 475 \text{ Hz}$$

$$v = \text{speed of sound} = 343 \ \frac{\text{m}}{\text{s}}$$

$$v_D = v_S = 50 \ \frac{\text{m}}{\text{s}}$$

Plugging these into the equation, we get:

$$f' = f\frac{(v + v_D)}{(v - v_s)}$$

$$= (475 \text{ Hz})\frac{\left(343 \ \frac{\text{m}}{\text{s}} + 50 \ \frac{\text{m}}{\text{s}}\right)}{\left(343 \ \frac{\text{m}}{\text{s}} - 50 \ \frac{\text{m}}{\text{s}}\right)}$$

$$= 475 \times \frac{393}{293} \approx 480 \times \frac{4}{3} = 640 \text{ Hz (actual} = 637.1 \text{ Hz)}$$

5 Convert frequency to wavelength.

This question asks for the wavelength of the observed wave, not its frequency. We can use the relationship between wave speed, frequency, and wavelength to determine the answer:

$$v = f\lambda \rightarrow \lambda = \frac{v}{f}$$

$$\lambda = \frac{343 \ \frac{\text{m}}{\text{s}}}{637 \text{ Hz}} \approx 0.5 \text{ m} \left(\text{actual} = 0.54 \text{ m}\right)$$

Takeaways

As the detector approaches the source, the observed frequency will be higher than the emitted frequency, and when the detector moves away from the source, the observed frequency will be lower than the emitted frequency. The same rule applies to the motion of the source. Therefore, when determining the right sign convention of the Doppler equation, use the sign in the equation that will yield the appropriate observed frequency.

Things to Watch Out For

Always separate Doppler effect questions into two parts: the effect of the source and the effect of the observer. Be careful in problems where the object and the source are moving in the same direction. If the source is ahead of the detector, the source will be moving away from the detector while the detector is moving toward the source, regardless of their relative speeds. If the detector is ahead of the source, the detector will be moving away from the source while the source is moving toward the detector.

Related Questions

1. Suppose a policeman running at $5\,\frac{\text{m}}{\text{s}}$ is firing his gun at a rate of 20 bullets per minute while chasing a bank robber who is driving away at $50\,\frac{\text{m}}{\text{s}}$. At what rate do the bullets reach the bank robber? (Note: Use $500\,\frac{\text{m}}{\text{s}}$ for the speed of a bullet.)
2. A bungee jumper yells at 350 Hz as he falls off a bridge toward a river at a rate of $20\,\frac{\text{m}}{\text{s}}$. What are the frequencies heard by the observers on the bridge and a boat on the river? (Note: The speed of sound is $343\,\frac{\text{m}}{\text{s}}$.)
3. Some animals use echolocation to navigate three-dimensional space and find prey. During echolocation, what is the detector and what is the source? What signs would be used in the Doppler effect equation in this case?

High-Yield Problem-Solving Guide questions continue on the next page. ▶ ▶ ▶

Key Concepts

Physics and Math Chapter 8

Refraction
Snell's law
Index of refraction
Trigonometry

Snell's Law

A gold doubloon rests on a rock 1 m below the surface of the ocean. A glass-bottom boat passes over the area, and a passenger spots the coin at a 60° angle from the normal. If the glass layer is 3 cm thick, find the apparent depth of the coin. (Note: The indices of refraction are as follows: air, $n = 1$; glass, $n = 1.5$; ocean water, $n = 1.34$.)

1 Sketch the situation.

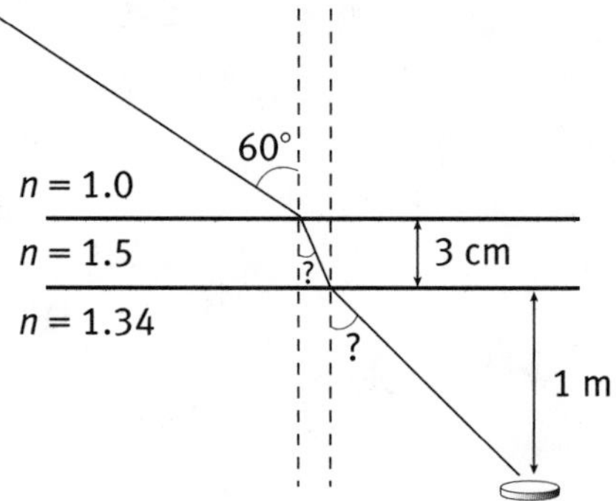

Light bends toward the normal when going from a medium with a lower index of refraction to one with a higher index of refraction. Your sketch need not be to scale; we use it to approximate what is going on and to keep track of the important data.

2 Apply Snell's law.

Snell's law shows mathematically that light bends toward the normal (decreasing θ) when it enters a medium with a higher refractive index. Here, we work through the formula to find the angles of light entry and exit for the glass and salt water.

$$
\begin{aligned}
n_{\text{air}} \sin\theta_{\text{air}} &= n_{\text{glass}} \sin\theta_{\text{glass}} \\
\theta_{\text{glass}} &= \sin^{-1}\frac{n_{\text{air}} \sin\theta_{\text{air}}}{n_{\text{glass}}} \\
&= \sin^{-1}\frac{1 \times \sin 60^\circ}{1.5} \approx \sin^{-1}\frac{0.866}{1.5} \approx \sin^{-1} 0.577 \\
\theta_{\text{glass}} &\approx 35^\circ
\end{aligned}
$$

While exact calculation of an inverse trigonometric function is outside the scope of MCAT math, we would be able to predict this value with reasonable accuracy on Test Day. If the sine of 30° is 0.5, then the inverse sine of 0.577 should be just a bit larger than 30°.

Now, plug into Snell's law for the second refraction step (from glass to salt water):

$$n_{\text{glass}} \sin \theta_{\text{glass}} = n_{\text{water}} \sin \theta_{\text{water}}$$

$$\theta_{\text{water}} = \sin^{-1} \frac{n_{\text{glass}} \sin \theta_{\text{glass}}}{n_{\text{water}}}$$

$$= \sin^{-1} \frac{1.5 \times \sin 35^\circ}{1.34} \approx \sin^{-1} \frac{0.866}{1.34} \approx \sin^{-1} 0.646$$

$$\theta_{\text{water}} \approx 40^\circ$$

Alternatively, realize that when light passes through multiple layers, the final angle can be determined merely by comparing the first and final media. The glass in this example alters the distance that the light travels in the x-direction but has no bearing on the final angle because the light enters and exits the glass at the same angle:

$$n_{\text{air}} \sin \theta_{\text{air}} = n_{\text{water}} \sin \theta_{\text{water}}$$

$$\theta_{\text{water}} = \sin^{-1} \frac{n_{\text{air}} \sin \theta_{\text{air}}}{n_{\text{water}}}$$

$$= \sin^{-1} \frac{1 \times \sin 60^\circ}{1.34} \approx \sin^{-1} \frac{0.866}{1.34} \approx \sin^{-1} 0.646$$

$$\theta_{\text{water}} \approx 40^\circ$$

3 Use trigonometry to determine how far the light goes in the *x*-direction.

We know the thickness and depth of the glass and water, respectively, so we can use that information to determine how far the coin is from the ray of light the passenger sees. Light travels through a total of three media, but the distance of the observer from the glass doesn't actually matter. As long as he is looking 60° from the normal, he will see the coin. The trigonometry here is direct, using the relationship:

$$\tan \theta = \frac{\text{opposite}}{\text{adjacent}} = \frac{x}{y}$$

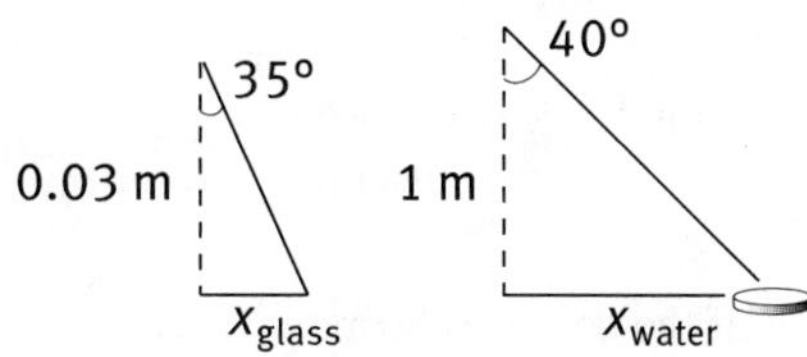

The value of x in the triangle within the glass can be determined as follows:

$$x_{\text{glass}} = y \tan \theta = 0.03\,\text{m} \times \tan 35^\circ \approx 0.02\,\text{m}$$

The triangle in the water is solved the same way:

$$x_{water} = y \tan\theta = 1\,\text{m} \times \tan 40° \approx 0.84\,\text{m}$$

The ray of light escapes the water and glass 0.02 + 0.84 = 0.86 meters from the coin.

4 Find the object's image.

When the passenger sees the coin, his brain interprets light as a straight line. In other words, his brain doesn't consider the bending of light due to the indices of refraction, and he perceives the coin to be closer than it actually is. We previously determined the x-component of the light ray from the air–glass interface to the coin to be 0.86 m. The observer sees the coin at a 60° angle from the normal, so set up a new triangle with this angle:

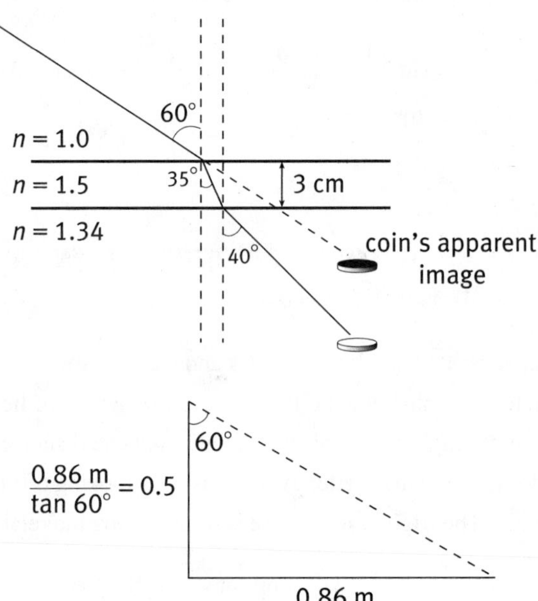

We are trying to find the apparent depth of the coin—the y-component of this triangle:

$$\tan 60° = \frac{0.86}{y} \rightarrow y = \frac{0.86}{\tan 60°} \approx \frac{0.86}{1.732} = 0.50\,\text{m}$$

Thus, the apparent depth of the coin is 0.50 m.

Takeaways

Complex problems can be solved with a little bit of ingenuity. Snell's law is a simple concept and is likely to be one of the first steps in any problem dealing with the refraction of light. When light passes through multiple layers, the final angle can be determined merely by comparing the first and final media.

Things to Watch Out For

Light reflects off of media boundaries, too. Because of this, the refracted ray of light is less intense than the incident ray. Different wavelengths also have slightly different indices of refraction—this difference is what causes light dispersion.

Related Questions

1. A firefighter shines her flashlight through a smoky room at a 45° angle to a window. What angle does the beam of light make with the pane of glass on the outside? (Note: The indices of refraction are as follows: air, $n = 1$; glass, $n = 1.5$; smoke, $n = 1.1$.)
2. A jeweler is appraising the stone on a ring. He aims a beam of light 35° from the normal at a flat edge of the gem. What angle would he observe in the gem if the stone were diamond ($n = 2.4$)? What angle would he observe if the stone were zircon ($n = 1.9$)?
3. If light were traveling from salt water into air, what would be the associated critical angle?

Key Concepts

Physics and Math Chapter 9

Atomic number

Mass number

Isotopes

Radioactive decay

Nuclear Reactions

A neutral U-238 atom absorbs a neutron and then immediately undergoes two alpha decays, three beta decays, one positron decay, and two gamma decays (not necessarily in that order). Describe the resulting nucleus using isotopic notation. The resulting atom is an isotope of what element?

1 Find the mass number and atomic number of the parent nucleus.

The notation U-238 indicates a uranium atom with a mass number (A) of 238. The letter is always the element's symbol, as listed on the Periodic Table. From the Periodic Table, the atomic number of uranium (Z) is 92: all uranium atoms, by definition, have 92 protons.

The mass number, A, is the sum of the number of protons and neutrons. The mass number is given in the question because a given element may have many different isotopes, which all have the same number of protons but vary in the number of neutrons they contain.

Isotopes may be written in shorthand notation as ${}^{A}_{Z}\text{X}$, where X is the element's symbol, A is the mass number, and Z is the atomic number. Here, this uranium isotope could be written as ${}^{238}_{92}\text{U}$.

2 Find the result of the neutron absorption.

A neutron has a mass number of 1 and an atomic number of 0 because it has no protons. In these problems, make sure to balance both the atomic numbers and the mass numbers in the decay equation:

$$
{}^{A}_{Z}\text{X} + {}^{1}_{0}n \rightarrow {}^{A+1}_{Z}\text{X}
$$

$$
{}^{238}_{92}\text{U} + {}^{1}_{0}n \rightarrow {}^{239}_{92}\text{U}
$$

The result of the absorption is the formation of a different isotope of uranium.

3 Find the result of the alpha decays.

An alpha particle is a helium nucleus: two protons and two neutrons. Thus, for a single alpha decay, A decreases by 4 and Z decreases by 2. Because there are two alpha decays, multiply these numbers by two to find the change in the values of Z and A:

$$^{A}_{Z}X \rightarrow {}^{A-4}_{Z-2}X + {}^{4}_{2}\alpha$$
$$^{239}_{92}U \rightarrow {}^{231}_{88}Ra + 2\,{}^{4}_{2}\alpha$$

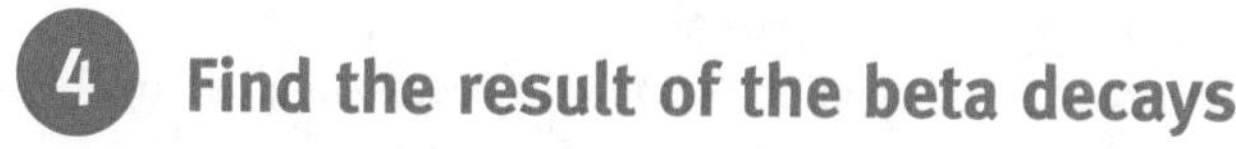

4 Find the result of the beta decays.

Beta decay comes in two forms: beta-minus and beta-plus (also called positron emission). In β^- decay, a neutron decays into a proton, a β-particle, and an antineutrino. The β-particle, which is nothing more than an electron, is ejected from the nucleus. Thus, the mass number stays the same, while the atomic number of the daughter nucleus increases by 1. There are three beta decays in this question:

$$^{A}_{Z}X \rightarrow {}_{Z+1}^{A}X + {}^{0}_{-1}\beta$$
$$^{231}_{88}Ra \rightarrow {}^{231}_{91}Pa + 3\,{}^{0}_{-1}\beta$$

5 Find the result of the positron decay.

Positron decay is the exact opposite of beta decay and is often called β^+ decay. In positron decay, a proton decays into a neutron, a positron, and a neutrino. The positron (an anti-electron—a particle with a positive charge and negligible mass) is ejected from the nucleus. Thus, the mass number stays the same, and the atomic number decreases by 1:

$$^{A}_{Z}X \rightarrow {}_{Z-1}^{A}X + {}^{0}_{+1}\beta$$
$$^{231}_{91}Pa \rightarrow {}^{231}_{90}Th + {}^{0}_{+1}\beta$$

Takeaways

It is important to know the decay types and the identities of the decay particles themselves. Once you have these down, these problems are relatively simple.

6 Find the result of the gamma decays.

In gamma decay, a gamma ray (an electromagnetic wave) is ejected from the nucleus. There is no change in atomic number or mass number:

$$^{A}_{Z}X^* \rightarrow {}^{A}_{Z}X + \gamma$$
$$^{231}_{90}Th^* \rightarrow {}^{231}_{90}Th + 2\gamma$$

The daughter nucleus of these eight decay processes is a thorium-231 atom, with 90 protons and 231 – 90 = 141 neutrons.

Things to Watch Out For

Fission occurs when a large nucleus splits into smaller nuclei. Fusion is the combination of smaller nuclei to form a larger particle. Transmutation, or radioactive decay resulting in a change of atomic number, is a specific type of fission reaction. β-particles (electrons) and positrons are very easy to confuse; make sure that you understand the differences between them.

Related Questions

1. Is it possible for neptunium to decay into an isotope of lead through a series of alpha decays?
2. How many β-particles are ejected when polonium-214 decays into radon-214?
3. Uranium-226 decays radioactively into radon-218 through two positron decays and an unknown number of alpha decays. How many alpha particles must be emitted in this reaction?

High-Yield Problem-Solving Guide questions continue on the next page. ▶ ▶ ▶

Key Concepts

Physics and Math Chapter 10

Dimensional analysis
Frequency
Density
Force
Surface tension

Dimensional Analysis

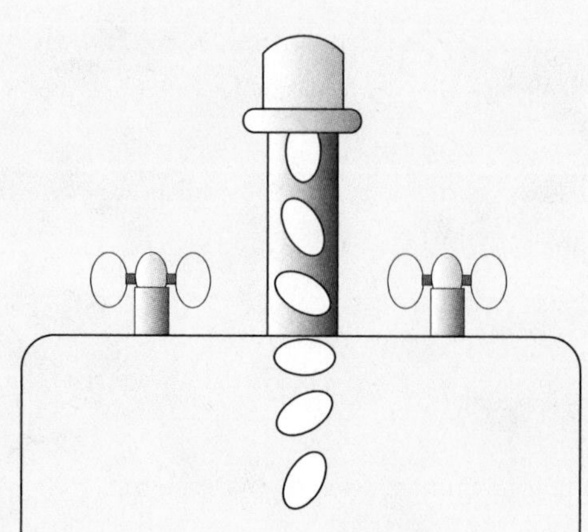

Water is dripping from a leaky faucet. As the drops fall, they oscillate as shown in the diagram above. Given that the frequency depends only on the surface tension T of the water (measured in $\frac{\text{N}}{\text{m}}$), the radius of the drops r, and the density of the water, use dimensional analysis to find a proportionality expression for the frequency f of the drops.

Identify all of the relevant physical quantities and their SI units.

As given in the problem, surface tension has units of newtons per meter. We can convert this to SI units by remembering that $1\ \text{N} = 1\frac{\text{kg} \bullet \text{m}}{\text{s}^2}$. Density can be given in the units of $\frac{\text{kg}}{\text{m}^3}$. Radius is a distance with the units of meters. Frequency has the units of Hz, or $\frac{1}{\text{s}}$. In summary:

$$T : \frac{\text{N}}{\text{m}} = \frac{\text{kg}}{\text{s}^2}$$

$$\rho : \frac{\text{kg}}{\text{m}^3}$$

$$r : \text{m}$$

$$f : \text{Hz} = \frac{1}{\text{s}}$$

2 Write a hypothetical formula for the frequency.

The frequency is related to the surface tension, T, the radius, r, and the density, ρ. Write an equation for these using variables (like x, y, and z) as exponents:

$$f = kT^x r^y \rho^z$$

where k is a unitless constant

3 Plug the units into the hypothetical formula.

Plug the units into the hypothetical formula from Step 2:

$$f = kT^x r^y \rho^z$$

$$\frac{1}{\text{s}} = \left[\frac{\text{kg}}{\text{s}^2}\right]^x [\text{m}]^y \left[\frac{\text{kg}}{\text{m}^3}\right]^z$$

4 Solve for the values of *x*, *y*, and *z*.

We know that the units on the left must equal the units on the right. Only the first term on the right side contains seconds, so we know x must be $\frac{1}{2}$; thus, we end up with $\frac{1}{\text{s}}$ on both sides.

Only the first and third terms contain kilograms; there are no units of kilograms on the left side of the equation. Therefore, the last term (density) must have an exponent of $z = -\frac{1}{2}$ so that the units of kilograms divide on the right side of the equation.

Finally, only the second and third terms contain meters; there are no units of meters on the left side of the equation. If the value of $z = -\frac{1}{2}$, then the middle term (radius) must have an exponent of $y = -\frac{3}{2}$ so that the units of meters divide on the right side of the equation.

Takeaways

It is often possible to determine an equation by concentrating on the units of the variables involved. This is a good approach on Test Day if you find yourself unable to remember a particular equation.

Things to Watch Out For

If you are short on time, you can at least determine general trends using a common-sense approach. The larger the radius, the slower the drop will oscillate. The denser the fluid, the slower the drop will oscillate. The surface tension is supplying the force to keep the drop oscillating, so if it is stronger, the drop will oscillate more quickly.

5 Convert these exponents to a simple equation.

All of our exponents are fractions, which means that a radical will be involved in the equation. Remember that a quantity raised to a negative exponent is the same as dividing by the same quantity raised to a positive exponent of the same magnitude. Putting this together, we can determine the equation:

$$\begin{aligned} f &= kT^{\frac{1}{2}}r^{-\frac{3}{2}}\rho^{-\frac{1}{2}} \\ &= k\frac{T^{\frac{1}{2}}}{r^{\frac{3}{2}}\rho^{\frac{1}{2}}} \\ &= k\sqrt{\frac{T}{r^3\rho}} \end{aligned}$$

Related Questions

1. What are the SI units of G in the universal law of gravitation?
2. An electric dipole is initially at rest in a uniform electric field. The torque provided by the electric field causes the dipole to oscillate back and forth. For the period of motion, the physicist derives the formula $T = kE^{\frac{1}{2}}$, where T is the period, E is the electric field, and k is a quantity with the appropriate units. Is this equation physically reasonable?
3. What are the units for the permeability of free space, μ_0?

High-Yield Problem-Solving Guide questions continue on the next page. ▶ ▶ ▶

Key Concepts

Physics and Math Chapter 11

Causality
Statistical analysis
Support for interventions
Study design

Study Design

A student wishes to document the effects of two different drugs in hypertensive patients. He obtains permission to contact all of the patients on propranolol and all of the patients on diltiazem from a certain pharmacy, and sends out written surveys asking for the patient's most recent blood pressure reading, age, and gender. Forty percent of respondents return their surveys. The student then compiles the diastolic blood pressure readings from each group. The mean systolic blood pressure in the propranolol group is 129 mmHg, and the mean in the diltiazem group is 127. The student concludes that diltiazem should be used as a first line treatment, rather than propranolol. Identify the errors that this student has made or the additional information that is needed to support his conclusion.

 Identify the steps in research design where error may be introduced.

Break the components of any study down into phases; the list of question design, experimental method, data collection, data analysis, conclusions, and execution is generally a good place to start. Next, determine where error is likely to be introduced. Question design is not likely to lead to errors, but should be kept in mind during a discussion of the experimental method. Data collection is also relatively unlikely to lead to erroneous conclusions (although it can with systematic bias and inaccurate instruments) and execution is almost always free from errors that impact the study. Therefore, we should focus our evaluations of most studies on the experimental method, data analysis, and conclusions.

 Compare the known execution of each step to ideal study design protocols.

To determine what errors have been made, we should compare the study to an ideal study of the same topic. Keep in mind that not all deviations from the ideal study are necessarily errors; some deviations may be deemed necessary because of practicality or financial concerns that may not substantially affect the data.

When considering the experimental method, one should always compare the study to the gold standard in biomedical research: the double-blind randomized controlled trial. The study that was conducted is not randomized, and does not have pre- and post-intervention data. The study was conducted from a single location and used self-report as the measurement instrument.

For data analysis, consider potential sources of bias. Studies with high response rates and sample sizes are ideal because they minimize selection bias. In this study, there was a very low response rate, which may have contributed to selection bias—only those who responded to the medication (or did not respond to the medication) may have replied to the survey, for example. Only one of the four collected variables was analyzed, and statistical findings were not provided. Whenever multiple variables may impact the measured outcomes, they should be considered as part of the analysis, and determinations of significance as well as p-values should be reported. This student did not account for other potential variables, such as severity of hypertension; demographic differences such as race, socioeconomic status, or access to healthcare; allergies to other study medications; and comorbid medical conditions.

To act upon a study, it should meet the requirements of the FINER approach and Hill's criteria. It should also demonstrate both clinical and statistical significance. In this study, we do not have sufficient information to draw the conclusions that the author makes for the reasons given above.

Takeaways

Research errors are pervasive and compound one another. It is not enough to look for sample size or an overt bias because there may be issues that arise before any data is even collected.

3 Determine whether the flaw is one of omission or design and consider appropriate ways to correct it.

The study is designed poorly, and requires a complete revision. However, there are several data points that could improve its relevance. An analysis that includes relevant p-values and adjusts for the collected variables could improve this study. Additionally, information about the clinical value of the different blood pressures would be worthwhile for study analysis in supporting the author's conclusion.

Things to Watch Out For

Statistical significance and clinical significance are often used interchangeably in common parlance, but they are two different topics. In study analysis we must look for errors in interpretation of data and experimental design, not just data analysis.

Related Questions

1. It is found that the number of shark attacks appears to correlate with the national gross sales of ice cream on a monthly basis. Why would it be a flawed conclusion to state that there is a causal relationship between purchasing ice cream and a shark attack?
2. How is respect for persons maintained in a study about the effects of electroconvulsive therapy?
3. How is causality established in an experimental study *vs.* an observational study?

Key Concepts

Physics and Math Chapter 12

Measures of central tendency
Measures of distribution
Charts, tables, and graphs
Comparative statistics

Graphical Analysis

Given the following data sets for age of mortality in these imaginary countries, construct a series of box-and-whisker plots. Use these plots to determine which countries have the best and worst life expectancies:

Physia	Orgostan	United Biology	GCS
69	65	91	56
74	87	56	89
52	55	82	65
63	69	44	47
70	66	62	85
71	59	53	39
65	72	68	98
81	72	85	71
64	58	65	52
70	71	59	65

1 Order the data sets and calculate meaningful statistics.

Median, mode, range, quartiles, and interquartile range (IQR) are easiest to calculate if the data are ordered, so this is the first step in generating comparisons. The reordered data are shown below:

Physia	Orgostan	United Biology	GCS
52	55	44	39
63	58	53	47
64	59	56	52
65	65	59	56
69	66	62	65
70	69	65	65
70	71	68	71
71	72	82	85
74	72	85	89
81	87	91	98

Now, it is possible to calculate the median, mean, and quartiles for this data. The median will be the average of the fifth and sixth data points for each set. Thus the medians are 69.5, 67.5, 63.5, and 65 for Physia, Orgostan, United Biology, and GCS, respectively.

We will calculate the mean by summing each column and dividing by ten. The means are 67.9, 67.4, 66.5, and 66.7 for Physia, Orgostan, United Biology, and GCS, respectively.

To find the quartile positions, we multiply the number of data points by $\frac{1}{4}$ and by $\frac{3}{4}$. If these are whole numbers, the quartiles are the averages of these data values and the ones above them. If they are not, then round up to find the positions of the quartiles. Here, $10 \times \frac{1}{4} = 2.5$ (round up to 3), and $10 \times \frac{3}{4} = 7.5$ (round up to 8). These data points are highlighted in green the following chart, with the median, mean, and IQR listed below the data.

	Physia	Orgostan	United Biology	GCS
	52	55	44	39
	63	58	53	47
	64	59	56	52
	65	65	59	56
	69	66	62	65
	70	69	65	65
	70	71	68	71
	71	72	82	85
	74	72	85	89
	81	87	91	98
Median	69.5	67.5	63.5	65
Mean	67.9	67.4	66.5	66.7
IQR	7	13	26	33

Already, this data is more accessible than the initial presentation, but using a graphical form is even easier to interpret.

2 Construct the appropriate box-and-whisker plots on the same axis.

Using an axis that contains the minimum and maximum data points (39 and 98, respectively), construct a box-and-whisker plot that is divided according to the quartiles and median for each data set. The box plots can be constructed with or without outliers. Including outliers is useful information, but does require additional mathematics:

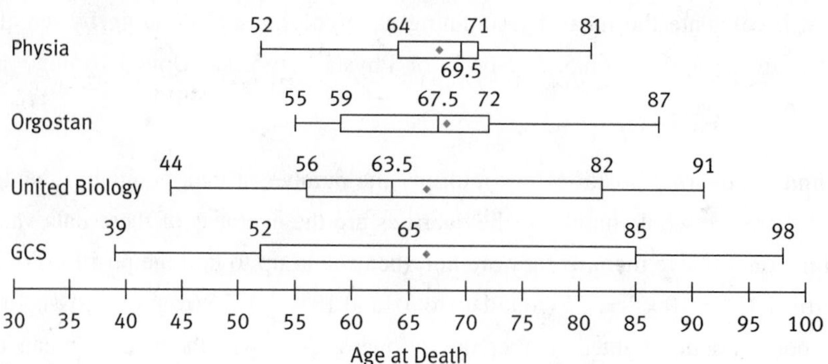

An outlier is any data point that is more than 1.5 × IQR away from the closest quartile. The one outlier in this data set is highlighted in red in the data table.

Takeaways

Graphical representations of data are generally more informative than text or tables. As long as the axes are the same between graphs, they provide comparative as well as absolute information.

Things to Watch Out For

Be careful not to rely on a single statistic or data point as a decision-making tool when evaluating graphs. In this case, outliers or erroneous data collection could cause a flawed result.

3 Compare the data using the constructed box-and-whisker plots.

Using the box-and-whisker plots, determine how countries compare to one another. For example, three quarters of the people in Physia live longer than half of the people in United Biology, so they have a longer life expectancy despite having similar mean and median values. In this data set, Physia has the best longevity outcomes when compared to the other groups; both United Biology and GCS are very similar and have the poorest outcomes.

Related Questions

1. Provide at least three criticisms of the following chart:

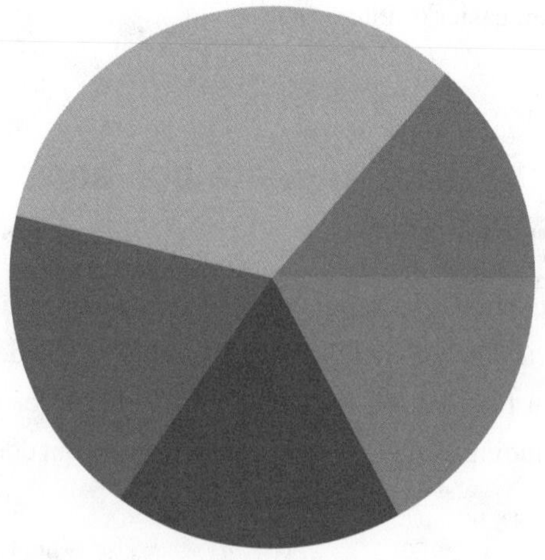

2. What are the appropriate first steps when analyzing any graph or table?

3. Determine the equations for the two lines below. At what point do they intersect?

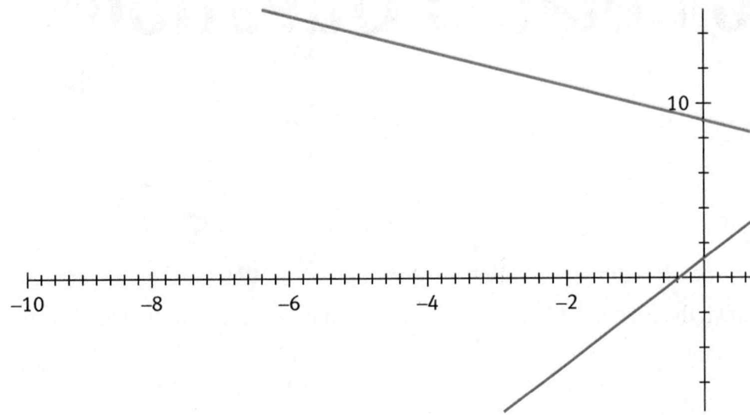

Solutions to Related Questions

1. Inclined Plane

1. The only two forces acting on this block in the parallel dimension are the force of static friction pointing up the plane and the parallel component of gravity pointing down the plane. If the block is at rest, then it is in translational equilibrium and the magnitudes of these two forces must be equal:

$$f_s = F_{g,\|}$$
$$\mu_s N = mg\sin\theta$$
$$\mu_s mg\cos\theta = mg\sin\theta$$
$$\mu_s = \frac{\sin\theta}{\cos\theta} = \tan\theta = \tan 45^\circ = 1$$

2. This question can be solved with kinematics equations, but it is actually easier to use conservation of energy to arrive at the answer. If the ramp is frictionless, then there are no nonconservative forces and all of the kinetic energy will be converted to gravitational potential energy. The initial gravitational potential energy can be assigned the value of zero because the question asks for the height above the initial point. The final kinetic energy is also zero because the block has zero speed when it reaches its highest point. Therefore, the initial kinetic energy and final gravitational potential energy are equal:

$$K_1 = U_2$$
$$\frac{1}{2}mv_1^2 = mgh_2$$
$$h_2 = \frac{v_1^2}{2g} \approx \frac{\left(2\ \frac{\text{m}}{\text{s}}\right)^2}{2\times 10\ \frac{\text{m}}{\text{s}^2}} = 0.2\ \text{m}$$

3. Start by determining the acceleration. Because the only force in the parallel direction is the parallel component of gravity, the acceleration will be g $\sin\theta = 10\frac{\text{m}}{\text{s}^2}\times 0.5 = 5\frac{\text{m}}{\text{s}^2}$. Now, use a kinematics equation:

$$v = v_0 + at$$
$$= 0 + \left(5\ \frac{\text{m}}{\text{s}^2}\right)(5\text{s}) = 25\ \frac{\text{m}}{\text{s}}\left(\text{actual} = 24.5\ \frac{\text{m}}{\text{s}}\right)$$

2. Projectile Motion and Air Resistance

1. The rock starts with zero kinetic energy and a gravitational potential energy of mgh_i. It ends with a kinetic energy of $\frac{1}{2}mv_f^2$ and zero gravitational potential energy. We are asked how much energy is lost, which would be the difference between these two terms:

$$\begin{aligned} W_{\text{nonconservative}} &= E_i - E_f \\ &= mgh_i - \frac{1}{2}mv_f^2 \\ &= m \times 10\,\frac{\text{m}}{\text{s}^2} \times 100\text{ m} - \frac{1}{2} \times m \times \left(30\,\frac{\text{m}}{\text{s}}\right)^2 \\ &= 1000\,m - 450\,m = 550\,m \end{aligned}$$

We cannot say an exact value for the amount of energy lost without knowing the mass of the rock, but 550m joules of energy have been lost, where m is the mass of the rock. We could also say that $\frac{550m}{1000m} = 55\%$ of the energy has been lost.

2. Let's call the speed of the slower rock v. This means that the speed of the faster rock is $1.3v$. The difference in kinetic energy between the rocks is:

$$\frac{1}{2}m(1.3v)^2 - \frac{1}{2}mv^2 = 0.69 \times \frac{1}{2}mv^2$$

The question asks how much more kinetic energy the faster rock has. We cannot give an exact value, but can compare it to the kinetic energy of the slower rock—the faster rock has 69% more kinetic energy than the slower rock.

3. First, find the difference in energy between the initial and final point:

$$\begin{aligned} W_{\text{nonconservative}} &= E_i - E_f \\ &= \frac{1}{2}mv_i^2 - mgh_f \end{aligned}$$

Now, divide that by the initial energy:

$$\frac{\frac{1}{2}mv_i^2 - mgh_f}{\frac{1}{2}mv_i^2} = \frac{v_i^2 - 2gh_f}{v_i^2}$$

$$\approx \frac{\left(30\,\frac{\text{m}}{\text{s}}\right)^2 - 2 \times 10\,\frac{\text{m}}{\text{s}^2} \times 44.1\text{ m}}{\left(30\,\frac{\text{m}}{\text{s}}\right)^2} = \frac{900 - 882}{900} = \frac{18}{900} = 0.02 = 2\%\ (\text{actual} = 4\%)$$

3. Thermodynamics

1. A minimum of three processes is required to have a closed cycle. This requires either an adiabatic or an isothermal process as well as an isobaric process (one with a constant pressure) and an isovolumetric process (one with a constant volume; also called an isochoric process). This creates a shape like a right triangle on a pressure–volume graph. While three-process cycles are seen, it is most common for closed-cycle processes to have four steps as seen in the Carnot cycle.

2. Entropy change can be given by the equation $\Delta S = \frac{Q_{\text{rev}}}{T}$. During an adiabatic process, $Q = 0$, thus $\Delta S = 0$. During an adiabatic process, there is no entropy change.

3. The liquid (usually mercury in older thermometers) is undergoing expansion. Because there is a change in temperature, this process is not isothermal. Because the change in temperature is accompanied by heat exchange, it is not adiabatic

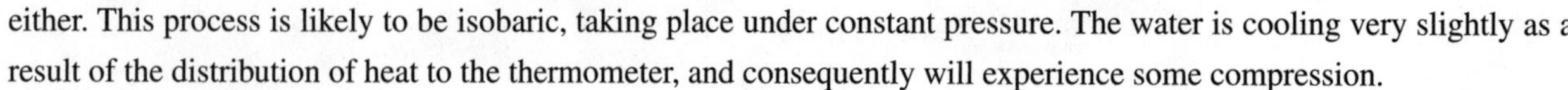

either. This process is likely to be isobaric, taking place under constant pressure. The water is cooling very slightly as a result of the distribution of heat to the thermometer, and consequently will experience some compression.

4. Fluid Dynamics

1. If the pipe is horizontal, then $h_1 = h_2$ in Bernoulli's equation. This simplifies the equation:

$$P_1 + \frac{1}{2}\rho v_1^2 = P_2 + \frac{1}{2}\rho v_2^2$$

We are told that $P_1 = 3P_2$. We can now solve for the linear flow speed at Point 1 in terms of the linear flow speed at Point 2:

$$3P_2 + \frac{1}{2}\rho v_1^2 = P_2 + \frac{1}{2}\rho v_2^2$$

$$\frac{1}{2}\rho v_1^2 = \frac{1}{2}\rho v_2^2 - 2P_2$$

$$v_1^2 = v_2^2 - \frac{4P_2}{\rho}$$

$$v_1 = \sqrt{v_2^2 - \frac{4P_2}{\rho}}$$

2. This question can be solved using the continuity equation. The radius at Point A is twice the radius at Point B, meaning that cross-sectional area at Point A is four times that at Point B:

$$A_A v_A = A_B v_B$$

$$\left(\pi r_A^2\right) v_A = \left(\pi r_B^2\right) v_B$$

$$\frac{v_A}{v_B} = \left(\frac{r_B}{r_A}\right)^2 = \left(\frac{1}{2}\right)^2 = \frac{1}{4}$$

Thus, $v_A : v_B = 1:4$.

3. We can solve this question with Bernoulli's equation again. In this case, the pressure is the same (atmospheric pressure) because the tank is open to the air. We can again assume the linear flow speed at the surface is essentially zero. Thus, Bernoulli's equation simplifies to:

$$\rho g h_1 = \frac{1}{2}\rho v_2^2 + \rho g h_2$$

$$\frac{1}{2}v_2^2 = gh_1 - gh_2$$

$$v_2 = \sqrt{2g(h_1 - h_2)} = \sqrt{2 \times 10\,\frac{\text{m}}{\text{s}^2} \times (1\,\text{m} - 0.5\,\text{m})} = \sqrt{10} \approx 3.16\,\frac{\text{m}}{\text{s}}$$

5. Electrostatics

1. The amount of work done is equal to the change in electrical potential energy:

$$\begin{aligned}\Delta U &= \frac{kQq}{r_2} - \frac{kQq}{r_1} = kQq\left(\frac{1}{r_2} - \frac{1}{r_1}\right)\\ &= \left(9\times10^9\ \frac{\text{N}\bullet\text{m}^2}{\text{C}^2}\right)(1\times10^{-6}\,\text{C})(-2\times10^{-6}\,\text{C})\left(\frac{1}{3\times10^{-2}\,\text{m}} - \frac{1}{1\times10^{-2}\,\text{m}}\right)\\ &= -18\times10^{-3}\left(\frac{1}{3\times10^{-2}} - \frac{3}{3\times10^{-2}}\right)\\ &= -18\times10^{-3}\left(-\frac{2}{3\times10^{-2}}\right) = 1.2\ \text{J}\end{aligned}$$

2. The amount of work can be determined by summing the work to move each charge into the configuration:

$$\begin{aligned}W_1 &= 0\ V\\ W_2 &= \frac{kQq}{r_1} = \frac{kQq}{1\times10^{-6}\,\text{m}}\\ W_3 &= \frac{kQq}{r_1} + \frac{kQq}{r_2} = \frac{kQq}{1\times10^{-6}\,\text{m}} + \frac{kQq}{1.4\times10^{-6}\,\text{m}}\\ W_4 &= \frac{kQq}{r_1} + \frac{kQq}{r_2} + \frac{kQq}{r_3} = \frac{2kQq}{1\times10^{-6}\,\text{m}} + \frac{kQq}{1.4\times10^{-6}\,\text{m}}\\ W_{\text{total}} &= \frac{4kQq}{1\times10^{-6}} + \frac{2kQq}{1.4\times10^{-6}} = \frac{kQq}{10^{-6}}\left(4 + \frac{2}{1.4}\right)\\ &\approx \frac{\left(9\times10^9\ \frac{\text{N}\bullet\text{m}^2}{\text{C}^2}\right)(5\times10^{-9}\,\text{C})(5\times10^{-9}\,\text{C})}{10^{-6}\,\text{m}}(5.4)\\ &\approx 225\times10^{-3}\times5.4 \approx 1.22\ \text{J}\end{aligned}$$

3. The initial potential energy of the system is:

$$\begin{aligned}U_{\text{i}} &= \frac{kq_1q_2}{r_{1,2}} + \frac{kq_1q_3}{r_{1,3}} + \frac{kq_2q_3}{r_{2,3}}\\ &= \left(9\times10^9\ \frac{\text{N}\bullet\text{m}^2}{\text{C}^2}\right)\left[\frac{(4\times10^{-6}\text{C})(-2\times10^{-6}\text{C})}{1\times10^{-3}\text{m}} + \frac{(4\times10^{-6}\text{C})(-3\times10^{-6}\text{C})}{2\times10^{-3}\text{m}} + \frac{(-2\times10^{-6}\text{C})(-3\times10^{-6}\text{C})}{1\times10^{-3}\text{m}}\right]\\ &= (9\times10^9)\left[-8\times10^{-9} - 6\times10^{-9} + 6\times10^{-9}\right]\\ &= -72\ \text{J}\end{aligned}$$

The final potential energy of the system is:

$$
\begin{aligned}
U_f &= \frac{kq_2q_3}{r_{2,3}} \\
&= \left(9\times10^9\ \frac{\text{N}\bullet\text{m}^2}{\text{C}^2}\right)\left[\frac{(-2\times10^{-6}\text{C})(-3\times10^{-6}\text{C})}{1\times10^{-3}\text{m}}\right] \\
&= (9\times10^9)(6\times10^{-9}) \\
&= 54\ \text{J}
\end{aligned}
$$

The change in electrical potential energy is therefore 54 – (–72) = +126 J.

6. Resistor Circuits

1. We know that the current through the circuit is 1.5 A and the equivalent resistance of the portion of the circuit including R_3, R_4, and R_5 is 15 Ω. Thus, the voltage across this part of the circuit is $V = IR = (1.5\ \text{A})(15\ \Omega) = 22.5\ \text{V}$. The same voltage drop will be seen across the branch including R_3 and R_4. The total voltage drop will be the sum of the voltage drop across R_3 plus the voltage drop across R_4. The current is the same through each resistor, so the ratio of their resistances will be the same as the ratio of their voltage drops. There is a 2:1 ratio of resistance, so the voltage drop must be 15 V across R_3 and 7.5 V across R_4.

2. Use the equation for equivalent resistance of resistors in parallel:

$$
\begin{aligned}
\frac{1}{R_p} &= \frac{1}{10\,\Omega}+\frac{1}{20\,\Omega}+\frac{1}{30\,\Omega}+\frac{1}{40\,\Omega} \\
&= \frac{12+6+4+3}{120} = \frac{25}{120} = \frac{5}{24} \\
R_p &= \frac{24}{5} = 4.8\,\Omega
\end{aligned}
$$

Now, use Ohm's law:

$$
\begin{aligned}
V &= IR \rightarrow I = \frac{V}{R} \\
I &= \frac{9\ \text{V}}{4.8\,\Omega} \approx 2\ \text{A (actual} = 1.88\ \text{A)}
\end{aligned}
$$

3. We know the current and voltage of the circuit, which allows us to find the equivalent resistance:

$$
V = IR \rightarrow R = \frac{V}{I} = \frac{20\ \text{V}}{10\ \text{A}} = 2\,\Omega
$$

Now determine the equivalent resistance of R_1 through R_5:

$$
\begin{aligned}
\frac{1}{R_p} &= \frac{1}{R_1}+\frac{1}{R_2}+\frac{1}{R_3}+\frac{1}{R_4}+\frac{1}{R_5} = \frac{5}{1\,\Omega} \\
R_p &= 0.2\,\Omega
\end{aligned}
$$

Because R_1 through R_5 are in series with R_6, the resistance of R_6 must be 2 – 0.2 = 1.8 Ω.

7. Doppler Effect

1. We are given all of the necessary variables to plug into the Doppler effect equation. Here, $f = 20$ bullets per minute, $v = 500\,\frac{\text{m}}{\text{s}}$, $v_D = 50\,\frac{\text{m}}{\text{s}}$, $v_S = 5\,\frac{\text{m}}{\text{s}}$. The detector (the bank robber) is moving away from the source, so a minus sign is used in the numerator. The source (the policeman's gun) is moving toward the detector, so a minus sign is used in the denominator, as well:

$$f' = f\frac{(v - v_D)}{(v - v_S)}$$

$$= \left(20\,\frac{\text{bullets}}{\text{min}}\right)\frac{\left(500\,\frac{\text{m}}{\text{s}} - 50\,\frac{\text{m}}{\text{s}}\right)}{\left(500\,\frac{\text{m}}{\text{s}} - 5\,\frac{\text{m}}{\text{s}}\right)} = 20 \times \frac{450}{495} \approx 20 \times \frac{9}{10} = 18\,\frac{\text{bullets}}{\text{min}}$$

2. In this question, $f = 350$ Hz, $v = 343\,\frac{\text{m}}{\text{s}}$, $v_D = 0\,\frac{\text{m}}{\text{s}}$, and $v_S = 20\,\frac{\text{m}}{\text{s}}$. There are two scenarios. In one case, the source is moving away from observers on the bridge, so a plus sign would be used in the denominator for this Doppler effect equation. In the other case, the source is moving toward observers on the river, so a minus sign would be used in the denominator for this Doppler effect equation:

$$f'_{\text{bridge}} = f\frac{v}{(v + v_S)} = (350\text{ Hz})\frac{343\,\frac{\text{m}}{\text{s}}}{\left(343\,\frac{\text{m}}{\text{s}} + 20\,\frac{\text{m}}{\text{s}}\right)} = 350 \times \frac{343}{363} = 331\text{ Hz}$$

$$f'_{\text{river}} = f\frac{v}{(v - v_S)} = (350\text{ Hz})\frac{343\,\frac{\text{m}}{\text{s}}}{\left(343\,\frac{\text{m}}{\text{s}} - 20\,\frac{\text{m}}{\text{s}}\right)} = 350 \times \frac{343}{323} = 372\text{ Hz}$$

3. During echolocation, the same animal serves as both the source and the detector. The sound wave bounces off of some surface and returns to the same animal that emitted the original frequency. In this case, as the animal flies toward some object, it could be said that the source is moving toward the detector and the detector is also moving toward the source. Thus, the top sign would be used in both the numerator (plus) and denominator (minus), and the general form of the Doppler effect equation would be:

$$f' = f\frac{(v + v_D)}{(v - v_S)}$$

8. Snell's Law

1. This is another application of Snell's law. Consider only the initial and final media because light enters and exits the pane of glass at the same angle:

$$n_{\text{smoke}} \sin\theta_{\text{smoke}} = n_{\text{air}} \sin\theta_{\text{air}}$$

$$\theta_{\text{air}} = \sin^{-1}\frac{n_{\text{smoke}}\sin\theta_{\text{smoke}}}{n_{\text{air}}}$$

$$= \sin^{-1}\frac{1.1 \times \sin 45^\circ}{1} \approx \sin^{-1} 0.778$$

$$\theta_{\text{air}} \approx 51^\circ$$

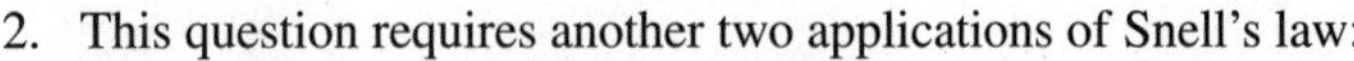

2. This question requires another two applications of Snell's law:

$$\begin{aligned} n_{\text{air}} \sin \theta_{\text{air}} &= n_{\text{diamond}} \sin \theta_{\text{diamond}} \\ \theta_{\text{diamond}} &= \sin^{-1} \frac{n_{\text{air}} \sin \theta_{\text{air}}}{n_{\text{diamond}}} \\ &= \sin^{-1} \frac{1 \times \sin 35^{\circ}}{2.4} \approx \sin^{-1} 0.239 \\ \theta_{\text{diamond}} &\approx 13.8^{\circ} \end{aligned}$$

and

$$\begin{aligned} n_{\text{air}} \sin \theta_{\text{air}} &= n_{\text{zircon}} \sin \theta_{\text{zircon}} \\ \theta_{\text{zircon}} &= \sin^{-1} \frac{n_{\text{air}} \sin \theta_{\text{air}}}{n_{\text{zircon}}} \\ &= \sin^{-1} \frac{1 \times \sin 35^{\circ}}{1.9} \approx \sin^{-1} 0.301 \\ \theta_{\text{zircon}} &\approx 17.6^{\circ} \end{aligned}$$

3. The critical angle is the angle at which light can no longer exit a medium, and instead is totally internally reflected. This implies that the refracted angle must be greater than or equal to 90°. The critical angle can be found as follows:

$$n_1 \sin \theta_c = n_2 \sin 90^{\circ} \rightarrow \theta_c = \sin^{-1} \frac{n_2}{n_1}$$

We are given the relevant indices of refraction in the original question:

$$\theta_c = \sin^{-1} \frac{1}{1.34} \approx 48^{\circ}$$

9. Nuclear Reactions

1. It is not possible for neptunium to decay into lead through a series of alpha decays. Each alpha decay reduces the atom's atomic number by two, but the difference between neptunium and lead's atomic numbers (93 – 82 = 11) is not divisible by two.

2. Balance the decay equation to determine how many β-particles are ejected:

$${}^{214}_{84}\text{Po} \rightarrow {}^{214}_{86}\text{Rn} + 2\, {}^{0}_{-1}\beta$$

Two β-particles are ejected during this decay reaction.

3. Balance the decay equation to determine how many α-particles are ejected:

$${}^{226}_{92}\text{U} \rightarrow {}^{218}_{86}\text{Rn} + 2\, {}^{0}_{+1}\beta + 2\, {}^{4}_{2}\alpha$$

Two α-particles are ejected during this decay reaction.

10. Dimensional Analysis

1. First, rearrange the universal law of gravitation to solve for G:

$$F_g = \frac{Gm_1m_2}{r^2} \rightarrow G = \frac{F_g r^2}{m_1 m_2}$$

Now, plug in the relevant units:

$$[G] = \frac{N \bullet m^2}{kg \bullet kg} = \frac{\left(\frac{kg \bullet m}{s^2}\right) m^2}{kg^2} = \frac{m^3}{s^2 \bullet kg}$$

2. The stronger the electric field, the stronger the electrostatic force. Because the electrostatic force is the restoring force in this question, we would expect that the larger its magnitude, the faster the dipole oscillates. Hence, the period should *decrease* as a function of the electric field—not *increase*. This makes the given equation unreasonable.

3. First, rearrange an equation that uses the permeability of free space:

$$B = \frac{\mu_0 I}{2r} \rightarrow \mu_0 = \frac{2rB}{I}$$

The units for r, a distance, are meters. The units for magnetic field are teslas, where $1\ T = 1 \frac{N}{m \bullet A}$. (If you did not remember this conversion factor, it can be determined from the equation $F = ILB \sin \theta$, where F is force in newtons, I is current in ampères, and L is length in meters.) Finally, the units for current are ampères. Now, plug in the relevant units:

$$[\mu_0] = \frac{[m]\left[\frac{N}{m \bullet A}\right]}{[A]} = \frac{N}{A^2} = \frac{\frac{kg \bullet m}{s^2}}{\left(\frac{C}{s}\right)^2} = \frac{kg \bullet m}{C^2}$$

11. Study Design

1. Correlation does not necessarily indicate causation. In this case, confounding likely explains the relationship between shark attacks and ice cream sales—namely, both of these variables are likely increased in summer months, when more individuals visit the beach, and when salt water climes may be more habitable for sharks. Ice cream sales also likely increase during summer months.

2. Respect for persons is maintained in any research context by providing the opportunity for informed consent, by allowing subjects to withdraw at any time, and by providing a debriefing at the end of the study period. Electroconvulsive therapy is still used in many psychiatric illnesses, including severe depression and suicidality, as well as psychotic disorders.

3. Causality in an experimental study is established through the use of at least one positive or negative control. Causality in an observational study cannot be proven, but can be supported through the use of Hill's criteria (temporality, strength, dose–response relationships, consistency, plausibility, consideration of alternative explanations, experiments, specificity, and coherence).

12. Graphical Analysis

1. Pie charts are generally poor at information dissemination with more than four categories, and for information that is not meant to add up to a whole. In addition, the colors have poor contrast and there is no written explanation or key. The chart is unlabeled, which leaves it uninterpretable.

2. For graphs, always start by checking the axes, including the relevant quantities, the units, and if there are any interruptions in the axes (indicated by wavy lines). Then, look for points of intersection, maxima, minima, differences in slope, or anything else noteworthy in the graph. For tables, always check for unusual values (zero, infinity, and so on) and make sure that the referenced categories are comparable.

3. These lines can be written in slope–intercept form. The slope of the red line is:

$$m_{\text{red}} = \frac{\Delta y}{\Delta x} = \frac{10-9}{-1-0} = \frac{1}{-1} = -1$$

This line's y-intercept is (0,9), so the equation of the line is $y = -x + 9$.

The slope of the blue line is:

$$m_{\text{blue}} = \frac{\Delta y}{\Delta x} = \frac{0-1}{-0.33-0} = \frac{-1}{-0.33} = 3$$

This line's y-intercept is (0,1), so the equation of the line is $y = 3x + 1$.

To determine their point of intersection, set the two equations equal to each other:

$$\begin{aligned} y &= -x + 9 \\ y &= 3x + 1 \\ -x + 9 &= 3x + 1 \\ 4x &= 8 \\ x &= 2 \\ y &= -x + 9 = -2 + 9 = 7 \end{aligned}$$

Thus, these lines intersect at the point (2,7).